Montagnard men in ceremonial combat dress at FULRO. Artillery hill in the background.

Left to right: Felix Jenkins, M.D., Tony Lindem, M.D., Stuart Poticha, M.D. and Larry W. Martin, M.D. standing in door of "Puff".

Montagnard woman cooking.

Street vendor in Pleiku.

Father and son in Pleiku.

A cartoon painted by Sgt. Steinberg at Camp Holloway.

D1287504

SOLDIERS
SAVING
SOLDIERS

Vietnam Remembered: A History of the 18th Surgical Hospital

Jerry W. Martin, M.D.

Jerry W. Martin, M.D.

Acclaim Press
MORLEY, MISSOURI

Acclaim Press
— Your Next Great Book —

P.O. Box 238
Morley, MO 63767
(573) 472-9800
www.acclaimpress.com

Book Design: Tiffany Glastetter
Cover Design: Tiffany Glastetter

Copyright © 2011, Jerry W. Martin, M.D.
All Rights Reserved.

No part of this book shall be reproduced or transmitted in any form or by any means, electronic or mechanical, including photocopying, recording or by an information or retrieval system, except in the case of brief quotations embodied in articles and reviews, without the prior written consent of the publisher. The scanning, uploading, and distribution of this book via the Internet or via any other means without permission of the publisher is illegal and punishable by law.

All photographs in the book are by Jerry W. Martin, M.D. unless otherwise indicated.

Library of Congress Cataloging-in-Publication Data

Martin, Jerry W.
Soldiers Saving Soldiers / Jerry W. Martin.
    p. cm.
ISBN-13: 978-1-935001-78-2 (alk. paper)
ISBN-10: 1-935001-78-7 (alk. paper)
1. Vietnam War, 1961-1975--Medical care--United States. 2. United States. Army. Surgical Hospital, 18th--Biography. 3. United States. Army--Medical personnel--Biography. 4. Vietnam War, 1961-1975--Personal narratives. I. Title.
DS559.44.M295 2011
959.704'37--dc23

2011018113

Second Printing 2018
Printed in the United States of America
10 9 8 7 6 5 4 3 2

CONTENTS

Definition of Freedom 4

Dedication 5

Foreword 6

Acknowledgments 7

Preface 11

Prologue 15

Chronology of World War II in the Pacific Theater 18

History of 18th (Portable) (Surgical) Hospital (Provisional) During World War II 20

Chronology of the Vietnam War 34

History of the 18th Surgical Hospital (MA) (MUST) (MA) During the Vietnam War 36

Emblems of the 18th Surgical Hospital 142

Emblems of Units Supported by the 18th Surgical Hospital 145

Lineage, Honors and Campaigns of the 18th Surgical Hospital 148

Surgical Procedures 151

Speech by Major General Vinh Loc at the FULRO Ceremony 172

Scientific Papers by Bob Hewitt, M.D.
    a. Acute Arteriovenous Fistulas in War Injuries 175
    b. Arterial Injuries at a Surgical Hospital in Vietnam 178

Personal Statements from Members of the 18th Surgical Hospital (MA)
    (Pleiku, Lai Khe, Quang Tri) 182

Reunions 211

Reflections at the Wall 228

Whither We Are Tending 235

Epilogue 244

Glossary of Medical Terminology 245

Glossary of Military Terminology 251

Bibliography 254

About the Author 256

Index 258

DEFINITION OF FREEDOM

Freedom is born of idealism; infused with patriotism; nourished by loyalty to a common purpose; upheld by faithfulness to the principles of liberty and self-determination; sustained by courage, bravery and dedication; paid for through sacrifice, suffering and often, death. Freedom is never achieved by a half-hearted effort or lip service to a cause. Freedom cannot be purchased by glib oratory, IOUs, cold checks or credit cards. The price for freedom must be paid in advance. Many hearts have stopped beating so that the heartbeat of this nation can continue, thereby preserving and guaranteeing our liberty and freedom.

—*Jerry W. Martin, M.D.*

DEDICATION

You who read,
Remember that these (this stranger) died in pain;
And passing here, if you can lift your eyes
Upon a peace kept by a human creed,
Know that they (one soldier has) have not died in vain.[1]

President John F. Kennedy said, "A nation reveals itself not only by the men it produces but also by the men it honors, the men it remembers." Inscribed on the World War II Memorial Monument are President Harry S. Truman's words, "Our debt to the heroic men and valiant women in the service of our country can never be repaid. They have earned our undying gratitude. Americans will never forget their sacrifices." On November 23, 1863, a Gettysburg newspaper editorial stated, "Every name…is a lightning stroke to some heart, and breaks like thunder over some home, and falls a long black shadow upon some hearthstone."

This book is dedicated to those who made the ultimate sacrifice for their country in America's Wars, especially in World War II and Vietnam, the two wars in which the 18th Surgical Hospital served. Abraham Lincoln wrote that we are left with "…only the cherished memory of the loved and lost…," those who "…laid so costly a sacrifice upon the altar of Freedom."[2]

———

Now slumbering in their graves.
How many homes made desolate,
How many hearts have sighed.[3]

———

O God of all Creation,
Let it not be in vain our sons have bled![4]

———

"Time will not dim the Glory of their deeds."[5]

—*Jerry W. Martin, M.D.*

---

[1] *Elegy for a Dead Soldier (paraphrased from the Epitaph),* Karl Shapiro
[2] *Letter to a Mother,* Abraham Lincoln
[3] *The Drummer Boy of Shiloh,* Will S. Hays
[4] *Four Voices from Shiloh,* Dr. Merrick F. McCarthy
[5] General John Joseph Pershing

FOREWORD

This book is the story the 18th Surgical Hospital, from its inception in 1928 through the war in Vietnam. In Washington, D.C., there is a deeply moving and beautiful monument to members of the U.S. Armed Forces who sacrificed their lives to preserve the freedom of South Vietnam. Other service men and women were luckier and survived, though they also sacrificed much. Some lived to return home because of the dedication and hard work by the 18th Surgical Hospital. Many medical personnel were a part of the hospital over the years, but it is of that group of doctors, nurses and medics who were located in Pleiku, South Vietnam, in August 1966 of which I will speak. At that time I traveled to South Vietnam under the auspices of the National Cartoonists Society and the U.S. Department of Defense with two other cartoonists, to do what we could to boost the morale of wounded U.S. and Vietnamese soldiers. In eleven locations in Vietnam, at Clark Air Force Base in the Philippines and in Oahu, Hawaii, we drew three thousand caricatures and did chalk talks—humorous sketches.

It was apparent immediately upon our arrival in Pleiku that the work of the 18th Surgical Hospital (a MASH unit) was an incredibly vital lifeline for many young servicemen. The nurses, doctors and medics, as must be the case with any combat hospital operation, worked admirably in spite of many difficulties. Two challenges mentioned in this book were obtaining enough blood when forty

Cartoonist, Don Orehek, drawing caricatures of 18th Surgical Hospital (MA) personnel attending our 5th reunion in San Antonio, Texas.

units was required for one patient, and making due with outdated anesthesia equipment.

It was thus surprising and gratifying that a nurse (2nd Lt. Pat Johnson) in Pleiku had kept her caricature for all the years from 1966. It now is in a museum in her home state of Michigan. Some other experiences that are foremost in my memory are: riding shotgun in a jeep in Ben Tre; meeting General Gilbert (Monk) Meyers, who actually did a caricature of me; visiting General William Westmoreland's office; and meeting South Vietnamese Premiere Nguyen Cao Ky. At

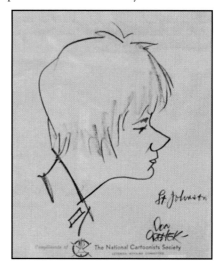

Caricature of Pat Johnson.

one location, as I set to work drawing, a soldier was wheeled out of the area designated for surgery. He was barely beginning to wake up from the effects of the anesthesia when I approached him and did a quick profile. (We only did profiles, as they were much quicker than full face drawings.) Close to a month later at a stop in the Oahu military hospital, this same soldier pulled out the caricature I had done, and asked if it was okay for him to get a second one. Of course it was. I was able to draw him with a smile on his face this time.

Forty-three years after my visit to Pleiku, I had the opportunity to reconnect with some of the people whom I had met there and also meet others that subsequently served in that location. The occasion was a reunion in the fall of 2009 of the 18th Surgical Hospital. I was asked to talk about my own Vietnam experience and share some highlights from my career in gag cartooning. As the weekend unfolded, I was reminded of the sacrifices that medical personnel, like fighting men and women, had made in Vietnam, and it was most gratifying to find that the passage of time had not diminished this quiet dedication to duty.

—*Don Orehek, Magazine Gag Cartoonist and Caricaturist*

ACKNOWLEDGMENTS

The information for this book was gleaned from many sources. The bibliography lists the numerous books that were consulted while searching for the historical facts necessary to reconstruct the movements, locations and activities of the 18th (Portable) (Surgical) (Provisional) (Reinforced) Hospital (MA) (MUST) (MA) as it migrated through World War II and the Vietnam War. In order to obtain the history of the 18th (Portable) (Surgical) (Provisional) (Reinforced) Hospital during World War II, it was necessary to review the history, movements and activities of the 32nd Infantry Division. In South Vietnam, the 18th Surgical Hospital (MA) (MUST) (MA) was a stand alone, or freestanding, hospital that supported numerous units but was not attached to a division.

I had access to the Army Medical Service Activities Reports of the 18th Surgical Hospital (MA) for 1966-1967. I also had copies of Lessons Learned, Headquarters, 18th Surgical Hospital (MA) from the Adjutant Generals Office (Army), Washington, D.C., covering the same years; but I was unable to retrieve any information from the military covering the years 1968-1971. The history for those years had to be pieced together from individual reports and personal accounts, many of which were posted on the Internet. Other information came from my personal notes and experiences, as well as the statements of others.

The most difficult challenge in compiling a list of acknowledgements is in being inclusive and expressing appropriate and adequate gratitude to those to whom that appreciation is due.

Mark T. Cenac, M.D. (Col., MC, USA, Ret.), our CO at the 18th Surgical Hospital (MA) in Pleiku, gave me his personal insights and important information through notes, letters, conversations and photographs.

Clarke M. Brandt (Lt. Col., MSC, USA, Ret.), the last XO at the 18th at Pleiku, sent information and a copy of his book, *Yeah Kids, I Really Did Go To Vietnam, My Vietnam War Memories 1966-1967*, covering his time in Vietnam and his few months with us at the 18th.

I was able to gather information concerning the last days of the 18th Surgical Hospital (MA) in Quang Tri Province through conversations with and written material and slides provided by Robert C. Fulton (Maj., MSC, USA, Ret.), the hospital's last XO.

Robert E. Spiller (Col., USA, Ret.) read the manuscript and wrote a brief synopsis, in which he presented his endorsement of the book.

Robert L. Hewitt, M.D. read the manuscript and provided constructive comments and helpful suggestions. He also gave me a copy of his book, *Supporting The Infantry Blue, Diary from a Surgical Hospital, Vietnam 1966-1967*. Bob's diary provided many details and assisted in keeping the correct chronological order, especially during the few months from my rotation to the States until the 18th moved from Pleiku.

A special thanks is also due a friend and fellow Literary Club (EQB) member, Dr. James Flynn (Ph.D., Retired Professor and Chairman of the English Department, Western Kentucky University). His critique provided many useful and valuable suggestions, and his personal comments are greatly appreciated.

Joy Downing, Richard Brannin and Kathy Macauley at Liberty Printing, provided excellent assistance with copying and reproducing documents used in the book. I appreciate their expert advice.

John Carmon, a friend and professional photographer in Bowling Green, Kentucky, blended and merged together two or three of my slides into a panoramic view of the area in the Central Highlands where the 18th Surgical Hospital (MA) was located.

I also wish to acknowledge the photographic skills of Tom Brown, another friend and a serious amateur photographer with professional ability, for providing the photograph of me used on the dust jacket as well as artifacts pictured in the book.

John, Tom and I have spent time together enjoying nature, photographing fall foliage, spring flowers and recording on film or disc the beautiful scenery here in Warren County, Kentucky. Their useful suggestions and expert advice are always genuinely appreciated.

I am grateful to Ray Buckberry for asking me to read *Reflections At The Wall* during the closing ceremonies when the *Wall That Heals* came to Bowling Green. Dr. Dwight Pounds (Ph.D., retired from Music Department, Western Kentucky University), also a friend and serious amateur photographer, digitally recorded scenes, activities, speeches, etc., of the closing ceremonies used in this book.

I also appreciate Larry Bailey's (broadcasting radio and tv, and banking) efforts in transferring my Vietnam radio programs from cassettes to CDs. Charles Wesley "Wes" Strader, a friend for nearly half a century now, deserves my thanks and gratitude. If he had not encouraged, enticed and coerced me into sending radio programs from Vietnam, I probably would not have kept notes or records concerning the history of Vietnam, nor would I have recorded any details of my activities during the year I was there. I would only have had memories from which to attempt to reconstruct the facts necessary to write this book. Memories always seem very real and genuine, but often are not accurate or reliable and are usually not substantiated by the true facts.

In September 2009, I called Harold G. "Hal" Moore (Lt. Gen., USA, Ret.) at his home in Auburn, Alabama and asked if he would consider writing a foreword for the book, especially since the 1st Cavalry troops that he commanded as a Lt. Col. in 1965 in the Ia Drang Valley were in Pleiku Province, only a few kilometers west of the location of the 18th Surgical Hospital (MA) that arrived a few months later in 1966. In our conversation, he was cordial and receptive to my request and seemed genuinely interested in undertaking the project. However, in February 2010 he sent me a letter in which he graciously apologized and explained that he was simply unable to complete the task after numerous attempts to do so. The General is now 89 years of age and lives a lonely and somewhat despondent life since his wife of 64 years died five years ago. His physical and mental activities have gradually and progressively declined. Although he was unable to complete the foreword, my appreciation to him is undiminished, and I extend my sincere gratitude for his willingness and the efforts he expended in attempting the project.

During our last reunion in San Antonio in September 2009, Don Orehek indicated that he would be delighted and honored to write the foreword. We were honored to have him speak at our reunion, and I am truly honored and sincerely grateful to have him write the foreword. It is difficult to adequately express my appreciation to him.

I must thank Pat Johnson Teranishi (Col., ANC [CRNA], Ret.) for her letters, emails, telephone calls and all her efforts in contacting, beseeching and prodding the members of the 18th to send their information, especially their personal statements and reminiscences for inclusion in the book. Obviously, I also must thank each individual who sent material, memorabilia, information and photographs.

Our granddaughter, Elizabeth Johnson Hathaway, was a tremendous help. Her suggestions increased immeasurably the quality of the book. Being an English major, she always made sure my commas were in the correct locations and that my spelling and grammar were correct. Her husband, Eric, a Bowling Green Intern Architect, did the drawing and map of the Pleiku 18th Surgical Hospital (MA) site, and served as an ongoing consultant during the process of scanning slides for reproduction in the book.

My wife, Jimmie, did all of the typing of the manuscript. I always wrote, corrected and rewrote the manuscript in longhand, and then dictated the material to her. A copy was run off, and together we made further spelling, punctuation and grammatical corrections. A new copy was made and given to Elizabeth for her to proof read. After she completed her corrections or suggestions, another copy was made and then shared with others. After further corrections and suggestions were received, a final copy was made, and that copy was then submitted to the publisher. As should be obvious, she did a lot of typing, correcting, rearranging and retyping before the manuscript was completed.

She was patient throughout the process, which, at times, was slow, exasperating and frustrating, especially on those occasions when the computer seemed to have a mind of its own. I truly appreciate her persistence and hard work.

The sine qua non of acknowledgments obviously must go to Publisher Douglas W. Sikes and Managing Editor Randy Baumgardner of Acclaim Press. Although the material for this book germinated from my personal experiences and research, his willingness to listen to my proposal and his immediate and genuine enthusiasm for the project allowed this book to develop and to ultimately be born in its current form. I appreciate their leadership in directing and overseeing its development and truly value their expertise and suggestions throughout the printing and publishing of *Soldiers Saving Soldiers: Vietnam Remembered: A Brief History of the 18th Surgical Hospital*.

It is imperative that I express my sincerest appreciation to William Bennett "Chip" Lawson, III, CEO of Hancock Bank and Trust Company and to the Board of Directors for their willingness to sponsor this book's unveiling reception and book signing hosted at the bank.

Initially, a decision was made to include a CD in the back of this book containing a few selected radio programs that I sent weekly from Vietnam, as well as a speech by Wayne F. Hosking, M.D. Dr. Hosking's lecture was recorded on cassette by Maj. Clarke Brandt, our XO. In Maj. Brandt's introduction, he stated that the speech was given at a "station hospital"; however, it was at the ARVN Hospital, situated adjacent to the site of the 18th Surgical Hospital (MA) on our northern boundary at a Pleiku Medical Society meeting. Later, it was decided to copyright the programs and place them on line so all would be accessible. The programs are not in chronological order. I did not prepare a script to assist me during the recording of the programs. Because they were done extemporaneously, numerous errors and misstatements occurred.

For example, Maj. Raymond Nutter (Col., USA, Ret.) was not from Lexington, Kentucky, but from Nicholasville, Kentucky, a smaller town nearby.

The Republic of Vietnam did not have a military award exactly equivalent to the U.S. Congressional Medal of Honor (CMH). When we first arrived in Vietnam, I was informed by someone that the Republic of Vietnam Gallantry Cross was equivalent to the CMH, but I soon discovered that was not true. The Gallantry Cross was given with four levels indicated by different devices. The highest level indicated by a bronze palm branch was for citation at the Army or Armed Forces level. That is the one we received at the 18th Surgical Hospital (MA). The Gallantry Cross was patterned after the French Croix de Guerre given in World War I and World War II, and had essentially the same significance. The Republic of Vietnam's highest award was the Grand Cross of the National Order, First Class.

A "gunship" was an armed Huey helicopter used for attack, transportation and air support of ground troops. In one broadcast, I referred to them as "gunboats."

There are no alligators in Vietnam, but there are four species of crocodiles.

Dragon Mountain was not eight to ten miles from the 18th. By air, the distance was only three to four miles away. In order to drive there, one had to drive south on Highway 19 two to three miles into Pleiku City, and then drive three to four miles westward to Camp Enari, the 4th Infantry Division's base camp located at the foot of the eastern slope of the mountain.

On one program I stated that we at the 18th had seen "more patients than any other hospital in Vietnam," but I should have said "more patients than any other surgical hospital in Vietnam."

When I stated that "Puff" fired its cannons at 18,000 rpm, I did not mean that each cannon fired at that rate. There were three guns, each firing up to 6,000 rpm, for a total of 18,000 rpm.

My statement that a large Montagnard village covered an area of about two to three square miles was inaccurate. I should have indicated that it was about two to three miles around the perimeter; however, most of their villages were smaller.

When the 4th Infantry Division moved into the Pleiku area, I misunderstood Maj. Gen. William Roy Peers' name and initially referred to him on the radio as "Gen. Pearson."

Brig. Gen. James A. Wier (USARV Surgeon) graduated from the University of Louisville Medical School in 1937, not in 1938 as I stated.

I also initially mispronounced Maj. Gen. Norton's name as "Horton" on a broadcast before I discovered my mistake.

On one program I mentioned the names "Johnny, Gene and Buck" without any explanation. Of course, the people in Bowling Green knew that I spoke of Johnny Oldham (former All-American, head basketball coach, and later athletics director at Western Kentucky University) and his assistant coaches, Gene Rhodes and Wallace "Buck" Sydnor. I also referred to the "Toppers" which is the commonly used abbreviation of "Hilltoppers," the appellation for the sports teams at WKU. Bowling Green is located on and around six or seven large hills, some of which were used as lookouts and forts during the Civil War. Western Kentucky University is situated on and around one of those hills referred to during the Civil War as "Vinegar Hill." There are remnants of Ft. Albert Sydney Johnson on the main part of the campus. Therefore, the athletic teams have always had the nickname "Hilltoppers."

I mentioned "antiaircraft fire" when Maj. Nutter was shot down. The VC used 50 caliber machine guns for this purpose since they did not have larger antiaircraft guns in the South; however, in the North the NVA had larger antiaircraft guns, as well as SAM missiles.

I also stated that the original physicians arrived at the 18th in Pleiku on June 26, when in fact it was June 25.

I mentioned that the 25th Division's base camp was northwest of the 18th Surgical Hospital (MA) site, when, in fact, it was northeast of us.

On a broadcast, I also mentioned that the time difference from Pleiku to CST in the U.S. was nine hours plus one day, when actually there was a thirteen-hour difference.

At the FULRO Festival, I stated that the Montagnards had broken away from South Vietnam during the Ky government. They had left a few years earlier and were returning during the Ky regime.

I mentioned that the Boeing 707, which we flew on to Saigon, traveled at nearly 600 miles per hour; however, I later learned that was a slight exaggeration. We flew at approximately 525 miles per hour.

"Peking Polly" often sounded as if she was saying "Peping" instead of Peking. On a broadcast, I imitated her by saying "Peping"; but after doing so, I realized that the radio audience did not understand what I was doing and probably thought I had mispronounced Peking.

I mentioned the sound of B-52's flying over our BOQ. I did not actually see one flying directly overhead. They flew at such a high altitude that they were not always visible; however, we heard the roaring, thunderous sound when they were overhead. We could hear their bombs exploding and, on a few occasions at night, could see the flashes of the explosions westward near the Cambodian border.

We were first told that the 12th Evacuation Hospital was coming to Pleiku, and I mentioned that on a broadcast. Later, we learned it would be the 71st Evac.

When I reported the incident of the 4th Infantry Division Colonel being shot by another member of the 4th Division while "cleaning his gun," I stated that he was shot in the side. There were multiple entrance wounds when the bullet fragmented upon striking the back of his chair. Some of the fragments entered at about the left posterior auxillary line, which was on the left lateral side of his back.

The length of the beach at the Leprosarium south of Qui Nhon was probably a little over a mile in length, not three miles as stated.

I mentioned that the Vietnamese language is the only Oriental language that uses the English alphabet. The Thai language uses the English alphabet, but they have a few additional letters.

On one program I mentioned "General Bedell," but I should have said, "General Bedell Smith."

When I described a Lambretta, I mentioned that the driver sat in the center of the seat with room for a "patient" on each side of him but should have said "passenger."

I trust that the aforementioned examples comprise a complete list of all the mea culpas that I made. These are the only ones I detected when I recently reviewed the broadcasts.

All photographs used in this book were made by me unless otherwise indicated. Photographs in which I am pictured were made with my camera (Leicaflex, using either a Summicron-R 50mm f-2 or an Elmarit-R 135mm f-2.8 lens) taken by whoever was accompanying me.

Most of the material contained in this book is not original with me. I have recorded and paraphrased historical information; inserted numerous literary and other pertinent quotes; organized and arranged the material into a concise, readable form; and organized it in chronological order. All thoughts and statements original with me should be obvious to the reader. As I began my research, what I had envisioned as a brief historical overview took on a life of its own and grew into something larger and more complex. Ultimately, it became a problem of elimination rather than inclusion. Every effort was made to designate the sources accurately and to attribute credit to those from whom I collected the data. I apologize for any failure to have correctly done so.

The writing of this book has been a challenging, laborious and, at times, frustrating task. Yet, the effort has been fulfilling and rewarding and one I have immensely enjoyed.

Shakespeare tells us that Hamlet once said, "Beggar that I am, I am even poor in thanks..." (Hamlet, Act II, Scene II). As I pondered the challenge of adequately expressing my sincere appreciation to all who contributed in the creation of this book, I could not help but feel a close kinship to Hamlet. Therefore, I can only echo Hamlet's further remarks, "...I thank you: and sure, dear friends, my thanks..." (Ibid).

—*Jerry W. Martin, M.D.*

Antoine's Restaurant, Japanese Room, Saturday evening, October 24, 1998. Pleiku Physicians. Front row, left to right: Joseph Juliano, M.D.; Tassos Nassos, M.D.; Orville Swenson, M.D.; Sheldon Brown, M.D.; Robert Engebrecht, M.D. Second row: Mark T. Cenac, M.D. (CO); Ted Stuart, M.D.; Wayne Hosking, M.D.; Terry McDonald, M.D.; Sam Gillis, M.D. Third row: Roger Ecker, M.D.; Eugene Chap, M.D. Fourth row: Michael Belinson, M.D.; Robert Hewitt, M.D.; Jerry W. Martin, M.D.

PREFACE

For many years I had recurring thoughts of writing a brief, succinct record of my activities, impressions and emotions while assigned to the 18th Surgical Hospital (MA) at Fort Gordon, Georgia and in the Central Highlands near Pleiku, Republic of Vietnam, in the event my descendants were ever interested in reading about them. Those thoughts remained intermittent and transient, and on each occasion, good intentions were always superseded by procrastination. Over the years, I sorted and labeled my photographs and gathered and consolidated all of the maps, charts, correspondence and memorabilia I had collected while in Vietnam, Hong Kong and Bangkok.

After being asked to write a history of our year in Pleiku at a reunion of the 18th Surgical Hospital (MA)'s staff that met in San Francisco in September 2007, I finally became interested and serious enough to undertake the challenge. Because of my lifelong interest in literature and history, I had already read a number of books about World War II and the Vietnam War, so using that as a starting point, I initiated the task by reviewing materials already in my library. I realized from having read the Lineage and Honors of the 18th that it had served with distinction in the South Pacific during World War II. As I pursued the investigation, pertinent historical material began to fall into place, and with sufficient military data available, I quickly decided to expand my research to include the entire history of the 18th Surgical Hospital from its creation in 1928 and its organization and activation in 1942 until its closure in 1971.

During my year in Pleiku, I sent back radio programs recorded on cassette tapes to radio station WKCT in Bowling Green, Kentucky. The 8-10 minute programs were played at 7:15 a.m. and 6:10 pm each Tuesday. My friend, Charles Wesley "Wes" Strader, then Sports Director at the station, asked me to undertake the project, which I initially declined using the excuse that I did not have a cassette recorder. Within a day or two, he purchased and brought me a portable recorder and a supply of empty cassette tapes; therefore, I began recording the programs out of a sense of both friendship and obligation. I recorded the programs extemporaneously, thinking that the information would seem more genuine and realistic; however, because of that, just as in everyday speech, poor grammar occasionally occurred.

The electrical voltage produced by the generators at the 18th frequently fluctuated, causing the speed and tone of my voice to change accordingly.

When I arrived in Pleiku, I asked our CO, Lt. Col. Cenac, if I could record and send the programs. He said he had no objection, but directed me to an office at MACV Headquarters located about one mile away, recommending that I clear the project through them. When I went to MACV and asked to speak to whoever was in charge of such matters, I was told that the Colonel was away for two or three days in Saigon, but his assistant told me to go ahead. He said that they had never had anyone ask for permission or clearance for such a project before. I was never asked to sign any papers and was never given written permission. I recorded the time and date of my visit, the name of the officer in charge, the major who gave his permission and kept that information in a file in the event I ever needed to confirm and document the permissibility of the broadcast.

As this book progressed, I noted numerous connections to Bowling Green, Warren County and Kentucky. I did not include details of those relationships in the text of the book since I wanted it to be about the unit and not about me. I always made an attempt to talk with every patient that came through the 18th who was from Kentucky. Time did not permit me to interview each individual for the radio programs, but I always mentioned their names. For those within broadcast range of WKCT, I gave a brief explanation of their wounds or illness, hoping to allay the worries, apprehensions and fears of their families back home.

The first connection to Bowling Green was encountered while writing the history of World War II. On Wednesday, April 22, 1942, the cruiser, USS *Indianapolis*, was one of the ships that escorted the convoy carrying the 32nd Infantry Division from San Francisco to Adelaide, South Australia. The personnel that later formed the 18th Portable Hospital (Provisional) on September 14, 1942, were also aboard ship in that convoy. The USS *Indianapolis*, commanded by Capt. Charles Butler McVay, III, later carried the atomic bombs, *Fat Man* and *Little Boy*, from San Francisco to Tinian Island, Mariana Islands. It was later sunk by a torpedo fired from the Japanese submarine, *I-58*, commanded by Lt. Commander Mochitsura Hashimoto on July 30, 1945, somewhere between

Guam and Leyte, Philippines. Joseph W. VanMeter was a crew member aboard the USS *Indianapolis* and was one of those who survived for four days while floating in the Pacific Ocean without food and water, miraculously escaping shark attacks, starvation and dehydration. The survivors were rescued by the USS *Cecil F. Doyle* on August 3, 1945. Mr. VanMeter (now deceased) worked for the Post Office in Bowling Green until his retirement. His son, Dr. Phillip P. VanMeter who currently practices Periodontics and Implant Dentistry in Bowling Green, came to my Literary Club (Ecce Quam Bonum [EQB]) a few years ago and related his father's experiences to us. Mr. VanMeter's widow, Marcheta VanMeter Skinner, is currently a member of First Baptist Church, Bowling Green, Kentucky.

At the time of his retirement, Raymond T. Nutter (Col., USA, Ret.) was one of the most highly decorated individuals in the U.S. Army. He was born in Nicholasville, Kentucky, and graduated from Western Kentucky University located in Bowling Green, where he played football. He served as the football coach at Ft. Campbell, Kentucky when Lt. Gen. William Westmoreland was Commander of the 101st Airborne Division. After retirement, he and his family returned to live in Bowling Green, where he was a successful businessman. Ray and I remained steadfast friends until his sudden cardiac death on October 25, 2006. I gave a brief eulogy at his funeral. He was interred on December 6, 2006, in Arlington National Cemetery. Every October 18, the anniversary date of his Vietnam surgery, Ray always came by the office or looked me up wherever I was, and either shook hands, gave me a hug or punched me on the arm and simply said, "Thank you," a tradition now perpetuated by his widow, Jean.

At Major Nutter's request, Martha Raye called me at the 18th Surgical Hospital (MA) at Pleiku, to inform me of his injuries; however, I was scrubbed in surgery and could not talk to her. I had met her when she visited the 18th in September 1966. On each of her other two subsequent visits to the 18th in 1967, we discussed the occasion of her call to the 18th. She remembered Ray and always asked about him. She was born Margaret Teresa Yvonne Reed on August 27, 1916, and was a Licensed Practical Nurse (LPN) before becoming an entertainer and comedienne. She was made an honorary Green Beret because of her frequent visits to, entertainment of, and work with the Special Forces. President Lyndon B. Johnson officially made her a Lt. Col. during a formal ceremony. After that, she was referred to by her military friends as "Col. Maggie." She died on October 19, 1994, and, because her request for an exception to policy had been granted in 1992, she is buried in the military cemetery at Ft. Bragg, North Carolina.

Harold G. "Hal" Moore (Lt. Gen., USA, Ret.) is a native of Bardstown, Kentucky, the site of My Old Kentucky Home and the Stephen Foster Pageant. The last time my wife, Jimmie, and I stopped to have lunch at the Old Talbert Tavern, I noticed that a street in Bardstown is now named for him, as well as a museum. Lt. Col. "Hal" Moore commanded the 1st Cavalry troops (1st Battalion, 7th Cavalry) that engaged the NVA on November 14, 1965, in the now-famous Battle of the Ia Drang Valley. Moore, along with co-author Joseph L. Galloway wrote, *We Were Soldiers*

Once…, And Young, about that battle. The battle demonstrated the need for a hospital in the area to provide quicker surgical support since continued heavy fighting was anticipated in the region. In June of the following year, the 18th Surgical Hospital (MA) was established just north of Pleiku City, a few kilometers from the Ia Drang Valley.

Moore and Galloway again collaborated and, in 2008, wrote the sequel to their first book, *We Are Soldiers Still*. The book describes the return visit of Moore, Galloway and two or three other Americans who were present in the battle, along with the NVA commander, Lt. Gen. Nguyen Hu An, and two of his company commanders to the Ia Drang battlefield. Joseph Galloway, who was a civilian war correspondent in the Ia Drang battle, was the only civilian to be awarded a Bronze Star for heroism by the Army in the Vietnam War. In the last chapter of the book they wrote, "…There is no such thing as closure for soldiers who have survived a war. They have an obligation, a sacred duty, to remember those who fell in battle beside them all their days and to bear witness to the insanity that is war…." Gen. Dwight D. Eisenhower also voiced his views concerning the "insanity" of war when he stated, "I hate war as only a soldier who has lived it can, as one who has seen its brutality, its futility, its stupidity." He added, "Every gun that is made, every warship launched, every rocket fired, signifies in the final sense a theft from those who hunger and are not fed, those who are cold and not clothed." H. Norman Swarzkopf (Gen., USA, Ret., of Gulf War fame, who had relatives in Bowling Green) noted that, "In my estimation Galloway is the finest combat correspondent of our generation—a soldiers' reporter and a soldiers' friend." Lt Gen. Moore's brother, J. William "Bill" Moore, a long time acquaintance and friend, was in the insurance business in Bowling Green for many years and, in retirement, still resides here.

Robert E. Spiller (Col., USA, Ret.) now resides in Oakland, Kentucky, near Bowling Green. As a Major (S-3) he accompanied Lt. Col. "Hal" Moore and entered South Vietnam with the 1st Cavalry Division in 1965, and a year later left Vietnam as a Lt. Col. (G-4). After retirement, he and his wife, Cora Jane, a native of Bowling Green and a niece of the late Duncan Hines (of cake mix fame, also of Bowling Green) returned to Warren County. We are currently members of the Military Officers Association of America (MOAA). He has been active in the VFW and the American Legion and is an active spokesman for VA affairs. He also was a former patient.

Lt. Gen. Heaton, the Army Surgeon General (1959-1969) attended the University of Louisville Medical School, graduating in 1926. While in Louisville he met and, upon graduation, married Sara Hill Richardson from Glasgow, Kentucky, which is located about 30 miles east of Bowling Green. When he toured the 18th Surgical Hospital (MA) at Pleiku, after learning that I was from Bowling Green, remarked to me about the numerous visits he and his wife made to Glasgow and Bowling Green.

The Reverend Othar O. Smith was Pastor and Jack Duval was Minister of Music at First Baptist Church, Bowling Green, while I was in Vietnam. The Duvals had been patients of mine, and I had delivered their daughter a few months before being drafted. When Chaplain Hollis needed recorded music for use in worship services at the 18th Surgical Hospital (MA)'s Chapel, I corresponded with Reverends Smith and Duval, explaining our need. I soon received two tapes containing appropriate church music recorded by First Baptist Church's choir. Chaplain Hollis was most appreciative and wrote a letter of thanks to the Church.

Airman First Class Spurrier O'Neal Harrell, a native of Leitchfield, Kentucky was assigned to the 619th Tactical Control Squadron as a radar operator. His unit was located probably less than a mile from the 18th Surgical Hospital (MA). Our tours in Vietnam coincided; however, we were not acquainted at the time. He was named Outstanding Airman of the Year in 1967. He and his family later moved to Bowling Green where he currently operates the South State Construction, Inc. He and I serve as deacons at First Baptist Church.

Patricia M. Smith, M.D., the Catholic medical missionary at Kontum (Pleiku Province) a few miles north of Pleiku City, worked briefly in an Appalachian Coal Miner's Hospital in Eastern Kentucky. It was a pleasure meeting and talking with her when she visited the 18th and when she spoke at the Pleiku Medical Association.

Robert L. Hewitt, M.D., grew up in Paducah, Kentucky and is a graduate of Paducah Tilghman High School (named for Lloyd Tilghman [1816-1863, Brig. Gen., CSA]). Two of his high school classmates, Delbert Reeder and Russell Morgan, are currently fellow members of First Baptist Church, Bowling Green. Bob did his undergraduate studies at the University of Louisville, before attending Medical School at Tulane University. Upon his retirement, he was Chairman, Department of Surgery, Tulane University, New Orleans, LA. During the 18th Surgical Hospital (MA)'s reunion in San Francisco in 2007, Bob and I slipped away for a few hours to a sports bar on Union Square to watch the University of Louisville vs. University of Kentucky football game.

Robert C. Fulton (Maj., MSC, USA, Ret.) and his wife, Virginia (whose home was here) retired and returned to Bowling Green in 1980. They were also patients of mine until my retirement from medical practice. We were aware that we both had served in Vietnam and quickly came to realize that we each had served with the 18th Surgical Hospital (MA), I in Pleiku when the hospital opened and he as XO during the hospital's second venture into Quang Tri Province. He was with the hospital when it stood down (closed) in 1971.

Even the American Legion was named by a Kentuckian. The American Legion was born in Paris, France in March 1919, at the end of World War I during a caucus of the American Expeditionary Force (A.E.F.). The caucus resulted from a proposal made by Lt. Col. Theodore Roosevelt, Jr. to a group of representatives of A.E.F. divisions and service units. Maj. Maurice K. Gordon of the 36th Division had the honor of naming and helping to establish the new organization. The blueprint of the American Legion and the Preamble to the Constitution of the American Legion were finalized at a meeting from May 8-10, 1919 in St. Louis, Missouri. Maj. Gordon was from Madisonville, Hopkins County, Kentucky and he later wrote a book, *Hopkins County History*.

Jerry Rosenberg, M.D., was a resident in surgery at the University of Kentucky Medical Center in Lexington, Kentucky at the same time that a Bowling Green Ob-Gyn, Nick Kafoglis, M.D., was in training there. Dr. Rosenberg was assigned to the 447th Medical Detachment (MILPHAP) and worked at the Pleiku Provincial Hospital in Pleiku City. He and the physicians at the 18th reciprocally offered medical and surgical assistance when circumstances permitted.

I was able to present to each of the original physicians at the 18th Surgical Hospital (MA) a Kentucky Colonel certificate, thanks to the efforts of State Representative Edward G. Brown. He, along with many members of his family, were patients of mine. His widow, Minnie Brown Coleman, still resides in Bowling Green.

All attempts at locating personnel rosters of the 18th Surgical Hospital (MA, MUST, MA) from 1966-1971, as well as World War II (18th [Portable] [Surgical] Hospital [Provisional]), were unsuccessful. Those lists must exist somewhere in military archives, but others, and I, were unable to retrieve them. I was able to reconstruct the list of officers, physicians and nurses at Pleiku from memory, but I could not remember the names of more than a few of the EM. When I review my photographs taken during the year, I recall faces but cannot recall their names. Almost without exception, each corpsman assigned to the 18th at Pleiku worked hard, was cooperative, competent in their work and often went above and beyond what their job description required.

For this book to be complete, every individual who came through the doors of the 18th Surgical Hospital (MA) as a patient should have their story told. Obviously it is impossible to remember each patient, and if it were possible, time and space does not permit the recording of details of each one. Every case was categorized according to their medical and/or surgical diagnosis and type of wounds, permitting quick and accurate statistical analysis; however, each case was peculiarly individual—their fears, pain, anxiety, loneliness and suffering could not be categorized or shared.

Many conversations among the 18th's Pleiku staff through correspondence, telephone conversations and, especially at reunions, frequently bring to mind cases long forgotten but medically and/or surgically unusual and interesting. I have chosen to list a few cases exemplifying some of the most serious or unusual ones. In doing so, I am not implying that the less severe, less ill or the more routine cases were any less important.

It is nearly impossible to write accurately about cases that did not involve me personally. Instead of listing an endless number of cases, I believe the reader will find this book more interesting by illustrating and documenting other cases with photographs accompanied by appropriate captions.

More historical details could have been included and various other political views, differing concepts concerning military strategies and tactics, as well as agreements or disagreements with each, could have been recorded, but for what purpose? Many similarities between Vietnam, Iraq and Afghanistan could be pointed out, but without definitive solutions, those comments would be of limited value. I concur with Aleksandr Solzhenitsyn who recently wrote, "The timid civilized world has found nothing with which to oppose the onslaught of a sudden revival of barefaced barbarity, other than concessions and smiles." How long before our leaders begin to listen, understand and believe the lessons history has already taught?

The second terrorist attacks on the World Trade Center on September 11, 2001, were just as real and violent as were the Japanese war mongers' bombs on Pearl Harbor, and just as egregious and threatening to the free world as were the German Nazis' and Italian Fascists' ominous intentions in Europe, and the world, during World War II. Terrorists are not protected under the Geneva Convention, so why should they be granted protection under the U.S. Constitution, the very Constitution they are intent on destroying? A trial in this country, especially in the city where the primary 9/11 attacks occurred, would demean the memory of the victims and be a slap in the face to their families and those who survived. All foreign terrorists found guilty should be executed and all terrorists who are U.S. citizens should be treated as traitors. Each terrorist will no doubt attempt to use their trial as a propaganda platform to proclaim to the world their perceived glory of jihad and as a venue to portray their imagined criminality of the "evil, infidel" Americans. Every jihadist's wish for martyrdom should be granted, instead of providing a global stage for anti-Western, anti-American and anti-Christian rhetoric. During the trial of the 1993 World Trade Center bombers, the defense, through cross-examination, forced the prosecution to turn over the list of the unindicted co-conspirators, including Osama bin Laden, and other intelligence information revealing highly sensitive materials as well as their sources to our enemies, thus hampering U.S. intelligence efforts. The only logic terrorists understand is the "logic" of force—a force more vicious, determined, overwhelming and unrelenting than the force they have available to use against us. Diplomacy and reason are languages they are unable, or unwilling, to speak. Enticements, counseling and deprogramming in an attempt to counter their extreme ideology will not be beneficial. Appeasement only postpones their ultimate goals and the impending, inevitable confrontation.

The United Nations will afford very little, if any, help in solving these problems since it has developed into, or perhaps always was, an impotent, exclusive, expensive international "club" subsidized to an inordinate degree by the U.S. taxpayer.

Much time is wasted while "experts" evaluate the problems and our politicians haggle over the most appropriate response. Sometimes "experts" are right, more often they are wrong and they are frequently self-serving. Political solutions are almost always self-serving. Politicians are often more concerned about their reelection probabilities than about our national interests.

The problems facing our world today are difficult and complex, just as those encountered before and during the Vietnam War, and for that matter, every other war the U.S. has encountered from the War of Independence through the Cold War until the present time. Abraham Lincoln's words delivered in a speech in 1858 remain appropriate today, "If we could first know where we are and whither we are tending, we could better judge what to do and how to do it." Sir Winston Churchill in a speech at Harrow School in 1941 stated, "Do not let us speak of darker days; let us rather speak of sterner days. These are not dark days; these are great days—the greatest days our country has ever lived; and we must all thank God that we have been allowed, each of us according to our stations to play a part in making these days memorable in the history of our race." Only when the free civilized nations of the world stand firmly allied against international terrorism will the words of Churchill again ring true, and reflect our situation and our future hope.

In presenting this brief history of the 18th Surgical Hospital I trust that the reader will get a cursory glimpse and a better understanding of the sacrifices made by so many as they struggled, and continue to struggle, to forge another link in the chain connecting the security of our Nation's past with its future, thereby providing each of us with the freedoms we enjoy.

My hope is that the material contained in this book will be informative and interesting. I would like to extend to each reader regardless of their personal philosophies, political persuasions, views on military strategy or religious beliefs, the traditional Vietnamese wish for perfect enjoyment, the Five Happinesses: PHUC (Happiness); LOC (Good Fortune); THO (Longevity); KHANG (Joy); and AN (Peace).

—*Jerry W. Martin, M.D.*

PROLOGUE

I concur with Helen Keller, who wrote, "I long to accomplish a great and noble task, but it is my chief duty to accomplish humble tasks as though they were great and noble. The world is moved along, not only by the mighty shoves of its heroes, but also by the aggregate of the tiny pushes of each honest worker." My thoughts regarding this effort parallels those of Harry S. Truman's comments concerning the success of his Presidency: "I never achieved greatness, but I had a great time while I was trying to be great." Readers of this brief history of the 18th Surgical Hospital will never attribute to it the accolades reserved for the "great" and the "noble," but perhaps they will conclude that I gave historiography a small, gentle, almost imperceptible nudge forward.

As I pondered writing this history, my first realization was that the ensuing forty-four years since our year at Pleiku (June 1966-June 1967) have seemingly sped by at an ever-accelerating rate. Some of the members of our hospital staff have already joined "…that innumerable, unending caravan marching toward the bivouac of the dead" (*Reflections At The Wall*). Our experiences during that year "…brought to each of us an indelible realization of our common mortality" (ibid).

We still have unforgettably engraved in our memory those audible and visual expressions of anguish and pain. We recall the fevers and chills that shook and weakened even the strongest. We continue to harbor mental images of charred, wounded and mangled bodies. We fondly recall the numerous examples of healing and near miraculous recoveries. Unfortunately, also in our recollections are memories that cannot be suppressed or forgotten. They creep into our consciousness, sometimes without provocation. On those occasions, we recall faces frozen emotionless and expressionless. We can see those staring, unseeing eyes and those lips permanently silenced and speechless, and as the poet, Karl Shapiro, noted, "…lips that shall no longer taste or kiss or swear…" (*Elegy for a Dead Soldier*), or pray.

Just as the book title, *We Were Soldiers Once—And Young*, reminds us, we, too, were young. Many years ago I wrote in a personal essay: "Youth hurries on without ever realizing it is going anywhere. Only after their yesterdays have melted into their tomorrows do the youth recognize the trick time has played on them. They have been lulled into an unworried, unhurried, carefree encounter with the present, never realizing that the past can only be revisited through reminiscent reflections. For them, like a child sledding down a hill, the future does not seem to be at the bottom of this hill, but rather at the bottom of some hill somewhere in the future. Ah, the masquerade of unrelenting time! If, when we get to the bottom of the hill of life, we could climb back to the top for another ride down, would it be more or less exciting and fun? Would we steer the same or a different course" (*A Morning Walk*)? Youth does not realize that life is as evanescent as the vanishing mist on a crisp, sunny October morning.

In July 1980, Wayne F. Hosking, M.D., and I, along with some of our children, rafted down the Colorado River through the Grand Canyon. In the essay I later compiled from a daily journal in which I recorded not only the sequences of daily experiences, but also my personal thoughts and emotions relating to those events, I noted: "As we shoved off, our state of expectancy and excitement steadily soared until it reached its apogee through the first few rapids. Approaching an unknown rapid for the first time carries with it a degree of apprehension and trepidation closely akin to those feelings one experiences when arriving in a war zone and, for the first time, being struck with the realization that 'war is hell.' I could not help but be impressed during the eight days spent in the canyon, that running the rapids of a river, especially one like the Colorado, is not unlike running the rapids of war, or for that matter, running the rapids of life, as one bounces and glides, churns and cascades through both the turbulence and calm of daily experiences. Thrust into life at birth, man flows along with the stream of time. Man, like the raft, once launched, is never able to move against the current, or against time" (*A River Rendezvous*).

Each of the original ten physicians assigned to the 18th Surgical Hospital (MA) at Fort Gordon, Georgia. were drafted from their private practices or residences and joined the nurses and enlisted men who had volunteered, had been drafted, or had chosen the military as a career. As we began our year's work in the Central Highlands, we sought no military honors, we envisioned no promotions and coveted no individual recognition. We only sought to carry out our duty to our country and responsibly fulfill our Hippocratic mission to treat the sick and wounded using our collective abilities and judgments.

In his address to the Cadets at West Point, General of the Army Douglas MacArthur eloquently espoused and reinforced the creed—Duty, Honor, Country. As physicians and nurses, we felt compelled to include in that creed the word—Profession.

DUTY

Ralph Waldo Emerson (*Voluntaries, III*) noted:

> So nigh is grandeur to our dust,
> So near is God to man,
> When Duty whispers low, *Thou must.*
> The youth replies, *I can.*

General Robert Edward Lee said: "Duty then is the sublimest word in our language. Do your duty in all things. You cannot do more. You should never wish to do less." Thomas Carlyle observed in *Sartor Resartus*: "Do the duty which lies nearest thee, which thou knowest to be a duty! Thy second duty will already have become clearer." Alfred, Lord Tennyson wrote: "The path of duty was the way to glory" (*Ode on the Death of the Duke of Wellington*). John Milton noted: "Real glory springs from the conquest of ourselves." We can each proclaim as did British Admiral Viscount Horatio Nelson: "Thank God, I have done my duty" (Battle of Trafalgar).

We were diligent in our pursuit of excellence, and never derelict in our responsibility to those entrusted to our care. Our personalities meshed compatibly into an unparalleled camaraderie and esprit de corps that resulted in an efficient and well-organized hospital, producing enviable and laudable results. Our noble intentions and our tireless efforts were sometimes not good enough; however, I trust that we earned the honor of having emblazoned on the marquee of our professional lives and inscribed as our personal epitaph—"We did our duty; we did our best."

HONOR

An anonymous writer once penned the truism: "The man that will not venture his all for his honor will be swept away on the first winds of adversity." Even in defeat, Francis I, King of France, proclaimed: "All is lost save honor." (Battle of Pavia, February 24, 1525)

———

> Unblemish'd let me live, or die unknown:
> Oh, grant an honest Fame, or grant me none!
> —*The Temple of Fame*, Alexander Pope

Honor is the achievable ideal which, when followed, makes an individual trustworthy. Honor is involved in everyday life and is the result of our living rather than in our dreaming. Character and honor are indivisible.

> Honor is purchased by the deeds we do:
> …honor is not won
> until some honorable deed be done.
> —*Hero and Leander*, Christopher Marlowe

Honor is not just a word; not even just an ideal or a goal. Honor is a state of being, a way of life to be lived moment by moment. John Greenleaf Whittier concluded: "When faith is lost, when honor dies—the man is dead."

Can we not, along with the others who served with the 18th Surgical Hospital, claim honor from the deeds we did?

COUNTRY

As Americans we should adopt the following as our National Creed:

> I believe in the United States of America as a government of the people, by the people, for the people; whose just powers are derived from the consent of the governed; a democracy in a republic; a sovereign nation of many sovereign states; a perfect union, one and inseparable; established upon those principles of freedom, equality, justice and humanity for which American patriots sacrificed their lives and fortunes. I therefore believe it is my duty to my country to love it, to support its constitution, to obey its laws, to respect its flag, and to defend it against all enemies.
>
> —*The American's Creed*, William Tyler Page

In his inaugural speech, John F. Kennedy said: "Let every nation know, whether it wishes us well or ill, that we shall pay any price, bear any burden, meet any hardship, support any friend, oppose any foe in order to assure the survival and success of liberty."

General Westmoreland testified to a national pride when he proclaimed to the world, "Never before in history has a nation so freely shared the treasures of its hard work; never before has a nation provided others with so much security; never before has a nation so responsibly shouldered the burden of world leadership, or combined both the material and human aspirations of man to such a reality."

Americans should always echo the comments made by U.S. Naval Commander Stephen Decatur in a toast given at Norfolk, Virginia, April 1816: "To our country! In her intercourse with foreign nations may she always be in the right; but our country right or wrong."

General MacArthur's observations during World War II are certainly valid today: "We stand today on a critical moment of history—at a vital crossroad. In one direction is the path of courageous patriots seeking in humility but the opportunity to serve their country, the other that of those selfishly seeking to entrench autocratic power" (*Revitalizing A Nation*).

As our nation continues to search for ways to thwart those "autocratic powers" that would fragment our unity and impose dictatorial regulations upon us, let us pray for bravery and courage when faced with danger and fear. Let us maintain a proud and unbending posture when we are right, yet exhibit a contrite and humble willingness to change when we have been wrong. Let us have the strength to stand firm in the midst of the storm and have sincere compassion toward those unable to withstand similar difficulties. We must be willing to accept any challenge and to prepare ourselves to be equal to any task that confronts us. Emerson wrote: "The reward of a thing well done is to have done it." We must jointly bear the burden, allowing our efforts to join in a spirit of unity with future generations and march on to victory.

PROFESSION

We in medicine have a long and illustrious heritage to uphold and defend. Although traditions, treatments and techniques are in a constant state of change, heritage is unchangeable. The heritage on which we stand today was bequeathed to us by those professional ancestors, who through the centuries, perpetuated and perfected the science and art of medicine. The foundation for modern medicine was securely laid by the Hippocratic school that ultimately broke the shackles of caste, superstition and witchcraft that had held captive the thinking of earlier medicine.

German pathologist Rudolf Virchow (1821-1902) stated: "...the duty of science is not to attack the objects of belief, but to stake out the limits of the knowable and to center consciousness within them." Throughout the centuries, innumerable giants— Galen, Harvey, Laennec, Jenner, Pasteur, von Leewenhoek, Sydenham, Hunter, Walter Reed, Osler, Rush, Oliver W. Holmes, Daniel Drake, Ephram McDowell, Jonas Salk—to name only a few, were dedicated to the task of tearing down the walls of ignorance that surrounded them. Contemporaneous colleagues are pioneers currently dedicated, through their research and discoveries, to similar efforts and will build new monuments for themselves and for medicine. Goethe remarked: "...mankind is always advancing; man always remains the same; science deals with mankind."

Sir William Osler wrote: "A physician may possess the science of Harvey and the art of Sydenham, and yet there may be lacking in him those finer qualities of heart and head which count for so much in life. The physician needs a clear head and a kind heart; his work is arduous and complex, requiring the exercise of the very highest faculties of the mind, while constantly appealing to the emotions and finer feelings" (*Counsels and Ideals from the Writings of William Osler*).

Herophilus (Greek anatomist, circa 300 BC) observed: "When health is absent wisdom cannot reveal itself, art cannot become manifest, strength cannot be exerted, wealth becomes useless, and reason is powerless."

"There is no process which can reckon up the amount of good which the science and art of medicine have conferred upon the human race; there is no moral calculus that can grasp and comprehend the sum of the beneficent operations" (ibid, Osler, chapter on the *Practitioner of Medicine*).

I, too, like Don Quixote (*Man of LaMancha*) and Martin Luther King, Jr., have a dream, but so much more than a dream. I have a conviction that we will always dare to do our duty to our profession and patients alike. I have a conviction that right does make might. I have a conviction that the art of medicine will be perpetually memorialized by the caring way we deal with our patients. I have a conviction that unprecedented monuments will continue to be erected by scientific medicine through research and unbelievable discoveries and cures. God grant to each of us the highest standard of professional ethics and the staunch moral character to always do our professional duty. The duty of medicine, the hallmark of both the art and the science, is succinctly condensed in the often-quoted phrase—To Heal Sometimes, To Relieve Often, To Comfort Always.

Perhaps old physicians, like old soldiers, never die but just fade into oblivion, joining that endless, unbroken chain connecting our Aesculapian ancestors with our Hippocratic descendents. May our colleagues of the future, as well as those who read about our combat experiences, always be able to hear echoing from the cryptic chambers of our forgotten lives, the undaunting, unrelenting, undying refrain—Duty, Honor, Country, Profession.

—*Jerry W. Martin, M.D.*

CHRONOLOGY OF WORLD WAR II
IN THE PACIFIC THEATER

1941

December 7-9
Japanese bomb U.S. military base at Pearl Harbor, Hawaii, also attack the Philippines, Wake Island, Guam, Malaya, Thailand, Shangai (China), and Midway Island (December 7). Both the U.S. and Britain declare war on Japan (December 8), as does China on December 9.

December 15
First Japanese merchant ship sunk by a U.S. submarine.

December 18
Japanese invade Hong Kong (the British surrender on the 25th).

December 23
General Douglas MacArthur begins a withdrawal from Manila, Philippines to Bataan; Japanese take Wake Island.

1942

January 27
First Japanese war ship sunk by a U.S. submarine.

February 1
First U.S. aircraft carrier offensive of the war as Yorktown and Enterprise conduct air raids on Japanese bases in the Gilbert and Marshall Islands.

February 23
First Japanese attack on the U.S. mainland as a submarine shells an oil refinery near Santa Barbara, California.

February 24
USS *Enterprise* attacks Japanese on Wake Island.

February 26
First U.S. carrier, the *Langley*, is sunk by Japanese bombers.

March 18
Gen. MacArthur appointed commander of the Southwest Pacific by President Roosevelt.

March 24
Admiral Chester Nimitz appointed as Commander in Chief of the U.S. Pacific theater.

April 6
First U.S. troops arrive in Australia.

April 9
U.S. forces on Bataan surrender unconditionally to the Japanese.

April 10
Bataan Death March begins as 76,000 Allied POWs, including 12,000 Americans, are forced to walk 60 miles under a blazing sun without food or water toward a new POW camp, resulting in over 5,000 American deaths.

April 18
Surprise U.S. "Doolittle" B-25 air raid from the USS *Hornet* against Tokyo boosts Allied morale.

1943

December 26
Full Allied assault on New Britain as 1st Division Marines invade Cape Gloucester.

1944

February 1-7
U.S. troops capture Kwajalein and Majura Atolls in the Marshall Islands.

February 24
Merrill's Marauders begin a ground campaign in northern Burma.

March 5
Gen. Wingate's groups begin operations behind Japanese lines in Burma.

April 17
Japanese begin their last offensive in China, attacking U.S. air bases in eastern China.

May 27
Allies invade Biak Island, New Guinea.

June 5
The first mission by B-29 Superfortress bombers occurs as 77 planes bomb Japanese railway facilities at Bangkok, Thailand.

June 15
U.S. Marines invade Saipan in the Mariana Islands.

June 15-16
The first bombing raid on Japan since the Doolittle raid of

April 1942, as 47 B-29s based in Bengel, India target the steel works at Yawata.

June 19
The "Marianas Turkey Shoot" occurs as U.S. Carrier-based fighters shoot down 220 Japanese planes, while only 20 American planes are lost.

July 8
Japanese withdraw from Imphal.

July 20
U.S. Marines invade Guam in the Marianas.

July 24
U.S. Marines invade Tinian.

July 27
American troops complete the liberation of Guam.

August 8
American troops complete the capture of the Mariana Islands.

October 11
U.S. air raids against Okinawa.

October 20
U.S. Sixth Army invades Leyte in the Philippines.

October 23-26
Battle of Leyte Gulf results in a decisive U.S. Naval victory.

October 25
The first suicide air (Kamikaze) attacks occur against U.S. warships in Leyte Gulf. By the end of the war, Japan will have sent an estimated 2,257 aircraft.

November 11
Iwo Jima bombarded by the U.S. Navy.

December 15
U.S. troops invade Mindoro in the Philippines.

1945

January 3
General MacArthur is placed in command of all U.S. ground forces and Admiral Nimitz in command of all naval forces in preparation for planned assaults against Iwo Jima, Okinawa and Japan itself.

January 9
U.S. Sixth Army invades Lingayen Gulf on Luzon in the Philippines.

January 28
The Burma Road is reopened.

February 3
U.S. Sixth Army attacks Japanese in Manila.

February 16
U.S. troops recapture Bataan in the Philippines.

February 19
U.S. Marines invade Iwo Jima.

March 2
U.S. airborne troops recapture Corregidor in the Philippines.

April 1
The final amphibious landing of the war occurs as the U.S. Tenth Army invades Okinawa.

April 7
B-29s fly their first fighter-escorted mission against Japan with P-51 Mustangs based on Iwo Jima; U.S. Carrier-based fighters sink the super battleship Yamato and several escort vessels that planned to attack U.S. forces at Okinawa.

April 12
President Roosevelt dies; succeeded by Harry S. Truman.

May 8
Victory Day in Europe.

May 20
Japanese withdrawal from China.

June 9
Japanese Premier Suzuki announces Japan will fight to the very end rather than accept unconditional surrender.

July 5
Liberation of Philippines is declared.

July 10
1,000 bomber raids against Japan begin.

July 14
The first U.S. Naval bombardment of Japanese home islands.

July 29
A Japanese submarine sinks the Cruiser Indianapolis, resulting in the loss of 881 crewmen. The ship sinks before a radio message can be sent out, leaving survivors adrift for two days.

August 6
First atomic bomb dropped on Hiroshima from a B-29 flown by Col. Paul Tibbets.

August 9
Second atomic bomb is dropped on Nagasaki from a B-29 flown by Maj. Charles Sweeney.

August 14
Japanese accept unconditional surrender.

August 30
The British reoccupy Hong Kong.

September 2
Formal Japanese surrender ceremony on board the Missouri in Tokyo Bay, as 1,000 carrier-based planes fly overhead; President Truman declares VJ Day.

October 24
United Nations is born.

HISTORY OF THE 18TH (PORTABLE) (SURGICAL) HOSPITAL (PROVISIONAL) DURING WORLD WAR II

The 18th Surgical Hospital was constituted in the Regular Army on Friday, December 21, 1928, as the 18th Surgical Hospital. I was unable to find a copy of the order, who gave the order creating the hospital, or the reasons necessitating the creation of the hospital during peace time.

When the war in Europe erupted, President Franklin D. Roosevelt proclaimed a state of National Emergency in September 1939, and in August 1940 Congress passed the legislation necessary to order National Guard units into active Federal service during peacetime. This initial legislative action stated that the National Guard troops could not be required to serve outside the Western Hemisphere or to serve for more than twelve months. One year later on August 12, 1941, Congress narrowly passed legislation allowing the Federal service of the National Guard to be extended from twelve to eighteen months, and also permitted the National Guard to serve outside the Western Hemisphere.

All of the existing National Guard divisions, plus countless smaller non-divisional units, were called up during the ensuing months, and the 32nd Infantry Division was among the first. The National Guard of the United States was activated in twenty increments between September 16, 1940, and June 23, 1941. The 32nd Infantry Division (Red Arrow Division) was a part of the second increment. (The 32nd Division had distinguished itself in World War I as the first division to pierce the German Army's Hindenburg Line, and the French gave it the sobriquet, "Les Terribles." The Division's symbol is a red arrow piercing a line. The World War I Division Commander, General William Haan, stated proudly, "I chose the Barred-Arrow as the Division symbol because we pierced every line the Boche [Germans] put before us.") On October 15, 1940, the National Guard units from Michigan and Wisconsin were called to active duty and together formed the 32nd Infantry Division. It was assigned to Camp Beauregard, Louisiana (near Alexandria), and in February 1941 was moved to Camp Livingston, Louisiana (about ten miles from Alexandria). In October 1941 the division organized the 128th Regimental Combat Team for maneuvers in

November. This combat team consisted of units from the 126th, 127th and 128th Infantry Regiments, 120th Artillery, 107th Engineers and the 107th Medical Regiment (the 18th Portable Hospital [Provisional] was later under this command). In January and February 1942, the 32nd Infantry Division, along with the Engineer, Medical and Quartermaster Regiments, reorganized into Battalions. When the reorganization was complete the 32nd Infantry Division consisted of the following units:

Division Headquarters and Headquarters Company
Military Police Company
126th Infantry Regiment
127th Infantry Regiment
128th Infantry Regiment
Division Artillery Headquarters and Headquarters Battery
120th Field Artillery Battalion
121st Field Artillery Battalion
126th Field Artillery Battalion
129th Field Artillery Battalion
107th Engineer Battalion (Combat)
107th Medical Battalion
107th Quartermaster Battalion
32nd Signal Company
32nd Cavalry Reconnaissance Troop
632nd Tank Destroyer Battalion

As the U.S. Army organized and professionalized, the Army Medical Department also began to plan and then mobilize for war. The first medical build-up was essentially based on expanding medical facilities, creating new hospitals and revising medical contingency plans.

The U.S. Medical Department faced immense obstacles throughout the war in the Pacific. Their supply lines were tenuous; environmental conditions almost intolerable; malaria was epidemic; logistical difficulties were nearly overwhelming; diseases took their toll; and medical support often broke down. Litter and amphibious medical evacuations had to be constantly revised.

Portable Surgical Hospitals were developed in Australia and later adapted to provide skilled surgical care in jungle fighting beginning in the Papuan Campaign. These "special" medical units were later attached to Task Forces for providing early frontline surgical care in amphibious operations. This kind of hospital was unique to the Pacific Theater.

Every combat Theater of World War II had its unique medical history, but nowhere did disease pose a greater threat to the American G.I., and to military operations, than in the bitter war against Japan. The extreme environments including rain forests, dense jungles, volcanic islands, steep mountain ranges and palm-fringed atolls resulted in medical consequences involving "jungle rot," "trench foot," malaria, dengue, scrub typhus, "swimmers itch" and other tropical diseases.

On March 24, 1942, the Combined Chiefs of Staff assigned the U.S. Commanders for the conduct of the war in the Pacific. The region was divided into separate Commands. On April 18, 1942, Lt. General Douglas MacArthur became Supreme Commander of the Southwest Pacific Area (SWPA) covering the Philippines, Australia, the Netherlands (Dutch) East Indies and New Guinea. On May 8, 1942, Admiral Chester W. Nimitz was named Commander Pacific Ocean Areas (CINCPAC), which comprised a large region stretching from the Bering Straits to Antarctica. The Command was further subdivided into three main sectors: the North Pacific Area (i.e. Aleutians), the Central Pacific Area (i.e. Hawaiian, Mariana, Palou, Caroline and Marshall Islands) and the South Pacific Area (i.e. Solomon and Gilbert Islands, Australia, the Philippines, the Bismarck Archipelago and New Guinea).

The war against Japan was fought over an immense area that covered roughly one-third of the earth's surface. After the attack against Pearl Harbor on Sunday, December 7, 1941, and the fall of the Philippines on Thursday, April 9, 1942 (Bataan fell to the Japanese followed by the infamous "death march" that resulted in thousands of G.I. deaths), Australia emerged as an Allied base and played a role in the Pacific War like that of Great Britain in the European War.

On Wednesday, March 25, 1942, the 32nd Infantry Division was notified that it was being sent to Australia to help halt the Japanese advances in the South Pacific. The Division boarded troop trains and headed for San Francisco. On Wednesday, April 22, 1942, the 32nd Infantry Division sailed from San Francisco (Fort Mason) on converted Matson Line cruise ships escorted by the cruiser USS *Indianapolis* bound for Australia and arrived three weeks later (8500 miles) at Adelaide, South Australia on Thursday, May 14, 1942. (The USS *Indianapolis* later carried the atomic bombs and afterwards was sunk by a Japanese torpedo.) There they were sent to Camp Woodside and Camp Sandy Creek, and later in July 1942 the Division was relocated to Camp Tamborine (renamed Camp Cable in honor of Gerald O. Cable, the first individual of the 32nd Division killed in New Guinea) near Brisbane on Australia's east coast. The divisional campaign responsibilities later involved New Guinea (Papuan Campaign), Southern Philippines (Leyte Campaign) and Luzon (Corregidor Campaign). In Australia, the 32nd Division, the U.S. 41st Division, along with the Australian 6th and 7th Divisions, became a part of I Corps under the U.S. 6th Army. The 18th Surgical Hospital was activated and organized in the U.S. Army in Australia on Monday, September 14, 1942, and was designated the 18th Portable Hospital (Provisional).

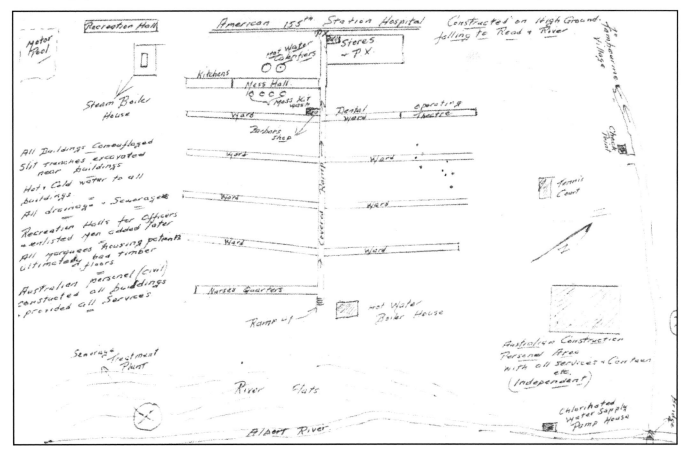

An Australian station hospital during World War II.

NEW GUINEA:

PAPUAN—BUNA CAMPAIGN

SEPTEMBER 26, 1942-FEBRUARY 28, 1943

The island of New Guinea was partitioned in 1884 by three Western powers. The Dutch claimed the western half (it passed to Indonesia in 1969), and the Germans and the British divided the eastern half. The southern section of the eastern half became a British Protectorate (British New Guinea Territory) and passed to Australia as the Territory of Papua (formerly Irian Jaya) in 1906. The northern section formed German New Guinea (Kaiser-Wilhelmsland). In World War I it was occupied by Australian forces, and in 1920 the League of Nations mandated it to Australia.

Sailing from the Malay Peninsula, the first European to encounter New Guinea was Jorge de Meneses, a Portuguese governor from the Spice Islands, who landed there during a monsoon storm in 1526 and christened it "Ilhas dos Papuas" from a Malay term "orang papuwah" meaning "fuzzy- haired man." Then in 1545, Ynigo Ortiz de Retes sailed by the island when returning from Moluccas to Mexico and named it Neuva Guinea.

The first combat exposure for the 18th Portable Hospital (Provisional) was in New Guinea. The history of the 18th Portable Hospital (Provisional) during World War II is inextricably enmeshed and intertwined with the history of the 32nd Division, especially the 128th and the 126th Infantry Combat Teams.

On September 15, 1942, General Douglas MacArthur issued orders alerting one combat team of the 32nd Division to prepare for action. The 126th Infantry Combat Team was alerted; however, they were involved in loading boats so the 128th Infantry Combat Team mobilized, assembled at Brisbane's Amberly Field and at Townsville's Archer Field and then were flown, along with the 126th Infantry Combat Team's 2nd Battalion, to Port Moresby (Papuan Capitol) on the Papuan Peninsula of New Guinea. The 126th Infantry Combat Team's 1st and 3rd Battalions followed in boats immediately; the entire transfer of both units was accomplished between September 18 and October 1, 1942.

The 128th Infantry Combat Team, with the 126th Infantry Combat Team's 2nd Battalion were transported by air to Wanigela on October 14, 1942, and the 126th Infantry Combat Team (two battalions) flew to Pongani and began hiking over the Owen Stanley Mountain Range following the trail of their own 2nd Battalion (*Ghost Mountain Boys*) that had crossed ahead of them through "…some of the harshest terrain ever faced by land armies in the history of the war." The U.S. 32nd Division and the Australian 7th Division constituted the main Allied force while the Imperial 17th Army Division was the Japanese main force.

The 2nd Battalion Aid Station section, a collecting platoon of Company A, 107th Medical Battalion, and the 19th Portable Hospital comprised the medical units on the trek over the mountains. The medical problems encountered, especially those of evacuation and supply, were almost insurmountable. The medical service for the 2nd and 3rd Battalions was furnished by two platoons of Company C, 107th Medical Battalion and their own aid stations. The 1st Battalion, 128th Infantry Combat Team, was accompanied by the 14th and the 22nd Portable Hospitals as they proceeded up the coast. On November 24, 1942, the 18th Portable Hospital (Provisional) joined the 128th Infantry Combat Team at Hariko and set up as an evacuation hospital. The medical evacuation problem settled down to an adaptation of a "funnel" chain of evacuation, with the 2nd Platoon, 2nd Field Hospital acting as the "neck" of the funnel in close proximity to the air strips at Dobadura, from which the sick and wounded were evacuated by air to the hospitals in the vicinity of Port Moresby.

The portable hospitals consisted of four medical officers and 25 enlisted men. Each hospital could be used as a surgical hospital, a treatment hospital or an evacuation hospital along the route of evacuation. The 18th Portable Hospital (Provisional), whose parent unit was the 174th Station Hospital, was first assigned to the 2nd Battalion, 128th Infantry Combat Team and then later assigned to the 1st Battalion, 126th Infantry Combat Team on January 7, 1943. From November 24 to December 14, 1942, the 18th Portable Hospital (Provisional) was at Hariko in conjunction with the 22nd Portable Hospital (the patients were credited to the 22nd Portable Hospital), and then from December 15, 1942, to January 20, 1943, was located at Sinemi Plantation. (Siremi, was mistakenly called "Sinemi" in military history accounts of the battle) The 18th Portable Hospital (Provisional) was set up at the main junction of two trails and received all patients from the Warren Front and also patients from the 23rd Portable Hospital, which was attached to the 1st Battalion, 126th Infantry Combat Team and located on the Sinemi-Buna Trail. At this site they treated 572 sick (mostly malaria), 161 battle wounds and 51 other injuries for a total of 784 U.S.; and 62 sick, 292 battle wounds and 5 other injuries for a total of 359 Australian; resulting in a total of 1,143 patients.

The medical service organized for each of the three Regimental Task Forces of the 32nd Division was essentially the same. It consisted of the Regimental Medical Detachment, three portable surgical hospitals, a collecting company and a platoon of the clearing company of the Division Medical Battalion. The medical detachment consisted of three battalion aid stations and a regimental headquarters medical section. The portable hospitals were organized out of a station or general hospital and attached to the division, one to each infantry battalion. The collecting company was broken down into three platoons of equal size, each one attached to an infantry battalion.

Medical supplies from the rear during the campaign were usually adequate and timely, although they occasionally were in critically short supply. The 126th Infantry Combat Team left the Medical Administrative Officer of the collecting company attached to the combat team in Port Moresby to forward medical supplies to the battalion aid stations and the 18th Portable Hospital (Provisional). The Medical Administrative Officer with the 128th Infantry Combat Team Collecting Company received supplies

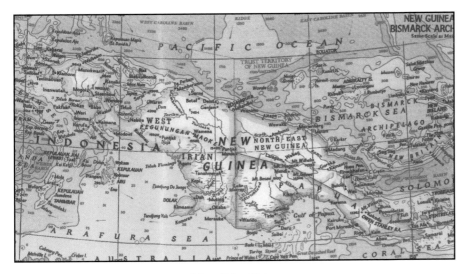

Map of New Guinea

by boat from Milne Bay. As the battle progressed, most of the medical supplies were flown from Port Moresby, so the Medical Administrative Officer left there with two men, became the division medical supply source. The Headquarters Detachment, Medical Battalion, had been left in Australia and never arrived in New Guinea. Requisitions were radioed from the front to the rear each night. The supplies were collected and packed usually between 2 and 5 a.m. and taken to the airport, to accompany ammunitions and rations on the day's supply flight schedules. The hospitals in the Port Moresby area cooperated, making and sterilizing dressings, operating sets, sponges, even occasionally depleting their own meager supplies, to guarantee that these items reached the front where they were most needed. All these supplies were dropped by parachute, landed by planes and/or boats or were carried by natives.

Patients were evacuated via returning supply boats, native outrigger canoes, or barges down the coast. The sick and wounded were taken by canoe from the beaches to boats off shore about one-half mile. During daylight hours, enemy bombing and strafing was a constant threat; therefore, almost all evacuations were accomplished during hours of darkness. The constant strafing of trail and ocean traffic became so hazardous that the engineers hacked a road through to Hariko from Sinemi Plantation, bypassing the Japanese positions on the Buna airstrips. From that time on, native bearers carried casualties from the front. The natives preferred to build their own litters, made from balsam wood and split bamboo. These litters were very comfortable and much cooler than our own, but were somewhat heavier. Eight natives were assigned to one litter patient, two teams of four which relieved each other. They were sure-footed, considerate of the patient and traveled rapidly.

In most cases portable hospitals were not very portable after their first setup. A tendency to acquire tentage, mess equipment and a large amount of supplies, as well as casualties among personnel, made them immobile, unless moved by motor transport or native carriers. The tentage issued could not be used under blackout conditions without improvisations. Too many items of medical supply were issued to the portable hospitals that were unnecessary, so they simply left them at their point of embarkation or abandoned them along the way. Sulfa drugs (later, penicillin), narcotics and Atabrine (anti-malarial drug, quinaerine) were constantly in high demand.

Portable hospitals were not issued any equipment or administrative personnel for official record keeping. Fortunately, they kept a log listing each admission's name, rank, serial number and diagnosis for their own information; otherwise it would have been impossible to later develop medical records.

The primary goal of these medical units was to save lives and to stabilize the patients in as good a condition as possible for evacuation. The war wounds were cleaned and hemorrhage controlled. Debridement of the wounds was done under general anesthesia. The anesthesia of choice was intravenous Pentothal Sodium since it provided prompt and adequate anesthesia with only rare instances of side effects (e.g. vomiting during recovery, etc.). Open mask drop ether was used in abdominal surgical cases. After exploration of the peritoneal cavity and repair of the injury, the abdomen was closed primarily in the usual manner. Sucking chest wounds were obviously also closed after debridement of the wound. The greatest percentage of wounds were of the extremities. These wounds were left open after debridement, packed with sulfanilamide powder, and covered with a sterile Vaseline gauze dressing and an outer bandage.

Primary closure was done only on scalp wounds after excisional debridement was accomplished, usually with local anesthesia. In cases of compound fractures, bone fragments were removed, the wound radically debrided, sulfa sprinkled into the wound, sterile Vaseline gauze dressing applied and the extremity immobilized in plaster molds. Splints and circular casts were not applied. When indicated, guillotine amputation was recommended while saving as much skin as possible. Amputations were left open, covered with sulfanilamide and Vaseline gauze and a plaster shell for protection. Wounds left open were later closed, when appropriate, as soon as possible after evacuation.

Blood plasma was used extensively, as was 5% and 10% glucose in normal saline. Whole blood was usually not available and rarely used.

The medical cases were in order of prevalence: Malaria, dehydration-exhaustion, gastroenteritis, dengue fever, acute upper respiratory infections and typhus fever. There were very rare cases of leishmaniasis, elephantiasis, yaws, yellow fever, typhoid, cholera and plague. The statistics were the same for both U.S. and Australian troops.

Medical units moved and fought with the infantry. They labored unceasingly, even performing major surgery while being bombed, strafed, machine gunned, sniped, killed and wounded. The Buna Campaign was the first Allied Ground Force victory in the Pacific and was purchased at a terrible price.

Every American unit that followed the 32nd Division into the islands and jungles of the Pacific would benefit from the lessons learned from their difficult experience. About 13,000 Japanese troops perished during the fighting, but Allied casualties were also heavy; 8,500 men fell in battle (5,698 of them Australians) and 27,000 cases of malaria were reported (in the battle for Buna and Sanananda, nearly 80% of the troops developed malaria). Besides devastating the Australian 7th Infantry Division and the U.S. 32nd Infantry Division, the campaign had severely damaged the Australian 5th Infantry Division and the U.S. 41st Infantry Division. The 32nd Infantry Division alone suffered 8,000 malaria cases in addition to heavy combat casualties. A total of 1,161 medical personnel, assigned or attached to the 32nd Division, were at one time or another furnishing medical services in the Buna Area.

From September 1942 to February 1943 two medical officers died (one of a myocardial infarction and one of typhus fever—no medical officer died as a result of combat). Twenty-nine medical corpsmen were killed in action and four later died of sickness or wounds received in action, one was missing in action, and forty-five were wounded in action. Thirty-six officers and 535 enlisted medical personnel were evacuated because of sickness or injuries.

The 32nd Division's casualties were higher than at Guadalcanal. On Guadalcanal 1,100 troops were killed, and 4,350 wounded. The loss in New Guinea's combined Buna-Sanananda-Gona Campaign was 3,300 killed, and 5,500 wounded. William Manchester noted in his book, *American Caesar*, "If the difference in the size of attacking forces is taken into account, the loss of life on Papua (New Guinea) had been three times as great as Guadalcanal's." Maj. Gen. Robert L. Eichelberger (I Corps Commander) wrote in his book, *Our Jungle Road to Tokyo*, "Buna was …bought at a substantial price in death, wounds, disease, despair, and human suffering. No one who fought there, however hard he tries, will ever forget it. Fatalities closely approach, percentage-wise, the

heaviest losses in our own Civil War battles." Historian Stanley Falk agreed, "…the Papuan Campaign was one of the costliest Allied victories of the Pacific War in terms of casualties per troops committed."

> I laid him down by the bend in the stream;
> And erected a cross at his head.
> His funeral song was a kockatoo's
> [cockatoo's] scream,
> As if they knew my buddy was dead…
>
> I've evened the score, yes, a dozen times
> o'er,
> But no matter the distance between,
> My mind wanders yet and I'll never forget,
> His grave by the bend in the stream.

—Bob Hartman, (Buna veteran, 32nd Infantry Division)

After the Papuan Campaign ended the 32nd Division and its attached units (including the 18th Portable Hospital [Provisional]) were sent back to Australia for six months to rest and to reconstitute and replenish the Division before their next combat operation. In Australia they were stationed at Camp Cable about 30 miles from Brisbane. The troops were in bad shape both physically and emotionally, and desperately needed a period of rest, relaxation and rehabilitation. All elements of the Division needed to be replenished, reorganized, resupplied and retrained before they could become combat ready again. The return to Australia was not completed until early April 1943 since there were only a limited number of planes to fly the troops back over the Owen Stanley Mountains to Port Moresby and also only a limited number of ships available to transport them to Australia.

Back in Australia under the Command of the U.S. 6th Army and I Corps, reorganization became a part of the restructuring and replenishing process. On April 1, 1943, the hospital's name was changed to the 18th Portable Surgical Hospital (Provisional). Three months later on July 1, 1943, the name was again changed to the 18th Portable Surgical Hospital. The Hospital's name remained unchanged throughout the duration of World War II.

After a period of rest, the 32nd Division began a difficult training period to fit new replacements into its ranks and pass on to them the hard won knowledge and experience of jungle fighting.

While in Australia the following order was received. General Orders Number 21, 6 May 1943, cited the Papuan Forces, United States Army, Southwest Pacific

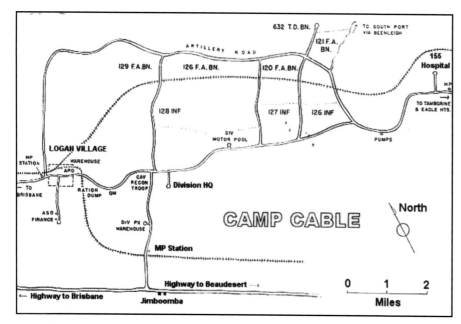

The 155th Station Hospital (U.S.) was located at Camp Cable. As many as 20,000 men were based at Camp Cable. The Camp was apparently evacuated during the Battle of the Coral Sea.

Area, for outstanding performance of duty in action during the period 23 July 1942, to 23 January 1943:

> When a bold and aggressive enemy invaded Papua in strength, the combined action of ground and air units, in association with Allied units, checked the hostile advance, drove the enemy back to the seacoast and in a series of actions against a highly organized defensive zone, utterly destroyed him. Ground combat forces, operating over roadless jungle-covered mountains and swamps, demonstrated their courage and resourcefulness in closing with an enemy who took every advantage of the nearly impassable terrain. Air forces, by repeatedly attacking the enemy ground forces and installations, by destroying his convoys attempting reinforcement and supply, and by transporting ground forces and supplies to areas for which land routes were non-existent and sea routes slow and hazardous, made possible the success of the ground operations. Service units, operating far forward of their normal positions and at times in advance of ground combat elements, built landing fields in the jungle, established and operated supply points, and provided for the hospitalization and evacuation of the wounded and sick. The courage, spirit, and devotion to duty of all elements of the command made possible the complete victory attained.

> Under the provisions of this order, the following units of the 32nd Infantry Division became entitled to the Distinguished Unit Citation (Army) with Streamer embroidered PAPUA (now called the Presidential Unit Citation): Headquarters and Headquarters Company, 32nd Infantry Division; 32nd Ordinance Detachment; 32nd Quartermaster Company; 32nd Reconnaissance Troop; 32nd Signal Company; 107th Medical Battalion (18th Portable Surgical Hospital); 126th Infantry Regiment; 127th Infantry Regiment; 128th Infantry Regiment; Battery A, 129th Field Artillery Battalion.

NEW GUINEA: SAIDOR CAMPAIGN
OCTOBER 1943-FEBRUARY 1944

By October 1943 the 32nd Division had been restored to combat status and preparations began for deployment back to New Guinea. Between October 16-30, 1943, the return of the entire Division to New Guinea was completed, a portion landing at Milne Bay on October 20 and the other portion on Goodenough Island (the 126th Infantry Battalion as well as the 18th Portable Surgical Hospital), which later on December 20 moved to join the other segments of the division. There they continued to train, prepare and strengthen until orders were received to resume combat operations.

New Guinea was essential to the U.S. and Allied forces across the Central Pacific and to the liberation of the Philippines from Japanese occupation. Although the U.S. controlled the air base at Port Moresby, the surrounding area was not considered to be completely secure. There were still many Japanese troops in the central and northern portions of New Guinea. At this time, Japan still held the preponderance of air, naval and ground strength in the Southwest Pacific and retained the strategic initiative in New Guinea. With these advantages, Allied intelligence assumed that the Japanese planned to strike again because failure to control the port and the air base at Port Moresby required them to divert much needed ships, planes and men who might otherwise have reinforced their slowly crumbling forces throughout the Central Pacific Theatre.

New Guinea is the second largest island in the world. From the northern coastline, the island extends nearly 1,600 miles from 12 degrees south latitude to just south of the equator. A major mountain chain cuts across the island's center from the eastern end of New Guinea to Geelvink Bay on the west, which made it nearly impossible for the movement of large units through the jungle. On the leeward side of the mountains, around the Port Moresby area, it is wet from January to April, but otherwise dry. On the windward side, the scene of most of the ground fighting during 1942-1945, rainfall runs as high as 300 inches per year with as much as eight or ten inches falling in a day. One veteran of the 32nd Division noted, "It rains daily for nine months and then the monsoon starts."

On December 17, 1943, the U.S. 6th Army was tasked with the mission to capture Saidor. The purpose was to strengthen the Australian 9th Division at Finschhafen. The American mission was to block the Japanese retreat from Finschhafen and trap the entire Japanese division at Sio. The task of establishing this blocking position near Saidor was assigned to the 32nd Division.

While on the island there was an outbreak of scrub typhus. The rickettsial disease was carried by fleas found on rats that lived in the kunai grass that grew in large meadows. Hundreds of GI's were infected and it was about 95% fatal. When they died or were evacuated, their clothing was burned.

On December 22, 1943, the Michaelmas Task Force was organized for the mission of seizing the airfield at Saidor (approximately 200 air miles west of Buna on the coast) and securing the surrounding area. The 32nd Division provided the majority of the units that made up the Task Force. The main combat power for this Task Force was the 126th Infantry Regiment (18th Portable Surgical Hospital). The scheduled D-Day for the Task Force was January 2, 1944. The main elements of the force embarked from Goodenough Island on January 1, 1944, in nine destroyer-transports, several LCIs (landing craft, infantry) and two LSTs (landing ship, tank) that began organizing during the last days of December 1943. Nine destroyers furnished the escort and gunfire support. The 126th Regiment, 3rd Battalion landed on Red (north) Beach, the 2nd Battalion at White (center) and Blue (south) Beaches. The 1st Battalion then came in on White Beach, passed through the 2nd Battalion and proceeded west to seize Saidor Village and the nearby airstrip.

The composition of the Michaelmas Task Force was as follows:

126th Infantry Regiment

120th Artillery Battalion

121st Field Artillery Battalion

Company A, 114th Engineer Battalion

Company C and 1st Platoon of Company B, 632nd Tank Destroyer Battalion

Company A and a Platoon of Company D, 107th Medical Battalion

Detachment of 32nd Quartermaster Company

Detachment of 732nd Ordinance Company

Detachment of Military Police Platoon, 32nd Infantry Division

Detachment of 32nd Signal Company

18th Portable Surgical Hospital

5th Portable Surgical Hospital

16th Signal Operations Battalion

191st Field Artillery Group, Headquarters and Headquarters Battery

Headquarters and Headquarters Battery, and Batteries A and D, 743rd Coast

Artillery Battalion

Batteries B and D, 209th Coast Artillery Battalion (Automatic Weapons)

Battery A, less one platoon, 236th Antiaircraft Artillery Searchlight Battalion

23rd Field Hospital

One section of Company C, 543rd Quartermaster Service Battalion

Shore Battalion, 542nd Engineer Boat and Shore Regiment

One Boat Company, 542nd Engineer Boat and Shore Regiment

One section of 2nd Platoon, 601st Graves Registration Company

670th Clearing Platoon

Company C (collecting), 135th Medical Regiment

Survey Detachment of 8th Engineer Squadron

21st Ordinance Company, plus attachments

Detachment of Company A, 60th Signal Battalion

863rd Engineer Aviation Battalion

One platoon of 189th Gasoline Supply Company

3rd Platoon of 453rd Engineer Depot Company

5th Malaria Survey Unit

15th Malaria Control Unit

27th Medical Supply Platoon (Aviation)

The combined strength of the units that comprised the Michaelmas Task Force consisted of approximately 450 officers and 8,500 enlisted men.

By late February 1944 the Michaelmas Task Force made contact with the Australian 5th Division that was advancing northwest along the coast. This link-up near Saidor concluded the Michaelmas Operation.

In early March 1944 the 2nd Brigade, 126th Infantry Regiment was selected as the principal combat team to make a landing at Yalau Plantation on the coast about 35 miles west of Saidor in order to intercept enemy stragglers from the 18th Imperial Japanese Army trying to bypass the Saidor area and escape to the west. On April 14, 1944, the force made contact with Australian units near Bogadjim, about 30 miles west of Yalau Plantation. The whole area was now firmly in Allied control.

NEW GUINEA CAMPAIGN: AITAPE AND DRINIUMOR RIVER APRIL 1944-AUGUST 1944

General MacArthur's next objective in preparation for the Philippine invasion was Hollandia, Netherlands (Dutch) New Guinea, situated 450 miles west of Saidor. This was an important Japanese air and supply base. The 32nd Division's 126th Regimental Combat Team was assigned this task, while the 127th and 128th Regimental Combat Teams remained in the Saidor

Green Hell in New Guinea: Allied forces led by General Blamey and General Eichelberger (below left, right) by the end of 1942 won a gruelling victory in Papua after the advancement over the infamous Kokoda Track (above).

area. The Japanese had occupied the Aitape area since December, 1942. Their primary force centered around the airbase near Tadji Plantation about eight miles east-southeast of Aitape. The initial U.S. invading force was the 163rd Infantry Division that landed on the beach on April 22, 1944, followed by the 127th that landed on April 23rd at Blue Beach (the main beach in the Aitape area). By June 10, 1944, the entire 32nd Division was in place, defending the airbase at Aitape with the 126th on the west, the 128th in the center and the 127th on the east. The 1st Battalion of the 126th Infantry Combat Team (which included the 18th Portable Surgical Hospital) was positioned on the Driniumor River, with the 3rd Battalion of the 128th Infantry Combat Team providing the main defense of the airfield, while the other units swept through the region cleaning out pockets of enemy resistance.

Throughout July and August 1944 nearly 10,000 Japanese were killed. Almost 3,000 Americans fell (440 killed) along the Driniumor River and the Tadji airfield. By August 25, 1944, the 43rd Infantry Division had relieved the 32nd Division, allowing it to return to Blue Beach to prepare for relocation elsewhere. The 32nd Division's participation in the New Guinea operations was at an end. In terms of American casualties, it was the most costly campaign since Buna. "Above all, New Guinea was the story of the courage of the GI who could always be counted on to move forward against a determined foe. It was the ordinary American soldier who endured the worst deprivations that the debilitating New Guinea climate and terrain could offer. It was the lowly GI who was the brain, the muscle, and the heart and soul of the great army that came of age in the Southwest Pacific Area in 1943 and 1944. In one tough fight after another, he never lost a battle to the Japanese. Those accomplishments and sacrifices are forever his and deserve to be remembered by all" (*New Guinea-The U.S. Army Campaigns of World War II*, Edward J. Drea).

NEW GUINEA CAMPAIGN: BIAK

AUGUST 1944-OCTOBER 1944

The island of Biak is 45 miles long and 23 miles wide and lies off Geelvink Bay near the western end of New Guinea. The Japanese had three airstrips on Biak large enough to support heavy bombers. The seizure of the island was important for the complete Allied dominance of all New Guinea, and also necessary to support operations against the Philippines and Borneo.

Apparently the 18th Portable Surgical Hospital remained at Aitape with the 32nd Division. The 121st Field Artillery Battalion of the 32nd Division was attached to the 41st Infantry Division for the Biak invasion. The Americans gained complete control of the island by late July. On September 11 the 121st Field Battalion was reequipped and resupplied. The battalion reverted to the 32nd Division on October 2 but it remained on Biak until November 13 when it sailed for Hollandia. On December 6, in company with some rear echelon elements of the 32nd Division, it sailed for Leyte. It put ashore on December 14 and was back with the main division by December 16. The main body of the 32nd Division, including the 18th Portable Surgical Hospital, had landed on the eastern beaches of Leyte on November 14, 1944.

MOROTAI CAMPAIGN

SEPTEMBER 1944-OCTOBER 1944

In the late autumn of 1944, with the New Guinea Campaign nearly complete, preparation began for the next phase of the war in the southwest Pacific, the liberation of the Philippines. The initial plan called for the invasion of Mindanao, about 650 miles north of New Guinea. For a large-scale invasion of the Philippines it was necessary to establish air and naval support bases about half way between existing Allied bases in New Guinea and the Philippines. Halmahera Island was the best choice since there were several operational airfields, but they were strongly defended by about 37,000 Japanese troops. Morotai, the second choice, is an oval island roughly 40 miles long and 25 miles wide and did not have significant existing facilities but was only weakly defended by the enemy.

The invasion assault force, named Tradewind Task Force, was comprised of the 31st "Dixie" Infantry Division plus the 126th Regimental Combat Team of the 32nd Division. The 126th Regimental Combat Team was assigned as the task force reserve and consisted of the 126th Infantry Regiment, 120th Field Artillery Battalion, plus detachment from the 32nd Division's engineer, quartermaster, ordinance, signal, military police and medical (107th Medical Battalion and the 18th Portable Surgical Hospital) units.

The 126th Regimental Combat Team boarded ships at Aitape on September 11, 1944, and arrived off Morotai on September 15 and went ashore on September 16. The 31st Division landed unopposed at Red Beach near Pitoe Airstrip. The 126th Regimental Combat team was tasked with establishing outposts and observation posts along the shoreline.

LEYTE CAMPAIGN

OCTOBER 20, 1944-DECEMBER 22, 1944

With the successful capture of Morotai, General MacArthur, Admiral Hulsey, Admiral Nimitz and the Joint Chiefs of Staff (who were attending the Octagon Conference in Quebec) decided to move directly against Leyte.

The main purpose of the Leyte Campaign was to establish an air and logistical base in order to support operations to nullify Japanese strength in Luzon.

"American Forces had fought their way across the Pacific on two lines of attack to reach a point 300 miles southeast of Mindanao, the southernmost island in the Philippines. In the central Pacific, forces under Admiral Chester W. Nimitz, commanding the Pacific Fleet and Pacific Ocean areas, had island-hopped through the Gilberts, the Marshalls and the Carolines. More than 1,000 miles to the south, Allied forces under General Douglas MacArthur, commanding the Southwest Pacific area, had blocked the Japanese thrust toward Australia, and then recaptured the Solomans and New Guinea and many of its outlying islands, isolating the huge Japanese base at Rabaul, New Guinea.

"The victories brought American forces to the inner defensive line of the Japanese, and in the summer of 1944 they pushed through that barrier to take the Marianas, Palaus and Morotai. With the construction of airfields in the Marianas, U.S. Army Air Forces were within striking distance of the Japanese home islands for the first time during the war. Yet, despite an unbroken series of defeats during two years of fighting, the Japanese showed no inclination to end the war. As American forces closed on Japan they thus faced the most formidable outposts of the Japanese Empire: the Philippines, Formosa and Okinawa" (U.S. Army Center of Military History, Charles R. Anderson).

A strong American beachhead in the Philippines would jeopardize Japan's internal communications within the archipelago, the location of the largest concentration of Japanese ground strength outside the home islands and China. Therefore, on September 8, 1944, the Joint Chiefs of Staff directed MacArthur and Nimitz to take Leyte and the Surigao Straits beginning December 20; however, after the quick capture of Morotai the invasion date was moved up two months.

The island of Leyte is a part of the Visayan Islands in the central Philippines, between the Philippines' largest islands, Luzon to the north and Mindanao to the south. Leyte extends about 115 miles from north to south and varies from 15 to 45 miles in width, the eighth largest of the Philippine Islands. A mountain range reaching 4,000 feet in elevation crosses the island from northwest to southeast and separates the Ormoc Valley to the west from Leyte Valley to the east. Most of the airfields, key roads and cities were located in the Leyte Valley. The 6th Army estimated Japanese strength to be about 21,000-22,000 troops: about half were the Japanese 16th Division, and the remainder were service and support troops.

The attack was October 20, 1944. All but one division were previous veterans against the Japanese: the 1st Cavalry Division in the Admiralty Islands, the 7th Infantry Division at Attu and Kwagalein, the 24th Infantry Division at Hollandia, the 32nd Infantry Division at Buna-Sanananda and Aitape, and the 77th Infantry Division at Guam; only the 96th Infantry Division had not yet faced the Japanese.

On October 20, the 6th Army forces (minus the 32nd and 77th Divisions) landed. Within an hour of landing, units in most sectors had secured beachheads deep enough to receive heavy vehicles and equipment and large quantities of supplies. Three and one half hours later General MacArthur made his dramatic entrance where he waded ashore and announced to the Philippine people that their liberation was near: "People of the Philippines, I have returned! By the grace of Almighty God our forces stand again on Philippine soil."

The 32nd Infantry Division was held at Hollandia and the 77th Infantry Division at Guam until the transports for the assault forces could be freed to pick them up. The 32nd Division (with the 18th Portable Surgical Hospital) landed on the eastern beaches of Leyte on November 14, 1944. On November 16 the 32nd Division began relieving the 24th Division at Breakneck Ridge in the vicinity of Hill 1525, about two miles east southeast of Lymon. All three Infantry Regiments (126th, 127th and 128th) of the 32nd Division were involved.

On December 22 General Gill issued General Orders 104, Headquarters, 32nd Infantry Division:

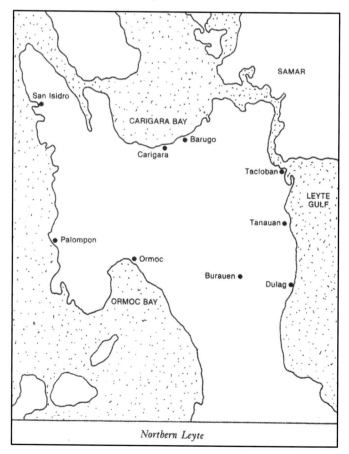

Map of Northern Leyte

Today the 'Red Arrow' Division successfully completed its primary mission of forcing a passage through the mountains from Pinamopoan to the Ormoc Valley. After thirty-six days of the bitterest hand-to-hand fighting yet experienced in this war the Division has annihilated the 1st Imperial Division (reinforced) and by this determined action has shortened the completion of the Leyte Campaign. Every officer and every enlisted man in the Division as well as those attached (107th Medical Battalion and the 18th Portable Surgical Hospital) played a vitally important part in the Division's success. I wish to compliment each individual and to express my personal appreciation for the splendid work accomplished by them in this Campaign. Without this coordinated effort of each individual the division could not have been successful. I extend the Season's Greetings to each of you, and in so doing, express my confidence in your continued success. May God watch over you and help you through the strenuous days ahead.

On January 1, 1945, the 77th Infantry Division was directed to relieve the 32nd Infantry Division. Shortly thereafter, the 32nd Division began assembling in the Carigara-Pinamopoan area on Carigara Bay for a brief period of much needed rest before its next mission—the invasion of Luzon. The 32nd Infantry Division suffered nearly 2,000 battle casualties during the 47 days of combat in the fight for Leyte, 450 had been killed, 1,491 wounded and 8 MIA.

The service units of the 32nd Division had about three weeks in which to get equipment together for another extensive campaign. The 107th Medical Battalion had to re-supply the battalion aid stations and hospitals (including the 18th Portable Surgical Hospital) before the Division's convoy departure scheduled for January 24, 1945.

The campaign for Leyte proved to be the most decisive operation in the re-conquest of the Philippines. The Japanese invested heavily in Leyte, and lost. The campaign cost their army four divisions and several separate combat units, while their navy lost 26 major warships, and 46 large transport and merchant ships (Battle of Leyte Gulf). The struggle also reduced Japanese land-based air capability in the Philippines by more than 50%, forcing them to resort to suicidal kamikaze ("Divine Wind") pilots. In the end, the Japanese decision to stake everything on the battle for Leyte only hastened their final collapse.

LUZON

JANUARY 9, 1945-FEBRUARY 15, 1945

While our forces were bringing the Leyte-Samar Campaign to a successful conclusion, the island of Mindoro, approximately 300 miles to the northwest, was also falling into American hands, setting the stage for the climax of the liberation of the Philippine Islands from Japanese domination. Even before the fighting on Leyte ended, MacArthur's forces had moved on to invade Luzon.

During the first week of January an American assault force gathered east of Leyte, slipped through the Surigao Strait, and passed into the Mindanao and Sulu Seas on its way to invade Luzon by landing on the beach in Lingayen Gulf. On January 9, 1945, the U.S. 6th Army, now composed of I Corps and XIV Corps, made the initial assault which included the 18th Portable Surgical Hospital (Arrowhead). I was unable to determine the unit to which the 18th Portable Surgical Hospital was attached during the invasion.

The 32nd Division first entered the planning for the Luzon Campaign on December 19, 1944, when General MacArthur (Commander in Chief SWPA) added it to the 6th Army's troop list along with the 1st Cavalry Division, three other infantry divisions and the 112th Cavalry Regimental Combat Team. The 32nd Division arrived in the Mabilao area of Lingayen Beach on January 27, eighteen days after the assault landing, and assembled in the Manaoog-San Vincente-Mapandan area. On January 30, 1945, the 32nd Division, less the 126th Infantry Battalion, passed to the control of I Corps. The 126th Infantry Battalion was placed in the 6th Army Reserve and the 18th Portable Surgical Hospital was probably reattached to the 126th Infantry Battalion at that time. The remainder of the 32nd Division advanced northeasterly astride the Villa Verde Trail. On February 15, the 126th Infantry Battalion was relieved from its Army reserve assignment and returned to Division control. Apparently while the 18th Portable Surgical Hospital was in reserve with the 126th Infantry Battalion it was again reassigned to the 503rd Parachute Infantry Regimental Combat Team for the invasion of Corregidor. The 126th Battalion was attached to the temporary operational control of the 25th Infantry Division on May 23, 1945, and remained attached to the 25th Division for the "mopping up" action in the Sante Fe-Imugan area.

CORREGIDOR

FEBRUARY 16, 1945-FEBRUARY 28, 1945

On February 6, 1945, the 503rd Parachute Regimental Combat Team, including the 462nd Parachute Field Artillery Battalion and C Company of the 161st Parachute Engineer Battalion, had completed its part in the invasion of the island of Mindoro in the northern Philippines. It was then alerted and given the mission to seize and secure the enemy-held island fortress of Corregidor, key to the important seaport in Manila.

Corregidor, officially named Fort Mills, is the largest of four islands protecting Manila Bay, the finest natural harbor in the Far East. The island bastion had a network of tunnels and a formidable array of powerful coastal artillery that had been installed prior to World War I. The tadpole-shaped island is 3.5 miles long and 1.5 miles across at its head, situated two miles from Bataan. The widest elevated mountainous area, known as Topside, contained most of the artillery installations. Middleside was a small plateau containing more battery positions and barracks. Bottomside was the low land and beach areas where the docks and the town of

San Jose were located. American service men referred to the island as "The Rock" or the "Gibralter of the East." Under Malinta Hill was the Malinta Tunnel that housed a hospital, offices, storehouses, etc., and served as MacArthur's headquarters prior to his evacuation, and the later surrender of Bataan (April 9, 1942) and Corregidor (May 6, 1942).

> Intrinsically, Corregidor is but a barren, war-worn rock, hallowed, as so many places, by death and disaster. Yet it symbolizes within itself that priceless, deathless thing, the honor of a nation. Until we lift our flag from its dust, we stand unredeemed before mankind. Until we claim again the ghastly remnants of its last gaunt garrison, we can but stand humble supplicants before Almighty God. There lies our Holy Grail.
>
> —General Douglas MacArthur
> Australia, 1942

From February 16 to February 26, 1945, American liberation forces spearheaded by the 503rd Parachute Regimental Combat Team along with Philippine Commonwealth troops swept into Corregidor and began the conquest to take back the island during the Battle for the Recapture of Corregidor.

Units of the 503rd Parachute Regimental Combat Team, the 462nd Parachute Field Artillery Battalion and C Company of the 161st Parachute Engineer Battalion parachuted onto the Topside area while the following units landed on the beaches (Field Order #9, Headquarters 503rd Parachute RCT):

1st Battalion, 503rd (Reinforced)
3rd Battalion, 34th Infantry (Reinforced)
Battery A, 950th AA AW Battalion
18th Portable Surgical Hospital (Reinforced)
174th Ordinance Service Detachment (Bomb Disposal)
Detachment 98th Signal Battalion
Detachment 592nd Engineer Boat and Shore Regiment
Detachment 1st Platoon, 603rd Tank Company
Detachment 592nd JASCO (A signal unit some of whom may have jumped)
Detachment 6th SAP (forward air controllers)
3rd Platoon Anti Tank Company, 34th Infantry Regiment
3rd Platoon, Cannon Company, 34th Infantry Regiment

The 18th Portable Surgical Hospital (Reinforced) was attached to the 3rd Battalion of the 34th Infantry Regiment during this invasion. This combined force was referred to as the "Rock Force," and the assault was called the "Rock Force Assault." "Three days after the jump, the 18th Portable Hospital (Reinforced) moved into the Topside Barracks beside us. They had come to Corregidor in the invasion barges on D-Day and had installed themselves on the beach; but down there they soon found they were subject to fire from hidden Jap squads …Not that they were unused to this sort of thing, for they had already seen fierce combat at 'Zig-Zag Pass' ("At the 18th Portable Surgical Hospital [Reinforced], loads

"…Villa Verde was the worst of all…" Above, an air view of the snakelike trail, built by a Spanish priest, which 9,000 Japs died to defend. It climbs 5,000 feet in twenty-four tortuous miles.

of wounded were coming back regularly. Six doctors …worked steadily for 48 hours.") on Luzon and had made the initial landing at Mariveles, as well as elsewhere" (Captain Charles M. Bradford, M.D., *Rock Force, Corregidor*).

In less than three hours after the hospital trucks rolled up to Topside, the wards and operating rooms of the 18th Portable Surgical Hospital (Reinforced) were functional. "We couldn't get the wounded back to the hospital fast enough so we brought the hospital up to the wounded" (ibid, Captain Bradford). There were many examples of lives that were saved because of the close proximity of the facilities to the fighting and the surgical skills and the exhausting hours of work put forth by the physicians and hospital personnel.

Few people now realize how completely the portable hospitals were integrated as functional parts of all combat teams and how fully they shared the experiences of battle. Many times they were pinned down in their foxholes like all front line troops by mortars, artillery, rifle and machine gun fire.

Black out curtains were draped across window and door openings in order to allow the surgical teams to work through the night. Portable generators produced electricity not only for illumination but also for autoclaves, which were able to keep adequate supplies of sheets, drapes, towels and instruments sterile to furnish two operating rooms. They also had portable refrigerators for serums, plasma and drugs (i.e. penicillin). Penicillin was routinely given to all surgical patients in three-hourly injections. Although army cots were used on the wards, patients received essential and excellent care. Oxygen tents were also available. Plasma, saline and glucose were available for intravenous use, and by this period of the war a plentiful supply of whole blood was available.

By February 28, the conquest of Corregidor was complete. The fighting was extremely intense, surprisingly brief, but very costly. The enemy lost about 4,500 men. The following is Major Thomas H. Stevens' (Regimental Surgeon) Regimental Medical Report:

APO 73
7 March 1945
Subject: Medical Section, Historical Report.
To: Commanding General, Sixth Army, APO 442.

1. 0700 hour 16 February 1945 members of the 503rd Regimental Combat Team loaded into transport planes at San Jose, Mindoro, Philippine Islands, in preparation for the jump on Corregidor, Philippine Islands. Members of the Medical Detachment jumped with the headquarters Sections and Platoons to which they were assigned. The first paratroopers jumped at 0833 hour. As the jump fields were small and rough and a high wind blowing, only seven or eight men were jumped at a time. Because of this precaution, jump casualties, though high were not as great as had been anticipated. Some few were shot by Japanese Marines while descending, but the jump caught the Japanese by complete surprise and unprepared to resist a parachute landing.

2. The Regional Aid Station was in operation by 0930 hour when the first jump casualties were brought in. The Regimental Aid Station furnished all medical care for the first thirty-six hours. The 18th Portable Surgical Hospital (Reinforced) which had made an amphibious landing with the 3rd Battalion, 34th Regiment, at 0930 hour, 16 February 1945, moved in and worked with us the rest of the mission. They administered excellent surgical and medical care to the members of the Rock Force. Through their untiring efforts, much suffering of the injured was alleviated and many lives were saved. The 503rd Regimental Combat Team owes a sincere debt of gratitude to the Officers and Enlisted men composing this hospital. List of jump casualties are as follows:

Jump Casualties, 16 Feb 45, 161
Jump Casualties, 17 Feb 45, 41
Later Reported, 7
Total 209

KIA and DOW by DAY

16 Feb 45 — 21	22 Feb 45 — 08	28 Feb 45 — 2
17 Feb 45 — 09	23 Feb 45 — 12	01 Mar 45 — 0
18 Feb 45 — 19	24 Feb 45 — 08	02 Mar 45 — 0
19 Feb 45 — 15	25 Feb 45 — 16	03 Mar 45 — 3
20 Feb 45 — 07	26 Feb 45 — 24	04 Mar 45 — 0
21 Feb 45 — 09	27 Feb 45 — 12	05 Mar 45 — 1

These figures represent 17 Officers and 148 Enlisted Men, a total of 165. Of these, those who died of wounds after receiving medical care, three were Officers and 20 were Enlisted Men.

3. The total of wounded in action included 15 Officers and 267 Enlisted Men by enemy action. Total injured in action included 17 Officers and 316 Enlisted Men. Total casualties for the entire mission includes 18 cases of Hepatitis, 48 cases of Dysentery, and 14 cases F.U.O. The majority of the F.U.O. cases were probably Malaria, as they responded to treatment with Atabrine. Of the total number of casualties, 613 were evacuated from the island, the rest being returned to duty. A total of 750 casualties occurred in the 503rd Regimental Combat Team.

4. The Medical Department suffered heavy casualties during the mission. Three members of the Medical Detachment were evacuated because of disease.

5. Casualties were relatively light throughout the mission as a result of enemy action. On 19 February an ammunition dump exploded causing numerous casualties. On 26 February another explosion occurred causing 196 casualties. These two explosions at least doubled all deaths and seriously wounded.

6. The members of the Medical Detachment worked tirelessly and efficiently, and the morale of all was excellent throughout the mission.

—Thomas H. Stevens,
Major MC.
Regimental Surgeon

On May 8, 1945, General Douglas MacArthur issued the following Distinguished Unit Citation (Army) with Streamer embroidered CORREGIDOR to the 503rd Parachute Infantry Regiment and the 18th Portable Surgical Hospital (Reinforced) as an attached unit:

HEADQUARTERS

UNITED STATES ARMY FORCES IN

THE FAR EAST

By direction of the President under the provisions of Executive Order 9396, the following unit is cited by the Commanding General, United States Army Forces in the Far East.

The 503rd Parachute Infantry Regiment, with the following units:

462nd Field Artillery Battalion
3rd Battalion, 34th Infantry Regiment
C Company, 161st Airborne Engineer Battalion
18th Portable Surgical Hospital (Reinforced)

3rd Platoon, Anti-Tank Company, 34th Infantry Regiment

3rd Platoon, Cannon Company, 34th Infantry Regiment

3rd Platoon, Company C, 3rd Engineer Battalion Company A, 34th

Infantry Regiment

3rd Platoon, Company C, 24th Medical Battalion Detachment, Service

Company, 34th Infantry Regiment

Battery A, 950th AAA (AW) Battalion

174th Ordinance Service Detachment (Bomb Disposal Squad)

Detachment, 592nd Engineer Boat and Shore Regiment

Detachment, 98th Signal Battalion

Detachment, 1st Platoon, 603rd Tank Company

Detachment, 592nd Joint Assault Signal Company

Detachment, 6th Support Air Party

Combat Photo Unit A, GHQ Signal Section

Combat Photo Unit Q, GHQ Signal Section

These units, organized as a task force, distinguished themselves by extraordinary heroism and outstanding performance of duty in action against the enemy from 16 to 28 February 1945. This force was directed to seize the enemy-held fortress of Corregidor, one of the most difficult missions in the Pacific War.

A long prepared and fanatical enemy, strongly entrenched in numerous tunnels, caves, dugouts and crevices, awaited the assault in commanding and extensively fortified positions. The small dropping area for parachutists was bordered extensively by sheer cliffs, with resultant variable air currents and eddies; and previous bombings and naval gunfire had cut trees and shrubs close above the ground, creating hazardous stakes which threatened to impale descending troops. The approach by sea, through shallow water known to be mined, led to a beach protected by land mines.

At 0830 on 16 February, the initial assault was made by parachute drop on terrain littered with debris and rubble. Heavy casualties were sustained. Two hours later the amphibious elements advanced by sea through the mine fields to the beach; and, though many lives were lost and much equipment destroyed by exploding mines, this element moving rapidly inland under heavy enemy fire seized Milenta Hill.

Meanwhile the airborne elements, though subjected to intense enemy fire and suffering increasing casualties, were organized into an aggressive fighting force as a result of the initiative of commanders of small units. Advancing doggedly against fanatical resistance, they had by nightfall, secured "The Top of the Rock," their initial objective.

On the following morning the entire task force began a systematic reduction of enemy positions and the annihilation of the defending force. Innumerable enemy tunnels and caves were sealed by demolition after hand-to-hand fighting, only to have the enemy emerge elsewhere through an intricate system of inter-connecting passageways. Direct fire of our supporting weapons, employed to seal tunnels and caves often resulted in the explosion of enemy emplaced demolitions and ammunition dumps, causing heavy casualties to our troops. Under increasing pressure the enemy, cut off from reinforcements, exploded demolitions in tunnels, destroying themselves as well as elements of our task force. At the completion of this desperate and violent struggle, 4,509 enemy dead were counted. Prisoners taken totaled 19.

Throughout the operation all elements of the task force, combat and service troops alike, displayed heroism in the highest degree. Parachuting to earth or landing on mined beaches, they attacked savagely against a numerically superior enemy, defeated him completely, and seized the fortress. Their magnificent courage, resourcefulness, tenacity and gallantry avenged the victims of Corregidor of 1942, and achieved a significant victory for the United States Army.

General Orders No. 112 8 May 1945
By command of General MacArthur

After the Corregidor Campaign ended, the 18th Portable Surgical Hospital was reattached to the 126th Infantry Regiment, 32nd Infantry Division. The military situation in northern Luzon had changed considerably during the weeks when the bulk of the 32nd Division was out of combat in a reserve capacity. The 37th Infantry Division and the 25th Infantry Division had captured Aritao on June 5, 1945; the next day Bambang was captured; and on June 7 Bayombong was taken. On June 9 the 37th Infantry Division overran Bagabac (Bagabog). The 33rd Infantry Division and the 6th Infantry Division were steadily advancing. Philippine Guerrilla Forces, under the command of I Corps, had cleared large areas across the northwestern part of the island. On June 23 paratroops from the 11th Division dropped near Aparri, captured two days earlier, and made contact with the 37th Infantry Division. By June 30, the Cagayan Valley was under American control but not yet completely cleared of enemy troops.

When the 32nd Infantry Division came back into the combat picture, its principal mission was to eliminate the remaining Japanese troops in its zone of action. The 32nd Division took responsibility for an area extending completely across the island from Bagabac to south of Balete Pass (the Villa Verde Trail area) and all of the Baguio area. The 126th Infantry Regiment, with the 18th Portable Surgical Hospital, took over the southeastern area of the Division's zone. During this period each of the regiments of the 32nd Division had Philippine guerrilla units attached to it.

On August 15, 1945, the 32nd Division received orders to discontinue aggressive action. Major General William H. Gill, Commander of the 32nd Infantry Division said, "I doubt if anyone, anywhere, is more profoundly moved by this news than the men of this Division, who have fought so hard, suffered so much and waited so long for this moment." The war ended on the 32nd Division's 654th day of combat, the longest of any unit in World War II. General Gill continued, "I'm proud of these men who fought at Buna, at Saidor, the Drimiumor, on Morotai, on Leyte and on Luzon. I also think this is an appropriate time to remember the sacrifice of the men who died in those battles. This is their moment too."

OCCUPATION OF JAPAN

OCTOBER 9, 1945-DECEMBER 1, 1945

On August 20, 1945, a Luzon Area Command was formed to assume tactical control of the remaining "mopping up" operations on the island of Luzon. A new headquarters was organized with the Commanding General of the 37th Infantry Division in command. This change was made in order to release XIV Corps and the 32nd Infantry Division for occupation duties in Japan. Before the Division left for Japan, General Tomoyuki Yamashita (Highest Commander, Imperial Japanese Army in the Philippines) surrendered to the 32nd Infantry Division on September 2, 1945. General Yamashita indicated that he considered the 32nd Division the best his troops had encountered on Leyte and on Luzon.

The 32nd Infantry Division was assigned to the 6th Army on September 7 and began to assemble at Camp Dagupan near the shores of the Lingayen Gulf in preparation for transfer to Japan.

On September 20, 1945, the 32nd Division took time out from its preparations for the move to Japan to dedicate a monument (erected by Co. A. 114th Engineers) to the 891 men of the Division who had been killed in the Villa Verde Trail operation. The monument was a cement Red Arrow bearing a plaque:

> Erected by the officers and men of the 32nd Division, United States Army, in memory of their gallant comrades killed along the Villa Verde Trail. January 30, 1945—May 28, 1945

Prior to leaving Luzon, the Philippine President Osmena recognized and honored the 32nd Infantry Division and all attached units, which included the 18th Portable Surgical Hospital. Those individuals serving with the unit received the Philippine Liberation Medal and the Philippine Independence Medal. In 1946, they were presented the Philippine Presidential Unit Citation for the time period of October 17, 1944—July 4, 1945, for their gallantry in action.

The 32nd Infantry Division had an early part in the occupation and disarming of Japan. The advance party sailed on October 9, 1945. During the next few days, the entire Division was transported by a 32-ship convoy to the harbor of Sasebo, a Japanese naval base. The 1st Battalion, 127th Infantry Regiment had been flown to Kanoya in southern Kyushu, the southernmost

of the four main Japanese Islands, to secure the Kanoya airfield for the staging and refueling of Allied aircraft until the rest of the Division arrived. The 128th Infantry Regiment and the 107th Medical Battalion moved into the Yamaguachi area; the 126th Infantry Regiment and the 18th Portable Surgical Hospital went to Kokura and Moji; the Division Artillery went to Oita; and the Division Headquarters, the 127th Infantry Regiment and the 114th Engineers went to Fukuoka.

The mission of the occupying forces was to supervise the demobilization and disarmament of the Japanese Armed Forces and to act as a surveillance force. Many thousands of Koreans, Chinese and other nationalities had to be repatriated and they, as well as the civilian population, had to be controlled, fed, housed and given medical attention. The water supply, food distribution, sanitation system, medical care and police and fire services had to be reestablished. Agriculture and manufacturing had to quickly meet the needs of a peacetime economy. The difficulties inherent in the occupation efforts were augmented, and the efficiency reduced, by the continual turnover of officers and noncoms as demobilization policies were applied. By December 1, 1945, the 126th Infantry Regiment had only 132 officers and 2,708 enlisted men in spite of a steady flow of replacements (the "old timers" had been returned to the States for discharge). For a brief period there were only 23 doctors available for duty in the entire 32nd Infantry Division. Housing for the troops was a constant problem, made worse by several fires. Smallpox also broke out among the troops resulting in some deaths that necessitated the initiation of a quarantine, which further slowed the effectiveness of the occupation force.

On December 31, 1945, the 32nd Division was transferred to the control of the 8th Army to relieve the 6th Army from occupation responsibilities in anticipation of its inactivation. On February 28, 1946, the 32nd Division was formally inactivated at Fukuoka, Japan. Back in the States, however, reorganization was soon in progress. On November 8, 1946, in Milwaukee, Wisconsin, the headquarters of the 32nd Infantry Division was again Federally recognized.

The 18th Portable Surgical Hospital was inactivated on December 1, 1945, at Kyushu, Japan and was not resurrected until it was re-designated as the 18th Surgical Hospital (MA) on March 1, 1963, and reactivated on March 26, 1963, at Fort Gordon, Georgia (3rd Army).

CHRONOLOGY OF THE VIETNAM WAR

1940s

1949
Vietnam made an Associated state of the French Union (March).

1950s

1950
President Truman sends 35-man military advisory group to aid French fighting to maintain colonial power in Vietnam.

1954
After French defeat at Dien Bien Phu (May), Geneva agreements (July) provide for withdrawal of French and Vietminh to either side of demarcation zone (DMZ) pending reunification elections, which are never held. Presidents Eisenhower and Kennedy (from 1954 onward) send civilian advisers and, later, military personnel to train South Vietnamese.

1954-55
Exodus of refuges from North Vietnam.

1955
Republic of Vietnam proclaimed (October).

1959
North Vietnam recommences effort to take the south.

1960s

1960
Communists form National Liberation Front (N.L.F.) in south (December).

1960-63
U.S. military advisors in South Vietnam rise from 900 to 15,000.

1963
Ngo Dinh Diem, South Vietnam's premier, killed in military coup (November 1). First Republic ends.

1964
North Vietnamese torpedo boats reportedly attack U.S. destroyers in Gulf of Tonkin (August 2). President Johnson orders retaliatory air strikes. Congress approves Gulf of Tonkin resolution (August 7) authorizing president to take "all necessary measures" to win in Vietnam, allowing for the war's expansion.

1965
U.S. planes begin combat missions over South Vietnam. In June, 23,000 American advisors committed to combat. By end of year over 184,000 U.S. troops are in the area.

1966
B-52s bomb DMZ, reportedly used by North Vietnam for entry into South (July 31).

1967
South Vietnam National Assembly approves election of General Nguyen Van Theiu as president (October 21).

1968
U.S. has almost 525,000 men in Vietnam. In Tet offensive (January-February), Viet Cong guerrillas attack Saigon, Hue and some provincial capitals. In My Lai massacre, American soldiers kill 300 Vietnamese villagers (March 16). President Johnson orders halt to U.S. bombardment of North Vietnam (October 31). Saigon and N.L.F. join U.S. and North Vietnam in Paris peace talks.

1969
President Nixon announces Vietnam peace offer (May 14) and begins troop withdrawals (June). Viet Cong forms Provisional Revolutionary Government. U.S. Senate calls for curb on commitments (June 25). Ho Chi Minh, 79, North Vietnam president, dies (September 3); collective leadership chosen. Some 6,000 U.S. troops pulled back from Thailand and 1,000 Marines from Vietnam (announced September 30). Massive demonstrations in U.S. protest or support war policies (October 15).

1970s

1970
U.S. troops invade Cambodia in order to destroy North Vietnamese sanctuaries (May 1).

1971

Congress bars use of combat troops, but not air power, in Laos and Cambodia (January 1). South Vietnamese troops, with U.S. air cover, fail in Laos thrust. Many American ground forces withdrawn from Vietnam combat. *New York Times* publishes Pentagon papers, classified material on expansion of war (June).

1972

U.S. President Nixon responds to North Vietnamese drive across DMZ by ordering mining of North Vietnam ports and heavy bombing of Hanoi-Haiphong area (April 1). Nixon orders "Christmas bombing" of North to get North Vietnamese back to conference table (December).

1973

President orders halt to offensive operations in North Vietnam (January 15). Representatives of North and South Vietnam, U.S., and N.L.F. sign peace pacts in Paris, ending longest war in U.S. history (January 27). Last American troops departed in their entirety (March 29).

1974

Both sides accuse each other of frequent violations of cease-fire agreement.

1975

Full-scale war resumes. South Vietnam premier Nguyen Van Thieu resigns (April 21). South Vietnamese government surrenders to North Vietnam; U.S. Marine embassy guards and U.S. civilians and dependents evacuated (April 30). More than 140,000 Vietnamese refugees leave by air and sea, many to settle in U.S. Provisional Revolutionary Government takes control (June 6).

1975

Saigon is captured and Republic falls (April).

1976

Election of National Assembly paves way for reunification of North and South.

"Dustoff" delivering wounded to the 18th Surgical.

HISTORY OF THE 18TH SURGICAL HOSPITAL (MA) (MUST) (MA) DURING THE VIETNAM WAR

Engraved on a black granite monument (Vietnam Veterans Memorial, dedicated November 13, 1982) in our Nation's Capitol are the names of 58,318 Americans who made the supreme sacrifice in the service of their country. The hostilities in Southeast Asia (Vietnam, Laos and Cambodia), the so-called "second Vietnam War," was the longest military conflict in U.S. history. In 1985, President Richard M. Nixon commented, "No event in American history is more misunderstood than the Vietnam War. It was misreported then, and it is misremembered now."

In order to understand more completely and to remember more accurately the Vietnam War, one must have at least a modicum of knowledge concerning the Vietnamese peoples and their culture. It is necessary that we have an understanding of the turmoil, political unrest, governmental instability, economic oppression and restless mood of the inhabitants of South Vietnam. We also must reflect on the more pertinent aspects of Vietnam's long and complicated history to become aware of the social, cultural and political milieu engaging and engulfing their society prior to the U.S. involvement and our military presence there. The Vietnamese were struggling toward independence, democracy, freedom and social justice; and each of those struggles was important, complex and vital to their ultimate national status.

North and South Vietnam combined is a narrow strip of mountains, hills, swamps and rice lands that flank the eastern portion of the Southeast Asian Peninsula. Long and narrow, it curves southwestwardly in roughly a S-shaped curve for approximately 1,100 miles from communist China in the north to the Gulf of Siam in the south. Each end of the country broadens somewhat, while along the waist at the 17th parallel of latitude it narrows to about 50 miles. To the east, Vietnam is washed by the waters of the South China Sea (the portion along the coast of North Vietnam is termed the Gulf of Tonkin), while it shares its western border with the kingdoms of Laos and Cambodia and, with those two nations, was known as French Indochina for about a century prior to World War II. The Annamite Mountain chain (Annamese Cordillera) stretches nearly the entire length of Vietnam, creating a narrow band of coastal lowland and a broad mountainous plateau (Central Highlands), and links the country's two large delta regions created by the estuaries of the Red River in the north and the Mekong River in the south. The land area totals about 127,000 square miles, approximately the size of New Mexico.

Politically, there were two Vietnams during the period of U.S. involvement. This division resulted from the International Conference in Geneva in 1954, which marked the end of a long period of French rule in Indochina and established an arbitrary demarcation line at the 17th parallel. This created the communist Democratic Republic of Vietnam (DRVN) to the north with approximately 17 million people (capital in Hanoi), and the Republic of Vietnam (RVN, South Vietnam) with approximately 16 million people (capital in Saigon).

In this predominately agricultural country, an estimated 80% of the 33 million people were farmers. They were concentrated mostly in the deltas, villages and hamlets scattered along the coastal lowlands. Rice was, and remains, the major food crop. Rubber and tea were important export products in the south, while the less fertile north was slightly more industrialized, possessing coal and ore reserves. Fishing was of great importance to

A typical, small Montagnard village viewed from a chopper.

Montagnard children

Montagnard men in their typical dress.

A group of Montgnard children. The young child in the left fore-ground has kwashiorkor, which is a severe protein malnutrition seen particularly in children 1–3 years of age due to a diet primarily of their mothers milk that usually clears when the child begins eating an adult diet.

Montagnard village meeting house

both. At least 85% of the population was ethnically Vietnamese (called Annamese in earlier centuries). There were several minority groups, the most notable being Chinese, Cambodians and Montagnards. These mountain people indigenous to the Central Highlands and collectively called "Montagnards" (French for "mountain people") were composed of two main ethnic groups: the Malayo-Polynesian and the Mon-Khmer. They numbered between 600,000 and 1 million and were divided into many tribes that lived a very primitive life. The Chinese, most of whom had Vietnamese citizenship, numbered well over 1 million and were congregated mostly in the cities of South Vietnam, especially in Cholon ("Pearl of the Orient"), a suburb of Saigon. The majority of the 400,000 people of Cambodian origin were farmers in the provinces near the Cambodian border in the Central Highlands and at the mouth of the Mekong River system. There were other minority groups including a few thousand Chams, Malays, Indians, Thais and French, and at one point, approximately 500,000 Americans. There were a total of fifty-three ethnic groups in Vietnam in the mid 1960s.

The religion of most Vietnamese is a mixture of Taoism, Shintoism, Mahayana Buddhism, Catholicism, Protestantism, Confucianism, Annamism (ancestor worship), Animism and Gao Dai (a mixture of all). In 1966, there were between 1.5 and 2 million Roman Catholics and small, scattered groups representing most Protestant denominations.

The ethnic Vietnamese are a mixture both genetically and culturally of Sino-Tibetan and early Malay or Indonesian ancestry, a very old people with a documented history of more than two thousand years and a legendary history of nearly five thousand years. According to legend the Vietnamese originated in the valley of the Yellow River in what is now the northern part of China in 2879 BC; however, historical documents record the Vietnamese as a tribal people inhabiting the Red River delta in what is now North Vietnam. They were gradually driven southward by the Chinese (early Chinese documents, circa 500 BC, refer to the Viet States to the south).

In 207 BC, a group of small states in the Red River Delta were conquered by a Chinese general and were combined with two Chinese provinces to form an independent kingdom called Nam Viet (Nan Yueh). This resulting kingdom was overrun in 111 BC by the armies of the Han Dynasty of China, and was incorporated as the southernmost province of the Chinese Empire, remaining under Chinese rule for more than one thousand years. Despite their exposure to Chinese customs and culture, the Vietnamese retained their national identity. In 39 AD an armed revolt led by two sisters, Trung Trac and Trung Nhi, succeeded in briefly defeating the Chinese. The Chinese soon regained control but, over the ensuing centuries, gradually liberalized their policies; and in 618 AD the province was made a protectorate and renamed Annam (An Nam, "pacified south").

Although the Chinese government adopted more liberal policies and the people enjoyed increasing prosperity, the Vietnamese continued to rebel. Finally in 938 AD, as China's Tang Dynasty tottered, a Vietnamese general drove out the Chinese army; thus the free and independent Great Viet State (Dai Co Viet) was born. With the exception of a twenty-year interlude of Chinese occupation in the 15th Century, the Vietnamese remained free for over 900 years. They drove off Chinese invaders in the 11th Century and three invasions by the Mongol armies of Kublai Khan in the 13th Century (1257 AD, 1284 AD and 1287 AD).

Vietnam prospered and expanded southward. Central governmental control was difficult; and, for much of the period between the 16th and 19th Centuries, the country was divided into northern and southern kingdoms, not for political reasons but because of administrative considerations. It was later unified again in 1902 under Nguyen Anh, a member of the southern aristocracy (who later became Emperor Gia Long), and the region was called Vietnam ("distant south"). Before the end of the 19th Century, the country was again ruled by foreigners, this time the French.

In August 1858, when a French naval squadron steamed into the port of Tourane (now Da Nang), France began an era of domination that was to continue for nearly a century. Saigon ("Paris of the Orient") was captured in 1861 and Vietnam's independence finally terminated in 1883 when French control was extended to the north. With the annexation of the southern part of the country as a colony in 1887, their control became complete, bringing together the north (Tonkin), the central section (Annam) and the south (Cochin, China).

Cambodia became a French Protectorate in 1867, and Laos was annexed in 1893. These countries, along with all of Vietnam, were finally merged into the Indochinese Union under a French Govenor-General in 1899.

The Vietnamese were no more satisfied to live under French rule than they had been under Chinese rule. Nationalistic feelings mounted, and extreme organizations were formed, the most notable among them the Association of Revolutionary Vietnamese Youths led by a young Moscow-trained communist known as Nguyen Ai Quoc (born Nguyen Tat Thanh [1890—1969], later called Ho Chi Minh ["He Who Enlightens"] and sometimes fondly referred to as Bac Ho [Uncle Ho]). The year was 1925.

As early as 1924, Nguyen Ai Quoc outlined his immediate task to be "…the unification of various Vietnamese nationalist groups under communist leadership …" and in 1927 declared, "I intend to form an Indo-Chinese national, revolutionary movement, whose leaders will bring its members step by step to orthodox Communism." This goal was realized when the Indochinese Communist Party, with Nguyen Ai Quoc ("Nguyen the Patriot") as its head, was organized in 1930.

On May 19, 1941, a congress of Vietnamese Nationalists (exiled groups) was held in Chinghsi, China, under the auspices of the Kuomintang government, resulting in the formation of the Revolutionary League for the Independence of Vietnam (Vietnam Doc Lap Dong Minh Hoi, later to become known as the Viet Minh) with Nguyen Ai Quoc as general secretary.

The Nationalist Chinese authorities soon became suspicious of Nguyen Ai Quoc and imprisoned him; however, in order to gain intelligence information about this subversive organization, he was released in 1943. It was at this time, in order to conceal his identity that Nguyen Ai Quoc took the alias of Ho Chi Minh. With the fall of France in 1943, Japanese occupation began, even though French officials were still permitted to administer the colonies. Later, with defeat imminent, the Japanese in March 1945 imprisoned the French authorities and granted independence to Vietnam under Japanese protection with Emperor Bao Dai (Nguyen Vinh Thuy) as Head of State (the last Emperor of Vietnam).

After Japan's surrender to the Allies on August 13, 1945, Ho Chi Minh acted swiftly, working through the clandestine Indochinese Communist Party and the Viet Minh National Front in order to seize as much Vietnamese territory as possible before the Allied forces could again occupy the country. Under an agreement by the Allies following the Japanese surrender, the Nationalist Chinese forces were to occupy Vietnam to the 16th parallel and the French were to control the remainder of the country to the south.

Only three days after the Japanese surrendered on August 16, the Viet Minh announced the formation of a National Liberation Committee for Vietnam; and by August 19, Ho Chi Minh's guerilla forces had taken control of Hanoi. Next he sent a mission to Hue, seat of Emperor Bao Dai's government, demanding immediate surrender. Bao Dai abdicated believing, as did most of the Vietnamese people, that the Viet Minh was a national front organization which enjoyed the support of the Allies. Saigon and

Majestic Hotel in downtown Saigon.

Street scene in downtown Saigon.

much of the countryside soon fell under the Viet Minh's control, and on August 29, in Hanoi, a provisional government was proclaimed. On September 2, 1945, Ho Chi Minh proclaimed the Democratic Republic of Vietnam with himself as President.

To win support of the Chinese and the French, as well as the Vietnamese people, Ho Chi Minh arranged the disappearance of the communist element in the Viet Minh by dissolving the Indochinese Communist Party. Instead, he encouraged all communists who wished to continue their "theoretical studies" to join the Association of Marxists Studies. Elections were held in January 1946 to select members to the country's first legislature, the National Assembly. The Viet Minh, as the major political organization, won most of the 444 Assembly seats; only 70 seats were allotted to the opposition parties. Throughout the ensuing months, negotiations between Ho Chi Minh and the French continued in spite of many inconsistencies and irregularities. Some legislators were arrested and imprisoned, others even executed, for "common law crimes." France agreed to recognize the Democratic Republic of Vietnam, and a referendum was to be held to determine whether Tonkin, Annam and Cochin China would be united. They further agreed that 15,000 French troops stationed in the north would be gradually withdrawn by 1952. Negotiations deteriorated, misunderstandings and hostilities developed, and incidents of armed violence culminated in a French cruiser shelling the port city of Haiphong. On December 19, 1946, President Ho Chi Minh retaliated by ordering a general attack against the French in Hanoi and throughout all of Vietnam, igniting the fires of the Indochinese War (the "first Vietnam war") that were to burn for the next seven and one-half years.

Ho Chi Minh's forces immediately adopted the strategy of guerrilla warfare advocated by Mao Tse-tung (Mao Zedong), resorting to sabotage, subversion and harassment but avoiding major battles. The French, meanwhile, tried to rally all non-communist nationalists to support one organized government and approve self-government for Vietnam with Bao Dai as Chief of State. After the communist government gained power in China in 1949, Peking began sending vitally needed equipment, supplies and advisors to train Ho Chi Minh's Army. For the first time, the Viet Minh forces were able to meet the French Army in large military confrontations. With the rising tide of communism in Asia, Ho Chi Minh announced in early 1951 that the Viet Minh was being absorbed by the new League for the National Union of Vietnam (Lieu Viet) and formed the Vietnamese Workers Party (Lao Dong) which was dedicated to the doctrines of Marx, Engels, Lenin and Mao Tse-tung. The guerilla forces under General Vo Nguyen Giap suffered reverses in 1951, but expanded their territory in 1952. The Democratic Republic of Vietnam's (DRVN) forces joined with the pro-communist's Pathet Lao Army in Laos, and in early 1954, the new communist offensives threatened southern Vietnam, as well as northeastern Cambodia and central and northern Laos. The French forces concentrated at Dien Bein Phu were overwhelmed by General Giap's forces resulting in the French surrender on May 8, 1954 (The French were closed off from the outside world under constant fire and taking heavy casualties. They appealed to the Americans, and some American advisors suggested the use of a nuclear bomb. President Eisenhower would not enter into the conflict without the British, and Winston Churchill refused, hoping the Geneva Peace Talks would resolve the situation.).

On the initiative of Britain, France and the United States, a foreign ministers conference, including the Soviet Union, was held in Berlin in February 1954. They agreed to hold a conference in Geneva with all interested parties to discuss the situation in both Indochina and Korea. The Geneva Conference opened in late April, first taking up the question of Korea, but failed to make progress. Negotiations on Indochina began on May 8 (the day Dein Bein Phu fell). The participants included the four conference originators along with Communist China, Cambodia, Laos, the State of Vietnam (South) and the DRVN (North).

The Geneva Accords were composed of two principal documents. First, was the "...agreement of the Cessation of Hostilities in Vietnam," signed on July 20, 1954, by the commanders of the French and the DRVN forces. Second, was the "Final Declaration" of the conference dated July 21, 1954, which remained unsigned. The Geneva Accords ended hostilities throughout Indochina; partitioned Vietnam at the 17th parallel pending a countrywide election by July 9, 1956; pledged France to grant complete independence to Vietnam; provided for the total evacuation of French and State of Vietnam military forces from north of the 17th parallel and total evacuation of DRVN forces from south of the parallel; banned the import of new weapons and any increase of troop strength; and provided for the free flow of refugees. The conference created a three-nation International Commission for Supervision and Control (ICC) for Vietnam, Cambodia and Laos. India was made chairman of the ICC with Canada and Poland as members.

The final declaration received the approval of all those represented at the conference, with the exception of the South Vietnamese and the American delegates. South Vietnam agreed to support the ceasefire but objected to the partitioning of the country. The U.S. representative, General Bedell Smith, also expressed concern about the partition but indicated that the U.S. would do nothing to disturb the agreement. He stated that the U.S. would view "...any renewal of the aggression in violation of the aforesaid agreements with grave concern as seriously threatening international peace and security." The Geneva Conference ended with a divided Vietnam, but the Vietnamese were at peace for the first time in nearly a decade and free from foreign domination for the first time in almost a century. The division of the country was to continue; peace, however, was not.

Immediately following the conclusion of the Geneva Accords, South Vietnam experienced a period of considerable confusion and uncertainty. Although Emperor Bao Dai had appointed a well-known nationalist figure, Ngo Dinh Diem, Prime Minister in July 1954, a national referendum was held in October 1955

that permitted the people to choose between Diem and Bao Dai as Chief of State. Diem won by an overwhelming majority, and on October 26, he established the Republic of Vietnam with himself as President. From the beginning, he had to contend with a country whose economy was ruined and whose political life was fragmented by rivalries among religious sects and political factions. During the ensuing nine years, Diem was able to consolidate his political position and eliminate the private armies of the religious sects. With substantial American military and economic aid, he built a national army and administration and made significant progress toward reconstructing a ruined economy.

By 1963, the communists had made significant progress in building a subversive organization in South Vietnam, organized a communist controlled National Front for the Liberation of South Vietnam (NFLSVN), and had recruited formidable guerilla units that made the countryside increasingly insecure.

In May 1963, religious unrest broke out among the Buddhists. On June 11, 1963, the Buddhist monk, Thish Quang Duc, burned himself to death in Saigon. The image of the burning monk emblazed the front pages of newspapers around the world. Following a revolt by Buddhists in the old Imperial City of Hue and the attack on the Buddhist Xa Loi Pagoda in Saigon, questions concerning Diem's leadership abilities and popularity surfaced. Other political and military groups, alienated by the Diem government, made common cause with the Buddhists. When a military coup developed to oust Diem, the U.S. backed the plot in a semi-clandestine fashion. On November 1, 1963, a military coup d'etat overthrew the government, which resulted in the death of Ngo Dinh Diem and his brother, Ngo Dinh Nhu. After Diem's death, chaos further destabilized political efforts, resulting in a purge in all levels of government. After Diem's death, General Minh purged thirty-five of the forty-four Provisional Governors and countless other key officials down to the village level. The politburo in Hanoi immediately began exploiting the weaknesses created by factional fighting in the rural areas of South Vietnam, with the deployment of North Vietnamese (NVA or PAVN [Peoples Army of Vietnam]) troops. Over Christmas 1963, Secretary of Defense, Robert S. McNamara, visited Saigon and noted, "The Viet Cong now control a very high proportion of the people in certain key provinces, particularly those south and west of Saigon." The assassination of President Kennedy just twenty-two days after Diem's death seriously complicated and changed the political climates in both Washington and Saigon, creating more aggressive war policies on both sides. Within forty-eight hours after being sworn in as President, Lyndon B. Johnson was facing the reality of the Vietnam situation. A National Security Action Memorandum (NSAM, 273) dated November 24, 1963, confirmed the U.S. commitment to the Saigon government.

The constitution of 1956, providing for a strong executive branch, an unicameral assembly and a strong judicial system, was abrogated with the overthrow of President Diem. On November 2, 1963, Provisional Charter No.1 was established

PAVN Officer Ranks: 1961

PAVN Rank	Translation	U.S. Equivalent	Level of Command
Dai-Tuong	Senior General	General	———
Thuong-Tuong	Colonel General	Lieutenant General	———
Trung-Tuong	Lieutenant General	Major General	———
Thien-Tuong	Major General	Brigadier General	CO, Division
Dai-Ta	Senior Colonel	None	XO, Division
Thuong-Ta	Colonel	Colonel	CO, Regiment
Trung-Ta	Lieutenant Colonel	Lieuenant Colonel	XO, Regiment
Thien-Ta	Major	Major	CO, Battalion
Dai-Uy	Senior Captain	None	XO, Battalion
Thuong-Uy	Captain	Captain	CO, Company
Trung-Uy	Senior Lieutenant	1 Lieutenant	XO, Company
Thien-Uy	Lieutenant	2 Lieutenant	Platoon Leader
Chuan-Uy	Aspirant[1]	None	———

Source: Department of the Army, 'Handbook on the North Vietnamese Armed Forces,' 1961.

[1] A PAVN Aspirant is not an officer but a 'combattant' or NCO who is to be promoted to officer.

stating that the country would remain a republic and authorized a Revolutionary Council to assume the function of the legislative and executive powers, pending adoption of a new constitution. On November 6, a Provisional Cabinet was installed with Prime Minister Nguyen Ngoc Tho as Chief of State and Major General Duong Van ("Big") Minh, along with a civilian Council of Sages (later renamed the Council of Notables), to advise the military government.

On January 30, 1964, another coup occurred. General Nguyen Khanh replaced General Minh as Chairman of the Military Revolutionary Council; and on February 8, Prime Minister Tho resigned. General Khanh became Prime Minister. In order to restore civilian leadership to the government, the Military Revolutionary Council dissolved itself on August 27, 1964. A triumvirate of generals composed of General Khanh, General Minh and General Tran Thien Khiem headed this caretaker government until a Provisional Charter was promulgated on October 20, 1964, establishing the statutes and institutions for the civilian government. Trang Van Huong, Mayor of Saigon, became Prime Minister on November 4, 1964, and Phan Khoc Suu assumed the position of Chief of State. A High National Council was appointed to act as a temporary legislative body. Opposition and public disenchantment caused the Vietnamese Armed Forces Council to abolish the High National Council on December 20, 1964, and Prime Minister Huong was asked to resign on January 22, 1965. Dr. Phan Huy Quat, a former Minister of Foreign Affairs, organized a new government on February 16, 1965. He retained Mr. Suu as Chief of State and created the National Legislative Council to act in a legislative capacity.

A constitutional crisis arose as to the meaning of the Provisional Charter and in order that no delay in the prosecution of the war would result, the civilian government dissolved itself on June 11, 1965. On June 19, the Congress of the Armed Forces composed of the General Officers of the Vietnamese Armed Forces was formed.

Subordinate to the Congress was the Directory (composed of 10 commissioners) who was entrusted with the exercise of power and the direction of the affairs of the government. Major General Nguyen Van Thieu was made Chairman of the Directory (equivalent to Chief of State), and Air Vice-Marshall Nguyen Cao Ky became Prime Minister. This government remained in office until the elected government of Thieu and Ky officially took office, along with the freely elected legislators.

It was, or should have been, glaringly apparent to everyone who bothered to inform themselves concerning the U.S. involvement in South Vietnam that communist aggression ran like a red thread throughout the problems encountered there. Political, economic and social developments were largely tied to the course of the war. The People's Liberation Armed Forces (PLAF), or Viet Cong (from Cong San, "Vietnamese Communist"), which was supplied and directed from Communist North Vietnam, was a most serious threat to the continued freedom of the Republic of Vietnam. North Vietnam and the Viet Cong, under the auspices of the National Front for the Liberation of South Vietnam, transported supplies not only via the "Ho Chi Minh Trail" through the Truong Son Mountains through Cambodia (the Ia Drang Valley region), but they also used the South China Sea route along the coast of South Vietnam (the "Ho Chi Minh Sea Route"). This effort to move supplies by sea was known by the code name "Market Time." The boats, usually trawlers (falsely registered as fishing vessels), took supplies into the coastal areas of the central and southern parts of South Vietnam, even as far south as the Mekong Delta.

Obviously, Vietnam has a long and complicated history. Throughout the centuries they maintained a national pride in spite of foreign domination, emperors, dictators, turmoil, corruption and poverty; and their repeated efforts to form a stable representative government are commendable. It is also necessary that we attempt to comprehend and understand the distrust, impatience and fears they felt toward their government. In spite of the many promises made to them by various governmental leaders, they continued to live in abject poverty; continued to observe destruction and death brought by war, pestilence and disease; and continued to witness their society as it deteriorated because of corruption, graft, sabotage and subversion. In some respects, this was technically a civil war; however, it primarily was a "...war of liberation..." in which the communist north was seeking to conquer and destroy the democratic freedoms of its southern neighbor.

Ho Chi Minh's activities and statements can only serve as evidence in favor of the decision by the U.S. not to support the Viet Minh movement. President Ho Chi Minh, writing in the Belgium Communist Party's publication, *Red Flag*, on July 10, 1959 stated, "...we are building capitalism in Vietnam, but we are building it in only one part of the country while in the other part we still have to direct and bring to a close the middle-class democratic and anti-imperialist revolutions." General Vo Nguyen Giap wrote in the January 1960 issue of the Lao Dong Party's journal, *Hoc Tap*, "...the North has become a large rear echelon of our Army..." and "...the North is the revolutionary base for the whole country." Le Duan (Lao Dong Party's First Secretary), in an address to a party congress held in October 1960, stated that Hanoi had two strategic tasks: "First, to carry out the Socialist Revolution in North Vietnam; second, to liberate South Vietnam ...these two strategic tasks are closely related to each other..." Then on January 9, 1961, Hanoi announced that the National Front for the Liberation of South Vietnam (NFLSVN) had been formed on December 20, 1960, to direct the Viet Cong guerilla forces in the south and had as its purpose the overthrow of the Saigon government and the establishment of a "...broad democratic coalition administration ..." with the announced objective of "...peaceful reunification of the country." In May 1962, the International Control Commission concluded an investigation of violations of the Geneva Agreements by pointing out that there was "...sufficient evidence to show beyond a reasonable doubt, ..." that Hanoi was sending arms and men into South Vietnam. By the end of 1964, it was estimated that in excess of 40,000 North Vietnamese military personnel had infiltrated into South Vietnam. It was stated in the *Red Flag* on May 4, 1965, that "... the Vietnam question is the focus of the present international class struggle and is a touchstone of the attitudes of all political forces in the world."

After World War II, the United States undertook significant responsibilities and commitments in Southeast Asia, beginning with the Truman administration. In 1950, the Chinese agreed to supply Ho Chi Minh with military aid. The same year (August 3, 1950), President Truman authorized 35 military personnel under the direction of the Military Assistance Advisory Group (MAAG) to instruct and train South Vietnamese troops and to coordinate U.S. aid. On February 27, 1950, the National Security Council's Memorandum 64 stated, "All practicable measures should be taken to prevent further Communist expansion in Southeast Asia." President Eisenhower was reluctant to increase military support; however, he and his successors, Presidents Kennedy and Johnson, believed in the "Domino Theory" and that South Vietnam was the key "domino." In May 1960, the United States, at the request of the South Vietnamese government increased the number of advisors to 685. On April 3, 1961, President Kennedy signed the Amnity and Economic Relations Treaty, and over the next three years, he increased the number of U.S. advisors in South Vietnam from 900 to 17,000 and committed U.S. helicopters (UH-1B [Huey]) to support the Army of the Republic of Vietnam (ARVN). In an attempt to counteract the VC (Viet Cong) and the North Vietnamese guerilla insurgencies, he expanded the Special Forces (Green Berets). On February 8, 1962, the Military Assistance Command Vietnam (MACV) was created, replacing the MAAG, and officially established America's commitment to the war effort. The first MACV Commander, General Paul D. Harkins, strongly supported Diem.

With Diem's assassination, corruption exacerbated, resulting in governmental chaos and instability, with political intrigue increasing among the military leaders. On June 20, 1964, General William Childs Westmoreland, who had assisted General Harkins, was appointed Commander of MACV. He inherited a troublesome, frustrating and deteriorating political and military situation (Westmoreland had been Commander of a Field Artillery Battalion in Europe [1944-45], Commander of an Airborne Combat Team [Korea, 1950s] and Base Commander, 101st Airborne Division, Ft. Campbell, Kentucky [early 1960s]).

Our Senate approved mutual defense treaties with South Korea, Japan, Nationalist China, the Philippines, Australia and New Zealand; and through our Southeast Asia Treaty Organization (SEATO) agreements, we were bound to defend Thailand, South Vietnam, Laos and Cambodia. These countries were assured that the U.S. would defend them against an attack by Red China or any other aggressor. Throughout the war, many of these countries demonstrated their willingness to help block the Red aggression in South Vietnam. South Korea sent nearly 50,000 troops; the Philippines, over 2,000; Thailand, slightly over 15,000; Australia, approximately 8,000; and New Zealand, about 1,000.

By 1964, the CIA was assisting the South Vietnamese in carrying out secret attacks on coastal targets north of the DMZ under the code name Operations Plan (OPLAN) using agents trained by the Special Forces. The U.S. Navy was conducting surveillance patrols regularly (code name DeSota) in international waters in the Gulf of Tonkin. On August 10, the North Vietnamese islands of Hon Me and Hon Ngu were hit by South Vietnamese troops. The North Vietnamese responded by sending five patrol boats into international waters and attacked the USS *Maddox*. The USS

121st Assault Helicopter Company, Viking Platoon.

Sampan on Mekong tributary in Soc Trang.

Mekong River Delta near Soc Trang.

The flash in the photo is the explosion of a Napalm bomb dropped by a F-4 Phantom Jet a few seconds earlier.

Can Tho in Mekong Delta.

My Tho in Mekong Delta.

```
              GUIDANCE FOR COMMANDERS IN VIETNAM
                               BY
               GENERAL W. C. WESTMORELAND, COMUSMACV

1.  Make the welfare of your men your primary concern with special
    attention to mess, mail, and medical care.

2.  Give priority emphasis to matters of intelligence, counter-intel-
    ligence, and timely and accurate reporting.

3.  Gear your command for sustained operations; keep constant pres-
    sure on the enemy.

4.  React rapidly with all force available to opportunities to destroy
    the enemy; disrupt bases, capturing or destroying his supply caches.

5.  Open up methodically and use roads, waterways, and the railroad;
    be alert and prepared to ambush the ambusher.

6.  Harass enemy lines of communication by raids and ambushes.

7.  Use your firepower with care and discrimination, particularly in
    populated areas.

8.  Capitalize on psywar opportunities.

9.  Assist in "revolutionary development" with emphasis on priority
    areas and on civic action wherever feasible.

10. Encourage and help Vietnamese military and paramilitary units;
    involve them in your operations at every opportunity.

11. Be smarter and more skillful than the enemy; stimulate profes-
    sionalism, alertness and tactical ingenuity; seize every opportunity
    to enhance training of men and units.

12. Keep your officers and men well informed, aware of the nine rules
    for personnel of MACV, and mindful of the techniques of communist
    insurgency and the role of free world forces in Vietnam.

13. Maintain an alert "open door" policy on complaints and a sensitivity
    to detection and correction of malpractices.

14. Recognize bravery and outstanding work.

15. Inspect frequently units two echelons below your level to insure
    compliance with the foregoing.

                                        /s/W. C. W.
                                        /t/W. C. W.      22/7/66


                        FOR OFFICIAL USE ONLY
```

Guidelines for commanders in Vietnam issued by General W. C. Westmoreland.

Maddox fired 5-in. guns in response to the North Vietnamese 12.5-mm machine gun attack. The USS *C. Turner Joy* was also involved in the attack. One of the North Vietnamese patrol boats fired two torpedoes; however, both missed their target. Four F-8E Crusaders took off from the carrier USS *Ticonderoga*, but by the time they arrived one of the patrol boats had taken a direct hit, and the North Vietnamese had withdrawn. Later on August 4, another attack took place some sixty miles off shore.

Under the Southeast Asia Collective Defense Treaty, our commitment to the South Vietnamese people was reaffirmed by both the Eisenhower and Kennedy Administrations and was reiterated by Congress with its approval of the Gulf of Tonkin Resolution on August 7, 1964, in response to Hanoi's naval attack on the USS Destroyers *Maddox* and *C. Turner Joy*. Those resolutions authorized "…all necessary measures…" the President might take "…to repel any armed attack…" against U.S. Forces and "…to prevent further aggressions." It also approved "…all necessary steps including the use of armed force …which the President might take to help any nation that requests aid …in defense of its freedoms…."

The position of the United States was expressed by Secretary of State Dean Rusk in a statement on August 3, 1965. He spoke first of America's role in defense of peace, freedom and the right of free choice everywhere. He cited our aid to Greece and Turkey in the face of Communist takeover threats following World War II; of the Marshall Plan in rebuilding a devastated Europe; NATO Defense Alliances in halting aggression in Korea; and support of the United Nations in preserving the Congo's independence. Then he stated "…had we not done these things—and others—the enemies of freedom would now control much of the world and be in a position to destroy us, or at least to sap our strength, by economic strangulation…For the same basic reasons that we took all those other measures to deter or repel aggression, we are determined to assist the people of South Vietnam to defeat this aggression."

The goals of the South Vietnamese and of the United States were made clear by Foreign Minister Tran Van Do on July 22, 1965, when he outlined them as follows: (1) Dissolution of the National Liberation Front and withdrawal of all North Vietnamese troops; (2) Self determination for an independent South Vietnam; (3) Withdrawal of foreign troops after aggression has ceased; (4) Guarantees for the independence and liberty for the Vietnamese people.

In a news conference on July 28, 1965, President Johnson succinctly stated the viewpoint of the U.S., "We do not seek the destruction of any government, nor do we covet a foot of any territory. But, we insist and will always insist, that the people of South Vietnam shall have the right of choice, the right to shape their own destiny in free elections in the south, or throughout all Vietnam under international supervision. And they shall not have any government by force and terror as long as we can prevent it." President Johnson on another occasion stated "…the U.S. is ready to hold 'unconditional discussions' with the governments concerned in the interest of arriving at a satisfactory peaceful settlement of the Vietnamese problems…." However, he cautioned in a speech on April 7, 1965, "…we hope that peace will come swiftly. But, that is in the hands of others besides ourselves. And, we must be prepared for a long continued conflict."

In May 1961, French President De Gaulle told President Kennedy, "I predict to you that you will, step by step, be sucked into a bottomless military and political quagmire."

General William C. Westmoreland repeatedly cautioned that, although military progress was being made, the United States would have to exercise patience, courage and perseverance in order to see the struggle through to a satisfactory conclusion.

On January 2, 1963, in the Mekong Delta 65 miles southwest of Saigon, two South Vietnamese Civil Guard Battalions (acting on a plan drawn up by Lt. Col. John Vann, a U.S. field advisor) attacked a VC radio transmitter between the hamlet (Ap) of Tan Thoi and the neighboring hamlet of Bac. The Army of the Republic of Vietnam (ARVN) was badly defeated. They exhibited a notable indecisiveness in battle, a lack of courage under fire and an unwillingness to engage the enemy.

Over the next two years the VC shifted their attention from ARVN units to American units in South Vietnam. On October 31, 1964, four U.S. servicemen were killed at Bien Hoa. On December 24, 1964, two people were killed and over 100 wounded in a bomb attack on the Brink Hotel (being used as a BOQ for U.S. military personnel) in Saigon.

On February 6, 1965, more than 300 VC attacked Camp Holloway at Pleiku, killing eight Americans and wounding many more. (Camp Holloway was dedicated on July 4, 1963, named for CWO Charles E. Holloway who was killed on December 22, 1962 [his 18th day in country], while piloting a CH-21 Shawnee ["Flying Banana"] helicopter from the 81st Transportation Company [later re-designated the 119th Aviation Company] carrying ARVN troops to an LZ near Van Hoa, north of Tuy Hoa in Phu Yen Province.)

In response to the Camp Holloway attack, President Johnson ordered air strikes on North Vietnam, code named Flaming Dart, and authorized the deployment of SAM missiles to a site near Da Nang.

On February 10, 1965, the VC hit Qui Nhon, killing 21 Americans and wounding many more. President Johnson responded with more air strikes (Flaming Dart II) and, then a few days later on March 2, initiated "…a program of measured limited air action…" against the North, known as Rolling Thunder. On March 7, 1965, the President ordered U.S. Marines to Da Nang to protect the air base there. This was the beginning of the "build-up" process that would ultimately bring the 18th Surgical Hospital (MA) to Vietnam a little over one year later.

On March 8, 1965, part of a Battalion Landing Team (BLT) went ashore on Red Beach a few miles northwest of Da Nang, and later that day, elements of the 1st Batallion, 3rd Marine Division landed at Da Nang, having been airlifted from Okinawa.

By April 1, 1965, General Westmoreland had persuaded President Johnson to increase the troop level to 33,000 in order to protect a top-secret Army Security Agency's communication complex at Phu Bai, farther up the coast, north of Da Nang. On April 22, a patrol from the Marine's Reconnaissance Batallion engaged a VC ("Charlie") force of about 100 men near Binh Thai, nine miles southwest of Da Nang. America's shooting war involving U.S. combat troops had begun. The ARVN troops were taking heavy loses, and the VC were constantly increasing their attacks. U.S. intelligence indicated that the North Vietnamese

Army (NVA) was increasingly entering the South to support the VC guerrillas.

On April 24, President Johnson officially designated Vietnam a "combat zone" for U.S. Forces retroactive to January 1, 1965. The 173rd Airborne Brigade was ordered to Vietnam and arrived at Bien Hoa on May 7. On July 1, more Marines landed at Qui Nhon, and on July 29, the 1st Brigade, 101st Airborne Division arrived at Cam Ranh Bay.

One day earlier, President Johnson had announced the commitment of the 1st Cavalry Division (Airmobile) to Vietnam (the lineal descendent of the unit Col. George Armstrong Custer led into another river valley at the Little Bighorn in Montana). The Division had been created in June with personnel from the experimental 11th Air Assault Division (Test) and from the 2nd Infantry Division (given cavalry designation) that were combined under the command of Major General Harry W. O. Kinnard. More than 400 helicopters (OH-13 Sioux for reconnaissance; UH-1A Huey "gunships" [in 1969, the U.S. began using UH-1B, making the UH-1A available for the ARVN forces] for assault and infantry lift; CH-47 [Boeing-Vertol] Chinooks and the CH-54 [Sikorsky] Tarhe Flying Cranes for heavy lifting, 16,000 personnel and 1600 vehicles) arrived in Vietnam in early September. The division began arriving at An Khe, 35 miles inland from the coastal town of Qui Nhon, on September 14 (their immense heliport at Camp Radcliff was dubbed the "Golf Course"). An Khe is located on Hwy. 19, which leads from Qui Nhon to Pleiku City (Central Highlands [Trung Nguyen]) and continues to Duc Co, then proceeds on into Cambodia (the Mang Yang Pass is a gap in the mountain chain through which Hwy. 19 passes from An Khe into the Central Highlands).

Intelligence sources indicated that NVA forces under the command of Brigadier General Chu Huy Man had infiltrated along the Ho Chi Minh Trail through Laos and Cambodia into South Vietnam. They were preparing to seize Kontum and Pleiku City and then capture An Khe and Qui Nhon, thus dividing South Vietnam through the Central Highlands (the Pleiku or Tay Nguyen Campaign). In order to capture Pleiku City successfully, they first needed to capture and destroy the Special Forces' camps at Plei Me and Duc Co. In July 1965, the NVA's 32nd Regiment surrounded Duc Co. The forces at Duc Co were ARVN and Montagnard troops, as well as U.S. Special Forces Advisors. The Montagnard troops were officially known as the Civilian Irregular Defense Group (CIDG). In late 1964, they were placed under MACV control through the 5th Special Forces Group (Airborne). Their long range patrols that, at times operated deep into enemy territory, were known as mobile strike ("Mike") forces. The Montagnards were primarily composed of the Muong and Jarai tribesmen. There

Red Beach ("China Beach") on Qui Nhon Bay.

were over 210,000 of the Muongs in the Central Highlands living throughout the area from Kontum in the northern section to Ban Me Tuot in the southern section with Pleiku City situated in the central region. Approximately 8,000 Montagnards had fled South Vietnam the previous year because of political differences, social prejudices and cultural ostracism. They returned in October 1966 and were welcomed back at a FULRO Festival. They used the Quoc Ngu script but also spoke Vietnamese. The attack was eventually thwarted by heavy U.S. air attacks, but not before the enemy had inflicted significant casualties.

The NVA's 32nd Regiment then joined with their 33rd Battalion and established a base camp on the eastern slopes of the Chu Pong Mountains (visible from the site of the 18th Surgical Hospital [MA]) near the Drang River, which is 37 miles west of Pleiku City. The 66th Regiment soon joined General Man's forces to provide him with the equivalent of a division.

The Special Forces camp at Plei Me (25 miles southwest of Pleiku) was attacked on October 20. The ARVN commanders at Pleiku were reluctant to commit their troops as backup support because of their concern that Pleiku might also be surrounded and attacked. General Westmoreland sent the 1st Brigade, 1st Cavalry (Airmobile) to Pleiku, relieving the ARVN forces to aid those trapped at Plei Me.

After the Plei Me attack on October 27, General Kinnard and the 1st Cavalry Division (Airmobile) was given responsibility for Pleiku, Kontum and Binh Dinh Provinces in II Corps Tactical Zone. On November 14, 1965, the 1st Battalion, 7th Cavalry (1st/7th) under the command of Lt. Col. Harold G. "Hal" Moore was airlifted into LZ X-Ray in the Ia Drang Valley in search of the NVA. They soon made contact with the enemy and a near tragedy ensued. When the fighting finally ended, the 1st Air Calvary Division had 304 dead and 524 wounded. The NVA had 1519 dead and 1178 wounded and the U.S. captured

157 prisoners. The NVA had been forced back over the border into Cambodia and a major attack in the Central Highlands had been repelled. The 1st/7th Cavalry won the Presidential Unit Citation for this action. Later, Lt. Gen. Harold G. "Hal" Moore wrote about this battle in his book, *We Were Soldiers Once—And Young*. During 1966 and 1967, the Division distinguished itself in battle against the NVA and VC units throughout II Corps in Operations Masher/White Wing, Paul Revere, Irving, Thayer II and Pershing I and II.

With an ever-increasing U.S. military presence and with the increasing VC and NVA attacks in South Vietnam, it is not surprising that the 18th Surgical Hospital (MA) was redesignated on March 1, 1963, and then activated on March 26, 1963, at Ft. Gordon, GA, for later deployment to the Republic of Vietnam in June, 1966.

About the time the 1st Cavalry Division was involved in the Battle of the Ia Drang Valley ("Battle of the Forest of Screaming Souls"), those of us originally assigned to the 18th Surgical Hospital (MA) were receiving our induction notices. At the end of 1965, there were 184,000 U.S. troops in South Vietnam and by 1968, there were 525,000 in country. We were a part of the nearly 400,000 sent during this buildup. We, along with many other physicians reported to the Medical Field Service School (MFSS), located near the Brooke Army Medical Center, at Ft. Sam Houston, San Antonio, Texas on Monday, February 7, 1966. While there we received classroom instruction and field training at Camp Bullis, and received our diplomas (Army Medical Service Officers Basic Course) on Saturday, March 5, 1966. We then had a few days at home before reporting to Ft. Gordon (U.S. 3rd Army) near Augusta, Georgia. for assignment to the 18th Surgical Hospital (MA).

As the 1st Cavalry Division (Airmobile) assumed responsibility for the Central Highlands (along with the 3rd Brigade, 25th

Graduating class of Army Medical Service Officer Basic Course, Class #5, Fort Sam Houston, Texas, February 1966. First row: A.S. Mufson, E.A. Merecki, R.H. Ulmer, J.E. Swink, B.B. Platt, C.H. Voncanon. Second row: J.W. Kramer, R.T. Shore, S.G. Pappas, E.W. Whalen, C.D. Morehead, D.B. Littman, R.E. Kleiger, R.M. Klaus, J.L. Vakas, H.E. Voss, R.M. Severino, S.H. Reid. Third row: G. Troiano, I.J. Weiner, J.W. Wall, S.H. Schachner, B.F. Sams, F.R. Weis, C.P. O'Riordan, T. Tomkiewicz, E.W. Till, B.G. Norwood, O.P. Swenson, M. Lefkowitz, T.J. McDonald. Fourth row: R.V. Munch, M.J. Pollak, J.W. Martin, C. Olsen, J. Vecchione, F. Swietnicki, H.L. Kilburn, M.C. Lindem, D.C. Moore, J.L. Parker, T.R. Woehler, Magim, H. Lieberman. Fifth row: H.K. Wirts, A.L. Kapsner, T.R. Watson, D.D. Nixon, I.J. Nelson, N.C. Spitzer, R.G. Kopff, Jr., R.E. Manicom, T. O'Callaghan, A.S. Kravatz, S. Tesser, J.A. Reichenberger, S.M. Poticha. Sixth row: H. Rohs, R. Schmidt, E.A. Nichols, W.L. Vandergriff, R.G. Neidballa, T.J. Stuart, Jr., B.C. Weber, P.E. Williams, Jr., H. Wechsler, H.M. Labiche, Jr., M.W. Phillips, T.J. Lord, A. Yogada, D. Lyerly. Underlined names are those who were assigned at one time or another to the 18th Surgical Hospital.

Infantry Division), they had the classic divisional support system that included a medical battalion of four companies, each with three platoons. A single medical company supported each brigade. The medical platoons, of three sections each, supported units of infantry or armored cavalry squadrons. The constantly changing conditions of warfare in Vietnam determined the deployment of combat units and resulted in a modification of the system. Probably no two medical battalions were used in the same way. The 2nd Surgical Hospital (deployed from Ft. Bragg in September 1965, boarded the USS *Buckner* at San Diego and landed at Qui Nhon 23 days later) moved into An Khe soon after the 1st Cavalry Division's arrival to provide additional medical and surgical support. Usually the air ambulances organic to the division evacuated patients in the division's area of operation from the battle site to one of the division's four clearing stations and then medical evacuation helicopters not organic to divisions (code named "Dustoff," the radio call signal used by an early pilot, Maj. Charles L. Kelly who was killed in action) evacuated the wounded from the divisional clearing stations to a surgical hospital. The clearing stations acted as a triage point, where an attempt was made to determine the priority of evacuation based on the location and severity of the wounds and the status of the patient. Those severely wounded requiring immediate surgical intervention were flown directly to the 2nd Surgical Hospital. Because of the distance involved and the prolonged turn-around-time for Dustoff medical evacuations, the need for a surgical hospital at Pleiku became obvious.

FORT GORDON

On Sunday, March 13, 1966, the following physicians arrived at Ft. Gordon, Georgia and reported for duty to the 18th Surgical Hospital (MA) on Monday, March 14, 1966:

1. Sheldon Charles "Charlie" Brown, M.D.
2. Robert Edward "Enge" Engebrecht, M.D
3. Wayne Frederick "Hoss" Hosking, M.D.
4. Felix Woodrow "Flix" Jenkins, M.D.
5. Joseph "Joe" Juliano, M.D.
6. Martin Carl "Tony" Lindem, Jr., M.D.
7. Jerry Wayne "Dai Uy" Martin, M.D.
8. Ted James "Ted" Stuart, Jr., M.D.
9. Orville Peter "Orv" Swenson, M.D.
10. John Henry Tatom, M.D.

I left Bowling Green, Kentucky on the morning of Sunday, March 13, 1966, and drove to Ft. Gordon, arriving later the same day. Many of our group had met at the MFSS before going to Ft. Gordon, and we quickly became acquainted with the others upon their arrival in Georgia. We were all assigned to the same Bachelor Officer Quarters (BOQ) and were soon introduced to the 18th Surgical Hospital (MA) personnel. The Hospital had been alerted for deployment to Vietnam on January 10, 1966. Major George W. Bierman, MSC, became the hospital CO on January 1, 1966, and continued in that capacity until his retirement on April 12, 1966. Capt. Thurman L. Shurtleff, MSC, was the acting CO from April 13, 1966, until May 17, 1966. Lt. Col. Mark Thomas "Tom" Cenac, MC (General Surgeon), our CO while at Pleiku, became CO on May 18; however, he did not join the 18th Surgical Hospital (MA) at Ft. Gordon, but joined the unit at Tacoma, Washington prior to deployment to Vietnam. On May 19, 1966, Capt. David A. Soberg, MSC, became the Executive Officer, and 1st Lt. John K. Walton became the Supply Officer on January 17, 1966. First Lt. Joseph F. Lazorchak became Adjutant on February 16, 1966, and MSG (E8) Russell W. Uselton became the First Sergeant on January 1, 1966. Capt. Bernard Nass was the Chaplain while at Ft. Gordon and accompanied the unit to Vietnam. Capt. Callie Carson was Chief, Nursing Service, while at Ft. Gordon. Military regulations require that an individual with the rank of Major fill that position; therefore, she was replaced on June 25, 1966, at Pleiku by Major Mary E. Berry, but remained as Assistant Chief until her rotation back to the States.

After being issued our combat gear, we joined the other members assigned to the 18th Surgical Hospital (MA) and underwent three weeks of intensive field training emphasizing specified requirements for overseas movement. This training included mock casualties and evacuation techniques, orientation regarding claymore mines and punji stakes, and a brief introduction to Vietnamese and Montagnard customs and culture. From Wednesday, April 27 to Friday, April 29, 1966, our unit was involved in an Army Training Test 8-1, and

Front, left to right: Standing on steps at our BOQ at Fort Gordon; Wayne Hosking, M.D., Orville Swenson, M.D., Bob Engebrecht, M.D. Second row: Ted Stuart, M.D., Jerry W. Martin, M.D. Third row: Felix Jenkins, M.D., Charlie Brown, M.D., Joe Juliano, M.D., and John Tatom, M.D. Tony Lindem, M.D. had left for Vietnam with the advance party, thus was not present for the photograph.

received a rating of excellent (I seriously doubt that we could have failed the test). A Readiness Inspection was conducted by the United States 3rd Army on Thursday, May 12, 1966. The 18th Surgical Hospital (MA) was considered operationally ready to perform its Table of Organization and Equipment (TO&E) mission.

When we were not involved in activities related to the 18th Surgical Hospital (MA), the physicians worked in the Clinics at the Eisenhower Hospital at Ft. Gordon. One day while working in the clinic, some of us met Corbett H. Thigpen, M.D., a consulting psychiatrist from the Cleckley-Thigpen Psychiatric Associates in Augusta, Georgia. He wrote the novel, *The Three Faces of Eve*, which was made into a highly popular, award-winning movie. Two or three of us accepted his invitation for dinner at his home one evening. Later, I saw a lady in clinic with an acute paranoid schizophrenic psychosis and attempted to contact him at his office. Dr. Thigpen was away lecturing, but his associate, Hervey M. Cleckley, M.D., admitted the patient to the Psychiatric Section at the University Hospital in Augusta.

While at Ft. Gordon, we were fortunate to have frequent opportunities to attend lectures, CPCs and Grand Rounds at the University of Georgia Medical School or at the University Hospital.

After completion of the field training exercises, Major Bierman and his wife hosted a picnic and cookout for us at their home.

My uncle, who was vice president of Wicks-Varina Lumber and Builders Supply, arranged for the manager of their Augusta store to have some of his employees construct footlockers for those of us who wanted one. They were sturdily built of rot-resistant 3/8-inch treated plywood, strongly braced and painted an army grayish-green color. They had sealing strips around the lid and were fitted with an interior socket for a small light bulb, plus latches to allow locking for security. Later, we found these to be ideal to keep our clothing, cameras, etc., dry during Vietnam's monsoon season. The lockers, filled with our gear, were shipped with the unit to

Vietnam. I shipped mine home when I returned to the States, and it is still used for storage.

Probably the highlight of our time at Ft. Gordon was the opportunity to attend the Masters Golf Tournament, won by Jack Nicklaus, in 1966. The CO of the Eisenhower Hospital had tickets and a reserved parking pass that he allowed us to use. We were able to attend the practice rounds, as well as each day of the tournament. MSG Uselton's house in Augusta was within walking distance of the Masters course. When he rotated back to the States for retirement on December 31, 1966, he invited us to visit him and attend future Masters tournaments. He offered us the opportunity of staying at his house at no cost, and he also offered to get tickets for us. Foolishly, we never took advantage of his offer.

The 18th Surgical Hospital (MA) was transported to Tacoma, Washington and then deployed to the Republic of Vietnam on Wednesday, June 1, 1966, aboard the U.S.N.S. *Walker*, arriving in Qui Nhon on Friday, June 17. The TO&E equipment did not arrive at Pleiku until July 12; however, the unit became operational on July 1. That was possible because we began working at the 542nd Medical Clearing Company, which was

Jerry Martin, M.D. taking a break while on maneuvers.

Jerry W. Martin, M.D. in combat gear while on maneuvers.

Eisenhower Hospital, Fort Gordon, Georgia. Front, left to right: Bob Engebrecht, M.D., Tony Lindem, M.D., Orville Swenson, M.D. Back row: Jerry W. Martin, M.D., Ted Stuart, M.D., Wayne Hosking, M.D. Not available for photo: Charlie Brown, M.D., Joe Juliano, M.D., Felix Jenkins, M.D., John Tatom, M.D.

The advanced party—Capt. Soberg, MSG Uselton, 1st Lt. Lazorchak and Tony Lindem, M.D. (Chief, Professional Services ["Our Fearless Leader"])—flew by USAF C-130 from Ft. Gordon on June 10, 1966 to Chicago, San Francisco, Honolulu, Wake Island, Guam, Manila, and landed at Nha Trang ("Riviera of the East"), before flying on to Pleiku.

The remaining nine physicians were granted a brief leave at home before flying to Vietnam. I flew out of Bowling Green, Kentucky on Eastern Airline at 9:50 a.m. on the morning of Tuesday, June 21, to Nashville, Tennessee. From there I flew to Dallas and then on to San Francisco on a TWA flight. We met at the San Francisco International Airport and spent the night at a hotel there. Our flight to Vietnam was delayed, so we spent the day touring San Francisco. Our Pan Am civilian charter flight (Boeing 707) did not leave San Francisco until about 8 p.m. on Wednesday, June 22. We arrived at Honolulu International Airport about 12:30 a.m. on June 23. We were allowed to deplane and after about a one- or two- hour delay, departed Hawaii headed for Wake Island. About 2/3 of the way between Hawaii and Wake, we lost a day upon crossing the International Date Line. As we flew westward, we were partially keeping up with the movement of the sun, so it seemed to remain morning for a much longer period of time than usual. We were served three breakfasts back to back, one near Wake Island, and another soon after leaving Anderson AFB, Guam. We were scheduled to land at Manila, Philippines; however, they were experiencing a typhoon. We flew over the storm by climbing to nearly the maximum allowable altitude for the 707. Through clear skies we could look down at the storm, but, nevertheless, it was a turbulent and exciting ride for a while. We had another breakfast before arriving in Vietnam.

On the flight to Vietnam the feature movie was *A Man Could Get Killed*, starring James Garner, Sandra Dee, Melina Mercouri and Anthony Franciosa. The song introduced in this movie as part of the score, *Strangers in the Night*, later became a number one hit for Frank Sinatra. The movie title seemed somewhat incongruent, considering our destination.

PLEIKU

We arrived at Tan Son Nhut International Airport in Saigon on the morning of Friday, June 24, at 10:20 a.m., and we had lost a day minus eleven hours (there was a 13-hour difference between Saigon and Bowling Green, Kentucky). We were bused from the airport to nearby Camp Alpha, a tent city with concrete floors built to accommodate temporarily incoming troops, where we spent the night. That evening, we went to the Champs Elysees Restaurant on the ninth floor at the Caravelle Hotel in downtown Saigon for dinner.

About midmorning on Saturday, June 25, Tony Lindem, M.D., and another member of the advanced party met us at Camp Alpha with flight orders to travel to Pleiku. That was the first time we knew specifically where we were going. We were bused back to Tan Son Nhut where we boarded a C-130 and then flew to Ban Me Thuot. After a brief stop there, we proceeded to Da Nang (we

Orville Swenson, M.D., Wayne Hosking, M.D., Bob Engebrecht, M.D. in San Francisco.

View over Pacific.

already operational. It was situated across a rice paddy less than 1/2 mile as the crow flies (approximately 3/4 mile by road) from our hospital site. We worked there in tents until our permanent facilities were completed. There was one surgical tent with two operating tables. Although we often had to fan mosquitoes away from the operative field, there were surprisingly few secondary wound infections. We ate at the 542nd Mess and, for the first two weeks, slept on cots in the partially completed Quonset buildings that eventually became the 18th Surgical Hospital (MA). Tents were soon set up and we moved there to allow the construction of the hospital to be completed.

arrived just as a mortar attack was ending). We de-boarded and waited while the plane continued on to Hue. Upon its return to the Da Nang Air Base, we re-boarded and flew to Kontum allowing a few troops to deplane, and then flew on to Pleiku, arriving there in the afternoon. From the New Pleiku Airport we were transported by jeep to the site of the 18th Surgical Hospital (MA) that was under construction a little over a mile away.

At the 542nd, we joined the 501st Medical Detachment (Dispensary) and the 240th Medical Detachment (Thoracic K-Team). The 51st Medical Company (Ambulance) transported patients to the New Pleiku Airbase (USAF) for evacuation from July 1 to December 5, 1966, and was replaced by the 1st Medical Company (Ambulance) on December 6, 1966.

The mission of the 18th Surgical Hospital (MA) was to provide resuscitative surgery and medical treatment necessary to stabilize the critically injured or ill U.S. Army Vietnam (USARV) and other Free World Military Assistance Forces (FWMAF) personnel located in Corps Tactical Zone II (CTZ II), for further evacuation. In addition, we provided dispensary medical services for non-divisional units located in CTZ II. We were under the command of the 44th Medical Brigade (Saigon) and the 55th Medical Group (U.S. Army Support Command [Qui Nhon]) and were located in Pleiku Province near Pleiku City.

During our year at Pleiku, the 18th Surgical Hospital (MA) provided both medical and surgical support for the 1st Cavalry Division (Airmobile); the 4th Infantry Division; the 25th Infantry Division (3rd Brigade); the 101st Airborne Division (1st Brigade); the 173rd Airborne Brigade (formed in Okinawa in June 1963 and was the first Army ground combat unit to arrive in Vietnam, landing on May 5, 1965) and all other units stationed in the Pleiku area. Those units included the 7th USAF personnel at the New Pleiku Airbase (Pacific Air Force); the American 5th Special Forces Group (Airborne), known as the Green Berets; Montagnard Special Forces; troops stationed with the 2nd Battalion, 9th Artillery at Artillery Hill; the 299th Engineer Battalion; MACV personnel; those assigned to Camp Holloway (52nd Aviation Battalion, 498th Medical Company [Dustoff, Air Ambulance]; 1st Battalion, 69th Armor; C Troop, 23rd Squadron, 4th Cavalry; 504th Military Police Battalion [Co. B]) and the 10th Detachment of the 619th Aircraft Control Squadron (ACS), a radar unit located a short distance from the 18th Surgical Hospital (MA). We treated many NVA and VC prisoners who were almost uniformly malaria-ridden, malnourished and most often dehydrated. As soon as their post-operative and/or medical status would allow, and after U.S. Intelligence had completed their interrogation, we were required to transfer them to the ARVN Hospital. After their full recovery, the ARVN were supposed to transfer them to the POW Camp, located on Highway 19 between the site of our hospital and Pleiku City.

I mentioned they were "supposed" to transfer the prisoners to the POW Camp after their full recovery. We received a NVA 1st Lieutenant POW at the 18th Surgical Hospital (MA) with a gunshot wound of the abdomen that required many hours of surgery to remove a portion of his liver and spleen and a resection

Airforce Base Da Nang

Ban Me Thuot

Air Strip at Kontum (on way from Da Nang to Pleiku).

POW camp located between the 18th Surgical Hospital (MA) and Pleiku City just off Highway 19.

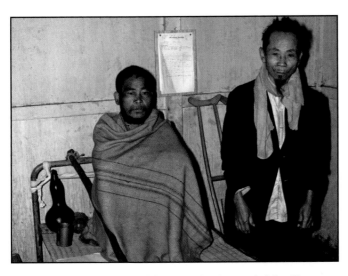

Provincial Hospital patients, a Montagnard patient on the left, a Vietnamese patient on the right, clearly depicting the ethnic and racial differences.

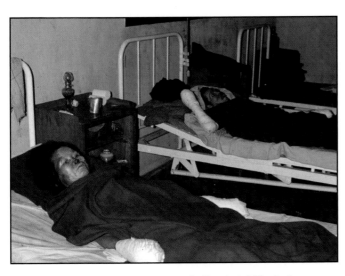

Vietnamese burn patients in the Provincial Hospital.

of a segment of his small bowel. He received many units of blood. After about six days, he was ambulatory on the ward (throughout his post-operative recovery period we had to post a guard on the ward to prevent some of the wounded GI's from killing him). We discharged him to the ARVN Hospital late one afternoon. The next morning, I commandeered a jeep to go to the PX at the 25th Division Base Camp, near Lake Bien Ho ("Sea Lake," an extinct volcano) to buy film. Tony Lindem, M.D., accompanied me. On the return trip, he suggested that we stop at the ARVN Hospital to check on the patient. An ARVN physician, who we knew through the Pleiku Medical Association, met us as we entered the hospital and when we inquired about the patient, he responded in broken English, "He died."

When questioned further, he responded, "He hemorrhaged." We were certainly mystified and puzzled since we did not believe that he had exsanguinated from post-operative complications resulting from the surgery. As we left, Tony asked if I knew the location of the morgue. I had been there once before while touring their hospital, so I drove around to the back entrance. We slipped in through a back door and found the morgue. There we found a body on a table covered with a sheet. When we pulled back the sheet, we saw that it was the NVA POW and saw that his throat had been slashed, severing both the jugulars and carotids bilaterally. Indeed, the patient had bled to death!

We sometimes operated on wounded ARVN troops who were then transferred to the ARVN Hospital as soon as possible. All ARVN medical cases were sent immediately to the ARVN Hospital for convalescence, usually after appropriate treatment had been initiated. On a few occasions we treated Australian, New Zealand, Thai, and South Korean (ROK) troops who were attached to the 173rd Airborne or to the 25th Division. We treated Vietnamese and Montagnard civilians at our hospital if they were injured by U.S. Forces. When we had free time, we often voluntarily went into Pleiku City (approx. population 30,000) and treated civilians at the Pleiku Provincial Hospital. Occasionally we went at the request of the U.S. Army physicians assigned to the Military Provincial Health Assistance Program (MILPHAP). In January 1963, the U.S. Army began the Medical Civic Action Program (MEDCAP) in an effort to improve outpatient care for the Vietnamese civilian population (and Montagnards in the Central Highlands). In 1965, the MILPHAP was formed as U.S. Forces increased, to help improve training for Vietnamese physicians, nurses and medical technicians in many of the Provincial Hospitals throughout South Vietnam. The 447th Medical Detachment (MILPHAP) was assigned to the Pleiku Provincial Hospital. We worked closely with the two physicians assigned there, Norig "Skip" Ellison, M.D., and Jerry Rosenberg,

M.D. They also helped at the 18th Surgical Hospital (MA). Occasionally we treated American civilian employees working for Raymond International, Morrison-Knudsen, Brown and Root, and J.A. Jones Construction (RMK-BRJ), who were involved in the construction of our hospital.

During the "big buildup" (23,000 U.S. troops in 1964; 185,000 in 1965; 385,000 in 1966), it was necessary to provide adequate infrastructure to accommodate the troops, equipment and all other forms of military aid. Neither South Vietnam nor the U.S. forces could quickly provide this essential infrastructure. That responsibility was given to RMK-BRJ. They referred to themselves as "The Vietnam Builders." For example, the construction demands outstripped the capacity of any one of the individual contractors. The equipment needs alone for the Vietnam Project far exceeded all equipment owned by M-K for all of its worldwide operations and all subsidiary companies. With the merger, RMK-BRJ entered into a highly lucrative, no bid, cost-plus-10% contract with the U.S. Federal Government, via the U.S. Navy, as exclusive contractors to develop South Vietnam into a modern integrated military installation that would allow the U.S. to adequately defend its ally.

Before 1962, construction and facility maintenance support for American advisors in Vietnam was provided by a management structure organic to the U.S. Naval Support Activity (USNSA) that was patterned after the utilities and public works organizations found on military installations in the U.S. In 1962, Lt. Gen. Paul D. Harkins (MACV), wishing to free more troops for advisory duties, requested that the U.S. Army and Japan negotiate a contract for facilities engineering services for installations in South Vietnam. In May 1963, a cost-plus-a-fixed contract was awarded to Pacific Architects and Engineers, which provided military installations at Tan Son Nhut, Da Nang, Pleiku, Qui Nhon, Nha Trang and the central office of MACV in Saigon.

Three of the four firms comprising RMK-BRJ ranked in the top ten of the top 400 U.S. corporations involved in international business in 1966. The Vietnam Builders employed 8,600 Americans (non-military) and over 51,000 Vietnamese. They built eight airstrips 10,000-feet in length, twelve airfields, six ports with 29′ deep-draft berths, six naval bases, twenty hospitals, fourteen million square feet of covered storage and twenty base camps, including housing for 450,000 service men.

In 1966, Rep. Donald H. Rumsfeld, (R, Illinois), among others, charged the Johnson administration with letting contracts that were "illegal by statute" and urged an investigation into the relationship between this private consortium and the administration, in particular the infamous "President's Club," to which Brown and Root had given tens of thousands of dollars that ultimately went to the Johnson campaign.

The government's Vietnam contract with RMK-BRJ ended in 1972. Brown and Root is now a subsidiary of Halliburton. Morrison-Knudsen now calls itself the Washington Group International.

The Australian and New Zealand Army Corps (ANZAC) first became involved in South Vietnam on August 3, 1962, when the

Entrance to the Pleiku Provincial Hospital.

Australian Army Training Team Vietnam (AATTV), which was comprised of thirty military advisors, arrived at Saigon's Tan Son Nhut Airport. Ultimately this small contingent of troops represented the vanguard of nearly 50,000 Australian and New Zealand troops ("Diggers" and "Kiwis") who would serve in Vietnam over the next decade. Although a relatively small number in comparison to American forces, their troop strength reached a peak of over 8,000 in 1968. They became involved in Vietnam because of a multinational mutual assistance pact against Communist aggression, the ANZUS Treaty, signed in 1951. They later joined the South

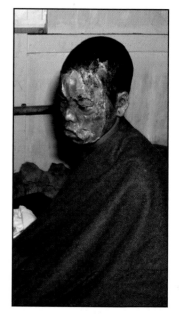

Montagnard woman with severe burn of her left face—note the tooth visible through the full thickness burn of the left cheek.

East Asian Treaty Organization (SEATO) in 1954. On April 29, 1965, Australian Prime Minister Robert Menzies decided to send an infantry battalion because of his deeply rooted belief that "… the take-over of South Vietnam would pose a direct military threat to Australia and all the countries of South East Asia." In late May and early June 1965, the 1st Battalion, Royal Australian Regiment (IRAR) and the 161st Battery, Royal New Zealand Artillery arrived and joined two battalions of the U.S. 173rd Airborne Brigade. The New Zealand Army Detachment Vietnam (NZADVN) arrived in June 1965. All of the Australian and New Zealand troops were handpicked, averaged thirty-five years of age and were experts in counter-revolutionary warfare (CRW), having served in Borneo and Malaya. They were under the control of MAAG and later MACV. As the war expanded, they worked with the Montagnards ("Yards") in the Central Highlands, the Regional and Popular

A panoramic view of Pleiku Province (Central Highlands), Republic of Vietnam taken from Camp Holloway looking North.

Forces (RF/PF, or "Ruff-Puffs"), the National Field Police Force, the U.S. Special Forces (CIDG and "Mike Forces"), the 173rd Airborne and the CIA-sponsored Provisional Reconnaissance Units (PRU, a secretive program concerned with identifying and eliminating the Viet Cong infrastructure); and in March 1966, they became an independent Australian Task Force (ATF).

A contingent of Republic of (South) Korea (ROK) soldiers arrived in South Vietnam in January 1965; and by that fall, their number had increased to a full division. The ROK ("Tiger" Division) was stationed near Qui Nhon where it was attacked in 1965. They were vicious and effective in combat and were highly respected and greatly feared by the VC and NVA. The ROK were accused of massacring Vietnamese civilians in December 1966, at Binh Hoa (a VC stronghold). The incident was similar to the attack involving the 1st Platoon, Company C (1st Battalion, 20th Infantry, 11th Brigade, American Division in the hamlet of My Lai, village of Son My, Quang Ngai Province, CTZ I) led by 1st Lt. William L. Calley on March 16, 1968, who was in search of the 48th VC Battalion. Reports circulated that after the ROK base camp was mortared by the VC, they immediately retaliated by making a circular sweep in a radius extending outward from the impact site. During the sweep they supposedly killed everything alive—pigs, chickens, water buffalo, men, women, children, etc. They were then convinced that those who perpetrated the attack had been eliminated. We heard this rumor from numerous sources, but never had any authoritative documentation. We did know, however, that anytime the ROK were in our area, the VC never attacked, and we were never under an alert; therefore, the rumor was generally accepted as true.

On July 16, 1965, the 299th Engineer Battalion, also from Ft. Gordon, Georgia ("Fighting 299th Engineer Battalion" of World War II), was alerted for movement overseas to Vietnam. During the next few weeks, the Battalion received new vehicles, equipment and personnel. The main body departed Ft. Gordon on September 27, 1965, by troop train bound for Oakland, California, and there, boarded the U.S.N.S. General Edwin D. Patrick. The advance party departed from Savannah, Georgia on two C-130 aircraft on September 28, 1965, and arrived in Qui Nhon on October 1, 1965, with the main body arriving at Qui

Nhon on October 22, 1965. They were assigned to the 937th Engineer Group and bivouacked in the Phu Tai Valley about ten miles southwest of Qui Nhon. Their first project was the repair of Highway 19 to An Khe, the main supply route to the 1st Cavalry Division. Other combat engineering projects quickly followed in support of the ROK near Qui Nhon, and later the 25th Division (3rd Brigade) at Pleiku. Their efforts in the Pleiku area involved the logistical depot complex at Artillery Hill, the aircraft maintenance facility at Camp Holloway and the 18th Surgical Hospital (MA). The Commanding Officer of the 299th was Lt. Col. Crowell; and the Executive Officer was Maj. Call. Although the work they did at the 18th Surgical Hospital (MA) at times seemed inordinately slow, they truly were spread pretty thin. The switch from base camp development projects to combat support began in August 1966, when the battalion participated in Operation Paul Revere II in support of the 1st Calvary and the 25th Infantry Divisions southwest of Pleiku. Operational support continued through October 1966, with the construction of a Special Forces camp at Duc Co. They continued upgrading and repairing Route 19 and expanded the airfields at Kontum and Dak To. After they began combat support of the 4th Division and the 173rd Airborne Brigade they continued to engage in general engineer support and the maintenance of roads, bridges and airfields in the Pleiku area until June 1967, about the time our initial group was rotating back to the States.

The 44th Medical Brigade arrived in country about three months (operational only two months) before the arrival of the 18th Surgical Hospital (MA).

The Headquarters and Headquarters Detachment, 44th Medical Brigade was constituted in the Regular Army on December 30, 1965, activated at Ft. Sam Houston, Texas on January 1, 1966, and was alerted for deployment to Vietnam on January 27, 1966. Readiness dates were set for April 1 for equipment and April 24 for personnel. Col. James A. Wier, already in Vietnam as Director of Medical Services, 1st Logistical Command, was designated Commanding Officer of the 44th Medical Brigade on January 26, 1966. On March 18, an advance party (8 officers and 10 enlisted men) arrived in Saigon to establish the Medical Brigade (Provisional). On March 24, Col. Wier assumed

Stores in Pleiku. I purchased lacquer ware, antique Chinese Vase, small brass vases and other items at the corner store.

Vietnamese peasant resting in the shade of a tree in Pleiku.

Former home of a French planter used as Pleiku mayor's home/office.

Home of Maj. Gen. Vinh Loc in Pleiku.

Shop selling false teeth with an adjacent restaurant in Pleiku.

Woman sorting prawns at entrance to their house.

One of three deep wells dug by engineers providing potable water in Pleiku.

Children mugging for the camera in Pleiku.

Peasants using don ganh to carry loaded baskets in Pleiku.

Clean, well-kept peasant's house with garden in front.

command of the 44th Medical Brigade (Provisional). The main body arrived at Tan Son Nhut Airport on April 21 and set up Headquarters at 24/8 Truong Quoc Dung, a group of villas in suburban Saigon. The "Provisional" designation was dropped, and the Brigade Headquarters became operational on May 1, and assumed command and operational control of all 1st Logistical Command medical units.

On June 10, 1966, Col. James A. Wier, MC, became USARV Surgeon and was promoted to Brig. General. Command of the 44th Medical Brigade was turned over to Col. Ray L. Miller, MC, by Maj. Gen. C. W. Eifler, Commanding General, 1st Logistical Command.

There were 58 medical units in the 1st Logistical Command in early 1966 and 65 under the 44th Medical Brigade when it became operational on May 1. Before the year ended, the Brigade had command and control of 121 units. Veterinary, Dental, Preventative Medicine, Medical Depot and Laboratory units, as well as the Medical Group Headquarters were organized directly under the Brigade Headquarters. The remainder of the units came under the further control of the Medical Group by geographic area. The strength of all of the 44th Medical Brigade units increased from 3,187 in May 1966, to 7,830 by December 31, 1966.

When we arrived in Pleiku, the ARVN and the 3rd Brigade of the 25th Infantry Division were involved in the operation code named Paul Revere I, which covered the time period from May 10 to July 30. This action was a border screening (Cambodia) and an area-control mission that claimed 546 enemy casualties with only moderate U.S. and South Vietnamese casualties. This was our initiation with combat surgery.

On Wednesday, July 13, while making rounds on both medical and surgical patients at the 542nd, I encountered Ron Nesson (NBC-TV, Saigon). He was brought in by Dustoff from a LZ near Dac To the evening before. He arrived at the 542nd within about 30 minutes following a chest injury caused by "friendly fire." He was with the 101st Airborne Division doing a story about the first anniversary of their activities in country. The reconnaissance platoon he was patrolling with had not made contact with the VC. As they came to a stream, the platoon fired into an area of dense jungle on the opposite bank. A M-79 grenade launcher was fired, the missile struck a tree and a shrapnel fragment ricocheted back and struck him in the chest. Tony Lindem, M.D., and Felix Jenkins, M.D., operated on him and inserted a left anterior chest tube to correct the hemopneumothorax (air and blood in the plural space).

Mr. Nesson later became a writer/editor at the UPI and VP for news of the Mutual Broadcasting System. He was President Gerald R. Ford's Press Secretary (1975-1977) and was VP for Communications at the Brookings Institute in Washington. He served for eight years on the Board (one year as Chairman) of the Peabody Awards for Excellence in Broadcasting and has written six books and co-authored a play, *The Presidents*. He currently is Journalist in Residence at the Brookings.

On Wednesday, June 11, 1975, I arrived home from making evening rounds at the hospital just in time to turn on the TV and

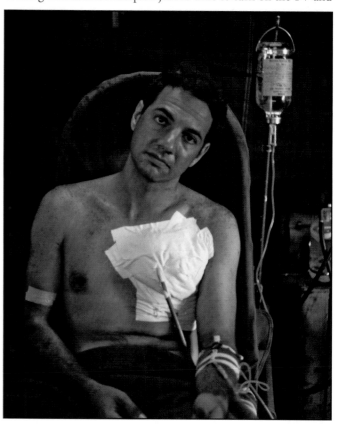

Ron Nesson, an NBC Correspondent, later President Ford's press secretary, at 542nd Medical Clearing Company. A left anterior chest tube in place correcting a pneumothorax caused by shrapnel.

View inside of the Medical Ward at Provincial Hospital.

watch the evening news. During the broadcast Mr. Nesson was introduced as the Press Secretary for President Ford. A few days later I rummaged through my Vietnam slides and found those I had made of him that day at the 542nd Medical Clearing Company, and sent prints to him at the White House. Even though his work schedule must have been very busy, he took the time to respond with a gracious letter of appreciation and thanks.

Samuel Peters Gillis, M.D., had arrived in Qui Nhon on March 13, 1966, and was assigned to the 67th Evacuation Hospital, although it did not become operational until September 1966. Because of that situation, he began working at the 85th Evacuation Hospital, also located in Qui Nhon. On Wednesday, June 1, 1966, two surgical teams (two surgeons [Sam and Ollie Beamon, M.D.], two assistant surgeons, one anesthesiologist, four male nurses and ten enlisted corpsmen) assigned to the 67th Evacuation Hospital were sent to the 542nd Medical Clearing Company at Pleiku. Roger Raymond Ecker, M.D., thoracic surgeon and CO of the 240th Thoracic K-Team, along with Capt. Leo "Ski" Plasczynski, R.N., (surgical nurse) and five surgical techs had already been assigned to the 542nd. The TO&E of a Thoracic K-Team is comprised of two thoracic surgeons, one anesthesiologist or nurse anesthetist, three surgical nurses and fourteen corpmen (sugical techs). As often happened, the TO&E were rarely completely filled so that the 240th Thoracic K-Team had only one surgeon, no anesthesiologist or anesthetist, one surgical nurse and five surgical techs. The TO&E for a Neurosurgical K-Team was, ideally, similarly constituted; however, they also usually did not have a full complement of personnel. This was the situation when the physicians with the 18th Surgical Hospital (MA) arrived in Pleiku. Control of the 542nd Medical Clearing Company and the 240th Thoracic K-Team, both equipment and personnel, were placed under the command of the 18th Surgical Hospital (MA) on Saturday, June 25, 1966. Within a few days, Sam and the other physicians went back to Qui Nhon. In August, Sam returned to Pleiku and was permanently assigned to the 18th Surgical Hospital (MA) and John Tatom, M.D., one of the original group at Ft. Gordon, was reassigned to the 67th Evacuation Hospital.

Left to right: Sam Gillis, M.D., Judy Dexter, R.N., Pat Sartorius, M.D. at the Provincial Hospital walking toward the Laboratory Building, with South Vietnamese flag flying in the background.

The Vietnam Counteroffensive Campaign that had begun on December 25, 1965, ended on June 30, 1966, the same day the female nurses arrived, five days after the physicians arrived and thirteen days after the main body of the 18th Surgical Hospital (MA) arrived in country. The Vietnam Counteroffensive Phase II began July 1, 1966, and lasted throughout most of the year while we were in Pleiku (ended May 31, 1967). The Vietnam Counteroffensive Phase III began on June 1, 1967 and ended on January 29, 1968. Those of us originally assigned to the 18th Surgical Hospital (MA) were, therefore, in country during all, or portions of, three Campaigns.

The lack of our TO&E equipment and the incomplete construction at our hospital site caused the first few weeks in country to be hectic, frustrating (sometimes exasperating) and unsettling. We all were in the process of quickly becoming adjusted to living in tents, becoming acclimatized to the mud and humidity associated with

View of the 542nd Medical Clearing Company taken from the site of the 18th Surgical Hospital (MA).

monsoon rains, while simultaneously accepting the reality of our combat environment. We shuttled back and forth from our hospital site, where we slept, and the 542nd Medical Clearing Company where we worked and ate (and slept when on duty). While the physicians and nurses were busy with patient care at the 542nd, our CO and XO (Executive Officer) were struggling to fit all of the necessary pieces together to expeditiously open a functional, and much needed, surgical hospital.

On Tuesday, June 28, the 18th Surgical Hospital (MA) received two 100 KW generators from Qui Nhon. Concrete pads had already been poured, so the generators were in place and operational very quickly; however, the electrical wiring in the hospital Quonsets had not been completed. A wooden shelter housing the generators was constructed later. The same day much other equipment and six 2x4 vehicles arrived. The hospital beds and mattresses, along with other equipment, arrived the day before. The incomplete construction created a transient, but significant, storage problem.

On Wednesday, June 29, Lt. Col. Cenac (CO) received orders to move the 542nd to the site of the 18th Surgical Hospital (MA). However, there was no electricity or water, and the buildings were still under construction. This was typical of some of the ridiculous, illogical orders sometimes given by individuals that had no understanding of the reality of the situation. Except perhaps in extreme emergencies, no individual, regardless of their rank, title, or position, should give an order or determine a strategy, whether in military, civilian or governmental life, until they first have a complete understanding of all the facts, have fully considered all of the possible ramifications, have comprehended the consequences of both success and failure, and are willing to accept full responsibility for the outcome, no matter what the results may be.

On the evening of Wednesday, July 6, Lt. Col. Cenac met with Major Mizell, CO of the 2nd Platoon, 498th Medical Company (52nd Aviation Battalion [Dustoff]) stationed at Camp Holloway, to establish the guide-lines for patient evacuation. We always treated all sick and wounded as they presented to us until we approached the hospital's bed capacity and/or the physical limits of the hospital's personnel. During the triage process we operated on the critically wounded first, while those with more minor wounds were made comfortable and observed until definitive surgery could be accomplished. Medical patients were started on appropriate therapy and placed in a large medical ward (Quonsets joined end to end) for continuing treatment until evacuation. Evacuations were scheduled as needed, sometimes daily if we were in the midst of a "big push." If we were at full capacity, Dustoff would fly over us and carry the casualties

on to the 2nd Surgical Hospital (MA) at An Khe for treatment and/or surgery. Those patients awaiting evacuation were carried by ambulances to the New Pleiku Airport and placed on C-130 Hercules or C-7 Caribou aircraft and taken to the 85th Evacuation Hospital or the 67th Evacuation Hospital in Qui Nhon. The surgical cases were kept there for a period of convalescence. If their injuries were minor enough to allow them to return to duty within about thirty days or less, they were kept there until their recovery was complete. The more severely wounded were further evacuated to military hospitals in Japan or to Clark AFB in the Philippines. Those who recovered within a few months were then returned to duty in Vietnam, while those debilitated beyond the possibility of returning to duty were further evacuated from Japan and Clark to hospitals in the U.S. For those severely burned patients, special C-140 flights were made directly to the Burn Center at the Brooke Army Medical Center at San Antonio. Severe medical cases that required a few weeks of recovery, especially malaria cases, ended up at the 6th Convalescent Center at Cam Ranh Bay and, upon recovery, returned to duty.

During the first few days of July, many visitors came to the hospital site. On Thursday, July 7, Col. Miller (CO, 44th Medical Brigade), Brig. Gen. Mark Meyer (CO, Logistical Command, Qui Nhon), Lt. Col. Zimov (Brigade S4) plus two Majors (Brigade S1

Orville Swenson, M.D. and Judy Dexter, R.N. at the Provincial Hospital.

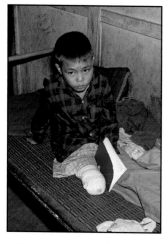

A Vietnamese boy with a right AK amputation at Provincial Hospital.

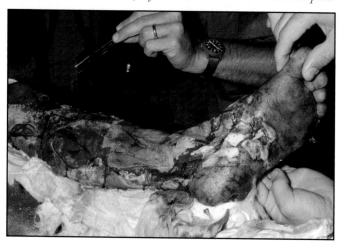

Montagnard patient with severe burn on left leg requiring skin grafts done by Bob Hewitt, M.D.; Orville Swenson, M.D. holding the foot.

and S3) toured the hospital construction site. Their well-intentioned visits offered no assistance to anyone, added no needed information or expertise, and simply slowed the construction efforts. The old adage "Too many cooks spoil the broth" became, for us, a truism.

On Tuesday, July 12, the TO&E equipment arrived. Two days earlier, Lt. Col. Ed "Digger" O'Dell (CO, 55th Medical Group) had given orders that the 18th Surgical Hospital (MA) would begin working in the new Quonsets within four days of receiving the equipment, even though there was still no electricity or water, another example of "brilliant" military strategy and planning. Lt. Col. O'Dell was replaced by Lt. Col. Robert Hall in December. Thereafter, our hospital's early struggle with the 55th Medical Group diminished significantly.

Lt. Col. Cenac received word on July 13, that RMK-BRJ would begin construction of six two-story Tropical Shell Billets the following day, to provide much needed housing for our enlisted men (EM) and officers.

Gen. Westmoreland visited our hospital on July 18, and asked to see the patients. There were no surgical patients (they were still at the 542nd Medical Clearing Company) but an annex of tents had been set up between the motor pool, the hospital-helipad area and the future site of our BOQ, for the medical patients. After talking with each patient, he spoke briefly with our staff, shook hands and left by chopper with Gen. Beyer (aide-de-camp, 4th Infantry Division), who had accompanied him.

That same day bulk lead was melted and poured into sheets to place in the walls of the X-ray room to provide proper shielding.

The following day the 55th Medical Group sent Lt. Witche, MSgt. Massey and a SSgt. to install an ANGRY 19 in lieu of a single sideband radio. Later that evening, a rumor began circulating that several bombs were found throughout the Pleiku area and that other unidentified bombs were suspected to go off later that night; therefore, we were on high (Red) alert.

Harvey Slocum, M.D., and Robert Dripps, M.D., Senior Consultants in Anesthesia to the Army Surgeon General, visited us on July 21. The same day Lt. Col. Cenac was elected President of the newly formed Pleiku Medical Association. We had bi-monthly meetings, with the site alternating between the 18th Surgical Hospital (MA) and the nearby ARVN Hospital. Interesting cases were presented and discussed through interpreters. The ARVN physicians, Vietnamese civilian physicians, the physicians at the Pleiku Provincial Hospital, and all U.S. physicians assigned to divisions and other units in the Pleiku area were invited to join.

By July 26, our hospital area was a sea of mud. It had rained with almost no letup day or night for a few days, which interfered greatly in the effort to move patients from the 542nd Clearing Company to the 18th Surgical Hospital (MA). The mud was even more ubiquitous than was the dust later encountered during the peak of the dry season. Maj. Gen. C. W. Eifler, (1st Logistical Command) flew in to evaluate the transfer and evacuation process. This was also the day we ate our first meals in the new Mess Hall at our hospital.

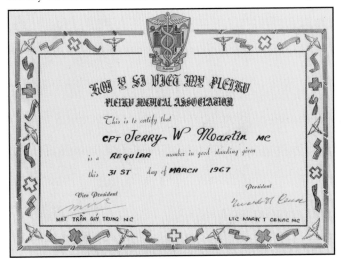

Certificate of the Pleiku Medical Association

Mud at the 18th Surgical Hospital in June, 1966.

Ubiquitous mud in the road beside the covered walkway.

The following day, Wednesday, July 27, 1966, the move to the 18th Surgical Hospital (MA) was completed in spite of the mud, and the 542nd Medical Clearing Company site was abandoned.

The first of four phases of Operation Paul Revere ended on Saturday, July 30. One of their forward base camps was referred to as the Oasis. These search and destroy operations finally ended on Sunday, December 26, 1966. The general Area of Operations (AO) was a few kilometers ("klicks") southwest, west and northwest of Pleiku. Paul Revere II (August l, 1966-August 25, 1966) continued as a search and destroy, ambush and blocking maneuver. Helicopter gunships, A1-Es (World War II-type planes with propellers and piston engines used for straffing and ground support bombing), artillery and mortar fire were used to support infantry troops when contact was made with the VC and/or the NVA. As soon as a firefight began, the unit radio operator would call Tactical Air Control Airborne (TACAIR) and transmit a call for help. Forward Air Controllers (FAC) flying over the area of operations in a light single-engine, two-seat Cessna 0-1 Bird Dog, after pinpointing the location, would call in AI-E Skyraiders or A-4 Skyhawks ("Scooter"). If the firefight began at night, the FAC would call in an AC-47 gunship (modified DC-3) known by the call name "Spooky." The Vietnamese thought that the "tongue" of red streaks of fire caused by tracer bullets from three 20-mm Gatling guns resembled the mythical fire from a dragon's mouth, hence the name "Puff, the Magic Dragon," shortened by the GIs to simply, "Puff." From the plane the target was viewed and the guns aimed using a Starlight night scope. When Puff fired, the speed of the plane and the rapidity of fire from the guns caused one round to land in each square foot of a space the size of a football field. Puff fired at an intermittent (6000 rpm per gun) rate to prevent melting of the gun barrels, carried 24,000 rounds of ammunition per gun and often dropped parachute flares. The C-47s were later replaced by AC-119s and AC-130s (Spectre, adapted from C-130 Hercules), which were equipped with 20-mm Gatling guns as well as 7.62-mm miniguns. The FAC would mark the enemy position with white phosphorus rockets to guide the fighter-bombers so they could fire rockets or drop napalm/conventional bombs with great accuracy. Because the enemy could at times shoot down the Cessna O-1 by hitting the engine, the twin-engine OV-10 Bronco became the preferred aircraft.

Operation Paul Revere II inflicted heavy casualties on the NVA. Although militarily successful, the U.S. forces sustained significant casualties. On August 1, we began receiving casualties from the Oasis. Dustoff was making regular trips, delivering the wounded to us. We were managing to keep our operative schedule in pace with the casualty flow until a Jolly Green Giant (HH 53 Sikorsky) landed, filled with 20-25 minor shrapnel wounds and three litter patients. Two of the litter patients had sustained fractures of their lower extremities. Medics had already applied dressings to the wounds and immobilizing splints to the fractures. The other litter patient was unresponsive and had no measurable blood pressure and only a weak, rapid, thready pulse. An IV was already running, but I inserted another IV line and immediately started a unit of blood in each IV, infusing them simultaneously. The only wound discernable was in his right axillary area (armpit). A nurse anesthetist intubated him, started oxygen and began

Dustoff helicopter leaving the 18th Surgical Hospital (MA) near Pleiku after dropping off patients. Photograph furnished by Michael Belinson, M.D.

assisting his breathing. The nurses were all busy evaluating and making comfortable the "walking wounded"; the corpsmen were occupied getting blood samples, bringing blood and IV fluids and retrieving needed drugs and supplies from the pharmacy and surgical supply; and the other physicians were busy in the operating rooms. I quickly cut away his jungle fatigue top and exposed the axilla. A baseball-size blood clot filled the large, jagged laceration caused by a mortar fragment. I began teasing away the clot to determine the source of the bleeding. After infusing 4-5 units of blood very rapidly, his blood pressure began to rise and he began to thrash about. The anesthetist gave him enough sedation to keep him from moving or experiencing pain. It was obvious that his brachial plexus (a large complex of nerves that supply the arm and hand) had not been damaged since he had moved his entire extremity. I completed the removal of enough of the blood clot to visualize the arterial tear caused by the shrapnel at about the junction where the axillary artery becomes the brachial artery. I was squatting beside the litter that rested on litter stands and had just asked a corpsman to get a vascular clamp so I could clamp the artery without causing further damage to the vessel. With the patient's slight movement, my removal of a portion of the blood clot and, mainly because of his rising blood pressure, the intraluminal clot (blood clot inside the artery) suddenly blew out. My head was about 15 inches away when the spurt occurred. The blood hit me in the face, and I could not see but was able to grab the artery with my hand. I could feel the blood spurting and was able to clamp the artery between my thumb and index finger. A nurse quickly wiped my eyes so I could respond by sight rather than by feel. I asked a nurse to see if another physician could break away from the case they were currently doing to come and help me. Fortunately, Tony Lindem, M.D., walked from the OR into R & E about that time and immediately came to help when he noticed my blood-drenched appearance. As we quickly moved the patient to the OR, I walked along and continued to hold the artery. Two more units of blood were rapidly infusing. Tony scrubbed, gowned and gloved and prepped the operative field, which included my hand. I had on surgical gloves but the field was obviously not sterile. As he prepared to drape the operative field with sterile sheets, I knelt under the drapes alongside the operating table. As soon as he placed a vascular clamp on the artery, I was then able to release my grip that had begun to weaken. It was difficult to hold the severed artery tightly enough to prevent bleeding, especially as his blood pressure rose to 100 mm of Hg (Mercury) or higher. I crawled from beneath the operative sheets and went to the BOQ, took a shower, put on clean clothes and then returned to scrub-in and assisted in finishing the case. Fortunately, the artery had been cleanly severed and could be anastomosed without a graft. The patient received a total of about 18-20 units of blood. The circulation to his arm was normally restored, and when evacuated two days later, he was doing well.

We operated in shifts and slept only enough to keep going. By the third or fourth day, we began receiving casualties who were in terrible, pitiful condition because of dehydration, hunger, exhaustion, and hypovolemic shock secondary to hemorrhage. They had been wounded thirty to forty-eight hours earlier, but Dustoff could not evacuate them because of the monsoon rains and/or the heavy enemy fire. During the first day or two of the "big push," a visiting electrical engineer (USARV) returned to Saigon and reported that two patients had died at the 18th Surgical Hospital (MA) because we had to operate with flash lights since there was no electricity in the operating room (OR). Obviously this was a blatant lie. As a result, on August 6, we were visited by a Major (Gates), four Colonels (Grove, Puleo, Wood, Price) and a General (Lollir) from Saigon, as well as others from the 44th Medical Brigade (Meyers) and the 55th Medical Group (O'Dell). As a consequence, we began receiving extra supplies and some needed equipment.

We usually had adequate surgical supplies. During the first few weeks we had difficulty obtaining enough refrigerators for hospital use, even though RMK-BRJ had stored a few hundred refrigerators, stacked two deep, in a field just off the road leading to the New Pleiku Air Base. After a short period of monsoon rains, the wood and cardboard shipping crates in which they were packaged deteriorated and collapsed. RMK-BRJ bulldozed the badly needed refrigerators, now unusable, into a ravine and covered them with dirt. With a cost- plus-10% contract, it was lucrative

View of Central Highlands during wet season.

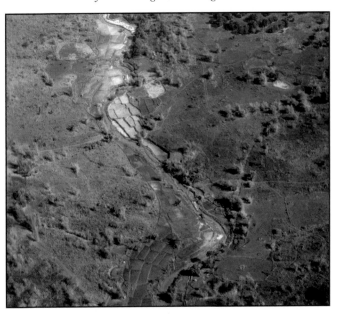

Same view of Central Highlands during dry season.

for RMK-BMJ, but it certainly did not help our situation. We finally did get an adequate number of refrigerators from RMK-BRJ's next shipment. Refrigerators had been requisitioned through military channels; however, I do not recall, during our year in country, ever receiving those requested through the Army's normal procurement process.

When U.S. troops arrived in Vietnam, they were required to declare the amount of U.S. currency ("greenbacks") in their possession, which was exchanged at face value for Military Payment Certificates (MPC). MPCs could be spent at PXs or exchanged for piasters, the Vietnamese currency, to spend in the local civilian economy (since 1976, their currency is called *dong*). Previously, 100 piasters were equivalent to one U.S. dollar. However, the value fluctuated and inflation had cheapened the piaster when, in 1966-1967, 100 piasters were worth only 70-80 cents; therefore, 400 piasters ("pi") were worth between $2.80-$3.20. When

Tony Lindem, M.D.

Military Payment Certificates (front).

Military Payment Certificates (back).

Piasters, the South Vietnamese currency.

leaving country on R and R, or returning to CONUS, the reverse process occurred, and each individual was reimbursed in U.S. currency in the amount previously relinquished. One "greenback" could be exchanged on the black market for about a ten-fold profit; however, it was illegal and would result in a court-martial, imprisonment and then a dishonorable discharge if caught. The black market usually operated through legitimate businesses.

In Pleiku, a clothing store selling tailor-made suits, dresses, etc., and operated by a family from India (usually they were Indian or Chinese) acted as a front for these clandestine transactions. I knew of a sergeant who had accumulated over 100,000 dollars through this process by having someone in the U.S. send cash in cards or letters. He received orders to leave country a few weeks early and was frantically trying to find individuals who would smuggle cash out of country—he was offering 50% to those who would take the chance, but I did not hear of anyone willing to take the risk. This practice of illegal currency exchange was not widespread, but certainly not uncommon.

The 1st Cavalry Division moved a large number of helicopters ("turkey farm") into an open field across Highway 19 from our hospital during the first few days of August. We awoke on August 6, to what seemed like a sky full of choppers taking off for the Ia (river) Drang Valley near the Chu Pong Mountains a few kilometers west of us. About noon they returned, reloaded more troops, ammunition and fuel and headed back to the Drang River Valley. By sundown, we began receiving casualties, the beginning of another "big push." Before midnight, we had received over thirty wounded.

During the first few days of August, there were two neurosurgeons at the 18th Surgical Hospital (MA) from a Neurosurgical K-Team at the 85th Evacuation Hospital in Qui Nhon. One of the neurosurgeons, Dr. Andrcus, assisted by Lt. Col. Cenac, successfully evacuated an acute subdural hematoma on August 6. On August 10, both Dr. Andrcus and the other neurosurgeon, Dr. Bob Andrews, returned to Qui Nhon. Except for those few days, we did not have a neurosurgeon at our hospital. One or two emergency burr holes were done; however, essentially all neurosurgical cases were over-flown or evacuated immediately to Qui Nhon.

Gen. Westmoreland returned to visit the wounded on August 7, and Gen. Hollis came on August 8. The same day the XO

from the Air Force's 7th Surgeons Office visited to discuss the possible placement of a Combat Surgical Unit (CSU) in our area. Col. McCullough (AF Squadron Commander) visited to offer further assistance. The Air Force had already provided eleven bomb canisters that were used as culverts, a few new under-wing fuel tanks used as water supply for the patients while we worked in tents, and also fabricated stainless steel tanks that were used to develop and rinse X-ray film. On the evening of August 8, intelligence issued our first area alert concerning a possible mortar attack by the VC; however, it did not materialize.

Maj. Gen. Robert R. Ploger, Chief of Engineers, U.S. Army, Vietnam, visited on August 9 to discuss further engineering needs at our hospital.

On August 10, the casualties we received included two Americans, six VC and forty-four Koreans ([ROK], attached to the 3rd Brigade [25th Infantry Division]). Communication was a problem, since we did not have a Korean interpreter. Since our hospital was filled to capacity, we operated on the most critical patients while the minor wounds were evacuated to An Khe (2nd Surgical Hospital) and Qui Nhon (85th Evacuation Hospital).

By August 11, we finally got a brief respite from the heavy casualty flow that had begun on August 1. Maj. Gen. Norton, CO of the 1st Cavalry Division, came to visit those in his command who had been wounded. He had replaced Lt. Gen Harry Kinnard, an aviator and paratrooper who first applied the concept of combining helicopter air assaults with infantry warfare when he brought the division to Vietnam. (Kinnard had parachuted into Normandy on D-Day, June 6, 1944 with the 101st Airborne Division. He was a Lt. Col. in the Belgian town of Bastogne and was the divisions' operations officer under Brig. Gen. Anthony McAuliffe, who was artillery chief and acting division commander. When a German commander, under a flag of truce, requested that the 101st surrender, Lt. Col. Kinnard remarked to Brig. Gen. McAuliffe, "Us surrender? Aw, nuts." McAuliffe then wrote a note to the Germans: "To the German Commander: NUTS! The American Commander." They were able to hold off the Germans and four days later the siege was broken with the arrival of Lt. Gen. George S. Patton and his tanks.)

Improvements at the 18th Surgical Hospital (MA) compound were evident almost daily. On August 14, Lt. George (R&U Engineers at Camp Holloway) brought a dozier and began spreading rock on roads throughout the compound. Heavy rains continued daily but slowly, progress was made toward conquering the mud. The following week the casualty flow was light, two American surgical cases and ten medical cases (mostly malaria) and one VC surgical and six medical cases. We usually admitted about ten medical cases for each surgical case.

On Labor Day, Wednesday, September 7, the Special Forces brought in three-month old Montagnard twins that we dubbed "James" (diarrhea and dehydration) and "George" (malaria) from the area near Kontum. They responded quickly to therapy and were released after about ten days of hospitalization.

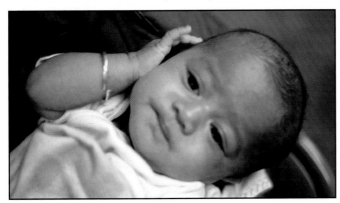
"George," the three month old Montagnard twin with malaria.

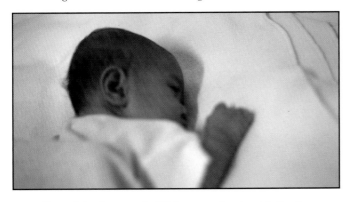
"James," the three month old Montagnard twin with diarrhea

By this time, the EM's first permanent billet was over 90% completed. The second was completed except for the roof, and the third was begun on Monday, August 22. By September 16, the Headquarters building, A&D building, latrines and showers had been completed. The same day, the 299th Engineers brought their crane and set poles for electrical power to the billets, and a second water tower was begun so that dual water systems could be designed, one for potable water and the other for a sanitary waste system.

In mid-September, Capt. David Soberg, MSC, the XO who traveled with the advance party from Ft. Gordon to Pleiku, was replaced by Lt. Col. James B. Ranck, MSC.

Eugene Joseph Chap, M.D., (birth name Eugene Boleslaw Czaplicki) came to the 18th Surgical Hospital (MA) from the 1st Cavalry Division (Battalion Surgeon, 2nd/8th) on Thursday, September 22. He became the Chief of Medicine and of the Laboratory. About the same time, Ted Stuart, M.D., one of our original group, was transferred to the 67th Evacuation Hospital in Qui Nhon and later reassigned to the 25th Infantry Division. By the last of September, the monsoon rains had significantly diminished. Vietnamese workers had completed sandbagging the hospital and Sgt. Evers was in charge of another Vietnamese crew laying sod around the hospital and heliport to prevent dirt and dust from blowing each time a helicopter landed. The dryer weather conditions allowed for more rapid improvements in our roads and drainage system.

At about this time, Col. Houlton from Qui Nhon came to visit. His purpose in the area was to establish a local Base Development Board, which meant no construction would be done without this Board's approval, following their guidelines and priorities. Fortunately, about 90% of our hospital complex had been built, and the remaining construction was rapidly nearing completion. With this system in place, any future construction could probably never be accomplished through the military's slow, laborious and tedious procurement system.

On October 14, 1966, while in Pleiku, I observed a rather large colorful parade composed of Montagnards in ceremonial battle dress, along with Montagnard and Vietnamese Special Forces and other military and local police units. The streets were lined with flags and banners; a large crowd was in attendance; and the mood seemed festive and celebratory. The next evening, nearly 1,000 Montagnards participated in a nighttime torch parade in

Montagnard parade in Pleiku City on the afternoon of October 14, 1966.

which they marched the two-to-three mile distance from Pleiku along Highway 19 to a designated area in an open field across the road from the entrance to MACV (II Corps) Headquarters (the location was no more than one half mile west from the site where the 542nd Medical Clearing Company had been located). The marchers camped that night in tents that had been erected earlier at the site. Flags and banners were in place and a temporary viewing stand had already been erected for the dignitaries and special guests that would later congregate for the FULRO (United Front for the Liberation of Oppressed Races—Front Unifie' de Lutte.de.la.Race Opprimee') Festival.

On Monday, October 17, 1966, I attended the FULRO Festival and Ceremony, photographed the event and recorded portions of it for use as a topic for one of my weekly radio programs. During the two-to-three hour ceremony, Premier (Prime Minister) Nguyen Cao Ky (former Air Vice-Marshall), Gen. Nguyen Van Thieu (Chief of Staff, the National Assembly elected him President with Ky as Vice President on October 21, 1967), U.S. Ambassador Henry Cabot Lodge (appointed as the U.S. Ambassador to the Republic of Vietnam by President Kennedy in June and arrived in Saigon in August 1963. He resigned the Ambassadorial post in May 1964, to seek the Republican Presidential nomination. He returned in July 1965, and was succeeded by Elsworth Bunker in 1967), the Australian Ambassador, the Mayor of Pleiku, Col. Lee (U.S. MACV-II Corps Commander), Maj. Gen. Vinh Loc (Vietnamese MACV-II Corps Commander) and many other U.S. and Vietnamese officers and numerous Vietnamese civilian dignitaries sat as honored guests. There was a series of speeches, including the Mayor of Pleiku and Premier Ky. Maj. Gen. Vinh Loc gave the official welcoming speech (copy included). At the conclusion of the speeches, following Maj. Gen. Vinh Loc's welcoming address, about 250 Montagnard rebel troops (FULRO) knelt before Premier Ky and pledged allegiance to the Saigon government.

A group of about fifteen Montagnard men wearing native ceremonial dress, some carrying long knives and spears, while others rhythmically beat on brass gongs, marched and paraded around a young water buffalo. Before the ceremony began, the water buffalo had been tethered to a bundle of small bamboo and wooden poles set in the ground a few yards in front of the reviewing stand. Colorful streamers and banners were attached to the poles. When they concluded the ceremonial dance, those with the long knives hacked the hamstring tendons and muscles just above the first joint (knee or elbow) causing the animal to flop and flounder about. Then those with spears stabbed the animal in the chest making it nearly impossible for the animal to breath. Finally, mercifully, one man stabbed the animal in the heart, killing it immediately.

The carcass was then ceremoniously butchered. Fresh blood was drained from a severed artery and collected in a glazed pottery bowl and given to the chief dignitaries (Ky, Thiu, Lodge, Vinh Loc, Australian Ambassador, etc.) who had by this time moved from the viewing stands to chairs set up near the ceremonial slaughter site. Each of the dignitaries was given a small saucer of fresh blood to drink and then a small piece of raw meat to eat. A small amount of blood was dripped or poured onto their boots

or shoes. The dignitaries were then relocated to chairs placed near 30 inch high vases or jars filled with rice wine and asked to drink. The Montagnards presented each of the "honored" dignitaries with a copper bracelet symbolizing brotherhood. Ambassador Lodge appeared nearly as pale as the off-white suit he was wearing. Initially, each dignitary exhibited an apprehensive restlessness interspersed with a disquieting queasiness, but ultimately they seemed to adopt a demeanor of resigned acceptance of their predicament.

For hundreds of years, the Montagnards lived in Vietnam, even before the ancestors of the Vietnamese people began migrating into the region from China. The Montagnards were considered

Front row, left to right: Gen. Nguyen Huu Co (Minister of Defense), Premier Ky, Gen. Thieu and Maj. Gen. Vinh Loc (only elbow showing). Back row unknown.

Henry Cabot Lodge (U.S. Ambassador) in hat and light suit near the viewing stand. Water buffalo sacrificed during the ceremony.

Ceremonial fire lit during FULRO opening ceremony.

a primitive, aboriginal race of people. The men wore loincloths and the women went topless and frequently smoked cigars. Their religion was both ancestor worship and Animism (a belief that all natural objects and phenomena have souls and that spirits and demons exist). As the Vietnamese migrated into the Indo-Chinese peninsula, they primarily occupied the rice-rich coastal and Mekong Delta regions, forcing the Montagnards more and more into the rugged mountains and open plains of the Central Highlands.

French Colonial policies kept the highland Montagnards and the lowland Vietnamese apart. Tribal courts were allowed to judge Montagnard civil and criminal cases and to judge moral and property disputes. The Montagnards are an intelligent people, and many spoke multiple dialects of their own language as well as French, Vietnamese and, in some cases, English.

Traditionally, the Montagnard and Vietnamese people interacted peacefully but remained segregated. They viewed each other with skepticism, suspicion and even prejudice. The situation became extremely difficult in 1954, when Ngo Dinh Diem, President of South Vietnam, attempted to assimilate the Montagnards into Vietnamese culture by resettling approximately 200,000 Vietnamese peasants from the coastal area onto land in the highlands that belonged to the Montagnards. He further attempted to impose Vietnamese laws and culture on them by eliminating their tribal courts, integrating their schools and disregarding their self-government.

As a result, over the next several months, many Montagnard tribes began organizing a resistance movement. What began merely as grumbling and complaining by the village elders as they sat around their long houses drinking rice wine, quickly metamorphosed into an organized resistance movement. By 1958, their tribal leaders had formed a group called "Bajaraka" (an acronym, a name derived from the initials of four powerful Montagnard groups—the Bahanar, Jarai, Rhade and Koho). They began working toward creating their own independent nation with their own army. When these organized efforts failed, and when numerous diplomatic missions and petitions to the Vietnamese government and the United Nations were ignored, they began demonstrating throughout the Central Highlands. This brought results, but not the ones hoped for: the Bajaraka leaders were arrested and jailed by President Diem. In Darlac, a Vietnamese Province chief decreed that Montagnards must wear shirts and slacks, and in Pleiku Province, they were forbidden to build houses on stilts.

After Diem's death, the government of Nguyen Khanh released the prisoners, and his Minister for Ethnic Minorities sought peaceful cooperation between the Vietnamese and Montagnards while preserving their culture and tradition. Y B'ham Enuol, the leader of a militant faction of FULRO, who wanted complete autonomy, fled to Cambodia. Another leader, Y Bih Alio even joined the Viet Cong.

The Communist strategy was to exploit the prejudices between the Vietnamese and Montagnards. They often terrorized the Montagnards, stole their crops and forced them to cooperate with the VC against the South Vietnamese.

On September 20, 1964, Montagnard CIDG in Quang Duc and Darlac Provinces revolted, killed seventy Vietnamese troops, marched on Ban Me Thuot (Montagnard Capital) and seized a radio station. With U.S. assistance, negotiations between the Montagnards and the Vietnamese improved the situation considerably. Gen. Nguyen Khanh's government began an assistance program that respected Montagnard traditions. They were allowed to choose their own representatives to the National Assembly, and their traditional court system was reinstituted. The Vietnamese government agreed to recognize Montagnard ownership of land, to build additional schools and granted them scholarships to high schools and universities. Except for autonomy, most of their grievances were recognized.

The Khanh government was replaced by a coup in 1965, and the promises made to the Montagnards were broken. On December 18, 1965, there was a second FULRO uprising in various places in Quang Duc, Darlac and Phu Bon Provinces. The leaders were imprisoned and/or executed, and the rebellion only lasted one day.

In 1966, the government of Premier Nguyen Cao Ky began implementing Gen. Khanh's programs. In February 1966, a Special Commissariat for Highlander Affairs was formed and a Montagnard was named to head it. Shortly thereafter, Premier Ky flew to Pleiku with a Bill of Rights which they had long sought: tribal lands were returned, a special Montagnard pennant was created to be flown along side the Vietnamese national flag and an elite Highland military force under Montagnard command was created. Tribal languages were again taught in their schools, and over 500 scholarships were granted to the Montagnard children. Nine Montagnard representatives were granted seats in the Constitutional Assembly.

In August 1968, Y B'ham Enuol returned to Ban Me Thuot for further negotiations. On December 12, 1968, arrangements were made for FULRO's permanent return from Cambodia. In January 1969, more than 1,300 FULRO soldiers and their families returned from Cambodia to Quang Duc Province. FULRO was formally dissolved and replaced with a new, non-militant Montagnard political party called the Ethnic Minorities Solidarity Movement (EMSM).

On October 18, while assisting on an abdominal laparotomy for a shrapnel wound of the abdomen, Lt. Col. Cenac came to the OR door and asked if I knew a Maj. Raymond Nutter. I acknowledged that I did, that in fact we were friends and that his family also resided in Bowling Green. Ray was a gunship pilot and CO of the Viking Platoon of the 121st Assault Helicopter Company in the Delta near Soc Trang in CTZ IV. He told me that Ray had been wounded when his chopper was shot down and that he was being evacuated to the 3rd Field Hospital in Saigon and had requested that I come down. Lt. Col. Cenac said that our intelligence reports indicated that there was no military activity planned in the next few days in the Pleiku area, so he cut orders for me to go to Saigon. As soon as we finished the surgery, I got my gear together and went to the New Pleiku Airport. When I arrived, I saw Col. Bonneaux, CO of the New Pleiku Airbase, whom I knew from having treated him at our hospital and also seeing him often at our Paradise Lost Officer's Club and the Air Force Officer's Club. He changed my flight order to "flight surgeon" status, and I was able to get on a C-130 flight leaving within a few minutes of my arrival. As a flight surgeon, I was able to sit in the cockpit with the pilot and copilot. In our conversations during the flight from Pleiku to Tan Son Nhut, they came to understand the purpose of my trip and my destination. The pilot said that a jeep and driver were coming to pick him up as soon as we arrived in Saigon and that he would drop me off at the hospital.

I arrived at the 3rd Field Hospital at about the same time that Ray arrived. I met the surgeon on call and told him of our friendship. He offered me the extra bed in his room where I quickly stashed my gear. We took Ray to the OR where I assisted with his surgery. He had sustained a deep laceration of the right lateral calf muscles but no nerve, bone or vascular injuries. He had been wounded on Monday, October 17 and had spent 18-20 hours in the muddy waters of the streams and rice paddies common throughout the Delta. We debrided the nonviable tissue and sutured his lip and hand wounds, but left the leg wound open for a later secondary closure. Numerous leaches had been removed at the battalion aid station, leaving red blotches over much of his body. His head was so swollen from mosquito bites that he was barely recognizable.

I stayed in Saigon about four days before returning to Pleiku. On the third day, we took him back to surgery to further debride the leg wound. Ray was evacuated from the 3rd Field Hospital to a U.S. Army Hospital in Japan on the same day that I returned to Pleiku. His leg wound was ultimately closed secondarily in Japan, and after adequate convalescence, Ray later returned to his unit in Soc Trang.

Later, I discovered while talking to Ray, that the battle had begun in the early afternoon and extended into the evening. One of the helicopter gunships in Ray's platoon was shot down while providing air support for an ARVN infantry unit engaging the VC. The downed pilot called for help because he and his crew were surrounded by VC. Ray and his crew went in to attempt a rescue and were also shot down. Ray's copilot was killed instantly with a GSW to the head. Ray and a gunner escaped the chopper and, while evading the VC, were involved in hand-to-hand combat on two or more occasions throughout the night. On the morning of the 18th, they were able to get back to an ARVN unit who took them to a battalion aid station. Martha Raye, the entertainer and comedienne, was working at the aid station and arranged for the call to be put through to me at Pleiku. His wounds were dressed, and after his condition was determined to be stable, he was then evacuated to the 3rd Field Hospital.

Ray was nominated for the Congressional Medal of Honor but instead received the Distinguished Service Cross. For this and other heroic actions during his military career, he also received the Distinguished Service Medal with Oak Leaf Cluster, the Silver Star, the Legion of Merit, the Distinguished Flying Cross, the Bronze Star with V, the Air Medal with Oak Leaf Cluster, the Meritorious Service Medal and the Purple Heart along with other medals specifically for Vietnam Service: National Defense Medal,

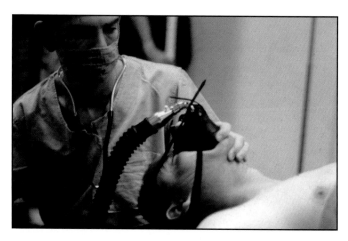

Maj. Raymond T. Nutter receiving anesthesia at the 3rd Field Hospital, Saigon, October 18, 1966.

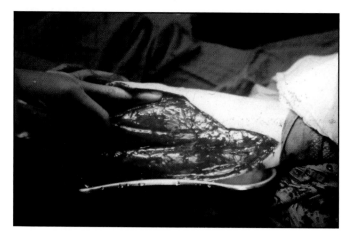

Irrigation and debridement of Maj. Raymond T. Nutter's leg wound at the 3rd Field Hospital, Saigon, October 18, 1966.

Vietnamese Cross of Gallantry with Palm, Vietnamese Service Ribbon and the Vietnamese Campaign Ribbon.

The Medevac helicopters provided a highly mobile and flexible medical evacuation system that responded to the constantly changing combat situation. These helicopters could transport four to six patients at a time, depending upon the number of litter patients, and each medical evacuation flight averaged about thirty-five minutes in duration. The speed of evacuation from the battlefield to the operating table meant the difference between life and death for unknown numbers of patients. The seriously wounded usually reached a hospital and were in surgery within one hour, or less, after sustaining their injuries. Of the wounded who reached medical facilities, over 97.5% survived. Obviously, this high survival rate was the result of decreasing the time lapse between injury and treatment. With the radio communications system, the severity of the wounds could be relayed to the hospital, and the hospital's bed availability and surgical backlog could be relayed to the helicopter while in flight. As a result, patients could be directed to hospitals for treatment; and hospitals, already overwhelmed with cases, could be overflown to other facilities that had adequate patient space and surgical availability.

An example of a typical radio transmission between Dustoff pilot, Capt. John Kreiner of the 2nd Platoon, 498th Medical

Dustoff delivering a stretcher patient and an ambulatory patient to the 18th Surgical.

Company and the Radio Operations at the 18th Surgical Hospital (MA) is as follows: "18th Surg Operations this is Dustoff 25, OVER." "This is 18th Surg Operations go ahead, OVER." "This is Dustoff 25, we are inbound with six patients; three litter, with gunshot wound of the chest, who is critical; one in the leg and the third in the abdomen. The ambulatory have wounds in the head, arms and hand. All patients are stable except for the chest wound, and an IV has been started on him. Our ETA (Estimated Time of Arrival) is ten minutes, please have litter bearers meet us when we arrive, OVER." "This is 18th Surg Operations, WILCO, we will meet you when you land, Dustoff 25, OUT."

Helicopter evacuations directly from the battlefield to a surgical hospital, usually bypassing battalion aid stations or medical clearing companies, allowed the surgical hospitals to become fixed medical facilities, enabling them to install better equipment, provide more comfort amenities (i.e. electricity, running water, flush toilets, air conditioning, better mess capabilities, etc.), and provide better and more effective post-op nursing care.

The buildup of air ambulance units paralleled the commitment of U.S. forces in Vietnam. The first air ambulance unit, the 57th Medical Detachment (Helicopter Ambulance), later nicknamed "The Originals," arrived in country in 1962, to support the 8th Field Hospital at Nha Trang. Initially, two of these aircraft were stationed in Qui Nhon, with the other three in Nha Trang. As fighting increased around Saigon and in the Mekong Delta, the helicopters were shifted from place to place. In November 1964, the 82nd Medical Detachment (Helicopter Ambulance) became operational in CTZ IV (the Delta). With an accelerated rate of

buildup, the 283rd Medical Detachment (Air Ambulance) arrived in August 1965, followed by the 498th Medical Company (Air Ambulance) in September. The 254th Medical Detachment (Air Ambulance) arrived in Vietnam before the end of the year, but did not become operational until February 1966, because a backlog at the port delayed the arrival of their equipment. Four detachments with six helicopters each, supported CTZ III and IV. The 498th Medical Company with twenty-five aircraft supported CTZ II.

By January 1966, there were forty nine air ambulances evacuating about 2,500 patients per month, but by the end of 1966, they were carrying over 7,000 patients a month. During 1967, the 45th Medical Company (Air Ambulance) and four air ambulance detachments arrived in country. The 571st Medical Detachment (Air Ambulance) and the 237th Medical Detachment (Air Ambulance) were in CTZ I. In 1968, four additional detachments were sent to Vietnam, which completed the buildup of aero-medical evacuation units. The 50th Medical Detachment (Air Ambulance) was assigned to the 101st Airborne Division in mid-1968. By 1969, there were 116 helicopter air ambulances in Vietnam.

These helicopters supported combat operations and gave general area support for all forces in country. In addition to evacuation of the wounded, they also transported medical supplies, blood and medical personnel.

A supply of stretchers was kept in a small wooden building near the heliport. As Dustoff delivered stretcher patients, our corpsmen met the chopper and carried the wounded into our R&E (Receiving and Evaluation, the Army's jargon for Emergency

Room) where the nurses and physicians immediately began their evaluation. We usually already knew the general nature of their wounds before their arrival.

The corpsmen would then re-supply Dustoff with an equal number of empty stretchers. The stretchers were recycled after being washed and cleaned. We often knew from intelligence briefings the size of the U.S. Forces engaged in each battle and the estimated size of the enemy involved; therefore, we could approximately predict the number of casualties we would ultimately receive. To gain a better insight into the actual situation, one of the physicians who was temporarily uninvolved in triage or surgery, would go out to the helicopter and talk with the pilots to get their perspective of the situation as well as their prediction concerning the status on the battlefield.

We became friends with many of the Dustoff pilots, especially Capt. John Kreiner. On one of his missions into an LZ to evacuate the wounded, he was shot through his foot. The floor and seats of the Huey had plate armor for protection; however, he had his left foot propped up on the glass area on the nose of the chopper. A bullet penetrated through the sole of the boot, traveled through his foot, and exited the top of his boot and then out the top of the chopper. Fortunately, there were no broken bones, therefore we had only to debride the entrance and exit wounds and apply an appropriate dressing. There was no secondary infection, and he was able to return to flying status within a short time.

When we arrived at Pleiku, our access to current news, both inside and outside of Vietnam, was limited and always a few days late. We were able to get *Newsweek*, *Time*, etc. within four to five days after their publication. We received delayed broadcasts of major athletic events (i.e., Bowl games, NCAA games, World Series, etc.), usually with a twenty-four-hour delay on the Armed Forces Radio and TV Network.

Military news inside Vietnam usually spread fairly rapidly by word of mouth, as well as in the *Pacific Stars and Stripes*, an authorized military newspaper published in Tokyo. By the spring of 1967, more than 95,000 free copies (each free copy was intended for five service men and women) and another 8,000 copies to be sold at newsstands were distributed throughout South Vietnam. The free copies were identified by a blue stripe, whereas the newsstand copies were printed without the stripe. The papers were loaded aboard an Air Force plane each morning, delivered to three major circulation offices, and then distributed to units by APO (Army Post Office) number.

The Observer, the official MACV Command newspaper was printed and distributed free each week to all units in Vietnam. When we arrived in country, *The Observer* was printed in Saigon, but by the time of our DEROS (Date of

Expected Rotation from Over Seas), it was published by the Stars and Stripes Press in Tokyo.

By April 1967, the Armed Forces Television stations in Saigon, Qui Nhon, Pleiku, Da Nang and Nha Trang were broadcasting on channel 11, and new stations in Hue and Tuy Hoa became operational within a few weeks. On average, there were about fifty hours of programming weekly.

Armed Forces Radio had 50,000-watt stations broadcasting 24-hour programming throughout the country from Saigon, Cam Ranh Bay and Pleiku and 10,000-watt stations at Da Nang and Qui Nhon. A well-organized and well-equipped News Department provided comprehensive coverage of U.S. and International news through the services of the Associated Press, United Press International, AP Wirephoto and ABC Newsreel. By the time we rotated back to CONUS (Continental United States) in June 1967, a direct cable communication with the Armed Forces News Bureau in Washington, D.C. made possible the immediate broadcast of major news, sports, and special events from the U.S.

We became acquainted with Anthony "Tony" Burgett, D.V.M., U.S. Army Veterinary Corps, under the command of the 44th Medical Brigade. He was with the 4th Medical Detachment based at Camp Holloway. He worked with both sentry (K-9 Corps) and scout dogs attached to the 25th Infantry Division (3rd Brigade).

Military Working Dogs have been used in the U.S. Military since World War I and were originally attached to the Quartermaster Corps. The breeds of choice were German Shepherd (most frequently used) and Doberman; however, the Labrador eventually replaced the Doberman. They were frequently referred to as "War Dogs"; however, the correct military name is "Working Dogs." It is estimated that the dogs and handlers saved thousands of lives. All four branches of the military used them in Vietnam: Army 65%, Air Force 26%, Marines 7% and Navy 2%.

By using the brand numbers (a tattoo placed in the left ear) of the dogs, the National Institute of Health in 1994, confirmed that

Front cover of the authorized military newspaper, the Pacific Stars and Stripes.

3,747 dogs were used in Vietnam. However, it is estimated that 4,900 dogs were used during the war between the years 1964 and 1975. The discrepancy in total numbers resulted because military records were not maintained prior to 1968. Only 204 dogs exited Vietnam during the ten-year period. A few dogs returned to the U.S., but none returned to civilian life. Most were euthanized, but some were turned over to the ARVN. Approximately 10,000 handlers served in Vietnam, which represented the largest number of dogs and handlers involving the U.S.

The dogs were used in four different ways: Scout Dogs, Combat Tracker Teams (CTT), Sentry Dog Teams and Mine/Booby/Tunnel Dog Teams.

A Scout Dog Team consisted of one German Shepherd and the handler. This team often joined an infantry unit and became its "eyes and ears." The team walked "point" (out front) for the unit, looking for snipers, ambushes, booby traps, trip mines, hidden caches of food, etc. When the dog alerted, the handler informed the patrol leader who then moved the troops forward. Scout dogs and handlers were generally trained at Ft. Benning, Georgia, but some handlers were trained in Vietnam.

The Combat Tracker Team consisted of a Labrador Retriever (sometimes Shepherds), a handler, a cover man, a visual tracker and a team leader. These teams were called on when an infantry unit wanted to locate and re-establish contact with the enemy. The dogs were able to trail ground and/or airborne scent (body odor, blood trails, etc.). They were used to locate the enemy, as well as wounded GIs, downed pilots, missing personnel, etc. Most of the Tracker Dogs and handlers were trained in Malaysia at the British Jungle Warfare School (JWS) or at Ft. Gordon, Georgia.

The Sentry Dog Teams (K-9) were used in every branch of the U.S. Armed Forces in Vietnam, including the Air Force in Thailand, and normally with a Military Police unit. They "walked the wire" (concertina wire, a coiled wire with razor-sharp barbs strung around the periphery of compounds, supply areas, ammo depots, communication centers, flight lines, naval installations, base camps, air strips, etc.). The handlers radioed the bunker guards or a quick response team if the dog alerted. These teams were comprised of one German Shepherd and one handler and generally worked at night. The majority of these dogs and handlers were trained at Lackland AFB, Texas.

The Mine/Booby/Tunnel Dog Teams were comprised of one German Shepherd and a handler and worked in support of an infantry unit or with combat engineers. Their mission was to detect mines, booby-traps, trip wires, tunnel complexes, etc. They also assisted in searching villages for hidden weapons and ammunitions.

Tony Burgett, D.V.M., occasionally brought dogs to the 18th Surgical Hospital (MA) for an X-ray to rule out possible fractures,

Anthony Burgett, D.V.M. holding a juvenile bear.

Dr. Burgett treating a Montagnard's cow in Central Highlands.

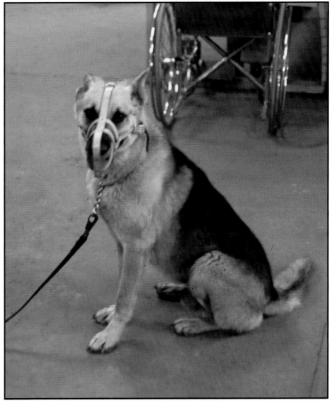

A dog (K-9) brought to 18th Surgical by Tony Burgett, D.V.M., for X-ray to rule out the possibility of a fractured foot.

shrapnel, pneumonia, etc. We often supplied him with medicines to treat the dogs since he sometimes had difficulty obtaining them through normal procurement channels. At times, he also worked with Montagnards in the surrounding villages treating their cattle (water buffalo) and hogs.

One day he came by the hospital and told me he was running a low-grade fever, aching and generally not feeling well. A malaria smear quickly determined that he had malaria (Plasmodium falciparum). Appropriate therapy was initiated but his response to treatment was slow, so after a few days, he was evacuated to the 67th Evacuation Hospital in Qui Nhon until his recovery allowed him to return to Camp Holloway. Because of limited bed space, we could not hospitalize patients for chronic treatment.

Thankfully, we lived in tents only about two months, although it seemed much longer. All of our equipment and personal items were kept off the ground because of the monsoon rains. Even though the tents had been trenched and sandbagged, water still flowed through them during the heaviest rains. Woven grass mats purchased in shops at Pleiku were placed on the ground beside our beds and in the aisle, which helped most of the time. We slept in hospital beds on mattresses that were very comfortable,

The bed and living space of Jerry W. Martin, M.D. while living in a tent. Paradise Lost is in the background. Everything was kept off the ground because of flooding during heavy monsoon rains even though the tent was ditched and sandbagged.

Our tent before Paradise Lost was added.

Contruction of Paradise Lost.

Left to right: Wayne Hosking, M.D., Felix Jenkins, M.D. and Jerry W. Martin, M.D. at Christmas party at Paradise Lost.

The initial Paradise Lost located in the end of our tent.

Page Communications antennae at MACV

Jerry W. Martin, M.D. at communications antennae.

at least when compared to the military cots we slept on for the first two weeks. We placed a stretcher on the cross braces of the legs of the bed, on which we placed our gear, thus keeping it out of the dampness. Those of us who had purchased footlockers in Augusta, Georgia set them on ammunition cans to keep them off the ground. We always slept with mosquito netting in place.

Bob Engebrecht, M.D., Tony Lindem, M.D., Orv Swenson, M.D., Wayne Hosking, M.D., Felix Jenkins, M.D., and I lived in the same tent. In the space remaining in one end of our tent, we reserved a small area with chairs and tables and a small refrigerator to keep ice and cold drinks. This portion of the tent was designated "Paradise Lost." During our leisure time, this became a hangout for everyone and gradually began to function as our Officers Club. After moving into our permanent BOQ, a tent was set up as our Officers Club until a permanent structure could be built. Later, the Air Force provided a metal building and RMK-BMJ did the construction. After completion, we were able to get a ping-pong table, pool table, TV, chairs and tables. The name "Paradise Lost" continued as the official name of our Officers Club. The building was not completed until January 1967; however, the degree of completion allowed it to be used for a Thanksgiving reception for officers from other units in the Pleiku area. The reception was organized and hosted by the nurses.

The 71st Evacuation Hospital arrived in the Pleiku area on Thanksgiving Day, Thursday, November 24, 1966. Their equipment was stored at the site where the 542nd Medical Clearing Co. had functioned, while awaiting completion of their facilities. The construction delay resulted because the original allocation of land was lost and disputes over land acquisition had to be resolved in a new contract with the Air Force. The location of the 71st was less than one mile northeast of the 18th Surgical Hospital (MA) on the road leading to MACV-CTZ II Headquarters, an ARVN compound and the site of the communication antennae constructed and operated by Page Communications, Inc. The new CO of the 71st was Lt. Col. Phillip H. Welch, MC, and his XO was Maj. Jerry Spurling MSC. He attempted to force a consolidation of personnel of the 71st and the 18th, with him as the CO of the combined unit. This arrangement could not

have worked efficiently for many reasons: namely, size and space requirements, mission goals and the practical day-by-day operations of a functional hospital and another under construction. Lt. Col. Cenac finally, and forcefully, rebuked his offer. As a distant observer, it was my impression that Lt. Col. Welch demonstrated only limited leadership skills, and his noblest attributes seemed to be the extremely high regard and the overly inflated opinion he had of himself. These personality traits were not peculiar to him.

The Pleiku area was a very active and hostile environment, frequently attacked by the enemy. After the original 18th Surgical Hospital (MA) personnel rotated home in June 1967, it remained operational at the Pleiku site until October 23, 1967, at which time it was relocated to Long Binh, Binh Dong Province in CTZ III, a few miles north of Saigon. When the 18th moved south, some of its personnel were re-assigned to the 71st Evacuation Hospital. The 71st admitted its first patient on May 29, 1967, and ultimately became a fully operational 400-bed facility on October 25, 1967. Just as we had experienced at the 18th, most of the casualties evacuated to the 71st resulted from fighting in the Dak To and Kontum areas. The 71st was very busy, as were all hospitals throughout South Vietnam, especially during the Tet Offensive in 1968. The 71st Evacuation Hospital was ultimately deactivated on December 15, 1970 and returned to the U.S.

Initially our chapel, The Chapel of the Good Shepherd, was housed in a tent. Chaplain Bernard "Ben" Nass (Capt.) came to Vietnam with the main unit from Ft. Gordon, GA and remained with us until about the early part of January 1967. The Chapel was used by Protestants, Catholics and Jews. Bob Engebrecht, M.D., played the portable organ for most services when he was not involved in surgery. Chaplain Nass (Lutheran, Missouri Synod) was replaced by Capt. William R. Hollis (Southern Baptist). When Bob could not play, there was no musical accompaniment for the services. Listening to a group of soldiers sing a cappella was not particularly inducive to a meaningful worship experience. I wrote the Pastor at my home church, First Baptist Church, Bowling Green, Kentucky, and asked if the choir would record a tape of appropriate worship music and send to us. The Music Director and the Sanctuary Choir responded with a beautifully recorded

Construction at 71st Evacuation Hospital Site.

Construction at 71st Evacuation Hospital Site.

tape, which was much appreciated, especially by Chaplain Hollis. A Quonset building with a concrete floor was erected in January-February 1967. At one end of the tent (or Quonset) was a small podium and a table covered with a white cloth, which served as an altar. A Cross and a Star of David were hung over the altar. On Sunday mornings, Catholic confession was held at 8:45 a.m. with Mass following at 9 a.m. Protestant services were held at 10 a.m. on Sundays and again at 6 pm on Wednesdays. Jewish services were conducted whenever a Rabbi could be present. Jews and Catholics often worshiped at other locations (i.e., Camp Holloway ["Tent City," Father Sullivan], Air Force, MACV, etc.). Our chapel was located near the hospital complex and close to the Mess Hall for the convenience of ambulatory patients.

In addition to conducting the scheduled services, the chaplain always tried to be present to meet, console and pray with the patients as they entered R&E. After surgery, he visited in the post-operative and medical wards to provide emotional comfort, to write letters, to allay their anxieties, to listen to their needs, to counsel and to pray with them. When possible, he went to the PX and picked up items that they might request, and he generally attempted to make their apprehensions, loneliness, misery and suffering a bit more bearable. Their altruistic efforts also included working with missionaries in the Central Highlands.

Prior to leaving for Vietnam, I contacted one of my patients, Ed Brown, a local businessman and a Kentucky State Representative, about getting Kentucky Colonel certificates for each of the physicians assigned to the 18th Surgical Hospital (MA). He agreed that it would be an appropriate gesture in demonstrating Kentucky's appreciation for their service to our country while simultaneously honoring each of them. I gave him the names and addresses of those originally assigned to the unit at Ft. Gordon and then after arriving in Pleiku, I obtained the names of those who were later assigned and mailed them to him. Gov. Edward T. "Ned" Breathitt signed them, along with Thelma L. Stovall, Sec. of State, on September 23, 1966. As soon as the certificates arrived, probably by mid-October, I presented them. I recorded my presentation of the Kentucky Colonelcy to Lt. Col. Cenac and used it as one of my weekly radio broadcasts. Kentucky obviously recognized Lt. Col. Cenac's potential and "promoted" him to "Colonel" before the U.S. Army did.

Paul Revere IV began on October 18, the day of the Montagnard Festival. In fact, a rumor spread throughout the Pleiku area that the

Chaplain Ben Nass conducting service at 18th Surgical while the chapel was still housed in a tent.

Chaplain Ben Nass

VC were planning an attack in an attempt to disrupt the FULRO Festival. During the FULRO Ceremony, helicopter gunships flew almost continuously one or two kilometers to our west, while units of the 25th Division were patrolling the same region. On October 21, the 2nd Platoon, Company A (3rd Brigade, 25th Infantry Division) made contact with 20-25 NVA at an enemy base camp. On October 23, they encountered a fifteen-man force composed of VC and NVA. On October 27, the 1st Platoon, Company B encountered a small NVA force. The 18th Surgical Hospital (MA) did not begin receiving casualties from Paul Revere IV until October 28 when the 1st and 2nd Platoons and Headquarters of

Company C were attacked by two companies of NVA at about 1845 hrs. (6:45 pm). Heavy fighting ensued, resulting in two KIA's (Killed in Action) and ten WIA's (Wounded In Action). At 2213 hrs., a USAF HH-43F Husky Medevac helicopter hovered to winch out the wounded through the heavy tree canopy. At 2237, just as three wounded had been loaded, the enemy successfully fired a rocket causing the helicopter to crash in flames inside of Company C's perimeter. The men of Company C were able to chop into the aircraft and retrieve the pilot and co-pilot, who were both injured. The wounded aboard the chopper were killed either by the rocket explosion or by the crash itself. One of the crewmembers was pinned inside the wreckage. Numerous attempts were made to get him out, but the fuel ignited, engulfing the helicopter before he could be saved.

About 0630 the next morning, another USAF Husky returned to the area and evacuated the pilot, co-pilot and some of the wounded of Company C. That afternoon Dustoff was able to land after a LZ had been cleared, and evacuated the other wounded.

During the periods when the 25th Infantry Division was not engaged in major combat operations, the battalion provided road security for Highway 19 east to the Mang Yang Pass and west to the Cambodian border. Throughout the early part of December, we had another "big push," resulting from unusually heavy fighting when the 4th Division joined the 101st, 25th and the 1st Cav in one of the biggest operations west of Pleiku. December was our biggest month (1250 patients) since our arrival in June. As previously mentioned, Paul Revere IV ended on the day after Christmas, Monday, December 26, 1966.

The 504th Military Police Battalion arrived in the Phu Tai Valley near Qui Nhon on August 31, 1965, under the command of the 16th Military Police Group. The battalion was comprised of A, B, C and Headquarters Companies. Company B, known by the sobriquet, "Roadrunners," deployed from the Phu Tai Valley to Camp Holloway, Pleiku in September 1965, and operated chiefly in the Central Highlands. The 504th Battalion provided direct combat support to the tactical units in I and II CTZs and, from 1965 to July 1966, provided military police support in twelve different locations.

The 504th received the Meritorious Unit Commendation for support provided for the buildup and deployment of three infantry divisions. It was cited specifically for its efforts during the Dak To fighting in November 1967 and its assistance provided to the 11th Infantry Brigade in December 1967. During the Tet Offensive in 1968, Company B was involved mainly in sealing off the Pleiku area and defending Camp Schmidt (on the northern side of Pleiku), where it had moved in December 1968 from Camp Holloway.

While town patrols were responsible for law and order in Pleiku City, the highway platoons conducted armed patrols on Hwy.14 (Pleiku to Khontum) and Hwy. 19 (Pleiku to An Khe through the Mang Yang Pass).

At the end of 1968, when the 504th MP Battalion was moved north, Company B remained in Pleiku and was attached to the 93rd MP Battalion. On February 20, 1970, Company B was reassigned to the 504th and moved to Da Nang. At maximum strength, the battalion had 650 men and operated 22 patrols daily. It was the only combat MP battalion (except for infantry MPs) operating in Vietnam. Those who served in the highway elements were eligible for the Combat Infantry Badge.

In August 1966, a concrete walk covered with metal roofing was constructed around the periphery of our hospital complex, which allowed for patient ambulation and movement of personnel about our hospital, even in inclement weather.

By early September, we moved out of tents and into a wooden Tropical Shell building. The physicians, male nurses and MSC officers occupied the top floor, while the female nurses lived on the ground level. Our living space was divided by approximately six-foot high partitions, creating cubicles with room for two beds. The resulting space was 8'x 20', with about a three-foot wide aisle down the center of the building. On both ends of the building, there was a single 8'x 10' cubicle on opposite sides of the aisle with only one bed each. This arrangement staggered the partitions along the aisle with the opposing cubicles, adding a bit more privacy.

Within four to six weeks, a new latrine was constructed next to our BOQ. The Quonset that housed the toilets and showers was partitioned and the facilities were duplicated in each half,

Mang Yang Pass (Hwy. 19 running from Cambodia through Pleiku and An Khe to Qui Nhon on the coast as it passes from the Central Highlands down to the coastal plain).

Jerry W. Martin, M.D. standing by a roadway sign showing directions and distances on Hwy. 14 as it continued to the south (Ban Me Thuot) and Hwy. 19 heading east (Mang Yang Pass).

to accommodate simultaneous usage by both males and females. Each half was further divided with lavatories and commodes on one side and showers on the other. Flush toilets and hot showers were luxuries that were long anticipated and greatly appreciated. With the construction of the latrines and the installation of the septic tank, two large water towers had been constructed to provide running water.

Fifty-five gallon drums, cut in half, with seats placed on them ("honey buckets"), constituted our first latrines. Periodically, diesel fuel was poured into the drums and ignited. While they were burning, we were always careful to stay up wind. The latrine was enclosed by a shoulder-high canvas curtain with no top. Because of the monsoon rains, a tent was later placed over them. We shaved in an unsheltered area where a crude, narrow, wooden table had been constructed. We used small, individual mirrors that could be hung or propped at the appropriate angle. Hot water was dipped into a washbasin from a barrel heated by a submersible kerosene heater. Initially, the shower was housed in a small 10'x12' building constructed with a wooden frame covered on all sides and roofed with corrugated metal. Two 55-gallon steel drums welded together, and placed on the roof, provided our hot water, which was also heated by a kerosene heater. The water from the tank flowed by gravity into the showerhead. During the monsoon rains, the heater frequently went out—on those occasions we had a brisk, but brief, cold shower.

When we lived in tents, there were only dirt, usually mud, walkways. We laid sandbags in areas that served as stepping stones. After showering, one probably could not tell it by looking. Even though we were clean underneath, our jungle boots were always muddy, and our jungle fatigues were usually splattered with mud.

By the time the new showers were constructed, the monsoon rains had greatly diminished, and gravel had been laid for walks. Walkways that began as dirt and mud soon became sandbagged stepping stones. They quickly changed to gravel and metamorphosed into ribbons of concrete. By this time the roadways were graveled. As the rain subsided and then ended, the walkways, roadways, drainage ditches and culverts were rapidly installed. Initially, trucks, jeeps, cranes and all other equipment frequently became mired in nearly knee-deep mud.

At first, the helipad was simply dirt and grass and then oil-covered gravel; but finally metal strips were laid and macadam was applied at the edges to create a hard surface with peripheral, recessed lighting, allowing safer night landings. A hard surface was essential; otherwise, each time a helicopter landed or took off, dust, sand, dirt, small rocks and other detritus blew everywhere. The patients and litter bearers could barely see or breathe, and dust blew into the A&D, R&E, etc. The area around the helipad was eventually sodded with grass, which helped tremendously in controlling the dust.

The numerous attempts at negotiation toward peace were always rejected by Hanoi. President Johnson suspended bombing of North Vietnam from December 24, 1965 to January 31, 1966. The United States contacted 115 governments around the world in an effort to start peace negotiations. Without a positive response, President Johnson and Premier Nguyen Cao Ky met in Honolulu, where they signed the Declaration of Honolulu on February 6-7, 1966, in which they agreed to continue the war. On October 17, President Johnson left Washington for a 17-day trip to visit seven Asian and Pacific nations and attend a Manila Conference (October 24-25, 1966) with Allied leaders. Prior to the Manila meeting, he visited New Zealand and Australia. At the conclusion of the Manila Conference, the seven participating nations (United States, Australia, New Zealand, South Korea, South Vietnam, Thailand and the Philippines) issued a communiqué, Declaration of Peace, in which they pledged to withdraw troops from Vietnam within six months if North Vietnam would agree to withdraw its forces to the North and cease the infiltration of South Vietnam. They stressed the need for a "…peaceful settlement of the war in Vietnam and for future peace and progress …" in the rest of Asia and the Pacific. As he left the Manila Conference, President Johnson flew to Cam Ranh Bay on October 26, for a surprise two and one half hour visit with U.S. troops.

The Thanksgiving season in Pleiku was not remarkable. We had a few IRHA's and a steady flow of NBI's (these acronyms are military parlance for "Injuries Resulting from Hostile Action" and "Non-Battle Injuries" [mostly malaria cases]). Most of the fighting during this period was in CTZ III and was known as Operation Attleboro (September 14 to November 24, 1966). This operation involved the 196th Infantry Brigade

Graduates of the University of Louisville Medical School, left to right: Capt. Jerry W. Martin (1963); Lt. Gen. Leonard D. Heaton (1926), Surgeon General; Brig. Gen. James A. Wier, (1937), USASV.

Lt. Gen. Heaton followed by Lt. Col. Cenac and Capt. Tony Lindem, our Chief of Staff, while touring our BOQ.

reinforced by a battalion of the 27th Infantry northwest of Saigon in the vicinity of Tay Ninh near Cambodia. In early October, they found a huge cache of enemy supplies south of the Don Dien Michelin plantation, and most of November was spent in search and destroy missions, which ended on Thanksgiving Day. Many did not have anything to be thankful for that day. We were thankful that we were alive and unscathed. Our noon meal on Thanksgiving was the usual fare: turkey and dressing, giblet gravy, mashed potatoes, green beans, sweet potatoes, cranberry sauce and rolls or cornbread—and of course, pumpkin pie.

During the first week of December, Lt. Gen. Leonard Dudley Heaton, Surgeon General of the U.S. Army (1959-1969), visited the 18th Surgical Hospital (MA) accompanied by Brig. Gen. James A. Wier, USARV Surgeon. They toured all portions of the hospital complex, even our BOQ, and then had lunch at our Mess Hall. They talked with the physicians and nurses, asked pertinent questions, made constructive comments and generally engaged in pleasantries and small talk. In a conversation, we serendipitously discovered that three of us were alumni of the University of Louisville Medical School: Lt. Gen. Heaton graduated there in 1926, Brig. Gen. Wier in 1937 and I in 1963. They requested that we have a group photograph taken, a copy of which I later sent to Donn L. Smith, M.D., Dean, University of Louisville Medical School, for placement in the Archives of the Health Science Center's Kornhauser Medical Library.

The same day, Maj. Gen. C. W. Eifler, Commanding General, 1st Logistical Command (Saigon); Brig. Gen. Mark Meyer, CO Logistical Command (Qui Nhon); Gen. Westmoreland, Commanding General-MACV and Maj. Gen. William R. Peers, Commanding General, 4th Infantry Division (Ivy) also visited us. At the end of the day, we added up the number of their stars—14 stars had visited the 18th that day. Maj. Gen. Norton, Commanding General, 1st Cavalry Division, intended to come to visit the wounded troops under his command, but had to cancel. He did visit the wounded the following day. Had he visited on the twelfth, there would have been a total of 16 stars present that day. We concluded that that was the day "the stars shown" on the 18th Surgical Hospital (MA).

Lt. Gen. Heaton, as a Major, was Chief of Surgical Services, North Sector General Hospital, Scofield Barracks when the Japanese

Chinook ferrying ambulatory patients from the 18th Surgical Hospital (MA) to the 4th Infantry Division Base Camp at Dragon Mountain for the Bob Hope Show.

attacked Pearl Harbor on December 7, 1941. In 1953, Maj. Gen. Heaton was appointed Commanding General, Walter Reed Medical Center, Washington, D.C. In June 1956, he operated on President Eisenhower for ileitis (ileocolic bypass) and later removed a colon cancer from Secretary of State, John Foster Dulles. He also operated on Generals of the Army, Douglas MacArthur and George C. Marshall. He was appointed Surgeon General of the Army on June 1, 1959 and retired from that position and the U.S. Army on September 1,1969. He was the first physician to receive three stars.

Robert Lee Hewitt, M.D., arrived at Tan Son Nhut International Airport about 2 pm on December 7, 1966, on a TWA charter flight. The flight left Travis Air Force Base, which stopped in Anchorage, Alaska and Kyoto, Japan. The entire trip from New Orleans was about thirty-six hours. Bob was originally assigned to the 17th Field Hospital in Saigon, but the orders were changed, reassigning him as the CO of the 240th Thoracic Surgery K-Team that had already been attached to the 18th Surgical Hospital (MA). He replaced Roger Ecker, M.D., CO of the 240th who was working at the 542nd Medical Clearing Company when the 18th arrived in country. Bob left Tan Son Nhut at 7 a.m. and arrived at the New Pleiku Airport about 8 a.m. on December 12, 1966. One of the ambulances of the 1st Medical Company (Ambulance), assigned to our hospital, served as the taxi that brought him from the New Pleiku Airport to the 18th compound. When he left Saigon (near sea level) that morning, the temperature was 85°, while in Pleiku (3,000 ft. elevation) at 11 a.m. it was 55°. At night in the Central Highlands during the dry season, the temperature often dropped to 40-45°, which is very cool considering that there was no heat. We usually slept under a sheet and two wool Army blankets to keep warm. Using a short extension cord, we often placed a burning light bulb between the sheets for a few minutes before going to bed. It was not only cool but also extremely dry. Quite a contrast, only a few months earlier we had had difficulty keeping cool and avoiding the dampness.

The following day, Michael Alan Belinson, M.D., came to Pleiku after having arrived in Saigon on December 7. Mike and Bob had first met at MFSS at Ft. Sam Houston, and their paths crossed again at Camp Alpha in Saigon. Mike was actually assigned to the 71st Evac; however, since they would not begin treating patients until May 1967, he, too, was assigned to the 18th.

On Monday, December 19, the Bob Hope Show came to the base camp of the 4th Infantry Division located at the foot of Dragon Mountain on the southwest side of Pleiku City, less than five air miles from our hospital. Ambulatory patients, physicians, nurses, EMs, etc. from the 18th were flown by Chinook helicopters to see the show. The stage was set up in a location at the base of a concave declivity in the mountainside. This area served as a natural amphitheater, allowing better audience visibility. Patients were positioned closest to the stage. Bob Hope had as his entourage: Les Brown and his Band of Renown, Anita Bryant, the Korean Kittens, Phyllis Diller, Joey Heatherton, Vic Damone and Rita Fera (Miss World from India). After leaving Pleiku, Bob Hope and his tour group went to Bangkok, Thailand. They then returned to Saigon, and finally stopped at Guam, before returning to the States.

About the same time, the Archbishop of New York, Cardinal Spellman, and the Rev. Billy Graham separately toured Vietnam. They stopped at Camp Radcliff (1st Cav) at An Khe, but did not come to Pleiku.

December was not only the busiest month for casualties to date; it was also an eventful month in other ways.

It was announced that new docks at Qui Nhon, constructed by U.S. Engineers, were dedicated on December 1. The port was now capable of receiving 10,000-ton ships.

On December 2, 1966, Prime Minister Nguyen Cao Ky asked the Education Minister to promote Vietnamese as the language of the Medical Schools throughout the Republic of Vietnam, beginning on January 1, 1967, thereby replacing French and English then currently used in teaching medicine.

Tan Son Nhut Airport was mortared on December 3 from two separate sites and then attacked by VC guerillas, eighteen of whom were killed and six were captured.

The Director General of the National Police, General Nguyen Ngoc Loan, defined the jurisdiction limits of VN police and U.S. MPs on December 8. Only Vietnamese police could arrest Vietnamese civilians and check papers of Vietnamese military personnel, and they had the authority to arrest U.S. civilians. The U.S. military police could only question and arrest U.S. military personnel.

The inauguration of a new U.S.-constructed, (27.5-million-dollar) Saigon metropolitan water supply system occurred on December 11, supplying 127.5 million gallons of potable water daily to Saigon, Cholon and the Gia Dinh area.

On December 16, the Constituent Assembly decided that the next year's civilian government would have a President, a Vice President and a Prime Minister, with the President having the power to appoint and dismiss the Prime Minister and the Cabinet. Four days later, it approved the process for the election of hamlet and district officials, as well as province chiefs and mayors. On the 28th, the Vietnamese National Leadership Committee decided to maintain its veto power over the Constitution being drafted by the Constituent Assembly. Decree Law No. 21 on Elections stipulated that the National Leadership Committee would retain the right to amend the future Constitution. The Constituent Assembly also approved a two-party system.

On Monday, December 12, just a few days after returning to Washington, D.C. after visiting the 18th Surgical Hospital (MA), Lt. Gen. Leonard D. Heaton, assisted by Col. Carl W. Hughes (Chief of the Department of Surgery at Walter Reed Medical Center) did a cholecystectomy (removal of gall bladder) on former President Dwight D. Eisenhower because of cholelithiasis (stones), which were confined to the gall bladder. Others who assisted were: Maj. Gen. Douglas B. Kendrick (Commanding General of Walter Reed), Capt. David E. Smith (resident in general surgery), Col. Jenicek and Maj. Hazel Outlaw (U.S. Army Nurse Corps). Mrs. Eisenhower, their son John, and Milton, the president's brother, were with the President before and after surgery.

As the infiltration by the NVA increased along the Laotian and Cambodian borders, the importance of the Pleiku Air Base increased, and the facilities were improved and expanded. In December 1962, it was designated by the South Vietnamese Air Force (SVNAF or VNAF) as Air Base 62. In March 1964, the tactical elements at Pleiku were formed into the VNAF 62nd Tactical Wing. The VNAF moved the 1141st Observation Squadron to Pleiku from Da Nang Air Base in January 1965, and also moved a detachment of Douglas A1-E Skyraiders from Bien Hoa Air Base. In 1965, the base was under the command of the VNAF 92nd Base Support Group and home of the SVNAF 6th Air Division's 72nd Tactical Wing and was used as a staging and emergency airfield. Units stationed there were the following: 118th Liaison Squadron Cessna O-2A, U-17; 530th Fighter Squadron A-1; 229th/235th Helicopter Squadron Bell UH-1H and 259th Helicopter Squadron (Det.B) Bell UH-1H (Medevac). On February 7, 1965, the NVA attacked the airfield at Pleiku, killing nine and wounding 127 Americans, and destroying 16 helicopters plus other aircraft.

After the attack, U.S. Army and Air Force civil engineering units resurfaced and extended the runways from 1829 m. (approx. 5872 ft.) to over 6500 ft. The base was then used jointly by the VNAF and the USAF. At that point it became known as the New Pleiku Air Base. Army, Navy and USAF personnel were stationed there. The USAF was a part of the 7th Air Force under the command of the U.S. Pacific Air Force (PACAF).

During World War II, the 7th Air Force was involved in the South Pacific, covering an area 3,000 miles north and south

A view of the 18th Surgical Hospital (MA), Pleiku, looking toward the southwest in June 1967. Photo furnished by Michael Belinson, M.D.

from Midway to Fiji and 5,000 miles east and west from Pearl Harbor to the Ryukus. It was activated on November 1, 1940, as the Hawaiian Air Force, and was almost completely decimated at Pearl Harbor. It quickly rebuilt and became active in the Gilberts, the Marshalls, the Carolines, the Marianas, Iwo Jima, Okinawa, Tokyo and everything in between. It was renamed the 7th Air Force on February 5, 1947. The 18th (Portable) (Surgical) Hospital (Provisional) (Reinforced) and the 18th Surgical Hospital (MA) (MUST) (MA) simultaneously served with the 7th Air Force both in World War II and Vietnam.

The Vietnam War prompted the USAF to activate the 7th Air Force on March 28, 1966, and to designate them a combat command at Tan Son Nhut Air Base—the Air Component Command of MACV. From April 1966 through 1973, the command assumed responsibility for Air Force operations in Vietnam and shared responsibility with the 13th Air Force for operations from Thailand. On March 29, 1973, the command transferred to Nakhon Phanom Royal Thai Air Base, Thailand prior to being inactivated on June 30, 1975.

The U.S. 21st Tactical Air Support Squadron (TASS), which had been activated on March 8, 1965, became operational on August 1, 1965, and was assigned to the 505th Tactical Control Group, headquartered at Tan Son Nhut. Its mission was to provide visual reconnaissance and airborne forward air control (FAC) in the support of tactical offensive operations. This unit played a key role in defense of the U.S. Special Forces Camp at Duc Co during an NVA attack, August 3-17, 1965. During the year that we were in Pleiku, the New Pleiku Air Base, commanded by Col. Bonneaux, was very busy. Later, the A1-E Skyraiders were placed under the 6th Air Commando Squadron and the C-47Ds ("Puff") were placed under the 9th Commando Air Squadron. The 6254th Air Force Combat Support Group was stationed there from July, 1965-July, 1966.

In January 1966, the 145th Air Transport Group (Heavy) became the 145th Military Air Lift Group with a worldwide airlift mission and a secondary aero-medical evacuation mission. It provided vital support for the Army, Air Force and Army National Guard in Vietnam, the United States and throughout the world. They airlifted over 23 million ton- miles of cargo to Vietnam, flew 8.5 million passenger miles and 1.1 million patient miles. The 145th Air Lift Wing is one of only four in the USAF equipped and trained to provide airborne fire fighting suppression, and since 1995, this unit has been working with the U.S. Forest Service.

As previously mentioned, Paul Revere IV continued during most of December. Throughout the month, sporadic encounters with the NVA and VC continued to occur. For example, on December 18, 1966 the 1st Platoon, Company A (3rd Brigade, 25th Infantry Division) made contact with a small NVA force while on a search and destroy mission. At the same time, U.S. B-52s from Guam bombed NVA supply bases and staging areas just south of the DMZ. On December 20, the Chinese Communist Party newspaper, *Jenmin Jih Pao* suggested that the NVA and VC should spurn negotiations with the U.S. and encouraged continuation of the war. On the 23rd, U.S. intelligence sources confirmed

reports that North Koreans were in North Vietnam training NVA pilots. There were no attacks in the immediate environs of Pleiku City during the month. We continued to receive a steady flow of medical patients (i.e., malaria, pneumonia, scrub typhus, etc.). Surgical cases numbered only three or four per day during the last week of the month. December was, to date, our busiest month.

Someone placed a Christmas tree adorned with lights and appropriate decorations near the edge of the helipad next to the "Bridge of Hope" welcoming the sick and wounded as they walked or were carried from Dustoff to R&E. The "Bridge of Hope" was a wooden bridge placed over a shallow drainage ditch between the helipad and the concrete walk leading to the entrance of the 18th Surgical Hospital (MA), so that litter bearers and/or ambulatory patients did not have to traverse this depression. After its construction, a sign was affixed to the end of the bridge facing the heliport with "Bridge of Hope" inscribed. One morning the rays emanating from a beautiful sunrise reflected a pink color instead of its original white. During the night a clandestine plot to assault the "Bridge of Hope" was stealthily accomplished, masterminded by some of the nurses and physicians, under the cover of darkness. Amused by this overnight transformation, Lt. Col. Cenac allowed this color change to remain permanent.

Christmas dinner was essentially a duplication of the Thanksgiving Dinner, except shrimp cocktails were added. The U.S. Defense Personnel Support Center in Philadelphia provided the following statistics: in order to provide the forces in Vietnam with a Christmas dinner of turkey and all the trimmings, it required 360,000 pounds of shrimp, 2.4 million pounds of turkey, 675,000 pounds of sweet potatoes and 360,000 pounds of cranberry sauce for a total cost of 2.5 million dollars. That comes to approximately $1.41 per person.

Construction of the "Bridge of Hope."

Christmas tree located beside the walk leading from our helipad to R and E near the end of "Bridge of Hope" at the 18th Surgical Hospital.

Oscar Valerio, M.D. standing on the "Bridge of Hope" reading the Stars and Stripes.

The food was delicious and thankfully appreciated, but food cannot replace family, especially at Christmas. It was an extremely lonely day. There seemed to be a lull in the fighting on Christmas Day. We never, ever wished for casualties; however, our involvement in patient care always superceded our personal emotions.

Around Christmas and New Years, we had numerous distinguished visitors at the 18th. One of those individuals was Col. Mildred Irene Clark, an Army nurse anesthetist who was the twelfth Chief of the Army Nurse Corps (ANC; 1963-1967). As a Major, she had been assigned to Gen. Douglas MacArthur's staff in Japan as the chief nurse, Far East Command. While working with the Navy, Air Force and U.S. Public Health Service Nurse Corps, she initiated efforts to gain "star" (General or Admiral) rank for the Chief of the Uniformed Services Nurse Corps. She retired before receiving a star, but her successor, Col. Anna Mae Hays, became the first woman in the military to be promoted to Brig. General. She was promoted on June 11, 1970, after being appointed by President Richard Nixon on May 14 and was Chief of the Army Nurse Corps from September 1, 1967 to August 31, 1971. The same day of Col. Hay's promotion, Elizabeth P. Hoisington was also promoted to Brig. General. Though legislation had been passed in 1955 to permit male nurses to be commissioned in the Reserve component of the Army Nurse Corps and serve on active duty, Col. Clark, working with the Army Surgeon General Lt. Gen. Leonard D. Heaton and the Secretary of the Department of the Army, managed to get Public Law 89-609 passed in 1966, authorizing them to acquire Regular Army commissions. A prayer written by Col. Clark became the official ANC Prayer, which reflects on her devotion to her profession and country and resonates as a commemorative to her:

The Army Nurse Corps Prayer

Hear my prayer in silence before Thee as I ask for courage each day.
Grant that I may be worthy of the sacred pledge of my profession.
And the lives of those entrusted to my care.
Help me to offer hope and cheer in the hearts of men and my country,
For their faith inspires me to give the world and nursing my best.

Instill in me the understanding and compassion of those who lead the way,
For I am grateful to You for giving me this life to live.

Col. Clark was accompanied by Col. Marian Tierney (USARV), Chief of Nurses in Vietnam. Colonels Clark and Tierney remained at the 18th Surgical Hospital (MA) for two days. Our nurses hosted a reception in their honor. The nurse anesthetists at the 18th at that time were Capt. Tom Goodwine, 1st Lt. Ron Thompson, 1st Lt. Ron Hatch and Major Pat Miller; while the nurses were Capts. Leo "Ski" Plasczynski (240th K-Team), Pat Weaver and Ann Stetcher, 1st Lt. Margie McGinnis, and 2nd Lts. Judy Dexter, Pat Dunn, Mary Lee Heath, Mary Hamilton (later married Joe Juliano, M.D.), Pat Johnson, Jim Jones and Bobby Gouldthorpe. Major Mary Berry was the Chief of Nursing and Major Margie Jaskowski was the Assistant Chief of Nursing. In August, nurses Dunn and Hamilton were promoted to 1st Lt.

A few days earlier Gen. Harold Keith Johnson, Chief of Staff of the U.S. Army (1964-1968) visited our hospital. He had survived the Bataan Death March, and in the Korean War, was awarded the Distinguished Service Cross. He created the position of Sergeant Major of the Army and selected William O. Woolridge to be the first to hold this post. Gen. Johnson also served as acting Chairman of the Joint Chiefs of Staff for a few months in 1967 during the convalescence of Gen. Earle Wheeler. Gen. Johnson was succeeded by Gen. Westmoreland as the Army's Chief of Staff on June 10, 1968. Gen. Wm. Westmoreland, in turn, was succeeded in Vietnam by Gen. Creighton W. Abrams, who had been his deputy since May 1967.

Within only a few days, Maj. Gen. Byron L. Steger, Surgeon Gen., Pacific Area Command (second in command under Lt. Gen. Heaton of the U.S. Army's Medical Corps) came to the 18th. He toured our facilities, visited with hospital personnel, talked with each patient and had lunch with us in our Mess Hall.

John Steinbeck, the American journalist and Nobel Prize winning author (*The Grapes of Wrath*) who had been awarded the U.S. Medal of Freedom by President Lyndon B. Johnson in 1964, came to South Vietnam in early December at the behest of *Newsday Magazine*. He

Left to right: Mike Belinson, M.D., Ron Hatch, CRNA, Wayne Hosking, M.D., Tom Goodwine, CRNA, Ron Thompson, CRNA and Pat Miller (seated), CRNA at Christmas party at Paradise Lost.

Left to right (back): Mark T. Cenac, M.D. (CO), Sam Gillis, M.D., Felix Jenkins, M.D. and Virgil Goforth, M.D. Left to right (front) Tassos Nassos, M.D., Jules Perley, M.D., Tony Lindem, M.D. and Bob Hewitt, M.D.

Left to right: Dave Bucher, M.D., Orville Swenson, M.D. at Christmas party.

Jerry W. Martin, M.D. and Lt. Col. Cenac (CO) sitting on Santa's knee in Paradise Lost, Christmas Eve, 1966.

stayed mostly in Saigon visiting with his son, John Steinbeck IV, but came to Pleiku just after Christmas and visited the 4th Infantry Division's Camp Enari' near Dragon Mountain. He was scheduled to visit the 18th; however, those plans were necessarily canceled because we received a large number of casualties.

Steinbeck's sons served in Vietnam. John Steinbeck IV was drafted in the U.S. Army in 1965 and worked as a journalist for the Armed Forces Radio and TV and was a war correspondent for the U.S. Department of Defense. *In Touch*, his book about his experiences with the Vietnamese, was published in 1969. His memoir, *The Other Side of Eden*, was published posthumously.

New Year's Day was a quiet day that came and went without significant celebration or fanfare. Only six more months to go! It seemed as if the New Year was reluctant about being born. In fact, quietness became the status quo throughout the first six days of the month. Then suddenly between 7-8 pm on Saturday evening, January 7, the status quo was shattered by the first explosion from a continuous and prolonged mortar attack in the Pleiku area. Most of the mortars struck the 20th Engineer Battalion (ARVN) and the U.S. Air Base at Camp Holloway. A few hit New

Pleiku Air Base, but the 18th was not hit. The attack destroyed numerous buildings, ignited a small ammo-dump, destroyed 20-30 helicopters, destroyed a large amount of equipment and supplies and resulted in several million dollars worth of damage. When the mortar attack ended, a company size VC ("Charlie") force attacked a section of Camp Holloway's eastern perimeter. They were able to penetrate their defenses and overrun about 100 yards of the compound before the U.S. Forces could adequately reestablish their defense. A large number of VC were killed, and the attacking force was quickly repelled and dispersed. There were 66 Americans wounded and six killed.

Soon after the initial attack began at Camp Holloway, casualties began arriving at the 18th and continued to come in over the next 24-36 hours. We operated throughout the night and all the next day. As we operated, we could hear the sporadic small arms fire and the explosion of additional mortars. There was constant activity of A1-E's taking off and landing at the New Pleiku Air Base. The air was filled with helicopters, and Puff was airborne.

The fighting closest to the 18th was in the rice paddy contiguous with Hwy. 19 on the west and the 18th Surgical Hospital (MA)'s motor pool on the east, which was about 150-200 yards from our hospital site. We were under Red Alert for many hours. Our perimeter guards were doubled, and we worked under black out conditions. If not scrubbed in surgery, everyone wore helmets and flack vests. Although our hospital did not receive a direct mortar hit, two buildings in our compound were hit by bullets.

These attacks were carried out by Viet Cong guerrillas from the Pleiku area. The hard core VC were full-time and commanded units organized into brigades and battalions on a provincial or regional basis. They were highly disciplined, well trained and experienced. They were led by individuals who lived locally but had been trained in North Vietnam. Part-time guerrillas were organized by districts into company or platoon sized units. These units guarded supplies and caches of ammunition stored throughout the region and were trained in small arms, grenades, land mines and mortars. The third category included those reserve guerrilla units who lived in the local villages and worked in civilian jobs during the day and then took part in night attacks, as directed by their leaders. The barber at MACV, who had cut my hair since we arrived at Pleiku, was captured that night firing mortars. He had been a professor of history at a university that was forced to close as a result of the war. In addition to Vietnamese, he was fluent in French and English and was keenly interested in U.S. sports, especially baseball. We frequently talked while he worked, about Vietnam, the U.S., sports and our families. He was articulate, gracious, affable and friendly. No one could have ever suspected his political persuasion or could have detected signs of traitorism.

The Viet Cong infiltrated many U.S. Military units, including MACV, and especially the ARVN units. Some were simply undercover "pro-American" employees (i.e., kitchen workers, housekeepers, barbers, secretaries, office workers, etc) who clandestinely worked on military compounds collecting valuable intelligence information. A few were officers in command positions.

A rumor began circulating that the 18th Surgical Hospital (MA) was a front organization and that we were concealing a stockpile of weapons. Intelligence traced this rumor to a kitchen employee who thought the cylinders containing oxygen were actually bombs.

In early 1967, we were told by troops of the 25th Division's 3rd Brigade that they had been instructed to consider all Vietnamese in the field during combat as the enemy, even those in ARVN units. Earlier while engaging the VC in a firefight some of the ARVN troops fighting alongside the 3rd Brigade, threw down their weapons and surrendered, some even joining the VC firing on the Americans.

After the initial surge of wounded, the pace slowed to a steady stream of casualties over the next two days. The physicians, as did all OR and R&E personnel, worked in shifts so our collective efforts could be continued indefinitely. After finishing a surgical procedure, we would break scrub and eat, take a shower and/or perhaps sleep two to three hours, before returning to allow others to get a brief rest.

About 2 a.m. on January 9, we finally finished the last case. The ORs were cleaned, restocked, and made ready for the arrival of future casualties. As soon as all of the patients were out of recovery and transferred to the post-op ward, and once it was determined that they were stable and comfortable, we began to relax and unwind. A few smoked cigarettes; others drank a Coke or coffee and generally engaged in small talk or listened as someone mentioned an aspect of a case that was unusual or of interest to everyone. After 15-20 minutes each person drifted off to bed. While others were relaxing, I got a cup of coffee and went into a small storage room located next to X-ray that doubled as a morgue. Six or eight bodies had been placed there, properly tagged, awaiting Graves Registration (located at Camp Holloway) who would pick them up about 7 a.m. for embalming and preparation for shipment back to the States.

I sat down in an open exterior door, leaned against the door facing, and placed my left foot against the opposite door facing, while resting my right foot on the top step exiting to the outside. The light in the room was turned off. The only light entered through the open door from one of the distant lights around our motor pool, and a dim light in X-ray also shined through an interior door. I suppose weariness and fatigue was greater than I realized; for as I drank my coffee, I was completely oblivious to both my surroundings and my thoughts. While repositioning myself, my left hand happened to strike something. The curiosity to know what I had hit reawakened me from my somnolence. When I turned to check, I realized that my hand had hit the head of one of the bodies lying there. As I looked, the dim light illuminated the face of a reddish-sandy haired, freckled faced, brown-eyed young man. It seemed as if he was looking at me. I sat for what seemed like a long time, perhaps staring back at him. Rhetorical questions ricocheted in my mind as I began a silent, private colloquy with myself. Who was this man? What was his name? Had he died cowardly or heroically, or had he simply been at the wrong place at the wrong time? Why was he now dead and I still alive? To what purpose had he lived? For what purpose had I survived? What might he have become? Might he have become president or pauper, minister or maverick, an acclaimed man of letters or an alcoholic or bum; or would he have had a professional career or been a derelict? What would have determined the direction his life would have taken, and what might the results have been? I could only wonder with Longfellow, did he leave permanent footprints on the sands of time? (*A Psalm of Life*) When I have "…shuffled off this mortal coil, …" (Soliloquy from *Hamlet*), will my footprints be visible? What might I become? A poem that I had read somewhere, sometime, interjected itself into the interstices of my thoughts:

> Across the fields of yesterday
> He sometimes comes to me,
> A little lad just back from play—
> The lad I used to be.
>
> And yet he smiles so wistfully
> Once he has crept within,
>
> I wonder if he hopes to see
> The man I might have been.
>
> —*Sometimes,* Thomas S. Jones, Jr.

As my inaudible, mental conversation continued, I wondered: Did he have a wife or a girlfriend? Who were his parents? Would they be saddened and deeply grieved, or would his death simply not affect them much? Was he Jewish, Christian, or of some other religious persuasion, or was he an atheist?

As I looked, it was as if his eyes were imploring me to do something more. What more could have been done? As fatigue tugged and prodded at my consciousness, I silently spoke one final, prayerful soliloquy, "God, let me, let us, always strive to do our best!"

An outgoing artillery round from Artillery Hill jolted me back to reality from my personal thoughts, as the sonic boom shook the building. I got up and wandered off to bed. I never consciously remembered this incident until one night, about six month after being discharged, I saw his face again in a dream. The dream was neither nightmarish nor horrifying, but it was a vivid replay of the experiences of that night.

Since then, each time I hear a sudden loud explosive-type noise (i.e., gunfire, fireworks, sonic boom, etc.), an instant replay flashes on the screen of my mind, and a vision of that face reappears. It never interferes with the activity or conversation in which I am engaged at the time, and no one is ever aware.

Years later, when I was asked to write an open letter from the 18th Surgical Hospital (MA)'s staff to those who died in Vietnam, to be read during our second reunion at the Vietnam Veterans Memorial Monument in Washington, D.C., I recalled and wrote about the "…staring unseeing eyes…," those "…faces frozen expressionless and emotionless…" and "…those lips permanently silenced and speechless." It was my memory of his face that inspired those words.

Each night for about a week following the January 7 mortar attack, we were under Red Alert from about 2100-2400 hours. However, no mortars fell, and no attacks came.

Not long after the mortar attack, after things had settled back to normal again, Bernard B. Fall visited the 18th. He was born in Vienna, Austria in 1926, of Jewish parents. The family fled to Nice, France in 1938. Four years later, the Nazis overran Southern France. His mother was deported to Auschwitz and died there, and his father was killed by the Gestapo. At age 16, Fall joined the French Resistance and fought in the mountains of Savoy.

In 1944, he served in the 4th Moroccan Mountain Division and was wounded in 1945. In 1946, at age 19, he became a research analyst at the Nuremberg Trials and then worked for the *Stars and Stripes* in Munich. In 1951, he was awarded a Fulbright Scholarship and attended Syracuse University. After obtaining his Master's degree and completing course-work for his PhD, he went to French Indochina in 1953, and did research for his doctoral dissertation. In 1957, he joined the faculty at Howard University. In 1959, under a SEATO fellowship, he wrote about the conflict in Laos. After the publication of his classic, *Street Without Joy* in 1961, he returned to Cambodia and North Vietnam and interviewed both Ho Chi Minh and Pham Van Dong. Two other books by Fall were *Viet-Nam Witness* and *The Two Vietnams*.

In a *Saturday Review* article (February 4, 1967), "*The American Commitment in Vietnam*," Fall wrote: "With all due reverence to the dead President (Kennedy), it will become part of the historical record that it was he, or men under him who made all the decisive mistakes in the Vietnam situation. Probably no Chief Executive in recent memory was so badly informed about an increasingly serious situation as JFK was about Vietnam. It was during his administration that the 'politics of inadvertence' blossomed into a full-grown commitment. As soon as American 'advisors' were engaged in combat operations, the fact that there were 20,000 under Kennedy and 400,000 under Johnson becomes of little importance; and perhaps some critics would be kinder to LBJ and his 'credibility gap' if they were fully aware of the huge 'information gap' that existed between JFK and his own Embassy in Saigon, and between both and Vietnamese realities on the ground."

On the evening of his visit, Lt. Col. Cenac and Bernard Fall were dinner guests of Brig. Gen. William Lee at MACV. A little over one month after his Pleiku visit, Fall was killed by a land mine while accompanying a Marine platoon in an area north of Hue, on February 21, 1967. He had produced nine books and hundreds of articles about Vietnam.

Operation Bolo began on January 2, 1967. The U.S. 8th Tactical Fighter Wing ("Wolfpack") sent three flights of four F-4C Phantoms each over North Vietnam posing as bomb-ladened F-105 Thunderchiefs ("Thuds"). The NVAF MiG-21s were lured into the sky to intercept the "Thuds" only to find themselves amid a superior force of Phantoms. The Phantoms were armed with AIM-9 Sidewinder missiles. Seven MiGs were downed in about fifteen minutes with no American losses.

On January 13, a Montagnard Chief, Nang Quan Knang, was brought to the 18th by Dustoff. He was from a village near Kontum and had sustained gunshot wounds in both feet and ankles. He had steadfastly refused to assist or cooperate with the enemy. When the VC entered his village, they used intimidation in an attempt to evoke a conciliatory response. They shot into the ground around his feet, making him dance and beg for lenience; however, rather than eliciting contriteness and a conversion to an obsequious cooperation, the Chief evinced a disdainful and haughty response. This attitude prompted the VC to shoot him in his feet. They also shot a village medicine man and the Chief's eight-year old granddaughter, Hai (the "Princess"), in both feet. They survived, but these egregious acts left the girl with a crippling deformity of one foot and the Chief with a stiff ankle requiring him to walk with a cane. They were operated on multiple times in order to save their feet.

The chief of a village was an individual who exhibited leadership skills based on spiritual insights, physical prowess, personal skills, courage, intelligence, wisdom and ingenuity. A chief was usually one of the older citizens, although a young man could be chief if he exhibited unusual or outstanding attributes. Their position of authority continued as long as they retained these necessary qualities. A village chief was frequently the victim of murder, assassination and kidnapping by the enemy. Decisions made by the village Elders and Chief were unchallenged by the population.

After being shot, the Chief was evacuated by U.S. Special Forces to their base camp, and then, he came by chopper to the 18th. He

Left to right: Bob Engebrecht, M.D., Lt. Joe Lazorchak, Orville Swenson, M.D., Lt. Ron Thompson, CRNA, Felix Jenkins, M.D., a physician from 4th Infantry Division, Bob Hewitt, M.D. and Fred Leacock, M.D. (back to camera).

Chaplain Hollis, who replaced Chaplain Ben Nass, presenting a sermon while the chapel was still housed in a tent.

Left to right: 2nd Lt. Mary Lee Heath, 2nd Lt. Pat Dunn, 2nd Lt. Jim Jones, Capt. Pat Weaver, 2nd Lt. Judy Dexter, 2nd Lt. Bobbie Gouldthorpe.

Maj. Gen Vinh Loc (left) and Brig. Gen. Lee (right) visiting Paradise Lost at the 18th Surgical Hospital (MA).

Left to right: Lt. Col. Cenac, MC (CO) and Lt. Col. Rank, MSC (XO).

Left to right: Oscar Valerio, M.D., Joe Juliano, M.D., Capt. Dave Soberg (XO).

Left to right: Oscar Valerio, M.D. (squatting), 2nd Lt. Pat Dunn, R.N., Sam Gillis, M.D., 2nd Lt. Jim Jones, R.N. (seated), Lt. Col. Ranck (XO), Lt. Col. Cenac (CO), back to camera, 1st Lt. Bill Hames (Supply Officer), Capt. Leo "Ski" Plasczynski, R.N., 1st Lt. Margie McGinnis, R.N., 1st Lt. Joe Lazorchak, (Adjutant), walking away, and Capt. David Soberg.

Ron Thompson (CRNA), Bill Hames (Supply Officer), Joe Lazorchak (Adjutant).

Time exposure of the 18th Surgical Hospital taken from the northern edge of the helipad. (Leicaflex, tripod, 135mm Elmarit-R, f-22, exposure 4 minutes).

was wearing only a black loincloth; however, his near nakedness did not evoke thoughts of salaciousness, since this was their native dress. He had multiple tattoos and was decorated with numerous bracelets and 15-20 necklaces, all of which were an indication of his important status among his people. He was very dirty with what seemed to be 1/4" of red-tan dirt covering his body and hair.

He and the "Princess" remained with us for over two months. While hospitalized, they saw themselves in a mirror for the first time. When asked about his injuries, he often demonstrated by using his cane or crutch and shouted, "Bang! Bang! Bang!" and then would fall to the floor. He was both an actor and a clown and enjoyed having the nurses around him. When Jayne Mansfield visited the 18th, she sat on the edge of his bed and put her arm around him. He quickly reciprocated her gesture by putting his arm around her. When he was discharged from our hospital, Bob Hewitt, M.D. who had operated on him numerous times gave him a photograph of himself with Jayne Mansfield.

By late January, the 101st Airborne Division had been moved to the Mekong Delta, and the 1st Cavalry Division had moved to the Qui Nhon area. The 4th Infantry Division, the 25th Infantry Division (3rd Brigade) and the Special Forces remained in the Pleiku area.

On January 28, we were all shocked to hear of the tragic accident involving three astronauts, Ed White, Roger Chaffee and Gus Grissom, when the Apollo I command module burned during a training exercise on January 17, 1967.

Bob Hewitt, M.D., observed that the VC seemed to plan most of their mortar and rocket attacks during the darkest nights of the month, just preceding the new moon. After corroborating this suspicion, he used an almanac to predict when future attacks would occur.

The 18th compound received mortar fragments on two or three occasions and rocket fragments on another occasion, with no real damage or injuries. The nearby ARVN Hospital did receive enormous rocket damage to the roof, which resulted in minor injuries.

We arrived in Vietnam during the Year of the Horse (January 22, 1966—February 8, 1967). In 1967, Tet fell on February 9, the year of the Sheep-Goat (February 9, 1967—January 29, 1968). The Vietnamese Lunar New Year (*Tet Nguyen Dan*) occurs on the first day of the first month of the Chinese lunar calendar and does not fall on January 1, as does our New Year using the Gregorian calendar (named for Pope Gregory XIII). Since the lunar month is 29.531 days in length, the date for Tet migrates from year to year but is usually near the end of January or the first few days

Jerry W. Martin, M.D. standing beside wheelchair of the Montagnard Chief, Nang Quan Knang.

The Chief's granddaughter, Hai, the Princess.

of February. Every four years an extra month—a leap month—is added to keep the lunar calendar in sync with the solar calendar. The Vietnamese (Chinese) system revolves on a sixty-year cycle of five elements (i.e. metal, water, wood, fire or earth) and a twelve-year cycle of animals from the Chinese zodiac (Gr. zodia, meaning animal). Each animal sign relates to their observations of the orbit of Jupiter.

Individual years are then named for an animal from the zodiac in the following sequence: rat, buffalo (or ox), tiger, cat (or rabbit), dragon, snake, horse, sheep (or goat), monkey, rooster, dog and pig. *Giao Thua*, refers to the turning over of time, from the old year to the new year.

For the Vietnamese, Tet (*Tiet*, meaning festival) is equivalent to our New Years, Thanksgiving, Fourth of July and Memorial Day all rolled into one. It also is the day on which all birthdays are celebrated, since in Vietnam individual birthdays are not celebrated—everyone is simply a year older at Tet. Tet also represents the start of spring and the concept of rejuvenation. It also is the time to forgive others, pay debts, correct one's faults and start the year with a clean slate. They exchange greeting cards, plant a tree (usually peach or apricot), wish each other Happy New Year (*chuc mung nam moi*) and eat more than usual. Women buy flowers and apricot or peach branches the day before Tet. Apricot and peach blossoms are reputed to keep demons out of their homes. Some families plant an apricot tree and display it, somewhat like a Christmas tree, decorated with greeting cards they have received. They spend a great deal of time cleaning the cemeteries and tombs of their ancestors. Their Dragon Dance is meant to ward off evil spirits and bring love and prosperity.

One week before Tet, at a family ceremony, they offer fresh fruit, cooked food, and homemade paper models to *Ong Tao*, the Spirit of the Hearth, who must travel to the Palace of Jade to hail the Heavenly Emperor and present his annual progress report on the family's affairs. The departure of the Spirit leaves the home unprotected for a week, until its return on New Years (Tet). They make a brilliant paper coat for him to wear on the trip and a

paper carp that he rides back to heaven (in South Vietnam, they usually provide him with paper storks and/or horses to ride on the return trip). These concepts reflect their Taoistic beliefs. Taoism (*Tao*, The Way) is a religious system extolling virtue and humility, founded by the great Chinese sage, Lao Tze, in the 6th century BC and brought into Vietnam by early Chinese invaders. They believe that through the study of Tao, one is able to gain insight into the mysteries of heaven and its influence on earthly activities. Taoism is often mixed with Buddhism, Catholicism, Protestantism, Animism, Confucianism, Anamism (ancestor worship), astrology, geomancy, numerology and other superstitions.

A thirty-foot long bamboo pole stripped of all leaves except for a small tuft on top (*cay neu*) is planted in the yard. An octagon of red paper (*bua bat quai*) bearing inscriptions signifying Buddhism's eight-fold path is attached. A small basket of betel and areca nuts are attached for good spirits. Small clay bells that tinkle in the wind and a square screen of woven bamboo act as a barrier to demons.

Houses are decorated in red and gold. Pictures of the animal appropriate for the New Year are hung. Everyone wears new clothes. All cooking, cleaning, sewing, arranging, decorating and other work must be completed before Tet begins—no work is supposed to be done during the holiday festivities. Most families serve the traditional *banh chung*, steamed sticky rice cakes filled with pork in bean paste and wrapped in banana leaves (symbolizing the earth).

On Tet Eve, everything closes early, allowing families to head home to celebrate the first dinner of Tet. An elaborate offering of chicken and glutinous rice is made to their ancestors, and everyone awaits the magic hour of midnight. Catholics attend pre-midnight Mass. Just after midnight, Buddhists go to their favorite pagoda to pray for a good year. The last pre-Tet undertaking is the *tat nien*, or year-end ceremony. This consists of a sacrifice to each family's deceased ancestors who are invited to take part in the jubilation and feasting of the New Year. Tet ends on the evening of the third day when the ancestral souls—who have returned to this world to participate in the holiday—must return to their own world. At a farewell dinner, the family burns fake gold and silver money (*giay*

Left to right: Virgil Goforth, M.D., Sam Gillis, M.D., Dave Bucher, M.D., Wayne Hosking, M.D., Tony Lindem, M.D., Felix Jenkins, M.D., Roger Ecker, M.D. sitting. Jerry W. Martin, M.D. sitting on the foot of his bed. The group was celebrating Jerry's 31st birthday, November 28, 1966.

Pleiku Medical Association meeting with Tet decorations. Lt. Col. Welch, CO of 71st Evacuation Hospital, seated on left.

vang giay bac), allowing the departing souls to hire a sampan to ferry them across the river that separates heaven and earth.

The first person to cross the threshold to their home after midnight must be a person of good character; otherwise misfortune could occur during the coming year. Not leaving anything to chance, some families discreetly arrange for the arrival of their first visitor.

In order to drive away evil spirits, firecrackers were traditionally used; however, in 1995 the manufacture of fireworks was banned because during the 1994 Tet celebrations, 71 revelers were killed, and 765 individuals were injured. Tape recordings of fireworks are now permitted.

On the first day of Tet, people dress in their finest new clothes and visit relatives. The traditional dress for a Vietnamese female is the *ao dai*, a long tunic with side slits from the waist down, worn over long silk pants. The second day involves visits to special people and close relatives. On the third day they visit teachers, friends and business associates. Visitors are served candied fruit, *banh chung*, rolls, sausage and drinks. Everyone is supposed to return to work on the fourth day of Tet, but they seldom do. It is usually not until the sixth day that people get serious about returning to work.

Whatever their basic religious beliefs, they generally engage in ancestor worship, which reflects the great importance that Vietnamese attach to strong family bonds and the belief of the existence of the extended family. They believe that the soul lives on to maintain a protective watch over those who follow in the family line. To neglect due care and attention of the soul is to condemn it to an aimless wandering around the Kingdom of the Dead, while inviting disaster upon its descendents. They harbor a fear that there are a great many lonely souls, who died in the Vietnam War, wandering around still unclaimed.

Prior to the communist takeover, the Buddhist calendar was used for religious purposes while the Gregorian calendar was used for political and commercial transactions. Because of its large Chinese population throughout Vietnam, the Chinese calendar is currently used for religious purposes.

The Vietnamese have two other big annual festivals: Wandering Soul's Day and the Mid-Autumn Festival.

Once a year, on the 15th day of the 7th month (August-September, by the Gregorian calendar) the Master of Hell opens the gate to purgatory, granting a full day's leave to all the guest souls (called *Trung Nguyen Day*). The Vietnamese believe they are accompanied by incalculable numbers of disembodied, vagrant, wandering spirits and metaphysical forces, both good and bad, resulting in inestimable spiritual uncertainties.

The good spirits are those deceased mortals who lived a good life and now in ethereal form protect their families, homes and villages. Those spirits are revered, honored and worshipped. The evil, or devilish, spirits (*ma guy*) are those representing the individuals who drowned or were orphans, prostitutes, criminals and other unfortunate creatures. Of course, no one worships those spirits. They, nontheless, are responsible for illness, bad crops and business failures. Women beat drums around the house to chase

them away. It is believed that evil spirits travel in straight lines like bullets; therefore, individuals build curved driveways and roads and hide pagoda entrances behind screens. In communist North Vietnam, many citizens remained terror-stricken of wandering souls of landowners massacred during the agrarian reforms until the commissars allowed relatives to build monuments, establish graves and build altars to worship their dead parents. It is not clear what, if any, provisions were made by the communists for the families of those massacred in South Vietnam (i.e. Montagnards, ARVN personnel, pro-U.S. sympathizers, etc.), when Allied Forces pulled out of South Vietnam in 1976 and the country was then united as the Socialist Republic of Vietnam.

Because the wandering souls released from purgatory on *Trung Nguyen Day* are terribly hungry, women in every household spend a great deal of time preparing roasted pig's head, sticks of sugar cane, sweet pork, bowls of rice and rice alcohol (*chum chum*). Women clad in black silk robes bow low before the prepared dishes, with burning incense sticks in hand, and invite their dead ancestors and all peripatetic souls to eat. They burn brightly colored papers simulating bank notes and currency. The smoke from these fires carries all of this wealth to the souls in heaven. These pantheists try to be sure

Our daughter, Melissa Martin Johnson, wearing a green robe over an ao dai and our grand-daughter, Elizabeth Johnson Hathaway, dressed in black pajama-type clothing typically worn by Vietnamese peasants. They are wearing the native Vietnamese woven straw hats. Photograph taken by Tom Brown.

that no visiting soul returns to heaven or hell without a proper feast. These epicurean rites begin on the last full moon of August and last until mid-September. Vietnam, the land of the Smaller Dragon, in comparison with the Big Dragon (China), is a spirit world where natives see occult celestial influences in every sequence of life. When Westerners say we have had good luck or bad luck, a Vietnamese sees the influence of psychic energy, evil spirits, good spirits, etc., emanating from an incarnated human. The fear of every Vietnamese male is leaving this world without being survived by a male heir to perform, or see that his widow performs, this propitiatory ceremony and not let his soul wander miserably for eternity.

The 15th day of the 8th month (September-October) of the lunar calendar is *Tet Trung Thu*, or Mid-Autumn Festival, a day of general celebration for the Vietnamese children. The origin of the celebration is buried in myth. A Chinese legend tells that about 713-735 AD, the 6th year of the Tang Dynasty in China, Emperor Tang Ming Huang, a lover of music and poetry, called a master magician, Lo Kong Yuang (on a full-moon night of the 15th day of the 8th lunar month) to help send him off to visit the moon. In the Emperor's dream, a rainbow-like bridge enabled him to set foot on the moon. While there, Fairies danced, and music flooded his soul. He was both bewildered and charmed beyond words. Back on earth, he ordered an annual celebration throughout the kingdom in commemoration of his trip to the land of Dance, Music and Poetry.

Another legend tells of a young boy, nicknamed Little Cuoi, who was exiled for life to the moon for disobeying a Fairy. Children are told that Cuoi is still there sitting at the foot of a banyan tree.

Another story tells that an evil genie lived in a carp but changed into a Casanova on the night of *Trung Thu* in search of women and pretty girls. To ward him off, carp-shaped paper lanterns are hung at front doors and dangle in the breeze along streets, market places and shops. In the evening, children and enthusiastic adults parade with candle-lit lanterns through the streets. Each group is led by an individual carrying a paper-form of a Unicorn head, as they dance along the streets. Shops sell moon-shaped cakes (*banh trung thu*) made of eggs, green bean paste, sugar and bacon wrapped in baked flour.

Jerry W. Martin, M.D. at city sign near the north edge of Pleiku on Hwy. 19 toward the 18th Surgical Hospital (MA).

The Unicorn is regarded as a sacred and benevolent animal, which, as the story goes, gambols in the moonlight at this time of year. In an effort to coax him to release rain down to earth, they make miniature imitations of the animal, as well as several kinds of fruit and fish to symbolize prosperity and peace. While the youths are celebrating, the grownups talk, recite poetry, play music, etc., as they drink hot tea and eat sugar-coated lotus seeds.

Sometime during late September or early October, Wayne Hosking, M.D., and I were invited by Bac Si (medical doctor) Hoang to join he and his wife and two children for an evening meal at their home during the Mid-Autumn Festival. I had met Dr. Hoang at the Pleiku Medical Association and again at the Pleiku Provincial Hospital. When visiting in a Vietnamese home during this Festival, it was not expected that the guest bring a gift for the family, but it was customary for the guest to give a gift (usually money, custom called Li Xi) to the children. We gave each child a few piasters (about the equivalent of a U.S. dollar). They served hot tea, rolls, *banh chung*, shrimp salad and water buffalo steak. For dessert, they served candied fruits and sweet cakes made of bananas, nuts and steamed rice that had been deep-fried.

On January 10, 1967, Gene Chap, M.D., Oscar Valerio, M.D., Joe Juliano, M.D., and Mary Hamilton, R.N., were dinner guests of Bac Si Ty, his wife and four children at their home during the Tet Celebration. Dr. Ty spoke English fluently; however, his family understood only a few words. Dr. Ty often translated during the Pleiku Medical Association meeings.

The Ty family served a typical Tet meal. Tea and the traditional sweets, consisting of candied turnips, pumpkin and dates were served before dinner. In addition, there were lotus flower seeds and peanuts in fish sauce (*nuc maum*), butter and coconut. For dinner, they served "…rice cakes boiled in banana leaves which made the rice turn green…," while "…within the cake…were bean sprouts and pork sausage." Also served were cabbage and chicken salad in vinegar, scallions in fish sauce, pork, boiled eggs in fish sauce, chicken and chicken soup, plus pickled bean sprouts with lettuce and cowslip and mint leaves. The bread was thin, flat and crisp and made of rice, resembling a large potato chip. Tangerines were served for dessert.

They also gave each child a 100-piaster note (red in color worth about 82 cents) placed in a red envelope, since the color red was considered to bring good luck during Tet.

The Ty house was a combination office/home, as was the Hoang home Wayne and I had visited. Upon entering, the guests proceeded through the waiting room into an examining room that doubled as the dining room. The next two rooms were bedrooms, with a kitchen contained in a small room that seemed to have been added on. The Vietnamese were always courteous, very cheerful and most gracious hosts.

Perhaps other nurses and physicians from the 18th were guests on similar occasions at the homes of Bac Sis Huong, Ty, Bui-Trong-Can or other Pleiku physicians. The Pleiku Medical Association meeting during Tet was at the ARVN Hospital. The dining area was elaborately decorated and the meal served was traditional Vietnamese fare.

Yellowstone Bar—protective screen preventing grenades or Molotov cocktails from being thrown through the doors. Doors were also offset.

A Lambretta approaching from the direction of Camp Holloway on Hwy. 14 at junction of Hwy. 19 in Pleiku.

A theatre in Pleiku.

Basketball at Catholic school in Pleiku.

Vietnamese peasants squatting in street in Pleiku.

Vietnamese woman cooking pork in street in Pleiku.

Pleiku City, situated at the crossroads of Hwy. 14 (north and south) and Hwy. 19 (east and west) was the capitol of Pleiku Province. However, there was no capitol building; in fact, there was not even a city hall. It seemed to be more of a village than a city. There were officially (1966 Rand McNally Vietnam map) 7,500 inhabitants, mostly peasants, but the population swelled to approximately 20,000-30,000 due to the migration of refugees displaced by the war. The various socioeconomic stratas of society were readily apparent by observing the method used for individual transportation. The poorest simply walked, while the majority rode bicycles. Farmers often rode in ox carts pulled by water buffalo. The middle class rode motorbikes, while the upper class had automobiles, usually 1950s, or older, French models. Their taxi system utilized Lambrettas almost exclusively. Lambrettas were tri-wheeled vehicles made in Italy and probably modified by the Vietnamese. These vehicles were covered by a metal roof, both front and rear. The driver sat in the mid-portion of a bench seat, leaving room for a passenger on each side, and guided it by using handlebars rather than a steering wheel. Passengers rode in the back on bench seats along each side, sitting facing inward toward the opposite passengers. There was no rear door or side doors on the front. There were side curtains that could be unfurled when it was raining. There was a windshield with wipers but no rear window between the driver and the rear passengers. The ride from Pleiku City to the 18th Surgical Hospital (MA), a distance of between two and three miles, cost only a few piasters (equivalent to about 15 to 20 cents).

Most of the businesses and shops in downtown Pleiku were housed in two-story buildings. The proprietors operated their businesses downstairs and lived with their families upstairs. Except in the central part of town, most other businesses were located in single level structures. There were no buildings taller than two stories. There were concrete sidewalks throughout the main part of town, and all streets were paved, except the roads on the outskirts of town which were graveled.

There were two service stations, probably eight or more bars, two to three barber shops, and about the same number of drug stores, numerous laundries, two hardware stores, probably

A Lambretta taxi carrying me to 18th Surgical Hospital (MA) situated in the distance to the right just below MACV-II Corps HQ. Artillery Hill in the distance to the left.

three to four physicians offices, two to three dental offices, five to six small hotels and numerous restaurants in addition to the ubiquitous venders who cooked on the sidewalk. Some of the bars and hotels doubled as brothels. There were two open-air markets selling vegetables, fruits and sugar cane, along with fish, shrimp, chickens, pork, etc. All buildings where fairly large crowds gathered (i.e., restaurants, bars etc.) had small-mesh wire screens extending from the sidewalk to the roof or overhanging awning with a zig-zag maze, allowing patrons to enter but preventing the VC from tossing grenades or Molotov cocktails through an open entrance door.

I visited at least three public grade schools, a private grade school and a high school, including an outdoor basketball court, associated with a Catholic Church. In addition to the Catholic Church, I saw two Protestant Churches. There were many Buddhist pagodas and a Shinto Shrine.

There were two movie theatres in the downtown area. The city did not have an indoor facility that could accommodate large crowds. There were two open areas used as soccer fields, and there was a two-block square in the main part of town that served as a park, and as a gathering place during parades, rallies, etc.

There was no running water or sewage system. U.S. engineers had dug three deep wells scattered throughout the town and installed hand pumps, providing the population with fresh, potable water for drinking and cooking. The citizens came regularly to these water sites with containers placed in straw or wicker baskets that hung by ropes from a pole about five feet long (*don ganh*) and carved to fit behind the neck and over the shoulders, balancing the weight to carry the water more easily. The *don ganh* was commonly used by Montagnards and Vietnamese to carry almost everything. Often women, especially Montagnards, carried lighter things on their head.

Most of the homes were small, modest, clean and neat with small yards and vegetable gardens, a few fruit trees and even small flower gardens, which demonstrated each family's pride in their home.

Throughout the town, there were numerous walled and gated villas that had been built by French tea and rubber plantation owners during more provincial times. These houses had been converted into ARVN military headquarters, various offices and homes for the Pleiku Mayor and the Pleiku Province Chief (or Govenor). Madame Nhu's summer home was in Pleiku. Major General Vinh Loc lived in a two-story house on a walled and gated lot just a few blocks from the central part of town. Most streets were tree lined, even throughout the downtown area.

The Pleiku Provincial Hospital was located a few blocks from the main business area. It was in a beautiful area in the midst of a grove of trees. The hospital lawn was clean but appeared unkept since the grass was only occasionally trimmed by a sickle and rarely by a power mower. Apart from the setting, there was nothing else of beauty. When entering from the street through the gates and into the hospital campus, one quickly approached the main clinic building. One's attention was immediately drawn to the rusted-out remnants of a water tank still standing to the right of the clinic, obviously abandoned long ago. Beyond the clinic building was a building housing the obstetrical ward and delivery rooms. A short distance beyond was another building that housed the surgical suites and recovery room. Adjacent to it was a separate building where the post-op ward was located. Across the street from the main entrance was a building housing the medical ward and another building that served as the laboratory.

There were essentially no ancillary services. There was no running water or sewage waste disposal and no kitchen or dining facilities, even for the

Washing clothes in stream with Dragon Mountain in background.

patients. Food was brought by families or friends, or was cooked by them over a small fire built in the yard outside the wards. They often cooked what appeared to be soup or broth in large sized tin cans that was then poured into smaller cans and distributed to the patients.

Sanitation was a constant problem. When operating at the Provincial Hospital, one had to constantly be vigilant and closely monitor the nurses and surgical assistants to avoid contamination. It was extremely difficult to preserve the sterile process. Trained Vietnamese technicians, nurses and even physicians had an inadequate knowledge of sterile technique or simply ignored proper sterile protocol. Whatever the reason, the results could have been catastrophic if due diligence had not been observed.

Also, isolation of contagious diseases apparently was not well understood, or at least not followed. For example, on the medical ward a patient with active pulmonary tuberculosis might be in the bed adjacent to a malaria or pneumonia patient, or even in the same bed, when the hospital was crowded and no other bed was available. It was not uncommon to see two patients occupying the same bed. To make matters worse, the patients' families often hovered around them and even slept on woven straw mats placed on the floor beneath the hospital bed.

There was very little housekeeping or cleaning of the facilities. The floors were occasionally swept, usually by women, using a typical Vietnamese broom. These brooms were made of straw stems about three feet long tied together in a bundle that left a curved tuft on one end. They swept using only one hand.

The delivery room had three delivery tables side by side, with no screen or partition between them. The rubber sheets on the tables often had dried bloodstains still present. The OR looked a bit better. It appeared clean; however, I doubt that disinfectants, or any type of sterilization, had been used. All of the buildings in the hospital complex had electricity, but the lighting was poor. The OR light was an old model, adequate, but not ideal.

The anesthesia machines were older models, yet they too were adequate. While operating, the OR window was usually open for ventilation, and on one occasion, a water buffalo stuck his head in the window during surgery. They had a limited supply of clean surgical instruments; however, we were dubious of the autoclave used for sterilization. Therefore, when we operated there, we took sterile instruments, masks, gowns, gloves, surgical drapes and sponges from the 18th.

It was truly amazing how different Pleiku and the Central Highand area appeared when comparatively viewed at the extremes of the monsoon and dry season. The lush green vegetation during the wet season contrasted notably with the stark and dusty conditions of the dry season.

A small stream ran through the southeastern side of Pleiku during the wet season. Women often did their washing at the creek bank. One day, I observed a group of women washing their clothes, while less than 100 yards upstream, an outdoor toilet was visibly situated on the stream bank. The stream flowed from the southwest toward the northeast, crossing under Hwy.14 between Pleiku and Camp Holloway. It must have run between Camp Holloway and the New Pleiku Airbase before meandering through the Central Highlands, ultimately flowing into the Drang River or one of its tributaries.

In Pleiku, most men and women wore black pajama-like clothing, although women sometimes wore various other colors. Businessmen, shop owners, etc., usually wore conventional pants and shirts, and women wore the traditional *ao dai*. When in the sun, both sexes wore the traditional conical straw hats. The dress in larger cities (i.e., Nha Trang, Qui Nhon, Saigon, etc.) was the same as in Pleiku, except the percentage of those wearing pajamas decreased, and the trend shifted toward the opposite end of the spectrum.

On Wednesday, January 6, 1967, Gene Chap, M.D., presented a few patients at the Pleiku Medical Association meeting. Patricia M. Smith, M.D., was a guest at that meeting. We all had heard of her, primarily through missionaries and

Montagnards who came to the 18th, and many of us had wanted to visit her hospital near Kontum. While in the Pleiku area, she visited the 18th. It was a pleasure to meet and talk with her. After graduating from the University of Washington Medical School, she had begun her medical career on the staff of a miners' hospital in the Appalachian Mountains of Eastern Kentucky. An Australian journalist told her about medical needs in other parts of the world. She joined the Grail, an international organization of Catholic women, and, eight months later in July 1959, arrived in Vietnam. She first worked at a leprosarium outside of Kontum not far from Laos and Cambodia.

The Montagnards had one of the highest incidences of leprosy in the world—7-10% of the population. Three out of four children did not reach adulthood and the life expectancy of those who did survive was only 35-40 years. Tuberculosis affected 30-40% of the people. Additionally, they frequently had malaria, cholera, scrub typhus, plague and acute forms of dysentery (many causes). The entire population was malnourished. Dr. Smith noted, "We take it for granted that they're all malnourished, especially protein malnourished. They all have malaria, whether it is active or not, and they all have intestinal parasites. We presume they have these three things when they come in. After that we ask them what acute disease really brought them into the hospital." They had "...absolutely zero knowledge of sanitation, or any concept of infection diseases.... They still believe in evil spirits, so they go to a sorcerer when they're sick." They blamed infection or disease on *deng*, an evil spirit.

She established a primitive dispensary in the area. At first the people would not come, but after a few lives were saved through modern medicine and surgery, they gradually overcame their apprehensions and suspicions.

During the Tet offensive of 1968, NVA and VC attacked her hospital and killed a few patients and shot others in the legs. These atrocities forced her to move the hospital to a Catholic school in Kontum. Later a 40-bed facility, the Minh-Quy Hospital, was constructed from funds contributed by the German Bishop's Relief Fund and was named for two priests who had been killed by the Viet Cong.

Dr. Smith received a substantial amount of help from the U.S. Military, particularly the 4th Infantry Division, who regularly sent volunteer physicians to her hospital for two-week tours of duty. Other physicians came to her hospital through the American Medical Association's Volunteer Physicians for Vietnam program. In addition to the U.S. Army, supplies were sent by the USAID program and through the Kontum Hospital Fund, a non-profit organization. The Montagnards came to affectionately refer to her as *Ya Pagang Tih* ("Big Grandmother of All Medicine").

The 4th Infantry Division gave a dinner in her honor at Camp Enari, at which time she gave a memorable talk about the ethos of the Montagnard people. (Camp Enari was named as a memorial to 1st Lt. Mark N. Enari, Company A, 1st Battalion, 12th Infantry, 4th Infantry Division on May 14, 1967, at Dragon ["Titty"] Mountain Base Camp).

The hospital remained operational until 1975, but she was forced to abandon it and leave the country in 1972, because the VC sought to kill all Americans. She turned the hospital over to Sister Gabriel, who was her most experienced Montagnard nurse.

She took two Montagnard children, Det, whose mother had been killed by the Viet Cong, and Wir, who had been abandoned in a burned-out village, with her to the U.S.—they became her adopted children. They settled in Bellevue, Washington where she worked for Group Health Cooperative for twenty years, before retiring in 1997. She then settled on Lake Cushman near Hoodsport, Mason County. She died on December 26, 2004 in Providence St. Peter Hospital in Olympia, at age 78.

In January 1967, Virgil Goforth, M.D., was reassigned as a Battalion Surgeon to the 9th Infantry Division in the Delta, and Tassos Nassos, M.D., went to the 1st Cavalry Division. Terry McDonald, M.D., was a "short timer" when he arrived in Vietnam. He was initially assigned to the 6th Convalescence Center at Cam Ranh Bay in December 1966, but was reassigned to the 18th in January, 1967. He returned to CONUS on July 4, 1967, for discharge.

Throughout our year at Pleiku, numerous physicians from other hospitals visited the 18th. Dick Jones, M.D., visited twice, and a few from the 18th visited him at the 8th Field Hospital in Nha Trang. Philip Freedman, M.D., and Arthur "Art" Waltzer, M.D., visited us from the 85th Evacuation Hospital in Qui Nhon. I had not seen Art since we first met as undergraduate freshmen at Vanderbilt University.

In early February 1967, we received many wounded Montagnard CIDGs from near Kontum, following an ambush in which two Special Forces officers were killed.

On Sunday, February 10, 1967, Maj. Clarke Max Brandt, MSC, came to the 18th (from the Headquarters Company, 15th Medical Battalion, 1st Cavalry Division) as XO, replacing Lt. Col. James B. Ranck, MSC, who went to the 67th Evacuation Hospital in Qui Nhon as their XO. By this time, 1st Lt. Bill Hames had replaced 1st Lt. John Walton as the supply officer, and soon Maj. Margaret Canfield replaced Maj. Mary Berry as Chief of Nursing. The 18th Surgical Hospital (MA) had approximately 140 medical, administrative and support personnel: 19 MCs (physicians), three MSCs (administrative), 16 ANCs (nurses), one chaplain and 98 EMs. Between July 1966 and March 1967, approximately 2500 operations were done with less than 5% being elective (i.e., hernias, circumcisions, lymph node biopsies etc.).

Patrick Sartorius, M.D., joined the 18th on Monday, February 15, 1967, coming to us from the 1st Cavalry Division in An Khe (An Tuc). Two other physicians, Dave Bucher, M.D., and Stuart Poticha, M.D., were assigned to the 18th for varying periods of time; however, I was unable to determine when they came and/or where they were reassigned.

In mid-February 1967, while triaging in R&E, I encountered a young man who had a superficial laceration with ecchymosis and hematoma over the precordial area of his chest (a shallow cut with bruising, discoloration and blood clotting over the left anterior chest in the general area of the heart). Auscultation of the chest was normal and a chest X-ray indicated there was no internal trauma. As I began debriding the wound, I discovered pieces of paper with words printed on them that, on closer inspection, were noted to be from the Bible. When I questioned the patient, he said he always carried a New Testament in the shirt pocket of his jungle fatigues. The velocity of the bullet that hit him had been partially absorbed and its direction deflected by the multiple layers of paper, turning what probably would have been an instantly mortal wound into a relatively minor one.

So many dignitaries visited the 18th Surgical Hospital (MA) that it was difficult to remember all who came. Most of them came through the auspices of the USO. As previously mentioned, when Jayne Mansfield visited, she was accompanied by a long-haired male hair dresser and her lawyer/agent, Sam Brody. He was arrogant and demanding, but everyone just seemed to ignore him. Jayne seemed to be just as usually portrayed—a dumb blonde. She and Sam Brody were killed in an automobile accident about four months later on June 29, 1967.

Roy Rogers and Dale Evans visited the 18th on three occasions. The first visit was probably in September 1966; the second, in February 1967; and the third, about May 1967. They were probably the most popular of the visiting celebrities.

Tony Martino and Elaine Stewart (who costarred with Kirk Douglas in *The Bad and The Beautiful)* visited in February 1967, just after Jayne Mansfield. Robert Mitchum came a few days later, but his visit was a complete flop. He stayed for most of two days and one night but remained intoxicated the entire time. He looked and acted more like a drunken bum than an acclaimed movie star. Everyone was quite disillusioned by his actions and his character, or the lack thereof.

In August 1966, Don Orehek, along with Jack Rosen and Jon Nielsen, highly recognized and respected members of the National Cartoonist Society came. They drew caricatures of each patient and presented them as individual gifts. Arthur Godfrey visited about the same time. He was very friendly and personable, giving the

impression that he was a long-time friend. He was extremely short of breath as the result of having had a pneumonectomy (lung removal) for treatment of lung cancer. His exertional dyspnea (shortness of breath) was so severe he could walk only a few steps before stopping to catch his breath. He later died of emphysema in 1983.

Martha Raye came on three occasions and was always in uniform. Jonathan Winters was a big hit. He was always joking

Jayne Mansfield at the 18th Surgical Hospital.

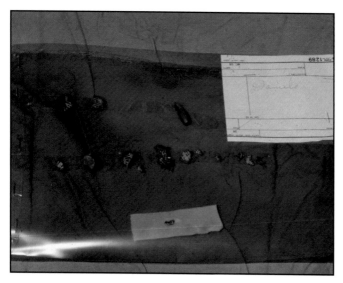

Fragments of New Testament removed from a chest wound. The New Testament which he carried in the breast pocket of his jungle fatigues deflected the trajectory of the bullet, thus avoiding a penetrating wound of the heart.

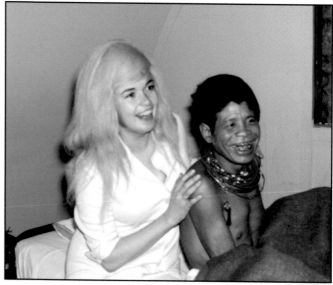

Jayne Mansfield with Montagnard Chief, Nang Quan Knang who was shot in his feet by the Viet Cong.

A self caricature of Don Orehek.

Caricature of Jerry W. Martin, M.D. by Don Orehek.

and kept the patients, and everyone else, continuously laughing.

"Dandy" Don Meridith (former quarterback with the Dallas Cowboys) was a really personable individual and related well with the patients. He stayed overnight and joined us in a game or two of touch football. I can make a truthful claim that I caught one of "Dandy" Don's touchdown passes. He was a lot of fun to be around.

Chet Huntley accompanied Gen. Westmoreland on one occasion.

Nancy Sinatra gave a performance before a large crowd at the New Pleiku Airbase. She included in her repertoire of songs her big hit, *These Boots Are Made for Walkin'*. It was very cold that night (in the low 40s). She had on white boots and wore a mini-skirt, but apparently the stage lights kept her warm. The audience was dressed in sweaters and heavy coats.

The Australian Broadcasting Company Orchestra performed at the nearby Special Forces base camp. Some of the individual members of the orchestra came to visit patients.

On separate occasions, Congresswomen, one from Texas and another from New York, visited the 18th.

Operation Junction City began on February 22, 1967, and ended on May 14, 1967. The Operation was conducted in two phases. It was located northwest of Saigon at War Zone C near Tay Ninh City in CTZ III, close to the Iron Triangle. The 25th Infantry Division, the 1st Infantry Division, the 173rd Brigade (the unit there made the only major combat parachute jump of the war), the 11th Armored Cavalry Regiment, the 65th Engineer Battalion and supporting units of gunships, artillery, etc. were involved in the effort.

The 4th Infantry Division was deployed from Ft. Lewis, Washington in August 1966, with Maj. Gen. Arthur S. Collins, Jr. commanding. The 3rd Brigade of the 25th Infantry Division, operating in the Pleiku area, was attached to the 4th Infantry Division, and the 3rd Brigade of the 4th Infantry Division was attached to the 25th Infantry Division near Saigon. This command structure lasted until August 1967. The two brigades were then

moved, on paper, back to their parent divisions. This arrangement always seemed very strange, but I quickly discovered that logical reasoning could not always be applied to military decisions.

In January 1967, Maj. Gen. William R. Peers assumed command of the 4th Infantry Division. He came to the 18th Surgical Hospital (MA) each evening to visit the sick and wounded troops under his command. He was always considerate of others and seemed to have a genuine interest in his troops, always exhibiting a gracious and understanding attitude when conversing with them. He talked, empathized, laughed and joked with each soldier who was able to communicate with him. For those unconscious or too sick to communicate, he still visited each bedside and, there, silently stood for a moment. We did not witness in him the vain, arrogant and condescending attitude that so many other generals seemed to have in abundant quantities. Gen. Westmorland, although exhibiting an arrogant persona, was always gracious and cordial to the physicians and nurses at the 18th. Throughout the year that we were in Vietnam, he visited the 18th innumerable times. He, too, always seemed to be concerned about the wounded, especially if they were paratroopers, but he only occasionally visited the medical patients. He was often accompanied by Lt. Gen. Stanley (Swede) Larson (Commander of I Field Force, Vietnam [Corps]), a very capable and gracious man.

Arrogance cheapens character and hauteur undermines the individual's leadership ability. An effective leader, whether civilian or military, must project confidence, inspire hope, exhibit wisdom and fairness and show concern for others while maintaining authority—very difficult attributes to achieve. These individual qualities, not the insignia on the uniform or the title on the door, are the traits that command respect. There were many good and competent leaders, but only a few who were truly outstanding.

Maj. Gen. Peers had assigned one of his administrative sergeants from the personnel casualty section to live at the 18th. I do not recall his name, but he went by the nickname "Red." Maj. Gen. Peers' pilot would always radio from the chopper to alert the 18th of his impending arrival, and "Red" was immediately notified. He would hustle to meet the General's helicopter when it landed and escort him throughout the hospital. "Red" kept a personnel list of all members of the 4th Infantry Division who were patients at the 18th, listing their individual problem and condition. The physicians or nurses who were in the hospital at the time of his arrival also accompanied him to answer any medical or surgical questions he might have. Lt. Col. Cenac and/or our hospital XO, often made rounds with the generals and other visiting dignitaries. It made no difference to Maj. Gen. Peers whether the soldier was a medical or surgical patient. One day he stopped at the bedside of a young man and inquired about his condition. The fellow responded that he was dehydrated from severe diarrhea. Maj. Gen. Peers replied, "I had the same thing in World War II, it began the day I arrived in combat and lasted until the day I left." Everyone on the ward began laughing. It broke the ice and allowed each patient to relax. This indicated to that particular patient, and to everyone else, that regardless of the reason they were hospitalized, their service to their country was important and appreciated.

Another patient was hospitalized with a fractured leg and a crushed pelvis. When Maj. Gen. Peers inquired about his injury, the patient told him that he was helping chop a LZ when a tree fell on him. The General asked, "Were there any enemy in the area, son?" "Yes, Sir!" was the reply. Maj. Gen. Peers then reached over to the box that "Red" held and pulled out a Purple Heart medal and pinned it on the patient's hospital gown, saying, "Well, I guess if there were enemy around, you deserve this, and since I am giving it to you, no one can take it away."

A few weeks later, a Colonel in the 4th Infantry Division was shot one evening while sitting in his tent. A soldier in a nearby tent "accidentally" shot him while "cleaning" his M-16. This explanation was implausible and nearly unbelievable. As Tony Lindem, M.D., and I were operating on him, Maj. Brandt, speaking from the OR door, said that the 4th Infantry Division had called, requesting that we plot the entrance and exit wounds, enabling them to calculate the trajectory angle of the bullet's passage through the chest. The bullet had fragmented when it struck the back of the metal chair where the Colonel was seated. There were, therefore, multiple entrance wounds but no exit wound. Fortunately the fragments missed the spinal cord, heart, aorta and major bronchi, and their velocity had decreased so that post-operatively he did not develop traumatic (wet) lung syndrome. He recovered without complications.

Over the next few days, we asked other soldiers from the 4th Infantry Division about the circumstances surrounding the shooting. Although some denied any knowledge or declined to comment, others stated that the Colonel was tremendously unpopular and highly disliked, even hated, by those serving under him. Those relating this information included a Major, a Captain, two or three Sergeants and four or five PFCs. One told me, "I wish he had been a better shot," and another said, "I would like to have killed the SOB myself." They all made similar types of comments. We never heard if they were able to prove that the shot was intentional, or whether or not the soldier was court marshaled.

Before the Colonel was evacuated, some of us witnessed Maj. Gen. Peers when he presented him with a Silver Star and a Purple Heart. This certainly greatly deflated our image of Maj. Gen. Peers, and it diminished our confidence in his judgment. When the circumstance involved in this situation was compared to those individuals who earned them in combat, the significance of these prestigious awards was sadly cheapened. Later, in November 1969, Lt. Gen. Peers, then serving in the Pentagon, was appointed to conduct an investigation of the My Lai incident.

Perhaps the best known, but least understood, military tactic employed during the Vietnam War was the use of herbicides and growth hormones. Between 1961 and 1971, as part of Operation Ranch Hand, the U.S. military sprayed 20 million gallons (72 million liters) of toxic chemical defoliants over 10% of Vietnam. Based on the advocacy of Gen. Layman L. Lemnitzer (Chairman, Joint Chiefs of Staff), President Kennedy approved the use of herbicides in Vietnam in 1961. Operation Ranch Hand was inaugurated in 1962, when USAF C-123 Providers equipped

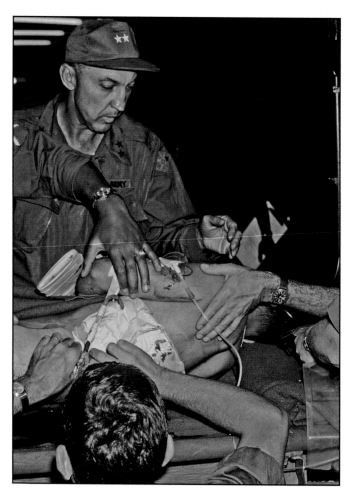

Maj. Gen. Peers helping to hold a patient from the 4th Division in position while Tony Lindem, M.D. evaluates his wounds.

with tanks began spraying portions of the Ho Chi Minh Trail, Laos and Cambodia. Initially, they flew exclusively out of Tan Son Nhut in Saigon. MACV announced on September 23, 1966, that defoliants were being used to destroy jungle cover in Vietnam.

Agent Orange (comprising about 2/3rds of the total volume of defoliants sprayed), as well as Agents Purple and Pink, contained dioxen (abbreviation for dibenzo 1, 4 dioxen [2, 3, 7, 8-Tetrachlorodibenso 1, 4 dioxen and 2, 4, 5-T which are highly toxic, teratogenic and carcinogenic contaminants]). The intention of herbicidal warfare was to kill vegetation and deny the enemy "cover." Agent Blue, used predominantly for crop destruction was mainly of an organic arsenic compound. These chemical agents were known by the identifying color of the stripe painted on the storage containers. During the period of time in which the chemicals were used, well over 2.5 million U.S. service men and women and American allies served one-year tours in South Vietnam. Additionally, there were millions of Montagnard, Vietnamese, Laotian and Cambodian populations who were exposed.

The U.S. dropped leaflets to warn local peasants prior to all impending sprayings. At first, the U.S. government and military officials believed that Agent Orange was harmless, or relatively so, to human and animal life. Teams even went into villages and ate bread dipped into the chemical to show the population that

Effects of Agent Orange on foliage. Landsat TM 1989 satellite image of a region 45 miles (72 km) north of Ho Chi Minh City; orange represents forested areas, blue human-dominated ones.

to be potential health risks. The Department of Veterans Affairs (VA) Cooperative Studies Program, the National Academy of Science (NAS, nongovernmental), the National Academy of Science's Institute of Medicine (IOM), the Office of Public Health and Environmental Hazards and the Department of Defense were involved. These groups have concluded that the following conditions should be recognized as service-connected for Vietnam veterans based on exposure to Agent Orange or other herbicides:

1. Chloracne (must occur within one year of exposure to Agent Orange)
2. Non-Hodgkins lymphoma
3. Soft tissue sarcoma (other than osteosarcoma, chondrosarcoma, Kaposi's sarcoma, or mesothelioma)
4. Hodgkin's disease
5. Porphyria cutanea tarda (must occur within one year of exposure)
6. Multiple myeloma
7. Respiratory cancers, including cancers of the lung, larynx, trachea, and bronchus (must occur within thirty years of exposure)
8. Prostate cancer
9. Acute and subacute transient peripheral neurophy (must appear within one year of exposure and resolve within two years of date of onset)
10. Type 2 diabetes

Conditions recognized in children of Vietnam Veterans:
1. Spina bifida (except spina bifida occulta)
2. Eighteen other birth defects are specifically included and others not specifically excluded are covered.
Agent Orange Review, Vol.22, No. 1, October 2005

The National Academy of Science's Institute of Medicine concluded there was "...limited/suggestive evidence of an association between herbicides used in Vietnam and a rare childhood leukemia, acute myelogenous leukemia (AML)." Australian researchers reported, "...new calculations show that the prevalence of these conditions in the children of Vietnam veterans, while higher than normal and suggestive of increased risk, is not raised to a statistically significant extent."

Medical researchers recently released a study from the Institute of Medicine, sponsored by the Veterans Affairs Department, in which they report an increased incidence of "...serious heart disease and Parkinson's Disease..." secondary to Agent Orange exposure (Richard Lardner, AP, July 25, 2009). On Monday, October 12, 2009 the VA announced that ischemic heart disease, Parkinsonism and hairy cell leukemia are caused by Agent Orange and considered compensable conditions.

An official survey has not been done on the individuals who served at the 18th Surgical Hospital (MA); however, through routine communications and correspondence, I am aware that just among the original physicians and nurses who were in Pleiku, one has had lung cancer (pneumonectomy), one had a small bowel

it was not dangerous. Obviously, they must have been aware of Rachael Carson's *Silent Spring*, published in 1962. The conclusion indicating non-toxicity and the relative safety of these herbicides was based in part on U.S. Army research done toward the end of World War II. This truly was an example of "the blind leading the blind."

As early as 1963, the President's Science Advisory Committee warned of the toxicity of these compounds. During the 1960s, scientists in the U.S. and abroad, along with opponents of the Vietnam War, denounced the use of Agent Orange. In 1967, petitions signed by prominent scientists were sent to President Johnson calling for a halt in the use of Agent Orange and similar compounds in the war effort. A United Nations resolution was passed, which accused the U.S. of violating a 1925 Geneva Protocol concerning the prohibition of chemical and biological weapons. After 1970, the U.S. military discontinued the use of Agent Orange, but continued to employ Agents Blue, White, Green, Pink and Purple. In 1969, the U.S. National Cancer Institute determined that dioxins in amounts as small as five parts per trillion caused cancer and birth defects when placed in constant or regular contact with animals and humans.

The U.S. Congress in 1991 required that an ongoing U.S. Government study be initiated to evaluate all issues considered

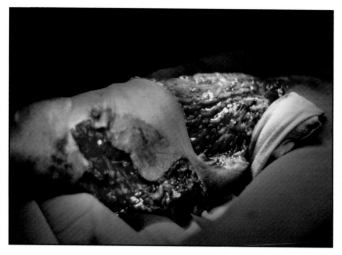

Vietnamese woman's ao dai caught on the rear of a military truck and was dragged along the pavement. The skin on her right leg was pulled downward as if it were a stocking. We were able to pull the skin back into its proper location and suture it in place. The wound healed quickly and without infection.

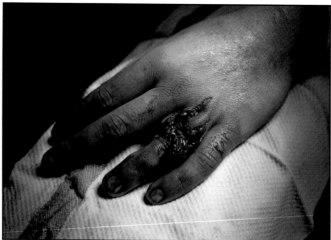

This man caught his ring on a bolt as he jumped from the back of a deuce and a half (large military truck) nearly severing his finger.

Closing the small bowel after segmental resection necessitated because of a gun shot wound to the abdomen.

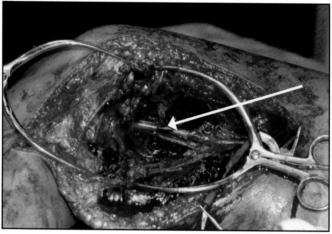

Thrombosis of right femoral artery.

tumor with lung metastasis (partial small bowel resection and a lobectomy), three have had prostate cancer (radical prostatectomy) and eight have developed type 2 diabetes. This represents a higher statistical incidence than would otherwise have been predicted.

When the 18th arrived at Pleiku, we used the equipment available at the 542nd Medical Clearing Company. The anesthesia equipment shipped with our unit was outdated but usable. The first of these machines was replaced with a requisitioned Fluotec (anesthesia) machine on August 18. Felix Jenkins, M.D., obtained another Fluotec through David Jones, M.D., an anesthesiologist at the 8th Field Hospital in Nha Trang, and I believe we received another machine loaned to the 18th by the Special Forces.

General anesthesia was used about 75% of the time. Initially, ether and nitrous oxide (NO_2) were used, following induction with Pentothal (thiopental sodium). As soon as newer equipment became available, Penthane, and then Flurothane, was used along with Anectine (succinylcholine). Pentothal was given slowly to avoid a vasovegal reflex and cardiac arrest, which fortunately did not occur at our hospital. A few cardiac arrests did occur secondary

to other causes (i.e., shock, hypoxia, etc). One piece of equipment that was desperately needed was a cardiac defibrillator. There were defibrillators in country; however, we were told that we could not get one until there was a sufficient number to allow each hospital in Vietnam to have one. By this time, the 18th had become the busiest surgical hospital in Vietnam, regularly seeing more acute combat wounds than any of the other surgical hospitals. On one of my weekly radio programs, broadcast over WKCT in Bowling Green, Kentucky, I mentioned our desperate need for a cardiac defibrillator. After hearing the program, the Bowling Green-Warren County Jaycees offered to donate a defibrillator. The Chairman of the Warren County Republican Party reported this to a friend in Washington, D.C., Rep. Gerald R. Ford, (R. MI), Minority Leader in the House of Representatives. Rep. Ford quickly requested a copy of the tape on which the radio program had been recorded to document our needs in his presentation to Congress. We received a defibrillator shortly thereafter. Whether receipt of this equipment was due to the Army's concern for patient safety or if it resulted from the attention given to our needs by Rep. Ford will never by known. It really does not matter, however, since we got the needed equipment, allowing us to save lives that otherwise would have been lost.

Nearly all (99%) of the cases done under general anesthesia were intubated using an endotracheal tube with an inflatable cuff because most of the wounded had either eaten or drunk water shortly before arriving at the 18th.

About 25% of cases were done using local anesthesia, spinal anesthesia, epidural blocks or axillary blocks. Spinal anesthesia or epidural blocks (Xylocaine 1.5%) were used on lower extremity cases, while brachial blocks (axillary approach; superclavicular approach could result in a pneumothorax) were used on the upper extremities, with local blocks sometimes used at the wrist or elbow.

There were two operating rooms: one with two operating tables and the other with three operating tables. The third table was usually reserved for patients with wounds requiring only local anesthesia.

In the U.S., most surgical cases do not require blood transfusions, and those that do require no more than five or six units (450 ml). The average adult has approximately five quarts of blood, or the equivalent of about ten units. During our year at Pleiku, we had approximately twenty cases that required forty or more units, and one patient received sixty-five units (the patient was shot through the liver, requiring the removal of about one-half of his liver, spleen, and one kidney and a resection of a portion of his small bowel). Fortunately, he survived both the injury and the surgery.

By the time we received whole blood through military channels, it was usually nearing the expiration date. Based on our early experiences and because of electrolyte imbalance and potential renal problems, we asked for fresh blood donors when it was estimated that a patient would require more than ten units of blood. Word was sent to various units, usually the Air Force, or occasionally the 4th Infantry Division, who would round up those individuals with the needed ABO blood types and bring them to the 18th, where their blood was drawn and processed for immediate transfusion.

We neither had the laboratory facilities nor the equipment necessary to do serum electrolytes or blood gases; therefore, one ampule of bicarbonate was given routinely for every four units of blood. Calcium (Ca++) was given, not so much to control hemorrage (whole blood is anticoagulated with citrate which binds calcium ions), but for the positive ionotropic effect on the heart muscle, to prevent cardiac arrest. Manitol was given if the patient was in shock on arrival or if signs of shock developed during surgery, in an attempt to prevent renal (kidney) failure. The only irreversible renal failures we saw were in patients with phosphorous poisoning. We quickly realized that phosphorous burns had to receive quick and radical treatment (amputations, radical debridement, etc.) to prevent irreversible renal tubular necrosis and certain death. There were no dialysis units available.

Every major case had one or more large IV tubes inserted prior to surgery via a cut-down (surgical placement of IV tube directly into a large vein). Central venous pressure was monitored, using the jugular vein. If a patient had a pneumothorax, a chest tube was always placed before anesthesia was begun.

I recall one patient that had a "sucking chest wound" (a hole in the chest allowing air to enter and exit through the chest wall) on the right side associated with a "flail chest" (fractures of ribs resulting in instability of the chest wall allowing the chest to move paradoxically with each breath, thus making it impossible to exchange gases properly in the lung) and a pneumothorax of the left chest. All of the operating rooms were busy, and there were no chest bottles available. The patient was unconscious and hypoxic (dark-ashen color due to a decreased O_2 level) even though nasal O_2 (oxygen) was flowing. I quickly plastered the hole in the chest wall with a sterile Vasoline gauze dressing, sealing the leak. To prevent the flailing, I used a sterile towel clip, clamped it onto a rib and tied it to an overhead IV stand, thus preventing the inappropriate chest wall movement. Since there were no chest bottles available, I asked the nurse assisting me to retrieve two empty Coke bottles setting on the floor by the wall near the door entering R&E. She put water in each bottle, and as I inserted a tube into the chest, she placed the other end of the tube into the bottle below the water level, one tube on each side. Within a minute or less, after taking a few breaths, his color pinked and within three to five minutes, he was awake enough to begin complaining of pain. In order to breathe normally, there must be negative pressure in the chest cavity; therefore, the chest must be sealed to outside air, thus the need for a water seal. I did all of these things without using any type of anesthesia. As soon as he awoke, we gave him enough morphine to ease his pain, and when chest bottles had been sterilized and were available, they were substituted for the Coke bottles. The chest bottles were then hooked to an Emerson suction machine. An IV, using a needle, was going when he arrived by Dustoff, but after stabilizing the patient, I did a cut-down on an ankle vein and started another IV. By the time the operating room was available, he was experiencing only mild pain and was asking for a cigarette and something to eat and drink. Surprisingly, he had very little hemorrhage. He was taken to the OR, and the injuries necessitating these temporary remedies were surgically corrected. He did well post-operatively and was evacuated in good condition a few days later, after the chest tubes were removed. It is truly amazing the amount of punishment a young, healthy human body can endure and still survive.

Unfortunately, we saw many cases of acute respiratory distress syndrome (ARDS) formerly recognized as shock, traumatic, or wet lung syndrome. This condition may result from trauma created by high velocity bullets. The damage caused by the passage of the missile through lung tissue was usually less than the complications secondary to the high frequency sound waves. Obviously, some pulmonary edema (swelling) always occurred, but the shock waves resulted in consolidation of lung tissue and impaired perfusion (decreased blood flow or circulation) and caused a reduction in alveolar space due to the collapse of alveoli (collapse of the air sacs that are unable to fill with air, preventing O_2 and CO_2 exchange). When this consolidation of lung tissue occurred, often times, all efforts at resuscitation were futile (i.e. diuretics, O2, suction, assisted ventilation, steroids etc.). A clear, pinkish secretion (not mucus or blood) would develop very quickly and begin oozing from the endotracheal tube, requiring frequent suction. We had one Bird and three Bennett respirators available to assist these patients.

One case demonstrates the lethality of this traumatic lung syndrome. A bullet struck the patient's rib at about the left anterior axillary line, followed the rib for a few inches and exited the skin just beyond the posterior axillary line. Although the rib sustained multiple fractures, the bullet did not enter the chest cavity. During surgery, we commented on how lucky the patient was to have escaped a penetrating chest wound. Within an hour or two, while still in the recovery room, the telltale secretions began to develop, and he quickly became extremely short of breath while his respiratory effort became difficult and labored. Suctioning did not help. Therefore, he was sedated; an endotracheal tube was reinserted; and he was placed on a respirator. In spite of all efforts, the patient died five to six hours later of respiratory failure. Later, Wayne Hosking, M.D., (our anesthesiologist) gave a lecture on March 31, 1967, at the Pleiku Medical Association meeting, in which he discussed these complications. Earlier, the Pleiku Medical Association had hosted the Vietnamese Armed Forces Chief Surgeon, Col. Vu-Ngoc Hoan, at its February 11, 1967, meeting located at the ARVN Hospital.

On February 13, 1967, Bob Hewitt, M.D., did the first angiocardiogram and aortogram in Pleiku on an ARVN soldier who was suspected of having a ruptured thoracic aorta following a jeep accident. Soon thereafter, using mercury obtained from a dentist friend, Bob made a mercury manometer for direct blood pressure recordings. A manometer was needed because a cardiologist assigned to MACV had seen a forty-year old Vietnamese patient at the Pleiku Provincial Hospital with congestive heart failure caused by mitral stenosis (heart valve failed to open completely) and was near death. On April 13, after consulting and evaluating the patient, Bob did a successful mitral valvulotomy (commissurotomy) on the Viet Cong POW. The surgery had been postponed until after we received a defibrillator. Fortunately, it was not needed in this case.

A similar operation had been performed by Navy surgeons on the aircraft carrier, *Repose*, and was reported in *Time Magazine*

in late 1966. Although the 44th Medical Brigade and the 55th Medical group were complimentary in their comments, they determined that no further similar procedures would be done since negative criticism had been received following the *Repose* incident. Accusations were made and reported in the press that the U.S. was doing experimental surgery on POWs, even though this was a well-documented and approved surgical procedure that was beneficial in saving lives. There were quite a few other patients in the Central Highland area that needed similar surgery in order to avoid an imminent and untimely death. I found it difficult to understand the military's rationale. If proper procedures are carried out using acceptable surgical techniques in order to save human life, what difference does it make what anyone says, or thinks, or writes?

Unfortunately, decisions in our society are too often made based on what the perception may be or what others may think or say, instead of doing the right thing. "Political correctness" is not necessarily based on moral or ethical criteria and is usually more detrimental than beneficial.

The first few days of March were very busy. The 4th Infantry Division made contact with the enemy southwest of Kontum, a little northwest of Pleiku. On March 4, we received over thirty wounded, necessitating our operating throughout the day and night. Two of the patients had thrombosis of their femoral arteries, each requiring a saphenous vein graft. On March 8, a forward base camp of the 4th Infantry Division received a heavy mortar attack resulting in about 36 casualties. We, again, operated continuously for the next twenty-four hours, and more wounded were received the following night. On March 11, another mortar attack hit the 4th Infantry

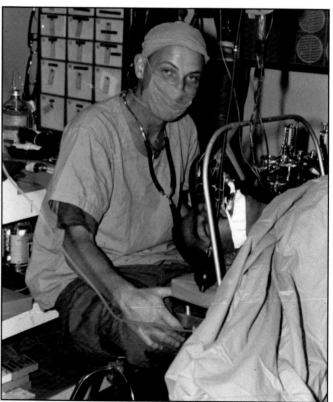

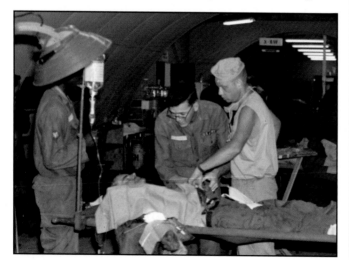

Bob Hewitt, M.D., with two medics evaluating a patient in R & E.

Wayne Hosking, M.D. giving anesthesia.

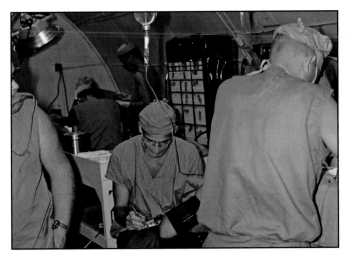

Wayne Hosking, M.D. giving anesthesia, Bob Hewitt, M.D. with back to camera.

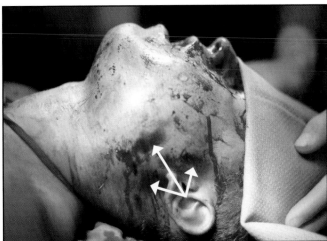

Self-inflicted gunshot wound of left jaw. Powder burns on skin surrounding a small entrance wound. The small caliber bullet penetrated through his neck and exited on the right side miraculously without significant damage to vital structures.

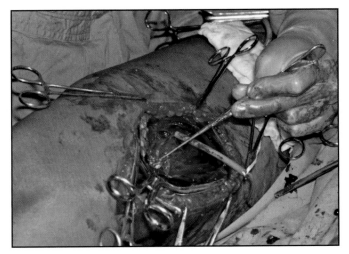

Gunshot wound of right thigh.

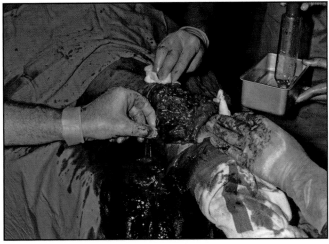

Posterior popliteal area (behind the knee) right leg wound.

Division's forward base camp, called Three Tango. We received over eighty casualties, and as soon as those cases were finished, Three Tango was hit again. Another 35-40 wounded were evacuated to the 18th, resulting in another "big push," requiring twenty-four hours of continuous surgery. On March 15, Dr. Hewitt wrote in his diary about this night: "Operated all night, caught a couple of hours of sleep and operated all morning. General Westmoreland visited the hospital this morning and passed out awards. Gen. Larson, second in command, was with him and mentioned that our hospital is really going to stay busy from now on and that activity in this area is going to continue at a terrific pace."

Occasionally, some of the wounded, especially those with the 1st Cavalry Division, were seen at a battalion aid station before being evacuated to the 18th. The following is a medic's description of triage at an aid station: "…in the aid tent we worked on the wounded men. One was critical. He'd lost a lot of blood from numerous wounds. Blood from his thigh wound spurted into my face before I got a bandage on it. I pressed tightly but soon the bandage was red-soaked and running through my fingers, onto my clothes, and splattering onto the floor. I called for another dressing, put it on top

of the others, and pressed harder. Even with pressure and elevation I couldn't control the bleeding. Sidney finally got an IV going, but the soldier was going into shock. Where was a real doctor when you needed one? There was blood everywhere. My arms were covered. I had blood on my face, in my hair, in my mouth. I must have looked like I had been wounded. But I was the lucky one. It wasn't my blood. We were told a Medevac was on the way. It couldn't get there soon enough for me. The other men were patched up and sitting on a stretcher on the floor. Outside someone yelled, Dustoff! I could hear the now familiar whopping sound of an inbound chopper. We picked up the stretcher, knocking over the litter stands, and hustled it outside. The walking wounded followed. The chopper settled on the ground and we hurried toward it with the wounded man. We lifted the stretcher onboard where another medic took over. The walking wounded climbed aboard. We picked up the litter with the poncho-wrapped body and hoisted it aboard, picked up two folded litters they dropped off and ran back toward the aid tent. The chopper's engine revved up. It slowly lifted off the ground, swung around, and raced off toward the 18th Surgical Hospital in Pleiku. The noise of the chopper faded in the distance and all was quiet again. It was out of our hands now. …When dealing with death there is heightened awareness of life among those who remain. You know how fragile life can be, how it can disappear in the blink of an eye. Life goes on, but not with the same 'There's always tomorrow' feeling" (*Vietnam Journal*, 1966, Howard Sherpe).

Recorded in Dr. Hewitt's diary, "I had just finished operating throughout the night and early into the morning. We were all exhausted after this 'big push.' I walked into the triage area, the receiving area, to survey the present, overall status. Only a few men, ones with lesser wounds awaited their turn in surgery. They were in order (of severity) on hospital cots adjacent to the operating area. Several cots were unoccupied beyond, indicating that no new casualties had arrived and only a few remained awaiting surgery. Yet, at the very end of the aisle on the right lay a soldier in obvious respiratory distress and unattended. I dashed toward him thinking 'why in the hell isn't someone with him!' No wounds were readily apparent at that distance only dark stains on his jungle fatigues. When I reached him, I understood why he was alone. The gunshot wound of his right temple was relatively small compared to the exit wound on the left side of his head. He was in deep and profound coma, agonal (terminal) and opisthotnic (hyperextended neck and back secondary to muscle spasm often seen in brain trauma). Triage had determined that he had a fatal injury and therefore no attempt toward resuscitation had been made, and they had made the correct decision. A nurse informed me that he was a platoon leader and point man of a patrol ambushed a few hours earlier. As I stood there, alone with him, I noticed that he was a young 1st Lieutenant. On his left ring finger was a handsome gold class ring with a light blue stone—infantry blue. I lifted his hand and read the inscription 'United States Military Academy.' I just stood in a few moments of silence to offer my complete respect. The truth was that I was momentarily immobilized and needed those moments to myself. Through my mind ran a mental picture of this young man as a cadet parading in the long gray line at West Point—thoughts of what was and what possibly could have been. For the first time, and only time, in Vietnam tears rolled down from my eyes. Those few minutes represented the most moving experience of my year in Vietnam. I have handled tragedies before and after, but this particular experience still brings tears after nearly thirty years. I think it is because, to me, the young lieutenant represented our finest. I ordered an attendant to stand by him as I returned to the operating room." (*Supporting the Infantry Blue, Diary from a Surgical Hospital (MASH). Vietnam, 1966-1967* Robert L. Hewitt, M.D.).

The rapid build-up of U.S. forces in response to the increased infiltration of NVA troops into South Vietnam quickly overloaded the telecommunication circuits linking South Vietnam with Hawaii and Washington, D.C., rendering this system inadequate and unreliable. Sunspots caused intermittent interruptions in the high-frequency radio circuits, as did occasional transmitter failure in Saigon.

An experimental satellite ground terminal providing one telephone and one teletype circuit to Hawaii became operational in August 1964. Signals were relayed from Saigon to Hawaii through a communication satellite launched into a stationary orbit 22,000 statute miles above the Pacific Ocean. This experimental synchronous satellite communication system (SYNCOM) was the first time a satellite communication system was used in a combat zone. This system was operated by the U.S. Army's Strategic Communications Command. The system was improved in October 1964, when the Commander in Chief,

Total Number of Patients Evacuated From Vietnam, U.S. Army, by Month, 1965-69

Month	1965	1966	1967	1968	1969
January	164	832	1,469	2,417	3,224
February	227	1,330	1,851	3,576	3,099
March	226	1,062	2,178	2,471	4,166
April	252	853	1,780	2,782	3,210
May	300	1,298	2,367	3,952	4,334
June	480	1,256	2,072	2,701	3,951
July	471	766	1,595	2,569	2,879
August	821	957	1,521	2,700	3,308
September	999	942	1,431	3,401	2,187
October	1,978	983	1,851	2,856	1,890
November	2,361	1,331	2,435	2,790	1,789
December	1,885	996	2,152	3,176	1,879
Total	**10,164**	**12,606**	**22,702**	**35,391**	**35,916**

Source: Army Medical Service Activities Report, MACV, 1965; Army Meidcal Service Activities Reports, 44th Medical Brigade, 1966, 1967, 1968, and 1969.

Pacific, validated requirements to the Joint Chiefs of Staff for additional communication service. These requirements became known as Phase I of the Integrated Wideband Communications System. Phase II was completed in October 1965, and Phase III, in December 1965. The Department of Defense decided to use permanent installations rather than a transportable system.

In September 1965, the U.S. Army, as the contracting agency, awarded the contract for the Vietnam portion of the system to Page Communications Engineers, Inc. The Page Communications' complex at Pleiku was about three-fourths of a mile from the site of the 18th Surgical Hospital (MA) on the road leading to MACV. The 2nd Signal Group assigned the responsibility of CTZ I and II to the 41st Signal Battalion and assigned CTZ III and IV to the 39th Signal Battalion. The 362nd Signal Company was placed directly under the 2nd Signal Group to operate the tropospheric scatter system used throughout the country.

On August 13, 1965, the necessary signal corps troops and equipment were airlifted to Pleiku, and by the following day they were able to link-up the communication system of the 173rd Airborne Brigade with the large fixed system at Pleiku, for the 173rd Brigade's Central Highland operations.

There was an undersea cable to the Philippines that connected the U.S. Army Strategic Communications Command Facility at Phu Lam, Clark Air Force Base, Tan Son Nhut Air Base and the Army's 27th Data Processing Unit in Saigon. This system was referred to as WET WASH.

Relay antennae were placed on top of Niu Lang Bian, a 7,000-foot high mountain peak a few miles north of Dalat, in the southern part of the Central Highlands.

The 595th Signal Company arrived in May 1966, to support the 1st Infantry Division, and the 13th Signal Battalion was deployed to An Khe in support of the 1st Cavalry Division.

When the 1st Cavalry Division was involved in the battle of the Ia Drang Valley, each brigade had direct telephone and message contact with both the division's forward tactical operations center at Pleiku and the division's base at An Khe. These sole-user circuits proved invaluable during this and other battles.

The short-range voice radios being used could not cope with the distances involved and the fact that the thick jungle undergrowth absorbed electrical energy. The problem was solved by placing combat radios in U.S. Army Caribou aircrafts, and then orbiting them above the ground units. The optimum altitude turned out to be 9-10,000 feet above ground, thereby, extending the effective range fifty to sixty miles.

Prior to 1966, operators at switchboards located throughout the country had to place all long-distance calls through eight exchanges: MACV, Vietnam, in Saigon; Tan Son Nhut; Can Tho; Bien Hoa; Nha Trang; Qui Nhon; Pleiku; and Da Nang. Because of inadequate trunk lines this arrangement proved ineffective.

The Department of the Army then placed the Strategic Communications Command under the Commanding General, U.S. Army, Vietnam. They further directed the Commander in Chief, U.S. Army, Pacific, Gen. John K. Waters, and Commanding General, U.S. Army Strategic Communications Command, Maj.

Gen. Richard J. Meyer to develop a system whereby all Army Signal elements down to field force level be placed under a U.S. Army Signal Command, Vietnam. This gave communications responsibility in Vietnam a new direction. The 1st Signal Brigade soon grew larger than a division and became the largest signal operation in the history of the U.S. Army. On July 1, 1966, Brig. Gen. Robert D. Terry established the responsibility of CTZ III and IV to the 2nd Signal Group and CTZ I and II to the 21st Signal Group. By the end of 1966, Brig. Gen. Terry assigned a signal battalion to support the U.S. advisory elements in each of the four CTZs: the 37th Signal Battalion in CTZ I at Da Nang; the 43rd Signal Battalion in CTZ II at Pleiku; the 44th Signal Battalion in CTZ III near Bien Hoa; and the 52nd Signal Battalion in CTZ IV at Can Tho in the Mekong Delta.

Three types of communication systems evolved during 1966. All were eventually interconnected and technically integrated. These three systems were: the Defense Communications System, the Corps Area Communications System and the Combat Communications System. The communication system operated and maintained by the signalmen of the 5th Special Forces Group was independent of any other U.S. system in Vietnam.

As mentioned, Page Communications Engineers, Inc. was awarded the contract for Vietnam, while the Philco-Ford Corp. received the contract for Thailand.

By mid-1967, the 1st Signal Brigade had developed and implemented the highly sophisticated Automatic Secure Voice Communications System, and by the end of 1967, a system actually existed that allowed continuous, high-quality communication from the firebase to the White House.

The presence of civilian communication controllers, maintenance technicians and operators in a war zone was something new in the U.S. Army's communications experience and was unique to Vietnam. Both Page and Philco-Ford opened signal schools at the U.S. Army Signal School, Ft. Monmouth, New Jersey.

The communications systems developed rapidly and responded brilliantly despite operating under severe geographical conditions and tactical equipment limitations. More communications services were provided than in any previous war. No combat operation in Vietnam was limited by a lack of communication.

We became acquainted with some of the Dustoff pilots soon after arriving at the 542nd Medical Clearing Company, and as our work at the 18th Surgical Hospital (MA) continued, our acquaintances increased while our friendships grew. The CO of the 498th Medical Company when we arrived at Pleiku was Maj. Mizell, who later was seceded by Maj. Medford. Each week the 498th sent a chopper and crew to Nha Trang to file a report at their 52nd Aviation Battalion Headquarters.

On Friday, September 8, Ted Stuart, M.D., and I accompanied them on such a trip. We were able to get away because of a brief lull in the flow of casualties to the 18th. We left about midday on Friday and returned Sunday afternoon. The crew flew over from Camp Holloway and picked us up at the 18th helipad. The helipad was about twenty to thirty feet higher than our motor pool and thirty to forty feet higher than the rice paddies between our hospital and Hwy. 19. Choppers usually took off from our helipad toward the west. As choppers climbed a few feet off the ground and as their forward motion carried them across the edge of the helipad, the pilots nosed them down and generally paralleled the terrain as it declined toward the nearby motor pool. This maneuver increased the forward air speed remarkably, allowing the choppers to ascend rapidly and achieve their flying altitude more quickly. To the first-time passenger, however, it seemed as if the chopper would end up in the motor pool on top of a deuce and a half or in the middle of the rice paddies just beyond.

Leaving the 18th, we followed the path of Hwy. 19 toward Pleiku, and passed over the northeastern edge of town, just southwest of Camp Holloway. At that point our altitude was about 1,500 feet, but as we proceeded beyond Pleiku we climbed to about 5,000 feet and then generally followed the path of Hwy. 19 eastward, crossing the Central Highlands toward the Mang Yang Pass. The end of the monsoon season was nearing, and the rains had diminished. However, the streams were still flowing, and the highland area was extravagantly covered in a beautiful verdant carpet. Before long, during the dry season, the streams would become parched, dusty gullies and would be drably clothed in various shades of browns. It was a clear day except for patches of small cumulus clouds floating effortless toward the horizon, silhouetted against a purplish-blue sky.

Soon after traversing over Mang Yang Pass, we landed at the 2nd Surgical Hospital's helipad at An Khe. We all remained aboard except for the co-pilot who ran in and picked up some papers to be delivered to Nha Trang. Within three or four minutes we were airborne again. Over open country choppers either flew close to the ground at about treetop level to decrease the accuracy of small arms ground fire or at about 5,000 feet which was out of range of the VC's fifty caliber machine gun fire. In secure areas choppers flew at various altitudes.

As we neared Qui Nhon, we dropped down to about 1,500-2,000 feet and then moved about one-half mile out over the South China Sea to be out of range of VC gunfire along the coast. The beaches southward from Qui Nhon to Nha Trang were snowy white, washed by the South China Sea whose color ranged from deep blue to azure, turquoise, pale green and back to blue again, obviously determined by the various depth of the water. It truly was beautiful.

Just before we arrived at the Nha Trang Airport, the pilot radioed for a vehicle from the 52nd to meet us, and by the time we landed and gathered our personal gear, they had arrived. On the way to the 52nd Aviation Battalion Headquarters they dropped Ted and me off at the 8th Field Hospital. There we found Dick Jones, M.D., who had space available for us to sleep at his villa.

Nha Trang was situated in a beautiful setting with low mountains extending to the coast. Long ago it had been dubbed the "Riviera of the East" or the "Vietnamese Riviera." French influence was notable everywhere, especially in the architecture. The beach was lined with coconut palms and other smaller trees that resembled either cypress or tamarisk trees, which are indigenous to the southern and southwestern part of the U.S. Nha Trang Bay was dotted with small islands that protected it from the open sea, and created a calm and peaceful bay. The beach curved for two or three miles along the bay and was gently washed by its calm waters. A narrow park ran along the portion of town contiguous with the beach and, in turn, was paralleled by a divided, tree-lined street. Madame Ngo Dinh Nhu's winter residence sat atop a hill on a peninsula extending into the bay.

That evening, Dick Jones, M.D., Ted Stuart, M.D., and I went to the Hostellerie La Fregate and enjoyed a dinner of French cuisine—onion soup and lobster thermador. For most of Saturday morning, we toured the 8th Field Hospital. Later, we stopped at a small restaurant on the beach for a seafood lunch. Saturday afternoon, we drove around town, photographing and sightseeing, and spent a couple of hours relaxing on the beach. That evening we returned to La Fregate since it was the best place in Nha Trang to eat. We were not disappointed on either occasion. Sunday morning was a slow and peaceful time. It seemed strange not to hear choppers bringing in the wounded. We had brunch at the beach house restaurant again and then met the Dustoff crew at the Nha Trang Airport around 1 pm for our return to Pleiku.

In early March, I accompanied Maj. Medford and Capt. Kreiner on another one of the weekly trips of the 498th to Nha

A sign on road paralleling the beach in Nha Trang.

Pharmacy in Nha Trang.

Menu from Hostellerie La Fregate

Dick Jones, M.D. and Ted Stuart, M.D.

Trang; however, on this occasion I stopped in Qui Nhon. Just before we reached the Mang Yang Pass region, I noticed unusual cloud formations below us. Using the intercom system, I asked what was causing them to form, since it was a clear day. They began laughing and explained that they were 50 cal. shells exploding. I immediately responded, "Don't you all know how to fly this chopper any higher?" Laughing louder, John said, "Don't worry. They are exploding a few hundred feet below us. We are out of their range." My rebuttal was, "How do you know that someone in the munitions factory didn't put too much powder in some of those shells?" Their laughter escalated even more and I reluctantly laughed along with them, but it was not until those "clouds" quit forming before I was truly able to see the humor of the situation. They dropped me off at the helipad of the 67th Evacuation Hospital. I quickly looked up Ted Stuart, M.D., who had been transferred from the 18th to the 67th Evac., and stayed with him.

We toured the 67th and the 85th Evacuation Hospitals soon after my arrival. On Saturday morning we drove around the town, sightseeing and photographing. Qui Nhon was a busy town very much like Pleiku, except larger and much hotter. It was dirty

and dusty, partially because of such a large military presence. Although, also located on the South China Sea, it did not favorably compare with Nha Trang. Even the water in the large bay seemed dingy, and the color was subdued. Many ships were anchored offshore waiting to be unloaded. There was a large area adjacent to the beach where supplies were stacked, awaiting distribution to the appropriate units. Planes were taking off and landing frequently and choppers seemed to be in the air constantly. We stopped briefly on "China" (or "Red") beach and walked a short distance. The beach was hot, humid and uninviting, especially considering the fact that about three hundred yards farther down, a section of beach was referred to as "stool beach," an undesignated area where many villagers regularly defecated, allowing the tides to flush their excrement out to sea. I often wondered how many other "stool" beaches existed along Vietnam's coast, or for that matter, throughout the world.

On Saturday, Ted and I, accompanied by another physician from the 67th, traveled by jeep to a leprosarium about three miles south of Qui Nhon on the South China Sea. As we left Qui Nhon, the shacks and hovels constructed on the outskirts of town by refugees displaced by the war, seemed to vanish as quickly as the paved road. The road became a narrow ribbon of white sand as it penetrated the countryside. As we drove along, I questioned our safety regarding the potential for VC attacks. I was reassured that there should not be a concern, since the Vietnamese population, including the VC, were frightened of contracting and developing leprosy. About two and one-half miles out of town, we approached a low mountain, probably about 800-900 ft. in height. The road inclined steadily at a slight angle to the mountain until we passed through a gap near the top. At the crest, we stopped for a panoramic view of the valley where the leprosarium was located. From this vantage point, it was clear that we were looking down into a valley completely enclosed by a horseshoe shaped mountain, the open ends of which jutted to the sea, isolating a beautiful mile-long beach. Without knowing anything about the geology of the region,

Qui Nhon

Helicopter we flew on to Qui Nhon from Pleiku.

Photograph of a woman on "China Beach" which I named, A Beach Peddler. This photograph won numerous ribbons and trophies in various juried contests.

Left to right: Arthur "Art" Waltzer, M.D. and Philip "Phil" Freedman, M.D. at the 85th Evac. Hospital.

I concluded that this was probably an extinct volcano with one rim eroded away over thousands of years by the sea's relentless attack, leaving this isolated valley. The depth of the valley from the South China Sea to the mountains, at the farthest point, was slightly over a mile. A small stream slowly trickled down from the mountain, bisecting the valley as it ran to the sea. As we descended into the

valley the temperature was notably cooler. The breeze from the ocean blowing into the valley rose when it hit the surrounding mountains, pushing the hot air up and over them. The road crossed the mountain and entered the valley near the left rear of the horseshoe. We drove a brief distance before the road turned sharply to the left onto a white sand, tree-lined street with a white statue at the end. As we approached, we saw that it was a life-sized statue of the Virgin Mary standing on a three-foot high pedestal. A small cross was painted over the letter "M" on the front of the pedestal. The road to the left led to a workshop and storage buildings. We turned right and almost immediately encountered on our right, a magnificent white Church. Just beyond was an administration building with a parking area in front. The entire area was deeply shaded. The ocean was about fifty yards from where we parked. The path leading to the beach passed from the parking area through a thirty or forty-foot wide swath of trees and bushes before opening onto an indescribably beautiful beach.

Beyond the administration building were streets of firm white sand laid out very precisely into blocks. There were both dormitories as well as individual houses. The individual houses were single story structures no larger than twenty by thirty feet with small porches or patios and very small yards. The two-story buildings provided dormitory-type housing on both floors, or some provided living quarters above with a patio beneath. The buildings were durably constructed using concrete blocks with an exterior coating of plaster, and some were partially covered with ceramic tile. All of the buildings had Spanish-type tile roofs. The doors, windows, trim,

Crossing the rim of the extinct volcano as we entered the pristine valley where the Leprosarium was located. The rim of the crater is unbroken except the portion to our left eroded over the millennia. The area is located two or three miles south of Qui Nhon.

shutters etc. were colorfully painted, mostly in pastel or muted shades of red, green, pink, orange, blue and brown. The tile work was artistically done while the windows and other decorations were distinctively appointed. The plaster was universally painted white. There were a lot of flowers, and all "lawns" were hard white sand, as were the streets. The entire village had been constructed in a large grove of coconut palm trees that covered many acres. A steady ocean breeze blew through the trees creating an enclave of cool, pleasant comfort. From the village, one could look out on the South China Sea, or looking in all other directions, there was nothing visible except tree-covered mountains. Throughout the valley, there were pasture fields, vegetable gardens, orchards, pineapple and banana groves and a few rice paddies. We were told that those residents who were able-bodied worked as caretakers, keeping the buildings maintained and the grounds clean.

The leprosarium, named the Qui Hoa Leprosarium, had been founded by the Maryknoll Order, who sent missionaries throughout Southeast Asia to China, Korea, Vietnam, Hong Kong and Indonesia where they established orphanages and leprosaria. Three French nuns, assisted by a few Vietnamese nuns, ran the leprosarium. In addition to the leprosarium, there was a Catholic-run orphanage in Qui Nhon, the Vien Duc Anh Bae Ae Orphanage. The Qui Hoa Leprosarium was the cleanest, quietest, most peaceful and beautiful place that I encountered in Vietnam. Over 900 hundred men, women and children lived there. If an individual developed leprosy, the entire family accompanied them when they moved to the leprosarium. Some were disfigured, having no nose, fingers or toes. Some had lost partial function of their extremities, secondary to neuritis. These deformities occurred before treatment was initiated because of delayed diagnosis, or in some cases, inadequate treatment. In some individuals the bacteria may have, rarely, developed drug resistance. Even more rarely, they may have developed complications caused by a drug reaction necessitating discontinuance of the treatment.

More than twenty cottages in the leprosarium had been constructed with donations from American troops and involved many military units. The revenue received from these donations was managed by a civic action fund council made up of representatives from each participating unit. A newsletter was

Road entering the Leprosarium with a statue of Mary.

Apartments upstairs with patio below.

regularly distributed to keep the donors informed. For example, by the spring of 1967, members of the 41st Signal Battalion had paid for two houses. Dedication plaques were appropriately attached, designating the contributing units.

We took time to spend an hour or so swimming and relaxing on the beach before returning to Qui Nhon. I could not help but make mental contrasts between the solitude, safety and peace of this place and the pain, suffering and carnage associated with the destruction of war. I was reminded of James Dickey's comments, "It is clean here, and empty. But no one would come who did not believe. There is an intensity of gentleness beyond any description and in silence a sense of congregation like layers of souls, close to each other, caring" (*Jericho: The South Beheld*). All sound seemed dampened and muffled. Even the gently swaying palm fronds seemed respectful and reverent. Was this nature's way of preparing us for requiem or for worship? The quietness and veneration of the moment created an inner conflict over leaving. As we gathered our personal belongings and headed for the jeep, I paused and looked back again and again. It was as if I were being helplessly, magnetically drawn back toward this beautiful place. Thoughtful circumspection occurred without effort or intent, and I felt reluctant, almost remorseful, about leaving.

As we exited down the drive, it seemed as if we were saying a permanent goodbye to an old friend. James Dickey further noted, "It is truth enough for mortal creatures that landscapes, seascapes, mountains, rivers and people can quite literally flow in the blood. These things are our significance, and will stay with us as possessions if we deeply open up to them" (*Ibid*). All human life has meaning and purpose. Each individual must determine what meaning and what purpose. I was reminded of Henry David Thoreau's words, "The setting sun is reflected from the windows of the almshouse as brightly as from the rich man's abode; the snow melts before its door as early in the spring" (*Walden*).

Soon after descending from the mountain, heading back to Qui Nhon, the distant noises of airplanes and helicopters steadily became more audible. The reality of war quickly resurfaced in our conscious awareness as we prepared again to face the daily tasks before us and, for me, to return the next day to Pleiku via Cam Ranh Bay on a C-130.

The popular thing to do in our leisure time during our year in country was recording music on reel-to-reel tape. The "ultimate" machine was a TEAC Automatic Reverse Model A-4010. Most of us got one from Hong Kong or Bangkok or through a PX. We then purchased tapes of our favorite recording artists and shared them with each other. We generally used earphones so we would not disturb our BOQ neighbors. I suppose that we took to heart Walt Whitman's words, "The subtlest spirit of a nation is expressed through its music—and the music acts reciprocally on the nation's very soul."

Felix Jenkins lived in the cubicle next to me and across the aisle from Tony Lindem and Wayne Hosking. We could always tell who Felix was listening to. If he was listening to Lou Rawls' music, he tapped his foot; but if he was listening to Nancy Wilson, he tended to rock back and forth in his chair, as well as pat his foot and even occasionally laugh or chuckle to himself. One evening we knew he was listening to Nancy because of his antics, but this time he started humming along and was badly out of tune. After a few minutes of this "torture," Wayne looked over at me and said, "Damn, isn't that the gawd awfullest noise you've ever heard?!" It was both an exclamation and a question; however, no particular response was expected.

After a while, Felix turned off his music and began reading. It was at that point that I retaliated by putting on a country-western

A family dwelling. All houses were colorfully decorated, clean and well kept.

Street scene showing houses and apartments.

Jerry W. Martin, M.D. on the beach at the Leprosarium.

tape of Eddie Arnold, but instead of using my earphones I turned on the speakers. With that, Wayne covered his head with a pillow, but did not comment. On one of the songs, Eddie Arnold began yodeling, and I attempted to sing along. Felix said, "I can't take anymore of that, I am going to the club and have a Scotch." Wayne flipped the pillow off his head and said, "Wait up, Felix, I'll join you. Anything would be better than this." Having succeeded in my vindictive amusement, as soon as they left, I turned off the speakers and started listening with my earphones. Everything was then quiet and peaceful.

After serving six months in Vietnam, all military personnel were entitled to a five day R and R (Rest and Recuperation) plus travel time to various places throughout the Orient: Hong Kong, British Crown Colony (B.C.C.); Bangkok, Thailand; Kuala Lumpur or Singapore, Malaysia; and Honolulu (Oahu), Hawaii.

My passport was issued by the U.S. Embassy in Saigon on Tuesday, April 18, 1967. The photograph I used was a self-portrait made in the BOQ one evening. I set up my camera and flash on a tripod and used the timer. I put on a shirt, tie and sport coat but no pants, only boxer shorts, for the picture. This made for some interesting comments. A photo shop in Pleiku developed the black and white film and printed the appropriately sized picture. I took the photo and the necessary paperwork to an office at MACV, who forwarded it to the Embassy. Within about two weeks, I received the passport via the military mail system.

On Tuesday, April 11, I flew on a C-130 from Pleiku to Cam Ranh Bay. An Air Force bus shuttled us from the airport to the R and R Processing Center (22nd Replacement Battalion). As soon as the paper work was completed, the shuttle process was reversed back to the airport, where we boarded a chartered commercial airline (PanAm Clipper) under contract to the Military Airlift Command (MAC). From Cam Ranh Bay, we flew NNE to Hong Kong, missing the air space over the Communist Chinese Island of Hainan. The distance from Cam Ranh to Hong Kong International (Kai Tak) Airport was a relatively short three-four hour flight since it was only about 900 miles; however, we did lose one hour between Vietnam and Hong Kong. The 8,350-foot runway (completed in 1958) at the Hong Kong Airport had been constructed by filling in a portion of Kowloon Bay extending out from the mainland. When making the approach for landing, it seemed as if we were going to set down in the bay. In fact, a few weeks after I was there, a plane did just that on June 30, 1967. All on our flight were military personnel in uniform with immunization records, so processing through customs was brief and simple.

Hong Kong (derived from "Heung Kong" meaning "Isle of Fragrant Waters" or "Fragrant Harbor") was comprised of Hong Kong Island (acquired in 1842), Kowloon Peninsula (acquired in 1860), the New Territories (leased by China to Britain in 1898 for 99 years), Lantou (Lantao) Island and numerous small islands covering a total of 398 sq. mi. The Japanese conquered and controlled the Colony during World War II.

Hong Kong Island is eleven miles long with an area of twenty-nine square miles. Victoria (the Capital, named for the Queen, is often referred to as Hong Kong) is located on Hong Kong Island with a population of slightly over one million (1967) and separated from the mainland by Victoria Harbor. The island is approximately 90 miles south of Canton.

I stayed on the Island at the Hong Kong Hilton at the corner of Queen's Road Central and Garden Road, located across the street from the Hong Kong Cricket Club, just four blocks from the Star Ferry Pier. The room rates were $10-18 single and $14-21 double. The rate for military personnel on R and R was $9/night. The view from my window looked out toward Victoria Peak, but I could also see a portion of the Central District

The Air Terminal at Cam Ranh Bay.

Barracks at Cam Ranh Bay for those going on R and R or returning to CONUS.

Tiger Balm Gardens

Waiting for boat transportation to the Sea Palace Floating Restaurant in Aberdeen Bay.

Aerial view of Tiger Balm Gardens.

Children diving for silver coins thrown into the water by tourists while waiting on the pier to take a boat to Sea Palace Floating Restaurant.

Children on boat on Aberdeen Bay.

View from Hong Kong Hilton Hotel looking toward the tram going to the Peak.

(Capitol Building, Government Buildings, and Commercial Center [Banks and "Wall Street" of Hong Kong]). Every afternoon the Chinese in Canton turned off Hong Kong's water supply, so it was necessary to plan ahead for bathing. In each bathroom there were three faucets: one for hot, one for cold, and one for potable water. A thermos bottle was supplied, allowing drinking water to be kept in reserve during the water stoppage. The Hilton had numerous restaurants: the Jade Lotus (main dining room), The Grill, the Eagle's Nest (on the 25th floor with harbor view), and The Den (lounge). Oriental, Continental and American menus were available.

Two blocks inland from the Hilton on Garden Road was the Peak Tram terminal. The Tram is a funicular cable car to Victoria Peak that rises 1,305 ft. above sea level. The two cars were capable of carrying seventy-two passengers and were pulled by separate 5,000-ft. steel cables, each wound on separate drums. While one car ascends the other descends on interlocking tracks, except for passing about midway. The view from Victoria Peak is spectacular, especially at night. The ride cost $.60 HK, departed every ten minutes and took eight minutes to reach the top. It opened in 1888, and, in 1967, there had not been an accident.

Other points of interest on Hong Kong Island were Repulse Bay (named for the HMS Repulse) and Shek-O (on Dragon's Back Peninsula), two well-known beaches, and the "boat people." Aberdeen is Hong Kong's main fishing village and has 26,000 people living on 3,500 vessels in Aberdeen Harbour. In Yaumati Typhoon Shelter there were 8,700 people on 1,200 boats, and Causeway Bay Typhoon Shelter had 2,000 people on 750 vessels. It was estimated that upwards of 100,000 people lived on 13,000 vessels in Colony waters. The tour I was on (Lotus Tours, LTD.) stopped at the Aberdeen Floating Restaurant for a Chinese dinner. We were taken from shore to the restaurant by small boats rowed by women. Another well-known sight on the Island was Tiger Balm Gardens constructed in 1935 by Aw

Boon Haw on eight acres in his backyard for a reputed cost of $16,000,000 HK. It consisted of grottos, grotesque statues and pavilions displaying effigies of Chinese mythology. The oldest Chinese Temple on the Island, Man Mo Meal (meal=temple), was constructed in 1848. The Suzie Wong Hotel (named for the movie, *Suzie Wong*, starring William Holden) and William Holden's house were located on the southwestern part of the island near Repulse Bay.

Tsimshatsui, the shopping district on Kowloon Peninsula, was about ¾ of a mile across Victoria Bay from the Star Ferry Pier. The Star Ferry ran from 6 a.m. until 3 a.m. daily, carrying automobiles and approximately 100,000 people daily. Passengers were first or second class, costing $.25 or $.10 HK respectively. If one missed the last ferry, the Walla Wallas (motor launches) operated continuously between the Kowloon Public Pier and Blake Pier on Hong Kong Island, but were more expensive.

The New Territories included 365 square miles, in addition to the 3¼ square miles of Kowloon Peninsula. It was a 65-mile drive through both industrial and farming areas to the Communist Chinese border. Upon arrival, the tour stopped at the Lok Ma Chau Police Station. There was a park with an observation area on a hill overlooking the Shumchum River in Communist China. On the way to the border, we stopped at the Kam Tin Walled City, built in the 1600s by the Tang people. The two five-or six-foot diameter concrete pipes carrying water from Canton to Hong Kong ran alongside the highway and were used as a sidewalk by pedestrians. On the return trip, we had lunch at the Sha Tin Floating Restaurant. Almost all of the 13% of arable land was in the New Territories, with over half of the acreage devoted to rice grown normally in two annual crops.

The population of Hong Kong was over 3,750,000, with over 99% being Chinese (mostly Cantonese), British (15,000), Americans (3,500), Portuguese (2,100), Japanese (1,700), Filipinos (600) and a few thousand others of various nationalities. The primary languages were English and Cantonese, but Shanghaiese and Mandarin plus several dozen other Chinese dialects were also spoken.

Hong Kong is just within the tropics, and the climate is monsoonal. The temperature rarely dips below 60° F or above 80° F, and the annual rainfall averages 85″, falling mostly between May and September.

The Portuguese Province (Colony) of Macao (Macau), located on the peninsula of Chung Shan, Kwangtung, plus a few islands, was located about 40 miles WSW of Hong Kong and could be reached by a fifteen-minute flight or about an hour boat ride. Located there was the Guia Lighthouse, the oldest on the China coast. Unfortunately, military personnel could not travel there at that time because of the Red Guard uprising throughout China.

Jerry W. Martin, M.D. at Hong Kong International Airport.

Tiger Balm Garden

View of Victoria Peak from my window in the Hong Kong Hilton.

In addition to the religions of the Far East, the Church of England, Roman Catholic, most all American Protestant denominations, and a Jewish Synagogue were available for worship.

The Hong Kong dollar was worth 62 yen and the U.S. dollar exchanged for 5.71 Hong Kong dollars. Most banking and business was conducted in Victoria; most of the shopping was done in Kowloon; and most of the farming and industry was confined to the New Territories.

There were hundreds of stores in Victoria and Kowloon. The well-known Lane Crawford British Department Store (established shortly before Abraham Lincoln became President) was in Victoria and was known for Mikimoto Pearls. Other stores included Oriental Galleries, Kung Brothers Clothing, Hong Kong Fur Company, the Ocean Terminal (Noritake China) and the Lien Hing Ivory Factory (where I purchased an ivory chess set).

Hong Kong reverted back to China on July 1, 1997.

When I reflect on Hong Kong, many images come to mind. The most vivid recollection is of a night view from Victoria Peak looking out over Victoria Bay and Kowloon. I can certainly relate to the Cantonese scholar, who sailed past Hong Kong Island into Victoria Bay in 1100 AD and later wrote,

Approaching Victoria Island on the Star Ferry.

> Across the waters when tis dark a million lights shall glow,
> And in their paths ten thousand ships go passing to and
> fro.

When I returned to Pleiku from Hong Kong, I learned that the 2nd Surgical Hospital at An Khe was being sent to CTZ I to support the 1st Cavalry Division, who was also moving north to give support to the 3rd Marine Division.

On Monday, March 28, 1966, Maj. Gen. William Peers, CO of the 4th Division invited the officers of the 18th Surgical Hospital (MA) to be his dinner guests at their Dragon Mountain Base Camp on Friday, April l. During the night of March 31, we were extremely busy. As the time for the dinner at the 4th Division neared, we began receiving more casualties. Needless to say, Lt. Col. Cenac had

Sha Tin Floating Restaurant, New Territories, Hong Kong.

to call and cancel the trip. Thankfully, we were granted a rain check. The casualties were not Americans, but were Chinese Nationalists from Formosa working as civilian guerrillas in Cambodia and Laos. The day I returned from R and R we were able to accept Maj. Gen. Peers' invitation for dinner. He sent 4th Division helicopters to pick us up. At the end of a delightful meal, the 4th Division presented the 18th with a certificate of appreciation:

> The Fourth Infantry Division in recognition of faithful and efficient performance of duty this Certificate of Achievement is awarded to The Doctors, Nurses, and Medical Corpsmen of the 18th Surgical Hospital for outstanding service to the United States Army's 4th Infantry (IVY) Division.
>
> We who wear the Ivy patch are soldiers, and, as such, are prepared to face the enemy and pay the price of victory. As we go to battle, we know that the price of victory might be paid in our own blood or that of our comrades. It is a comfort to us at times like this to know that dedicated medical personnel of your caliber will be there to help us in time of need. Through your renderence of medical aid to our wounded and sick you have displayed a devotion to duty far exceeding that normally accepted as the standard, a devotion to duty that we of the 4th Division respect, admire, and appreciate. The professional quality of your care is incomparable and reflects great credit upon you, the Medical Corps, and the United States Army.
>
> Given at Dragon Mountain Base Camp, Pleiku Province, Republic of Vietnam this 16th day of April, 1967.
>
> W. R. PEERS
> Major General, USA
> Commanding

One of our surgeons, Jules Perley, M.D., received orders to report to Chu Lai (CTZ I) within twenty-four hours to relieve another surgeon. The week before, another physician in the 1st Calvary Division was killed. On May 7, a Chinook helicopter carrying forty wounded was shot down, and many of the wounded were killed. We ultimately received over twenty casualties from that chopper and worked continuously for over eighteen hours.

One evening a Montagnard man was brought in with a puncture wound of the abdomen, sustained a few hours earlier when a land mine exploded in a field where he was working. By the time he arrived, his abdomen was very tender with involuntary guarding, indicating peritonitis. We quickly prepared him for surgery. When his abdomen was opened, we found the peritoneal cavity crawling with Ascaris (parasitic intestinal round worms) that had crawled through a perforation in the small bowel. After scooping out the parasites with our hands, a segment of damaged small bowel was resected, and the shrapnel fragment removed. We had to remove many intraluminal worms in order to anastamose the bowel. With abdominal drains and antibiotics he did well postoperatively and was discharged in about a week. We discussed treating his parasitic infestation; however, since he would return to the same environment and since we could not treat all of his family, nor could we quickly educate them concerning personal hygiene, it was decided that a one-time cure would really not help. He would become re-infected immediately upon his return to his family and their way of life.

Sometime earlier, a Special Forces Sergeant brought in a four or five-year old Montagnard girl that had received a perforating shrapnel wound of the abdomen that had occurred about twenty-four hours earlier. She was dehydrated, in severe pain and had a rigid abdomen consistent with severe peritonitis. Her heart rate was very rapid, and her blood pressure was extremely low. She was nearly in shock. We explained through an interpreter to her father, who had accompanied her that she was near death from the severe infection. We further explained that her only hope would be to have surgery; however, it was also our belief that even with surgery she would not survive. The father very reluctantly, but stoically, decided to take her back home to die in their village among her family. It was their belief that if she died outside of the village, her spirit would wander

Closure of small bowel of Montagnard man wounded by a penetrating shrapnel wound of the abdomen. Round worms (Ascaris lumbricoides) had escaped through perforations in the small bowel and were crawling throughout the peritoneal cavity when we opened his abdomen.

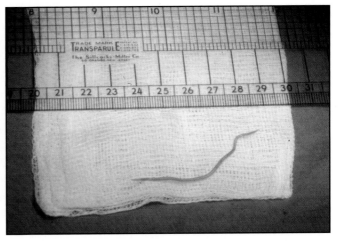

A round worm from the Montagnard man shown to the left.

for all eternity. A small house was constructed and set on a pole at the edge of each Montagnard village so that wandering spirits, who happened by, could find temporary lodging. Their Animistic beliefs were very strong. We later heard that the child had died within a few hours after leaving the 18th.

The Air Force had a hangar at the New Pleiku Air Base where A1-E Skyraiders were repaired and/or rebuilt. Those that had been shot down or crashed were picked up by CH-47 Chinooks or CH-54 Tarhe Flying Cranes and flown back there. They were disassembled, repaired and rebuilt. A few of the A1-E's that were not repairable were kept as a source for parts.

The Vietnamese alphabet is the only Oriental language that uses the English alphabet; however, they have more, and different, diacritical marks than English, resulting in inflexions and intonations which give a singsong cadence to their speech. A word with different diacritical marks will sound differently and have a completely different meaning, although spelled the same. Most signs, storefront advertisements, slogans, banners, etc. were written in Vietnamese, Chinese and English (frequently) though rarely in French and, depending on the location, even more rarely in a Montagnard dialect.

We saw a large number of splenic injuries but they were more frequently seen in Vietnamese and Montagnards than Americans. Bob Hewitt, M.D., reviewed our records and discovered that the incidence of splenic injuries in Vietnamese and Montagnards was 22% as compared to 12% in Americans. L.H. Wolff, M.D., reviewed abdominal injuries from World War II and reported to the Surgeon General in 1955. He determined that the frequency of wounding any given abdominal organ was directly proportional to the space that it occupies, which is what logical reasoning would dictate. Since essentially all Vietnamese and Montagnards had enlarged spleens due to malaria, Wolff's conclusions proved to be true at the 18th.

On May 8, the perimeter guards at the New Pleiku Air Base exchanged fire with VC infiltrators, foiling an apparent planned mortar attack. The next morning the civilians who worked at the Air Base were searched and examined upon their arrival for work. Some had wounds inflicted by the skirmish the night before.

The day before, Sunday afternoon, I went over to Paradise Lost to see if there was a football game being televised. Lt. Col. Cenac and Col. Bonneaux were seated at a table engrossed in the game. Maj. Clarke Brandt was seated at a nearby table, so I sat with him. He mentioned that he was going on R and R to Bangkok on Tuesday. In our conversation, I mentioned that I had been to Hong Kong on R and R and was trying to go to Bangkok, but all the R and R flights were already booked beyond my date to return to CONUS.

Because the flights were already booked, there was no hope of going standby. I gave him some money to buy a Princess dinner ring (Star Sapphires) for my wife, in case I was not able to go.

The day after Clarke left, I got a call from Col. Bonneaux. He told me that he had a C-130 flight going to Bangkok on Saturday, May 13, and thought that I might like to go. I gladly accepted his offer.

Saturday morning, I went over to the New Pleiku Airport and signed in for the flight. We flew to Saigon to pick up a few Air Force personnel. From there we flew over the southern part of Cambodia and arrived at the Bangkok International Airport (Donmuang) in the early afternoon. The plane was flying on to Rangoon, Burma so those with Bangkok as their destination disembarked. An Air Force van carried us to the Fortuna Hotel where the Air Force kept a block of rooms rented since they had regular flights to Bangkok. I had no reservation, so I used one of their empty reserved rooms.

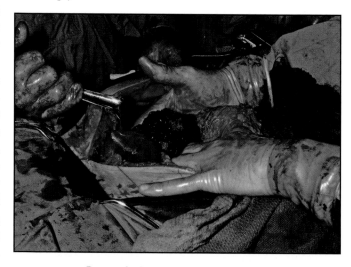

Ruptured spleen, blood clot being removed.

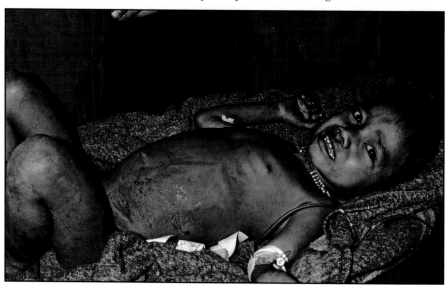

Montagnard girl with an intra abdominal shrapnel wound hours old. She had developed severe peritonitis (BP↓, P↑, rigid abdomen, pain, fever). We told her father that her only hope was surgery but even with surgery she probably would die. He refused the operation and chose to allow her to die in their village so that her soul would not wander throughout eternity. We were told that she died a short time later at her home.

The Fortuna Hotel was situated in an Embassy section of Bangkok at the corner of Sukhumvit Road and Nana Tai. It was located near the Pakistanian Embassy and three blocks from the American Embassy. The location was between three or four miles from the Grand Palace and the Chao Phraya River. I knew that Maj. Brandt was staying at the Rama Hotel (Hilton), so I decided to go there for dinner that evening, hoping to see Clarke and check about the ring. The Rama was a luxurious hotel, beautifully decorated. On the stairs leading to the mezzanine, Thai mythology was depicted in stained glass. The Rama Hotel was on Silom Road about three miles from the Fortuna Hotel. Clarke was out when I arrived. I ate dinner in the Chiengmai Room. I had Roast Prime Rib of Beef (Hellaby Beef from New Zealand). I checked after dinner and Clarke had not returned, so I hailed a cab and returned to my hotel. The next morning (Sunday) I called Clarke early around 7 a.m. I wanted to catch him before he left for the day to find out if he had purchased the ring, before I started shopping. I woke him up, which wasn't all-bad. He told me later that since he was awake, he decided to go to Mass. He left the ring and my surplus money remaining after the purchase, at the front desk for me to pick up later in the day. I took a morning tour (Mother's Day) with the Alisa Thai Tour (English Speaking Guide) to the Temple of the Emerald Buddha (or Chapel Royal of the Emerald Buddha, Wat Pra Keaw) and The Grand Palace, built in 1782, by King Rama I. One group of buildings on the Grand Palace Grounds was the Mah amontien where the Coronation Ceremony takes place. Another hall was The Audience Hall (Hall of Amarindra) and the Royal Dressing Chamber in Cakrapatipiman Hall. We also visited the Royal Ceremonial Barges (ancient, highly decorated barges made of teak wood), especially the Soupanahonges, on which the King journeys once a year in October, from the Noi Klong, and along the Chao Phraya River to Wat Arun for the presentation of Kathin gifts. Since Sunday is the Buddhist Sabbath, we could not enter the main gate, but entered through the Swadisopa Gate, in front of the Defense Ministry. Photography was not allowed inside the Main Chapel (Ubosodhi) and I had to get a special card from the Officer at the Temple of the Emerald Buddha Office, granting me permission to photograph outside the Temple. Over 600 years old, the Emerald Buddha is a two-foot high statue of Buddha carved out of emerald. It was placed about 20 feet above the floor on a base covered with gold leaf and under a gold leaf canopy.

After lunch, I joined the Temple Tour that visited three Buddhist Temples (Wat Tri Mit). The first was the Golden Buddha (Sukhothai Era). It stood three meters high, weighed 5.5 tons and was made of solid gold (with gold at $950 per ounce, the value would be slightly more than 150,000,000 U.S. dollars). The second was the Wat Po (or Wat Phra Chetuphon) that included The Mondop (Library) and the Reclining Buddha (160 ft. long and 30 ft. high). The third was the Gallery of Buddhas and the Statue of Lord Buddha in Wat Benchamabophit (Marble Temple) that was a perfect example of Thai architecture.

As soon as the Temple Tour ended around 4 p.m., I took a taxi to the Rajadamnoen Stadium for a ringside seat at a Thai boxing match. There were eight bouts of five rounds each. I ate there during the bouts. Everything in Bangkok was very inexpensive since a U.S. dollar exchanged for 20.65 Baht (1 HK $=3.65 Baht). The boxing matches cost about $3.80 U.S.

On Monday, May 15, I took the Floating Market tour, which was a boat tour on the Chao Phraya River and numerous klongs (canals). It exposed tourists to a portion of the Thai culture that vividly revealed their traditional way of life, uninhibited for hundreds of years. We also stopped at Jim Thompson's Silk Market. Jim Thompson was an American OSS (Office of Strategic Services, a U.S. government intelligence agency during World War II) agent in Southeast Asia during World War II. After the war, he returned to Bangkok, built a silk factory and soon opened his own retail outlet store. I had not heard of Jim Thompson until about February or March 1967. While visiting in Malaysia, he went for a walk one evening and was never heard of again. His disappearance was widely reported by the press. He had combined three or four Thai teak houses into one large, rather luxurious home on one of

Grand Palace Temple Complex.

Left to right: Lt. Col. Cenac (CO), Maj. Gen. Vinh Loc, II Corps Commander, Col. Bonneaux, CO of New Pleiku Airbase. In the background Maj. Mary Berry (Chief of Nursing) greeting "Max", an employee of RMK-BRJ.

the klongs. After his death his house became a museum to house his large Oriental art collection. His Silk Market was a popular tourist attraction. Silk of every color and pattern imaginable was available at his store and sold for three dollars a yard.

We also visited the Temple of Dawn (Wat Arun), a 218-ft. high temple situated on the Chao Phraya River. It was covered with small porcelain tile creating a very distinctive design. I climbed to near the top for a panoramic and truly spectacular view of the city.

Bangkok is located about 17 miles up river from the Gulf of Siam. Formerly known as Siam, Thailand means, "Land of the Free." It has always been independent and is the only country in Southeast Asia that has never been colonized. The Thai people originated in 650 AD in the Yangtze Valley of Southeast China, known as the Kingdom of Nanchao. Kublai Khan conquered Nanchao in 1253 AD, resulting in a mass migration of the people southward where they settled in the fertile Chao River Valley and founded the capital city of Sukhothai. The most important Sukhothai ruler was King Rama (1275 AD), who introduced the Thai alphabet. In 1350 AD, the capital moved to Ayudhya under a new King, Rama Tibodi. Ayudhya fell to the Burmese in 1767. A General, Phya Tok Sin, drove off the invaders and was crowned King. He established the capital at Dhonburi, which is across the Chao Phraya River from present day Bangkok. His successor, a General named Chao Phya Chakri, became King Phra Buddha Yod Fah Chulaloke (Rama I) who established the capital in Bangkok in 1732. In 1967, the King was Bhumibol Adulyadej (he was born in Boston, Massachusetts in 1927), who married Queen Sirikit in 1949. They had three daughters and one son, Crown Prince Vajiralongkorn (born July 28, 1952).

That evening I went to the Sala Norasingh Restaurant on Sukhumvit Road, a dinner-theatre known for good food and Classical Thai Dancing. We sat on comfortable cushions on the floor. A triangular cushion was provided for each person to lean on. The cushions were red with a gold design. The eighteen-inch high gilded tables were of the same color and similar design. The orchestra sat on floor cushions and played drums, hollow bamboo rods, flutes and something that resembled a marimba or

Golden Buddha.

Temple of Dawn.

View of temples taken from a boat on a klong.

Kanchanaburi War Cemetery near the Kwai River.

Floating residence on the Kwai River.

Monuments on the grounds of the Grand Palace.

Marble Palace

Monuments viewed from outside the walls of Grand Palace.

xylophone. The dancers, mostly female, were dressed in traditional ancient-style Thai costumes. Every movement was highly stylized and exaggerated to depict a story. Their dances were graceful and portrayed love and romance, war and struggle, peace, merriment and happiness. These emotions were dramatically captured. Their rhythmic movements were choreographed in tempo with the instrumental accompaniment. Their headwear was tall and conical, rising to a sharp point and ornately designed. Many, usually males, wore grotesque, but colorful, masks depicting demons from their cultural mythology.

On Tuesday, May 16, my tour traveled about seventy miles west of Bangkok to Kanchanaburi. At the bridge over the River Kwai, we boarded a long, narrow motorized boat and traveled on the Kwai River for two or three miles to a large cave that housed a Buddhist Temple. When we returned to the bridge, we were served a box lunch. Afterwards I walked out onto the bridge and photographed. Scenes from the movie, *The Bridge Over the River Kwai*, starring Sir Alec Guiness flashed through my mind as I stood there. Near the bridge, we visited the Kanchanaburi National Cemetery containing the remains of the British, Dutch and Australian prisoners who died during the Japanese construction of the notorious railroad and bridge.

During the afternoon, I visited numerous stores, shops, jewelers, etc. At the Star of Bangkok on Silom Road, near the Rama Hotel, I found another Princess dinner ring with black star sapphires and matching earrings, a ring with a large solitaire sapphire stone and other items. The story of the Princess ring dates back to early Sanskrit literature, in which the ring was called "NA VA RA TA NA." Originally, there were nine different gems. However, they are currently made using only one type of stone, but the stones are tiered so as to resemble a Princess' Crown. Since I was near the Rama Hotel, I went back there for dinner.

We were supposed to have returned to Vietnam on Wednesday the 17th, but the plane was delayed until Thursday. Upon discovering the delay, I quickly scheduled a City Tour. We visited Lumpini Park, Pasteur Institute with its Snake Farm, Chulalongkorn University, China Town, the National Assembly Hall and the Zoo. In the early afternoon, I walked around the Embassy area, photographing, and spent the remainder of the afternoon, reading and resting. That evening I ate in the dining room of the Fortuna Hotel, which was rather unusual. One wall of the room was glass that served as one end of the swimming pool. Diners were on the level of the bottom of the pool and could watch guests as they dived and swam.

We left Bangkok about midmorning on Thursday, May 18, and arrived in Saigon in the early afternoon. At Tan Son Nhut, I called Major Raymond Nutter who had recovered from his previous wounds and had returned to duty as CO of the 121st Assault Helicopter Company (Viking Platoon) at Soc Trang in the Delta about ninety miles SSW from Saigon. He told me to wait in the terminal, and he would send a chopper to pick me up. I had already checked with Lt. Col. Cenac at the 18th who gave the okay for me to visit Ray for three or four days. In a little over an hour, I was paged and one of the gunners on the gunship

Classical dancer at Sara Norasingh Theatre.

Bridge over the River Kwai.

came into the terminal looking for me. I grabbed my camera and gear and followed him to the helicopter. They had not turned off the engine, so we were quickly airborne. I stayed with Ray until Sunday, May 21. Ray drove me around Soc Trang so that I could see the town and get a few photographs. One evening, the only remaining member of the original Three Sons, Marty Nevins, entertained by playing the accordian and singing many of their hit songs from the late forties and early fifties, including their theme song, *Twilight Time*. Sunday morning, I boarded one of the Viking Platoon's choppers for the return trip to Saigon. On the way, we observed a firefight near the small village of Can Tho on the Song Hau Gian, the southernmost tributary of the Mekong River. Phantom F-4s were dropping napalm and strafing and were followed by helicopter gunships giving additional air support. At Tan Son Nhut I boarded a C-130 and arrived at Pleiku in mid-afternoon.

Casualties had begun arriving at the 18th on Saturday, May 20, after being transferred from the 2nd Surgical Hospital at Chu Lai (CTZ-I), which was overwhelmed by the large number of wounded. I quickly stashed my camera and gear in our BOQ, changed from khakis into scrubs and went to work. By the time I was able to get to bed, near midnight, I was truly fatigued.

On Monday morning May 22, we received another seventy-five casualties from an ongoing battle, in which the 4th Division was

Dust storm at 18th Surgical Hospital (MA).

Dust storm approaching. ARVN Hospital in foreground with MACV-II Corps on hill to the right.

Left to right: Pat Weaver, R.N., Bob Engebrecht, M.D. and Ann Stetcher, R.N. at 542nd Medical Clearing Company.

engaged a few kilometers west of Pleiku. Many of the wounded had vascular injuries of the lower extremities. Most often, it was the femoral artery that was involved. The bullet frequently passed through the thigh without touching the artery, but the high-frequency waves caused arterial thrombosis (clotting), stopping the flow of blood. When that occurred, the involved section of the artery had to be resected, and a section of saphenous vein was used as a graft. An extensive fasciotomy (the muscle covering was opened surgically to accommodate excessive swelling and was closed secondarily in a few days) was done, and the patient's pulses were monitored regularly, especially during the early post-op period. We operated on the most critical, while all who were stable were transferred to Qui Nhon.

The incidence of acute arteriovenous fistulas in penetrating arterial injuries at the 18th was about 6%, which is consistent with later analysis of arterial injuries from the entire Vietnam War (Vietnam Vascular Registry).

On Tuesday, May 23, the NVA disengaged from the battle and slipped back into Cambodia to celebrate Buddha's birthday (Buddha, Prince Siddhartha Gautama, born in 563 BC in Lambini [now Nepal], son of the Rajah of the Sakya clan). The VC took only one day off for the celebration, so by early Wednesday, May 24, our work began again when we received a few Montagnard

civilians wounded by NVA mortars. Then, by late afternoon, more wounded from the 4th Division arrived. It was a very busy few days.

Around the first of May, South Vietnam experienced a severe dust storm. We were told that it began in Burma and Thailand and then blew across Cambodia and Vietnam before going out into the South China Sea. The sand and dust came as a wave or cloud, almost in monsoonal fashion, from the west. Even with the windows and doors closed, everything was permeated with dust. Visibility was limited, the sky darkened, and breathing was difficult despite the use of surgical masks. Our bedding and clothing had to be washed, and everything, thoroughly cleaned. I even had to clean sand from my "sealed" footlocker.

By the end of the year we were in Vietnam, Pleiku became a burgeoning center, or hub, for the Central Highlands. Most everyone who came wanted to visit a Montagnard village.

My first visit to a Montagnard village was in July 1966. I accompanied Ann Stetcher, R.N., Pat Weaver, R.N., Bob Engebrecht, M.D., and one or two others to a village a few miles west of Pleiku. Our invitation came because we had treated a few patients from this village at the 18th. Earlier engineers had dug deep wells, providing them with fresh, potable water. When we arrived the mood was festive. As a greeting, a sign written in Montagnard had been placed over the gate entering the village, and the gateposts were elaborately decorated with banana leaves. We parked the jeep near the entrance and walked into the village under the sign. We were then greeted by a young man, the village Chief, and a few Montagnard Special Forces. The men and boys of the village stood on one side, while women and girls stood on the other side, forming a human corridor through which we walked.

Before leaving the 18th, we obtained a supply of cigarettes to give to the adults and candy for the children. After dispensing these handouts, we were led to chairs set up in a place of honor. The chairs on which we sat were draped with a white cloth, colorfully designed with reds, greens and blues, in an unusual pattern. Placed before each chair was a large urn filled with rice wine. Before the ceremony began, we were entertained by a young woman who sang, accompanied by a young man who both sang and played a guitar. The duet was very pretty, even though we could not understand them. Then a quartet of teenage girls sang, accompanied by the same young man.

After the entertainment concluded, remarks of greeting were made by the Chief, without the benefit of an interpreter. We were encouraged to drink the rice wine through cane straws from the urns set before us, while a man broke off chunks of chicken that had been roasting over a small fire on a makeshift rotisserie. The chicken still had its head and feet and a few feathers. I was not concerned about the rice wine since the alcohol content was high enough to kill parasites and bacteria; however, the chicken, broken off by a fellow with grimy hands, was a different matter. I placed a piece of chicken in my mouth and pretended to chew and swallow it. Then I took a mouth full of rice wine and held it for a while before swallowing, hoping to kill any organisms that might have been present. I kept the chicken between my gum and cheek until I could discreetly remove and dispose of it. As we drank the wine, one of the villagers kept refilling the urns with wine from a nearby storage vessel, using an old tin can. After this portion of the ceremony, we were each presented with a copper bracelet, indicating that we were brothers with this village.

I visited other Montagnard villages in August 1966, February 1967, and again in March 1967. On these occasions we were not honored guests, nor were we made "brothers" with the villagers. In February 1967, Maj. Pat Miller, Joe Juliano, M.D., Gene Chap, M.D., Orville Swenson, M.D., and I drove to a village just beyond Lake Bien Ho near the 25th Division. On the March visit, I purchased a crossbow from a Montagnard man who spoke English, French, and Vietnamese, as well as two or three dialects of Montagnard, yet he was uneducated. He was very friendly and eager to learn about Americans. Later I was told that he had been killed by the VC for being pro-American.

We saw a few cases of bubonic plague (*Yersinia pestis*) in Montagnards at the 18th. I do not recall having seen plague in GIs or Vietnamese.

It is interesting to note that the man for whom the plague bacillus is named lived much of his life in Vietnam, specifically in Nha Trang. Emile John Alexandre Yersin (1863-1943) was born

Jerry Martin, M.D. drinking rice wine. We also received a piece of chicken. After the ceremony, I was given a copper bracelet, making me a "brother."

in Lavaux, Switzerland. His father had died three weeks before his birth, and his mother soon moved to Morges and opened a finishing school for girls. Alexandre received his primary and secondary education in Lausanne.

In 1883, he enrolled at the Academy of Lausanne for his first year of medical school. The next year (October 1884), he registered for his second year of medical school at Marburg University in Germany. He excelled in surgery and pathology and was noted by Professor Marchand (1846-1928) to be "a very gifted" student in histology.

In November 1885, he presented his Swiss and German Diplomas to the Faculty of Medicine at the University of Paris, where he completed his third and fourth years of study. A family friend in Morges wrote a letter of introduction to the eminent pathologist, Professor Andre' Victor Cornil (1837-1908). After learning of Alexandre's work with Marchand, Cornil admitted Yersin to his laboratory as an assistant. It was there that Yersin met Louis Pasteur (1822-1895), Charles Edouard Chamberland (1851-1908) and Emile Roux (1853-1933), who had collaborated in developing an antirabies vaccine in Pasteur's laboratory in the Ecole Normale Superoeire in Rue d'Ulm. Dr. Roux later employed Yersin for two years as a paid assistant. During this time, Yersin did independent research on an experimental form of "septicaemic" tuberculosis. Yersin used the results of this work as the basis for his doctoral thesis, for which he was awarded the Bronze Medallion by the Faculty of Medicine of the University of Paris in 1889.

Roux and Yersin began work in 1886 on the bacillus described by Theodor Klebs (1834-1913) and Friedrich Loëffler (1852-1915) and soon confirmed that it was the causative agent for diphtheria (*Corynebacterium diphtheriae*).

In 1888, the French Academy of Science opened a new, larger Pasteur Institute. Dr. Roux sent Yersin to the University of Berlin to attend a two-month bacteriology course given by Robert Koch (1843-1910). Upon his return and after teaching five courses, Dr. Yersin, who did not enjoy teaching, resigned from the Pasteur Institute and joined the Compagnie des Messageries Maritimes as a doctor on a ship sailing between Saigon and Manila, rendering medical services to the crew. He quickly learned Vietnamese in order to communicate with the sailors. He soon changed ships and began sailing between Saigon and Haiphong, the port of Hanoi. As he sailed up and down the coast of Vietnam, he saw the Annam Mountain range (now the Truong Son range). Yersin landed at Nha Trang and immediately started hiking toward Saigon, but with only a ten-day leave of absence from the ship, had to return soon. He did, however, have an opportunity to meet Montagnards who had never seen a European and acquired his first severe attack of malaria.

Shortly thereafter, Yersin met Dr. Albert Calmette (who had also attended Roux's course in bacteriology at the Pasteur Institute) with the French Colonial Health Service who persuaded Yersin to likewise join (Yersin held the rank of Colonel in the French Army).

His second trek through the Central Highlands was better planned and equipped. He spent ten weeks hiking from Nha

Montagnard village near a river in the Central Highlands.

Trang to the Mekong River in Cambodia, photographing and mapping the mountains and villages. Quinine helped to combat malaria, but he suffered a severe attack of dysentery. Based on his survey and recommendations, a health resort was begun at Da Lat (the ancient capital of the South Vietnamese Highlands).

In 1894, Yersin spent four months exploring from Nha Trang to Attopeu in Laos. He returned to the coast at Da Nang. His expedition provided the first systematic geographical knowledge of the Central Highlands.

In May 1894, he was ordered by the Chief Medical Officer in the Colonial Health Service to Hong Kong to study an outbreak of plague. At the same time Shibasaburo Kitasato (1852-1931), an eminent bacteriologist, headed a Japanese Commission from Tokyo for the same purpose. Dr. Kitasato had studied and worked in Berlin with Emil von Behring (1854-1917) in the laboratory of Robert Koch, helping to develop the first anti-tetanus serum. This team was welcomed in Hong Kong on June 12, by Superintendent Dr. James A. Lowson (1866-1935) and offered facilities in a hospital. Yersin arrived on June 15, but was not offered the use of facilities in the hospital or access to autopsy material for examination.

Working on his own in a makeshift hut, he quickly concluded that the bacteria in patients' blood had spread there from another source. He sought bubos (infected lymph nodes) to study but was stymied by bureaucracy. Father Vigano, an Italian missionary, was successful, by bribing English sailors who were engaged in burying the dead, to divulge the location where the coffins awaiting burial were temporarily stored. Yersin was able to clandestinely open the coffins and get bubo samples from the dead. Subsequently, a request from the French Consulate to the Governor of Hong Kong resulted in Yersin being provided laboratory facilities and adequate samples of autopsy specimen.

Through his microscopic examinations, cultures, stainings and reproducing the disease by injecting laboratory mice, he was convinced that he had identified the microbe responsible for plague. He sent specimens (sealed in glass containers placed inside bamboo) to Paris and regularly corresponded with the Pasteur Institute. On July 30, 1894, Dr. E. Duclaux (1840-1904), Director of the Pasteur Institute, at a meeting of the Academy of Science in Paris, read excerpts from Yersin's letters announcing his discovery.

A controversy developed among bacteriologists as to who first identified the plague bacillus, Yersin or Kitasato. As Chairman of the Congress of the Far Eastern Medical Association in 1925, Dr. Kitasato conceded that Dr. Yersin was the discoverer of the cause for the dreaded disease.

Using the samples Yersin sent to Paris, Drs. Calmette and A. Borrel (1867-1936) began investigating the possibility of immunizing animals and developing an anti-plague serum and, after six-weeks, the results of animal studies produced hopeful results. However, anti-plague serum was ultimately proven to be ineffective.

Upon his return to Nha Trang from Hong Kong, Yersin was commissioned to establish a laboratory to develop an anti-plague serum for use in the Far East. In 1896, he was sent to Bombay, British India to test the anti-serum during an outbreak of bubonic plague there, and again it proved to be ineffective.

In 1897, in Nha Trang, Yersin began an institute to provide medical services for the local population, as well as a setting for his personal research.

Paul-Louis Simond found that infected rat fleas served as vectors for transmission of bubonic plague. Simond and Yersin presented a joint paper on plague at the 13th International Congress of Medicine in Paris in 1900. The French Government asked him to found a medical school in Hanoi, where he served as Director from 1902-1904. In 1904, the Bacteriology Institutes in Saigon and Nha Trang were changed from the Colonial Health Services to the Pasteur Institutes of Indonesia with Dr. Yersin serving as Director.

In 1915, he began growing *Cinchona ledgeriana* trees from seeds he had brought from Java. Eventually Indochina, especially Vietnam, became a large producer of the quinine-containing cinchona bark for malaria treatment.

In 1919, Yersin became Inspector of the Pasteur Institutes of Indochina; and upon his retirement in 1923, he was given the honorary title of Inspector General. France recognized his remarkable achievements by electing him to the Academy of Medicine, the Academy of Colonial Sciences and the Academy of Science. In 1934, Yersin received the high honor of being appointed Honorary Director of the Pasteur Institute of Paris and a member of the Scientific Council (a building constructed at the Pasteur Institute in the 1980s was named for him).

During his fifty years in Indochina, Yersin led a life of monastic simplicity, yet he always kept abreast of current events and the latest scientific research. Nha Trang remained his home throughout his life. His house was modest; however, he installed the most expensive instruments and equipment in his laboratory. The villagers and neighbors viewed him with the highest regard and called him Monsieur Nam.

Dr. Alexandre Yersin died at Nha Trang at the age of 79 in March 1943. The name "Yersin" remains on buildings, streets, parks, etc., in Nha Trang, Saigon (Ho Chi Minh City), Hanoi and other areas throughout Vietnam. His tomb at Suoi Dau is a national shrine, and his house in Nha Trang is a museum, named Lau Ong Nam.

In 1949, the French changed the genus name from *Pasteurella* (for Louis Pasteur) to *Yersina*. In the English-speaking world, a detailed analysis of the Yersin-Kitasato controversy was published in the *Bacteriological Reviews*; and in 1980, the genus and species names, *Yersinia pestis*, were officially entered in the *Approved List of Bacterial Names*, replacing, *Pasteurella pestis*.

All of the physicians in our BOQ shared the cost of two mama-sans. They were dependable, efficient, always pleasant and happy and addressed each of us as "Bac-si" (Doctor) or "Dai-uy" (Captain). They changed our beds when needed, made the beds each day, swept the floor, dusted the furniture and polished our boots. For this work, we collectively paid each of them 4,000 piasters a month ($35-$38). Lan was tall and thin, while Mai was shorter and slightly heavier. Both of their husbands were in the Vietnamese Military. Lan's husband was a sergeant in the South Vietnamese Air Force, and Mai's husband was with an ARVN unit. They both had children, but I have forgotten the number or their names. In January 1967, my wife sent me photographs of our children playing in the snow. As I sat looking at the pictures, Lan and Mai walked by, and I showed the pictures to them. They could not speak English, but I was able to make them understand

that this was my family. They finally made me understand that they had never seen snow but that they knew what it was. They would touch their finger to the snow in the picture, jerk it back; act like they were shivering and make a noise like "Brrr." Some of us paid them extra to wash and iron our clothes; in fact, Lan's husband, Sgt. Dinh, frequently was the one who came by to pick up the laundry. I have often wondered if they were killed, imprisoned, or were able to escape when the NVA conquered the area and established the communist government.

While engaging an NVA unit near the Cambodian border, a platoon of the 4th Division became isolated and overrun in an ambush. They were taking heavy casualties and attempted to withdraw to rejoin their company. The radio operator sent a radio message for help, but reinforcements did not arrive in time to prevent a massacre. All in their platoon had been killed except for the 1st Lt. platoon leader and the radioman. The two wedged themselves back-to-back between two large rocks and continued fighting, hoping to stay alive until help arrived. The Lt. soon was killed, and the radio operator was hit, although not too seriously. He lay still and played dead.

The NVA checked all of the dead and began gathering the American weapons and equipment they wanted. When they came to the radio operator, although he kept his eyes closed and tried not to breathe, they quickly realized that he was still alive. The commander of the NVA unit directed one of his troops to pick him up and carry him with them. They cut the radio's microphone cord and bound his hands behind his back. One of the NVA picked him up and started carrying him back to Cambodia. Being too heavy to carry, however, he was soon dumped on the ground. As he lay on his back, he looked through slits in his eyelids and saw the NVA who had been carrying him reach down, take his 45 cal. pistol from the holster on his pistol belt, then stand over him pointing his own pistol at his head. Another NVA shouted something from a short distance away, and then he heard a shot and felt something sting along the side of his head. The NVA quickly left him for dead and headed back toward their Cambodian sanctuary. He lay very still, not daring to move until another U.S. platoon, arriving too late to provide support, reached the area. He

Lan, one of our mama-sans.

Mai, one of our mama-sans.

then called out to his buddies. They were startled since he was the only one alive. They immediately radioed for Dustoff, and he arrived at the 18th a short time later. He had sustained a glancing wound of his shoulder and posterior chest wall and had the 45 cal. wound along his left temple.

When he was relating his story to Maj. Brandt, a patient in a nearby bed was listening and chimed in, "But you guys told us to pull back." The radio operator responded, "Yeah, but not that damned far back."

It seems impossible that an infantryman trained in the use of firearms could have missed a stationary target only a few feet away. Had this young North Vietnamese man refused to follow orders to kill his helpless, unarmed opponent or in his haste had he simply missed thinking that he had hit his target? Was this event Omnipotently determined or did it simply reflect the vagaries of the battlefield? This young man was only one of a number of other wounded that we treated who played dead to narrowly escape death. One survivor had come face-to-face with an NVA on a jungle trail, but as he attempted to fire, his M-16 jammed. The NVA took careful aim at him, and as the American watched helplessly, expecting to be shot at any moment, the NVA's head suddenly exploded. His American buddy had fired just in time.

While at Ft. Gordon, Georgia on maneuvers, the instructors talked at length about and demonstrated for us Punji stakes, graphically describing the horrible wounds that resulted. Punji stakes were usually made of bamboo spikes sharpened to a point, whose tips were contaminated with animal or human feces. The Viet Cong placed them in concealed and camouflaged traps, hoping to inflict deep, penetrating wounds to unwary GIs who stepped on them. Fortunately, we saw relatively few of these wounds, but those we did treat required wide debridement and thorough irrigation to prevent the intended devastating, even life threatening, wounds.

Soon after arriving in Pleiku, some of us compiled standard order forms listing treatment protocols for malaria, Plasmodium falciparum and P. vivax. At times, we admitted thirty or more malaria patients per day. These standard orders saved a lot of time and effort that would have been needlessly wasted had we written complete orders on each patient. Any additional necessary orders, peculiar to a particular patient's needs, were simply added to the routine orders. Orders on other medical patients were individually written (i.e. patients with scrub typhus, pneumonia, dengue fever, dysentery, etc.). Orders on each surgical patient were individually written correlating with that particular patient's injury and condition.

Near the end of July or the first of August, a twenty-five or twenty-six year old sergeant was brought in by Dustoff, along with five or six other wounded. Their platoon had made contact with "Charlie" about twenty miles west of the 18th. The 3rd Brigade (25th Infantry Division) was maneuvering near the Ia Drang Valley close to Cambodia. As patients were brought into R & E, a physician would assume the responsibility of evaluating the next patient as they presented on a rotating basis. The sergeant was the patient that I began evaluating. From a short distance away, as his stretcher was carried into the room, I observed that he was

tachypnic (rapid breathing). As soon as his stretcher was placed on the stretcher stands, I felt his pulse and noted that he also had a tachycardia (rapid heart beat). The corpsman who took his blood pressure told me that it was low. I noted that his external jugular veins (neck veins) appeared to be slightly distended. His breath sounds were fairly normal on the right but somewhat diminished on the left. There was a small hole in the front of his jungle fatigues and as his top was cut away, I noted a small entrance wound in the left precordial (front mid-chest) area and a slightly larger wound in the infrascapular (below the shoulder blade) region on his left back where the bullet exited. I do not know the caliber or type of weapon used, but the wounds were too small for it to have been an AK-47. He was obtunded and moaning occasionally, but was neither awake nor comatose. Oxygen was started immediately, and blood was drawn for a type and cross-match. An Hct was requested, while I began doing a cut down on his ankle to start an IV. I called across the aisle to Tony Lindem, M.D., a vascular and thoracic surgeon, who was evaluating a leg wound on another patient, and asked him to let someone else take that case because this patient had a cardiac tamponade (increased pressure in the pericardial sac compressing the heart, preventing normal heart function) and needed to go to surgery immediately. After opening the patient's chest we quickly suctioned the blood from the pleural space, and the small hole in the pericardium (sac around the heart) was enlarged, exposing the heart. The bullet had penetrated the heart, but there was no bleeding from the myocardium (heart muscle). The bullet had torn away a portion of the wall of the left anterior descending artery (the main artery running diagonally downward across the front of the heart, a very critical artery) supplying the anteroinferior (lower front) portion of the myocardium.

Repeated attempts at suturing the defect in the artery were unsuccessful. The beating of the heart caused the sutures to tear through the wall of the artery when we attempted to tie them. Two other surgeons joined us and attempted to close the defect but were also unsuccessful. We were infusing blood as rapidly as possible and were barely able to maintain his blood pressure. A graft or patch would have presented identical suturing problems. At that point our only choice was to tie off the artery, resulting in an iatrogenically induced (caused by a physician) myocardial infarction (MI=heart attack). By doing this, we postponed an immediate certain death, hoping he would survive the massive heart attack. Obviously, we did not have equipment for cardiopulmonary bypass surgery or hypothermia and did not, at that time, even have a defibrillator.

He tolerated the surgery well and went to the post-op ward in stable condition. At his age, his body had not formed any collateral circulation. He began very limited ambulation on the third day but was kept mostly on bed rest. An EKG documented his MI. He experienced no cardiac pain or shortness of breath. A nurse found him dead in bed on the morning of the fifth day. His death probably resulted from a rupture of the weakened heart muscle.

Late one afternoon, while I was in R & E admitting the last of eight or ten malaria patients, Dustoff brought in a young man with abdominal pain. His pain had begun about twenty-four hours earlier and had slowly, but progressively, worsened. He had a very low- grade fever and had not felt bad until his pain began. He was experiencing slight nausea, but no vomiting or diarrhea. He did give a history that about two months earlier, after eating in a local restaurant in Pleiku, he had had a few days of cramping and diarrhea. When I checked his abdomen he had mild voluntary guarding and tenderness in his periumbilical (navel area) region and right lateral abdomen. The remainder of his examination was normal or negative. His WBC (white blood count) was only slightly elevated. I admitted him to the surgical ward, started an IV and made him NPO (nothing by mouth). His pain was mild enough that he did not require medication for pain relief. After checking him again on the ward a short time later, I went to the Mess Hall for supper. I joined Bob Hewitt, M.D., who was already eating, and told him that I had admitted a young man with probable early appendicitis or an amebic abscess of the liver and asked him to stop and evaluate the patient after supper. When we had finished eating, I accompanied Bob to the ward as he examined the patient. He agreed that he probably did have an early acute appendicitis. The plan was to repeat the WBC in the morning, and we left instructions with the nurse to monitor him closely during the night and to let us know if his symptoms changed or his condition deteriorated. There were no new arrivals at the hospital, so we walked up the hill to our BOQ. I read for a while and, about 9 p.m., decided to go back down to the hospital and check on him. He was slightly uncomfortable, but his condition had not changed significantly. Near the end of my examination, I pressed firmly on his abdomen and quickly withdrew my hands to illicit rebound tenderness or other localizing signs. As soon as I withdrew my hands, the patient immediately said, "Doc, you cured my pain—it's all gone." He thought that I had worked a miracle; however, I knew that most likely either his appendix or liver abscess had ruptured. I told a corpsman to notify Dr. Hewitt that we needed to go ahead and operate. I also explained the circumstances to the patient that, although his pain had subsided, his improved symptoms were transient and that his life would be in jeopardy if we did not operate. At surgery, we discovered a ruptured hepatic (liver) abscess. The content from the abscess was sterile, whitish-yellow of creamy pudding-like consistency rather than the darker, thicker greenish avocado-paste consistency described in textbooks. The color and consistency of the abscess' contents apparently depended on the age or duration of the abscess. The ones that we saw were all of short duration. He probably became infected by consuming food contaminated with *Entamoeba histolytica* (Phylum Protozoa) at a Pleiku restaurant two months earlier. This was the first amebic abscess of the liver that we encountered at the 18th; however, others were seen throughout the ensuing year.

He did well postoperatively and received medication to eliminate any remaining parasites. We instructed him never to eat food or drink water in a local restaurant, to drink soft drinks or beer only if he opened the bottle or can himself and not to use ice cubes in coke, tea, water, etc.

Toward the end of August, during the final days of Paul Revere II, a sergeant with the 3rd Brigade (25th Infantry Division) was brought to the 18th by Dustoff with a gunshot wound (GSW). His platoon had been overrun by NVA. Most members of the platoon were killed. When he was wounded, he fell among the bodies of his dead friends. As the NVA troops swarmed the area, he lay still and played dead. First, they took his weapon (M-16) and then proceeded on pursuing the retreating U.S. troops. After a few minutes, another NVA stopped and removed his watch and ring. Soon the Americans regrouped and counter-attacked. As the retreating NVA again passed the area where he lay, someone paused long enough to take his wallet and his dog tag. Quickly, the Americans overtook the area and routed the enemy. At that point, he called out to a medic who bandaged his wounds and, although weakened by blood loss, was able to hobble with the medic's assistance, back to the nearby LZ. A radio operator called in Dustoff to pick him up along with four or five other casualties. They were quickly loaded and within about twenty minutes were in the R & E at the 18th. At surgery, he was found to have a thrombosed femoral artery. A saphenous vein graft was inserted to replace the resected portion of the artery. The circulation to his leg was fully restored. Postoperatively, he did well without complications and was evacuated to Qui Nhon on the third day. He told us about his ordeal and described the associated fear and his final acceptance of an almost certain impending and imminent death. He said he had never thought seriously about death before, although he had been in combat numerous times. "You always realize it could happen, but I always told myself it wouldn't happen to me." He went on to say, "I prayed more than I ever had before. It sure caused me to get my priorities straight." He added, "The hardest part was laying still and not attempting to defend myself." I feel certain that he retained vivid memories of that day throughout his entire life.

One case of carcinoid of the appendix was seen. The patient presented with classical, clinical symptoms of acute appendicitis. I assisted Bob Hewitt, M.D., with the surgery. The appendix was approximately 2-3 times as long and about 3-4 times its usual diameter. After surgery, we opened the appendix longitudinally and from the gross appearance it appeared to be carcinoid; however,

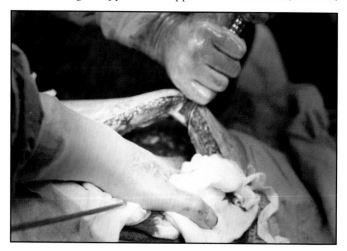

View into the right upper abdominal cavity toward the liver showing the yellowish, creamy contents of a ruptured liver abscess resulting from the intestinal parasite, Entamoeba histolytica.

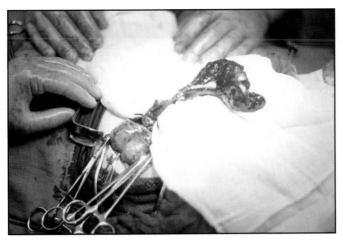

Secum of colon visible with large inflamed appendix.

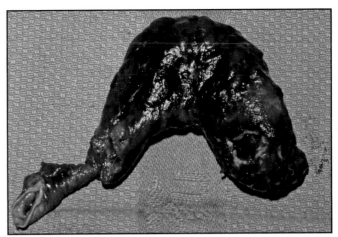

Appendix removed.

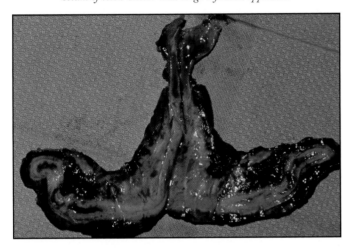

Appendix sectioned longitudinally revealing a carcinoid tumor. There was no evidence of intra-abdominal metastasis.

we did not know definitively until we received a report from the U.S. Army Pathology Laboratory in Japan a few weeks later. There was no evidence of metastasis (spread) in the patient. Over 90% of these low-grade neoplasms (cancers) occur in the appendix, and the remainder are located chiefly in the ileum (distal small bowel) but may occur anywhere throughout the GI tract. Those that have metastasized to the liver frequently secrete serotonin and large quantities of 5-hydroxyindoleacetic acid that results in flushing and irregular mottling of the skin, diarrhea, bronchial spasm and rarely heart valve involvement. These symptoms are referred to as the "carcinoid syndrome."

So many other stories could be told about our experiences during the year we were with the 18th Surgical Hospital (MA) at Pleiku. Each individual member could perhaps relate a hundred interesting events that they remember. Innumerable anecdotes of narrow escapes and harrowing experiences could be described. There are multitudinous, unreported memories that could be recalled and recorded, although among them are those unpleasant and unwanted memories which are intentionally left untold.

By the last part of May, the monsoon rains had returned in full force. Bob Hewitt, M.D., recorded in his diary, "It pours torrents of rain all night, and the wind sounds as if the roof is about to blow off." Then it drizzles all day with intermittent torrents."

Sam Gillis, M.D., left the 18th on emergency leave on Friday, February 17, 1967. The Red Cross notified him that his son was critically ill. It turned out that the illness was not as serious as the initial diagnosis had presumed.

Oscar Valerio, M.D., left for home on Wednesday, May 24, soon after I returned from Bangkok and Soc Trang. Everyone became apprehensive a few days before leaving country. It was called the "short timers syndrome." Gene Chap, M.D., left on Friday, June 2, for Cam Ranh Bay and then for the States on Saturday, June 3. The eight remaining original Ft. Gordon physicians left the 18th within three or four days of each other around the third week of June, except Tony Lindem, M.D., who left about the first of June since he had gone over with the advance party.

Lt. Col. Cenac left for CONUS on Sunday, May 28, 1967. The physicians contributed to a fund to buy him a going-away gift. He had not purchased a reel-to-reel tape deck during the year, so everyone decided that that would be an appropriate gift. Maj. Clarke Brandt was able to obtain one for us through his friend at a PX. At Saturday night's farewell party, Tony Lindem, M.D., presented it to him. The evening was a pleasant occasion, and he was both surprised and pleased with the gift.

We were fortunate to have had Lt. Col. Cenac as our CO. He was a fair and decent individual, possessing both character and integrity, and was a man of his word. He was even-tempered and exhibited his leadership skills in an efficient and low-key manner. He was always gracious and thoughtful of others, and his judgments were well thought through and logical.

Soon after arriving at Pleiku, at a physicians' staff meeting, Lt. Col. Cenac layed out for us his ideas and expectations. We reciprocated by giving him our thoughts. Everyone was candid, honest and straightforward in their comments with each other. In our discussions, we reminded him that each of us had been drafted from our residences or private practices and sent to Vietnam for one purpose—to treat the sick and wounded, and that in fulfilling this Hippocratic mission, we were simultaneously serving our country and meeting our military obligations. We stressed that we sought no promotions, individual recognition, decorations or awards and were unconcerned about efficiency reports. Since he was Regular Army, with a goal toward a successful military career,

Monsoon rain clouds approaching from Cambodia.

Jerry W. Martin, M.D. at 25th Division PX. The monsoon rains "melted" the cardboard/paper cases allowing cans of soda and beer to scatter.

Left to right: Jerry W. Martin, M.D. and Sam Gillis, M.D.

we pledged that through our collaborative efforts, we would always strive to make him, as CO, look good, thus providing him with an outstanding efficiency report, which for him, was necessary. While at Ft. Gordon, except while working in the clinics, we had already been exposed to military inefficiency. All of the military maneuvers, mock casualty exercises, visits to replicas of Montagnard villages, etc., had been a complete waste of time and effort; and the only thing it achieved was in meeting some military requirement.

When the first chopper landed at the 18th with the first wounded patients, we automatically tossed "all that stuff" out the window and immediately began triaging and treating the casualties, as we instinctively knew how to do, based on our medical/surgical training and previous experiences.

Lt. Col. Cenac was wise enough to allow us the latitude to perform at our medical and surgical best, unencumbered by unnecessary and unreasonable military restrictions, regulations and protocols, while guiding us and keeping us within appropriate and acceptable military parameters. He always supported us in our work. As a result we achieved enviable results. During our year at Pleiku, we evaluated and treated more acute combat casualties than any other surgical hospital, or possibly all others combined. All of the physicians had an unreserved respect for each other and for Lt. Col. Cenac, which he always reciprocated.

Since we all planned to resume our careers, which the draft had interrupted, our efforts were always cooperative without any thought toward self-aggrandizement or personal gain. We all pitched in to the extent necessary to serve the needs of our patients and to meet the exigencies as they presented to us.

During my time in the military, I did not experience or even witness, another unit that even came close to exhibiting the voluntary cooperative spirit, camaraderie and esprit de corps that existed among the original group of physicians at the 18th Surgical Hospital (MA) in Pleiku, and this attitude permeated throughout the entire unit. I never heard a word spoken harshly or angrily among the physicians or toward the nurses or EMs, either openly or privately. This military-medical milieu resulted because of Lt. Col. Cenac's support and guidance, because of the willingness of the physicians and nurses to work unselfishly together and because of the shared mutual respect we had for each other. Friends never

have difficulty working unselfishly together in a unified mission when they seek to accomplish a common goal, if it is done without any desire for personal accolades.

Unfortunately, this esprit de corps did not long continue after Lt. Col. Cenac's departure. A sub-area Surgeon had not been designated; however, Lt. Col. Welch, CO of the 71st Evacuation Hospital, "appointed" himself as temporary CO of the 18th, pending the arrival of Lt. Col. Kaku. Maj. Brandt recorded in his book, "It wasn't but fifteen minutes (after Lt. Col. Cenac left) when Welch came into the headquarters, obviously upset. He started ragging on me, and I had no idea why he was so upset. In jest, I said, 'What's wrong, didn't I get Cenac's name off the front gate fast enough?' Welch practically shouted, 'That's right! He's been gone fifteen minutes and his damned name is still up there!' I couldn't believe what I was hearing! Well, maybe a little since he was such a despised jerk, but making a federal case over a sign within fifteen minutes of Cenac's leaving was just too much." The deterioration obviously began immediately. Those of us who were the original physicians remained at the 18th until our rotation back to the U.S., but to his credit, Lt. Col. Welch did not bother us. Beginning on May 26th, all medical cases were admitted to the 71st Evac, and the medical ward at the 18th was closed. Because all surgical cases continued to be done at the 18th, we were still very busy. One could not help feeling revulsion and extreme repugnance observing an individual, as insecure and frustrated as Lt. Col. Welch must have been, reacting in such a paranoid and egomaniacal way. I would have hated to have been assigned to the 71st Evac, and felt sorry for those who were.

In early June, many of the EM began leaving for home. Many of the older medics who had served in Korea as well as Vietnam, voluntarily stated that the 18th had the most cooperative, cohesive, congenial, outstanding and dedicated group of physicians of any hospital they had been involved with. The medics had certainly been a dedicated, highly competent group and their work was very commendable.

On the evening of June 2, we received four Americans whose tank was hit by an NVA rocket near Cambodia. With the monsoons intensifying, the worsening mud caused tanks to have difficulty maneuvering. I believe these were the first, and only, casualties involving a tank crew that we saw while at the 18th.

Col. Bonneaux had arranged for me to accompany an Air Force flight to Sydney, Australia for five days, leaving on Friday, June 9.

I had to cancel that trip because we began getting casualties early that morning. The enemy mortared nearby Artillery Hill, and we received forty American wounded and eight severely wounded Montagnards. Most of the mortars landed in a Montagnard training camp, killing thirty-five and injuring seventy-five more. We operated all day and all night. On June 11, two or three of us visited Artillery Hill to view the damage and talk with some of those stationed there.

The 18th Surgical Hospital (MA) had meager laboratory facilities, which resulted in very limited capabilities. Malaria smears were done usually many times per day and type and x-match for blood transfusions were done frequently. Total white blood counts (WBC) and differential counts were done. Hematocrits (Hct) were also available. Sputum smears could be done to assist us, along with chest X-rays, in differentiating between bacterial and viral pneumonia. Blood sugars were not done. However, we had urine dip sticks that allowed us to screen the urine, and, if it tested strongly positive, we at least could make the presumptive diagnosis of diabetes mellitus (Gene Chap, M.D., had physician friends in the States send the dip sticks, the military did not supply them). Electrolytes, bilirubin, liver function studies, antibody titers etc., could not be done. VDRLs could be done to test for syphilis, and uretheral discharge smears were done to document gonorrhea. Dengue was presumptively diagnosed when a patient had a low WBC, severe aching and joint pains and fever spikes occurring on alternate days giving the typical "saddle curve" on the temperature chart. Scrub typhus was diagnosed by noting an eschar (scab) and erythemia (redness) on the skin. When patients arrived with jaundice, we generally considered the diagnosis to be hepatitis if their malaria smears were negative. We listed our presumptive

Artillery Hill with living quarters and statue on top.

and differential diagnosis on the patients' charts before transfer, trusting that the ultimate definitive diagnosis would be made at the evacuation hospitals, or even later in Japan, Manila or the U.S.

In the evenings we sometimes amused ourselves by listening to "Freedom Radio" or "Liberation Radio." These were thirty-minute propaganda broadcasts from Peking ("Peking Polly") or Hanoi ("Hanoi Hannah"). Trinh Thi Ngo joined the Voice of Vietnam in 1955 after the communists under Ho Chi Minh defeated the French at Dien Bien Phu. She was selected as an announcer on the radio's new English-language shortwave service, broadcasting outside of the country. She had learned English, in addition to French and her native Vietnamese, by attending private schools and employing private tutors during the early 1950s. "I always preferred American movies to French films. The French talk too much. There was more action in American movies. I remember *Gone With the Wind* with Clark Gable and Vivien Leigh. It was so popular in Hanoi. I remember we took bread and sausages with us because it was a long film."

The Americans dubbed her "Hanoi Hanna," the Vietnam War's counterpart to World War II's "Tokyo Rose." The alias she used when broadcasting was Thu Huong (meaning, Autumn Fragrance). She spoke English without an accent and in a clear, soft voice. "I was not political, I was patriotic. I wanted to join the Voice of Vietnam because it was a good opportunity to help my country." Her broadcasts took an anti-American turn after the first American troops landed in South Vietnam in 1965. The scripts for the programs were written by North Vietnamese Army personnel and sanctioned by the Hanoi Government. "I was never tempted to alter a word, no matter how strident the tone. I agreed with the scripts. We were trying to make the Americans understand that it was not right for them to be in Vietnam, that they were an aggressor, that this was a problem for the Vietnamese to sort out."

She often read clippings from American magazines and newspapers about anti-war demonstrations in the U.S. and occasionally read the names of GIs who had recently been killed in action. "We wanted to make them a little bit sad." However, she said she never felt aggression or anger toward the Americans as a people except during the 1972 Christmas bombing of Hanoi. "When the bombs came, I did feel angry. To the Vietnamese, Hanoi is sacred ground. But even then, when I spoke to the GIs I tried always to be calm."

After Saigon was captured in 1975, she and her husband, a retired engineer originally from South Vietnam (a communist since his college days), moved to Ho Chi Minh City where she worked in Vietnamese television. Their home was near the former Presidential Palace ("den of the puppets").

During early June the 173rd Airborne, the 101st Airborne and the 1st Cavalry moved back into the Pleiku area. We were very much aware, even before any intelligence briefings, that something big was about to happen from Pleiku westward to Cambodia. On June 16, the 18th began receiving numerous casualties, almost all of which were shrapnel wounds. I helped with an abdominal wound that required a laparotomy and resection of a segment of small bowel, as well as a splenectomy. That was my last surgical procedure in Vietnam.

Finally, the long anticipated day arrived. My DD 214 lists the duration of my tour in Vietnam as eleven months and twenty-four days. I arrived in Saigon on Friday, June 24, 1966, and left for home on Sunday, June 18, 1967. I left New Pleiku Airport in the early afternoon on June 17, and flew by C-130 to Cam Ranh Bay. Everyone from our area going on R and R or returning to CONUS went through the Processing Center at the 510 Replacement Company, 22nd Replacement Battalion located in Cam Ranh Bay. After checking in and completing the paperwork, I was assigned to a BOQ in a Tropical Shell building. The latrine and showers were located in an adjacent building. The Mess Hall was only three or four buildings away. The 6th Convalescence Center was located nearby, so I spent a little time there touring their facilities. About nine a.m. the next morning, those of us returning to the States gathered at the Processing Center and boarded an Air Force bus, which transported us to the passenger terminal at the Cam Ranh Airport. We boarded a Pan Am (Boeing 707) chartered commercial flight ("Freedom Bird") and were soon airborne headed for Tokyo, Japan.

As the plane left the ground, my last contact with the Republic of Vietnam ended. As we rapidly gained altitude my thoughts and emotions also soared. I was engulfed by a sense of freedom, as if being released from a year's imprisonment. The exhilaration of this "freedom" brought the anticipation of being reunited with family and friends, but superimposed were those fresh memories of the brutality and often finality of war.

The words of Henry Van Dyke's poem, *America For Me*, came to mind:

> So it's home again, home again, America for me! My heart is turning home again, and there I long to be, In the land of youth and freedom beyond the ocean bars, Where the air is full of sunlight and flag is full of stars.

As elated as I was, my thoughts drifted back to a young man lying on a stretcher one day in R & E at the 18th awaiting evacuation. I often went from stretcher to stretcher and asked the patients if they were in pain or if they needed anything. I came upon one patient who asked if I would light him a cigarette. I was momentarily taken back, but quickly realized that he was a quadriplegic. A shrapnel fragment had fractured two vertebra and severed his spinal cord at about C-3—C-4, making it impossible for him to move anything below his neck. I did not smoke, but I bummed a cigarette and a light from someone and lit it for him. Obviously, I had to hold it and put it to his lips whenever he asked. Considering that his physical status would now make it difficult for him to handle his pulmonary secretions adequately, I suggested that he should give up smoking. His reply was, "Doc, what other pleasures do I have left?" I did not have a suitable answer to his poignant and cogent comment, which was more of a statement than a question. They soon came to carry him

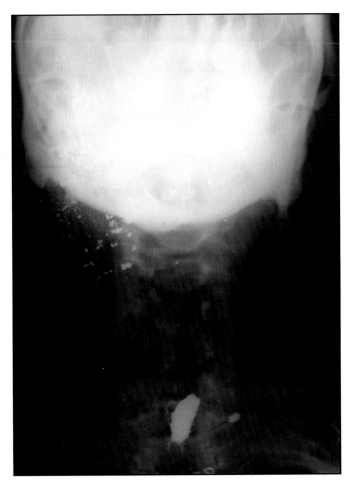

Shrapnel fragments at base of skull with large piece in spinal canal that severed the spinal cord at C-3 level, resulting in quadraplegia.

to the awaiting ambulance. As they lifted his stretcher, he took one last draw from the cigarette, turned his head toward me and said, "Thanks, Doc. At least I'm not going home in a black body bag." With that comment, he was gone. I said a silent prayer for him; then I, too, moved on to other patients. I realized that he had a very poor prognosis and a much- shortened life expectancy. He would face many difficult problems over the ensuing months and years. Among them were skin breakdown and decubitus, joint contractures, muscle wasting, and recurring urinary tract infections secondary to an indwelling suprapubic catheter. Over the years, I have thought of him hundreds of times and wondered if he died of pneumonia, septicemia, aspiration or some other cause.

Many good things had occurred during our year in Vietnam. Personal relationships had been forged, and lifelong friendships established. One cannot work closely with others for a year, laboring in a unified mission through difficult, trying, and even frightening conditions, sharing in the horrors and uncertainties of combat without having, at least to a degree, an inextricable intertwining of emotions, thoughts, expectations and fears. The opportunity for travel and the exposure to other cultures and customs had enriched each of our lives. Our endeavors were beneficial for our patients; the results of our work were personally gratifying; and our medical/surgical encounters were irreplaceable experiences that were professionally enhancing. Enmeshed in those feelings, however, were those unsolicited and non-repressable memories of the carnage and ravages of war that we had witnessed. My thoughts echoed Lincoln's words in his Second Inaugural Address: "Fondly do we hope—fervently do we pray—that this mighty scourge of war may speedily pass away."

"Freedom Bird" over the Pacific on flight home.

Flight over Pacific on "Freedom Bird."

127

I skimmed through a magazine before the stewardess served our lunch. After lunch I had a brief nap and was awakened by the "fasten seat belt" announcement, preparatory to landing in Tokyo.

We were at the Tokyo International Airport slightly over an hour and were allowed to deplane, but had to remain in the gate area to avoid renegotiating customs. Soon we began the fifteen and one-half hour trip to Seattle, Washington. Because we were moving against the sun's motion, the sun set and rose again quickly, resulting in a shortened night. When we crossed the International Date Line, we recaptured the day we had lost nearly a year ago, thus allowing us to arrive home the same day we left Vietnam.

It was raining when we landed at the Seattle-Tacoma International Airport at about 8 a.m. on June 18. My connecting flight to Nashville did not leave until about 10:30 a.m. Since my luggage had been checked through, I had no way of showering, shaving or changing clothes. While awaiting the flight, I stopped in a barbershop for a shave. The flight stopped in St. Louis for about thirty minutes, but we did not deplane. I arrived in Nashville about 4:30 pm CST where my wife, Jimmie, met me. The following day we drove to Western Kentucky to pick up our children, who were staying with their grandparents.

After a two-week leave, I reported to the hospital at Ft. Campbell, Kentucky (U.S. 3rd Army), about seventy miles from Bowling Green. When I reported in, the CO of the hospital was Col. Jules J. McNurney, M.C. He appointed me Director of the Out-Patient Clinic. Because I had served in Vietnam, I did not have to work on weekends. I made up the work schedule, which he approved. I left Bowling Green each Monday morning early enough to arrive for the nine a.m. clinic. I stayed in a BOQ at Ft. Campbell on Monday, Tuesday and Wednesday nights, then returned to Bowling Green after the last clinic on Thursday, and remained home with my family until the next Monday morning. After his retirement, Dr. McNurney lived in Hopkinsville, Kentucky, and I saw him again two or three times at medical meetings after I returned to practice. I was at Ft. Campbell from Wednesday, July 5 until my Honorable Discharge on Monday, December 11, 1967.

As we returned to the U.S., the physicians that had taken the 18th Surgical Hospital (MA) to Vietnam each went our separate ways to new assignments and to reunite with our families; however, we have stayed in touch through visits, telephone calls, correspondence and reunions.

My former associate, L. Jack Scott, M.D., and I had to contact our U.S. Senator, John Sherman Cooper (R.-KY), because the military attempted to draft Dr. Scott while I was in Vietnam, which would have destroyed our practice. Through Sen. Cooper's efforts, Dr. Scott was granted a six-month deferment, and I was granted a six-week early release. As soon as I was discharged, I resumed practicing, and Dr. Scott was drafted almost immediately. Since I had practiced for a year and one-half before the draft, it was almost as if I had never been away.

In November 1967, a few weeks before my discharge, I received a call from Dr. Robert Mills, President of Georgetown College (Georgetown, Kentucky), asking me to participate in a three-day Symposium on Southeast Asia ("Southeast Asia—A Christian Dilemma") in January 1968 during the College's World Awareness Week. He became aware of my Vietnam experiences through friends and alumni who had listened to my weekly radio programs recorded in Vietnam and broadcast over radio station WKCT in Bowling Green.

At 10 a.m. on Tuesday, January 30, 1968, I presented an hour-long lecture, *Whither We Are Tending*, to an audience of between 300-400 faculty and students. After lunch, I participated in a panel discussion with the other guest lecturers to answer questions from the conference attendees. Later, I spoke at Western Kentucky University in Bowling Green to a slightly larger audience, discussing the same material and answering similar questions. For many years, I spoke annually at Alpha Epsilon Delta, the honor pre-med fraternity at WKU, where I showed slides of war wounds and talked about Vietnam. I made similar presentations at various civic and church groups, medical meetings and literary clubs.

About the time the original group of physicians left country, military activities in the Central Highlands increased, especially west and north of Pleiku. The 71st Evacuation Hospital still did not have any surgeons, only internists and general medical officers. All medical cases were going there, while all surgical cases were still being routed to the 18th. Just one week after I left, the 503rd Infantry of the 173rd Airborne Brigade sustained thirty-five casualties, and the 4th Division sustained over thirty casualties. Both units were ambushed in different locations, but in both instances, the enemy toll was extremely high. While many had multiple wounds, only a few were critical.

Two days later, Saturday, June 24, the 173rd took heavy casualties, probably the heaviest they had sustained during the war. It seemed that real progress was not being achieved in the Central Highlands. The NVA were repeatedly decimated and routed, but they kept returning from their sanctuaries in Cambodia. The war would have ended quickly had the U.S. mounted a sudden massive attack on those sanctuaries, while simultaneously bombing the oil storage, power stations, dams, key railroad terminals, bridges and harbors in the North. However, decisions made by the U.S. Congress and the President often thwarted military efforts.

The military activities continued into July, then decreased somewhat as the monsoon rains returned in force. Sometimes the temporary lull or decrease in the flow of casualties to the 18th was because the heavy rains and/or the heavy fighting prevented Dustoff from quickly evacuating the wounded. On Friday, July 7, the 173rd sustained twenty more casualties.

On Wednesday, July 12, at about 4 p.m., wounded from the 4th Division began arriving and continued into the next day. The remainder of July was slower, only a small steady stream of wounded, until July 27-29, when the 173rd and 4th Division took heavy casualties again. By August 1, the 173rd had moved into the Duc Co area. Two surgeons at the 18th were admitted to the 71st Evacuation Hospital with pneumonia, so it was fortunate that the fighting remained light.

On Monday, August 7, at the Pleiku Medical Association meeting, South Vietnamese physicians discussed Viet Cong and NVA medical and surgical treatments. They used cobwebs to aid in blood clotting of wounds. Leeches were used to evacuate hematomas (blood clots), and maggots were used to help debride dead and badly damaged tissue. Their facilities in the jungle were often in caves or in excavated tunnels.

The casualty flow increased significantly during mid-August and then tapered off again. Some of the wounds resulted because of "friendly fire," mostly misdirected artillery or air support.

Charleton Heston visited the 18th Surgical Hospital (MA) on Sunday, September 10. Everyone found him to be a most gracious and interesting individual who was sincerely concerned about the welfare of the patients.

On September 14, a Montagnard was admitted to the 18th with tetanus. His progress was slow; however, his condition progressively improved, and he ultimately recovered. The same week, a GI was treated for a Bamboo Viper snake bite, the third in one week. During the year, there were only two cobra bites treated at the 18th.

On September 22, the 18th Surgical Hospital (MA)'s CO, Lt. Col. Michio Kaku (arrived July 23) and his XO, Maj. Robert A. Massey (replaced Maj. Clarke Brandt, July 18) received word that if a MUST (Mobile Unit, Self-contained, Transportable; manufactured by the Garrett Corp.) unit could be obtained in November, then the 18th Surgical Hospital (MA) would become the 18th Surgical Hospital (MUST) and would either move north to Chu Lai in CTZ I, or possibly to the Delta. If a MUST unit was not available, then the 18th would probably go to An Khe in late November (in April, the 2nd Surgical hospital had already moved from An Khe to Chu Lai). The 55th Medical Group further directed that, in addition to all medical patients, all

minor wounds were now to go to the 71st Evacuation Hospital, and the 18th would continue receiving the seriously wounded. From mid-September through early October, the casualty flow slowed significantly. The NVA had pulled back into Cambodia, apparently waiting to see what would develop in regard to the political situation and the social unrest in the U.S.

A MUST hospital consists of "buildings" which are inflatable. There already were two MUST hospitals in South Vietnam, the 3rd Surgical Hospital and the 45th Surgical Hospital.

A MUST hospital has multiple arched air tubes attached together that can be inflated in about 30-40 minutes by an air compressor run by a turbine engine. If alternate tubes are punctured during an attack, it would still remain standing and functional; however, if more tubes are punctured then the unit could, and probably would, eventually collapse. For transportation, the unit was collapsed and placed into a large aluminum, shipping container. The hospital complex consisted of a surgical suite, recovery room and postoperative wards. The turbine engine provided electrical power for the vacuum, air pressure, hot air heating, water pumping and air conditioning. Should the engine become disabled during combat, the hospital would be rendered useless. MUST-equipped surgical hospitals were operated for a few years in Vietnam with mixed success. This type of hospital would have been great during World War II, when the hospitals had to move frequently with their divisions; however, the technology was not available then. Now with the technology available, this type of hospital was not practical, especially with Dustoff available for rapid evacuation of the wounded. Hospitals in a fixed location were able to provide more services and more comfort to the patients. Fixed units were usually in a more secure location, thus providing more safety for both the patients and hospital personnel.

Pleiku Medical Association meeting at ARVN Hospital. 1. Dr. McCloud (MACV) (left), 2. Jerry Rosenberg, M.D. (MILPHAP), 3. Lt. Col. Cenac, 4. a physician from the 4th Infantry Division, 5. Bob Hewitt, M.D. (right). All others are unknown.

In late September, the 18th Surgical Hospital (MA) received word that it would be awarded the Republic of Vietnam's Gallantry Cross Unit Citation (the appurtenances of the Gallantry Cross: Brigade, Regiment or Unit, Bronze Star; Division, Silver Star; Corps, Gold Star; Army or Armed Forces, Bronze Palm; 9 August 65-19 May 69, DAGO 59, 1969) for courage under fire against an armed enemy, as well as the U.S. Army's Meritorious Unit Commendation for the work we had done and the successes we had achieved during our year at Pleiku.

The Meritorious Unit Commendation was awarded by direction of the Secretary of the Army, DAGO 43, 1968:

THE 18TH SURGICAL HOSPITAL (MOBILE ARMY) AND ATTACHED UNIT: 240TH MEDICAL DETACHMENT (KF) with citation as follows:

> The 18th Surgical Hospital (Mobile Army) and its attached unit distinguished themselves in support of military operations in the Republic of Vietnam during the period 1 June 1966 to 14 October 1967. Shortly after arriving at Pleiku, Republic of Vietnam, the unit established the first operational hospital in the Central Highlands, immediately providing the area with much-needed medical support. Operating initially under tentage and later in a semipermanent facility, the Hospital provided the epitome of surgical care services to the combat and support troops operating in its area of responsibility despite being handicapped by not having its full complement of authorized equipment. Through the skill of the Hospital's surgeons and the advanced medical techniques being utilized, hundreds of wounded, both military and non-military, were operated on, with the result that numerous lives were saved and countless limbs preserved. The 18th Surgical Hospital (Mobile Army) not only provided surgical care, but the unit was augmented by other subordinate elements to provide a medical clinic as well. This organizational innovation was of great significance in that it partially relieved the division-level medical service of its cumbersome load. This multifaceted medical situation was met with the enthusiasm and diligence, which characterized the Hospital's unique overall performance. The exceptional professional treatment rendered by the Hospital in the Central Highlands fostered a warm rapport between personnel of the United States and the local populace. The remarkable proficiency and devotion to duty displayed by the members of the 18th Surgical Hospital (Mobile Army) are in keeping with the highest traditions of the military service and reflect distinct credit upon themselves and the Armed Forces of the United States.

On Monday, October 2, 1967, Brig. Gen. Collins, Commanding General of the 44th Medical Brigade informed Lt. Col. Kaku that the 18th would relocate and become a MUST unit.

On October 17, Bob Hewitt, M.D., received word that his paper on vascular injuries had been accepted for presentation at a Military Surgeon's Meeting from November 15-19 in Tokyo. That same day, Martha Raye visited the Pleiku area again and, that evening presented a show for the troops at nearby Camp Schmidt. (Camp Schmidt was named in honor of Maj. Richard Herman Schmidt of Scranton, Pennsylvania, Civil Affairs Officer, Qui Nhon Support Command. On May 17, 1966, he and four enlisted men delivered health items to villagers of Phy My in Binh Dinh Province. On their return to Qui Nhon, the convoy was ambushed by the Viet Cong. Maj. Schmidt was posthumously awarded the Silver Star for valor in a ceremony on June 1, 1966, and Camp Schmidt, headquarters for the 45th General Support Group, was dedicated November 3, 1966. Camp Schmidt was located on Hwy. 19 between II Corps headquarters and Artillery Hill.)

Bob Hewitt, M.D., CO of the 240th Medical Detachment (Surgical K Team) received orders on Sunday, October 22, for the transfer of his detachment to the 71st Evacuation Hospital. The transfer of all equipment was finalized on Wednesday, November 1. The 18th Surgical Hospital (MA) closed at Pleiku on Monday, October 23, 1967, in preparation for air movement to Long Binh, only a few miles north of Saigon in CTZ III near an area referred to as the Iron Triangle.

About 11 p.m. on Friday, October 27, the NVA hit the Pleiku area with sixty rounds of Russian-made 122-mm rockets. One round hit the ARVN Hospital adjacent to the 18th, destroying a portion of the roof. Shrapnel fragments from the explosion hit the Paradise Lost Club and other areas of the recently closed 18th (some physicians and a few other military personnel [chopper pilots] were still billeted in the BOQ). The rockets hit all around the Air Force Officers Club, Mars Station (communication center) and MACV-CTZ II Headquarters, but no real damage was done. The 71st Evacuation Hospital was not hit. Only ten individuals sustained injuries during the attack, and these were only minor wounds. They were apparently attempting to hit the New Pleiku Air Base, the Page Communications complex, Artillery Hill and other strategic locations. Luckily, a Phantom F-4 from Cam Ranh was in the air over Pleiku and witnessed the flash at the sight where the rockets were fired. The pilot quickly received radio confirmation and then blasted the area with rockets, causing the VC and NVA to flee. U.S. artillery and air support from the New Pleiku Air Base responded immediately. An NVA Captain who had defected to the U.S. earlier that same day said that another attack had been planned to hit the area the next night. He also revealed the hiding place where seventy-five more rockets were cached. It must have taken them weeks to carry 135 rockets from North Vietnam down the Ho Chi Minh Trail to the Pleiku area.

By early November, the 173rd Brigade and the 4th Infantry Division had moved into the Dak To area, a border outpost manned by Montagnards and U.S. Army Special Forces (Kontum Province) about forty-five miles NNW of Pleiku and about fifteen-twenty miles NW of Kontum. From November 4-13, a steady flow of seriously wounded were evacuated to the 71st Evacuation Hospital (more than 500 total, over 200 during the first four days and about 200 more on November 12). The NVA broke off contact at about 7 pm on November 13. A sweeping operation of the area (Operation MacArthur) under the command of Maj. Gen. Peers, involving the entire 4th Division, all of the 173rd Brigade, a portion of the 1st Air Cavalry Division and a Brigade of ARVN, continued for many days.

On November 18, the 173rd Airborne Brigade engaged the NVA's 1st Infantry Division's 66th Regiment, and both sides sustained heavy casualties. Two companies of the 173rd Brigade's 503rd Regiment were wiped out the next day, and the fighting was so fierce that the wounded could not be evacuated for many hours. It was estimated that there were 4,000 NVA fighting in the Dak To battle. Their 1st Infantry Division's Headquarters (24th Regiment, 32nd Regiment, 66th Regiment and the 174th Regiment) was safely situated in Cambodia. The U.S. should have been bombing and attacking those reserve forces in Cambodia and Laos from the onset. The American troops in Vietnam were generally not anti-war, but they gradually came to disagree with the prosecution of the war. In our political system, civilian politicians must be the ones to decide if a war is to be fought, but once that decision is made, the management of the war must be left to military expertise with Congressional oversight, but without political meddling.

The Battle of Dak To resulted in 376 Americans killed in action (KIA) and 1,441 wounded. The NVA sustained 1,445 KIA and about 2,500 wounded.

The 173rd Airborne Brigade's 503rd Regiment was the same unit as the 503rd Parachute Infantry Regiment who arrived at Port Moresby, New Guinea from Australia on Sunday, September 5, 1943. They were at Dobodura, Hollandia, Wakde, Biak and Geelvink Bay. In September 1944, the unit was reinforced by the 462nd Parachute Field Artillery Battalion and the 161st Parachute Engineer Battalion, and its name was changed to the 503rd Parachute Regimental Combat Team (RCT), a designation it retained for the remainder of World War II. In November, it was shipped to Leyte. On Friday, February 16, 1945, the 503rd RCT left Mindoro Island for the assault of Corregidor Island. The 18th Portable Surgical Hospital (Reinforced) was a part of the 503rd Parachute RCT assigned to the 3rd Battalion, 24th Infantry Division (the combined force was referred to as the "Rock Force"). It is ironic that the 18th Portable Surgical Hospital (Reinforced) supported the 503rd Parachute RCT at "Topside" on Corregidor, Philippine Islands; and then twenty-two years later, the 18th Surgical Hospital (MA) at Pleiku supported the 503rd Infantry Regiment of the 173rd Airborne Brigade in the Central Highlands, Republic of Vietnam.

LONG BINH—LAI KHE

The first flight carrying the 18th Surgical Hospital, (MA) to Long Binh departed Pleiku at 6:30 pm on Wednesday, November 15. A total of seventeen flights were required to move all personnel and equipment to Long Binh, the last one leaving on Friday, November 17, 1967.

While in Long Binh, the unit married-up with its MUST elements, and a two-week period of intensive training was conducted to familiarize all personnel in the establishment of a MUST unit. Officers and enlisted personnel were trained in erecting, inflating, loading, transporting and off-loading of MUST equipment. During the final days of this training period, an Advanced Party was dispatched to commence the process of establishing the 18th Surgical Hospital (MUST) in the Lai Khe area to support the 1st Infantry Division.

Lai Khe was located on Hwy. 13 at the 1st Infantry Division's Base Camp about twenty miles north of Saigon and about thirty-five miles south of An Loc, in Binh Duong Province.

Bob Hewitt, M.D., left for CONUS on Tuesday, December 5. Mike Belinson, M.D., left Vietnam at approximately the same time. They were the last physicians who worked at the 18th Surgical Hospital (MA) at Pleiku to leave country. Probably the last officer to leave Vietnam who had worked at the 18th was Capt. Clive "Skip" Winslow, a Certified Registered Nurse Anesthetist (CRNA). He arrived in Pleiku in January 1967 and was assigned to the 71st Evacuation Hospital with temporary duty orders (TDY) for the 18th. He went to the 71st when the 18th closed at Pleiku and then returned to CONUS in January 1968.

Left to right: Pfc. Martin Casarez and Sp/5 Al Garcia standing at a bunker near the showers at Lai Khe.

Showers and bunkers at Lai Khe.

Med-Evac Unit (Dustoff) at 18th Surgical Hospital (MUST) at Lai Khe.

Mess Hall at Lai Khe.

Inflatable ward at the 18th Surgical Hospital (MUST) at Lai Khe.

Thursday, December 7, 1967, the main body minus the MUST elements convoyed to the Lai Khe site. Within three days, the construction of all tent floors and billet accommodations were completed. Over the ensuing nine days, bunkers were dug; billets sandbagged; supply, storage, mess and chapel facilities finished; and the MUST site was prepared. On the morning of Wednesday, December 20, the MUST equipment was convoyed to the site from Long Binh. By nightfall the following day, all elements were in position and erected. During the next week, the interior equipment and all supplies were in place and made ready for use as a functional hospital.

The 18th Surgical Hospital (MUST) had a sixty-bed capacity, the same as the 18th Surgical Hospital (MA) at Pleiku, minus the medical ward. On Monday, January 1, 1968, the relocated 18th Surgical Hospital (MUST) received its first patient at Lai Khe. There were ninety-six EM and thirty officers (nine MC [physicians]), five MSC [administrative] and fourteen ANC [nurses and anesthetists]) assigned to the 18th Surgical Hospital (MUST). There were no female nurses at Lai Khe. The nurses assigned to the 18th Surgical Hospital (MA) in Pleiku had rotated back to the U.S. or were reassigned to the 71st Evacuation Hospital. Capt. Teddy L. Hildebrand was Chief Nurse from November 15 to December 1, 1967. Maj. Thomas J. Wetsch

replaced Capt. Hildebrand and continued in that capacity at Lai Khe. The 18th Surgical Hospital (MUST) was operational at Lai Khe for only about one month. Following the 1st Infantry Division to CTZ I, the 18th Surgical Hospital (MUST) closed about February 1 and was redeployed to a site at Dong Ha just north of Quang Tri, Quang Tri Province, thirty-five miles south of the DMZ, where it reopened about March 1, 1968.

QUANG TRI—CAMP EVANS—QUANG TRI

The U.S. strength in South Vietnam was approximately 473,000 by the beginning of 1968. That number included: combat infantry, 10.46%; artillery and engineers, 12.0%; aviators and airmen, 2.0% and other logistical and Headquarters support, 75.0%. Actual combat strength consisted of about 49,500 men comprising 90 combat infantry battalions (about 700 men each). The NVA and VC strengths included an estimated 152 battalions of 320 men each, with an approximate total of 63,000.

By this time, a strictly defensive strategy had been imposed on the military by our politicians. They were unwilling to provide adequate combat forces to complete the job and win a victory. They were unwilling to remove the restrictions that prevented attacks on the NVA's "safe havens" in Cambodia and Laos. Their decisions converted a winnable war into a war of attrition. Too many had already given their lives to abandon the cause at this late stage; however, that is what President Johnson and his advisors chose to do in order to appease U.S. public opinion.

The policy, which called for the minimal movement of hospitals, was modified in 1968 and, to a greater extent, in 1969. The hospital was operational at Dong Ha for one year. Around March 1, 1969, the 18th Surgical Hospital (MUST) was again relocated, this time to Camp Evans at Cia La, to support the 101st Airborne Division. Lt. Col. Malcolm T. Fishback, M.C. was the CO of the hospital at that time. Camp Evans was located SE of Hue, NW of Phu Bai in Thua Thien Province (CTZ I), west of Hwy.1. After working there five months, female nurses were again assigned to the 18th, sometime in August. In November 1969, the MUST equipment was withdrawn from the 18th, and in December 1969, the hospital was once more returned to Quang Tri Province, this time in support of the remaining Marines of what had been the III MAF (3rd Marine Amphibious Force), specifically the 1st Brigade, 5th Mechanized Infantry, 3rd Marine Division. The III MAF's Tactical Area of Responsibility (TAOR) was a 30 to 70 mile-wide zone that stretched southward about 175 miles from the DMZ to the northern part of the Annamite Mountain chain. There were four Corps (not to be confused with the four CTZs) operating in Vietnam during the war: I Field Force, Vietnam; II Field Force, Vietnam; III Marine Amphibious Force; and XXIV Corps.

The frequent movement of the 18th and other hospitals defies logic. While in Quang Tri Province (CTZ I), the 18th Surgical Hospital (MA) was a part of the 67th Medical Group, headquartered at Da Nang. The hospital was reestablished in semi-permanent facilities that had been a III MAF Hospital. The 3rd Marine Division had entered South Vietnam in June 1965, to protect the airbase at Da Nang and later fought valiantly at Khe Sanh and at Hue. In late 1969, the 3rd Marine Division began withdrawing to Okinawa. By April 15, 1970, 12,900 U.S. Marines departed South Vietnam to complete the third phase of U.S. Troop withdrawals announced by President Nixon. The U.S. completed the turnover of the DMZ to the South Vietnamese, as the 1st Brigade, 5th Mechanized Division transferred the responsibility of the area to ARVN troops.

The 18th Surgical Hospital (MA), using the abandoned hospital, was located a few miles from the DMZ. The female nurses lived in a restricted compound within the hospital compound. The physicians were housed in wooden barracks ("hooches"). The hospital compound included Officers and Enlisted Clubs, a small Chapel, barbershop, motor pool, mess hall, helipad and a supply warehouse. A medivac detachment from Medical Group Headquarters and a Mortuary (Graves Registration) unit from the U.S. Army Vietnam Headquarters were also located there.

The Mission of the 18th was to provide resuscitative surgery and medical treatment necessary to prepare critically injured or ill United States Forces, Free World Forces (FWMAF), civilian war casualties (CWCP), suspects, detainees or prisoners of war (POW), and Vietnamese civilians as directed, located within Military Region I Tactical Zone, for further evacuation and to also provide area medical support to units without organic medical capabilities.

In addition to its primary mission, the 18th Surgical Hospital (MA) had a forty-bed Vietnamese Pediatric hospital. The Children's Hospital had previously been located at the Dong Ha Combat Base and was operated by Company D, 3rd Marine Medical Battalion as a one hundred-bed facility. When the 3rd Marine Division withdrew from the Republic of Vietnam, the Children's Hospital was relocated to the 18th Surgical Hospital (MA) at Quong Tri Combat Base as a twenty-bed facility (expanding to a forty-bed facility in mid January 1970) until the 18th closed. The Marines had begun the construction of a cinderblock building to house the Pediatric Hospital, but construction was abandoned when the Marines left country.

The CO of the 18th Surgical Hospital (MA) during its second venture into Quang Tri Province was Lt. Col. William Keeling, MC. Maj. Robert Fulton, MSC, who had come to the 18th on December 22, 1970, from the 25th Medical Battalion, 25th Infantry Division at Cu Chi was XO; and Lt. Col. Jane Johnson was the Chief Nurse. The 18th Surgical Hospital (MA) was deactivated in September 1971. The pediatric section was transferred to the Quang Tri Provincial Hospital. In December 1971, following the deactivation of the 18th, a fifteen-member MACV Advisory Team moved into the abandoned facilities. Robert J. Wells (Maj., U.S. Army, Retired) stated, "My senior adviser Col. Metcalf and I personally selected the compound for our headquarters/living area because of the helipad and of course, the wonderful generators that provided electricity and running water. When we got there…, every building in the area was totally deserted." It was "…totally intact, but no Americans were within one hundred miles except the handful of us American Advisers. All hell broke lose on March 30, 1972, when the NVA surprised us, and the world, by coming across the DMZ only a few miles away. We held out for two days, and got orders to escape and evade to the coast …but, thank God, the choppers came at the last minute and saved us." On Easter Sunday, April 1, 1972, "…before we left we destroyed the hospital. We were completely surrounded by 20,000 NVA. Col. Metcalf gave the order to destroy everything we could. We had been under constant artillery fire for two days and took several hits, so there was not much to destroy. We mainly used thermite grenades to burn everything down. We put sand in the oil of the generators and turned them on high. I remember using my M-16 to shoot up the Officers/EMs Clubs—bottles were flying everywhere. The mess hall had taken a direct hit and food was everywhere. I just remembered the syrup—it was everywhere and we were cleaning our boots off when the choppers came in. We lost two advisers…" About two weeks later, "I went with a small team and walked through the compound to check things out and to look for any bodies of Americans. The entire place had been sacked by the NVA Army looking for loot. To make sure they got nothing of value, our higher headquarters ordered a B-52 bombing raid over the entire base, a week later. I got to see some of the aerial photos of the raid …there in the middle of the mess was the helipad with the big red cross saying 'We Came, We Served'." Then in May 1972, the 366th Tactical Fighter Wing out of Da Nang blew up what remained of the 18th Surgical Hospital (MA). The 18th Surgical Hospital (MA) was again awarded the Meritorious Unit Commendation for 1 Jan 70-31 July 71, DAGO 43, 1972. The 18th (Portable) (Surgical) Hospital (Provisional) (Reinforced) (MA) (MUST) (MA) was probably the most decorated Surgical Hospital in Military history.

The Tet Offensive became the most controversial journalistic event of the war. In his pontifical reporting, Walter Cronkite, who had been exalted to a demagogic position by the liberal press, compared the siege of South Vietnam with Dien Bien Phu. He wrote and narrated a "speculative, personal" report advocating negotiations leading to the withdrawal of American troops. Cronkite concluded, "We have been too often disappointed by the optimism of the American leaders, both in Vietnam and

Left to right: Lt. Col. Johnson, Chief of Nursing, Maj. Sylvester, Asst. Chief of Nursing, February 1971.

Dustoff on helipad at Quang Tri, June 1971.

Christmas 1970. Left to right: A cook, a physician, Lt. Col. Keeling (CO) and other physicians.

Christmas 1970 at the 18th Surgical Hospital, Quang Tri.

18th Surgical Hospital at Quang Tri, December 1970. The "wishing well" with hooches in background.

Vietnamese boy (amputee) at Pediatric Hospital at the 18th Surgical Hospital (MA), May 1971.

Capt. Suorez with pediatric patient at the 18th Surgical Hospital, February 1971.

ANC Anniversary Party, February 1971.

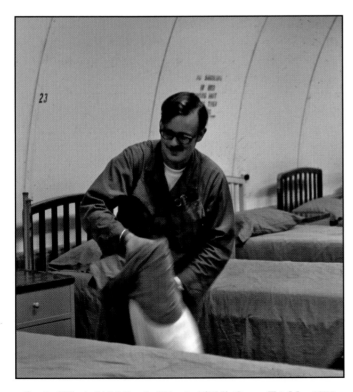

Surgical Ward of 18th Surgical Hospital (MA), Quang Tri, May 1971.

One of the officer's hooches at 18th Surgical Hospital (MA), Quang Tri, May 1971.

Army Nurse Corp's Anniversary Party at Mess Hall at the 18th Surgical Hospital (MA), Quang Tri, Lt. Col. Keeling in background with camera, February 1971.

Aerial view of 18th Surgical Hospital (MA) in May 1971.

Washington, to have faith any longer in the silver linings they find in the darkest clouds. We are mired in stalemate."

Gen. Vo Nguyen Giap, Commanding General, North Vietnamese Armed Forces, had hoped that there would be an uprising of the citizens of South Vietnam against their own government; however that situation did not materialize. The U.S. Army, Air Force and Marine Corps responded to the surprise attacks swiftly and thoroughly. When the dust from the battles had settled, the Tet Offensive was a total defeat for the Communist Forces with some 100,000 Viet Cong guerrillas and 45,000 NVA killed, effectively destroying the VC as a military force. The anti-war news media misreported and misinterpreted the 1968 Tet Offensive to the American public. They reported their personal opinions rather than facts and told the anti-war element of the American public what they wanted to hear rather than what they should have been told. When Cronkite told the American people, "And that's the way it is," they unfortunately accepted it as truth. Then, as with current events, we must always question the truthfulness and validity of the news we hear or read and ask the most pertinent question, "Is that really the way it is?" The U.S. had been mauled but, in fact, had achieved a stunning victory, yet Cronkite, Walter Kalb and others reported that the U.S. had been badly defeated and that the war was in a stalemate. This type of broadcasting was responsible for the loss of American political resolve and undermined our military efforts.

Gen. Giap in his *Memoirs* stated, "What we still don't understand is why you Americans stopped the bombing of Hanoi. You had us on the ropes. If you had pressed us a little harder, just another day or two, we were ready to surrender. It was the same at the battles of Tet. You defeated us! We knew it, and we thought you knew it. But we were elated to notice your media was definitely helping us. They were causing more disruption in America than we could in the battlefields. We were ready to surrender. You had won!"

"Do not fear the enemy, for they can take only your life. Fear the media far more, for they will destroy your honor" is an often-quoted phrase that proved to be true.

The turmoil on college and university campuses arose because of student apprehension over being drafted. If there had been an all-volunteer military at the time, there would have been far fewer, if any, demonstrations. The possibility of having to go to war was a sacrifice many were unwilling to make. The press portrayed their championing of counter-cultural ideas and the public voicing of anti-administration slogans during their demonstrations as political and philosophical statements, instead of portraying their vociferous efforts as simply a means of avoiding and evading the draft. A few no doubt, held sincere and genuine philosophical and political differences. Most students, like the average U.S. citizen, did not understand our SEATO Treaty obligations and certainly had no understanding of Vietnamese history and culture.

Fuel bladder explosion following a rocket and mortar attack adjacent to the 18th Surgical Hospital (MUST) at Quang Tri.

During that time period, most Americans were more interested in the stock market and the good life than in treaty obligations and more concerned about making money than pursuing a war. They gave little, if any, thought to the freedom they enjoyed or who provided that freedom and at what cost. This indifferent attitude and actions caused numerous GIs to lose their lives by encouraging the enemy. On October 11, 1967, the Speaker of the U.S. House of Representatives, John W. McCormack (D-MA) declared, "If I was one of those (whose descent heartened the enemy), my conscious would disturb me the rest of my life." A few months earlier on April 28, 1967, Gen. Westmoreland stated in an address to a joint session of Congress, "Backed at home by resolve, confidence, patience, determination, and continued support, we will prevail in Vietnam over the Communist aggressor." The public gave no heed to these comments made by Gen. Westmoreland and Speaker McCormack, if they heard them at all.

Hanoi calculated that there was a reasonable possibility of a change in U.S. policy before the collapse of the Viet Cong and the NVA. The North Vietnamese were correct in predicting that the American public did not have the patriotic loyalty, the determination of spirit, or the will to make the necessary sacrifices needed to win the war. The general public neither understood, nor were willing to discover, the political and military issues involved. Most could not have located Vietnam on a world map. Ho Chi Minh's prediction concerning U.S. public apathy and Gen. Giap's understanding of U.S. political indecisiveness were proven to be true. The U.S. and Allied Forces won every battle on the battlefields of South Vietnam, only to lose the war in the United States. In 1917 Theodore Roosevelt, our 26th President (1901-1909), summed up his observations and reflectively recorded his predictions which are still valid today, "The things that will destroy America are prosperity-at-any-price, peace-at-any-price, safety-first instead of duty-first, the love of soft living and the get-rich-quick theory of life." William Wordsworth wrote, "...Getting

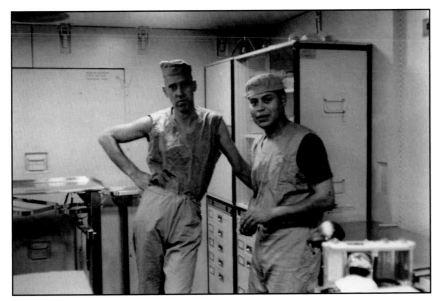

Maj. Ron Kirkland, MC and Sp/5 Garcia inside expandable OR (MUST) at Quang Tri.

and spending, …We have given our hearts away, …we are out of tune; …" (*The World Is Too Much With Us*).

President Dwight D. Eisenhower stated in his farewell address to the nation on January 17, 1961, "We…must avoid the impulse to live only for today, plundering for our own ease and convenience the precious resources of tomorrow. We cannot mortgage the material assets of our grandchildren without risking the loss also of their political and spiritual heritage. We want democracy to survive for all generations to come, not to become the insolvent phantom of tomorrow."

When the mood in the U.S. increasingly demonstrated a willingness to surrender and get out of South Vietnam at any cost, the North Vietnamese simply waited for the American public opinion to give them the victory. How tragic! In his inaugural address (January 20, 1965) President Lyndon B. Johnson stated, "Our destiny in the midst of change will rest on the unchanged character of our people—and on their faith."

As these political realities played out, the NVA and VC were, unfortunately, more and more able to call the shots about when and where the next battle would be fought, rather than those decisions being determined by U.S. military strategy. The U.S. political strategy was often counterproductive and even countermanded some of the military's effort to win. The American public did not realize, nor apparently did they care, about the executions, murder, pillage and destruction which would later result in South Vietnam because of the political decision to pull out and abandon those we had pledged, through treaties, to support. Hundreds of thousands were ultimately massacred! Almost all of the Montagnards were slaughtered; and multiple thousands of the South Vietnamese were killed or languished in prisons for years. Anyone who had sympathized with, worked for or supported the U.S. and/or ARVN forces had to flee before they were murdered or imprisoned.

On January 18, 1969, President Nguyen Van Thieu confirmed that he had requested the withdrawal of some troops from South Vietnam. He did not initiate this request; rather, he was responding to U.S. pressure and the realities of the expanded Paris Peace talks. Technically, South Vietnam lost the war; however, they, and the U.S., realized that when our forces left the country, they could not win the war alone.

About two months after being inaugurated as our 36th President, Richard M. Nixon stated on January 20, 1969 that, "…after a period of confrontation, we are entering an era of negotiations." This was political double talk, indicating that the U.S. was abandoning their commitment to South Vietnam. In spite of this political position, a Gallup Poll reported on March 22, 1969, that 32% of Americans favored greatly expanding the war, 19% favored continuation of the current policy, 21% had no opinion and only 20% favored an immediate pullout. This demonstrates how a vociferous minority, with the continued bombardment by a sympathetic media's never-ending desire to create the news, was able to sway public opinion and create political pressure for change.

The Department of Defense Vietnam War Service Index reported that 9,097,000 military personnel served on active duty from August 1964 to May 7, 1975 (official Vietnam era). The report also stated that 2,710,276 U.S. military personnel served in South Vietnam (The War Library); however, a census done in August 2000 indicated that 13,853,027 falsely claimed to be Vietnam veterans.

Although a draft was in place, two-thirds of those who served in Vietnam and approximately 70% of those killed were volunteers. Of those who died in Vietnam, 86% were Caucasian; 12.5% were black; and 1.2% were other races. It was reported by the anti-war press that a disproportionate number of blacks were killed in Vietnam, which is false. The 12% who died represent a percentage proportional to the number of blacks in the U.S. population at the time and is slightly "…lower than the proportion of blacks in the Army at the close of the war" (*All That We Can Be,* by Charles C. Moskos and John Sibley Butler). The first American who died in Vietnam was James Davis, 509th Radio Research Station, in 1958. Davis Station in Saigon was named in his memory. There were 75,000 severely disabled; 23,214 were 100% disabled; 5,283 lost limbs; 1,081 sustained multiple amputations. Of those killed, 61% were younger than 21 years of age; 11,465 were younger than 20; while five who were killed were only 16 years old. The oldest man killed was 62 years of age. As of January 15, 2004, there are 1,875 Americans still missing in action (MIAs).

The Combat Area Casualty File (CACF) that provided information for the Vietnam Veterans Memorial (The Wall), list the average age of the 58,267 who were killed to be 23.11 years. Enlisted personnel numbered: 50,274 (22.37 years); Officers: 6,598 (28.43 years); Warrant Officers: 1,276 (24.73 years); E1: 525 (20.34 years) and Infantrymen: (MOS11B), 18,465 (22.55 years).

Aerial view of Quang Tri base camp showing the Han Giang River, May 1971.

Sandbagging at 18th Surgical Hospital (MA), Quang Tri, May 1971.

Maj. Robert C. Fulton, MSC (XO) at 18th Surgical Hospital (MA), May 1971.

Above: Areial view of 18th Surgical Hospital (MA) at Quang Tri.

Right, left to right: Maj. Jim West (Chief of Staff), unknown, Lt. Col. Johnson (Chief of Nursing), Lt. Col. Keeling (CO), Maj. Sylvester (Asst. Chief of Nursing), Capt. Joe Allen, May 1971.

Chapel at 18th Surgical Hospital (MA), Quang Tri, May 1971.

Barber Shop at 18th Surgical Hospital (MA), May 1971.

Headquarters of 18th Surgical Hospital (MA), Quang Tri, May 1971.

Above: Pharmacy technician and X-ray technician at 18th Surgical Hospital (MA), Quang Tri, May 1971.

Left: Acquiring a tan at 18th Surgical Hospital (MA), Quang Tri, January 1971.

Approximately 2.5% of the wounded died; however, of those wounded who survived the first twenty-four hours, only 1% died. Approximately 304,000 of the 2.7 million who served in Vietnam were wounded. These excellent statistics reflect the effort of the Dustoff pilots and crews. Medevac helicopters flew nearly 500,000 missions and airlifted over 900,000 patients to medical and surgical treatment. The average time lapse between being wounded and arriving at a hospital was less than one hour and often was only a few minutes.

Ninety-seven percent of Vietnam veterans were honorably discharged. There is no statistical difference in drug usage between Vietnam veterans and non-veterans, and only 0.5% of Vietnam veterans have been jailed for crimes.

The little nine-year old Vietnamese girl, Kim Phuc, shown burned by napalm bombs and running naked down a road was reported by the anti-war press on TV in the U.S. as a horrible event caused by careless Americans when, in fact, no American military personnel were involved. The bombing occurred on June 8, 1972 near the village of Trang Bang. ARVN troops were attempting to recapture the area recently overrun by the NVA. A Vietnamese pilot in the VNAF (Vietnamese Air Force) flying air support for the ground troops dropped the bombs (he later moved to theU.S.). The AP photographer, Nick Ut, who took the pictures, was Vietnamese. Lt. Gen. (Ret.) James F. Hollingsworth (Commanding General of TRAC) stated, "We (Americans) had nothing to do with controlling the VNAF." It was also reported that two of her brothers were killed. They were her cousins, not her brothers. The incident in which the South Vietnamese Air Force General, Nguyen Ngoc Loan, photographed using his pistol to execute a Viet Cong prisoner, was widely shown on TV and throughout the print media directly suggesting, or at least indirectly implicating, the Americans of condoning atrocities and brutality. What was not mentioned by the press is that Gen. Loan was Commander of the 70,000-man National Police Force. The VC prisoner had been found guilty at a court martial of slaughtering and methodically killing families and dependents of the members of the National Police. The .38-caliber revolver Gen. Loan used was a gift from the U.S. Air Force Office of Special Investigation (OSI), the Air Force counterpart to the Naval Investigative Service (NIS). So much for objective reporting!

We were told of a similar incident that occurred while the South Koreans (ROK) were fighting in the Pleiku area. A South Korean enlisted man was accused of raping a South Vietnamese woman and a military court martial determined that he was guilty. The commanding officer carried out the execution by shooting him in the head with a .45-caliber pistol. Obviously we did not witness the execution; however, we heard the rumor from numerous individuals on various occasions and assumed it to be correct. It was generally known that there were no disciplinary problems among the South Korean troops.

The domino theory was accurate. Ambassador Henry Cabot Lodge II stated in an essay (for publication in *Foreign Affairs*), "Foreign Affairs is widely commented on by columnists, editors and so-called 'opinion makers' generally—Undoubtedly the single most factor in the whole Vietnam problem is support from the American home front." He continued, "Vietnam is the keystone for all Southeast Asia. The conquest of South Vietnam would immediately disturb Cambodia and Laos, and bring strong repercussions farther west in Thailand and Burma. It would shake Malaysia to the south. It would surely threaten Indonesia. Then, if Indonesia were unable or unwilling to resist, the Chinese Communists would be on the doorstep of Australia. Finally, eastward, the repercussions for the Philippines and Formosa would be severe." Even though we left Vietnam too soon, our efforts in South Vietnam provided courage and support for the Association of Southeast Asian Nations to thwart the efforts of communism. The Philippines, Indonesia, Malaysia, Singapore and Thailand have remained free because of U.S. commitments.

Wars should not be fought except as a last resort, after diplomacy and all other efforts have failed. When the decision is made to fight, our efforts must be stealthy and unexpected, sudden and forceful and unrelenting until victory is complete. Corporate "whiz kids" should never be placed in the position of directing a war! The terms "attrition," "stalemate" or "limited" are words that should never be used in the vocabulary of war. Wars using seek and destroy battlefield tactics that are intensified incrementally in an effort to quell insurgencies allows the enemy to understand your strategy and allows time for them to adjust their counter-forces accordingly. Such an open-ended, progressively prosecuted war is always nearly impossible to win and, according to Ambassador Lodge, would put the U.S. "…onto a slope along which we (will) slide into a bottomless pit." He, therefore, encouraged a forceful and rapid escalation of the war effort in order to accomplish a complete and decisive victory.

The Provisional Revolutionary Government (PRG) was established on June 8, 1969, and represented political and military forces in South Vietnam (after U.S. withdrawal) at the Paris Peace Talks. The PRG received diplomatic recognition from communist states. Its Foreign Minister was Madam Nguyen Thi Binh, who headed the PRG delegation at the Paris Peace Talks. On April 30 1975, the PRG assumed power as the Republic of South Vietnam for fifteen months until the South and North were officially reunified as the Socialist Republic of Vietnam (SRV) on July 2, 1976. The SRV reorganized and redistricted what had been the Republic of Vietnam (South) into new districts. The Provincial Governments were abolished, and Districts were formed. The Pleiku Province is now a portion of the Gia Lai District.

We often hear the slogan, "Eternal vigilance is the price of freedom." It is a wise and true statement; however, liberty and freedom require so much more than vigilance. "Freedom is the right to be free, and then the obligation to accept responsibility" (*America's Prophet*). The cost of freedom is enormous. The price is more than some are willing to pay, yet those same individuals are never reluctant to accept and enjoy the benefits resulting from the sacrifices of others. Freedom is born of idealism; infused with patriotism; nourished by loyalty to a common purpose; upheld by faithfulness to the principles of liberty and self-determination; sustained by courage, bravery and dedication; and paid for through sacrifice, suffering and often death. Freedom is never achieved by a half-hearted effort or lip service to a cause. Freedom cannot be purchased with glib oratory, IOUs, cold checks or credit cards. The price for freedom must be paid in advance. Many hearts have stopped beating so that the heartbeat of this nation can continue, preserving and guaranteeing our liberty and freedom.

In a speech to the House of Commons in May 1940, Sir Winston Churchill remarked that he could offer nothing except "…blood, toil, tears and sweat." A few days later, he said, "…whatever the cost may be, …we shall never surrender." Still later he stated, "This was their finest hour." Unfortunately, the same cannot be said about the U.S. public's response during the Vietnam War.

The words and thoughts of the anonymous writer must always be remembered:

> It is the veteran, not the minister, who has given us freedom of religion. It is the veteran, not the reporter, who has given us freedom of the press. It is the veteran, not the author/poet, who has given us freedom of speech. It is the veteran, not the liberal protestors, who has given us freedom to assemble. It is the veteran, not the lawyer, who has given us the right to a fair trial. It is the veteran, not the politician, who has given us the right to vote. It is the veteran, who salutes the flag, who serves under the flag. Let us honor them all.

Stanley Swenson wrote a poem about his brother, Orville P. Swenson, M.D., one of the original physicians with the 18th Surgical Hospital (MA) at Pleiku. "I worried about his safe return. One sleepless night I wrote this poem, relating to him. This poem may tell the story of many of our men and women preparing to defend our country at this time. Our thoughts and prayers are with them and may God bring them safely home."

I AM A SOLDIER

This land of mine, I love it so.
It gave me birth, it let me grow.
It gave me happiness and joy,
and carefree days while a young boy.

But now I've reached a turning tide,
those carefree days lie at my side.
I'm on my way to a distant shore,
to preserve the freedom I adore.

I'm looking back on those days I knew,
before I crossed those waters blue.
My home, my family, my bride-to-be
all these, and more, are part of me.

They are my hope, my strength, my joy,
that helped me grow beyond a boy.

But I'll hope, I'll pray, I'll try to go
on living while many may die.

"Why am I here," many will ask,
"Doing this dangerous daring task?"
I'm here, I think, to keep men free
from an ever-pressing tyranny.

The job may be long, a struggle for me
but maybe I'll form our destiny.
A land ever free from want and fear
this , I believe, is why I'm here.

The time has come, the day is near
to return to this land I love so dear.
My family, my home, my joy, my pride,
they all will be there at my side.

I've served her well, both day and night
but still there's unrest—and endless fight.
Many more will die that we might be free.
God help us find a lasting liberty.

We Came, We Served. We served under the flag and we "…served her well." We did our best. We not only helped to "…form our destiny…", but also the destiny of others.

> Ask ev'ry person if he's heard the story;
> And tell it strong and clear if he has not:
> That once there was a fleeting wisp of glory—
> called Camelot.
> Don't let it be forgot
> That once there was a spot
> For one brief shining moment that was known,
> as Camelot.

From a military-professional perspective, perhaps the 18th Surgical Hospital (MA) at Pleiku was, at least at times, our Camelot. There was nothing paradisiacal or idyllic about our hospital. Our experiences certainly were not imaginary, nor were our efforts legendary or glamorous. There were numerous "shining moments" of patient's survival and recovery, resulting in us collectively experiencing a sense of pride and "a fleeting wisp of glory" each time our collaborative endeavors were successful. We provided survival and hope for many. The prayer of Maimonides became our unconscious and unspoken creed: "Inspire me with love for my art and for Your creatures." We upheld our Hippocratic Oath, fulfilled our military obligations and did our part to preserve "…this land we love…" and guarantee our liberty and the "…freedom we adore." In the process, we truly were *Soldiers Saving Soldiers.*

—Jerry W. Martin, M.D.

EMBLEMS OF THE 18TH SURGICAL HOSPITAL

The emblem (shown below) of the 18th Surgical Hospital (MA) was created by Robert Lee Hewitt, M.D., who came to the 18th Surgical Hospital (MA) at Pleiku, Pleiku Province (Central Highlands; II Corps) on December 12, 1966 as Commanding Officer of the 240th Medical Detachment (Thoracic Surgical K Team) to replace Roger Raymond Ecker, M.D. who was rotating back to the states. He drew the emblem in February 1967, and by April it had been approved by our hospital staff and our Commanding Officer, Lt. Col. Mark Thomas Cenac, MC, and we were informed that it was officially sanctioned and accepted by the 55th Medical Group and the 44th Medical Brigade. Dr. Hewitt returned to New Orleans after military discharge and later retired as Chairman of the Department of Surgery at Tulane University Medical School.

The emblem consists of a shield divided into four quadrants. The left upper and the right lower quadrants are dark blue. The right upper and the left lower quadrants each consist of alternating red and white vertical stripes (five red, four white), totaling 18 stripes. The left upper blue field contains a red cross (Cross of St. George) outlined in white. Two white stars are honoring the fact that the hospital served in two wars; the 18th (Portable) (Surgical) Hospital (Provisional) served in World War II and the 18th Surgical Hospital (MA) (MUST) (MA) served in the Vietnam War. That quadrant also resembles the Australian Flag and symbolizes the hospital's activation in Australia during World War II. The right lower quadrant consists of a caduceus, the Army Medical Corps insignia. The upper shield has a sword with five maroon and five white turns on the handle, signifying the 55th Medical Group, and is topped with the maroon and white insignia of the 44th Medical Brigade. This emblem was displayed with pride in our Officers Club, on wall plaques, uniform patches, and even on Zippo cigarette lighters.

The hospital apparently did not have a unit insignia during World War II since it was always attached to an infantry division or an infantry combat team, as a part of the 107th Medical Battalion.

While researching this book, I discovered another insignia for the 18th Surgical Hospital that was designed when the 18th Surgical Hospital (MA) was located in Quang Tri Province (about three years after the first emblem had been created and supposedly accepted), as part of the 67th Medical Group (Military Region I Tactical Zone; I Corps), a few miles south of the DMZ.

The call sign, "Eagle Landing," and the motto, "We Came, We Served," were presumably initiated there also; however, the Institute of Heraldry lists, "Soldiers Saving Soldiers" as the motto for the 18th Surgical Hospital.

"A gold color medal and enamel device consisting of a maroon enamel heptagon bearing overall a Philippine Sun with seven rays, the disc of the sun of blue enamel and the rays [of] gold and surmounted by a seven-pointed star of [white] enamel charged throughout by a scarlet enamel Geneva cross, the points of the star extending over the blue disc and between the gold rays of the sun. Symbolism: the seven-pointed white star, suggested by the Australian flag, and bearing a scarlet Geneva cross refers to the activation of the organization in Australia as the 18th Portable Hospital (Provisional), September 14, 1942. The seven points of the star further allude to the 4 battle honors: Papua, New Guinea, Leyte and the assault landing at Luzon, (the point of the star bearing the scarlet arm of the cross simulating an arrowhead) and three decorations: Distinguished Unit Citation for Papua, Distinguished Unit Citation for Corregidor and Philippine Presidential Unit Citation for the period October 17, 1944 to July 4, 1945, awarded the organization in World War II. The two Distinguished Unit Citations are symbolized by the blue disc of the sun and the Philippine Presidential Unit Citation by the colors blue, white and red, the rays of the sun illuminating and glorifying the achievements of the unit. The number of rays of the sun (7), of the [points] of the star (7) and arms of the cross (4) also add up to 18, the unit's numerical designation. The colors maroon and white are those used for the Army Medical Department." (Military.com: 1SG Charles W. Aresta, The Hawaiian Military Insignia Collectors and Study Group.)

This Distinctive Insignia for the 18th Surgical Hospital (MA) was authorized in accordance with a Directive from the Chief of Staff, U.S. Army, dated March 27, 1968. It was officially authorized by the Institute of Heraldry on February 10, 1969.

Because of administrative negligence, error or oversight, "our" unit insignia was never officially processed. Although those of us who served with the 18th Surgical Hospital (MA) at Pleiku will always consider "our" emblem as the "official insignia," it apparently is not the one officially sanctioned.

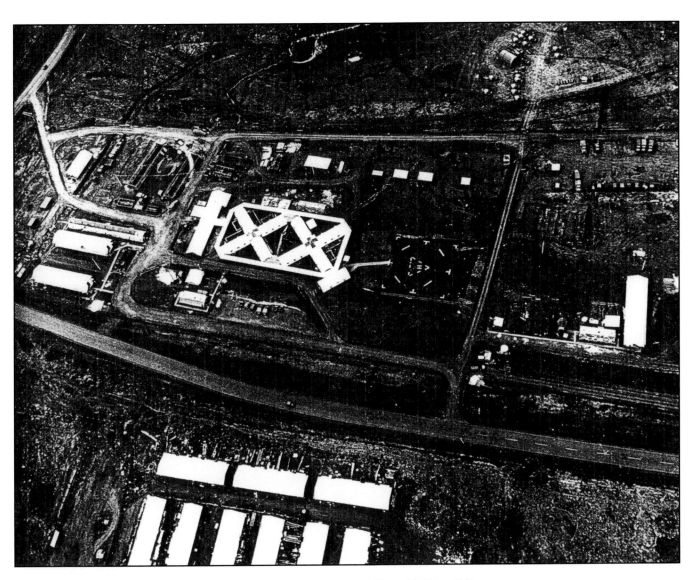

An aerial view of the 18th Surgical Hospital (MA) at Pleiku..

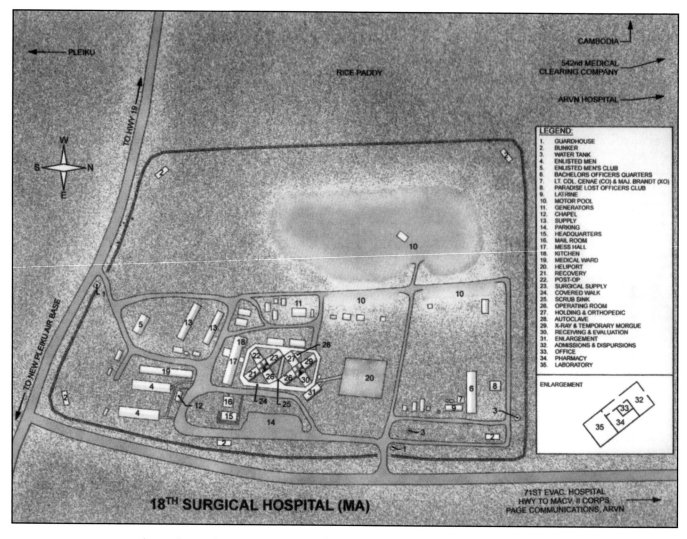

An aerial view of the 18th Surgical Hospital (MA), Pleiku, drawn by Eric William Hathaway.

EMBLEMS OF UNITS SUPPORTED BY THE 18TH SURGICAL HOSPITAL

The following insignia are unit patches representing those units to which the 18th (Portable)(Provisional) (Surgical) Hospital (MA)(MUST)(MA) was attached, served under or provided medical/surgical support for in World War II and in the Vietnam War.

6th Army

7th Airforce

3rd Army

32nd Division

8th Army

24th Division

I Corps

PACAF

3rd Marine Division

44th Medical Brigade

4th Division

WWII Meritorious Unit Citation

1st Division

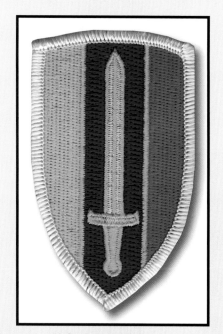

U.S. Army Vietnam

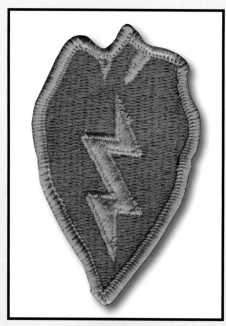

25th Division

MACV

173rd Airborne Division

101st Airborne Division

5th Special Forces

1st Cavalry Division

503rd Infantry Regiment, 173rd Airborne Brigade (503rd Parachute RCT, 34th Infantry Division)

LINEAGE, HONORS AND CAMPAIGNS OF THE 18TH SURGICAL HOSPITAL

Vietnamese Service Medal

18th Surgical Hospital (MA), Pleiku
Vietnam Counteroffensive
Vietnam Counteroffensive II
Vietnam Counteroffensive III

"Extremism in the defense of liberty is no vice, moderation in the pursuit of justice is no virtue."
—*Senator Barry Goldwater (R. Arizona)*

"If we are strong, our strength will speak for itself. If we are weak, words will be of no help."
—*John F. Kennedy*

World War II Campaigns

18th (Portable) (Surgical) Hospital (Provisional) (Reinforced)

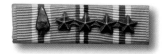

(Asiatic-Pacific Campaign Ribbon)

Papuan Campaign (New Guinea)
New Guinea Campaign
Southern Philippines Campaign (Leyte)
Luzon (Corregidor Campaign [with Arrowhead])

Vietnam Campaigns

18th Surgical Hospital (MA) (MUST) (MA)

(Vietnam Service Ribbon)

The 18th Surgical Hospital (MA) (MUST) (MA) served in the Republic of Vietnam (South Vietnam) during 13 military campaigns. Since the hospital moved numerous times, there were four instances where it served in different locations during the same campaign.

Pleiku

Vietnam Counteroffensive
Vietnam Counteroffensive, Phase II
Vietnam Counteroffensive, Phase III

Lai Khe-Long Binh

Vietnam Counteroffensive, Phase III

Quang Tri

Vietnam Counteroffensive, Phase III
Tet Counteroffensive
Vietnam Counteroffensive, Phase IV
Vietnam Counteroffensive, Phase V
Vietnam Counteroffensive, Phase VI
Tet 69 Counteroffensive

Camp Evans

Tet 69 Counteroffensive
Vietnam Summer-Fall
Vietnam Winter-Summer

Quang Tri

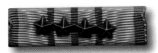

Vietnam Winter-Summer
Vietnam Counteroffensive, Phase VII
Sanctuary Counteroffensive
Consolidation I

18th Surgical Hospital

World War II Asiatic Pacific Campaign
(1942-1945)

World War II Occupation
(1945)

U.S. Vietnam Service
(1966-1971)

18th Surgical Hospital Lineage

- Constituted December 21, 1928 in the Regular Army as the 18th Surgical Hospital
- Consolidated July 1, 1943 as the 18th Portable Surgical Hospital (Provisional), organized September 14, 1942 in the Army of the United States in Australia as the 18th Portable Hospital (Provisional); re-designated April 1, 1943 as the 18th Portable Surgical Hospital (Provisional) and consolidated unit designated as the 18th Portable Surgical Hospital.
- Inactivated December 1, 1945 in Japan.
- Re-designated March 1, 1963 as the 18th Surgical Hospital.
- Activated March 26, 1963 at Fort Gordon, Georgia.
- Inactivated August 31, 1971 at Fort Lewis, Washington.
- Activated November 18, 1991 at Fort Lewis, Washington.

Philippine Presidential Unit Citation
(1944)

Presidential Unit Citation
(Papua; Corregidor)

Vietnam Service Medal
Seventeen campaigns were designated:

1. Vietnam Advisory	March 15, 1962–March 7, 1965
2. Vietnam Defense	March 8, 1965–December 24, 1965
3. Vietnam Counteroffensive*	December 25, 1965–June 30, 1966
4. Vietnam Counteroffensive Phase II*	July 1, 1966–May 31, 1967
5. Vietnam Counteroffensive Phase III*	June 1, 1967–January 29, 1968
6. Tet Counteroffensive*	January 30, 1968–April 1, 1968
7. Vietnam Counteroffensive Phase IV*	April 2, 1968–June 30, 1968
8. Vietnam Counteroffensive Phase V*	July 1, 1968–November 1, 1968
9. Vietnam Counteroffensive Phase VI*	November 2, 1968–February 22, 1969
10. Tet 69 Counteroffensive*	February 23, 1969–June 8, 1969
11. Vietnam Summer-Fall*	June 9, 1969–October 31, 1969
12. Vietnam Winter-Spring*	November 1, 1969–April 30, 1970
13. Sanctuary Counteroffensive*	May 1, 1970–June 30, 1970
14. Vietnam Counteroffensive Phase VII*	July 1, 1970–June 30, 1971
15. Consolidation I*	July 1, 1971–November 30, 1971
16. Consolidation II	December 1, 1971–March 29, 1972
17. Vietnam Cease Fire	March 30, 1972–January 28, 1973

*Indicates campaigns involving the 18th Surgical Hospital (MA) (MUST) (MA)

Meritorious Unit Commendation
(1966-1967; 1970-1971)

Republic of Vietnam Gallantry
Cross Unit Citation (1965-1969)

18th Surgical Hospital Honors

Campaign Participation Credit
- World War II: Papua; New Guinea; Leyte; Luzon (Corregidor [arrowhead])
- Vietnam: Counteroffensive; Counteroffensive, Phase II; Counteroffensive, Phase III; Tet Counteroffensive; Tet/69 Counteroffensive; Summer-Fall 1969; Winter-Spring 1970; Sanctuary Counteroffensive; Counteroffensive, Phase IV; Consolidation I

Decorations
- Presidential Unit Citation (Distinguished Unit Citation [Army]), Streamer embroidered Papua
- Presidential Unit Citation (Distinguished Unit Citation [Army]), Streamer embroidered Corregidor
- Meritorious Unit Commendation (Army) for Vietnam 1966-1967
- Meritorious Unit Commendation (Army) for Vietnam 1970-1971
- Philippine Presidential Unit Citation, Streamer embroidered, October 17, 1944 to July 4, 1945
- Republic of Vietnam Gallantry Cross Unit Citation, 1965-1969

Recognitions
- Certificate of Achievement, 4th Infantry Division, April 16, 1967

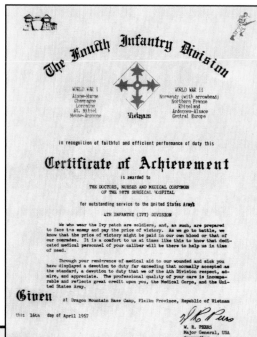

Republic of Vietnam Gallantry
Cross with Palm
Unit Citation

National Defense
Service Medal

Republic of Vietnam
Campaign Medal

SURGICAL PROCEDURES

Hundreds of photographs showing wounds and surgical procedures could have been included in this book. The 18th Surgical Hospital (MA) was extremely busy during our year at Pleiku (June 1966-June 1967). During the year our original group was in country, a total of 17,576 patients were evacuated from Vietnam and during the entire time the 18th Surgical Hospital (MA) was located at Pleiku, the total number of evacuees from Vietnam totaled 26,966 (all hospitals in Vietnam). From July 1966-October 1967 the 18th Surgical Hospital (MA) admitted 10,531 patients, transferred 7,835 and returned to duty 2,699. During the first six months of operation, we had 1,273 IRHA (injuries received during hostile action) and 5,168 NBI (non-battle injuries) for a total of 6,441.

For each surgical case admitted to our hospital, we also admitted approximately 8-10 medical cases (i.e., malaria, scrub typhus, hepatitis, pneumonia, FUO, dengue, gastroenteritis with diarrhea, etc.).

The majority of surgical cases encountered were of the extremities, with abdominal wounds a close second, chest wounds were third and burns fourth. We received only a few patients with head wounds since most of those injuries were instantly fatal or the wounds were mortal when they occurred.

Of the extremity wounds, most were of the lower extremity usually involving the thigh and often involving the femoral artery. Hand wounds were of second frequency while shoulder and arm wounds were third.

Most chest wounds involved hemo/pneumothoraces (puncture wounds of the chest with collapse of the lung and/or internal bleeding caused by shrapnel fragments from grenades, mortars, etc.). Gunshot wounds of the chest were the next most prevalent injury resulting in a high number of acute respiratory distress syndrome (ARDS [wet lung]).

Burns were usually the result of chopper crashes; however, we saw a few cases of phosphorus burns from grenades, a few of which died of renal (kidney) failure.

Human achievement is measured by successes rather than failures. Those stories are best told by showing the people where they live, work and play. There were too many untold stories in Vietnam, as I am sure there are in all wars. The following photographs illustrate some of the problems that we encountered during surgery as we attempted to alter almost certain catastrophe into the renewed hope for life.

Hospitalization

The following chart is presented to indicate the workload of this hospital for calendar year 1967.

18th Surgical Hospital (MA)

	Admissions		Dispositions	
	Direct	Transfer	Duty	Transfer
January	154	551	199	556
February	131	463	147	433
March	165	667	155	629
April	194	543	229	548
May	198	671	215	665
June	212	286	160	317
July	117	408	158	389
August	114	128	139	149
September	174	107	146	133
October	60	24	68	49
November	0	0	0	0
December	0	0	0	0

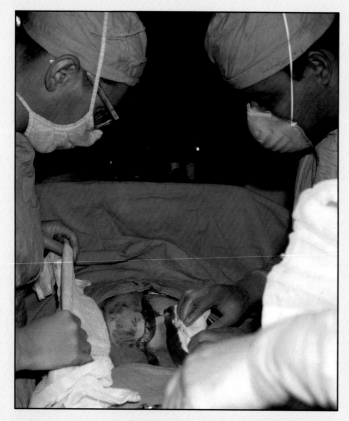

Jules Perley, M.D. and Oscar Valerio, M.D. making the incision in order to explore an abdominal wound.

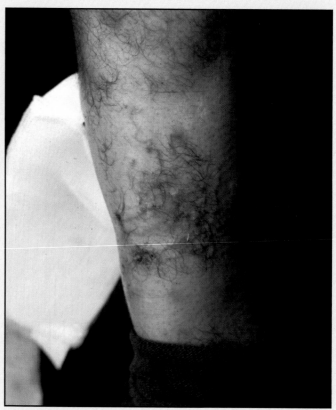

Cutaneous larvae migrans, right leg. Subcutaneous larvae of the dog hookworm.

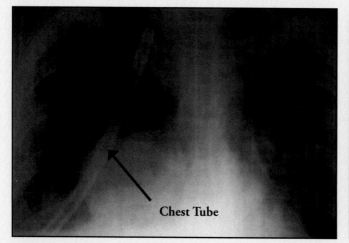

Collapsed right lung with chest tube in place before tube hooked to chest bottle.

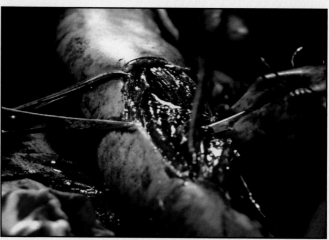

Right posterior calf wound, muscle exposed.

Hematoma (blood clot) of transverse mesocolon (the fold of peritoneum attaching the colon [large bowel] to the posterior abdominal wall and through which pass the nerves, veins, arteries and lymphatics).

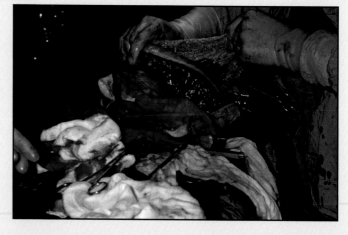

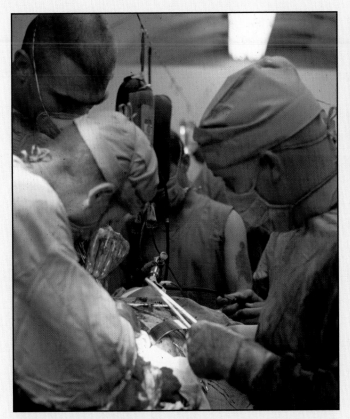

Left to right: Roger Ecker, M.D., Sam Gillis, M.D., Ron Hatch, CRNA and Bob Engebrecht, M.D. operating on right lung gunshot wound.

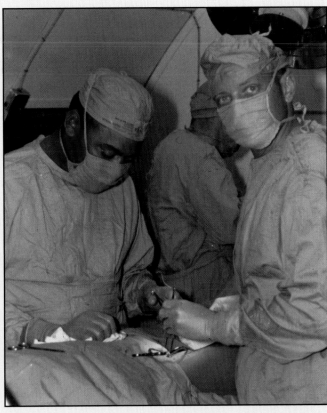

Left to right: Felix Jenkins, M.D. and Bob Hewitt, M.D. exploring an abdominal wound.

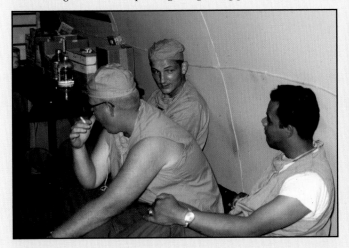

Left to right: Wayne Hosking, M.D., Ron Thompson, CRNA and Oscar Valerio, M.D. in R & E resting between cases.

Gunshot wound to right jaw and mouth with lower teeth blown away.

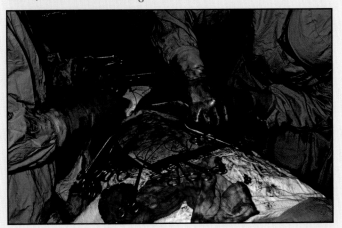

Closure of abdominal incision following eploration of an abdominal wound.

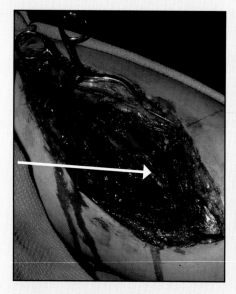

Thrombosis (clot) of right femoral artery.

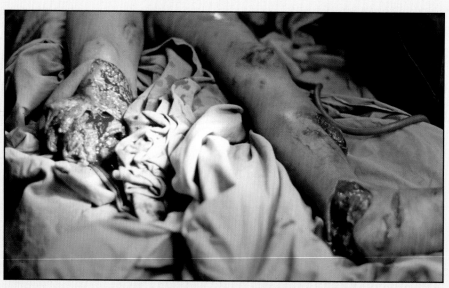

Montagnard boy with right leg blown off by a claymore mine.

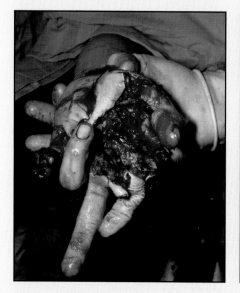

Blast wound of left hand.

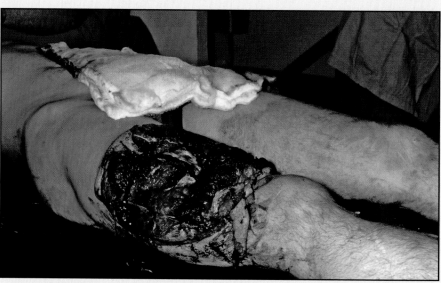

Blast injury of right thigh.

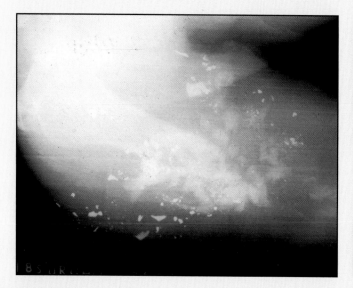

Gunshot wound right humerus near the shoulder showing both shrapnel and bone fragments.

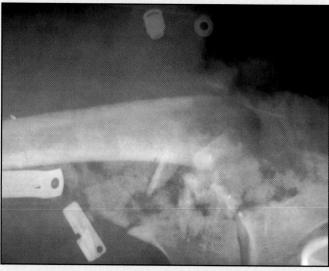

Fracture of hip and pelvis due to gunshot wound. The metal items (i.e. can openers) were in his pocket.

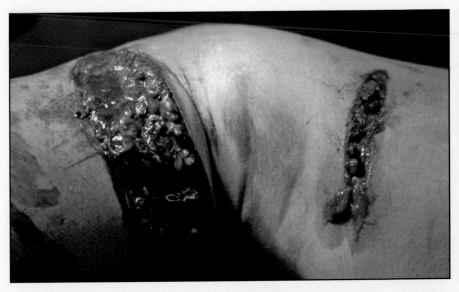

Medial and posterior thigh and upper calf wounds caused by propeller blade on a boat at Lake Bien Ho.

Laceration and thrombosis of right popliteal (behind knee) artery.

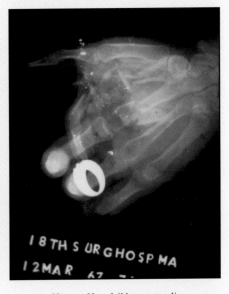

Left tibia and fibula blown away (foot to left, knee to right).

X-ray of hand (blast wound).

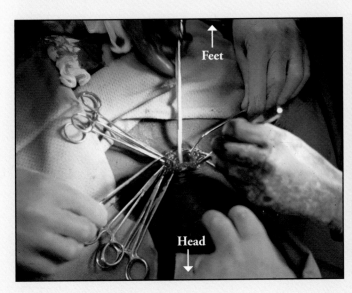

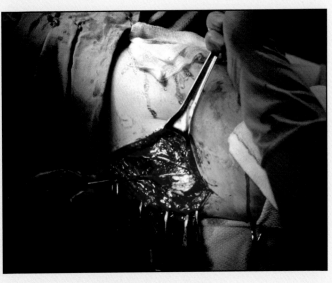

Performing a tracheostomy.

Right posterior hip wound.

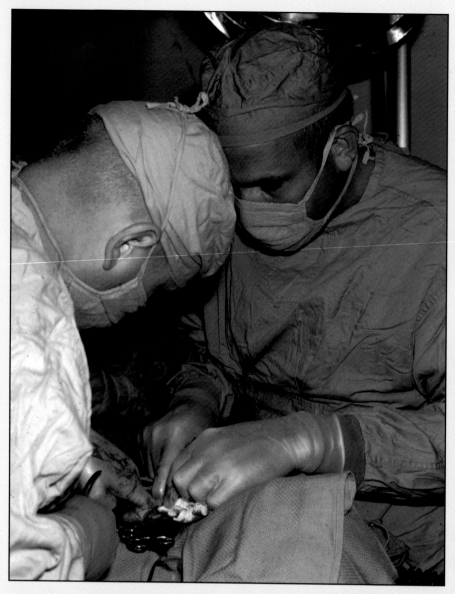

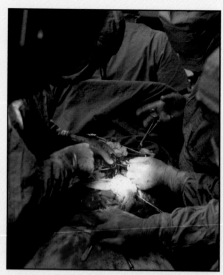

Stuart Poticha, M.D. exploring the abdomen following a penetrating shrapnel wound.

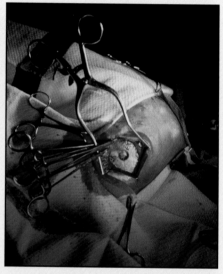

Left to right: Bob Hewitt, M.D. and Bob Engebrecht, M.D. searching for shrapnel fragment inside the abdominal cavity.

Burr hole in the left posterior temporal area with bulging dura (covering of brain) caused by gunshot wound of the head. He died a short time later.

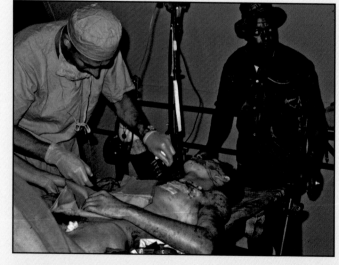

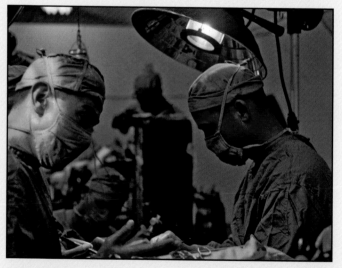

Sam Gillis, M.D. evaluating a patient. Sandy Rameriz is standing at the end of the stretcher.

Left to right: Tony Lindem, M.D., Jerry W. Martin, M.D. and Wayne Hosking, M.D. giving anesthesia. Thoracotomy to repair damage of left lung caused by gunshot wound.

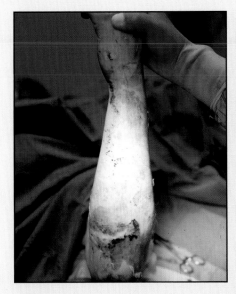

Phosphorus burn of left forearm. Patient died of renal tubular necrosis (kidney failure).

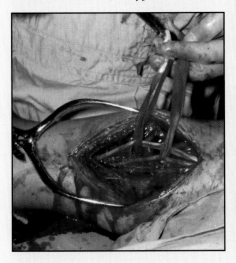

Right brachial artery injury. Upper arm near the axilla (arm pit).

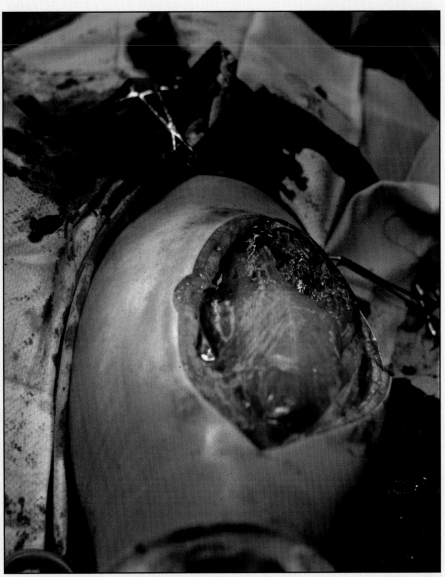

Gunshot wound of left thigh demonstrating the associated marked edema (resulting from high frequency missile) and the fasciotomy (incising the fascia or covering over the muscle to allow muscle to swell outward to preserve circulation).

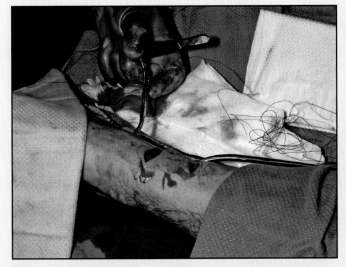

Harvesting a segment of the left saphenous vein for a graft to replace a segment of resected femoral artery thrombosed by high frequency waves caused by AK-47 missile.

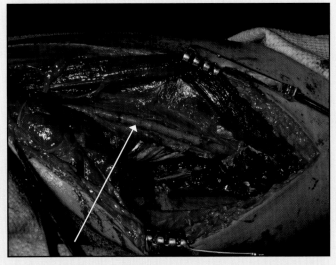

Resected segment of thrombosed femoral artery with saphenous vein graft in place.

157

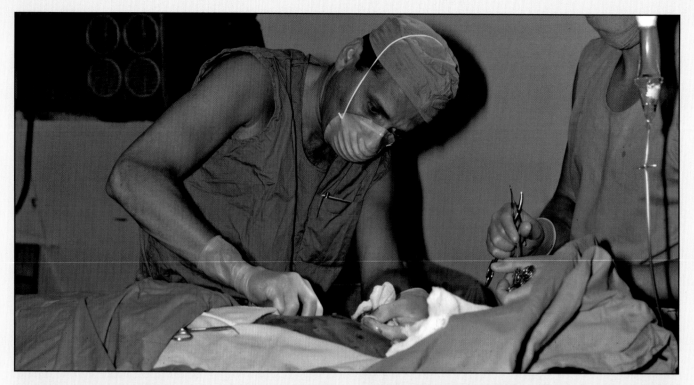

Jerry Rosenberg, M.D. operating at 18th Surgical Hospital, exploring a superficial chest wound.

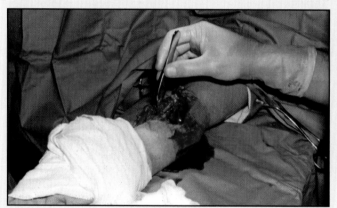

Debridement gunshot wound of left forearm.

Thrombosed right femoral artery secondary to gunshot wound.

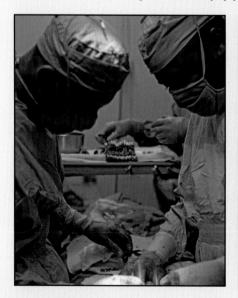

Lt. Col. Cenac, M.D. and Felix Jenkins, M.D. exploring the abdomen.

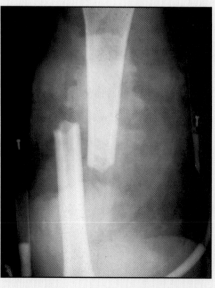

X-ray of femoral fracture.

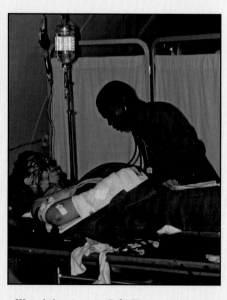

Wounded patients in R & E awaiting surgery.

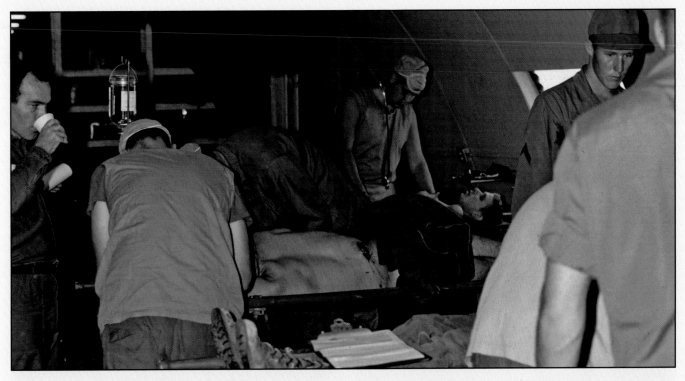

Left to right: Joe Juliano, M.D., Tony Lindem, M.D., (leaning over) and Bob Engebrecht, M.D. in the distance to the right evaluating wounded patients.

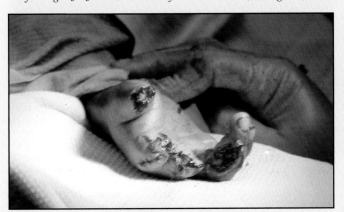

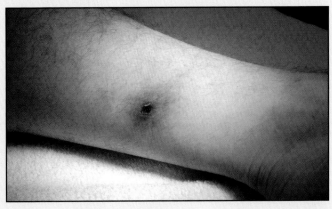

Blast wound of right hand.

Eschar on left leg typical of scrub typhus.

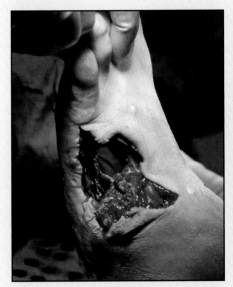

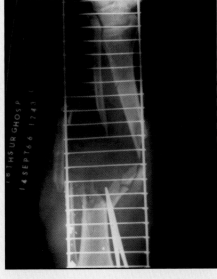

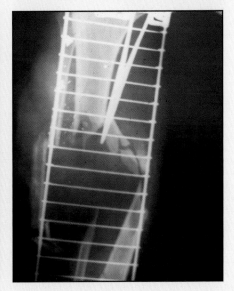

Viet Cong prisoner with old gunshot wound of foot.

High velocity AK-47 bullet wound of leg with fracture of tibia and fibula.

AK-47 bullet wound of leg resulting in fracture of tibia and fibula.

Blast wound of right hand showing macerated muscle and tendons.

Saphenous vein graft of right brachial artery. Note the wide spread hematoma of muscle caused by high frenquency sound waves.

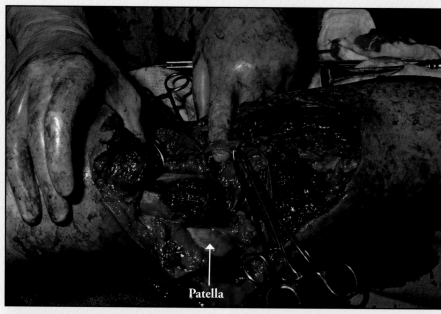

Patella

Repair of shrapnel wound on medial side of right ankle.

Left knee blown away; proximal tibia (leg) to the right, distal femur (thigh) to the left and the patella (knee cap) are visible. Finger is under the popliteal artery.

Viet Cong prisoner with old, dirty, infected wounds.

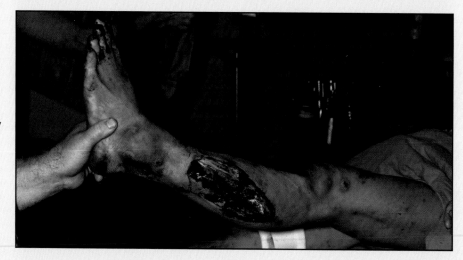

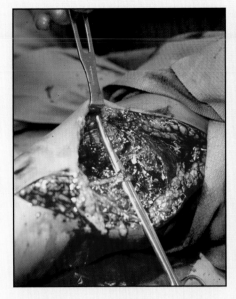

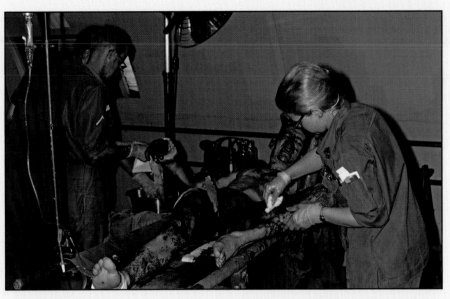

Right arm wound just superior to the antecubital (front of arm at the elbow) space showing the brachial artery and median nerve.

A chopper pilot badly burned in a crash receiving 3rd degree burns to his hands and feet as well as his pelvic, perineal and lower abdominal area. His injury was terminal and he expired within a short time. Lois Wilderman, R.N. attending the patient.

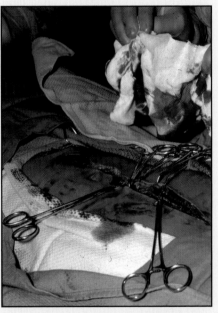

Roger Ecker, M.D. starting IV on Viet Cong prisoner.

Making an abdominal incision.

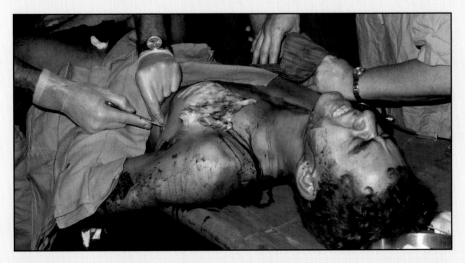

Gunshot wound to the chest with hemopneumothorax. Although sedation and local anesthesia were used, it is painful when the pleura is punctured (i.e. placement of chest tube), unless the patient is completely anesthetized. Note his left chest wound. All penetrating chest wounds had chest tubes before anesthesia.

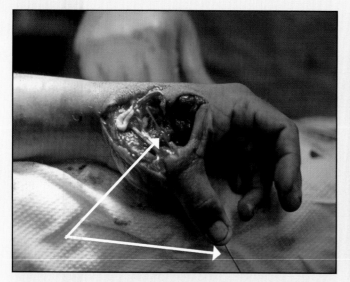

Gunshot wound of left hand. Metal rod used to stabilize multiple thumb fractures.

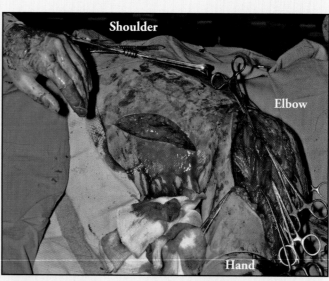

Wound of left arm, elbow and forearm.

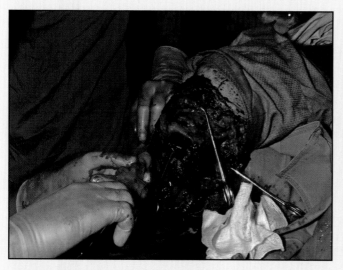

Right leg blown off requiring a BK (below the knee) amputation.

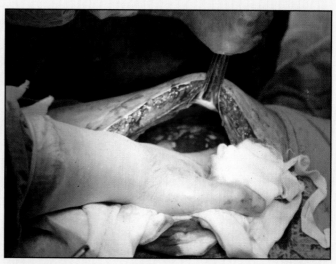

Ruptured amoebic abscess of the liver—content of abscess was yellowish, creamy pudding–like consistency.

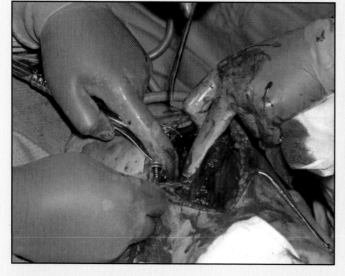

Gunshot wound of left thigh, exploring femoral blood vessels for possible damage.

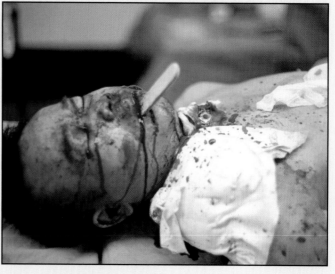

Viet Cong prisoner with head injury and tracheostomy. Tongue blade was in place since he was seizuring intermittently even with heavy sedation. He died within two to three hours. He also had a right shoulder, chest and abdominal wounds.

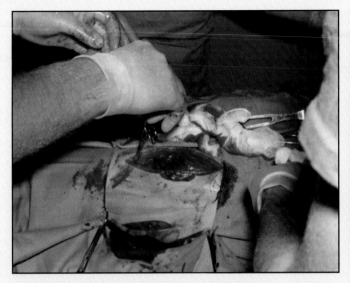

Superficial left thigh wound.

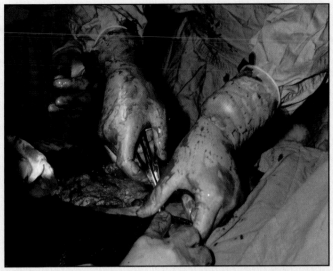

Gunshot wound of thigh, exploring the femoral blood vessels.

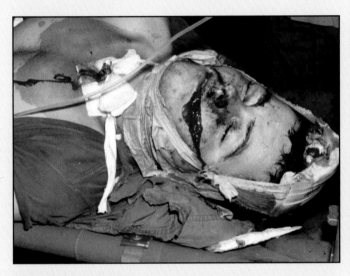

Mortally wounded patient with gunshot wound to the head (brain tissue protruding). He lived only one or two hours.

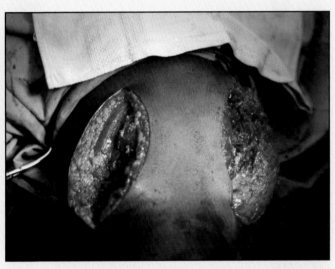

Gunshot wound of left thigh. All such extremity wounds had to have a faciotomy due to extensive swelling and the wound later closed secondarily.

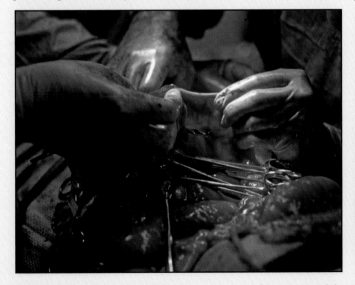

Resection of a section of small bowel to remove perforations caused by gunshot wound.

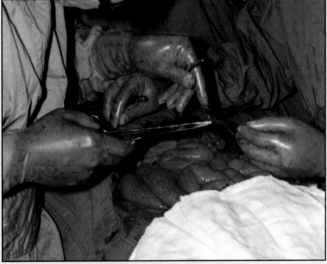

Exploratory laparotomy for shrapnel wound to the abdomen, preparing to "run" the small bowel to inspect for possible perforations.

163

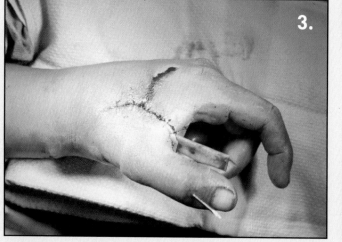

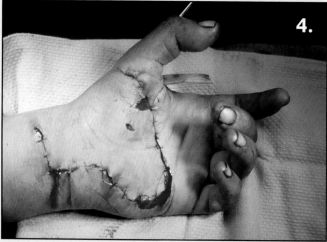

These photographs are of the same hand. We had no way of knowing the outcome, i.e. infections, hand function, etc. We attempted to salvage as much viable tissue as possible to save for reconstructive plastic surgery later. Clockwise: 1. Grenade exploded prematurely (defective ordinance) resulting in hand injury. 2. Same hand, different view. 3. Same hand after repair. 4. Same hand after repair, different view.

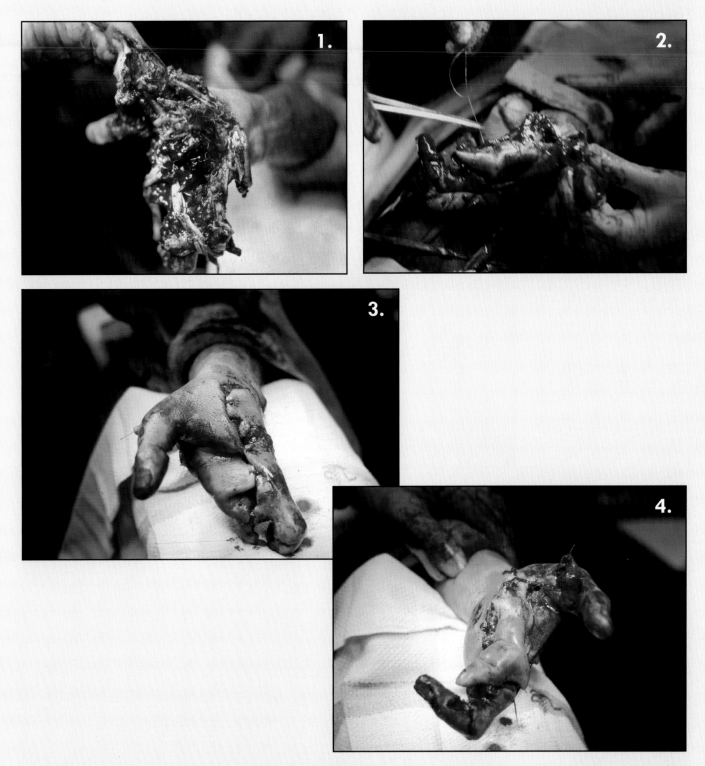

These photographs are of the same hand. Left to right: 1. Blast injury of hand due to premature detonation of grenade—there were too many of these. 2. Attempting to cover all bone, muscle, tendon, etc., with skin. 3. Post-op view. We attempted to save all viable tissue so that later under elective conditions plastic and reconstructive surgeons would have as much tissue as possible to attempt some type of repair to achieve the maximum amount of function. 4. Post-op view.

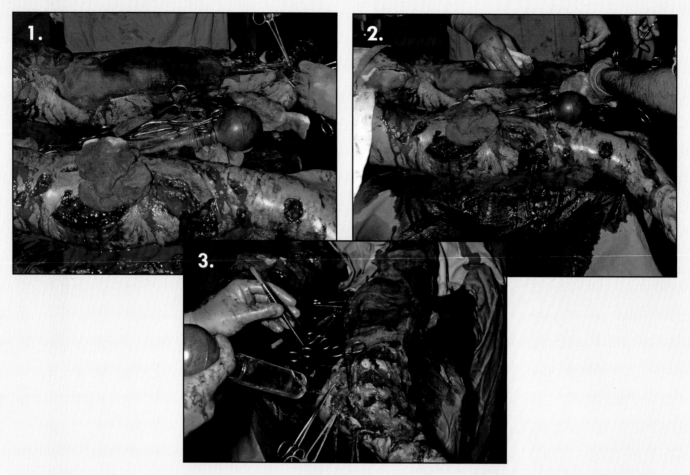

Clockwise: 1. Claimore mine blast damage. This man was second in a patrol. The first man was killed instantly, this man injured below the knees. The next two or three men received lesser injuries while the remainder of the platoon were not injured. 2. Blast wounds below knees. 3. Blast wounds below knees.

This man received 65 units of fresh whole blood and was anesthisitized for many hours—we rotated surgical teams. He survived both his wound and our surgery. Right: Gunshot wound involving the liver—right lobe resected. Below: The resected right lobe of liver.

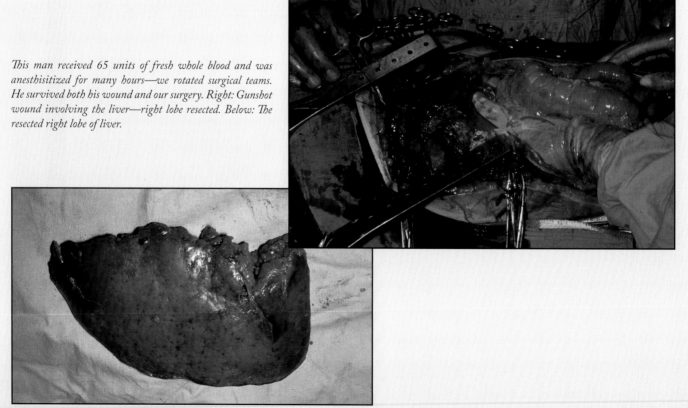

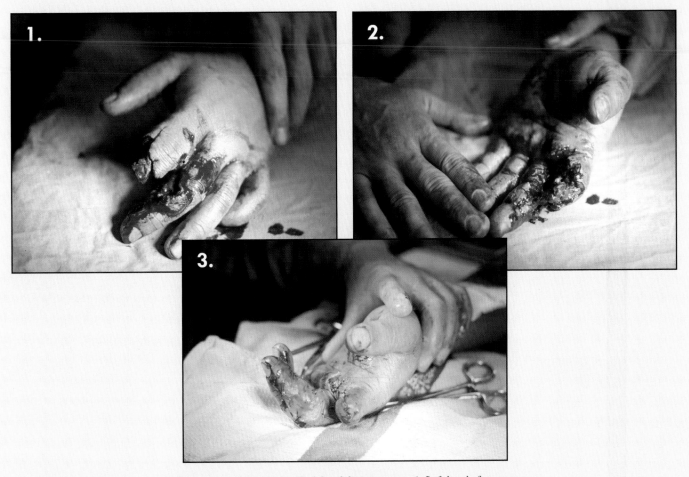

1. Blast injury of left hand. 2. Left hand during surgery. 3. Left hand after surgery.

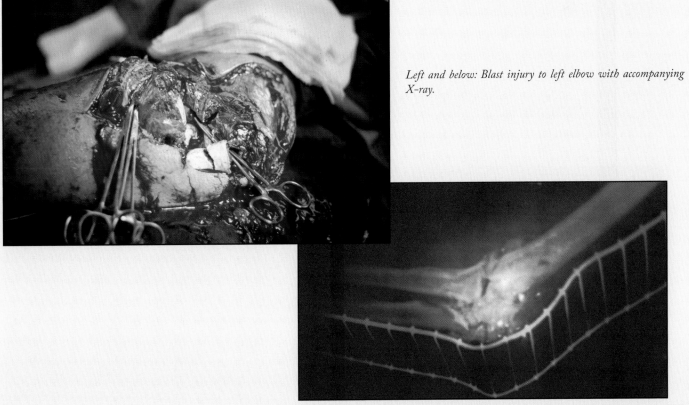

Left and below: Blast injury to left elbow with accompanying X-ray.

This series of wounds depicts injuries sustained by the patient when a bullet entered the patient's right lateral abdomen, perforated the small intestine, stomach and spleen before passing upward through the left hemidiaphragm, punctured the lower left lung and then lodged in the plural space next to the left chest wall. When we opened the chest, we encountered the everted gastric mucosa (lining of the stomach) with the tip of the nasogastric tube (NG) protruding. When we initially put down the NG tube we noticed on X-ray that the tip of the tube was in the left chest (picture #2). We replaced the stomach into the abdominal cavity through the hole in the diaphragm which we sutured and then repaired the lung damage and closed the chest. As we worked on the chest, another surgical team simultaneously made an exploratory incision into the abdominal cavity where they sutured the stomach by re-approximating the margins appropriately, removed the damaged spleen, closed the peritoneum at the bullet's entrance, resected the segment of damaged small bowel and then closed the abdominal incision and the external entrance wound. The chest tube placed at surgery in the left chest was removed on the third day and on the fifth day the patient was evacuated, with some of the surgical drains still in place, to Qui Nhon (85th or 67th Evacuation Hospital). The IV's had been removed and the patient was afebrile, ambulatory and tolerating a soft diet at the time of his transfer.

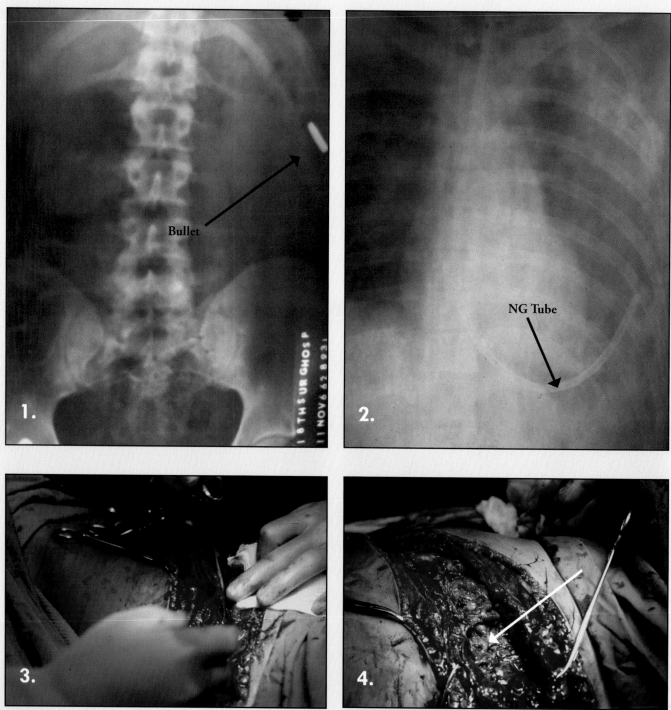

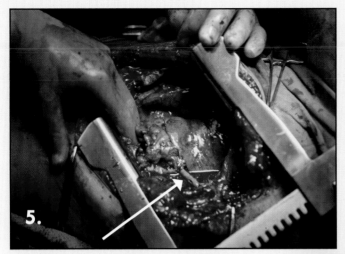

5.

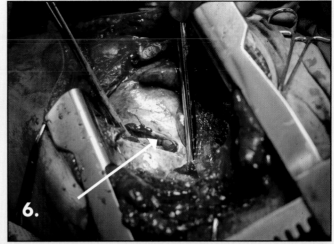

6.

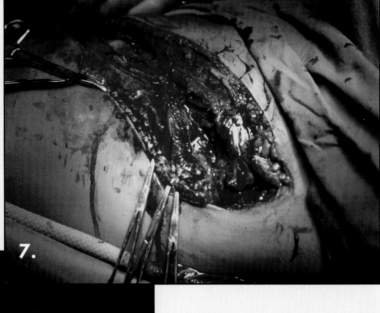

7.

Clockwise, both pages: 1. X-ray showing bullet in left chest, haziness of left lung and free air in the abdomen. The entrance wound was in the right lateral abdomen with no exit wound. 2. X-ray shows a nasogastric tube passing through the esophagus, through the diaphragm into the abdomen (where the stomach should be), then through the left diaphragm into the left chest. 3. Opening left chest. 4. Chest opened with gastric mucosa and tip of NG tube visible. (Stomach everted) 5. NG tube visible. Fingers inside the stomach. The visible lung is left upper lobe and right lobe, tip of heart barely visible. 6. The stomach replaced into the abdominal cavity through the tear in the left diaphragm which was then closed. 7. Closing chest. 8. Hole in left diaphragm viewed from the abdomen. The stomach was then closed. 9. Ruptured spleen with bullet.

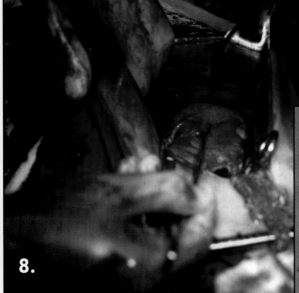

8.

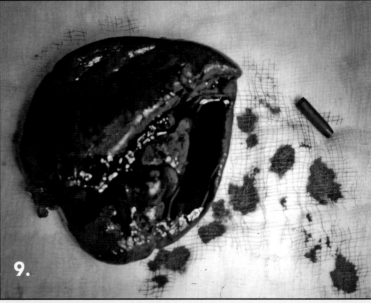

9.

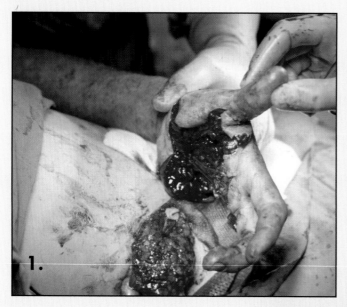

1.

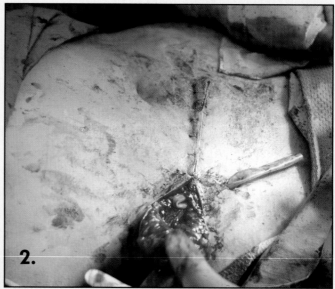

2.

1. Skin denuded from palm of left hand—tendons, blood vessels, nerves etc. intact. 2. Flap of skin from right abdomen created for use as a pedicle graft. 3. Pedicle graft sutured to palm of left hand. 4. View of pedicle graft in place. 5. Approximately three weeks later wounds were well healed. 6. Approximately three weeks later—another view. 7. Pedicle graft amputated from donor site on abdomen. 8. Donor site closed. 9. Palmer surface closed. 10. Approximately two weeks later—wound well healed. Later plastic and reconstructive surgeons could mold and modify his hand to appear more normal. 11. Approximately two weeks later—a different view.

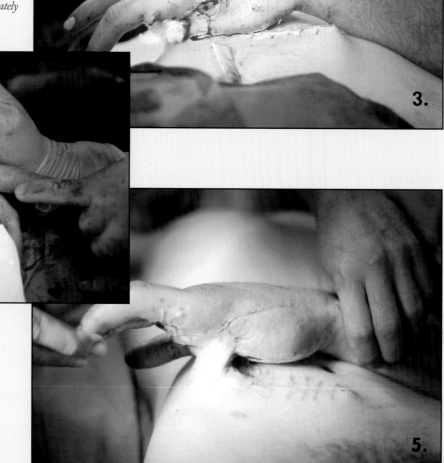

3.

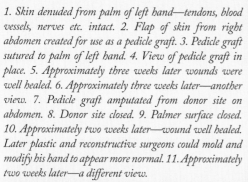

4.

5.

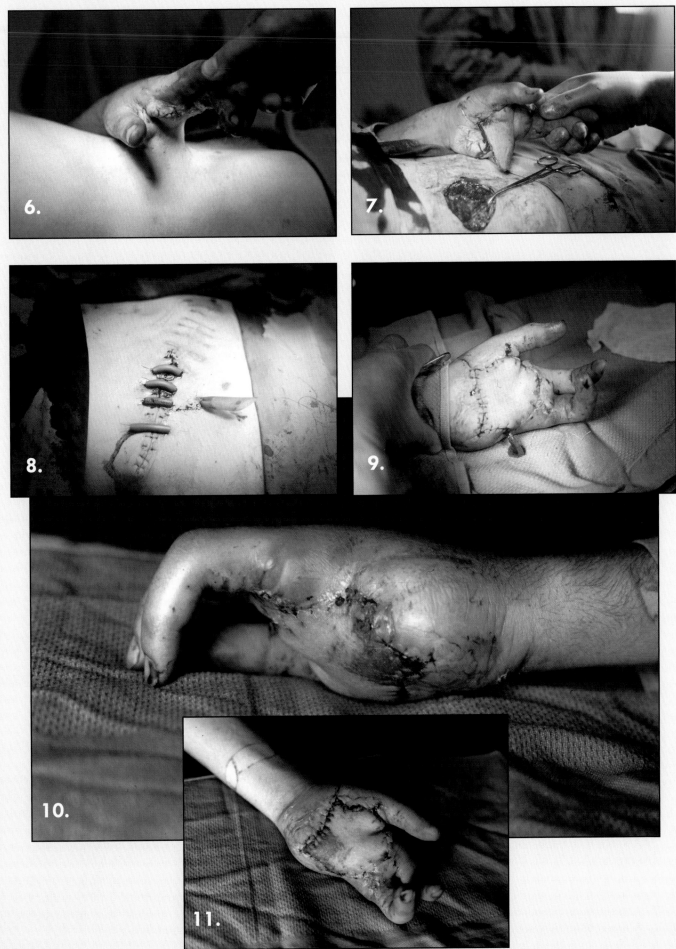

SPEECH BY MAJOR GENERAL VINH LOC AT THE FULRO CEREMONY

Major General Vinh-Loc
Commanding General H Corps and II CTZ
Government Delegate in the Central Highlands
at
The Oath-taking Ceremony of FULRO Returnees
Pleiku, Vietnam

17 October 1966

General Thieu, Chairman of the National Leadership Committee; General Ky, Prime Minister; Excellencies, the Members of the Constituent Assembly; Excellencies, the Ambassadors and Members of the Diplomatic Body; Distinguished Guests.

It is a great honor for all the population and troops in Second Army Corps Tactical Zone to have the opportunity to welcome you to this ceremony, which is an historic event of the Central Highlands.

By its meaning, this ceremony wholly differs from previous celebrations in glory of military victories gained by ARVN and Allied Forces at Plei Me, Plei-Djereng, Ia Drang and Taumorong in the 1966 rainy season for inauguration ceremonies of new political, economic and cultural installations.

This ceremony is of particular importance because it celebrates solemnly the return of Highlander rebels who have finally realized their obligation as citizens and decided resolutely to return into the national ranks in order to make their contribution in the struggle against Communists; the reconstruction and development of the country; and the improvement of the welfare of the population in the Highlands.

This ceremony also celebrates the success which, despite difficulties, the population and troops in II Corps Tactical Zone have gathered in the recent elections of the Constituent Assembly. By their devotion to democratic principles, they have performed the highest ratio of voters all over the country and elected two FULRO representatives into the Assembly. These results prove that the elections have been held in complete honesty and liberty, in accordance with democratic procedure and with full support of the population.

This ceremony by its environment also bears a special meaning. Throughout the 1966 rainy season the VC have gathered only defeats and in harmony with friendly success on every front throughout the Highlands, the FULRO rebels have decided to return to the Government's side. Along the coast in Binh Dinh and Phu Yen provinces, the ARVN and Allied Forces have gone from one victory to another, defeated the VC "Autumn-Winter Campaign," killed and captured thousands of VC guerillas and regulars, seized over one thousand VC weapons, emancipated thousands of people who so far have been reduced to live under VC control.

The present Convention between Lowlanders and Highlanders is organized with two main objectives:

1. To mark a turning point in history, to introduce a new concept in the policy of the Government toward Highlanders, and to welcome the return of FULRO dissidents.
2. To conduct a seminar for the Truong Son Cadres, who for the last year have done their best in every corner of the Central Highlands, so that from experiences learned, their activities become more effective in the reconstruction of the Central Highlands.

Based upon these lessons of experiences, the Program of Instruction at the Truong Son Training Center shall also be revised and improved in order to keep the Pacification and Rural Reconstruction activities in the Highlands abreast of, and in harmony with, those now being conducted successfully by Rural Reconstruction Teams in provinces along the coast in II CTZ.

Today's ceremony also occupies a particular place in our present struggle because it marks the failure of the Colonialists, Communists and saboteurs in their plot to use the FULRO in the subversion of the Central Highlands.

Everyone knows that the so-called FULRO Movement, through its various changes and appellations during the last ten years, was instigated by Colonialists. By their candid ingenuousness, some Highlanders have believed in the Colonialists' fallacious promises and secretly set up "Committees for Autonomy" in some provinces in the Highlands. Then in 1957, by its compulsory and coercive resettlement of the population, the former Ngo regime provided the theme for the subversive propaganda of the Colonialists and Communists and pushed them to incite the Highlanders to oppose the "occupation of land" by Lowlanders.

During the second period, of 1960-61, together with the overt terrorism conducted by the VC, some cadres of the Highlanders' Autonomy Movement were lured by Communists to participate in their ranks and Y BIH ALIO, alias AMAJAP was invested in the so-called Vice-Chairmanship of the VC Committee for the Liberation of South Vietnam. The plan was also devised to attack and occupy some provinces in the Highlands, especially Ban Me Thuot, by VC units disguised as bands of the Highlands' Movement.

In view of a larger expansion, the Communists also organized "tours in North Vietnam" in early 1960 for delegations of Highlanders. They hoped that once back to their tribes, these Highlander delegates would serve as Red propaganda agents and so, the support of the Highlanders to the VC would be increased.

It was partly due to this propaganda that in late 1960, some Highland tribes joined the VC. But only one year after, these tribes began to suffer the harsh realities. Defeated by friendly forces and deprived of food by friendly economic blocks, the VC demasked themselves and made their living with the fruits of the Highlanders' labor. For this reason, in 1961, while the VC coerced the Highland Tribes to join them, the Highlanders also began to strive to escape from their control and in 1962, there was quite an exodus of Highlanders from VC-held areas into Government-controlled territory.

The Highlanders have since realized the truth about VC atrocities. Those who still lived in unsecured areas under VC control looked for opportunities to take refuge in government-controlled zones. The Colonialists and Communists fomented rebellions and incited Highlanders into massacres of Lowlanders last year, at the CIDG Camps of Buon Sarpa, Buon Miga, Buprang, Bandon, Buon Brieng, Buon Ho and Phu Thien.

Toward all these odious atrocities, the Government continued to keep its clemencey and to do whatever possible to settle the problem. Although having committed serious mistakes, the rebels have been given the opportunity to redeem their misdeeds, provided the help necessary for improving their capabilities and the chance to take part in the reconstruction of the Highlands.

It is this perseverance and leniency of the Government, which finally has shown to the rebels the right way which caused them to decide to return. I am proud to report that up to now, the total number of FULRO armed rebels having surrendered amounts to 1479 men with 788 crew-served and individual weapons.

To the FULRO returnees,

Your return is full of significance, not only to your families but also to yourselves because for a long time you have been the victims of the Colonialists and Communist machinations. You have been misled into hazardous ventures and wrong doings.

đại-hội

kinh-thượng

vùng 2 chiến-thuật

từ 13.10 đến 19.10.1966
Pleiku

Thiệp Mời   **INVITATION**

Trân trọng kính mời

quang-lâm tham dự Ngày « ĐẠI HỘI KINH-THƯỢNG » *vào lúc* 08 *giờ* 00 *ngày* 17 *tháng* 10 *năm* 1966 *dưới quyền chủ tọa của* TRUNG - TƯỚNG CHỦ-TỊCH UBLĐQG.

You are cordially invited to attend the « Lowlanders and Highlanders Convention » presided over by NLC chairman at Pleiku the 17th October 1966 0800 hours.

Thiếu-Tướng **VĨNH - LỘC**
TƯ-LỆNH QUÂN-ĐOÀN II – VÙNG 2 CHIẾN-THUẬT
KIÊM ĐẠI-BIỂU CHÍNH-PHỦ

Major General **VĨNH - LỘC**
COMMANDING II CTZ
GVNT. DELEGATE IN CENTRAL HIGHLANDS

Left: The front cover of the invitation for the FULRO Ceremony. Above: The inside of the invitation.

Opening ceremony, raising of flags, lighting of flame, etc. at FULRO.

Maj. Gen. Vinh Loc delivering the welcoming speech at FULRO.

Today, in the solemn atmosphere of this ceremony, permeated with the presence of the Spirits of the Sun and of the Yang, we sincerely share your sorrows and repentance from your past misdeeds as well as your will to redeem your mistakes.

In the presence of the statesmen and all distinguished guests, I should like to stress that this ceremony has been celebrated solemnly because the Government wants to keep its promise that clemencey will be granted to all of you.

The Government has done whatever possible to develop the Highlands and to improve the welfare of the Highlanders. But the Government will not refuse to take hard measures against those who try to breach our national sovereignty.

I sincerely hope that you shall participate in the common struggle against Communists and again we can write together the glorious pages which our ancestors in the Ly and Nguyen Dynasties achieved with the harmony between Lowlanders and Highlanders.

I am sure that all of you are aware of the efforts which our Armed Forces are now making in order to restore peace on our Fatherland and to quickly defeat the enemy. I am satisfied that

you have returned on time because as long as you persist in ignoring the good will of the Government and the aspirations of the Highland tribes, you remain tools of the Communists, your sacrifices completely vain and your struggle as well.

In the Battles of Duc Co, Pleime, PleiDjereng, Buprang, together we Lowlanders and Highlanders as a whole, have shed our blood to defeat the Communists. Our common sacrifice has shown that a real harmony exists between us. I firmly believe that with the present policy and devotion of the Government, the complexes among Highlanders as well as the prejudices among Lowlanders, shall be erased. The reconstruction of our country needs lots of skilled cadres and I sincerely hope that a larger contribution to the prosperity of our nation will be made by capable Highlander cadres.

Excellencies,

Distinguished Guests,

Along with victories on the battlefields, today's ceremony has consecrated the political success which is achieved in the rear by the population and troops in the Central Highlands.

Once again, I sincerely present my heartfelt thanks to you, General Thieu and General Ky, for having honored this ceremony with your presence, in spite of the busy schedule which lies ahead at the next MANILA Conference.

I also should like to present my warmest thanks to you, Excellencies and Distinguished Guests for having so kindly accepted our invitation.

I also should like to take this opportunity to thank deeply the US AID Representatives and MACV Advisors for the tremendous material help they have given us in the organization of this Convention and Ceremony. Without their support, it would be a hard task for us to celebrate today's event with all the pomp and solemnity it deserves for such a historic occasion.

Please accept our deep gratitude for the tremendous contribution to the common struggle for the welfare of the large and rough High Plateaus.

SCIENTIFIC PAPERS BY BOB HEWITT, M.D.

Acute Arteriovenous Fistulas in War Injuries*

by Robert L. Hewitt, Capt., MC, USAR,
Daniel J. Collins, Capt., MC, USAR

From the Division of Surgery, Walter Reed Army Institute of Research, Walter Reed Army Medical Center, Washington, D.C. 20012

Acute arteriovenous fistulas frequently result from and follow vascular injuries. Chronic arteriovenous communications were frequent during World War II, because arteriovenous fistulas seldom were treated in forward hospitals.[1] Repair was delayed intentionally until the patient reached an established vascular center.[2] As recently as the Korean conflict, selected injuries of the carotid and subclavian vessels were not operated upon during initial treatment.[3]

Experience with arterial injuries in Vietnam emphasizes the practicality of prompt repair at forward hospitals of all major acute arterial injuries except those requiring partial or total cardiopulmonary bypass. This is a report of arteriovenous fistulas which immediately followed war injuries and which were repaired at the time the patient was first admitted to the hospital.

Clinical Material

Six of 60 patients with arterial injuries treated from December, 1966, through October, 1967, at the 18th Surgical Hospital (MA) and during November, 1967, at the 71st Evacuation Hospital, Vietnam, were operated upon for acute arteriovenous fistulas. The hospitals, located at Pleiku in the Central Highlands, treated a large number of injured patients from the II Corps area during the months indicated.

Five U.S. Infantrymen had acute arteriovenous fistulas, and one Montagnard Striker was referred with a chronic fistula. The acute fistulas were noted upon admission of the patients to the hospital, which ranged from 1 to 6 hours following injury. The patient with a chronic fistula was admitted two months following injury.

Cause of Injury

The injuries in all six patients were caused by fragments from grenades, artillery, or mortar. During the same period the causes of all arterial injuries at those hospitals were equally divided between gunshot and fragment wounds. The association of arteriovenous fistulas with small arterial wounds caused by low velocity fragments was noted in World War II.[2]

Location of Fistula

Table 1 lists the sites of the six arteriovenous fistulas. The carotid, external iliac, superficial femoral, and popliteal fistulas were acute, whereas the brachial fistula was chronic and associated with an aneurysm. (Figure 1).

Diagnosis

Diagnosis was established by physical examination in all instances. A distinct thrill was present in all but one patient; a popliteal fistula had no detectable thrill, and its murmur could be detected only by careful auscultation. The site of injury often was unimpressive (Figure 2A). A moderate amount of hematoma was usual, and peripheral pulse were present in all patients. Arteriography was used to demonstrate the precise location of a popliteal arteriovenous fistula on one occasion (Figure 2B) and to demonstrate the chronic brachial fistula and false aneurysm.

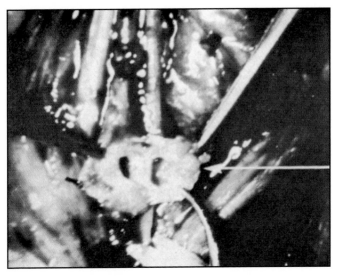

Figure 1. Chronic arteriovenous fistula and aneurysm of brachial artery.

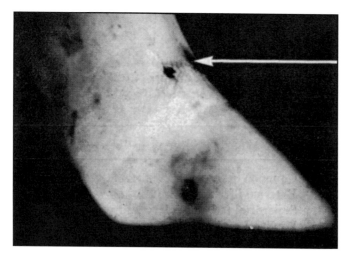

Figure 2A. Fragment wound popliteal space resulted in acute arteriovenous fistula. Diagnosis made by the presence of a murmur.

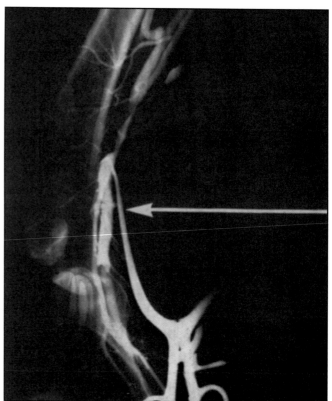

Figure 2B. Arteriogram showing popliteal arteriovenous fistula in same patient.

Operation

The artery and vein routinely were isolated proximally and distally to the fistula. At least 500 ml. of fresh hematoma was present in each acute injury, but proper proximal and distal control of the vessels prevented further blood loss (Figure 2C).

Vein grafts were used for arterial reconstruction in the common carotid, superficial femoral, and both popliteal fistulas (Figure 2D), but the external iliac artery was repaired by direct suture. Although repair of all veins was attempted, extensive and multiple venous injuries required ligation of the external iliac, the superficial femoral and one popliteal vein. The brachial repair, because of the small size of the artery, was accomplished by endoaneurysmorrhaphy, and the vein was ligated.

Table 1. Arteriovenous Fistulas, 18th Surgical Hospital, MA and 71st Evacuation Hospital, Vietnam, December 1966-November 1967	
Patient	Location of Fistula
1.	Common carotid artery, internal jugular vein
2.	External iliac artery and vein
3.	Superficial femoral artery and vein
4.	Popliteal artery and vein
5.	Popliteal artery and vein
6.	Brachial artery and vein; false aneurysm

Following thorough debridement of the wounds, the arterial reconstructions were covered by a layer of muscle. The subcutaneous tissues and skin were not closed initially in patients with acute injuries, but were closed by delayed primary technic 4 to 5 days later.

Results

All patients had satisfactory results with excellent peripheral pulsations immediately following operation. A single complication,

transient leg edema, occurred in the patient who required ligation of the external iliac vein. The edema subsided, and 6 months later the patient was active with no edema or disability. These results compare favorably to an approximate 83 percent success rate for arterial injuries treated at the 18th Surgical Hospital (MA) during this same period.

Discussion

Restorative arterial surgery at Surgical Hospitals has become routine in Vietnam. Arterial injuries receive highest priority and are operated upon whenever the patient reaches the hospital. The development of chronic arteriovenous fistulas and pulsating hematomas thus should be largely prevented.

A surprising number of arteriovenous fistulas develop almost immediately and are diagnosed upon admission to the hospital. All penetrating wounds which are near major arteries should be carefully examines by palpation and auscultation. Auscultation is all too frequently omitted in the examination of extremity wounds. The reasons for considering such injuries as emergencies are obvious. The presence of continued blood flow through the artery and absence of ischemia favor an excellent prognosis for this particular vascular injury.

Summary

Six among 60 arterial injuries at the 18th Surgical Hospital (MA) and 71st Evacuation Hospital, Vietnam, were treated for arteriovenous fistulas. Five of six fistulas caused by war injuries were acute, and one was chronic.

All injuries were caused by fragments, and diagnosis was obvious at time of admission. The importance of auscultation of all penetrating wounds near major arteries is emphasized. Patients with carotid-jugular, femoral and popliteal arteriovenous fistulas had their arteries repaired with autogenous vein grafts, while an external iliac injury was repaired by direct suture and a brachial artery fistula and aneurysm was repaired by endoaneurysmorrhaphy. All patients had satisfactory results.

Acute arteriovenous fistulas, like other acute arterial injuries, should be operated upon promptly. The presence of continued blood flow through the artery and absence of ischemia favor an excellent prognosis in this injury.

References

1. DeBakey, M.E. and Simeone, F.A.: Acute battle-incurred arterial injuries, Medical Department, United States Army, Surgery in World War II, Vascular Surgery, Office of the Surgeon General, Department of the Army, Washington, DC, 1955, p. 60.

2. Elkin, D.C. and Shumaker, H.B., Jr.: Arterial aneurysms and arteriovenous fistulas. General Considerations, same p. 149.

3. Hughes, C.D.: Arterial repair during the Korean War. Ann. Surg., 147:555, 1958.

*From the 18th Surgical Hospital (MA) and 71st Evacuation Hospital, Vietnam.

Reprinted from Annals of Surgery, Vol. 169, No. 3, March 1969, Copyright © 1969 by J.B. Lippincott Company

1. Fisher, G.W.: Acute Arterial Injuries Treated by the United States Army Medical Service in Vietnam, 1965-66, J Trauma 7:844-855 (Nov) 1967.

2. Eiseman, B.: Combat Casualty Management, J Trauma 7:53-63 (Jan) 1967.

Reprinted with permission from the Archives of Surgery, March 1969, Volume 98, American Medical Association © 1969.

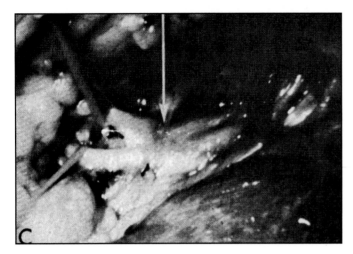

Figure 2C. Popliteal artery and vein isolated proximally and distally to fistula.

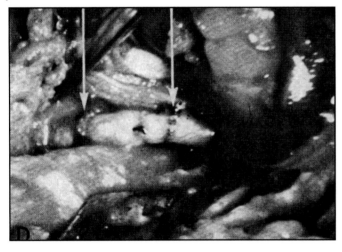

Figure 2D. Autogenous vein graft in popliteal artery repair.

Arterial Injuries at a Surgical Hospital in Vietnam

by CPT Robert L. Hewitt, MC, USAR;
CPT Daniel J. Collins, MC, USAR; and
COL Harold F. Hamit, MC, USA, Vietnam

Experience in Vietnam has confirmed the practicality of repair of arterial injuries at forward hospitals. Air evacuation by helicopter directly to Surgical, Evacuation, or Field Hospitals has resulted in an increased number of patients having repair of injured arteries. Certain problems related to extent of injury and delay in treatment still exist and contribute to loss of life and limb. The following report is based upon the experience of a Surgical Hospital (MA) during the 15 months of its location in the Central Highlands of Vietnam.

Clinical Material

A review of arterial injuries treated at the 18th Surgical Hospital (MA) in Vietnam from July 1966 through September 1967 included 62 patients who required arterial repair. The 18th Surgical Hospital (MA), located at Pleiku, treated a large number of patients from the II Corps area and performed over 2,500 operations during this period. Omitted from the series are patients in whom only arterial spasm was found at operation.

Injuries

Cause of Injury—The majority of wounds were caused by either gunshot (30) or fragment (28) from grenades, mortar, or artillery. There were three wounds caused by puncture, and one injury was due to blunt trauma. Fisher,[1] in a recent survey of vascular injuries in Vietnam found 64.8% of the wounds to be caused by fragments and only 30.6% due to gunshot.

Type of Injury—Fifty-one injuries consisted of either penetration, perforation, lateral laceration, or transection of the artery. Occlusion without penetration was seen in five patients and was caused by fracture of the intima with a variable degree of disruption and subsequent thrombosis. While the artery appeared intact, subadvential hematoma was usually present.

Five patients presented with arteriovenous fistulas. One patient sustained a laceration of the external iliac artery from blunt trauma resulting in fracture of the pelvis.

Arteries Injured—The most commonly injured arteries were the superficial femoral, 24; brachial, 21; and popliteal, 10. Other arterial injuries included two of the external iliac and one each of the common femoral, innominate, common carotid, internal carotid, and radial arteries.

Associated Fractures—Fractures were associated with approximately one-half of the 62 arterial injuries. Among patients with popliteal injuries, fractures were usual, occurring in eight of ten. Among 24 patients with superficial femoral injuries, there were ten who had fractures, and nine of the 21 patients with brachial artery injuries had fractures. Fractures were more frequent in this series than in the recent report by Fisher,[1] who

found fractures to be associated with 32% of vascular injuries in Vietnam.

Associated Injuries—Thirty-two patients had other major injuries, and 30 patients had primarily vascular injuries. Table 1 lists the sites of associated injuries. Eight of ten patients requiring abdominal exploration were found to have intra-abdominal injury.

Diagnosis—The diagnosis of arterial injury was generally prompted by location of the wound, presence of hematoma, or evidence of impovished blood flow to the part. A considerable number of patients with injuries to the brachial or the superficial femoral arteries had a palpable pulse in the respective wrist or ankle of the injured limb.

Arteriography was rarely used initially, although it was frequently used following repair (Figure 1). Because all wounds required debridement, direct exploration of the artery usually circumvented the unnecessary delay of the arteriography. Arteriovenous fistulas may accompany minute and innocent appearing fragment wounds, and, thus, may be overlooked. Ascultation of such wounds is indicated.

Management

Arterial Repair—Autogenous vein grafts were used in 38 repairs, direct suture in 21, venous patch angioplasty in two, and a Dacron graft was used once. Table 2 illustrates the type of repair done for the most commonly injured arteries; superficial femoral, brachial and popliteal.

The decision to use a vein graft rather than direct suture is one which generally must be based on experience. Since it is most often necessary to resect 2 cm or more of artery in war injuries, vein grafts are usually required to prevent tension This is particularly true for wounds of the popliteal artery where vein grafts were used almost routinely (nine of ten patients).

The greater saphenous vein is taken from the uninjured leg in femoral and popliteal injuries. For repair of the brachial artery, a superficial vein from the injured arm is usually satisfactory (Fig 2). Plastic sutures rather than silk should be used for arterial repair in war wounds.

Direct suture repair is adequate in instances where extensive arterial debridement is not required and where tension is not required and where tension is not a problem. Venous patch angioplasty is useful in the repair of small arteries such as at the brachial bifurcation, the radial, and the ulnar arteries, but should not be used for repair of larger arteries in war injuries. Radial and ulnar arterial injuries of the forearm should be repaired in all instances when time permits.

Dacron grafts are used in instances where autogenous veins are too small. A Dacron graft was used in one instance to repair a severed external iliac artery.

Injuries of the common carotid or internal carotid arteries must be repaired promptly. When the artery is not transected and is assumed to be still perfusing the brain, the use of an internal shunt and systemic heparinization should be considered during temporary occlusion. The use of hypoventilation to assist cerebral

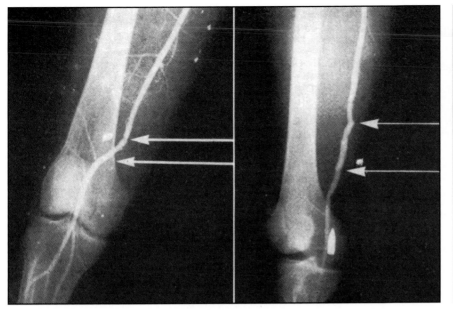

Figure 1. Left, Femoral arteriogram showing femoral popliteal autogenous vein graft following fragment wound. Right, Operative arteriogram showing autogenous vein graft in distal femoral artery following high velocity missile (AK-47) wound.

Figure 2. Autogenous vein graft in distal brachial artery.

vasodilatation and the prevention of hypotension are further important adjuncts.

Table 1. Sites of Associated Injuries

Associated Injuries	Number of Injuries
Abdomen	10
Chest	9
Neck	6
Head	5
Upper extremities	7
Lower extremities	5
Total	**42**

Following any arterial repair, the vessels should be covered with at least one layer of viable, healthy tissue. Muscle usually is used. The subcutaneous tissue and skin were not closed initially but were closed by delayed primary technic, four or more days later.

Stabilization of Fractures—Internal fixation of fractures of the femur with an intramedullary nail was done whenever possible (Fig 3). Although balanced suspension following internal fixation of the femur or balanced skeletal traction, when intramedullary nailing is impossible, are preferable to plaster immobilization, spica casts were used because of the necessity for early evacuation. All casts and circular padding should be bivalved to the skin as soon as possible after application.

Adjunctive Measures—Debridement of devitalized tissue should be completed at the initial operation, but suspicion of inadequate debridement should prompt another inspection of the wound in the operating room with care not to expose the arterial repair.

Decompressing incisions in the fascia of the leg are indicated in most war wounds of the popliteal and lower superficial femoral artery. The anterior, lateral, and posterior compartments can be decompressed through separate anterior, posterolateral, and posteromedial incision through skin and fascia. Decompression of the deep posterior compartment is often indicated. Development of edema or tenseness in the leg following operation should prompt a second inspection of all muscle groups.

Prevention of edema begins with the prompt restoration of arterial and venous flow. Concomitant venous injuries should be repaired whenever possible. Following operation, a limb should be elevated if significant venous injury, fracture, or extensive soft tissue injury exists. Elevation of a limb following arterial reconstruction does not interfere with arterial flow, provided the repair is satisfactory, the arterial tree is patent, and the perfusing pressure is adequate.

Results

There were three deaths among 62 patients; two patients died from cerebral edema and coma following repair of transected common and internal carotid arteries, and one death occurred in a patient requiring bilateral above knee amputation following repair of one superficial femoral artery. Extensive muscle destruction and infection were considered contributory to his death.

Five patients with arteriovenous fistulas were operated upon, and all had excellent results. Included were acute arteriovenous fistulas of the external iliac, superficial, and popliteal arteries. A chronic brachial fistula with aneurysm in a Montagnard Striker was also repaired (Fig 4).

There were 11 amputations in this series, only three of which were performed at the 18th Surgical Hospital. The results of the three most common arterial injuries, superficial femoral, popliteal

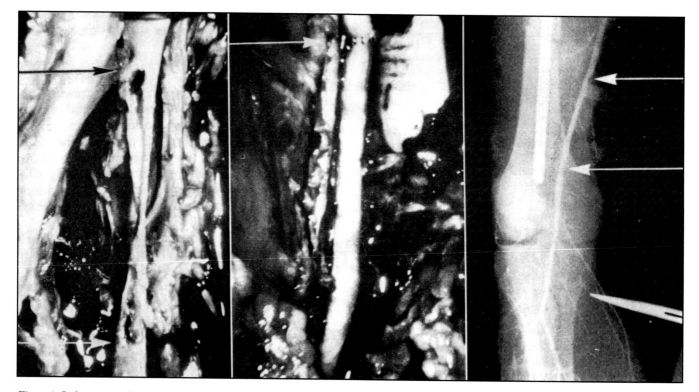

Figure 3. Left, extensive laceration of superficial femoral artery and open fracture of femur. Center, autogenous vein graft in same patient. Right, femoral arteriogram demonstrating long vein graft and intramedullary nail in femur in same patient.

and brachial, are shown in Table 2, which includes the 11 patients who required amputation. Four patients requiring amputation following repair of the superficial femoral artery had sustained injuries to the distal superficial femoral. The seriousness of popliteal artery injury in Vietnam has been emphasized by Eiseman,[2] who found that estimates of success following repair ranged from ten percent to fifty percent.

Table 3 illustrates several interesting features about those patients who eventually required amputation of an extremity. Fractures were present in ten of 11 of these patients. Eight of 11 injuries were due to high velocity gunshot wound, and eight of 11 injuries were associated with massive muscle destruction. Four patients in the series were admitted in profound shock, and all four were among the patients ultimately requiring amputation. Three of them were among the four failures of repair of the superficial femoral artery. At least six of 11 patients had either palpable pulses distal to the repair or arteriographic evidence of blood flow past the repair at the time of amputation.

Comment

The repair of arterial injuries in a forward Surgical Hospital is now routine. The limiting factors in success are related to extent of accompanying soft tissue injury, presence of fractures and delay in treatment.

The most curious phenomenon is that of necrosis of muscle in spite of arterial repair and evidence of blood flow through the reconstructed artery. Such eventual necrosis may be an irreversible change initiated at the time of injury through ischemia, extensive soft tissue, and smaller vessel damage. These changes are to a great extent enhanced by the development of swelling of the muscular tissue in tight fascial compartments with subsequent interference with arterial inflow, especially capillary circulation.

Death, following repair of the carotid artery, might be attributed to ischemia before and during repair and cerebral edema following revascularization. Data are not sufficient for further speculation.

Summary

Experience with arterial injuries at Surgical Hospital (MA) in Vietnam during a 15 month period included 62 patients who required an arterial repair. Cause of injury was approximately equally divided between gunshot and fragment wounds from grenades, mortar, or artillery.

The superficial femoral, brachial, and popliteal arteries were the most commonly injured arteries. Five patients with arteriovenous fistula and five patients with occlusion without penetration were included. Over one-half of the patients had fractures associated with vascular injury, and most had multiple injuries.

Repair included 38 autogenous vein grafts, 21 primary repairs, and two venous patch angioplasties. Internal fixation of femoral fractures was used whenever possible.

Two patients died following carotid artery injuries, and one died with massive wounds of the lower extremities. Eventual failure was known to occur in four of 24 superficial femoral, in one of 21 brachial, and in six of 10 popliteal repairs, although patency of the repair at the time of amputation was usual. Failure was related to high velocity of the missile, presence of shock, delay in treatment, fracture, and extent of soft tissue injury.

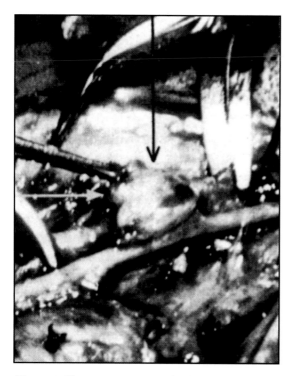

Figure 4. Chronic arteriovenous fistula and aneurysm of brachial artery.

Prompt arterial repair and restoration of blood flow are most important. Emphasis must also be directed toward satisfactory debridement of devitalized tissue, decompression of muscle, stabilization of fractures, prevention of edema, and prompt treatment of shock.

References

1. Fisher, G.W.: Acute Arterial Injuries Treated by the United States Army Medical Service in Vietnam, 1965-66, *J Trauma* 7:844-855 (Nov) 1967.

2. Eiseman, B.: Combat Casualty Management, *J Trauma* 7:53-63 (Jan) 1967.

Table 2. Type of Repair and Results in Injuries of Superficial Femoral, Brachial and Popliteal Arteries

Artery	Type of Repair			Total	Eventual Amputation
	Autogenous Vein Graft	Direct Suture	Venous Patch Angioplasty		
Superficial femoral	14	10	0	24	4
Brachial	14	6	1	21	1
Popliteal	9	1	0	10	6*

* Includes one popliteal to posterior tibial arterial graft.

Table 3. Arterial Repairs Resulting in Amputation

Artery Repaired	Eventual Amputation	Patent Repair at Amputation	Factors Favoring Amputation			
			High Velocity Gunshot Wound	Profound Shock	Fracture	Massive Muscle Injury
Popliteal	6	3	4	1	6	4
Superficial femoral	4	3	3	3	3	3
Brachial	1	0	1	0	1	1

PERSONAL STATEMENTS FROM MEMBERS OF THE 18TH SURGICAL HOSPITAL (MA) (PLEIKU, LAI KHE, QUANG TRI)

Pleiku History
by Sam Gillis, M.D.

On March 9, 1966, I left the United States by air. I arrived in Qui Nhon about March 13, 1966. I was assigned to the 67th Evacuation Hospital, which opened September 1966, six months after I arrived. The 85th Evacuation Hospital was already in Qui Nhon and was set up in Quonset Huts with air conditioning. I was in a GP large tent with two other physicians and six male nurses. We slept on canvas cots. We were cooled by a large space fan. We had a refrigerator on our wooden floor. A married couple shared a small tent just 20 feet from our tent. We had a shower platform that had plenty of fresh clean water. Wooden sides about 4 feet high were there for privacy. The South China Sea was 500 meters to the East. A nice beach about 200 meter wide with barbed wire extending out into the water on each side was guarded by soldiers with M-16 weapons. Nurses, male and female, doctors and enlisted men all enjoyed the beach. An outside movie theater

Sam Gillis, M.D. delivering the mail.

showed movies every night. Take your lawn chair and watch the movie, old TV program or replay of a 3-week-old baseball game.

We saw a fair number of wounded, but also did some pacification work. I was taught and repaired several cleft lips. I did little else. We could eat at the mess hall or walk to one of several officers' clubs in the area. A refrigerator ship in the harbor was filled with steaks that needed to be eaten. We obliged.

In early May 1966, I went to Nha Trang to the 5th Field Hospital to fill in while the surgeon was on R&R. We had a private dining room and a nice beach. The nurses in Nha Trang were much prettier than the nurses in the 85th or 67th. I enjoyed my week in the 5th Field Hospital but did little surgery.

Back in Qui Nhon it was a little busier. About June 1, 1966, two surgical teams were taken from the 67th and sent to Pleiku to help a clearing company. We took two trained surgeons, two assistant surgeons, one anesthesiologist and about four male nurses, and ten enlisted corpsmen. We were busy. We would start operating about 5 pm every day and finish about 11 or 12. We had a generator. We had a water truck and scrub sinks that had to be filled frequently. We would go to bed after our last patient and get up about 8 or 9 a.m. We did not make rounds because all of the patients that had surgery had already been evacuated by the clearing company doctors. There was also a Surgical K team there. (Ecker???). The 18th MASH arrived in late June 1966 and took over our equipment. I returned to Qui Nhon by helicopter. The remaining 67th personal remained several days and also returned to the 67th.

With little to do in the 85th, we had two sets of hospital personal; I made a quick trip to the USA. I accompanied a wounded patient with an eye injury to Washington, D.C. to Walter Reed Hospital and then made a quick trip to Mississippi. I got back about two weeks later and found out I was being transferred to the 18th in Pleiku. I didn't know why except they told me they needed an experienced battle surgeon in Pleiku. (The only experience I had was the four weeks in Pleiku in June.)

In August 1966, I moved permanently to the 18th MASH— my lucky day. Let it be known that the landscape and weather in Pleiku is much like September and October in Mississippi. I felt like I was home. The 18th was also so much smaller than the 67-85th that it felt like family.

You know my history from there. I was in Bangkok in January 1967 when the hospital area was mortared. I left for home on emergency leave on February 17, 1967. I left so quickly that few knew I was gone. I gave Goodwine my poncho liner and took off. I missed my going away party. When I got home my ill son was completely well. The case had been overstated to get me out early. I am still not happy about that. I wanted to serve my time (and I wanted to say good-bye.)

447th Medical Detachment (MILPHAP)
by Skip Ellison, M.D.

Why did USA go into Vietnam and how did I end up in Pleiku?

There are many possible answers to the first question involving decisions made by Presidents Truman, Eisenhower, Kennedy, and Johnson. The net result of this series of decisions was a major war costing thousands of American lives and considerably more Vietnamese. Johnson made the major decision in 1965 to commit American combat units—not just advisors as Eisenhower (who first articulated the Domino theory) did with "noncombatant advisors" and Kennedy with "combatant advisors"—and with those combat units, medical units were sent to provide direct in country support.

Although I integrated into the Regular Army (RA) to qualify for a family practice (FP) residency at Fort Dix, NJ, I was not interested in a prolonged separation from my family and so in Sept '65 I went to Washington and volunteered for an accompanied overseas tour in Pakistan. Even though accompanied, the tour was so undesirable it was only two years instead of the usual three-year overseas tour. The assignment officer was delighted (and incredulous?) that I would volunteer for that assignment and hastily agreed to my request. I returned to Fort Dix confident that nine months later I and my family would head to Pakistan. Two weeks later I was summoned to the C.O.'s office, informed that I was going to Vietnam, and given two weeks to clear post and relocate Mary and our children (15 months and 3 years). So much for advance planning in the Army! The FP residency had already convinced me that I wanted to be an anesthesiologist and the abrupt change in orders convinced Mary and me that we were not RA-material.

Fort Sam Houston, Camp Bullis, & the 447th Med Detachment

In October 1965, three Army, two Air Force, and two Navy detachments, each consisting of three physicians, one administrative officer, and twelve medics were activated at Fort Sam, the vanguard of twenty-five such units, and underwent two weeks training and orientation to Vietnam, including an evening E&E (escape & evasion) training exercise in the cactus jungles of Camp Bullis. Very little of our training had any applicability to what we experienced in Pleiku!

MILPHAP

In Jan 1963 the Army began a Medical Civic Action Program (MEDCAP) to improve outpatient care for the Vietnamese civilian population. With the force escalation in 1965 there was a significant increase termed the Military Provincial Health Assistance Program (MILPHAP) with the major objective to improve the training of Vietnamese MDs, RNs, & medical techs. In reality what happened was that the US medical units began to provide the major portion of direct care to the civilian patients in eventually 25 of the 44 provincial hospitals.

One of the major limitations to care provided was the limited experience of the physicians—most of us were just out of internships. While I had performed some minor surgical procedures as an FP resident, I was reluctant to do anything more than urgent C-sections. The C.O. of the 1st Cav Medical Company had been an OB/GYN resident at Tripler Army Hospital in Honolulu when I was an intern (in time of war gynecologists become trauma surgeons) and I recruited him to do a hysterectomy for me—but it was the arrival of the 18th Surg in Spring 1966 which provided the 447th with real surgical support for our patients. During quiet periods their willingness to come down and help was much appreciated. In turn during periods of peak casualty flow I would take a portion of the 447th to assist the triage officer.

There were two personal benefits for me from the 18th being in Pleiku. Shortly after their arrival Dr. Robert Dripps, the senior consultant in anesthesia to the Army Surgeon General, visited the 18th Surg. During his visit I confirmed a residency at Penn whenever I was discharged from the Army. The second was that Wayne Hosking knew of my interest in anesthesia and went out of his way to educate me about the unique requirements of trauma anesthesia. Wayne and I have had the opportunity to meet since both at the Hartford Hospital, where he trained and to which he returned, and at national anesthesia meetings.

Patients and their Diseases

Malaria was endemic in the civilian population, but fortunately the resistant strains, which were to plague both GIs and civilians later, were just beginning to emerge in 1966. Plague (bubonic, not pneumonic) was also seen in many patients and responded well to treatment. Fallout from the war (bombs, artillery, etc) on civilians was rare in Pleiku compared to the Delta and III Corps areas. What was a problem was motor vehicle accidents. Adults, as well as children, just were not used to looking left-and-right before crossing the street or path. Regrettably, GI drivers did not exercise restraint behind the wheel.

There was a Viet Cong (VC) ward in the hospital and I marveled that the VC remained an effective fighting force for they were uniformly malnourished and malaria-ridden. While the VC seemed grateful for the care we provided, they also made it obvious that they did not welcome Americans. For one week I was asked to hold sick call for an NVA POW compound. In contrast to the VC, I was impressed that they were well nourished, did not suffer on their hike down the Ho Chi Minh Trail from North Vietnam, and were not hostile to Americans.

There were two distinct populations in Pleiku, the Vietnamese who lived in the towns and the Montagnards who were an extremely primitive people living in villages outside of the towns. We had a

Vietnamese interpreter who would translate what our Vietnamese patients said, but to interview a Montagnard my interpreter had to speak to a Montagnard who spoke Vietnamese. I felt there was much substance (as well as time) lost in this double translation.

Two Memorable Patients

A young girl (about 14, age was always a guess, especially with the Montagnards) entered the "French Valley" outside of Pleiku—so named because a French battalion had been badly mauled there during the 1954 French-Indochina War. As part of their defense the French troops had placed land mines and twelve years later they were still there and active. This child stepped on a mine, destroying her left leg. Before I took her to the O.R. to complete a left B-K amputation, my interpreter told me her mother said, "You must save her leg because she is not yet married." Apparently, I was dooming the child to being a spinister. When she emerged from anesthesia both she and her mother were inconsolable. I do not believe in forcing patients to do something, but six months later I coerced them (mother and daughter) to go to the British Red Cross prosthesis lab in Saigon where she received a prosthesis that was nicely hidden by the customary ao dai dress females wore. When she returned from Saigon with her prosthesis and visited me at the hospital I finally saw her smile.

The second patient was about four years old. I diagnosed meningococcal meningitis on the basis of gram negative rods in spinal fluid. (We had no culture capability.) Treatment was started with a good response, but the next day the patient was gone. Why? His father dreamed of a red monkey, which meant the child was going to die. The father wanted the child to die in his village or his soul would not rest and so he took him home where he died.

Conclusion

The year in Pleiku was fascinating professionally, but I missed my family greatly. With the benefit of forty years hindsight I think our efforts were not only futile, but not necessary. Ike's domino theory did not prevail. Historian Arthur Sclesinger, Jr. called the Vietnam War (called the "American War" in Vietnam) "the most useless, most mysterious war." I agree!

I hoped American troops would never again be put in a similar situation. Regrettably, I believe that today they are in an even worse situation in Iraq—worse because the Islamic concept of a jihad makes suicide a very real possibility whenever an Iraqi approaches a GI.

Vietnam—1966-67

by Anthony Burgett, D.V.M.

My background information is: On July 6, 1966, I arrived at Tan Son Nhut and left Vietnam July 1, 1967 from Cam Ranh Bay. I was technically assigned to the 4th Medical Detachment based in Saigon. A Col. Quigley was my CO, although I only saw him four or five times.

While in country the U.S. Army Vet Corps had one mindset—food inspection! I and my other DVM conscripts could not

Terminal at Tan Son Nhut International Airport, Saigon.

Airport terminal at Cam Ranh Bay.

comprehend this! It still makes no sense! I never food inspected! Rather I worked with Sentry and Scout dogs, plus a lot of Montagnard cow work (peace corps with a paycheck). To do the work, I had to beg drugs and equipment from (1) 18th Surgical Hospital (MA) (chloramphenicol and instruments) (2) 52nd Aviation Battalion (the same) (3) Civilian classmates and friends (4) Old civilian mentors-but no help from the Vet Corps.

If my slides are still good, I will send pictures of me scrounging from the 18th; plus, when I had malaria (falciparum) you treated me for a while and then sent me to the 67th Evacuation Hospital at Qui Nhon. I have not experienced any malarial symptoms since returning to civilian life.

Although I could have lived at various places, I chose to live at Camp Holloway, since it seemed to be the most logical with the sentry dogs located there and readily available helicopter transportation out to the scout dogs (25th Infantry Division, 3rd Brigade) and to the Montagnard villages. Camp Holloway had a very nice bunch of people, albeit some of the pilots were a little nuts.

A work detail sitting outside the new Paradise Lost Club ready to start painting: Left to right: 2nd Lt. Ron Thompson, CRNA, the next two are unknown EMs, Maj. Margaret Jaskowski, R.N., Felix Jenkins, M.D., 2nd Lt. Barbara "Bobbie" Gouldthorpe, R.N., 1st Lt. Bill Hames, Lt. Col. Cenac, CO.

Paradise Lost
by Barbara A. Gouldthorpe (LTC., ANC, Ret.)

I arrived in Pleiku, Vietnam at the 18th Surgical Hospital (MA) on June 30, 1966 with the first group of nurses. We were set up in tents, both the hospital and living quarters, for the first few months and then advanced to Quonset huts for the hospital and tropical buildings for living quarters. We worked at least twelve hours on and twelve hours off seven days a week. The sound of helicopters still brings back memories of those days. The wounded arrived at our location that was in sight of Cambodia usually within half an hour of injury. Our job was to triage, operate, stabilize and evacuate to the next level of care. The biggest push I recall was working nonstop for thirty-six hours. One of the tents was converted into our Officers Club, "Paradise Lost." It was there that we spent most of our time between working and sleeping where lifelong friendships were established.

There are several vivid memories that I have: the sounds of helicopters, patriotic events with fireworks or gunshots will bring them to the forefront of my mind. The only time I ever fainted in my life in receiving one day when I was positioning a young GI's head for a better airway and when I removed my hand there was some tissue on it and I asked Felix Jenkins, M.D., what it was and he said grey matter and I keeled over. Another time that comes to mind was once when all the surgeons and OR nurses were busy and another case needed to be done and I was asked to assist Jerry Martin, M.D., with the surgery. Although I had not been in the OR since I was a student nurse, I figured if a medical physician could do the surgery then I should be able to assist— the outcome was ok. Since I had been assigned to recovery/ICU and open heart team in my most recent prior duty at Letterman

General Hospital, San Francisco, I was one of the R.N.'s picked to go with head trauma cases during evacuation to the next level of care (usually Qui Nhon, 85th and 67th Evacuation Hospitals). Some of those trips were most challenging.

In 1967 when I would have been returning to the States I agreed to extend my tour in Vietnam since we would have to return after two or three months anyway. I finished my second tour with the 71st Evacuation Hospital since the 18th Surg moved from that area and took only male RNs.

When I returned to the States, being a career Army Officer, I was assigned to Ft. Sam Houston, Texas for the Advanced Officers Course that provided quite a bit of deprogramming for us and I credit this time in helping me to deal with the trauma of war, even to this day. Vietnam was a rewarding experience for me and prepared me for just about anything else I would have to face in life.

Proud to Have Served
by Robert L. Hewitt, M.D.

I arrived at the 18th Surgical Hospital in Pleiku from Saigon on December 7, 1966, as a new captain. I had completed my surgical training in general, vascular, thoracic and cardiac surgery at Tulane, six months earlier. I was appointed Commanding Officer of the 240th Medical Detachment, KF, a Thoracic Surgery K Team attached to the 18th Surgical Hospital. I performed general, vascular and thoracic surgery during my entire time at the 18th Surgical Hospital until November 1, 1966, when my K Team was then attached to the newly opened 71st Evacuation Hospital in Pleiku, just up the road, adjacent to the Pleiku Airfield compound. Actually, we gradually shifted the surgical activities from the 18th Surgical to the 71st Evacuation throughout the summer and early Fall of 1967. I continued at the 71st Evacuation Hospital throughout the Battle of Dak To and left Vietnam to return to CONUS December 1, 1967.

When I arrived at the 18th Surgical Hospital in December 1966, I was highly impressed with the organization, discipline, function and efficiency provided by well-trained surgeons, physicians, nurses and technicians and with the leadership of Lt. Col. Mark Cenac, Hospital Commander.

I could tell from the very onset that the environment was conducive for us to achieve the highest level of surgical care for our soldiers, and that perception led to a feeling of confidence and pride, which was contagious. The esprit de corps was proven to be based upon genuine quality, energy and commitment. From the onset, I determined that I had never been associated with a more outstanding group of individuals and was grateful to be able to

Left to right: Bob Hewitt, M.D. and Jerry W. Martin, M.D. scrubbing for the next surgical case.

serve with this unit. We intended to make it the best, and I feel confident that no unit surpassed us. I conveyed all of these feelings in letters to my wife, which were later abstracted into a diary of all of my activities in Vietnam. I continue to cherish the friendships of my colleagues and associates of the 18th Surgical Hospital of nearly a half-century ago and always shall.

Our 18th Surgical Hospital was destined to become the busiest surgical hospital in Vietnam during the most intense period of the war. In 1965, enemy attack upon Camp Holloway in Pleiku and the North Vietnamese Regular Army activities in the Ia Drang Valley signaled an ambitious plan by the enemy to take Pleiku and Route 19 to the sea, thus, cutting South Vietnam into two parts. Whoever controlled Route 19 controlled the Highlands, and whoever controlled the Highlands controlled Vietnam. In late 1965 and early 1966, our government planned to counter such an enemy offensive, and our 18th Surgical Hospital was part of that plan.

By January 1967, an estimated four to six NVA regiments were in the Central Highlands. Cambodia was saturated with NVA

units, which regularly invaded the Highlands, and our troops were restricted from violating their sanctuaries in Cambodia. A series of aggressive search-and-destroy operations by the Fourth Division in early February, OPERATION SAM HOUSTON, included eleven or more major engagements with well-trained, well-equipped North Vietnamese Regulars. Although the NVA retreated to Cambodia, our forces were not allowed to exploit the enemy. OPERATION SAM HOUSTON ended on April 5 and the next day, April 6, OPERATION FRANCIS MARION began. Although OPERATION FRANCIS MARION was very effective, our casualties prompted deployment of the 173rd Airborne Brigade to the Central Highlands under the command of General William Peers and the Fourth Division. That deployment was recommended by General Stanley Larson to General Westmoreland, who ordered the maneuver. General Larsen along with General Westmoreland were frequent visitors to our 18th Surgical Hospital as they visited the wounded soldiers. General Peers also visited frequently. On June 15-16, the NVA attacked Dak To Special Forces Camp, and our ultimate response was OPERATION MACARTHUR. OPERATION FRANCIS MARION ended October 11, and OPERATION MACARTHUR began immediately.

Ultimately, the Battle of Dak To evolved into the largest single battle of the Vietnam War to that point. The battle was essentially over by Thanksgiving Day, 1967, and my K Team and I were part of the 71st Evacuation Hospital during those times.

Despite the restrictions imposed upon our soldiers to execute a purely defensive war (with exception of search-and-destroy and bombing of North Vietnam as the only offensive strategies), results of the 1966-1967 tactical operations gave reason for optimism toward successful conclusion of the Vietnam War. As General Giap admitted to Colonel Harry G. Summers years later, we won every battle and every tactical engagement, and North Vietnam was forced to contemplate surrender as result of the attrition on the ground and bombing of infrastructure in the North. But, our public in the United States decided that they could not take it any longer and demanded our withdrawal. As result of our failed strategy in Vietnam, the Weinberger-Powell Doctrine evolved.

Counterinsurgency doctrine has also evolved and improved from the transient inflexible dogma that lured us into a nation-building commitment and a land war in Asia with such imposed restrictions that victory remained elusive. Those imposed restrictions were primarily based upon possible risks of war with China, the Soviet Union or even nuclear war if the balance of containment policy became unstable. Although such risks were possibly overestimated, the possibility also exists that they were not. We will never know. Even a clear win without materialization of such risks could have resulted in a lingering compromise attended by continuing danger as we have in Korea. That compromise had set the stage for the result in Vietnam just as Douglas MacArthur predicted.

We served, and we are proud of our Nation and our Armed Forces and of the brave soldiers who fought in Vietnam and Southeast Asia!

Helicopter Ambulance Support

by John Kreiner, Dustoff Pilot

"18th Surg Operations this is Dustoff 25, OVER."

"This is 18th Surg Operations go ahead, OVER."

This is Dustoff 25, we are inbound with six patients, three litter with gunshot wounds of the chest, who is critical, one in the leg and the third in the abdomen. The ambulatory have wounds in the head, arms and hand. All patients are stable except for the chest wounds and an IV has been started on him. Our ETA is ten minutes, please have litter bearers meet us when we arrive, OVER."

"This is 18th Surg Operations, wilco, we will meet you when you land Dustoff 25, OUT."

This was a typical radio transmission between a Dustoff medical evacuation helicopter from Pleiku Dustoff and the 18th Surg Operations every day during the support of the Pleiku area U.S. Forces by the 18th Surgical Hospital.

The 18th Surgical Hospital arrived in Pleiku during the rainy season of 1966 and Pleiku Dustoff, the only other medical unit in the area, made sure they were welcomed in the proper manner when they arrived as a number of the pilots went over to the hospital to meet them and welcome them to the area and tell them about what was going on there. They were living in tents then so we had a meet and greet party with a few adult beverages and one of our pilots strumming a guitar so we sat around in the tent singing songs. Everyone had a good time meeting each other and developing the initial rapport that was needed to work as a team in the evacuation and treatment of our wounded soldiers

Pleiku Dustoff was the second platoon of the 498th Medical Company (Helicopter Ambulance), which was stationed in Nha Trang. The mission of the 2nd Platoon was to provide Air Ambulance support in the western II Corps area from North of Dak To to the North to Ban Me Thuot in the South, and West to the Cambodian border. Many of those evacuations were to Medical Clearing Companies in the U.S. Brigades but most were directly to the 18th Surgical Hospital. During heavy casualties periods the Dustoff ships would overfly the clearing companies and take their on board patients straight to the 18th Surg.

During the years of 1966-67 the majority of enemy actions came from the Dak To area to the North and West of Pleiku out near the Cambodian border. Dustoff would send support ships to the engaged brigades for evacuation of causalities from the battlefield to the Brigade Clearing Companies and then other Pleiku Dustoff helicopters would evacuate many of the wounded to the 18th Surg. The more severely wounded, since there were many, would be evacuated by Army Caribou and Air Force C-130 planes, if there was an airfield close by, directly to Evacuation Hospitals on the coast of Vietnam.

One of the most harrowing missions conducted by the 2nd Platoon DUSTOFF was the using of an on board hoist to extract severely wounded patients from a jungle location where no LZ existed to land the helicopter. The D Model Huey was too under powered to adequately do many of the missions we were required to accomplish. The field elevation of the Pleiku area was 4,000 feet above sea level so the air was much thinner than on the coast. We could not fill the helicopters full of fuel because of the density altitudes so we only kept about 1,000 pounds of fuel when we started our mission which would give us about 1 hour, 30 minutes of flight time. One of our ships cut it too close one day and ran out of fuel on the way back from a mission. The pilot did an autorotation and landed the helicopter without breaking it. Some fuel was brought to them and they continued on their mission.

Back to hoist missions, many of these missions started out at a hover at about 125'-150' and when you came to that high hover you usually had only ½%-1% of power left. When the patient was on the hoist you were usually at maximum power so if you had a change in wind or something went wrong with the helicopter, it could waffle down through the trees, and we haven't even mentioned enemy fire, which was a distinct possibility.

The only Pleiku Dustoff pilot that was killed during the 1966-April 67 time frame in country was during a night hoist mission when an enemy B-40 rifle grenade shot down the helicopter and their brave crew. The Aircraft Commander, Bob Bradley was killed and the pilot lost his left leg. This crew was evacuated to the 18th Surg for their initial treatment and they did a wonderful effort on all crewmembers.

An incident that happened to the writer was the failure of an engine while enroute to a brigade LZ near the Cambodian border. While enemy action was not a threat, the need to have security after completing an autorotation was supplied by a tank that was nearby so everyone felt good after leaving the aircraft.

Preparing for flight back to Pleiku. Maj. Bill Medford in the truck, Capt. John Kreiner standing to the right with hand to his face.

One of the interesting facts of this flight was a Doctor that was on board and this was his last day before going to Cam Ranh Bay to catch the Freedom Bird home. He was going to the Brigade LZ in order to have the Brigade Surgeon sign his clearance papers. He was so happy to be on the ground in one piece after the engine failure that when I joined the other seven people that had been on the flight that he kissed me.

The writer was also wounded and evacuated to the 18th Surg. While the wound was not severe, it did require debriding and suturing and there was always the danger of infection in Vietnam. The care I received while a patient was outstanding as it was for all of their patients. All of us that served with the 18th Surgical Hospital either as a member, support, or a patient will always cherish the memory of this hospital and of the scores of soldiers they treated and the many, many lives they saved.

Now the 18th Surgical Hospital and the 498th Medical Company (Helicopter Ambulance) are no longer units in the Army force structure but the people and spirit of their service lives on in the memory of each one of us that served in them or were associated with them.

Anecdotal Story

by Leo "Ski" Plasczynski, R.N.

One day the missionary brought in a young Montagard boy, about ten or twelve years old, who had a distended bladder. Our doctors diagnosed it as a tumor inside the bladder. It was a calcified tumor about the size of a small grapefruit, and it showed up clearly even on the old Picker field unit X-ray. The decision was to operate, but we had to take him to the Provincial hospital for the operation. Tony and Inge, the two surgeons, asked me to go along as the scrub nurse, so I threw a few sterile packs into the jeep and went along with them. Here is where the fun began.

The operating room was very warm, so the windows were left open and they had no screens on them. A three bladed wobbly Singapore fan hung from the ceiling over the operating room table. It ran very slowly, rotating about every three to five seconds. Whrr! Whrr! Whrr! was very audible. In operating room gowns, we all perspired profusely.

I stripped down to my t-shirt and went into the scrub room to scrub up and set up for the operation. There was a fairly modern well-used scrub sink with foot pedals to control the water flow. A soap dispenser could be operated with the elbows. The soap was similar to our old Phisohex, so I lathered it on my hands and arms. I stepped on the foot pedal to get water and only about three or four drops came out. I asked the little Vietnamese nurse, "What's up with the water?" She said it was after one o'clock in the afternoon and we usually run out of water. The only place that has any water is the maternity building. I finished scrubbing up with pure soap and rinsed with a little alcohol.

The Vietnamese nurse was holding up a sterile gown by the shoulders for me to slip into. It was suppose to be a white gown but it was full of brown, dried red and other colored stains. They did their laundry in the river, and that river was used for many other purposes by both humans and animals. It was the only water supply for bathing, toileting and who knows what else. The gowns were sterilized, but still gave off strange odors. Fortunately, I did think ahead and brought some sterile packs of gowns, gloves and linens with me. I sent the little nurse out to the jeep to get them.

After donning my gown, I had to put on my sterile gloves. The nurse opened the pack and held the first glove up by the cuff for me to slip into. Whoa! As I pushed my handy into the glove the whole thing disintegrated. They must have been washed and sterilized a hundred times before. I instructed the nurse how to open the sterile glove pack and donned the gloves myself.

Now it was time to set up my table and Mayo stand, and we used the linen packs I brought with us. I had everything neatly arranged on the table, and since there was no sterile water, pure alcohol was poured sparingly into my sterile basins. I also draped and neatly arranged the instruments on the Mayo stand tray. Just as I finished, a big black fly landed in the middle of the tray and was marching around on some of the instruments. I turned and looked at the nurse. She promptly responded with a fly swatter and brought it down in the middle of the sterile tray, disposing of the intruder. Opening my eyes widely and surveying the situation, there was nothing I could do but dump all the instruments in the alcohol, spread a couple of clean towels over the Mayo tray, dry the instruments as best I could and replace them back on the tray.

As we were operating we had an intruder. I looked over the anesthesia screen at the open window behind the Vietnamese anesthesiologist, and there

Left to right: Lt. Lazorchak, Oscar Valerio, M.D., "Ski" Plasczynski, R.N., unknown, Terry McDonald, M.D., Tom Goodwine, CRNA working on Paradise Lost.

was a big water buffalo with his head inside the operating room. Signaling to the Vietnamese nurse, I pointed out the intruder to her. She hurriedly picked up a broom and proceeded to hit the animal over the head. He went scurrying off, but the window remained open for ventilation.

The rest of the operation went well and the surgeons removed the calcified tumor from the open bladder. There was no sign of attachment to the wall of the bladder. It appeared to be like a giant kidney stone. Now it was time to close the patient. Normally when it is time to suture, the patient is put into a deeper anesthetized state to relax the muscle and tissue. Tense muscle and tissue may cause the suture needle to tear through.

The Vietnamese doctor was administering GOE (gas, oxygen and ether) through an old regulated mixing machine and could regulate the lightness or depth of the anesthetic induced sleep. The surgeon was having a hard time closing the muscles over the bladder. He asked repeatedly for the gas doctor to put the patient down deeper to relax the muscle. There was no answer. This was a little strange. I rolled back to back behind the surgeon and looked behind the high ether screen. There was no one there. The machine had been set on automatic feed. I assumed that the Vietnamese doctor had probably stepped outside for a smoke. When I asked the nurse where the doctor was, she replied it was after three o'clock and the doctor always went home at three o'clock. It was a shock to me. I only knew a little about administering anesthesia, but I had to break scrub and take over the regulator. This was done by careful step-by-step directions from the surgeon. The assisting surgeon had to thread the needles and place them in the needle holder while retracting the suture area. It was a nightmare of an ending, but the amazing thing was that the patient recovered very well with not even an infection. The boy returned to his village in just a couple days.

Reclassifed 1-A
by Felix Jenkins, M.D.

While I attended medical school at Meharry Medical College, I wanted to do my surgical residency there as well. However, the doctor in charge of the program was hesitant to take candidates without solid draft deferments, because he had been short of residents due to the draft. I had a 2-S deferment, which did not guarantee that I wouldn't get drafted, so I went to Hurley Hospital in Flint, Michigan instead.

Toward the end of 1964, I received a call from the draft board, stating that I would be reclassified 1-A and to look out for my draft notice. I went to the Navy, Air Force and Marines to see if I could join the reserves and complete my residency, but in the end I was allocated to the Army. In January 1966 the Army conducted the largest draft of doctors in U.S. history. Everyone passed, even four with cancer and disabilities. I passed, and was reclassified with 1-A, and began my way into the 18th Surgical Unit.

I had a great surgical experience with the 18th. I worked with world class surgeons, especially Robert, whose experience at Charity was not dissimilar from what we had at Pleiku, save

for the volume. I had done a great number of surgical cases prior to being inducted, but being a D 3150, I was extremely lucky in not being transferred to Battalion Aid Station. It was also a tremendous pleasure to watch a first class anesthesiologist work. I distinctly remember essentially "stealing" two Fluotechs in Nha Trang with the assistance of Dick Jones. Those in charge of medical support for the combatants should have been ashamed for sending a MASH unit such antiquated equipment. Some of the anesthesia equipment was probably used in World War I. I think that Jerry almost got court marshaled for reporting the same.

There were many poignant and happy moments during my tour. I will mention a few of the former. John Walsh (a 19-year-old who could not be resuscitated after open chest cardiac massage in spite of course fibrillations just begging for some direct current), three GIs in a half-filled laundry bag, an Air Force husky pilot who was rocketed while hovering at night and had fractures of all of the long bones as well as multiple rib fractures with flailing and finally, debridement in the dim light to remove white phosphorus fragments. A few of the happy moments: Joe Juliano delivering my Provolone and Chianti to mother earth, Charlie Brown hiding an abdominal pedical flap from the head honchos, and lastly, assisting Robert Hewitt doing what was probably the first heart procedure on a Vietnamese. Brent Burgoyne's death was one of the most tragic incidents during all of my years in medicine.

Left to right: Felix Jenkins, M.D., Wayne Hosking, M.D. and Jerry W. Martin, M.D. resting between cases.

Felix Jenkins, M.D. listening to music.

Memoirs—18th Surgical Hospital
by Joseph Juliano, M.D.

After taking my residency in Radiology at Philadelphia General Hospital, I was drafted into the Army. After being commissioned as a Captain, I was assigned to the 18th Surgical Hospital while in basic training at Fort Sam Houston, Texas. I joined the other original members of the hospital at Fort Gordon, Georgia, where the unit was organized and trained for the coming duty at Pleiku, Vietnam.

I was the sole radiologist at the 18th while stationed in Vietnam. After leaving the 18th, I was assigned as a Radiologist at Fort McArthur, San Pedro, California, until my discharge from service.

Following discharge, I practiced radiology with the Western Radiological Group in Los Angeles, California, and became boarded in General Radiology and in Nuclear Medicine.

Memoirs
by Mary Hamilton Juliano, R.N., J.D.

While completing my last year of nursing school in Ottumwa, Iowa, I enlisted as a PFC E-3 in the Army USA WAC as a part of the Army Student Nurse Program. Upon starting basic training at Fort Sam Houston, I was commissioned as a Second Lieutenant in the Army Nurse Corps.

The duty assignments included Fort Wolters, Texas; Operating School in Fort Benning, Georgia; Vietnam; and Fort Carlson, Colorado.

On September 9, 1967, I was promoted to the rank of Captain, which is the rank I had upon discharge from the service.

Since the G-I bill was available, I started night classes while working in the operating room at St. John's Hospital in Santa Monica, California. During my second career I transferred to the University of Southern California, where I received a B.S. degree

in Business. In 1977 I graduated from Loyola Law School in Los Angeles, and was admitted to the California State Bar. After working for two years in the Tax Department at Arthur Young and Company, I retired to raise our four children.

Memories of Pleiku, 18th Surgical Hospital, 1967
by Kenneth Wayne Hancock

Pleiku. The Highlands. I was only there about a month or two. Seemed longer at the time, like a short lifetime. As it turned out, many lifetimes ended there. I arrived in Pleiku the last week of October 1967. I was in Saigon for med. lab training the month before, learning to test for malaria—something they didn't teach us stateside.

I remember that it was so cool there. It was up out of the steaming coastal areas where you could definitely breathe better.

The hospital physically looked like it had been there for many years. The buildings were semi-permanent wooden structures that gave it an air of stability. I can say that because the 18th Surg. would go MUST in Nov-Dec 1967.

I was just getting my bearings, green as heck, 20 years old, learning under a 30-year-old Spec. 5 lifer who knew what he was doing. I didn't, of course, but I learned the ropes fast—obtaining blood samples from the wounded and then cross-matching units of blood for them. That is what I did 95% of the time during my tour. The hundred other lab tests that I was taught to do seemed insignificant, superfluous busy work discarded in the face of bloody ordeals. That ought to tell you something about how many casualties we took in. We worked a 12-hour shift, seven days a week, always on call.

Many enlisted men (and a Major) turned to marijuana to ease the tension of the brutal toll taken on our nerves. Yes, I was weak and succumbed to the temptation to forget everything chemically. Just getting back home to the "world" was all that mattered at the time, in one piece, physically and mentally. I am pleased now with the work we all did in saving lives. That part makes me feel good.

I remember one night in Pleiku, I was walking back to our barracks at night, very stoned. A big ruckus came blowing out the door and onto the front lawn. I peaked in and saw a boot flying in slow motion through the air. Excited yells echoed off the walls. "I hit him! There he is! He's still alive! Let me have him!" It turned out to be a rat that McDonald, our company clerk, had stunned.

He then picked it up, took it outside, and commenced to douse it with lighter fluid. Soon the Zippo was out and a writhing animal bonfire was ignited. Everyone was laughing maniacally. I guess the tension was being relieved like when some of us laugh during a horror movie. It was pretty crazy.

Funny how you remember stupid things like that. The mind has a way of forgetting the truly traumatic incidences in our lives. God allows us to forget those times when we either did dark things or had them done to us. I suppose it allows us to continue on, to walk on toward sunshine.

Joe Juliano, M.D.

I, of course, have forgotten the faces of suffering I saw every day—the dying young men at the 18th Surgical Hospital during my year there in 1967-68. Hundreds, thousands were treated. If I could remember them now, I would be so heartbroken all the time that I wouldn't be much good for anything else.

I remember that I was welcomed by my brothers-in-arms because I was a professional barber before I was drafted. Oakland, California Barber College. It was the family business; Dad was a barber, Uncle Dale and others. They told me that the Vietnamese barber who had been cutting their hair at the hospital had been captured, and was a Viet Cong. He was holding scissors and razors against the heads of our men by day and raining down mortars on them by night. So, I was a big hit as I set up shop in our barracks during my free time. The C.O., other officers, and many enlisted men were my clients. I actually made more money cutting hair than I made in Army salary.

Being in Pleiku was a pretty nice gig, except for the bloodshed. We had a nice club and had bands come in—GI dudes who were very good rock musicians, working for the USO special services, making their rounds to the different NCO clubs. I remember a trio—elec. guitar/lead vocals, bass, drums—that were dynamite. In fact, they played "Mr. Dynamite" James Brown songs, cape and all, plus the wicked Pickett, Otis, Temptations…a big hit for us.

It was there in Pleiku that I got my nickname that stuck with me the whole year—"The Groove." It was a difficult name to live up to, but I tried very hard. A short-timer named Tenant saw me on my cot playing the Martin guitar that I hauled all the way from home. He came over and says very loud and sarcastically, "Hey, everybody, look at this guy. That's just groovy, man. He is so groovy," and it stuck.

My one to two months at Pleiku, working at the 18th Surg. proved to be the best months during my tour. We would move the hospital to Lai Khe/Long Binh in November 1967, be overrun during the Tet Offensive and have to move again, finally winding up 15 miles from the DMZ in Quang Tri, where the salty red stuff flowed more abundantly, and a thousand personal insanities cried out for Mom, apple pie, and a good bed.

My Time with the 18th
by Michael Alan Belinson, M.D.

I became associated with the 18th Surgical Hospital (MA) in December 1966, after being in Vietnam three days. After being delayed in beginning my overseas assignment for about three or four days because of bad Midwestern weather, I eventually flew from Travis Air Force Base to Saigon's Tan Son Nhut on December 6, 1966. A trip that was "advertised" as going through Honolulu, Hawaii, was actually via Anchorage, Alaska (-16° F) and Tokyo before "dropping out of the sky" into Saigon via the alternating, sequential runway lights used to keep us out of danger. I sat next to Warrant Officer Sellers returning for his third tour, and he had said the flight always stopped in Hawaii. When the doors opened and we were exposed to the 90 F temperature and high humidity, it actually "rained" inside the plane. This was December 7 in Saigon.

Prior to my Ft. Sam experience and our introduction to the Army, I had been allowed to begin my anesthesia residency (delayed induction) and spent 3 ½ months at the University of Virginia Hospitals being prepared for my expected assignment. I had been informed that I would be assigned to the 71st Evacuation Hospital from Ft. Campbell in Kentucky. We visited in the area prior to our trip to San Antonio in mid-October 1966, and were informed by Maj. Sperland not to look for housing as the 71st would be on its way to an "unspecified" location. "Ah, Hah," I exclaimed to my wife, "looks like I'm headed for Vietnam."

After staying with three of my medical school classmates, all activated before me, and sharing a Saigon apartment, I was finally sent to Pleiku to the 18th Surgical (attached being the correct terminology) as I waited for the 71st Evac to be completed. After many construction delays, I finally did work at the 71st, built about one mile north of the 18th, the last 2-3 weeks of my Vietnam tour. Compared to the warmth of the closely knit "family" at the 18th the Evac was an open, cold, "machine-like," surgical factory and I was so glad to finally leave.

When I arrived at the Pleiku Airport (AFB) and jeeped to the 18th Surgical (December 13) I met Col. Cenac and others in HQ and then went to the living quarters. A familiar face, Dr. Bob Hewitt, appeared; familiar, because we had met at Ft. Sam and again crossed paths at Camp Alpha, the processing camp in Saigon. As time passed at the 18th and it became obvious that the 71st was a non-entity, at least in the immediate future, I requested and was assigned (by Army Anesthesiology Advisor/Consultant) to the 240th K-Team, under the leadership of thoracic surgeon, Robert Hewitt, M.D. Leo Placzszynski, R.N. was the K-team's scrub nurse. Thus the "web of attachments" was further woven and the 18th Surgical's family, a closely knit group of medically motivated career military and civilian turned military men and women became one of the busiest military hospitals in the entire Vietnam theatre. I personally felt very comfortable and adapted well to this tight knit group of nurses, doctors and enlisted corpsmen. The hospital's leadership was exemplary, even with Col. Kaku as our second hospital CO, and the network of care and skillful maintenance of our command, led us through many stressful and hectic periods. Stress was so felt during one period, that Dr. Richard Fields, the fully trained anesthesiologist who succeeded Dr. Wayne Hosking, spent his non-OR time "ditch digging" as he prepared a large foxhole outside our barracks. Speaking of Dr. Hosking, Wayne was a great mentor for me especially after just 3 ½ months of training. As the Department Chief, he taught and guided me in many aspects of anesthesia and patient care.

My experiences in the operating rooms of Vietnam at the 18th Surgical Hospital (and the following several months in the U.S. held me in good stead and allowed me, while caring for our injured U.S. soldiers (some Montagnard soldiers) to gain great experience before heading back to my residency and reduced by six months my time for the Board Certification process. As I finish with a few specific memorable incidents, I wish to say, "God Bless to all of you" who served at the 18th Surgical-Vietnam, a "very special, comfortable family." The 18th Surgical Hospital (MA) and my

Equipment of the 71st Evacuation Hospital stored on the site formerly used by the 542nd Medical Clearing Company until their hospital was completed.

"comrades in scrub clothes" remain a great memory of a time and a place where we were all thrown together and came out as good friends, who did a job as well as anybody ever has.

Specific Items of note: (1) First Vietnam cardiac procedure was performed by Robert Hewitt, M.D. in early 1967 on a sick Vietnamese man (a mitral vavulotomy). (2) Bob Hewitt and I drove our jeep on a road that we later learned was allegedly mined, in order to shortcut our trip to a required shooting test. (3) Bob Hewitt and I had our last trip to see our crossbow maker in a nearby Montagnard village cut short when we were informed by his neighbors, that he had been kidnapped by the Viet Cong. (4) On my trip to Hong Kong I was "tailed" by Party Members in a Chinese Communist department store. (5) I visited Mai and Lan, our two barracks housekeepers, at their homes and met their families and was shown by Mai that her wall paper was all the pages from the New York Times Magazine *Fashion* sections that she took home. My aunt sent me the Sunday *New York Times* each week while I was in Vietnam. She was so proud! I took over their "handling/supervising" when Felix Jenkins, M.D. headed home in June of 1967. (6) The final coup de gras was when I observed in October 1967 (I have a picture) the once very busy 18th Surgical Hospital (MA)'s helipad being used as a grazing area by a couple of water buffalo; this occurred after the 18th closed (later became a Helicopter Company's base HQ) as the 71st finally opened.

Personal Statements
by Orville P. Swenson, M.D.

Wars and Stress

It is interesting to note the amount of Post Traumatic Stress Disorder (P.T.S.D.[up to 20%]) along with readjustment disorders and anxiety disorders in troops returning to the U.S. from Iraq/Afghanistan and the use of antidepressants and/or sleeping pills or anti-anxiety drugs.

Wars are different, but I wonder if an even bigger difference is the "ambivalence" of home support the troops hear from all the communication overseas with satellites, computers, text messaging, etc. World War II, Korea and Vietnam troops didn't have access to this extent—mostly we only learned via letters from home, *Stars and Stripes* newspaper and Army radio stations.

Additionally, the current wars involve civilian areas more (who is the enemy?) and fears of the unknown and the unexpected. Yet, the support of comrades and commanders sounds good. With those thoughts I transition to the 18th Surgical Hospital (MA).

18th Surgical Hospital (MA)

The camaraderie and cooperative efforts of our group evolved out of duty, "busyness" and leadership. There never seemed to be ill will among the medical personnel. There were lots of medical and tropical diseases: e.g. diarrhea, Dengue, plague, leptospirosis, scrub typhus, amoebic dysentery, venereal diseases and especially malaria. The sickest patients we saw were severe malarial attacks (paroxysms of chills, high fever, etc.) and especially those who died with cerebral malaria. I have always been grateful that our anesthesiologist, Wayne Hosking, M.D., brought along a comprehensive textbook on Tropical Diseases (being from Minnesota I had had zero experience with tropical diseases). The several weeks of orientation at Ft. Sam Houston in 1966 did not include a significant amount of tropical disease information.

As a General Medical Officer I was involved with medical patients, emergencies and triage. It seemed that there was a disproportional number of spinal cord injuries and I woefully pondered each of those soldiers' futures. The wounds we treated had various causes: e.g., gunshot wounds (GSW), shrapnel, claymore mines, land or air vehicle accidents, burns, etc. We saw a few self-inflicted wounds—interestingly a right-handed shooter would always shoot off a left toe, usually not the big toe, but the second toe. I also did a lot of assisting in surgery and debridement of minor wounds. The injured usually came to us by helicopter. From the time of injury to medical care ("golden hour") was fortunately very brief; however, in a jungle war this time could be prolonged since the landing zones (LZ) were sometimes difficult to establish and secure because the enemy was always nearby. The Medevac pilots really had a dangerous job.

We were thankful for the relatively secure location of the 18th, away from the jungles with other military installations nearby. We were also thankful for more favorable weather conditions in the Central Highlands.

Patriotism and Living

The real positive of the 18th Surgical Hospital (MA) at Pleiku was the camaraderie, patriotism, mission, humor, recreation and the mix of personalities—we were close emotionally (as well as in our living quarters) with a strong sense of purpose. Our living arrangements evolved from tents to a frame building. The Officers Club, "Paradise Lost", evolved from a tent with a wooden crate bar with a couple of tables and chairs to a much larger metal building with concrete floor and adequate furnishings. Our showers evolved from water heated with kerosene heaters to modern shower and toilet facilities. Our chapel also evolved from a tent to a Quonset building that accommodated Protestants, Catholics and Jews. In our free time we enjoyed tag football, volleyball and basketball as well as bridge, cribbage, photography, musical tapes, etc., and of course chitchat sessions. I have fond recollections and memories of all the many varied and interesting personalities. We all appreciated the leadership of our CO, Lt. Col. Mark T. Cenac, M.C., and our Chief Medical Officer, Tony Lindem, M.D. (aka "our fearless leader").

Orville Swenson, M.D. at airport terminal in Qui Nhon.

Personal

The policy of drafting physicians up to the age of thirty-five was known. After one year of practice in northern Minnesota (Cloquet near Duluth) with three other General Practitioners, I received a four-day notice to report to Ft. Sam Houston, San Antonio, Texas in early 1966. It was a scramble to get ready. My wife, Sandy and our five-month old son, Craig, went to live with her folks at Ely, Minnesota about two hours north. This was a blessing and provided them with a sense of security. They drove down to Augusta, Georgia (Ft. Gordon) and took the train back. My wife and son stayed a while and we then drove back to Minnesota for a brief leave before embarking to Pleiku, Vietnam. I was able to see Sandy again on R&R in Hawaii. I won't ever forget seeing the plane come in and her walking across the tarmac. I got some good photos in Hawaii, thanks to the photography instructions given to me by Jerry Martin, M.D.

We always ate at the Mess Hall except when we infrequently ate at the Pleiku Medical Association meeting at the ARVN Hospital. Although our food was high in calories (carbohydrates) I still managed to lose thirty pounds of excess weight while in Vietnam, no doubt due to eating fewer snacks, being more active and eating less because of the heat.

I will never forget the sound of the helicopters, especially those flying their approach for landing at our helipad bringing in the wounded.

My brother, a farmer and non-poet, had a dream and wrote a poem, which was as much of a surprise to him as it was to me.

Summation

As a General Medical Officers I always felt fortunate to have been assigned to the 18th Surgical Hospital (MA) for the many reasons I have alluded to—camaraderie among the staff, our collective accomplishments, lifelong friendships and the opportunity of helping our troops and serving our country.

18th Surgical Memoirs
by Patricia Johnson Teranishi, C.R.N.A.

I felt I could put my experience as an emergency room nurse to more use. I heard that a MASH unit was coming into the country and was going to be headquartered in Pleiku. I asked the head nurse on my ward how I would go about having my assignment changed to the 18th Surg., and she said only the Chief Nurse could make that decision. I figured my chances were pretty slim, because I was a newcomer and had not yet paid my dues. Later, in the Officer's club I spoke with one of the physicians and he said that Col. Ed Odell, the 55th Med Group Commander, was really the guy to talk to if you wanted a change of assignment.

I waited a few weeks until I got my courage up and one night, when he was seated at the bar in the Officer's Club, I slid into the empty seat next to him and started a conversation. He was very cordial and asked a few questions about my background and asked how a nice girl like me wound up in the Army and in Vietnam. I proceeded to tell him the whole story about how I volunteered for Vietnam and had been seduced by the posters of nurses on a battlefield doing what I thought all combat nurses did. He laughed and said the Army recruited a lot of nurses with those posters. He seemed pretty friendly, so I figured it would not hurt to ask to be assigned to the 18th Surg. in Pleiku. His tone changed almost immediately and he said, "You and every other nurse here would like to be assigned to the 18th Surg." I thanked him for his time and slid off the stool and headed back to my hooch, thinking the whole idea of the 18th Surg. was a dead deal. First, I had gone out of the chain-of-command and second, I was one on a long list.

Three days later the Chief Nurse called me and said I was wanted in her Office. I figured she had heard what I had done and I was in for trouble. She wasn't very friendly, but told me I had been re-assigned to the 18th Surg. and should pack my bags and be ready to leave on the first plane in the morning.

I will never forget my first impression of the 18th Surg. The hospital was operating in tents while the actual hospital facility was being constructed of Quonset huts at a site a ways down the road. The afternoon I arrived there had been many surgeries performed and all of the patients were on litters in a tent. Most seemed very ill to me, and the whole scene rather chaotic. There were medics running all over the place, physician's shouting out orders and an

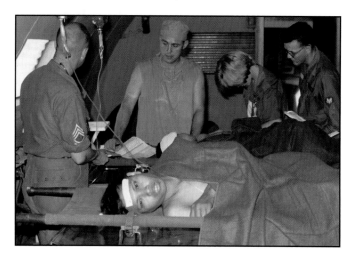

Viet Cong prisoner with abdominal wound. Jerry W. Martin, M.D. assisted by Pat Johnson, R.N. preparing patient for surgery.

Air Force Officer who was coordinating an air-evac of the wounded to the 85th Evac Hospital in Qui Nhon.

Within a few days of my arrival we moved to what would be our permanent hospital site, which was located between the Air Force base on the hill and the airstrip. Major Berry, the Chief Nurse, put me on one week of orientation during the day shift and then assigned me to work in the R&E (emergency room) during the 7:00 p.m. to 7:00 a.m. shift. Except for an occasional trauma or medical patient, we were not very busy initially. I actually spent a good part of each night visiting on the hospital perimeter with the MP who had a guard dog.

We lived in tents on the hill across the helicopter pad. Our tents were really rather cozy. We each personalized our space with rugs, various wooden boxes, shipping trunks and blankets brought from home. My space was near the door, so on sunny days we would roll up the sides and leave the doors open, making the tents homelike and welcoming.

The shower had an immersion heater and initially it had no roof. We soon learned that low flying helicopters could see us as we showered, so a roof was quickly added. The latrine was down the hill and down wind, a rather long trek, especially during the night and the monsoon season.

From the moment I arrived I felt welcome and a sense of camaraderie with the others assigned to the 18th Surg. Most of the enlisted personal had been assigned to the unit stateside and knew one another prior to arrival in country. They worked extremely hard, because they had their medic or other assigned duties as well as pulling guard duty and helping to build and set up the hospital. I was always so impressed with their cheerfulness and willingness to help in light of the terrific burdens placed on them. Many of our doctors and some of the nurses had also been assigned to the hospital prior to deployment. The nurses who were previously assigned were regular Army as opposed to others like myself who had joined just to go to Vietnam. I felt the seasoned nurses were really very supportive and tolerant of the rest of us. We didn't especially like to play by the rules and we were not worried about our long-term careers. Many of the physicians had been drafted out of residency programs and shortly after setting

up their practices. Except for those assigned to the 18th prior to deployment, none of us knew one another. We all realized soon after arriving in Vietnam that our job was not about us or any of the hardships we may have been experiencing, but rather to take the very best care of every soldier who arrived on our doorstep.

For me, to this day, the miracle of the 18th Surg. was the cohesiveness and sense of dedication displayed by every one assigned to this wonderful little unit. We came from all walks of life, rich, poor, urban, rural, young and more mature, single, married, enlisted, officer, professional soldier, inductee and volunteer. We knew why we were there, we never lost sight of our real mission, we helped one another during personal crisis, we shared family stories and delighted when good news came from stateside for one another and provided a shoulder to cry on when the news wasn't so good. We laughed together, drank together, and hung out together for an entire year. We worked extremely hard when duty called, volunteered to care for the locals on our off-duty time, played hours of volleyball in diversion and spent hours sharing stories in the officer's and enlisted club. We waited for mail call, marked off our short-timer calendars, attended USO shows, at times babysat the performers and threatened to spend our last two weeks in a conex container safe from "Charlie." We all jumped for joy when our DEROS finally arrived and had our ticket in hand to take the "Freedom Bird" home.

The friendships and respect we felt for one another was almost universal and is shared to this day. No one who hasn't experienced war can ever begin to understand these relationships. We lived and worked with one another day in and day out under the most stressful conditions. I never, not once, called for one of our doctors in the middle of the night to come and see a patient when I sensed any hesitation on their part. We nurses and medics, for the most part, worked 12 hour shifts, seven days a week. When mass causalities arrived we worked until the work was done. No one complained, it was just the way it was.

The others may have written about the patients we cared for and their bravery and courage. There aren't words really to express our admiration and respect we felt for the soldiers who passed through our doors. I have chosen instead to try to explain the relationships between us that contributed to our success as a hospital. There was a special group chemistry that only happens once in a lifetime. I am so honored to have been a part of this outstanding group.

When the time came for each to rotate home there was certain sadness. Because we had arrived at different times and some of us had volunteered to serve extended tours in Vietnam, we all left at different times. When our replacements arrived we welcomed them, but at the same time felt as though they were intruders. We were all accustomed to working together and had developed a comfort level with one another. Our replacements wanted to change all of our routines and, even though they had no experience, started making changes that affected working relationships.

I remember when Tony Lindem's replacement arrived. Tony was our Chief of Professional services, and an experienced surgeon whom we affectionitally nicknamed, "Our Fearless Leader." He inherently knew what was important, what was not, and what would work in mass causality situations. Everyone knew what to do and we all went about our jobs so efficiently it all worked like clockwork. Tony's replacement decided during mass causality situations we should tie a red flag on the foot of each litter when the patient was critically injured. That lasted for about a week until he discovered that before he could tie his red flag on the litter we would have the soldier through X-ray and into the operating room.

I had signed up for an additional six-month tour in Vietnam so I stayed actually for nine months after the last of the original crew for the 18th Surg. had gone home. The camaraderie was not the same.

Eventually the 18th was dismantled and sent to another location further up country. They had built the 71st Evacuation hospital nearby and all of the female nurses and others were assigned there rather than being deployed with the 18th. As to what serving with the 18th Surg and serving in Vietnam has meant to me, it is hard to imagine how my life would have been had I not had that experience.

When I arrived home in March 1968 the war was still going strong. I went to work in a civilian hospital in Grand Rapids, Michigan, and I realized that unless someone had a family member in Vietnam no one cared. I soon learned that people despised the war and those of us who had served there as well.

I eventually joined the reserves and spent many rewarding years in the military. Often after I became a Chief Nurse I would think back to Col. Cenac, our Hospital Commander, and Mary Berry and Marge Canfield, our Chief Nurses and marvel at their leadership. I know now what a tremendous responsibility leadership is. I believe they knew that we were professionals and left alone we would all surpass their expectations.

I never forgot all of my friends from the 18th and am so happy that we have been able in the recent years to see one another again at reunions. The thing that has amazed me the most is how little everyone has changed. Everyone is a little grayer but the goodness, sincerity and compassion is still there. We have all had productive, successful and seemingly happy lives. One thing I know for sure, we all contributed equally to making the 18th Surg. the best hospital in Vietnam.

Titi

by Phillip M. Leonard (MSG, USA, Ret.)

I entered active military service 16 January 1959 at Salt Lake City, Utah. I received basic training at Ft. Carson, Colorado and Ft. Riley, Kansas. Medical training was received at Ft. Sam Houston, Texas and Ft. Sill, Oklahoma. My first permanent assignment was at Ft. Jackson, South Carolina. From there I went to Tripler Army Hospital, Hawaii, then to Dugway Proving Ground, Utah. I then went to Ft. Douglas in Salt Lake City, Utah and thence to Ft. Benning, Georgia, and Heilbronn, West Germany. After serving in clinical laboratories and a biological warfare research lab, 1966 found me doing my second year in the 761st Medical Detachment in Karlsruhe, West Germany where I received orders

transferring me to the Republic of Vietnam. In March 1967, I arrived in Pleiku, in the Central Highland of Vietnam. My new home was the 18th Surgical Hospital (MA).

The hospital unit was setup on a slight slope a couple of miles north of Pleiku. Specialist 5th Class Bob Lee and Chuck Slabisak ran the lab under the supervision of Capt. Gene Chap. My impression of Bob and Chuck was that they were both skilled and efficient. Both techs were ready to rotate back to the United States, and I was the Specialist 5th Class replacement for Bob Lee. Dr. Chap was an easy going but knowledgeable manager. He would check to insure men and equipment were ready to respond whenever needed. He did not want to, nor did he have to, micro-manage the laboratory. It was my view that personnel throughout the hospital were skilled and efficient at what they did. From the beginning it was clear this hospital was about patient care above all else. The degree to which the hospital succeeded at patient care testifies to that fact. I had a legacy to live up to.

We treated both medical and surgical patients. Our days were occupied caring for patients or preparing supplies and equipment to care for those patients. Everyone worked long hours to see that they did not disappoint the patients who counted on them with their lives.

Many of the medical patients were men with malaria or other tropical diseases. They were usually kept at the hospital until initial treatment had been established. It was routine to perform the necessary surgery on the wounded casualties and then ship them to Qui Nhon on the coast for additional treatment or further evacuation.

One of the most memorable people outside of the military staff was a young and quite diminutive Vietnamese girl who went by the name of Titi (I have been told it means "small"). She was about 13 years old in 1967. As I recall, her parents had been killed by the Viet Cong and she had no other relatives. The unit "adopted" her and let her work in our dining facility cleaning and doing odd jobs. Each month we all contributed to provide her with a living wage. She had a very cheerful personality and was quite a moral builder. In November 1967 when the unit moved to Long Bihn to re-equip, we had to leave her in Pleiku. She was very distraught over not being able to accompany her only "family" to their new location. By early December, we had relocated to Lai Khe about forty miles north of Saigon. It wasn't long after that Titi showed up at the unit. She had walked and hitchhiked from Pleiku to Qui Nhon then south to Saigon where she was able to find out where we had moved. Unhappily, when she arrived at the unit, our Commander would not let her stay with us. I don't know what happened to her after that.

The 18th Surgical Hospital
by Roger Ecker, Capt. MC

Now I had to serve my Army duty. Having completed my residency in General and Thoracic Surgery at the New York Hospital-Cornell Medical Center in New York City, I entered the Army as a Captain. I was in the "Berry Plan," which allowed for deferment for medical school and residency training. I was offered a position at West Point but declined because I wanted to return to the western U.S., my home. Maybe because of turning down this plum, I was assigned to Fort Wolters, Texas. This was a helicopter pilot training facility west of Fort Worth, which gave me very little opportunity to practice surgery, but needed a surgeon in case of an aircraft accident. My family and I settled in, lived on-base, played golf, went to the pool, grew tomatoes and generally relaxed after a demanding residency.

After I had been there 15 months, some officer from Washington, D.C. came through and interviewed me. He asked me how I would like to go to Vietnam. I replied that my wife was six months pregnant with our second child, and it was not opportune for me. Six weeks later I got my orders to activate the 240th Medical Detachment (KF) (Thoracic Surgery) for duty in Vietnam. In early summer, 1966 I went to Walter Reed Medical Center and got the paperwork done. The 240th met in San Francisco. The TOE called for two surgeons, an anesthesiologist, two nurses and six enlisted men. Instead it was me, Capt. Leo Plasczynski, R.N., and three enlisted men, Sgt. Doner, a corporal, and PFC Harkless. We requested to travel to Vietnam by air, but they said they didn't need us that soon because the 4th Infantry Division that we were to support was still on its way. We stayed in a hotel on Geary Street across from the theatres and had a last stateside dinner together.

We boarded the MSTS *Gordon*, a smallish troopship, at the Oakland Army Terminal and headed out under the Bay Bridge and the Golden Gate Bridge. "I Left my Heart in San Francisco" was our theme song from then on. It was 21 days until we saw land again. That would be Naha, Okinawa. No one was allowed to leave the ship except the crew, who returned in an inebriated state. Through some ruse, I managed to get off the ship, walked

up the road to the Marine base and had a beer at the OC. The other officers asked whether I was "going South" and I allowed that I was. I also bought a camera at the BX.

The crew on the *Gordon* was civilian, and they guarded their rights jealously. When one of our group used their clothes washer, the only one available, they threw his clothes overboard when they found them there.

The days on the *Gordon* were monotonous for the officers, but positively awful for the enlisted men. We had two-man staterooms, they had triple or quadruple bunk beds in the hold, with no natural light. We had the officers' mess and wardroom above deck. Do you remember seeing old war movies where the soldiers or sailors are lining the rails all the time? That is exactly what happens, because it is better to be out in the open looking at the featureless ocean than in the hold or in a stuffy bunkroom. You could watch the flying fish, always a big event. We played chess. No radio, TV or newspapers. Bor-r-r-ing!

Then one morning we pulled into Da Nang harbor. A contingent got off. We went on to Qui Nhon where we disembarked. We immediately boarded a convoy and went by road to An Khe and on to Pleiku to join the 18th Surgical Hospital (18th Surg).

We were welcomed cordially by the 18th, its CO, Col. Mark Cenac, and all the Officers and Enlisted men. This comradeship was helped by the fact that our detachment had a 4x4 truck that had survived the pilferage at the docks in Qui Nhon and which was handy for going into Pleiku, a few miles away. Of course we were more than willing to give rides. We quickly settled in to our quarters, a large tent housing about a dozen officers. This had been set directly on the grass, and they didn't mow it first, so you often lost your boots near your cot. It was quite damp in the tent and leather tended to mildew, so we built armoires equipped with a large light bulb to provide enough heat to counteract it. Our tent was

one of four, three housing personnel and the fourth used for the malaria patients. This led us to be scrupulous in taking our malaria prophylaxis and keeping the mosquito netting around our bunks closed. Showers were in another tent for a while, until the engineers built us a wooden building with a concrete pad floor, with showers and a clothes washer and dryer. Before that we gave our clothes to the Vietnamese ladies to wash and iron. The first time I put my uniforms in the washer I was amazed how the water turned brown, supporting the rumor that these ladies washed them in the local ditch. Those same great engineers later built us a 2-story barracks, making life much more civilized.

There were other semi-permanent units in the area: MACV, II Corps, the nearby airbase, Special Forces and

Left to right: Dave Bucher, M.D., Roger Ecker, M.D., Joe Juliano, M.D., and Felix Jenkins, M.D. (squatting) near our BOQ. MACV-II Corps HQ on hill in background.

others. When they had a party, the officers of the 18th Surgical Hospital were always invited. This might have been due to the fact that we had the only women officers in the area, but the host organization couldn't very well send an invitation that said *Women Officers only*, so we male officers enjoyed a certain advantage in the invitation department. The only other American women in the area were Red Cross workers.

We had very little security on our compound. Vietnamese kitchen workers and other workers came and went with little scrutiny. We did not feel threatened, but we avoided being out on the roads or in Pleiku after dark. There were reported incidents of satchel bomb attacks on the air base but I heard no gunshots in our area the entire time I was there. Others may have had different experiences. A party of our doctors played golf at the only nearby course close to a lake, and reportedly were fired upon. I have no details about that. I was reminded of our security when a General Medical Officer/Battalion Surgeon accompanied a couple of wounded soldiers by helicopter to the 18th. He was in helmet and full battle gear. He carried a .45 caliber automatic. He had been there in the midst of the battle, supervising his corpsmen and treating the wounded. When his usual day was over, he slept in a tent, ate in a field kitchen and shared the dangers of the troops. After turning over his wounded soldiers he re-boarded the chopper and went back to duty. We enjoyed civilization and security, while he was in the thick of things. My respect for him was unbounded.

The routine came to an end when the First Airborne and the 4th Infantry, along with other units built up and began engaging the Vietcong and North Vietnamese Army (NVA) west of us along the Cambodian border. After a battle, the Dustoff helicopters would begin arriving on our helipad, the wounded were quickly brought into the triage area and those in need of immediate surgery were taken to the Operating Rooms. A wounded soldier on a gurney shouted across the room, "Hey, Sarg, we kicked their butts, didn't we?" We had two OR's with two operating tables each. We used other treatment areas for less involved cases, operating on gurneys. My physician colleagues, the nurses and corpsmen were superb. We all worked together until the casualties were all taken care of. This might require 48 hours. Sometimes you could grab a bite to eat or a catnap. A Surgical Hospital was supposed to keep a patient for not more than three days. By that time he was either returned to duty or evacuated to the next stage. Some were sent down to the 85th Evacuation Hospital, some to the Philippines, and some to Tachikawa Air Base in Japan. Severe burns went to Brooke Army Hospital at Fort Sam Houston, San Antonio, Texas. Four or more ambulances would line up and the wounded would be tenderly put on board for the short trip to the Air Base, where they would be airlifted to their next treatment site.

An artillery officer was brought in with blast injury of the lungs. He had been a forward observer and had called in rounds too near his position, perhaps by necessity. He was intubated and because we had no mechanical ventilator, we took turns bagging him to keep him alive. We sent to Qui Nhon and a Bird pressure-regulated ventilator was sent by air, along with an enlisted man who had instructions to bring it back with him or else! Unfortunately the officer died of respiratory failure in spite of our care.

There was a contingent of the South Korean Army fighting alongside our troops. I had occasion to operate on a Korean officer who had a gunshot wound in the right lower quadrant which had gone through and through his cecum. In the process of doing a cecostomy, *Ascaris lumbricoides* began exiting the bowel into the field. We policed them up and threw them in the bucket.

A local soldier and his buddies came in with a 6-inch long centipede that had bitten him. He was pale and sweating profusely, obviously near anaphylaxis. He recovered with epinephrine. All of us hospital personnel gathered around to look at the huge insect.

More seriously, a battle casualty arrived with a large compression dressing on his right groin. In the OR, we immediately encountered massive bleedng from a gunshot wound, got exposure and clamped bleeders as encountered. When bleeding was controlled and we could assess the damage, we had four clamps on the femoral artery and the femoral vein, separated by about six inches of lost tissue. We used the saphenous vein as a graft for the artery and tied off the femoral vein. Skin coverage was impossible without a flap, and because it was a dirty wound we simply dressed it and sent him on to the Phillipines. I greatly regret the lack of feedback that this patient illustrates. To this day I have no idea how he fared. Did he get a good vascularized flap to cover the area and allow the graft to succeed? Or did it all end up in infection and amputation? Some efforts were made to communicate with stations down the line at different times, but these were informal and uncommon, so we really did not know how our efforts and our treatment could be improved.

The first meeting of the Pleiku Medical Association was held in the mess hall at the 18th Surg. Our Vietnamese colleagues presented a case of leprosy. The middle-aged man had the signature leonine facies and had lost the distal parts of a couple of fingers, but was in generally good condition. I don't recall what the Americans presented. It was a cordial but formal meeting.

The Vietnamese government organized a festival in a field in the Pleiku area (FULRO). A large covered stage was set up, tents were pitched in the large grassy area, flags flapped in the breeze. ARVN (South Vietnamese Army) units arrived. Several Montagnard tribal units of probably 50 men each took part, each unit dressed in its own colorful tribal costume, carrying spears and swords. A number of dignitaries took their seats on the stage. My memory fails me, but they may have included General Nguyen Van Thieu, then the President of South Vietnam and Henry Cabot Lodge, our Ambassador to the country. General William Westmoreland was not present. He had visited our hospital on one occasion previously. Other II Corps and American officers were in abundance. Speeches over the loudspeaker system were interminable. Then the beautiful and adorned water buffalo tethered in front of the viewing stand was ceremonially hamstrung, slaughtered and cut up into pieces. The band played. The ARVN units and the tribal units marched. Dignitaries departed. The soldiers took down the pavilion and tents.

A group of 18th Surg doctors visited a local Montagnard village. They were well prepared to accept our visit. They invited us into one of the houses where we sat on the ground and talked. A tall earthenware vase was fermenting and bubbling with their beer. A bamboo straw was set upright in it, held in place by other strips of bamboo. We were invited to drink. My recollection of a small sip was a murky liquid akin to dishwater, with no noticeable alcohol. It won't replace Heineken. Then we went outside for a demonstration of the crossbow. They showed us how it is cocked, an arrow placed and shot. Crossbows were for sale, and several changed hands. A young lady of the village offered her charms and services, which were politely declined.

At Fort Wolters, Texas there was a General Medical Officer named Capt. James Wittenberg who preceded me to Vietnam. We had kept in touch and he was then working in a northern village whose name escapes me, on a MILPHAP (Military Provincial Health Assistance Program) Team. I flew out in a helicopter one sunny day and we landed on top of a fortified hill about 5 miles from the town. C-130s were landing and taking off constantly. I was informed that it was too late in the day to go to Jim's town, so I hunkered down in the sandbagged fortifications for the night. All night long our artillery fired interdiction rounds out into the surrounding area. I suppose it made everyone feel safer, but I cannot imagine this almost random fire to have been effective. They also shot off flares regularly, turning the hilltop and its perimeter as bright as day. This seemed more logical to me at the time. Dawn broke, we convoyed into town and I met Jim. He told me that their compound at the end of the street, near the river, took occasional rounds. The bridge on that street had been blown up by the Vietcong the week before. We visited the hospital, a one-story structure set in a large open treed area and was attractive but very basic. In the clinic I saw the only civilian casualty that I encountered in Vietnam, a child of about three years with a gunshot wound of the shoulder. This was not fresh; she was receiving outpatient dressing care and it was healing well. No one seemed to know whether it was accidental or the result of military action. Patients occupied hard beds, surrounded by family who tended to them. There was a roofed area behind the hospital where they cooked for their relative over the charcoal fire. Jim took me to the maternity hospital, a similar building about 100 yards away. He said it was not safe to walk from one to the other without carrying your sidearm. I was not able to stay overnight, so departed with the last convoy and flew out from the hilltop landing strip.

I accompanied several evacuees on a C-141 to Tachikawa Airbase in Japan, and took the opportunity to take the high-speed train into Tokyo. I had borrowed a suit and tie, important at that time, and hooked up with another officer on the flight. We took a bus tour of Tokyo, saw a traditional Japanese wedding in the garden of the

New Otani Hotel, had a beautifully-served sukiyaki dinner at a multistoried restaurant, visited the Ginza, stayed in a traditional Japanese hotel with a wooden bathtub in which one soaked *after* bathing thoroughly. The Japanese were exceptionally friendly. Two drunk young businessmen we met in the Ginza took us to their favorite snack counter in an arcade underground, where we tried to converse, mostly with sign language. They were irrepressible. One of them absently reached over and took a drag on the cigar I had been smoking, all the time laughing, talking and gesticulating. We parted like old friends.

Somehow I managed to go on R and R (Rest and Recreation) to Hong Kong. Because I was one of the first to be thus blessed, I was deluged with a shopping list by the other personnel. Of course, Hong Kong was a thrilling place to visit. While others in our party (not from our unit) had suits and shirts made, I took in the sights on both sides of the bay, did the shopping for myself, my wife and children, and my colleagues back in Vietnam. Without boring the reader with other wonderful experiences on the trip, let me say that it was memorable. However, it was to cost me what would have been an even more memorable surgical case. While I was in Hong Kong, the only penetrating injury of the heart came in. I do not remember which surgeon operated on him, but he found a right atrial wound of some magnitude, and was able to get to it and repair it successfully. I certainly applaud his work.

As the thoracic surgeon for the 18th Surg I had operated on a number of chest wounds. Some were major, often gunshot injuries. Others consisted of low-velocity "plinkets," resulting in hemo-pheumothorax. Plinkets were small pieces of shrapnel from NVA (North Vietnamese Army) grenades, or some of the smaller mortars. These resulted in a spray of small wounds with imbedded pieces of metal. The surgeons at the 18th Surg. spent hours

Montagnard girl. Women originally went topless but slowly had begun to adopt Western style clothing.

picking out plinkets. Sometimes there were wounds from large mortars, which were more powerful. One such patient I saw was in very stable condition with a wound to his lower leg. On X-ray there was an astonishingly large piece of shrapnel in the posterior aspect of the leg. At operation, a half-cylinder of metal six inches long, three inches wide and 1/4 inch thick had entered the skin through a minimal wound and lay in the subcutaneous space over the gastrocnemius. We all marveled at how little damage this huge piece of shrapnel had done.

Land mines were a different story. We seldom saw survivors of land mines. One day the word spread around about a land mine victim whose body had been brought in, and was lying on a gurney in the hospital. We silently gathered to gaze on what had been a young soldier, his feet gone and his uniform and underlying body shredded in a pattern of decreasing fury as it went from feet to waist and above. It was a horrific sight which is ever etched on my mind.

My military obligation came to an end while I was in Vietnam. I was offered the opportunity to extend my active duty time, which I politely declined. A month later my family and I were living in Mill Valley, California, and I was commuting to my research fellowship at the Cardiovascular Research Institute of the University of California, San Francisco. While there I put together a movie of some footage I had taken in Vietnam, and I was asked to present it to the fellows and residents at a regularly-held conference. They watch and listened to my talk (home movies in those days had no sound) and were very attentive. When questions time arrived, I was taken by surprise. How many civilians did I see burned by napalm or injured or killed by bombs? What about the destroyed villages? I had seen peaceful Pleiku, had seen only the one civilian casualty and tended to primarily American military. They left the auditorium grumbling and frustrated. This was, after all, San Francisco in the 1960s. The corner of Haight and Ashbury was just down the hill from UCSF, about 12 blocks away. One of my professors said privately, "Serves them right."

It makes me proud to remember the 18th Surgical Hospital and my unit, the 240th Medical Detachment (KF). The doctors, nurses, corpsmen and other personnel were well-trained, conscientious, hard-working and dedicated. We worked like a team at all times. Perhaps time has idealized it, but I cannot remember any serious conflict or disagreements within the unit. I give due credit to our CO, Col. Mark Cenac and to our Executive Officer. Their fine management of all the personnel made for a well-regulated hospital with high morale. I am fortunate to have been able to meet with many of these fine individuals over the years since the fateful convergence of our lives in Vietnam.

The Last MASH
by Leo "Ski" Plasczynski, R.N.

The 240th K (Thoracic Surgical) Team was hastily formed in 1966 to be attached to the 18th Surgical Hospital (MA) in Pleiku, Vietnam. I had just enrolled as a graduate student at Boston University to complete the final steps of my thesis on a Monday

morning. The Executive Officer called me in on Thursday morning of that same week to tell me I was being transferred from Fort Devens, Massachusetts. My first question was, "Where am I going?" I was hoping there was another University near there where I could continue on with my studies. His answer was, "I cannot tell you, but you are leaving tomorrow.

The next day I arrived at Walter Reed Army Medical Center in Washington, D.C. Our Thoracic Team and a Neurosurgical Team were being formed at the same time and both teams would be traveling together, the Neurosurgical Team ending up in Qui Nhon. The T. O. & E. of our team is usually comprised of two thoracic surgeons, one anesthesiologist or nurse anesthetist, three surgical nurses, and fourteen corpsmen (Surgical Techs). As often happens, the T. O. & Es are rarely completely filled so we shipped out with one surgeon, no anesthesiologist nor anesthetist, one surgical nurse and five surgical techs. The only difference the Neuro Team had was two surgeons.

We received a short briefing on Saturday morning and were sent home for the rest of the weekend. Sunday afternoon one of the surgical techs and I flew out of New York to San Francisco. The two of us made quite a sight boarding the plane, dressed in combat fatigues, wearing holstered Army 45's and each carrying two metal boxes of ammunition. We had to turn our weapons over to the pilot in flight.

Arriving in San Francisco, we were taken to the United States Army Recruiting Center and then billeted in a regular hotel. I do not even remember the name of it. The next day we were free to visit the city, but all I can remember is riding the trolley up one of the hill streets and Fishermen's Wharf.

Left to right: Mike Belinson, M.D.; Pat Sartorius, M.D. standing in Paradise Lost. The coat of arms of the 240th K Chest Team is noted on the wall, and the emblem of the 18th Surgical Hospital (MA) is hanging on the chimney over the fireplace.

Coat of Arms of the 240th KTeam (Thoracic Surgical Team) that was commanded by Roger Ecker, M.D. and later by Bob Hewitt, M.D.

Our real Army routine started the next morning as we were awakened at 0500 hours and transported by bus to the pier for boarding. The Army "hurry up and wait" syndrome kicked in as it was late afternoon before we got on the ship. It did give me time to meet the neurosurgical team. My counterpart on that team was another male nurse, Jack, who carried the nickname of Red. I do not understand why because he did not have red hair but he did have a ruddy complexion. I did not meet any of the enlisted men, but the two neurosurgeons were Bob Anderson, M.D. and Raquel Hernandez, M.D.. If you meet the latter, do not play chess with him because he always won in just a few moves.

The trip to Vietnam took twenty-one days and was somewhat boring after the first two days. The officers' quarters were crowded but comfortable. I would have hated to see the troop ship compartments, for there were nearly a thousand men aboard. The Navy does know how to serve and feed their officers. We were given the same amenities.

The port of Qui Nhon had no piers or docks so the ship had to anchor about five hundred yards out in the harbor. There was another troop ship there with about a thousand more men aboard, so all the unloading had to be by Landing Personnel Craft (LCP's).

The unit supplies had to be unloaded first before the troops could be put ashore. The large equipment and ammunition was sent to Long Binh and Saigon by cargo ships where they had docks to unload them.

Since all the equipment was to be unloaded on the beach, an armed guard was needed to protect the supplies. Ironically, both ships had lots of personal weapons but no ammunition. Our two medical teams were the only one with ammunition because we were deployed at the last minute. The troop Commander wanted us to give our ammunition to a guard force, but our team Commanding Officers refused to do this by terms of Army regulations. The only solution was to send our two medical teams in first to guard the supplies. We boarded the LCP and were the first of the troops to land on Vietnam soil. Right across from the supplies was a Vietnamese bar, so we left one man outside with the supplies and the thirteen of us tasted our first (ugh) Vietnamese booze.

A couple of hours later we were relieved by some armed combat troops, so we headed out to the airstrip to await our transportation to Pleiku. The neuro team was staying in Qui Nhon as part of the Evacuation Hospital already set up there. Our thoracic team sat under the palm trees for several hours sipping warm beer (ice is a premium in Vietnam) until the C-47 arrived to whisk us to our new home.

The 18th MA was in the middle of a circle surrounded by a number of combat units and the air base. Pleiku Air Field was directly east of us; the Special Forces Camp was directly south; Camp Holloway, the helicopter base, was southwest and the 169th Infantry Regiment, which had not yet arrived, was to be due west of us. On the Northeast was a Vietnamese Red Beret unit. An Artillery unit, with 175 mm. Howitzers that were so accurate they could hit a target about twenty-three miles away, was on the NNW, just a short distance from II Corps Headquarters, which could track mortar fire and return fire to the exact spot within minutes. The US Air Force billets were due north and the 25th Infantry Division rounded out the circle to the northeast.

A Better Man
by Wayne F. Hosking, M.D.

I embarked on the trip that would last two years and met the greatest bunch of friends that would prove to be excellent in every possible way. It was with fear and trepidation that I left my family in West Hartford, Connecticut. I said goodbye to my new car, new home, wife and two babies.

It was a great learning experience, since it showed quality in a group of young physicians and surgeons, nurses and soldiers who were experiencing many of the same things.

I had the privilege of attending the Masters Golf Tournament in Augusta, and we worked in the Army Hospital named for the great American General, Dwight David Eisenhower.

On our plane trip to Vietnam on a Pan Am 707 we watched a movie entitled, *A Man Could Get Killed,* which made one hope that it was not prophetic.

On arrival in Saigon, I had my first meal "in country" on the sixth floor of a downtown hotel. This was supposed to be safer in case someone threw a grenade. On our return to our overnight accommodations near the airport, we were informed that we were not supposed to be out that late.

In my training as an anesthesiologist, I had not been prepped for a tent with sand blowing through it; however, we were all young, energetic, enthusiastic and inventive.

I met one of the best chefs in Felix. I listened to music that I literally heard in my sleep—Nancy Wilson and Eddie Arnold!

I found out that humans can go from a basketball court to an operating room and save a life in seconds!

Our bar, thanks to Charlie Brown, was a great place to relax, talk about our work and meet some of the Air Force—who really came to meet our nurses.

We all perfected our jobs, but at times we seemed proudest of our photographs!

One of the things that we were able to do for the Vietnamese people was to take medicine to their hospitals as well as perform operations on many of their sick and injured people. We even did open heart surgery!

While I would never want to repeat it, I can honestly say I would not be the same person that I am today without those experiences.

Because of this call up, Georgi and I had one of the best trips ever, with Tony and Peggy Lindem in Hong Kong. Thank you Col. Cenac.

I also appreciate what the best nurse in the Army did in Vietnam and then did getting us together here in the best country in the world! Thank you, Pat!

542nd Clearing Platoon
by Martin Casarez

I was assigned to the 542nd Clearing Platoon assigned to the 18th Surgical Hospital. The 542nd (known as the 54duece) was assigned to the 18th at Lai Khe and at Quang Tri in Vietnam. The 18th was set up in the midst of a rubber tree plantation, and in support of the 1st Infantry Division. I was one of the medics assigned to the sterilization of medical supplies, and maintained the four autoclaves in our CMS area. I was also asked to assist during surgical procedures that were on going.

I arrived in Vietnam in October 1967. In November we traveled with the 18th to Lai Khe and set up the hospital there. Alfredo (Al) Garcia, whose hometown is 17 miles away from my home town, and I became fast friends.

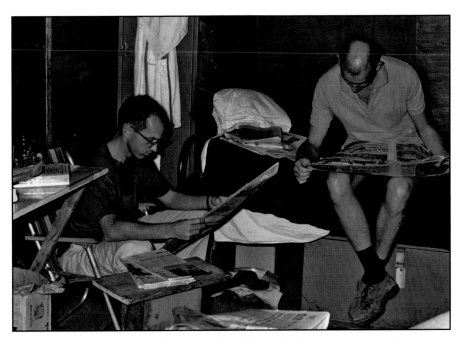

Orville Swenson, M.D. in chair, Wayne Hosking, M.D. sitting on Orv's bed.

While in Lai Khe, I remember observing an aircraft on the outside of the perimeter, spraying what we thought to be mosquito spray. Later we found it was Agent Orange. This was occurring within a half-mile from where we were operating. Shortly after the spraying and after a rain storm, I developed a terrible rash on the lower portion of my legs that I still have today. I was given some type of white, powdery medication to put on my legs.

I also remember a wounded American soldier brought in for surgery. Half of the soldier's torso was blown away. All that was left of his body was from the waist up. Blood was being administered from a bag held above his head, yet a steady stream of blood was coming out the bottom portion of his torso. The surgeon and his tech cut away much of the mangled flesh. I was asked to hold a container close to where the cutting was taking place so the surgeon could throw out pieces of the flesh and bone he was cutting. When that container got full, I would run outside to an incinerator of sorts, and throw in the flesh and bones. The smell of burning flesh, bones and blood I carry with me today. After dumping out the container, I would go back into the surgical room and proceed to have the container filled again. We sloshed around in 1-2 inches of blood and water. It is hard to explain the smell of blood; like death, maybe. I don't know the exact number of hours that we worked on that soldier, I just know that it seemed to last forever. I don't know if he lived or died.

At the beginning of the TET offensive in January 1968, the perimeter nearest us was being overrun. We prepared our unit to move further into the compound. While standing beside our deuce and a half we could all see and hear the artillery and mortar fire along the perimeter; it seemed like daylight. There was a small-framed doctor who had a bag in one hand and a .45 caliber pistol in the other. He kept screaming, "I don't want to die." I asked him to stay close to me. We never did evacuate, as the NVA, VC intrusion was repelled.

Personnel of the 18th Surgical (MUST) and the 542nd Medical Clearing Company waiting for a convoy to move to Quang Tri. Pfc. Martin Casarez, right front.

During the TET Offensive, while preparing to eat inside our mess hall, we began receiving mortar and rocket fire. Breakfast trays were flying every which way, as everyone was trying to exit the mess hall and find a hole to hide in. We already had water leaks in the mess hall before the mortars and rockets began to fall. In fact, we used to find containers to catch the rain to prevent flooding in the mess. The shelling made the leaks worse.

During the TET Offensive we had wounded soldiers brought in by medevac, and Chinooks. Reports would say that we had 12 or so casualties, but we had many more…hundreds!

One of the duties was also to wrap up the KIAs. The first KIA that I had to "plug up" was already in a black bag. I unzipped the bag and saw the destroyed body of an American soldier…an image that I still see today. We would place gauze over the eyes and nose, stuff the mouth, tie a knot on the penis, and place gauze in the rectum.

We set up in Quang Tri in March of 1968, in support of the 3rd Marine Division. We found that the Marines had a PX on the compound. Several of us went into the PX in an attempt to make purchases but were refused by the Marines.

Al Garcia and I decided to go to Pa Nang, Malasia on R&R in June of 1968. We spent five days of "fun times" before coming back to Quang Tri. I still have some binoculars that I bought in Malasia.

Monsoon started around September of 1968. It rained so much that big rats started coming out of their holes and started eating on "our" toenails. It was no surprise to wake up and find your toenails chewed on.

I remember that both the fuel dump and ammo dump placed around the 18th compound were hit by rocket fire during the time I was there. I know that beside American soldiers, we also received wounded Viet Cong, ARVNs, and Vietnamese civilians to including many, many children.

Female nurses started arriving at the 18th Surgical around August of 1968. I finished my tour in October 1968. I caught a C-130 to Saigon, from where I got on a commercial flight. I travelled from Saigon to Japan, Alaska, and arrived in Ft. Lewis, Washington. We were fed a 2" steak with baked potato. Yes, I ate it all.

I wonder sometimes how these soldiers, the ones that we worked on and made it, are doing today. What were their names? How many we saw die! How many we packed up! How many children we saw die or left crippled.

I now live in O'Donnell, Texas. I have had a battle with colon cancer, triple bypass, and total knee replacement on both knees. I still have the lower leg rash that I developed in Lai Khe, without any type of cure. I also have my memories, or better described as nightmares, and flashbacks that accompany me every day and probably will until the day I die.

PERSONAL STATEMENTS

Pfc. Martin Casarez and Sp/5 Al Garcia standing at a bunker near the showers at Lai Khe.

Pfc. Martin Casarez (542nd Medical Clearing Company) sitting on a bunker at Quang Tri (March 1968 to November 1968).

Notes from Letters Written Home, Vietnam 1966-67

by Eugene J. Chap, M.D.

26 September 1966

I am settling in Pleiku and the 18th Surgical Hospital (MA). Four of us bought a small Japanese refrigerator for our sodas and perhaps ice cubes. It cost $89.50, which we split four ways. I bought a chair for my cubicle for 650 piastres, or about $5.75. Capt. Leo "Ski" Plaszyczynski and I went downtown to Pleiku to purchase a chest of drawers.

2 October 1966

My first on call for 24 hours began today. I am the Chief of the Medical Section of the hospital. Last week I flew to Qui Nhon with 40 patients who had malaria, fevers and/or injuries. They were settled into the 85th Evacuation Hopital there. While in Qui Nhon, several of us were invited to dinner on board a Navy ship, the *Corpus Christi Bay* (I am not sure who was invited). We left shore to the ship via a launch and had a view of the mountains, shore, villages and ocean. All were beautiful. After touring the ship

with Dr. Charles Truluck, a South Carolina native, we enjoyed dinner of prime ribs and had cheesecake and pears for dessert. We returned to shore at 1930 hours. The next day was spent on ward rounds.

15 October 1966

Last night the Montagnards began FULRO celebration. It lasted about one week. It began with a torch light parade, in which nearly 1,000 people took part and ended up at a camp site about one mile from the 18th Surg.

7 November 1966

I flew by helicopter to Qui Nhon with a patient a few days ago. I have probably been approved for an R&R in Hong Kong, probably in December. Usually as our staff all go on these trips, a list of items and the necessary cash goes with the traveler. I guess we can call the trip a relaxing one, but also a shopping trip.

We have had runs of malaria patients, at times 30 per day. We have a standard treatment list for the diagnosis and treatment of our patients. These were developed when the staff of the 18th Surg. (MA) first arrived in Vietnam. Since I came to the hospital via other means, I inherited the treatment schedules and was mighty pleased to have them.

Martha Raye visited a while ago, but as I was on call, I did not meet her. I understand she was a joy to party with.

8 December 1966

Martha Raye visited the hospital again yesterday. She entertained the troops and then met with about eight of us in Lt. Col. Ranck's tent. We had a great chat and enjoyed her vibrant personality. I understand she spends about four to five months a year traveling and entertaining the troops at various camps in Vietnam. She is an R.N., I believe, but am not sure about this. She is a Lt. Col. as well, but again, I am not sure of this. She does travel in combat garb.

We had another visitor from the 1st Cav. (AM), Maj. Ron Gooding. He has been assigned to the 101st Division (The Screaming Eagles) and is the Brigade Surgeon.

I leave tomorrow for my R&R in Hong Kong. We leave Pleiku, fly to Da Nang and then on to Hong Kong.

13 December 1966

Hong Kong is great. I am staying at the Hong Kong Hilton. I have enjoyed the trip up Victoria Peak as well as the mainland. Getting around is quite easy. Purchased a few items for the folks back home but also for the guys and gals at the Surg. Now if only they will be received in good shape. I enjoyed a wonderful meal at the Four Seasons Restaurant at the foot of the tram that goes up Victoria Peak. Kobe steak from Japan with blue cheese on top. The Japanese strawberries were huge and absolutely delicious, and, I might add, cost more than the steak. I took pictures all over the place, including the Tiger Balm Gardens, but later found out that my camera was on the fritz and none of the great sights were captured on film.

203

Gene Chap, M.D. in laboratory.

26 December 1966

Christmas was busy, but we did have time to have a small Christmas party and even exchange a few gifts. I received a calendar and gave a deck of cards. The docs and the nurses pooled our collected goodies from home to help make the party a proper one. I did attend Midnight Mass last night. It was very crowded, so I stood in back of the chapel with a few troopers who certainly had partied a hellova lot more than I had.

29 January 1967

Summer, in quotes, is now here in Pleiku. It is rather hot. Insects abound. And while the work of the hospital continues, some news from CONUS comes in, usually thru old newspaper or magazines or personal letters. There was a report of rioting in Chicago, together with looting. Since I had family in Chicago, I sent a letter to a paternal aunt, Wanda Kotlarz, to ask whether the family is safe. Some time later, I did receive a note from her and she said that the rioting did not come close to their area.

One of the mainstays of life in Vietnam is the camera. My German made camera bit the dust, as I found out when my mother and father advised me that all of the rolls I had up to then sent for development were blank. It turned out that the shutter mechanism was broken. I made plans to purchase a Pentax Spotmatic camera one day, when they were available, since some of the doctors and nurses at the hospital were quite happy with their Pentax cameras.

10 February 1967

Tet began yesterday in Vietnam. It is the year of the goat. I think that last year was the year of the horse, but I am not sure.

Dr.'s Valerio and Juliano, Nurse Mary Hamilton and I were invited to dinner at Doctor (Bac-si) Ty's home in Pleiku. While he speaks English quite well, his wife and four children do not speak it at all. We had traditional sweets and tea before dinner. The sweets consisted of candied turnip, pumpkin and dates. In addition, there were lotus flower seeds and peanuts in fish sauce butter and coconut. Dinner was quite extensive and consisted of rice cakes boiled in banana leaves, which made the rice turn green. Within the cake, which by the way, is traditional fare for Tet, were bean sprouts and pork sausage. We had cabbage and chicken salad in vinegar, scallions in fish sauce, pork, boiled eggs in fish sauce, chicken and chicken soup, plus pickled bean sprouts with lettuce and cowslip and mint leaves. The bread was flat and crisp, made of rice, and appeared like large potato chips. Tangerines were served for dessert.

Since we were honored guests, we were not expected to bring gifts for Dr. and Mrs. Ty, however, in Vietnamese tradition we gave each child a 100 piastre note (red in color). The note is worth about 82 cents. Each note was placed in a red envelope. This is a must since the color red is considered to be good luck on the first day of the new year, Tet.

We wore our best civilian clothes, since even the poorest person would attempt to wear their best on that day, but would purchase new clothing if at all possible. Apparently, too, the first guests in the new year, Tet, must be important and wealthy and fortunate. Many Vietnamese refuse to see poor or unfortunate persons at this time. We had to assume that we fit the fortunate category.

The Ty home was a combination of office and home. The entrance led to the waiting room, which in turn led into the examination room and doubled as the dining room. The next room was a combination of sleeping quarters and kitchen. Whatever was lacking in worldly things in the home, our hosts more than made up by their courtesy and cheerfulness. We were made to feel quite at home.

5 March 1967

The rainy season is threatening to come around soon and the heat is still with us. I understand, and later found out, that the rainy season in our area was a strange one, with rain coming in torrents around 1700 hours but clearing a few hours later. The doctors and nurses advised me that they had gone thru an earlier rainy season.

There is, apparently, television in Pleiku now. Last month a sending station was built and programs are beamed in to the area.

Jayne Mansfield and Robert Mitchum visited the hospital a few weeks ago. Jayne looked worse for wear. Mitchum became quite drunk. I did meet him and even shook his hand. It was difficult to believe that this was the famous actor whom I had seen in several movies in the past.

14 May 1967

There has been serious fighting about 20 miles from Pleiku. Planes are busy carrying troops to the front. We are getting new doctors, nurses and technicians, too. I am still waiting for orders especially since I have only 25 days left in country, theoretically. Am getting more and more nervous.

24 May 1967

My orders have arrived. I am to be assigned to the Kenner Army Hospital at Ft. Lee, Virginia and I should be leaving Pleiku around the 8th of June.

2 June 1967

I left for Cam Ranh Bay as directed and am now waiting for travel availability to the west coast. Met with one of the doctors here and as we sat high above the port having a drink, he pointed out the ships and the unloading far below us. He noted that nearly 50% of material being unloaded gets "lost." I hope to catch a flight tomorrow and cannot wait to depart. I am anxious to meet with my family and civilization.

A Memoir of 18th Surg.

by Robert Engebrecht, M.D.

I vividly remember that cold winter day when I received a manila envelope containing about 100 pages of orders telling me to report to Fort Sam Houston, Texas by February 1, 1966. I called the Army HQ in Chicago and told them I only needed one sheet of orders to tell me where to go. I told them where to go with the other 99 sheets! A young lieutenant, anxious to calm me down, assured me I would need them all. Early on I was exposed to the inefficient way the Army did business. Turned out I needed only about twenty-five percent of them, as I recall. The orders said our second stop would be Fort Gordon, Georgia, with our final destination… "unknown." I asked where that would be and the good lieutenant told me he "couldn't say." It was pretty obvious from the content the destination would be a newly activated hospital, the 18th Surg. setting up for business outside of Pleiku, South Vietnam.

Several of us met for the first time at Fort Gordon and started friendships that continue to this day. Our trip to Vietnam flew from San Francisco to Hawaii, to Wake Island, to Guam, to 47,000 feet above the Philippines. The pilot said he could not go any higher in his attempt to avoid the typhoon raging around us. I watched as the wings of the commercial aircraft went up and down where they joined the cabin of the plane. The pilot decided to fly directly to, what was then, Saigon. We were met by Tony Lindem, our head surgeon. Tony was ahead of us in arriving in Vietnam by about three weeks. He knew how to get to places and was no happier to be there than any of us. That evening he took us to a hotel in old Saigon for dinner. That night was spent in an Army camp of tents near the only golf course in South Vietnam. Weather in Vietnam was calm when we arrived.

Our arrival, by plane, the next day at Pleiku, showed us immediately that we were there way too soon. The Army was not ready for us. There were some partially assembled Quonset huts and a few tents. Sam Gillis and his surgical team had been working out of tents and with limited supplies. We operated out of those

Barracks at Cam Ranh Bay.

same tents for several weeks, with equipment left over from the Korean War. The instruments were sent from the states packed in a viscous oily substance just like the medical personnel from Korea had packed them after they last used them. Vascular instruments were rudimentary, near antiques. The X-ray capabilities were outdated. There were no respirators. Ether anesthesia was all there was available. The only antibiotics were penicillin and streptomycin, and each surgical patient received them.

The monsoon season was to begin in those first few weeks. It rained and rained every day, all day. Everything was wet and all the same color, mud, water, sky. The tents were all trenched to divert the water. Despite the trenches, I remember standing in water as I cleaned wounds and operated in those tents. Regardless of the hardships, we all recognized that we still had it much better than the guys out in the field.

I remember several things that occurred while we were still working in tents. Since we had received only limited training in wound debridement at Fort Sam Houston, I had wondered what our first casualties would be. It turned out they were from a group of Armored Personnel Carriers, ambushed at night. There were about thirty men, all with multiple fragment wounds and burns, none of which were life threatening. Wound debridement was to become one of our specialties. Our "fearless leader," Tony, had trained at Peter Brent Brigham under Francis Moore, M.D.. Tony knew all about electrolyte replacement for burns and could write the orders for the burn case needs in about three minutes, something that would have taken me quite awhile. So in the interest of quick response to patient needs, I wrote for all my burn patient's IV orders to be gotten from Tony.

A personally memorable case was a patient with multiple head and chest injuries. The crew had him all draped and prepped when I got there. After surgery, we removed all the drapes and found his pants were still on, along with four live hand grenades. I'm sure I was leaning on those grenades all during the surgery. This shows how new we all were and how in a hurry we all were to help our young soldiers. The enlisted men were supposed to have removed all weapons and clothing as the patients came in.

One case turned exciting in a hurry, a patient with a gunshot would to the right side of his chest. X-ray showed a bullet on the

Left to right: Sam Gillis, M.D., Bob Engebrecht, M.D., foreground, Jerry W. Martin, M.D. standing between.

left side of his chest. Tony, our head and chest specialist, started the surgery but soon hollered for help. I was close by so ran and found Tony with an index finger in the entry wound to stop the blood loss. I was not as adept as Tony, but finally got the chest open and exposed, to see that Tony had his finger in a hole in the innominate artery. Eventually, Tony was able to debride the arterial edges and repair the innominate artery. We closed the chest and within 48 hours the patient was transferred to the 85th Evac Hospital in good condition. We always said the youthfulness and good health of the men we served was what really helped them recover from their wounds.

A fourth patient I remember from the days in tents was a North Vietnamese who was brought to our hospital. Regulations did not allow us to operate on them. They were transferred to the nearby South Vietnamese Hospital. That hospital was better supplied and had newer equipment that we envied. I was doing surgery on another casualty in the same tent. This North Vietnamese and I did make eye contact several times. You could imagine his fear. His mandible was completely shot off, probably by an M-16. We both knew, if rumors were true, he would not survive long at the next stop.

Finally the contractors were done and we moved from our tents into barracks with indoor toilets and hot showers. We were fortunate to have asphalt put on the heli-pad. The dust from the landings had been horrible during the dry season. The landing pad was near and the patients were carried in on litters from the helicopters to the triage area. The choppers would not take off again until they had received as many empty litters as we had received patients. The enlisted men kept a stock of empty litters by the buildings for quick exchange.

The hospital consisted of Quonset huts arranged in an X. There were two X formation buildings. The helicopter pad was just outside the first arm of the first Quonset; that was the

triage area. All the patients went through there first. A few steps from there was a single Quonset that housed the Lab and Pharmacy. If X-ray was needed it was right next to triage, occupying the second arm of the X. The nurse's station was in the center of the X, available to all areas. The most serious patient went to the first operating room nearest triage in the third arm of the X. The others went to pre-op, a busy area where patients were readied for surgery. The door of the pre-op/holding area opened toward the second set of x-shaped Quonsets. In order of the seriousness of the injury, patients were transported a short distance to the other operating rooms in the second set of X Quonsets. Two post-op units, where patients were cared for after surgery, completed the second X shaped Quonsets. Most patients were brought in by helicopter and flown out on C-130s. There was an air base just across the road from the hospital. An Army ambulance would back up to the door of post-op and the enlisted men would load patients for air transfer. Four patients on litters were all that could fit in an ambulance. If there were wounded who could sit up, the Ambulance could transport eight or ten at most.

Before the second monsoon season came, someone thought to build a cement walkway with a roof over it around the perimeter of the hospital. Sometimes we had so many casualties the patients had to wait outside. This provided them some cover from sun or rain.

We seldom got to follow up on our patients, there was one, though. He was working with a crew that were bulldozing trees for a landing zone (LZ) for helicopters. He was spraying jet fuel on a pile of trees and stumbled as the pile burst into flame. He came in with fourth degree burns everywhere except the soles of his feet and a tiny area on his abdomen the shape of his belt buckle. He was in no pain and wondered why we were so busy on him, putting in cut-downs to start IV fluids and antibiotics. After consulting with proper Air Force and Army officials it was decided to emergency evac. him to the U.S. Army Burn Center in San Antonio, Texas. We later learned that he died half-way across the Pacific Ocean.

Another casualty came in with a GS (gunshot wound) to his spine and was paraplegic. Our orthopedist operated on him and lowered his level of paralysis by two levels. That improved the soldier's ability to breathe more completely on his own. When I returned to Hines, VA to resume my residency, I rotated through the Spinal Cord Injury Service. While talking with a young paraplegic, I found out he was the one who we operated on at the 18th Surg. He did not remember any names of people there who cared for him. He and I spent a long time talking about Vietnam. At the time we spoke he was happy to be alive and had no ill will concerning the wounds he had received at war.

The year in Vietnam passed slowly. Everyone had a calendar marked with the number of days to their rotation out. Christmas was probably the hardest time of year for me. Our work load was sporadic and other times continuous for 36 to 48 hours straight. We eventually got very adept at triage, surgery and post-op. That came only with experience.

The best thing in my personal life that I took home from Vietnam was the friendship of comrades. That has lasted to this day: Mark, Tony, Sam, Wayne, Felix, Joe, Roger, Orv, "Charlie Brown," Ted, Bob, Jerry, Special Friend John and his fellow "dust-off" pilots, Pat, Skip, and all the other First Class nurses of the 18th Surg.

Many of us kept in contact loosely, usually with Christmas cards or an occasional letter. Then Pat Johnson decided to take it upon herself to get us together for a reunion. Thanks to her hard work and great planning skills, we met in New Orleans in 1998. It was a delightful time! I was amazed that each of us remembered things the other had forgotten. It was also obvious that thirty years had slowed most all of us down. We could never accomplish all the good things we previously did. However, we do have the memories.

My History with 18th Surgical (MA)
by Ted Stuart, M.D.

I first heard of the 18th Surgical (MA) when I met Wayne and Tony at Fort Sam Houston for basic training. We were then sent to Fort Gordon, Georgia for further training. The original ten of us were at Fort Gordon and participated in field maneuvers, which were not exactly like what we experienced in RVN.

When we shipped out, we were given a brief leave, then went to Travis AFB. Tony went with the advance party to RVN. I was separated from the group due to contracting a flu-like illness and was confined for three days in the hospital.

I finally made my way to the 18th Surgical (MA) via Camp Alpha and Qui Nhon. The accommodations were not what I was used to. I was in a tent with a mud floor. Inge was a fellow tentmate. We took over the facilities of the 542nd Clearing Company. There was one operating room that had two portable tables. The anesthesia machines used ether. I remember that several of the patients had seizures when inducted under anesthesia and broke

Ted Stuart swimming in the South China Sea at the Leprosarium near Qui Nhon.

Ted Stuart, M.D. and Dick Jones, M.D. in recovery ward at 8th Field Hospital at Nha Trang.

the arm and leg straps. I recall that Sgt. Crispa-Vega was sent on a mission to secure modern anesthesia machines with no questions asked. He was successful.

The sink for handwashing was outside the tent. After washing one's hands, one would grasp the tent flap to enter. Everyone got gloves, but only chest and abdomen cases were given gowns and masks. The mud in the tent was only six inches deep in comparison to that outside (10"). There was no duty roster. Whenever helicopters came in the whole crew responded.

This was the essence of the spirit of the 18th MASH. I had never experienced it before, nor since. After three months, I was transferred to the 85th Evacuation Hospital and then to the 25th Infantry Division. I sorely missed the ambience of the 18th Surgical (MA).

Experiences in Lai Khe and Quang Tri, South Vietnam

by Alfredo Garcia

I was ten days short of my twentieth birthday when I landed in Bien Hoa, Vietnam on November 16, 1967. It was around noon or a little after. The sun was yielding its best heat of the day. As I walked out of that plane, the smell of burning diesel, burning feces, the helicopters flying to and fro, seemed like a very well-prepared welcoming. The song of welcome was, "White Rabbit" by Jefferson Airplane. To this day, it remains the song that has the closest attachment to "my Vietnam."

Someone directed me to where I was to go and I got my first briefing. Not since basic training had I drunk water from a water bag. This time, I used it to chase a salt pill I was ordered to take. I and several other soldiers were boarded on a bus that had mesh wire on the windows, and were transported to what I now believe to be Long Binh. I don't recall what we were fed that evening; however, I do remember not getting much sleep that night. The howitzers going off, and flying helicopters kept me up most of the night.

The next day we helped load the 18th onto duece and halves. The first part of the convoy left, leaving several of us waiting for the next day. That night was spent in the metal bed of the duece and a half. I was really kept awake by the outgoing artillery rounds, as they seemed to resonate inside the metal bed.

Tired from lack of sleep, and from doing manual labor the day before, hot and sweaty, and not having a shower available, we began our journey to a place they called Lai Khe. I was driving the truck I was assigned to. It was a hot, dusty trail with MP's driving back and forth along side us, adding dust to the air. When we arrived in Lai Khe and drove into the compound, we could see that it had been built inside a huge rubber tree plantation. We could see that the first part of the convoy was already there. I found out that this was a 1st Infantry Division Base of operations, and that we were here in support of the Big Red One. We set up our expandable surgical wards.

With generators ready to go, medical wards inflated, autoclave sterilzing our surgical supplies, and with me, a Spec-4, having trained four months in an operating room at Ft. Leavenworth, Kansas—appendectomies, D&C's and C-Sections—I felt I was ready to handle anything.

It is only fitting to mention that the 542nd Clearing Platoon was attached to the 18th from as far back as I can remember. The NCOIC for this platoon was a Sergeant E-6 Luna. PFC Martin Casarez, member of the 542nd, turned out to be from O'Donnell, Texas, home of "Hoss Cartwright" and only 17 miles from my hometown of Lamesa. We became fast friends.

It is now my third or fourth day in country, and our first casualty is brought in, a young, 19ish year-old soldier, blue eyed, still with peach fuzz on his face covered by dried blood and dirt. The GI was covered with metal fragments, mostly on his back. I didn't train for this type of surgical procedure in the States. We debried the wound, cleaning out the back of this wounded soldier, and everything was going well. When we turned him over to debrie the front portiotn of the body, he went into cardiac arrest. After working on him for what appeared to be an hour, the attending doctor pronounced him dead. I was in shock. I had never seen a dead man, let alone one where I had just been the surgical assistant. A lifer came over and told me to get used to it. "This is going to happen again and again." He was so right.

That was how my tenure in Lai Khe got started. It did get worse with every traumatic amputation, abdominal cavities torn open, and heads blown away. I cannot count the number of our soldiers that came in blown in half, yet still alive. I remember seeing them and wondering about the one's that did not survive; what would their lives be like? It was a continous stream of casualties that never seemed to end. Many a day I wadded in 1-2 inches of blood and water, inside the surgical room, as a result of the surgical procedures that took place.

I drank some alcohol before I went to Vietnam, but nothing compared to the way I was drinking now. Every minute away from the O.R. I would drink a beer or take a sip of whiskey. It got to where I would always drink myself to sleep. That was to continue even after I left the Army.

When TET started, our wounded and deceased soldiers increased tremendously. We also treated a lot of Vietnamese civilians, soldiers, and young children—some wounded, some dying. It was during this period that we had about 3-4 young children in the receiving area. One of the young wounded female children, who was seriously wounded, hugged me around the neck as I picked her up, and refused to let go. She died after I placed her on the surgical table. Now when I go visit my grandchildren, the oldest, who is now eight, holds me around the neck, crying because Grandpa has to leave, I break down and flashback to the scene of this Vietnamese child (this is hard to write about).

My records show we packed up and left Lai Khe in February 1968 for Quang Tri—a dusty and barren place, much like west Texas. During our stint in Quang Tri we got shelled pretty often. We had a field, full of fuel bladders for helicopters, located to the east side of the compound, and an ammo dump to our north. Both places got hit by rockets and mortars at different times.

I have not been able to remember my last couple of months in Vietnam. I can't remember how I got (mode of transportation) to where I departed the country from, may have been Da Nang, or what time I left Vietnam. I remember landing in Ft. Lewis, Washington, after which I deplaned, changed to civilian clothes, and traveled the rest of the way home in civvies.

Surprises at the 18th Surgical Hospital
by Robert C. Fulton

After standing down the 25th Medical Battalion, 25th Infantry Division at Cu Chi, and following a two week R & R to CONUS, I reported to duty with the 18th Surgical Hospital (MA) at Quang Tri on 21 December 1970.

It was a physical and psychological shock going from the humid tropics of the Vietnam southern latitudes into the cold rains of the Northern provinces. I was assigned as the Executive Officer.

The hospital compound was at the north end of the Quang Tri base camp and about seven or eight miles from the DMZ. The north and west boundaries of the hospital compound were also the base camp perimeter. So, in addition to patient care duties, our enlisted personnel also had to perform base camp security functions (guard duty) every night. The female nurses lived in their own restricted compound within the hospital compound. I was only allowed on the female compound once at the inviation of the chief nurse to attend the ANC anniversary celebration. The male staff were housed in wooden barracks, called hooches. Field grade officers and senior NCO's had their own rooms in a hooch, but the more junior people generally had to share quarters with one or more roommate.The compound also included Officers and Enlisted Clubs (no food service), a small chapel, a barber shop and the assorted medical and military support buildings typical to a military unit, i.e. motor pool, supply warehouse, mess hall, etc. We had two attached units: a medical evacuation helicopter detachment from the Medical Group HQ, and a Mortuary (Graves Registration) unit from US Army Vietnam HQ.

Basically the compound consisted of seven separate sets of collocated buildings, which allowed us to function as an integral complex: 1) Hospital, 2) Pediatric Hospital, 3) Unfinished Hospital, 4) Mortuary, 5) Female Compound, 6) Male building area (to include air crews, 7) Support buildings and helipad.

I arrived at Quang Tri late in the afternoon of 22 December 1970 and had been there only a short time when the main transformer for the compound burned out. There was no replacement available in country, and the engineers said it would take several days to have a new one shipped in. The patient care areas had emergency power sufficient to perform at a minimal level, and power had to be conserved. Nurses made their rounds by flashlight, and we were lucky that inbound patients were slack so the O.R. was basically on standby. The billeting, mess hall, and support areas were without electricty. Most of the unit TOE equipment had been returned to Depot, but inexplicably a 15KW field generator was still in the motor pool. We moved the generator to the mess hall and the engineers rigged it so at least we could have power to

feed the patients and staff and have a real Christmas dinner. As I recall, we used that "field expedient" for two weeks before the transformer was replaced. We were truly "in the dark" for much of that time.

By the time the Christmas excitement was over I had realized there was a serious security issue that somehow had to be redressed. Our compound entrance gate was just yards from the north gate of the base camp. The pediatric hospital drew many indigenous visitors, plus we had indigenous staff members on the compound during daylight hours. These folks pretty much came and went as they pleased with only a very brief "lookover" at the base gate. Almost all visitors carried multiple packages and even bedding rolls since parents of seriously ill children often remained on the grounds for days or even weeks.

After bringing the security issue to the attention of LTC Keeling, he merely said, "Fix it." I developed a wild idea and asked the supply officer to visit and bring his NCO and a Spec. 4 that worked for him. I had known the Sp4 in Germany several years earlier. He was a person who was absolutely untrustworthy if permitted temptation, but totally dedicated when given a mission and responsibility. I explained the security situation, and the Sp4 immediately suggested a solution. His officer and NCO were very relunctant with the plan, but we went ahead with it.

There was a hooch on the compound that had blown or fallen down and was not useable. I instructed the specialist to salvage the materials, move them to the front gate and construct a new building where visitors could be segregated by gender and receive a body and property search. Destroying a building and constructing a building were absolutely contrary to rules, but we went ahead. As the project advanced, I tried to figure out how to staff this extraneous operation. Again, the specialist had the answer. He had taken a Vietnamese wife and learned the language. So, I put her on payroll and put him in charge of security for the indigenous personnel. It worked very well. A few weeks later the engineer showed up, wanting to know about this new building. He never did discover the missing building. The procedure worked very well and my concern for illicit commodities or bombs was much reduced.

Once this problem was solved and the gate search working well I again called in the supply officer, his NCO and the specialist. This time I asked them to find a solution so the male officers could have hot water showers. Everyone else on our compound had hot water, except the male officers. Regretfully, our immaginative and ingenuous E4 could not solve this problem, and so cold showers continued. This was bad news, because the ambient temperature in the rainy season was around 40 degrees. I thought it was supposed to be hot in Vietnam! We had to keep light bulbs turned on in our clothes chests to reduce mold and mildew, but the clothes never really dried out. I would have promoted this young fellow immediately if I could have obtained an E5 promotion quota, but he probably would have screwed up in his next assignment and lost the stripe. I often wonder what ever happened to him and his Vietnamese wife.

I am, indeed, indebted to the officers and enlisted personnel of the 18th Surgical Hospital (MA) during my time with them. Most didn't want to be there, but they did their duty to their country and to the sick and injured soldiers to the best of their ability. Many men are here to tell their stories to their grandkids who otherwise might not have been.

Job Well Done

by Mark T. Cenac, Col., MC, USA, Ret.

To: Hospital staff and all personnel 18th Surgical Hospital M.A. of Pleiku RVN

I am delighted to take this opportunity to praise each and every one of you for your constant and superior performance of duty at the 18th Surg. in Vietnam in 1966-67.

I will always remember those days, as I'm sure that you too will, day after day (and night) carrying out your prodigious efforts to save life and limb of all the wounded. Then reorganizing and cleaning up to be ready should additional casualties arrive. At other times, while not at work, you were friendly in relaxing and in recreational pursuits, as appropriate for any society however large or small.

We have heard so many comments these last forty plus years on how bad or terrible our military presence in RVN was that it

seems we were uniquely spared such a fate and even managed to enjoy that eventful year.

You have my profound gratitude for a job well done.

Lt. Col. Cenac working at his desk in the new HQ building.

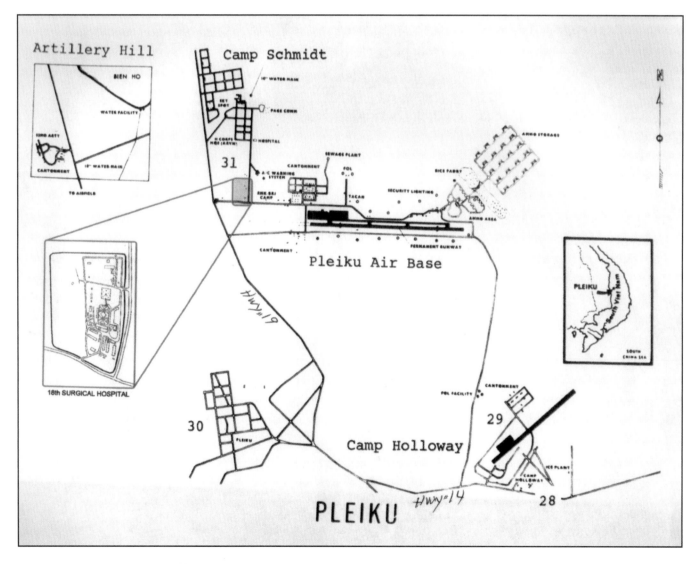

REUNIONS

The first reunion of the members, spouses and friends of the Pleiku 18th Surgical Hospital (MA) occurred from Friday, October 23 to Sunday, October 25, 1998. The Le Meridian Hotel, 614 Canal Street, New Orleans, Louisiana served as the headquarters for both our lodging and meetings.

Most attendees arrived Thursday afternoon or evening and very quickly began meeting, greeting, talking and reminiscing. Although some of us had visited over the years, this was the first organized reunion since we departed South Vietnam a little over thirty-one years earlier. The nucleus of our group (most of the original physicians, two or three other physicians who came to the 18th during the year and a few nurses) had communicated via letters, Christmas cards, and telephone conversations (later by email) throughout the years. Robert L. Hewitt, M.D. and his wife, Pat, lived in New Orleans where he served on the surgical staff at Tulane Medical School (in 1998, he was Professor and Acting Chairman of the Department of Surgery). He and Pat Johnson, CRNA (Col., ANC, Ret.) collaborated to arrange the reunion.

During the day on Friday, after breakfasting either at our hotel, the Cafe' du Monde, Brennan's or various other popular and notable sites, we gathered into unorganized groups and toured around New Orleans, especially the French Quarter (Vieux Carre'); browsed in old bookstores and antique shops; and visited museums of historical interest, St. Louis Cathedral and Jackson Square. Our group ate lunch at the Chartres House on the Square.

By five o'clock that evening, rested and refreshed from the day's touring and shopping, we met in a private banquet room at the Le Meridian Hotel. The bar for happy hour was decorated with an old parachute and camouflage material in an attempt to duplicate and simulate Paradise Lost, the Officers Club at the 18th. Many brought photographic prints to view, and a projector and screen were set up for those who brought 35mm slides. Around 7 p.m., we enjoyed a salad bar and a buffet of Cajun and Creole foods, notably crawfish jambalaya and numerous other splendid seafood delicacies.

On Saturday morning, we were bused from the hotel to Tulane University School of Medicine for Surgical Grand Rounds. Bob Hewitt, M.D. called me at home one evening about eight

weeks before the reunion and said that it was necessary for him to conduct the Grand Rounds conference Saturday morning and wondered if the physicians and nurses of the 18th would be interested in attending. Since we were all in private practice and away from academic medicine, I responded that I felt the group would find it enjoyable, as well as enlightening. After thinking it over, Bob called again a few nights later and asked if we—members of the 18th—should present acute combat trauma cases that we encountered at the 18th Surgical Hospital (MA) in Pleiku instead of having the Department of Surgery present cases. I agreed that the students, residents and staff would no doubt find our experiences in Vietnam of interest. He then said, "Jerry, I remember that you took a lot of photographs of wounds and surgical procedures in Vietnam, so why don't you present some of your slides at Ground Rounds?" I acquiesced to his suggestion and, over the next few days, assembled about 100 Kodachrome 35 mm slides from my collection, organized them in a viewable and logical sequence and began attempting to recall those cases long submerged in my memory from those experiences thirty-one years earlier.

Upon arrival at Tulane Medical School, Bob directed our group to room #7062 for the Surgical Ground Rounds that convened at 11 a.m. For almost an hour, I presented a photographic review of our experiences at the 18th and gave a brief explanation of the wounds and the corrective surgical procedures. After my presentation, Clarke Brandt (Lt. Col., MSC, USA, Ret.), our last XO at Pleiku, gave a brief report regarding the total number of cases we saw during our year in country and presented a statistical summary of medical and surgical facts from the Vietnam War. These presentations were followed by audience participation in a question and answer session. The questions and comments indicated their genuine interest in trauma surgery and our experiences in Vietnam.

The afternoon was spent relaxing and further reminiscing with each other about our Vietnam experiences.

That evening the Japanese Room on the second floor of Antoine's Restaurant on St. Louis Street was reserved for our dinner meeting. Bob Hewitt, M.D. served as the Master of Ceremonies. After the invocation and the Pledge of Allegiance to the American Flag, Bob read a letter from William C. Westmoreland to the 18th

A S P E C I A L
Department of Surgery Grand Rounds

A Vietnam Surgical Hospital Revisited

Reunion of the Officers of the 18th Surgical Hospital, M.A., Pleiku, Vietnam 1966-1967

Saturday, October 24, 1998
11:00 am

ROOM 7062
TULANE UNIVERSITY SCHOOL OF MEDICINE

PROCLAMATION

City of New Orleans

WHEREAS, former members of the United States Army's Vietnam-based 18th Surgical Hospital have organized and will gather in the City of New Orleans for a first-time reunion of the hospital's doctors, nurses corpsmen, dustoff pilots and crews, along with hospital staff; and

WHEREAS, this gathering will reunite men and women who served together with the 18th Surgical Hospital in Vietnam's central highlands during the period April 1966 through August 1967; and

WHEREAS, it is realized that most soldiers in the 18th's area of medical support never had the opportunity to personally say to these gallant men and women: "...thanks for being there for me"; and

WHEREAS, the city of New Orleans, on behalf of those soldiers, takes this moment in time to be their surrogate. By this **PROCLAMATION**, the Crescent City formally acknowledges and thanks the reunited members of the 18th Surgical Hospital for their past guardianship of our American fighting men in Vietnam. Our citizenry salutes your professionalism, dedication, and the unselfish patriotism shown when each of you answered our Nation's call to serve; and

WHEREAS, this 31st year reunion of the men and women of the 18th Surgical Hospital will serve as a forum for the assembled to remember comrades past; to renew friendships misplaced; and to refresh memories faded of those tumultuous times and, yes, some good times experienced during the bloom of their youth, and

NOW, THEREFORE, I, MARC H. MORIAL, by the authority vested in me as Mayor of the City of New Orleans, Louisiana, do hereby proclaim the days of the 18th Surgical Hospital's reunion, Friday, October 23rd, 1998 through Sunday, October 25th, 1998, as:

18th SURGICAL HOSPITAL DAYS

IN WITNESS WHEREOF, I have hereunto set my hand and caused the seal of the City of New Orleans, Louisiana to be affixed this 23rd day of October, 1998.

Marc H. Morial
Mayor

in which the General recalled and graciously complimented our medical and surgical efforts at Pleiku. Bob then read a Proclamation from Marc H. Morial, the Mayor of the City of New Orleans, proclaiming the days of our reunion, October 23-25, 1998, as: 18th SURGICAL HOSPITAL DAYS. For dinner we were served our choice of trout or steak and enjoyed Baked Alaska for dessert. All spouses and guests were introduced and the physicians and nurses who served at Pleiku made brief remarks. The evening was delightful and extremely conducive to excellent conversation. The setting was beautiful, conveying an extraordinary ambience.

The Japanese Room was decorated with materials obtained in Japan. The walls were covered with hand-painted rice paper on which Japanese scenes were depicted. The tables, chairs, table decorations and other furnishings were of Japanese origin and the curtains and drapes, made of Japanese silk, complimented the décor. When the Japanese bombed Pearl Harbor on December 7, 1941, the room was closed to the public. Not until about 1980, almost forty years later, was the Japanese Room refurbished and reopened for public use.

Sunday morning after breakfast, everyone was involved with preparations to check out for return home early in the afternoon.

Shortly after the New Orleans reunion, Pat Johnson recorded her thoughts and submitted them to *Newsweek Magazine*. The Editor replied saying, "No one cares about Vietnam anymore." The following are her words:

I have just returned from what arguably has been the most emotionally expensive and, at the same time, the most exhilarating experience of my life. What is it about reunions, and this one in particular, that makes me want to shout so that the whole country can hear?

The year was 1966, and the massive troop buildup in Vietnam had just begun. Early in the spring I had responded to the Army's urgent call for nurses to care for the sick and wounded in Vietnam. By mid-June I was in Qui Nhon at the 85th Evacuation Hospital caring for soldiers with malaria and learning to care for a fungal skin infection of my own.

I had heard that a small sixty-bed surgical hospital was soon arriving in the country, and would be situated near Pleiku in the Central Highlands.

Marge McGinnis, who was another recruit from Michigan, and I volunteered to go to Pleiku and the 18th Surgical Hospital. We were eager to escape the heat from the coast and anxious for another challenge (at twenty-two my life was a series of challenges).

This essay is not about our work (though there was plenty to go around) nor is it about the hardships that we endured (at the time we hardly noticed). Rather, it is about the folks assigned to that wonderful little unit who exhibited total dedication and selflessness.

The entire hospital staff was comprised of three groups of people with the exception of the Commander, the Chief Nurse, the Executive Officer, and a few of the senior enlisted soldiers. The first group was the physicians who had been drafted out of their residency programs or who had only been in practice for a short period of time after having just set up their practice in a community setting. The second group was the nurses like myself who responded when a need for their services became apparent. The third group was the enlisted soldiers whose draft number had been selected.

The vast majority of these caregivers did not volunteer. All of us though, came to the same conclusion both individually and collectively, after having compared stories. Despite this being a great inconvenience perhaps and a disruption of our families for sure, we were totally dedicated to give the very best of care to the soldiers in our hospital. For they, like most of us, had not volunteered to serve in Vietnam either.

As the year progressed, we settled into a routine that got us through each day, each week and each month. We worked extraordinarily hard during periods of heavy casualty influx performing our own job responsibilities as well as helping with whatever else needed to be done.

More than once I witnessed doctors doing what ordinarily would be described as "nurses work." Yes, they even gave patients bed baths. Cooks helping to organize blood drives and distributing juice and cake to the volunteer donors was also a common occurrence.

We bonded emotionally to one another as well. I believe as much from the sense of desperate souls making the best of an awful situation, to an awesome respect for the professionalism and capabilities of one another. We deeply admired the dedication of the field medics and the Medevac helicopter crews who so courageously tended to and delivered our patients quickly and safely.

As our year drew to a close and individuals received orders returning them home, we never really talked about seeing one another again. Everyone was eager to return to his or her families, pick up the pieces, and move on with their lives. The fact that we were returning to a country that demonstrated hostility not only about the war, but also towards the reluctant participants of the war was never discussed.

The years have passed, most memories have faded, and attachments now seem less important. I learned only last month that this code of silence that I have maintained has been adopted by most all of us to some degree. A few of us have seen one another occasionally at professional meetings and talk of a reunion was mentioned briefly but never gained momentum.

Then last fall I received a call from Dr. Bob Hewitt as he had done from time to time throughout the years. He is the Professor and Acting Chair of the Department of Surgery at Tulane University School of Medicine. He promised to help me if I would co-chair a reunion for everyone assigned, attached, or affiliated with the 18th Surgical Hospital. His enthusiasm was contagious. Within a few months I had located forty-six of our long lost colleagues and friends with the help of the Internet, medical and nursing association rosters, and unbelievably patient long distance operators. Everyone was so surprised and happy to hear from me and delighted about the prospect of a reunion.

After months of arrangements and almost unbearable anticipation, we finally met in New Orleans in late October of this year. We had gone to great pains to reconstruct our Officers Club in Vietnam from the beaded doorway to the parachute canopy over the bar. We played Roy Orbison tapes in the background. As everyone assembled, it seemed as though thirty-one years had washed away. The magic had returned. The people were slightly grayer, but just as gracious and genuine as they had been in Vietnam. Every one of us had returned from our

Antoine's Restaurant, Japanese Room, Saturday Evening, October 24, 1998. Pleiku Physicians and Nurses. Front row, left to right: Clive "Skip" Winslow, CRNA; Orville P. Swenson, M.D.; Sheldon "Charlie" Brown, M.D.; Margaret Jaskowski, R.N.; Ruby Britsch Schueing, R.N.; Margie McGinnis, R.N.; Margaret Canfield, R.N.; Lois Wilderman Baird, R.N.; Sally Dawson Borja, R.N. Middle row: Pat Johnson, CRNA; Ron Thompson, CRNA; Joe Juliano, M.D.; Mary Hamilton-Juliano, R.N., J.D.; Leo Plasczynski, R.N.; Tassos Nassos, M.D.; Mark T. Cenac, M.D. (CO); Clarke Brandt, MSC (XO); Ted Stuart, M.D.; Wayne Hosking, M.D.; Terry McDonald, M.D.; Judy Dexter Richtsmeier, R.N.; Robert Engebrecht, M.D.; Samuel Gillis, M.D. Standing on steps: Roger R. Ecker, M.D.; Eugene J. Chap, M.D. Back row: Michael Belinson, M.D.; Robert L. Hewitt, M.D.; Jerry W. Martin, M.D.

experience with the understanding that we had answered the call when our country had needed us, practiced our professions to the best of our ability, and had taken the very best care of every soldier rendered to us.

Many of our colleagues have risen to the pinnacles of their professions, and every one of us has continued to serve our country as educators, administrators, and practitioners. We are proud of being Vietnam Veterans, and now, as then, we consider caring for fellow American Soldiers a privilege and honor.

Our second reunion was organized, and arrangements were finalized by Marge McGinnis, R.N., (Lt. Col. ANC, Ret.) and Pat Johnson. We met in Washington, D.C. from Thursday, September 6 to Sunday, September 9, 2001. We arrived on Wednesday, September 5. Reservation were made (contract SHR 501) for us to stay at the Mologne House on the campus of the Walter Reed Army Medical Center (WRAMC) located at 6825 16th Street N.W., Building 20, Washington, D.C.

On Thursday morning, we took the subway to the FBI Building and joined a 10:30 a.m. tour, followed by lunch at one of Union Station's many restaurants. Union Station is a beautiful building of the Beaux-Arts style of architecture designed by Architect, Daniel Burnman, and was completed in 1908 at a cost of $125 million. With the decline in train travel, the station was transformed into the "National Visitor Center," which opened on July 4, 1976, for the Bicentennial, but failed to draw sufficient crowds and was closed in 1978. It rapidly deteriorated but was resurrected by Congress with the passage of the Union Station Redevelopment Act of 1981. Three years of renovation and restoration at a cost of $160 million brought it back to its original glory, and it was reopened on September 29, 1988. It is a living and working museum, as well as a retail center and a transportation facility. It now has over 130 unique shops and restaurants and serves as the hub for Amtrack's headquarters and executive offices. It now is the most visited destination in the Nation's Capitol with over 32 million visitors per year.

On Friday, we toured the Walter Reed Medical Center Complex. We were met and welcomed in the main lobby where our tour began. We were shown the Eisenhower Suite, the Omnicell (a prescription dispensing system using barcodes, robotics, and dispensing cabinets for automated inventory control and distribution of drugs), the Center for Prostate Disease Research, the Comprehensive Breast Center, and the Pharmacy; and we had a briefing about the Walter Reed Health Care System (WRHCS).

Friday evening, we enjoyed a cocktail buffet at Delano Hall across the street from the Malogne House from 7-9 pm. Saturday morning we were bused to the Bethesda, Maryland campus of the National Naval Medical Center, where we attended a lecture and conference at the F. Edward He'bert School of Medicine, Uniform Services University of the Health Sciences. We then returned to the Mologne House briefly to change into more comfortable clothing for our visit to the Vietnam War Memorial, where I read the letter,

Reflections At The Wall, and a wreath was placed at the section of the Monument listing those who died during 1966-1967.

We returned to the Mologne House from the Vietnam Veterans Memorial about 3:45 pm and quickly refreshed and dressed for our dinner meeting that evening in the McNair Room at Ft. McNair. We left the Malogne House at about 6 pm and arrived at the Officers Club at Ft. McNair about 6:45. For dinner we enjoyed Maryland crab cakes, salad, beef wellington with duchesse potatoes, asparagus and rolls, followed by chocolate raspberry palet cake and lemon sorbet. Music was provided by the U.S. Army Band. Bob Hewitt, M.D. again served as Master of Ceremonies. The guest speaker was Richard A. Stratton (Capt., USN, Ret.), a former POW for over six years and a sometimes cell mate with Senator John McCain. Bob introduced the speaker with the following remarks:

I have never had an honor more appreciated by me, than in introducing our most distinguished guest speaker, Richard A. Stratton. Dick Stratton is a great American—a Patriot and a Hero. Most, if not all of us, have felt as though we have known him since 1967. During the dark days of his captivity, our hearts and prayers were with him, his fellow prisoners and with their families. But before I tell you more about our honored guest allow me to recall January 1967, when most of us were at the 18th Surgical Hospital in Pleiku. By January 1967, an estimated four to six North Vietnamese Army regiments were in the Central Highlands, and adjacent Cambodia was saturated with NVA units, which regularly invaded the Highlands. Their strategy was to reach the coast and divide South Vietnam, and the units we supported prevented that. Our forces were under strict orders not to violate those sanctuaries in Cambodia, and our Secretary of Defense vigorously denied that North Vietnamese troops were in Cambodia and even chastised Lt. Gen. Stanley "Swede" Larsen, who pointed out that they were. You remember Lt. Gen. Larsen, who regularly visited the 18th Surgical Hospital with General Westmoreland. Troops under Lt. Gen. Larsen's command later captured several hundred of the NVA and exposed that their origin was indeed Cambodia before international television to prove the point. In January 1967, the 4th Infantry Division under the command of Maj. Gen. William (Ray) Peers, whom you also recall, started a series of aggressive search-and-destroy operations called Operation Sam Houston, which took the 4th Infantry Division into southwestern Kontum Province and west of Plei Djereng Special Forces Camp near Pleiku, and within two weeks of February, the 4th Division had eleven or so major engagements with well-trained, well-equipped North Vietnamese Regulars. I wrote in my diary about the mortar attack on Camp Holloway, January 7, 1967, when we received 35 or more casualties, just days before the aforementioned operations resulted in massive casualties received by the 18th Surgical.

On January 4, 1967, Lt. Cmdr. Richard Stratton, A4E pilot and the maintenance officer of Attack Squadron 192 on board the carrier, USS *Ticonderoga*, launched in his "Skyhawk" attack aircraft at 0703 hours, for his 22nd Mission, an armed reconnaissance mission over Thanh Hoa Province in North Vietnam. After launching his rockets at the target, he experienced engine malfunction and fire—his plane had been hit. He had to eject and was captured later. He was held in the Hanoi prison system, but they could not arrest his courage or his leadership. We all came to know of him and prayed for his safe return. Our POWs agreed among themselves that none would accept release until all were released—an example of their discipline. But in 1969 they decided upon three to accept release in order to provide an accurate list of prisoners to our Nation and so that the story of torture would become known. Lt. Cmdr. Stratton told them "…go ahead, blow the whistle. If it means more torture for me, at least I'll know why and will feel it worth the sacrifice."

Lt. Cmdr. Stratton was released in March 1973 during Operation Homecoming, along with a total of 591 American POWs. He had been held six years, three months—2,251 days—which he later referred to as "shore duty." He was awarded: the Silver Star; the Legion of Merit for Valor; the Bronze Star for Valor; the Navy Commendation Medal for Valor; the Purple Heart; the Air Medal; the Combat Action Ribbon and the POW Medal.

He continued his Naval Career and retired with the rank of Captain in 1986 after 31 years of service. Capt. Stratton is a native of Quincy, Massachusetts and a graduate of Georgetown University in 1955 with an A.B. in History. He became a Commissioned Naval Officer that year and then a Naval Aviator. He graduated from Stanford University with a M.A. in International Relations in 1964 and now also holds a MSW degree from Rhode Island College School of Social

Work. Following retirement from the Navy, he trained and commenced practice as a clinical social worker, specializing in working with trauma victims, Vietnam Veterans and substance abusers. He has served as Chairman of the Department of Veterans Affairs Advisory Committee on Prisoners of War and maintained a supportive lead for our POWs and their families.

He has been married for over 40 years to Alice, who was the First Deputy Assistant Secretary of the Navy for Force Support and Families and served in the Pentagon from 1985 to 1989. Alice, too, is a social worker, and together they were counselors, but they recently retired approximately five weeks ago, and now make their home in Atlantic Beach, Florida. Two of their sons and a daughter-in-law are former Marines and combat veterans of Desert Storm.

I hope that most of you were able to watch the recent television program "Return With Honor" narrated by Tom Hanks, which was a splendid tribute to our Vietnam POWs—their courage, their endurance, their conviction and honor. Their military discipline is unsurpassed in our history and should serve as examples in our U.S. history textbooks along with Valley Forge and subsequent operations that have made our Nation what it is.

I am honored to present Capt. Stratton.

As we listened intently to his speech, it was impossible not to imagine what the torture and loneliness must have been like. I am sure the hardest part was not allowing hopelessness to creep in and take control of his thoughts and behavior. We were impressed with his seeming lack of vindictiveness, anger or self-pity. He was extremely interesting to talk to, and he projected the persona of a sincere, humble, honest and trustworthy man that seemed to possess a natural integrity and an impeccable character.

After dinner, I was again asked to read *Reflections At The Wall*. We departed Ft. McNair about 10:30 pm and arrived back at the Mologne House at approximately 11:15. The evening was memorable, cogent and unforgettable.

Most of our reunion group departed Washington on Sunday, September 9, 2001; however, two couples delayed their departure in order to sightsee and vacation a while longer. Orville Swenson, M.D. and wife, Sandy, flew out on Tuesday morning. When the terrorists struck the Twin Towers in New York and the Pentagon in D.C., all commercial flights were grounded. All in-air flights were allowed to proceed to the closest useable airport. The Swensons were fortunate since Duluth, Minnesota, their intended destination, was the nearest airport and were able to finish their flight as originally planned. Tony Lindem, M.D. and wife, Peggy, had to remain in Washington for three or four days before they were able to fly back to Salt Lake City.

After the Vietnam War ended and when the Communist government opened the country to foreign visitors, Clive "Skip" Winslow, CRNA, guided tours for friends who wanted to revisit the areas where they were stationed while serving in Vietnam. He had become friends with many Vietnamese while

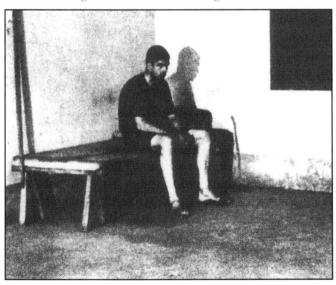

Lieutenant Commander R.A. Stratton U.S. Navy, sits glumly in his prison cell in North Vietnam. This was one of the more "luxurious" suites. Cells in the "Hanoi Hilton" were described by their inhabitnats as "tombsized."

Pleiku 18th Surgical Hospital (MA) Group at the Veterans Memorial Monument Saturday afternoon, September 8,2001. Front row, left to right: Clive "Skip" Winslow, CRNA; Roger Ecker, M.D.; Ruby Britsch Shueing, R.N.; Margie McGinnis, R.N.; Michael Belinson, M.D.; Tassos Nassos, M.D.; Orville Swenson, M.D.; Back row; Wayne Hosking, M.D.; Ted Stuart, M.D.; Robert Engebrecht, M.D.; Phillip Leonard, (Lab Tech); Pat Johnson, CRNA; Mark T. Cenac, M.D. (CO); Vivian Hanks-Rizzo, CRNA; Lois Wilderman, R.N.; Barbara Gouldthorpe, R.N.; Samuel Gillis, M.D.; Margaret Jaskowski, R.N.; Norig "Skip" Ellison, M.D.; Jerry W. Martin, M.D.; Eugene Chap, M.D.; Martin C. "Tony" Lindem, Jr., M.D.; Robert L. Hewitt, M.D.

Vietnam Tour Itinerary
May 1 – May 17, 2004

- April 30, Fri. Fly to L.A. Transfer to: Porto Fino Hotel Yacht Club Renondo Beach, CA 92077
- May 1, Sat. Dinner as a Group at Porto Fino Hotel Yacht Club
- May 2, Sun. All day in LA – meet at L.A. International Terminal @ 9 pm
- May 3, Mon. Flying
- May 4, Tues. Arrive Saigon about noon – transfer to Caravelle Hotel
  Free Afternoon – very good shopping one block away
  Meet for dinner to be ARRANGED ! !
- May 5, Wed. Tour Saigon and the Cu Chi Tunnel & Shopping Tour to
  Saigon Central Market – Visit War Museum, Art Museum
- May 6, Thurs. Fly to Nha Trang, Transfer to the Ana Mandara Resort on
  South China Beach – Afternoon Free to Rest or Shop
- May 7, Fri. Over Land to Pleiku – through Qui Nhon and AnKhe Pass
  Stay at Pleiku Hotel (the only hotel which is not 4 or 5 STAR)
  Tour Pleiku – Visit Pleiku Central Market
- May 8, Sat. Tour Pleiku, Kontom, Elephant Rides – Try to find 18th Surg.
  (The last time I was there the area of the 18th & 71st was a Military Base, plan a reunion
  dinner – I'll get in touch with some friends in Pleiku to help!!)
- May 9, Sun. Fly to Danang, Transfer to Furama Hotel & Resort at China Beach
  Afternoon at the beach or the Lagoon Pool (This is a 5 STAR Hotel)
- May 10, Mon. Visit Marble Mountain, in the center is a cave which was
  a V.C. Hospital, the mountain was a look out for the V.C., visit old Hoi An City – which
  was an ancient Sea Port, Tour Danang, shopping is everywhere!!
- May 11, Tues. Over Land to Hue through Hai Van Pass about 2.5 hours
  Stay @ Saigon Morin Hotel, visit the Imperial Citadel
- May 12, Wed. Boat Cruise on the Perfume River to Thien Mu Pagoda
  Then visits to the Royal Tombs
- May 13, Thurs. Fly to Hanoi, Over Land to Halong Bay, 3hours
  Stay @ the Plaza Hotel over looking Halong Bay
- May 14, Fri. Day Cruise on Halong Bay by Chinese Junk
  There are 3 tourist stops along the way
- May 15, Sat. Over Land to Hanoi, Stay @ Hanoi Hilton
  Visit Hanoi Hilton Prison, Ho Chi Minh's Home
- May 15, Sun. Tour Ho's Tomb, Afternoon free for shopping
- May 17, Mon. Fly to L.A.

serving with the 18th Surgical Hospital (MA) and the 71st Evacuation Hospital and met many others on subsequent trips. He told our group that he would take us back to Pleiku if we wanted to go. Such a trip was discussed, and planning began. A third reunion was planned in Los Angeles for two days prior to the beginning of the trip. Ultimately most of our group decided not to return to Vietnam. Pat Johnson Teranishi and husband, Irv, chose to go. They met Skip in Los Angeles on Friday, April 30 and on Sunday, May 2, 2004 departed L.A. International Airport for Ho Chi Minh City (Saigon).

After returning from the trip Skip, as well as Pat and Irv, wrote that the trip was exciting, interesting and very instructive. Pat mentioned that currently there is nothing where the 18th Surgical Hospital (MA) near Pleiku was located except an overgrown field. Skip died of colon cancer in 2008 (Wayne Hosking, M.D. died in 2010 and Tony Lindem, M.D. died in 2003.)

Arrangements for the fourth reunion of our hospital were planned and coordinated by Judy and Roger Ecker, M.D. and Pat Teranishi and Irv. We met in San Francisco, California, from Thursday, September 13 through Sunday, September 16, 2007, using the Marine Memorial Club and Hotel for our meetings and lodging. The hotel is located at 609 Sutter Street, only a block and a half off Union Square.

After check-in, there was a complimentary cocktail reception for our group in the Skyroom Restaurant from 4:00 to 6:00 p.m. At 7:00 p.m., we met in the Regimental Room where we were officially welcomed by Pat and Roger. Hors d'oeuvres and a cash bar were available. Presentation of the Colors by the Travis Air Force Base Color Guard occurred at 7:45, followed by a thirty-minute performance by the Travis Air Force Base Brass Quintet. Following the Quintet performance, Bob Hewitt, M.D. gave a review of Hurricane Katrina and the damage to New Orleans, especially regarding the damage to the hospitals, the devastation of physicians' offices and the destruction to clinics and other medical support groups. Around 9 p.m., the Colors were retired by the Color Guard.

On Friday, September 14, after enjoying breakfast in the Skyroom Restaurant, we loaded a bus for a private tour of three boutique wineries in Napa

18th Surgical Hospital (MA) Physicians at the Family Club in San Francisco, CA Saturday Evening, September 15, 2007. Left to right: Wayne F. Hosking, M.D.; Ted J. Stuart, M.D.; Robert E. Engebrecht, M.D.; Joseph Juliano, M.D.; Felix W. Jenkins, M.D.; Jerry W. Martin, M.D.; Sheldon Charles Brown, M.D.; Orville P. Swenson, M.D.

Drury Hotel Lobby, Saturday evening, September 19, 2009. Bob Hewitt, M.D.; Gene Chap, M.D.; Jerry W. Martin, M.D.; Michael Belinson, M.D.; Ted Stuart, M.D.

Drury Hotel lounge, Saturday Evening, September 19, 2009. Seated in foreground: Toni Stuart; Georgi Hosking; Lori Franklin. Seated facing camera: Gene Chap, M.D.; Orville Swenson, M.D.; Wayne Hosking, M.D.; Suzanne Orehek; Don Orehek (member, National Cartoonist Society); Mark T. Cenac, M.D. Standing: Janet Plasczynski; Roger Ecker, M.D.; Gary Franklin; Nancy Cenac and Pat Teranishi (back to camera).

Valley. At one of the vineyards we were served a picnic lunch. After returning to the hotel, there was an informal reception in the Skyroom. The evening was left free.

Saturday morning after breakfast there was time for sightseeing, touring, golfing or shopping. Arrangements for us to have a private tour of the "Dahlia Dell" were made by John Kreiner (Dustoff pilot) through his interests in the American Dahlia Society. The tour was conducted by Ms. Deborah Dietz of the California Dahlia Society. We were transported from our hotel to the Golden Gate Park, where the dahlia gardens are located, in open trolley-like motor vehicles. The afternoon was then free to watch ball games, reminisce, shop, etc. That evening we had a group dinner at The Family Club.

Sunday morning after breakfast we packed, checked our luggage at the hotel and were transported by taxi to a pier on the bay where we boarded a San Francisco Bay Cruise ship for a delightful brunch while cruising San Francisco Bay. Following the cruise we collected our luggage, went to the airport and headed for home.

The fifth reunion, from September 17-20, 2009, was in San Antonio, Texas. The Drury Hotel on the San Antonio River Walk (Paseo del Rio), 201 North St. Mary's Street, served as our hotel. Roger Ecker, M.D. and Judy, Pat Teranishi, CRNA and Irv, again jointly assumed responsibility of planning and organizing the meeting. Upon arrival on Thursday, September 17, after checking in and unpacking, we began congregating and greeting each other in the hotel lobby. That evening a dinner buffet was served in Drury's Milan Room. Following the meal, I discussed the progress of *Soldiers Saving Soldiers: Vietnam Remembered; A Brief History of the 18th Surgical Hospital (MA)*, the history I had agreed to write at our last reunion in San Francisco.

Each morning we enjoyed a complimentary breakfast at the hotel. Friday morning, we loaded a bus that transported us to the Army Medical Department (AMEDD) Museum at Ft. Sam Houston. We had a privately conducted tour by David Windsor (Command Sgt. Maj. [CSM], USA, Ret.). After completing the tour, we had box lunches in the AMEDD Museum cafeteria.

After lunch, we again boarded the bus for Brooke Air Force Base where SSgt. Daniel Stoner led us on a tour through the Altitude Chamber, the Centrifuge and the Research Center before returning to the hotel.

That evening, we walked a few blocks to Casa Rio Restaurant, 430 Commerce Street where we boarded two River Boats and enjoyed a Mexican dinner accompanied by a Mariachi Band.

Saturday morning after breakfast, we again boarded a bus and traveled to Fredericksburg, Texas (hometown of Adm. Chester W. Nimitz) for a few hours of shopping and browsing. Wayne Hosking, M.D. and I visited the National Museum of the Pacific War. The Adm. Nimitz Museum, George Bush Gallery of the Pacific War, the Plaza of the Presidents, Japanese Garden of Peace, Memorial Walk and the Pacific Combat Zone, all part of the Museum and Park.

In the evening, we walked a few blocks to Biga on the Banks, 203 S. St. Mary's Street for dinner. The dinner meeting opened with the presentation of the Colors. A wonderful salad was followed by an entrée of pan roasted red snapper or beef tenderloin medallions. Between dinner and dessert, there was a brief pause in our culinary pursuits to allow John Kreiner (Lt. Col., USA, Ret.) to make a brief presentation. He told of his hobby of cultivating and propagating Dahlias. At the conclusion of his talk, he showed a photograph of a new species developed and named by him.

We were surprised to learn that he had named it for our Pleiku hospital: *Dahlia 18th Surgical Hospital*. I am certain that the 18th Surgical Hospital (MA) is the only military hospital that has a flower named for it.

The meal concluded with a dessert of Praline Opera Torte with candied hazel nuts and chocolate sauce. Following dessert, Mr. Don Orehek, a respected and noted member of the National Cartoonists Society, who visited the 18th Surgical Hospital (MA) at Pleiku as a member of a USO show in September 1966, was our guest speaker. He, assisted by his wife, Suzanne, showed examples of his highly acclaimed work published in newspapers and magazines over the years. Don graciously agreed to write the forward to this book.

Sunday morning, we walked to the Historic Menger Hotel, 204 Alamo Plaza (adjacent to The Alamo) for a wonderful farewell brunch. The Menger Hotel, built in 1859 by W. A. Menger, has provided lasting impressions for over 130 years on visitors and guests with accommodations that exude opulence and elegance. Today the lush tropical courtyard remains very much as it was in 1882 as Oscar Wilde strolled there "...sipping spiked lemonade

DAHLIAS

These plants were discovered in the mountains of Mexico in the 16th Century by a Spanish physician sent by King Philip II to study the natural history of that country. They were first described under the native name of *acoctii* (the Aztecs called them *cocoxochitl*). About 1789, the Spanish sent plants back to Europe, some of them going to a Swedish botanist, Dr. Anders Dahl (a former student of Carolus Linnaeus [1707-1778]), for whom they are named.

One report states that dahlia tubers were stolen from the Royal Gardens in Madrid and taken to the Jardin du Roi in Paris. Another story says that they were imported directly to France by a Monsieur Menoville, who had been sent to Mexico by the French government to smuggle out cochineal insects (a precious source of red dye). Menoville reputedly sent the tubers home to Paris as food for the insects on the journey. Since this was not their main food source, the cochineal insects died. The tubers were then sent on to the Jardin du Roi, whose curator, Andre' Thouin, saw them as a possible edible substitute for the potato. It was soon discovered however, that they have a "... repulsive, nauseous peppery taste, which inspires equal disgust to man and beast."

The tubers also reached Dr. Johann Georgi of St. Petersburg, Russia, who studied and propagated them; and, in areas of Eastern Europe, they are still referred to as *Georginas*.

These plants, native to Mexico and Central America, are now cultivated around the world for their showy, variously colored flowers.

The original scientific name was D. variabilis, but it was later changed to D. pinnata. There are at least 13 classes, numerous

flowering forms (i.e., IV: Formal Decorative), 30 species and 20,000 cultivars. The dwarf varieties are D. coccinea and D. pinnata. Hybrids are officially classified into 14 groups based on flower shape. Synonyms are *Georgina* or *Georgina Wild*.

100 Flowers and How They Got Their Names
By Diana Wells

The Garden Encyclopedia
Edited by E. L. D. Seymour, B.S.A.

Botany: Principals and Problems
By Edmund W. Stinnott

Dahlia 18th Surgical Hospital

Kingdom: Plantae
Subkingdom: Tracheobionta
Phylum: Magnoliophyta
Class: Magnaliopsida (Dicotyledon)
Subclass: Asteridae
Order: Asterales
Family: Asteraceae (Compositae)
Subfamily: Asteroideae
Tribe: Coreopsideae
Genus: Dahlia
Species: 18th Surgical Hospital

Dahlia propogated and photographed by John Kreiner.

and smoking long foreign cigarettes." The Menger Bar is a replica of the House of Lords Pub in London, with French beveled mirrors, glass cabinets and a paneled cherry-wood ceiling. Teddy Roosevelt recruited Rough Riders from this bar to fight in the Spanish American War.

The sixth reunion of the physicians, nurses and spouses of the 18th Surgical Hospital (MA) who served at Pleiku, Pleiku Province (Central Highlands), Republic of Vietnam (II Corps) occurred from Thursday, September 15 to Sunday, September 18, 2011 at the U.S. Military Academy at West Point, NY. The year 2011 represents the 45th year since the original group organized the 18th Surgical Hospital (MA) at Fort Gordon, GA in the spring of 1966 and then accompanied it to South Vietnam in June of that year.

My wife, Jimmie, and I drove to NY in order to carry boxes of my new book, and arrived in the early afternoon Wednesday, September 14. Most attendees flew and arrived on Wednesday afternoon, in addition to a few Thursday morning, who arrived at the airport at either Stewart, NY or White Plains, NY and were then shuttled to the hotel in rented vans by Sam Gillis, M.D. and wife Sandra, Roger Ecker, M.D. and wife Judy, and Irv and Pat Teranishi, R.N.

Everyone stayed at the Hotel Thayer on the campus of the U.S. Military Academy. We breakfasted each day in small, spontaneously formed, groups in either the main dining room, the MacArthur Room, or the adjacent Poe's Riverview Room.

During the day, Thursday, we were free to talk, reminisce and wander around campus. That evening we met in the hotel lobby at 5:45 p.m.

Pat Terranishi, CRNA (right) responds after Jerry W. Martin, M.D., presents her with a Kentucky Colonel Certificate at the 6th reunion, West Point, NY. Jimmie H. Martin is seated.

Jerry W. Martin, M.D., presenting Mark T. Cenac, M.D., a certificate indicating that he was now an Admiral of the Kentucky Waterways.

and were transported by vans to the West Point Club where we enjoyed a buffet dinner in the Hudson Room. Following dinner, I briefly discussed my recently published book, *Soldiers Saving Soldiers*. Earlier I had given a copy to each of the members of the 18th Surgical Hospital (MA) in attendance. I then presented Pat Teranishi, CRNA (Col. ANC, USA, Ret.) a certificate designating her as a Kentucky Colonel in recognition of her efforts organizing and coordinating our reunions. I also presented Mark T. Cenac, M.D. (Col., MC, USA, Ret., our CO at Pleiku) with a certificate designating him as an Admiral of the Kentucky Waterways. These certificates were obtained for me by the Hon. Jodie Richards (KY Rep. [District 20], former Speaker of the House Representatives).

THE CULINARY INSTITUTE OF AMERICA
welcomes

18ᵗʰ *Surgical Hospital*

to

RISTORANTE CATERINA DE' MEDICI

Friday, September 16, 2011

~

Gamberetti con Caponata di Melanzane
Warm Salad of Shrimp with Classic Sicilian Eggplant Relish

~

Rotolo di Pasta con Spinaci, Ricotta e Prosciutto Cotto
Pasta Roll filled with Spinach, Ricotta and Ham

~

**Brasato di Vitello allo Spumante
con Polenta e Indivia Dolce Gratinata**
Asti Wine Braised Veal with Polenta and Endive Gratin

~

Torta Caprese
Flourless Chocolate and Almond Cake

Caffè, Tè, Tè Freddo
Coffee, Tea, Iced Tea

*Included in your package are the beverages listed above.
Please ask your server to purchase additional beverages.*

*Same day substitutions are not guaranteed and
will incur a surcharge.*

Gift cards are available through our Maître d'Hôtel

Alberto Vanoli, C.H.E.
Chef Instructor

Ezra Eichelberger, C.H.E.
Maître d'Hôtel Instructor

A key component of the education process at the CIA is learning how to deliver outstanding service. Students at The

Menu honoring the 18th Surgical Hospital at the Culinary Institute of America, September 16, 2011.

At the conclusion of a delightful evening, we returned from the Officers Club to Hotel Thayer.

Friday, September 16, was another interesting and exciting day. That morning we were free to visit museums, gift shops, etc., in West Point, NY and/or walk around campus, photograph, etc. At noon we boarded a bus at the hotel for a guided tour of the West Point Military Academy, during which we enjoyed a box lunch.

After returning to the hotel, our time was unorganized until we again boarded a bus at 4:15 p.m. to be transported to the Culinary Institute of America at Hyde Park, NY. Following a marvelous dinner from 6-8 p.m., we returned to the Hotel Thayer about 10:30 p.m.

Dinner at Culinary Institute of America, pictured l–r: Sandra Gillis and Sam Gillis, M.D.

Dinner at Culinary Institute of America, pictured l–r: Toni Stuart and Ted Stuart, M.D.

Dinner at Culinary Institute of America, pictured l-r: Pat Teranishi, CRNA; Felix Jenkins, M.D. and his daughter, Cheryl Haywood, J.D.; and Bob Hewitt, M.D.

Dinner at Culinary Institute of America, pictured l-r: Jean Marie McDonald; Terry McDonald, M.D; and Jerry W. Martin, M.D.

Dinner at Culinary Institute of America, pictured l-r: Judy Ecker, Nancy Cenac, and "Admiral" Mark T. Cenac, M.D.

Dinner at Culinary Institute of America, pictured l-r: Judy Dexter Richtsmeier, RN; Ron Richtsmeier; and Leo "Ski" Plascyznsi, RN.

On Saturday, after another free morning, we either walked or caught shuttle buses to the pre-game activities on The Plains (parade grounds) where we watched the cadets parade. At the conclusion of the Review of the Corps, we went to Michie Stadium (Hall of Fame Weekend) to attend the Army vs. Northwestern football game. Army's junior quarterback, Trent Steelman (#8) and Northwestern's senior safety, Jared Carpenter (#27) are both from Bowling Green, KY. Army's Black Knights upset the Northwestern Wildcats 21-14.

That evening we gathered for dinner at the Eisenhower Room (Hotel Thayer). After the Presentation of the Colors and conclusion of the National Anthem, we enjoyed an appetizer and salad. Our entrée

Reception at Thayer Hotel, West Point, NY, of the 18th Surgical Hospital (MA), September 15-18, 2011, with Pat Teranishi, CRNA, and Tassos Nassos, M.D.

Members of the 18th Surgical Hospital (MA), Pleiku, during their 6th reunion at the U.S. Military Academy at West Point, NY, September 15-18, 2011 in the Thayer Hotel. Back row, l-r: Leo "Ski" Plasczynski, RN; Ted Stuart, M.D.; Terry McDonald, M.D.; Mike Belinson, M.D.; Robert Engebrecht, M.D.; Roger Ecker, M.D.; Sam Gillis, M.D.; Tassos Nassos, M.D.; Orville Swenson, M.D.; and Robert Hewitt, M.D. Front row: Jerry W. Martin, M.D. (holding a copy of Soldiers Saving Soldiers, *which he unveilved at this reunion); Pat Teranishi, CRNA; Judy Dexter Richtsmeier, RN; Mark T. Cenac, M.D.; Marge Canfield, RN; Ruby Shueing, RN; and Lois Wilderman, RN.*

Pictured l-r: Mary Engebrecht; Bob Engebrecht, M.D.; and Orville Swenson, M.D., at Thayer Hotel, West Point, NY.

was served following the Keynote Address given by CSM Jose Powell, Garrison Command, West Point. Between the entrée and dessert, the West Point Knight Caps (West Point Glee Club) presented a most entertaining program. Following their presentation, the Glee Club members dispersed throughout the dining room and one or two sat at each table, thereby, allowing us to become briefly acquainted with them and they with us. Following the Retirement of the Colors, we adjourned.

At the Sunday brunch, also in the Eisenhower Room, "Admiral" Cenac presented me with a print made from an original Vietnamese painting given to him by Maj. Gen. Vinh Loc at Christmas, 1966. Group photographs were then made. The

Group picture of spouses of physicians and nurses of the 18th Surgical Hospital (MA), Pleiku, held at the U.S. Military Academy, West Point, NY. Back row, l-r: Mary Engebrecht; Irv Teranishi, J.D.; Mart T. Cenac, M.D.; Mary Ann Nassos; and Ron Richtsmeier. Front row: Jean Marie McDonald, Jimmie H. Martin, Toni Stuart, Nancy Cenac, Sandra Gillis, Sandy Sevenson, and Judy Ecker.

phrase, "Good friends are hard to find, harder to leave, and impossible to forget," is often quoted and very true. It is always an unpleasant task to break up something special, and it is never easy to say goodbye to long-time friends. Following our goodbyes, everyone began making preparations for departure to their respective homes.

We returned to the Drury Inn and Suites San Antonio Riverwalk Hotel for the 7th Reunion of the 18th Surgical Hospital (MA) from April 21-24, 2016. The reunion was both exciting and festive since it occurred during the final weekend of Fiesta San Antonio 2016.

We often congregated in the hotel's dining room for breakfast/brunch and occasionally for lunch and supper (dinner). We were on our own to shop, visit museums, or engage in other interesting activities. There were only two scheduled events: (1) our official group dinner in the Alamo Room at the Biga on the Banks (203 South St. Mary's) and (2) Sunday brunch at the historic Menger Hotel (204 Alamo Plaza) before departing for home. Because of aging, difficulty of travel for some, and dwindling numbers due to illness and death, there are no plans for additional future reunions.

A special group camaraderie and close personal relationships and friendships have been established among those of us who took the 18" Surgical Hospital (MA) from Ft. Gordon, Georgia, to a site approximately 2 miles north of Pleiku City, Pleiku Province, Republic of Vietnam from June 1966 to June 1967. We have visited and communicated innumerable times through letters, cards, photographs and by telephone, email, etc. throughout the years since leaving South Vietnam and being discharged from the army.

It has now been fifty years since our group left Vietnam. This 50th Anniversary Commemorative Edition is, therefore, very meaningful to us. We hope the readers will comprehend that

Reception during the 6th reunion of the 18th Surgical Hospital (MA) at West Point, NY, September 15-18, 2011. Pictured l-r: Judy Dexter Richtsmeier, RN; Jerry W. Martin, M.D.; Bob Engebrecht, M.D.; Mary Engebrecht; Pat Johnson Teranishi, CRNA; Judy Ecker; and Jimmie H. Martin.

Brunch at the historic Menger Hotel during the April 2016, 7th reunion of the 18th Surgical Hospital (MA), Pleiku, at San Antonio, Texas. Pictured l-r: Jimmie H. Martin; Jerry W. Martin, M.D.; Lori Franklin; Gary Franklin; and Phil Leonard.

significance and also appreciate and understand the wonderful interpersonal relations that have developed among our original Pleiku group.

—*Jerry W. Martin, M.D.*

Sheldon "Charlie" Brown, M.D., holding a "Paradise Lost" sign that was hung in the Officer's Club at the 18th Surgical Hospital (MA), located 2-3 miles northwest of Pleiku, Pleiku Province, Republic of South Vietnam, from June 1966-June 1, 1967.

Brunch during the 7th reunion of the 18th Surgical Hospital (MA), Pleiku, held at the Menger Hotel, San Antonio, TX. Pictured l-r: Roger Ecker, M.D.; Judy Ecker; Pat Johnson Teranishi, CRNA; Terry McDonald, M.D.; Jean Marie McDonald; Lois Wilderman, RN; Jimmie Martin; Jerry W. Martin, M.D.; Lori Franklin; Gary Franklin; Phil Leonard; and Sandy Ramirez.

REFLECTIONS AT THE WALL

"They gave their lives, the noblest of all offerings at duty's call, and fame will ever point with pride to this sacred place…"[28]
An open letter from the members of the 18th Surgical Hospital (MA) to the Vietnam War dead.
Saturday, September 8, 2001 at Vietnam War Memorial
Washington, D.C.

PROLOGUE

After practicing in Bowling Green, Kentucky for one and a half years, I was drafted and, along with nine other physicians, assigned the task of reorganizing the 18th Surgical Hospital (MA) at Ft. Gordon, Georgia, which we then took to the Republic of Vietnam (South Vietnam) in Pleiku Province (II Corps) in the Central Highlands about two miles north of Pleiku City toward the Ia Drang Valley, a few kilometers from Cambodia.

A few weeks before our second reunion of the 18th Surgical Hospital (MA) that was held in Washington, D.C. in September 2001, I was asked to write an open letter from our hospital staff to those who had died in Vietnam.

When asked to compile the letter, my first thoughts immediately reflected back to a poem I read in high school written by another Kentuckian. The first quatrain of the poem is inscribed on the stone arch at the McClellan Gate to Arlington National Cemetery; therefore, I quickly concluded that it would be most appropriate to open and close the letter with quotes from that poem, *The Bivouac of the Dead*.

When thinking of death and dying, one of my first thoughts always seems to reflect on *Thanatopsis*, thanks to a high school teacher of English and literature. Who can think of the military dead without remembering the words of Abraham Lincoln in his now-famous *Gettysburg Address*?

Many poems come to mind when philosophizing about bravery, courage, sacrifice and death. I used quotes from some of those in attempting to express our emotions and gratitude to the Vietnam War dead. I could never attempt to eulogize someone without reflecting on Tennyson's, *In Memoriam,* written over a twenty or more year period to memorialize the untimely death of his young friend, Arthur Henry Hallam.

Numerous Scripture passages from the Holy Bible are available, but I chose only two that I thought best expressed the mood of the occasion and best typified the symbolism that I was attempting to portray.

Large crowds are not permitted to gather on the walk in front of the Vietnam War Memorial. Permission was granted by the U.S. National Park Service for us to gather in a designated area near one end of the Monument. There I read the letter, *Reflections At The Wall*, to our group, plus the other tourists and visitors who stopped to listen.

We then selected the section of the Monument listing the names of those who died during the year we were in country (June 1966-June 1967), and our Pleiku CO, Mark T. Cenac, M.D. (Col., MC, USA, Ret.) and the Assistant Chief of Nursing, Marjorie Jaskowski, R.N. (Lt. Col., ANC, Ret.) placed a memorial wreath, and I placed a copy of the letter that had been transcribed in calligraphy, hard bound and signed by all of the 18th Surgical Hospital (MA) members in attendance.

All written material left at the Monument is regularly collected, cataloged and then placed in an archive at the Museum and Archaeological Regional Storage Facility. I have embellished the letter slightly from its original form by adding a few words and phrases to make it read more smoothly.

Although I had been to Washington numerous times prior to this occasion, I had chosen not to go to the Vietnam War Memorial Monument, I suppose to avoid recalling those unpleasant memories of war, combat, violence, suffering, sacrifice and death. I had seen photographs of individuals standing at the monument whose images reflected from the mirror-like granite surface. When contemplating the title, it was apparent that not only images reflect from the surface, but also many invisible and unspoken thoughts, emotions and memories reverberate from the Wall.

Completed in 1982, the Vietnam Veterans Monument is a National War Memorial located in Constitution Gardens adjacent to the National Mall. One end of the Monument points toward the Washington Monument, the other in the direction of the Lincoln Memorial. The Walls are 246.75 ft. long and the angle at the vertex is 125° 12′. There are 140 pilings with the average depth to bedrock being 35 feet. The height of the Wall at the vertex is 10.1 feet. The black granite came from Bangalore, India, but was cut and fabricated at Barre, Vermont. The names were grit blasted in Memphis, Tennessee. The height of individual letters is 0.53 inches and the depth is 0.035 inches. It was designed by architect Maya Ying Lin of Athens, Ohio, who at the time was a twenty-one year old student at Yale University. In 1984, a life-size sculpture by

Frederick Hart depicting three soldiers in combat gear was added, along with a sixty-foot flagstaff on a base containing the emblems of the five services. In 1993, a Vietnam Women's Memorial sculpted by Glenna Goodacre was added. The Monument honors those members of the U.S. Armed Forces who died during the Vietnam War or those who are still missing in action (MIA). "Each name is preceded on the west Wall or followed on the east Wall by one of two symbols: a diamond or a cross. The diamond denotes that the individual's death was confirmed. The approximately 1,150 persons whose names are designated by the cross were either missing or prisoners at the end of the war and remain missing and unaccounted for. If a person returns alive, a circle, as a symbol of life will be inscribed around the cross. In the event an individual's remains are returned or are otherwise accounted for the diamond will be superimposed over the cross." The Vietnam Veterans Memorial Monument is visited by approximately three million visitors annually.

The Moving Wall Vietnam Veterans Memorial, known as "The Moving Wall," or more often as "The Wall That Heals," is an approximate one-half size replica of the Monument in Washington. The first structure made of black Plexiglas panels mounted on plywood with wooden frames toured for three years. Because of weathering and deterioration, it was replaced by aluminum panels and supported by square tubular steel braces. The surface is painted with a polyurethane gloss black coating which gives a mirror-like finish that reflects images similar to the polished black granite in the permanent Monument.

The Wall That Heals came to Bowling Green's Aviation Heritage Park and was on display from September 24, 2009 through September 27, 2009. I was asked to read the open letter, *Reflections At The Wall*, as a part of the closing ceremony. I trust that the reader will find it engaging and meaningful.

Photograph of a view of *The Wall That Heals* in Bowling Green, Kentucky. Photograph by Dr. Dwight Pounds.

REFLECTIONS AT THE WALL

On Fame's eternal camping-ground
Their silent tents are spread,
And Glory guards, with solemn round,
The bivouac of the dead.[1]

Those words, written by a noted Kentuckian,[2] are carved in stone at the entrance to the Arlington National Cemetery.

Today we gather to pay tribute to each one whose name is inscribed on this wall. Individually and collectively, we memorialize your lives, recognize your unequaled bravery, commemorate your dedication to duty, verify your heroism, acknowledge your ultimate sacrifice and eulogize your death. The poet eloquently noted:

Close his eyes; his work is done!

As man may, he fought his fight,
Proved his truth by his endeavor;
Let him sleep in solemn night,
Sleep forever and forever.

Fold him in his country's stars,
Roll the drum and fire the volley!

Leave him to God's watching eye
Trust him to the hand that made him.[3]

We can only trust that a special Providence watches over your eternal welfare.

Tennyson noted:

Thou wilt not leave us in the dust:
Thou madest man, he knows not why,
He thinks he was not made to die;
And thou hast made him: thou art just.[4]

This monument stands erect and proud like a perpetual honor guard establishing and protecting this place as hallowed ground. In the quiet of our personal reflections the words of Abraham Lincoln echo, "…from these honored dead we take increased devotion to that cause for which they (here) gave the last full measure of devotion—that we here highly resolve that these dead shall not have died in vain."[5] All who shall walk this path must pause and pay homage to your devotion to duty and remember your unexcelled sacrifice. Tennyson also observed, "The path of duty was the way to glory."[6]

Thirty-five years ago the 18th Surgical Hospital (MA) entered South Vietnam. Our hospital was reorganized at Ft. Gordon, GA in 1966. It had served with distinction in the South Pacific during World War II, receiving the Philippine Republic Presidential Unit Citation and the U.S. Presidential Unit Citation (Oak Leaf Cluster). In Vietnam, it received the Meritorious Unit Citation (Oak Leaf Cluster), the Republic of Vietnam Gallantry Cross Unit Citation and a Certificate of Achievement Award from the 4th Infantry Division.

All of the physicians initially assigned to our hospital were drafted from their private practices or residencies and joined the nurses and enlisted men who had volunteered, had been drafted, or had chosen the military as a career. As we began our year's work in the Central Highlands near Pleiku (II Corps), we envisioned no promotions, coveted no recognition and sought no military honors. We sought only to fulfill our Hippocratic mission to use our "…ability and judgment, …for the welfare of the sick…"[7] and wounded. We strove always to keep that oath "…inviolate and unbroken."[8] We were diligent in our pursuit of excellence, and never derelict in our duty to our patients. Although not verbalized, our work epitomized the prayer of Maimonides, who prayed,

"Inspire me with love for my art and for Your creatures."[9]

Our personalities meshed compatibly and our efforts quickly resulted in an efficient and well-organized hospital that produced enviable results.

In spite of the intrepid spirit and the ebullient optimism of every person within our unit, our noble intentions and our tireless efforts were sometimes not good enough. Our collective remembrances and our individual recollections easily conjure up those mental images of your charred, wounded and mangled bodies. We recall those lips permanently silenced and speechless with faces frozen expressionless and emotionless, never again able to express your unachieved aspirations. We remember your staring unseeing eyes forever prevented from witnessing the wonder of the sunrises of opportunity or the beauty of the golden sunsets of achievement. With the arrival of each new casualty, we sensed "…The ticking of Eternity…" as did Edna St. Vincent Millay when she eloquently, but unknowingly, described our collective, unspoken emotions:

And every scream tore through my throat.
No hurt I did not feel, no death
That was not mine; mine each last breath
That, crying, met an answering cry
From the compassion that was I.[10]

You truly gave the "…full measure of devotion."[11]

Longfellow wrote:

Life is real! Life is earnest!
And the grave is not its goal;

Dust thou art, to dust returnest,
Was not spoken of the soul.[12]

Our service and sacrifice pale in comparison to yours, but our presence and our efforts qualify us to speak. Our efforts at times may have been inadequate; however, we can proudly claim that we did our best.

In September, 2000, while in Dallas, Texas, attending the American Academy of Family Physicians Scientific Assembly, I, quite by chance, encountered a man,[13] who had received an abdominal wound while fighting in the Ia Drang Valley and was operated on at the 18th Surgical Hospital (MA) on May 20, 1967. He expressed to me the gratitude, which he had been unable to express to our entire hospital staff for "…saving my life."

Ah! never shall the land forget
How gushed the life-blood of her brave—
Gushed, warm with hope and courage yet,
Upon the soil they fought to save.[14]

Our experiences brought to each of us an indelible realization of our common mortality, while our successes reinforced a profound intimacy with a higher calling.

Daily we move one step closer to joining that innumerable, unending caravan marching toward the bivouac of the dead. From the gaudiest epaulet to the simplest chevron, "…all that breathe will share your destiny."[15] When the bugle sounds the final reveille from the "…battlements of Eternity…"[16] and all wars have ended, we will form ranks with you for that final roll call when the Eternal Commander will present to each one accolades for the battles successfully fought.

"No man is an Island, entire of itself …Any man's death diminishes me, because I am involved in Mankind; and therefore, never send to know for whom the bell tolls: it tolls for thee."[17] John Donne's words penetrate deeply and meaningfully, for we all have been diminished. As we await the tolling of the bell and approach the benediction of our lives, I trust that we can go as one "…sustained and soothed by an unfaltering trust approach our (thy) grave, like one who wraps the drapery of his couch about him and lies down to pleasant dreams."[18] I further trust that we can echo the humble claim of the Apostle Paul who said, "I have fought the good fight, I have finished the race, I have kept the faith."[19]

No more shall the war-cry sever,
Or the winding rivers be red;
They banish our anger forever,
When they laurel the graves of our dead.
Under the sod and the dew,
Waiting the judgment day;[20]

We are the Dead. Short days ago
We lived, felt dawn, saw sunset glow,
Loved and were loved, …
If ye break faith with us who die
We shall not sleep, …[21]

"We cannot dedicate—we cannot consecrate—we cannot hallow—this ground."[22]

It is for us today to

"…here highly resolve that these dead shall not have died in vain—that this nation, under God, shall have a new birth of freedom—and that government of the people, by the people, for the people, shall not perish from the earth."[23]

Now rest in peace, our patriot band;
Though far from nature's limits thrown,
We trust you (they) find a happier land,
A brighter sunshine of your (their) own.[24]

We are reminded of Julia Ward Howe's (*Battle Hymn of the Republic*) well-known words:

With the glory in His bosom that
transfigures you and me;
(As) He died to make men holy,
you (let us) died (die) to make men free,…

Your hearts no longer beat, allowing the heartbeat of this nation to continue, preserving and guaranteeing our liberty and freedom. You gallantly marched to your "…rendezvous with Death."[25]

God bless the Flag and its loyal defenders,
While its broad folds o'er the battle-field wave,
Till the dim star-wreath rekindle its splendors,
Washed from its stains in the blood of the brave![26]

No more on Life's parade shall meet,
That brave and fallen few

Rest on, embalmed and sainted dead!
Dear as the blood ye gave;
No impious footsteps here shall tread
The herbage of your grave;
Nor shall your glory be forgot
While Fame her record keeps,
Or Honor points the hallowed spot
Where Valor proudly sleeps.[27]

"You (They) gave your (their) lives, the noblest of all offerings at duty's call, and fame will ever point with pride to this sacred place…"[28]

No time shall come, when your (Channing's) name
Shall grow less bright on Freedom's scroll.[29]

We, the nurses and physicians of the 18th Surgical Hospital (MA) in attendance, on behalf of the entire unit, salute your courage and the sacrificial devotion to duty that you exhibited in preserving our nation's freedom. Now, with profound respect and sincere gratitude, we honor your memory.

The friends of freedom slumber here![30]

Presented Saturday, September 8, 2001 Vietnam War Memorial Washington, D.C.

END NOTES

1. *The Bivouac of the Dead,* Theodore O'Hara

2. Theodore O'Hara was a journalist and soldier born in Danville, Kentucky (home of Centre College, host of Cheney—Lieberman debate, 2000). He graduated from St. Joseph College, Bardstown, Kentucky in 1839, and was admitted to the bar in 1842. In 1845, he worked at the Treasury Department, Washington, D.C. On June 26, 1846, he was appointed as a Captain in the Kentucky Volunteers serving in the Mexican War, ultimately attaining the rank of Brevet Major. He wrote *Bivouac of the Dead* in honor of the Kentuckians killed at the Battle of Buena Vista on the occasion of their re-interment in the Frankfort Cemetery, Frankfort, Kentucky in 1847. During the Civil War, O'Hara fought for the Confederacy as a Lieutenant Colonel, and served on the staffs of Generals Albert

Jerry W. Martin, M.D. reading Reflecions at the Wall *at the closing ceremony when The Wall That Heals was in Bowling Green, Kentucky. Phototraph by Dr. Dwight Pounds.*

Sidney Johnston (Fort Albert Sidney Johnston is currently a part of the campus of Western Kentucky University in Bowling Green) and John C. Breckinridge (Commander of the Kentucky "Orphan Brigade"). He died in Guerrytown, Alabama, on June 6, 1867, and was buried at Columbus, Georgia. On September 15, 1874, his body was re-interred in the Frankfort Cemetery.

3. *Dirge for a Soldier*, George Henry Boker was born in Philadelphia, Pennsylvania in 1823. He graduated from Princeton University and later served as United States Minister to Turkey and then Minister to Russia. He died in 1890.

4. *In Memoriam,* Alfred Tennyson, 1st Baron, English Poet Laureate (August 6, 1809—October 6, 1892).

5. *Gettysburg Address*, Abraham Lincoln

6. *Ode on the Death of the Duke of Wellington,* Alfred Lord Tennyson

7. Hippocratic Oath: Hippocrates is the most famous Asclepiad, a Greek physician who is called the "Father of Medicine" and was the most celebrated physician of antiquity. Tradition states that he belonged to the Asclepiadae, the sixteenth in descent from Asclepius (Asclulapius [L], Asklepios [Gr.]), and began his practice in the Asclepieion of Cos. He received his first medical instruction from his father, Nicomachus. He then studied at Athens and acquired extensive experience in travel and practice among the cities of Thrace, Thessaly and Macedonia (History of Medicine, Fielding H. Garrison, A. B., M.D.), and was a contemporary of Sophocles (495-406), Euripides (480-406?), Aristophanes (448?-385), Pindar (522-443?), Socrates (469?-399?), Plato (427-347), Herodotus (485?-425), Thucydides (460-400), Phidias (500-432?), Pericles (495-429), and Polygnotus (?-450-?) – truly an age that produced great men as well as great ideas. According to Soranus, he was born on the island of Cos (c. 460 BC) in the first year of the eightieth Olympiad and died at the approximate age of 90 (c. 377 BC) at Larissa. He disassociated medicine from theurgy and philosophy, crystallized the fragmented knowledge of the Coan and Cnidian Schools into a systematic science, and bequeathed to medicine the Hippocratic Oath which binds together all those who seek to practice the noble art of healing with the most vigorous bonds of honor and brotherhood. He pointed out for us the sacredness of life and the supreme obligation of the physician to serve humanity and to preserve life through careful observation, judicious restraint, transmission of knowledge and proper treatment.

8. Ibid.

9. *Prayer of Maimonides*: Maimonides (Moses ben Maimon; Moseh ben Maymun; a.k.a., Rambam, 1135-1204). Jewish philosopher, rabbi and physician (born in Cordoba, Spain), one of the major theologians of Judaism. In 1165, the Muslims drove him to Morocco, then Cairo, Egypt, where he later became physician to the Sultan, Saladin.

10. *Renascence,* Edna St. Vincent Millay

11. Op. cit., *Gettysburg Address*

12. *A Psalm of Life,* Henry Wadsworth Longfellow

13. Walter A. "Wally" Williamson, 1st Battalion, 1st Brigade, 8th Infantry, 4th Infantry Division. Co-owner/tour guide, Odyssey Tour and Travel International, 9243 Bentham Ct. #101, Dallas, Texas 75227.

14. *The Battle-Field*, William Cullen Bryant

15. *Thanatopsis*, William Cullen Bryant

16. *The Hound of Heaven*, Francis Thompson

17. *Devotions upon Emergent Occasions* (1624), John Donne (1573-1631)

18. Op. cit., *Thanatopsis*

19. 2 Timothy 4:7

20. *The Blue and The Gray,* Francis Miles Finch

21. *In Flanders Fields,* Lt.Col. John McCrae

22. Op. cit., *Gettysburg Address*

23. Op. cit., *Gettysburg Address*

24. *To The Memory of the Brave Americans,* Phillip Freneau

25. *I Have A Rendezvous with Death,* Alan Seeger

26. *God Save The Flag,* Oliver Wendell Holmes

27. Op. cit., *The Bivouac of the Dead*

28. A portion of the epitaph on the monument of Confederate General Felix K. Zollicoffer (May 19, 1812—January 19, 1862) who died at the Battle of Mill Springs near Somerset, Kentucky—the first major battle of the Civil War in Kentucky.

29. Poem by C. T. Brooks, read at the Unitarian Church at Newport on the ninety-ninth anniversary of the birth of Dr. William Ellery Channing (1780-1842), Unitarian clergyman and writer; from the book, *Channing—A Study*, by Thomas S. Matthews.

30. op. cit., *To The Memory of the Brave Americans*

EPILOGUE

Death be not proud, though some have called thee
Mighty and dreadful, for, thou art not so,
For, those, whom thou think'st, thou dost over-throw,
Die not, poor death, nor yet canst thou kill me.
From rest and sleep, which but thy pictures be,
Much pleasure, then from thee, much more must flow,
And soonest our best men with thee do go,
Rest of their bones, and soul's delivery.
Thou art slave to fate, chance, kings, and desperate men,
And dost with poison, war, and sickness dwell,
And poppy, or charms can make us sleep as well,
And better than thy stroke; why swell'st thou then?
One short sleep past, we wake eternally,
And death shall be no more; death, thou shalt die.

Holy Sonnets, X
John Donne

———

'Twas Resurrection morn,
And Gabriel blew a blast upon his horn…

———

To wake the dead, dead for a million years;
A blast to reach and pierce their dust-stopped ears;
To waken them, wherever they might be,
Deep in the earth or deeper in the sea.

———

From the four corners of all the earth they drew,
Their faces radiant and their bodies new.

———

Saint Peter Relates an Incident of the Resurrection Day
James Weldon Johnson

Weeping may tarry for the night, but joy comes with the morning.

Psalm 30:5

In 1801, Daniel Butterfield wrote a song entitled, *Last Post*. In 1862, the rather lengthy and formal piece was shortened to twenty-four notes and renamed, *Taps*. The original was written to be played with a bugle, but is now usually played with a trumpet.

TAPS

1. Day is done, gone the sun,
From the hills, from the lake,
From the sky.
All is well, safely rest,
God is nigh.

2. Fading light, dims the sight,
And a star gems the sky
Gleaming bright.
From afar, drawing nigh,
Falls the night.

3. Then good night, peaceful night,
Till the light of the dawn
Shineth bright;
God is near, do not fear,
Friend, good night.

Ode to Fallen Veterans

They shall grow not old, as we that are left grow old:
Age shall not weary them, nor the years condemn.
At the going down of the sun and in the morning
We will remember them.

(Returned Services League, Australia)

Mark T. Cenac, M.D. (CO); Margaret Jaskowski, R.N.; Jerry W. Martin, M.D. presenting the memorial wreath from the 18th Surgical Hospital (MA) and a copy of Reflections At The Wall *at the Vietnam Veterans Memorial Monument on Saturday, September 8, 2001.*

Vietnam Veterans Memorial Monument, Saturday afternoon, September 8, 2001. Left to right: Sandra Gillis; Sam Gillis, M.D.

Vietnam Veterans Memorial Monument, Saturday afternoon, September 8, 2001. Phillip Leonard, (Lab tech); Pat Johnson, CRNA.

HISTORIC KINGDOMS AND COLONIES

Except in the Chinese-influenced Viet kingdoms, the major realms and cultures of mainland Southeast Asia combined local customs with the religious and political influences of India. Through the centuries these cultures retained their essential Indian characteristics. The mixture inspired the building of unique religious and royal centers such as Angkor and Pagan.

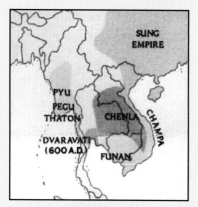

400-500 AD

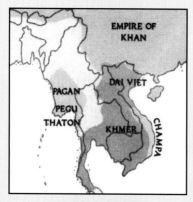

1100-1200AD

1450-1500 AD

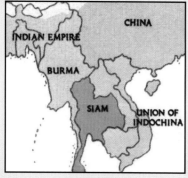

1900 AD

FUNAN - From its beginning in the first century, this state prospered by its position on the trade route between India and China. Funan exchanged embassies with both countries and at its zenith was the dominant state of the region. In the fertile marshlands of the Mekong Delta the Funanese built canals to control floods and limit the intrusion of salt water.

PYU - After the third century AD, Tibeto-Burman tribesmen migrated from the north into present-day Burma and in 638 founded the Buddhist capital of the Pyu Kingdom at Srikshetra (today called Hmawza). Early seventh-century urn inscriptions bear Hindu names of Pyu kings.

CHAMPA - The Hindu-influenced Kingdom of the Chams rose in the second century AD and for 1,200 years struggled to remain independent of the expanding Dai Viet and Khmer Kingdoms. In 1177 the Chams sailed up the Mekong, defeated the Khmers on the Great Lake, and sacked Angkor. A century later Champa joined forces with Dai Viet against Kublai Khan; 200 years later Champa succumbed to its former ally.

DVARAVATI, THATON and PEGU - These Mon kingdoms ranging from the 6th to the 16th century had a lasting influence upon the culture of mainland Southeast Asia. They spread the Buddhism that ultimately became the faith of the people of Burma, Thailand, Cambodia and Loas.

CHENLA - The Khmer people of Chenla overthrew Funan in the sixth century. Their realm was long split into two distinct regions, Water Chenla (Mekong Delta area and present-day Cambodia) and Land Chenla (upland area of the middle Mekong Valley). From this divided kingdom emerged the powerful Khmer Empire.

KHMER - In the ninth century the Chenla Dynasty set up its capital at Yasodharapura- the present site of Angkor- which became the center of vastly expanded Khmer Empire. Here its kings received Indian scholars, artists, and religious leaders. The Siamese ravaged Angkor in 1431.

DAI VIET - The Vietnamese gained independence by rebelling against the Chinese in the tenth century. Gradually, they expanded to the south at the expense of the Chams. Though traditionally hostile to Chinese interference, the Vietnamese absorbed much of Chinese character; industrial and agricultural techniques adopted from the north made them among the best farmers on the Southeast Asian mainland.

KAMBUJA - The Khmers abandoned Angkor in the 15th century and established a new capital at Lovek. Siam repeatedly invaded their once-mighty empire, but they held to their chief rice-farming lands around Tonle Sap.

BURMA - The Toungoo Dynasty united Burma in the 16th century after 300 years of divided rule under the Shan and Mon. From the 16th to the 18th century Burma repeatedly expanded its frontiers eastward into Siam. Britain annexed Burma as part of the Indian Empire in the 19th century.

SIAM - By the early 13th century the Thai had established a capital at Sukhothai. Then in 1350, the political center moved south to Ayutthaya. Siam, today called Thailand, remains the only kingdom of mainland Southeast Asia never colonized by the West.

LAOS - The Laotian Kingdom of Lan Xang, first established by a Lao monarch in the mid-14th century, encompassed all of present-day Laos and much of northern and eastern Thailand. In 1697 Lan Xang split into three rival states, which for nearly two centuries wrangled among themselves while fighting off outside invaders. In 1893 the region became Laos, a French protectorate.

UNION OF INDOCHINA - In the 19th century, as European nations competed to colonize Asia, the French organized the Union of Indochina. The protectorates of Cambodia, Laos, Tonkin and Annam, and the colony of Cochin China remained under French control until 1953, except for Japanese occupation during World War II.

WHITHER WE ARE TENDING

Author's Note—In November 1967 while director of the Outpatient Clinic at Ft. Campbell, Kentucky (U.S. 3rd Army), prior to my military discharge (December 11, 1967), Dr. Robert Mills, then president of Georgetown College (Georgetown, Kentucky), called and asked me to participate in a three-day Symposium on Southeast Asia (Southeast Asia—Christian Dilemma) during the college's World Awareness Week.

He had become aware of my Vietnam experiences through friends who had listened to my weekly radio programs recorded in Vietnam and broadcast over WKCT radio station in Bowling Green, Kentucky during my year with the 18th Surgical Hospital (MA) in the Central Highlands near Pleiku, Pleiku Province, Republic of Vietnam.

I was hesitant to accept his invitation, since I was just planning to resume my medical practice (I had been in the same practice for one and a half years before being drafted). Through the efforts of Senator John Sherman Cooper (R-KY), I was granted a six-week early discharge and my former associate, L. Jack Scott, M.D., was granted a six-month deferment so that our practice would not be destroyed. Two weeks after my return Dr. Scott was drafted. Because I did not have an associate at the time to provide medical coverage and since I would quickly become extremely busy, it would have been nearly impossible for me to attend the entire three-day conference. I, therefore, reluctantly agreed to participate for only one day.

I presented this lecture, "Whither We Are Tending," at 10 a.m., Tuesday, January 30, 1968 to an audience of three to four hundred faculty and students. After lunch I participated in a panel discussion with the other guest lecturers to answer questions from the conference participants.

It is often said that history repeats itself and, to the extent that certain corollaries can be made, I am sure that is true.

A little over one hundred years ago, just as today, many political factions were spreading rampantly across our nation and numerous solutions were being advocated by both responsible and irresponsible individuals when Abraham Lincoln addressed an audience in Springfield, Illinois in 1858 and delivered his famous House Divided speech, in which he suggested, "If we could first know where we are and whither we are tending, we could better judge what to do and how to do it."

Lincoln was able to comprehend that unless the nation reexamined its policies and a reestablished a logical common sense approach to government, then crisis, confusion and disaster would soon follow. I need not recall history to point out that Lincoln's judgments *then* are still valid today. He was confronted with the division of a nation, state against state and brother against brother; whereas, today we are faced with the division of a world, nation against nations and race against race.

How much more complicated and ominous is our predicament today in comparison to that of a century ago? Unless our government soon establishes more rational and responsible policies, I wonder how much more disastrous will be our future and how much more costly will be our reconstructive efforts. We as a nation cannot continue tolerating the ineptitudes, indecisions, grafts and extravagances in the present and past administrations that have allowed creeping socialism to undermine our democratic principles, have permitted chiselers on relief to deride and debase the diligent labors of honest people and have tolerated the erosion of our fiscal and military integrity both at home and abroad.

Paramount among our thoughts today, however, are the war efforts in Vietnam, the action that we are taking there, and where those policies will ultimately lead us. Our commitment to the struggle has from the first been confused, switching from advisory aid, to support, to full-scale war action. Our resolve to see the military task already initiated through to completion has been made abundantly clear; however, the political and economic situation remains confused and disorganized. Can we be confident that at some future date these efforts will not be obstructed, or even sabotaged, simply for the appeasement of world opinion? We should not waver from the projected course toward victory. We must not allow our leaders to make needless conciliatory gestures, compromise our national and international integrity, or alter the basic principles underlying our efforts in order to achieve a quick and empty peace simply for selfish political gains or for a favorable world image.

One can never correctly predict the trends of world opinion, the state of governmental diplomacy or the final goal of many of the world's ideologies. Past experience has very clearly demonstrated that final victory will be slow, painful, tedious, complex, and at time, even exasperating. Military victories will be accomplished by the overwhelming firepower of the Allied Forces, but I submit that the final, true victory of winning the peoples of Southeast Asia through economic aid, political freedom and social pacification will require many years of diligent, patient diplomacy, and a social reformation approaching utopianism. In order to see these goals through to completion our leaders, in conjunction with those of South Vietnam, must transcend the cheapness of petty politics and arrive at a plateau of diplomacy that is dignified, visionary and at the same time practical.

There can be no question that the U.S. Forces and our Allies are demonstrating a military competency and skillfulness unexcelled in history. All Americans can be proud of the courage, the determination of purpose and the noble dedication to duty that our troops in Vietnam are exemplifying daily in their efforts to abolish the malignancy in Southeast Asia, which we call communism. General William C. Westmoreland expressed this very succinctly and eloquently recently when he stated, "Americans believe in freedom and the dignity of man. They back that belief with action. The Americans in Vietnam know war at first hand. They see it for what it is. War is fear cloaked in courage. It is excitement overlaying boredom. It is close friendship with loneliness only a though away. It is compassion in the midst of destruction. It is dedication winning over weariness and frustrations. War is paying a terrible price today for a better tomorrow."

After being in Vietnam and witnessing first hand not only desolation, pain, problems, frustrations and even death, but also seeing the pride, the satisfaction victory affords, the compassion, courage and valor demonstrated by so many, I agree wholeheartedly. Although the price being paid is exorbitant, world peace is well worth the cost. We need, however, to establish a fresh new image before the mocking eyes of the world by clearly stating and outlying our purposes, goals and reasons for being there. We must indicate to the world the limits and bounds of our tolerance and vigorously reaffirm our intentions and demands, then adhere steadfastly without hesitation to those fundamental principles.

What are some of the problems, other than military considerations, that we face today and will continue to encounter years and perhaps decades to come? None of the problems are new. All are simply the age old enemies of man that today are wrapped in a cloak of the modern world, thereby blurring our vision and creating a confused impression that they are peculiar only to the generation in which we live.

The most prodigious of these problems is poverty. Although poverty is universal, it is particularly apparent throughout Vietnam and Southeast Asia. Poverty not only strips away physical needs, but more tragically it negates individual efforts, destroys personal initiatives, counteracts the efforts of freedom, deletes individual and national pride, stems social and economic progress, and literally tears apart the human soul. This obviously results in moral, spiritual, economic, social, religious, and governmental decay. I cannot envision significant improvement of the conditions in South Vietnam until we begin to diagnose and vigorously treat these social ills. There are no immunizations or preventatives available to us, thus we must begin work toward the eradication and abolishment of the needs and miserable conditions of an entire nation.

Obviously the countryside must be cleared of insurgents, the unpatriotic must be confronted and dealt with, and the population must be provided adequate protection before social progress can be anticipated. Military victories will surely come but conciliation will lag unless we adopt a platform of social reform as militant and vigorous against graft, deceit, fraud, and corruption as our combat efforts are against the enemy. Above all, these reforms must fulfill the needs of the total population!

It does little good to win a war militarily and then not provide the people with those things for which they fought. Does it do much good to fill an individual's mind with democratic ideologies and leave his belly empty? How can one learn pride if there is nothing to be proud of? Can agrarian reforms culminate satisfactorily without modern equipment and conservation methods? Will illiteracy be conquered with inadequate and/or insufficient schools and teachers? Hunger will never vanish spontaneously nor will disease eradicate itself. Will people continue to fight forever if goals are never achieved? Or will they long endure if we frequently alter or change our commitments and intentions? How can the unceasing miseries of the people of South Vietnam be so totally misrepresented by our press to allow condemnation to fall on the U.S. Armed Forces for a few unfortunate civilian deaths in the North, while mass murder, ambush, torture, and sabotage are completely overlooked, ignored and forgotten in the South? John Steinbeck denounced this attitude while discussing the truce by saying, "…they knew we would keep the truce and they knew they would not…" and then reflected angrily, "…and we observed this nonsense. And by observing it our so-called 'image' gets worse and worse." What allows our enemy to succeed in misleading public opinion around the world? Is it because our so-called "image" needs to be refreshed and redefined, or is it because the liberal press is attempting to create the news rather than reporting it?

The Vietnamese are struggling toward independence, democracy, freedom, and social justice. Each of these struggles is important, complex and vital to the outcome of the war.

In order to have an understanding of the turmoil, political unrest, governmental instability, economic oppression, and the restless mood of the inhabitants of South Vietnam, it is imperative that we take a cursory glance at the land and its peoples. We must briefly reflect on the more pertinent aspects of Vietnam's long and complicated history.

North and South Vietnam combined is a narrow strip of mountains, hills, swamps and rice lands that flank the eastern coast of the Southeast Asian Peninsula. Long and narrow, it curves southwestwardly in roughly an S-shaped curve for approximately eleven hundred miles from communist China in the north to the Gulf of Siam in the south. Each end of the country broadens somewhat, while along the waist at the seventeenth parallel of latitude it narrows to about fifty miles. To the east, Vietnam is washed by the waters of the South China Sea (the portion along the coast of North Vietnam is termed the Gulf of Tonkin), and shares its western border with the Kingdoms of Laos and Cambodia and, with those two nations, was known as French Indo-China for about a century prior to World War II. The Annamite Mountain chain (Annamese Cordillera) stretches nearly the entire length of Vietnam, creating a narrow band of coastal lowlands and a broad mountainous plateau (Central Highlands), and links the country's two large delta regions created by the estuaries of the Red River in the north and the Mekong River in the south. The land area totals about 127,000 square miles, approximately the size of New Mexico.

Politically there are two Vietnams. This division resulted from the International Conference in Geneva in 1954, which marked the end of a long period of French rule in Indochina and established an arbitrary demarcation line at the 17th parallel, creating a communist Democratic Republic of Vietnam (DRVN) to the north, with approximately 17 million people (capital in Hanoi), and the Republic of Vietnam (South Vietnam), with approximately 16 million people (capital in Saigon).

In this predominately agricultural country, an estimated 80% of the 33 million people are farmers. They are concentrated mostly in the deltas and in villages and hamlets scattered along the coastal lowlands, Rice is the major food crop. Rubber and tea are important export products in the south, while the less fertile north is slightly more industrialized, having coal and ore reserves. Fishing is of great importance to both. At least 85% of the population is ethnically Vietnamese (called Annamese in earlier centuries). There are several minority groups, the most notable being Chinese, Cambodians and Montagnards. These mountain people indigenous to the Central Highlands and collectively called "Montagnards" (French for "mountain people") are composed of two main ethnic groups—the Malayo-Polynesian and the Mon-Khmer and number between six hundred thousand and one million. The Chinese are congregated mostly in the cities of South Vietnam, especially in Cholon (a suburb of Saigon). The majority of the four hundred thousand people of Cambodian origin are farmers in the provinces near the Cambodian border in the Central Highlands, and at the mouth of the Mekong River system. There are other minority groups, including a few thousand Chams, Malays, Indians, Thais, French, and at present, approximately five hundred thousand Americans. There are a total of 53 ethnic groups in Vietnam.

The religion of most Vietnamese is a mixture of Taoism, Shintoism, Mahayana Buddhism, Catholicism, Confucianism, Anamism (ancestor worship), and Gao Dai (a mixture of all). There are between 1.5 million and 2 million Roman Catholics, and small, scattered groups representing most Protestant denominations.

The ethnic Vietnamese are a mixture both genetically and culturally of Sino-Tibetan and early Malay or Indonesian ancestry, a very old people with a documented history of more than two thousand years and a legendary history of nearly five thousand years. Legend says that the Vietnamese originated in the valley of the Yellow River in what is now the northern part of China in 2879 BC; however, historical records pick up the Vietnamese as a tribal people inhabiting the Red River delta in what is now North Vietnam. They were gradually driven south by the Chinese (early Chinese documents, circa 500 BC, refer to the Viet States to the south).

In 207 BC, a group of small states in the Red River delta were conquered by a Chinese general and were combined with two Chinese provinces to form an independent kingdom called Nam Viet (Nan Yueh). This resulting kingdom was overrun in 111 BC by the armies of the Han Dynasty of China, was incorporated as the southernmost province of the Chinese Empire and remained under Chinese rule for more than one thousand years. Despite their exposure to Chinese customs and culture, the Vietnamese retained their national identity. In 39 AD, an armed revolt led by two sisters, Trung Trac and Trung Nhi, succeeded in briefly defeating the Chinese. The Chinese soon regained control, but over the ensuing centuries gradually liberalized their policies and in 618 AD the province was made a protectorate and renamed Annam (An Nam, meaning "pacified south").

Although the Chinese government adopted more liberal policies and the people enjoyed increasing prosperity, the Vietnamese continued to rebel. Finally in 938 AD, as China's Tang Dynasty tottered, a Vietnamese general drove out the Chinese army, thus the free and independent Great Viet State (Dai Co Viet) was born. With the exception of a twenty-year interlude of Chinese occupation in the 15th century, the Vietnamese remained free for over nine hundred years. They drove off Chinese invaders in the 11th century and three invasions by the Mongol armies of Kublai Khan in the 13th century (1257 AD, 1284 AD, and 1287 AD). Vietnam prospered and expanded southward. Central governmental control was difficult and, for much of the period between the 16th and 19th centuries, the country was divided into northern and southern kingdoms, not for political reasons, but because of administrative considerations. It was unified again in 1802 under Nguyen Anh, a member of the southern aristocracy (who later became emperor Gia Long) and the region was called Vietnam ("distant south"). Before the end of the century, the country was again ruled by foreigners, this time the French.

In August 1858, when a French naval squadron steamed into the port of Tourane (now Da Nang), France began an era of domination that was to continue for nearly a century. Saigon ("Paris of the Orient") was captured in 1861 and Vietnam's independence finally terminated in 1883 when French control was extended to the north. With the annexation of the southern part of the country as a colony in 1887 their control became complete, bringing together the north (Tonkin), the central section (Annam) and the south (Cochin China).

Cambodia became a French Protectorate in 1867 and Laos was annexed in 1893. These countries, along with all of Vietnam, were finally merged into the Indochinese Union under a French Governor-General in 1899.

The Vietnamese were no more satisfied to live under French rule than they had been under Chinese rule. Nationalists' feelings mounted and extremist organizations were formed, most notable among them the Association of Revolutionary Vietnamese Youths led a young Moscow trained communist known as Nguyen Ai Quoc [later called Ho Chi Minh (Bac Ho=Uncle Ho)]. The year was 1925.

As early as 1924, Nguyen Ai Quoc outlined his immediate task to be "...the unification of various Vietnamese nationalist groups under Communist leadership…" and in 1927 declared, "I intend to form an Indo-Chinese national, revolutionary movement, whose leaders will bring its members step by step to orthodox Communism." This goal was realized when the Indochinese Communist Party, with Nguyen Ai Quoc as its head, was organized in 1930.

On May 19, 1941, a congress of Vietnamese nationalists (exile groups) was held in Chinghsi, China, under the auspices of the Kuomintang government, resulting in the formation of the Revolutionary League for the Independence of Vietnam (later to become known as the Viet Minh) with Nguyen Ai Quoc as General Secretary.

The Nationalist Chinese authorities soon became suspicious of Nguyen Ai Quoc and imprisoned him; however, in order to gain intelligence information about this subversive organization, he was released in 1943. It was at this time, in order to conceal his identity, Nguyen Ai Quoc took the alias of Ho Chi Minh. With the fall of France in 1943, Japanese occupation began, although French officials were permitted to administer the colonies. Later, with defeat imminent, the Japanese in March 1945 imprisoned the French authorities and granted independence to Vietnam under Japanese protection with Emperor Bao Dai (Nguyen Vinh Thuy) as Head of State (the last Emperor of Vietnam).

After Japan's surrender to the Allies on August 13, 1945, Ho Chi Minh acted swiftly, working through the clandestine Indochinese Communist Party and the Viet Minh National Front in order to seize as much Vietnamese territory as possible before Allied Forces could again occupy the country. Under an agreement by the Allies following the Japanese surrender, the Nationalist Chinese forces were to occupy Vietnam to the 16th parallel and the French were to control the remainder of the country to the south.

Only three days after the Japanese surrendered on August 16th, the Viet Minh announced the formation of a National Liberation Committee for Vietnam and by August 19 Ho Chi Minh's guerilla forces had taken control of Hanoi. Next he sent a mission to Hue, seat of Emperor Bao Dai's government, demanding immediate surrender. Bao Dai abdicated believing, as did most of the Vietnamese people, that the Viet Minh was a national front organization that enjoyed the support of the Allies. Saigon and much of the countryside soon fell under his control and on August 29th, in Hanoi, a provisional government was proclaimed. On September 2, 1945, Ho Chi Minh proclaimed the Democratic Republic of Vietnam with himself as President.

To win support of the Chinese and the French, as well as the Vietnamese people, Ho Chi Minh arranged the disappearance of the communist element in the Viet Minh by dissolving the Indochinese Communist Party. Instead, he encouraged all communists who whished to continue their "theoretical studies" to join the Association of Marxists Studies. Elections were held in January 1946 to select members of the country's first legislature, the National Assembly. The Viet Minh, as the major political organization, won most of the 444 Assembly seats, only 70 seats were allotted to the opposition parties. Throughout the ensuing months, negotiations between Ho Chi Minh and the French

continued in spite of many inconsistencies and irregularities (some legislators were arrested and imprisoned [some even executed] for "common law crimes"). France agreed to recognize the Democratic Republic of Vietnam and a referendum was to be held to decide whether Tonkin, Annam, and Cochin China would be united. They further agreed that 15,000 French troops stationed in the north would gradually be withdrawn by 1952. Negotiations deteriorated, misunderstandings and hostilities developed and incidents of armed violence culminated in a French cruiser shelling the port city of Haiphong. On December 19, 1946, President Ho Chi Minh retaliated by ordering a general attack against the French in Hanoi and throughout all of Vietnam, igniting the fires of the Indochinese War that were to burn for the next seven and one half years.

Ho Chi Minh's forces immediately adopted the strategy of guerilla warfare advocated by Mao Tse-tung (Mao Zedong), resorting to sabotage, subversion and harassment but avoiding major battles. The French meanwhile, tried to rally all non-communist nationalists to support one organized government, and approved self-government for Vietnam with Bao Dai as Chief of State. After the communist government gained power in China in 1949, Peking began sending vitally needed equipment, supplies and advisors to train Ho Chi Minh's army. For the first time, the Viet Minh forces were able to meet the French Army in large conventional military confrontations. With the rising tide of communism in Asia, Ho Chi Minh announced in early 1951 that the Viet Minh was being absorbed into a new League for the National Union of Vietnam (Lieu Viet) and formed the Vietnamese Workers Party (Lao Dong), which was dedicated to the doctrines of Marx, Engles, Lenin, and Mao Tse-tung. The guerilla forces under General Vo Nguyen Giap suffered reverses in 1951 but expanded their territory in 1952. The DRVN's forces joined with the pro-communist Pathet Lao army in Laos, and in early 1954 the new communist offenses threatened southern Vietnam, as well as northwestern Cambodia and central and northern Laos. The French forces concentrated at Dien Bien Phu were overwhelmed by General Giap's forces, resulting in the French surrender on May 8, 1954. (The French were closed off from the outside world under constant fire and taking heavy casualties. They appealed to the Americans and some American advisors suggested the use of a nuclear bomb. President Eisenhower would not enter into the conflict without the British, and Winston Churchill refused, hoping the Geneva Peace Talks would resolve the situation.)

On the initiative of Britain, France and the United States, a foreign ministers conference, including the Soviet Union, was held in Berlin in February 1954. They agreed to hold a conference in Geneva with all interested parties to discuss the situation in both Indochina and Korea. The Geneva Conference opened in late April, first taking up the question of Korea, but failed to make progress. Negotiations on Indochina began on May 8th (the day Dein Bein Phu fell). The participants included the four conference originators along with Communist China, Cambodia, Laos, the State of Vietnam (South) and the DRVN (North).

The Geneva Accords were composed of two principal documents. First was the "…agreement of the Cessation of Hostilities in Vietnam," signed on July 20, 1954 by the commanders of the French forces and DRVN forces. Second, was the "Final Declaration" of the conference dated July 21, 1954, which remained unsigned. The Geneva Accords ended hostilities throughout Indochina, partitioned Vietnam at the 17th parallel and total evacuation of DRVN forces from south of the parallel, banned the import of new weapons and any increase of troop strength, and provided for the free flow of refugees. The conference created an International Commission for Supervision and Control (ICC) for Vietnam, Cambodia and Laos. India was made chairman of the ICC with Canada and Poland as members.

The final declaration received the approval of all those represented at the conference with the exception of the South Vietnamese and the American delegates. South Vietnam agreed to support the ceasefire but objected to the partitioning of the country. The U.S. representative, General Bedell Smith, also expressed concern about the partition, but indicated that the U.S. would do nothing to disturb the agreement. He stated that the U.S. would view "…any renewal of the aggression in violation of the aforesaid agreements with grave concern as seriously threatening international peace and security." The Geneva Conference ended with a divided Vietnam, but the Vietnamese were at peace for the first time in nearly a decade and free from foreign domination for the first time in almost a century. The division of the country was to continue; however, the peace was not.

Immediately following the conclusion of the Geneva Accords, South Vietnam experienced a period of considerable confusion and uncertainty. Although Emperor Bao Dai had appointed a well-known nationalist figure, Ngo Dinh Diem, Prime Minister in July 1954, a national referendum was held in October 1955 that permitted the people to choose between Diem and Bao Dai as Chief of State. Diem won by an overwhelming majority and on October 26 he established the Republic of Vietnam with himself as President. From the beginning he had to contend with a country whose economy was ruined and whose political life was fragmented by rivalries among religious sects and political factions. During the ensuing nine years, Diem was able to consolidate his political position and eliminate the private armies of the religious sects. With substantial American military and economic aid, he built a national army and administration and made significant progress toward reconstructing a ruined economy.

By 1963 the communists had made significant progress in building a subversive organization in South Vietnam, and organized a communist controlled National Front for the Liberation of South Vietnam (NFLSVN), and had recruited formidable guerilla units that made the countryside increasingly insecure.

In May 1963, religious unrest broke out among the Buddhists. Other political and military groups alienated by the Diem government made common cause with the Buddhists and on November 1, 1963 a military coup d'état overthrew the government, which resulted in the death of Ngo Dinh Diem and his brother, Ngo Dinh Nhu.

The constitution of 1956 that provided for a strong executive branch, an unicameral assembly and a strong judicial system was abrogated with the overthrow of President Diem. On November 2, 1963 a Provisional Charter No. 1 was established, stating that the country would remain a republic and authorized a Revolutionary Council to assume the function of the legislative and executive powers (pending adoption of a new constitution). On November 6th a Provisional Cabinet was installed under Prime Minister Nguyen Ngoc Tho as Chief of State and Major General Guong Van Minh, with a civilian Council of Sages (later renamed Council of Notables), to advise the military government.

On January 30, 1964, General Nguyen Khanh replaced General Minh as Chairman of the Military Revolutionary Council and on February 8 Prime Minister Tho resigned and General Khanh became Prime Minister. In order to restore civilian leadership in the government, the Military Revolutionary Council dissolved itself on August 27, 1964. A triumvirate of generals composed of General Khanh, General Minh and General Tran Thien Khiem, headed this caretaker government until a Provisional Charter was promulgated on October 20, 1963, establishing the statutes and institutions for the civilian government. Trang Van Huong, mayor of Saigon, became Prime Minister on November 4, 1964 and Phan Khoc Suu assumed the position of Chief of State. A High National Council was appointed to act as a temporary legislative body. Opposition and public disenchantment caused the Vietnamese Armed Forces Council to abolish the High National Council on December 20, 1964, and Prime Minister Huong was asked to resign on January 22, 1965. Dr. Phan Huy Quat, a former Minister of Foreign Affairs, organized a new government on February 16, 1965. He retained Mr. Suu as Chief of State and created the National Legislative Council to act in a legislative capacity.

A constitutional crisis arose as to the meaning of the Provisional Charter and in order that no delay in the prosecution of the war would result, the civilian government dissolved itself on June 11, 1965, and on June 19th the Congress of the Armed Forces composed of the General Officers of the Vietnamese Armed Forces was formed.

Subordinate to the Congress was the Directory (composed of ten commissioners) who was entrusted with the exercise of power and the direction of the affairs of the government. Major General Nguyen Van Thieu was Chairman of the Directory (equivalent of Chief of State) and Air Vice-Marshall Nguyen Cao Ky became Prime Minister. This government remained in office until the elected government of Thieu and Ky took office, along with the freely elected legislators.

It is, or should be, glaringly apparent to everyone who bothers to inform themselves concerning our involvement in South Vietnam that communist aggression runs like a red thread throughout the current problems encountered there. Political, economic and social developments are largely tied to the course of the war. The People's Liberation Armed Forces (PLAF), or Viet Cong (from Cong San, meaning "Vietnamese Communist"), supplied and directed from communist North

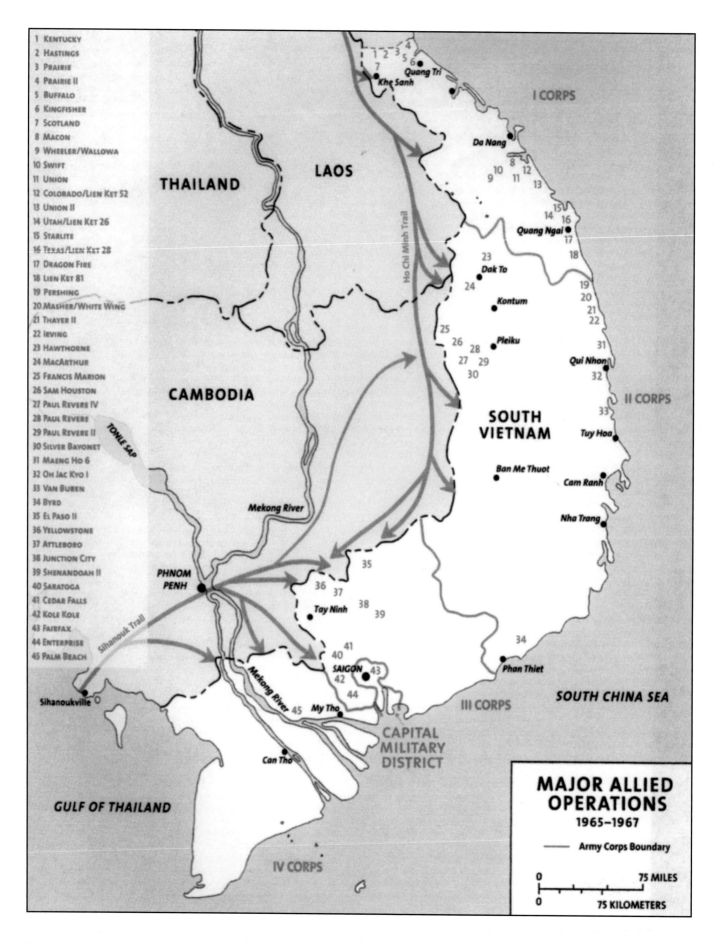

1 KENTUCKY
2 HASTINGS
3 PRAIRIE
4 PRAIRIE II
5 BUFFALO
6 KINGFISHER
7 SCOTLAND
8 MACON
9 WHEELER/WALLOWA
10 SWIFT
11 UNION
12 COLORADO/LIEN KET 52
13 UNION II
14 UTAH/LIEN KET 26
15 STARLITE
16 TEXAS/LIEN KET 28
17 DRAGON FIRE
18 LIEN KET 81
19 PERSHING
20 MASHER/WHITE WING
21 THAYER II
22 IRVING
23 HAWTHORNE
24 MACARTHUR
25 FRANCIS MARION
26 SAM HOUSTON
27 PAUL REVERE IV
28 PAUL REVERE
29 PAUL REVERE II
30 SILVER BAYONET
31 MAENG HO 6
32 OH JAC KYO I
33 VAN BUREN
34 BYRD
35 EL PASO II
36 YELLOWSTONE
37 ATTLEBORO
38 JUNCTION CITY
39 SHENANDOAH II
40 SARATOGA
41 CEDAR FALLS
42 KOLE KOLE
43 FAIRFAX
44 ENTERPRISE
45 PALM BEACH

THAILAND

LAOS

Ho Chi Minh Trail

I CORPS

Quang Tri
Khe Sanh

Da Nang

8
9 10 11 12 13
15
14 16
Quang Ngai 17
18

23
Dak To 19
24 20
Kontum 21
22
25
26 31
28 Pleiku
27 29 Qui Nhon
30 32

SOUTH
VIETNAM 33

Tuy Hoa

II CORPS

Ban Me Thuot
Cam Ranh

Nha Trang

CAMBODIA

TONLE SAP

Mekong River

PHNOM
PENH

Sihanouk Trail

35
36 37
Tay Ninh 38
39

41
40
42 SAIGON 43
44

34
Phan Thiet

Sihanoukville

Mekong River
45 My Tho

III CORPS SOUTH CHINA SEA

CAPITAL
MILITARY
DISTRICT

Can Tho

GULF OF THAILAND

IV CORPS

MAJOR ALLIED
OPERATIONS
1965–1967

——— Army Corps Boundary

0   75 MILES

0   75 KILOMETERS

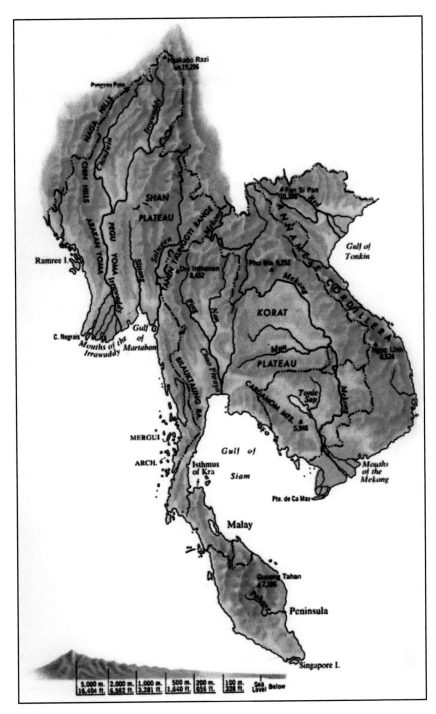

The topography of Southeast Asia.

Drawing facts from this brief general discussion of Vietnam's history and from current events, we are justified in forming some basic conclusions.

First, Vietnam has a very long and complicated history. While we boast of our national age in years, they can boast of a heritage and civilization covering many centuries. Throughout the centuries they have maintained a national pride in spite of foreign domination, emperors, dictators, turmoil, corruption and poverty and are to be commended for their repeated efforts to form a stable representative government. It is true that many of their efforts have fallen short or failed completely, but presently they are on the threshold of success and given time and continued military, economic and diplomatic assistance will enjoy the fruition of their efforts and sacrifices.

Secondly, we need to understand the distrust, impatience and fears they feel toward their government. In spite of the many promises made to them by various government leaders, they continue to live in abject poverty, continue to observe destruction and death brought by war, pestilence and disease, and they continue to witness their society as it deteriorates because of corruption, graft, sabotage and subversion.

The third and fourth considerations, which have to do with the question of whether or not this is a civil war and if we should or should not have backed the Viet Minh, can be grouped together for the purposes of this discussion. One can unreservedly conclude that this is not a civil war among the Vietnamese people, but rather it is a "...war of national liberation..." in which the communist north is seeking to conquer its southern neighbor. Ho Chi Minh's activities and statements can only serve as evidence in favor of the decision not to back the Viet Minh movement. President Ho Chi Minh, writing in the Belgium Communist Party's publication, *Red Flag*, on July 10, 1959 stated, "We are building capitalism in Vietnam, but we are building it in only one part of the country while in the other part we still have to direct and bring to a close the middle-class democratic and anti-imperialist revolutions." General Lo Nguyen Giap wrote in the January 1960 issue of *Hoc Tap* (Lao Dong Party's Journal), "The North has become a large rear echelon of our Army..." and "...the North is the revolutionary base for the whole country." Le Duan (Lao Dong Party's First Secretary), in an address to a party congress held in October 1960, stated that Hanoi had two strategic tasks, "First, to carry out the Socialist Revolution in North Vietnam; Second, to liberate South Vietnam...these two strategic tasks are closely related to each other...." Then on January 29, 1961 Hanoi announced

Vietnam are a most serious threat to the continued freedom to the Republic of Vietnam. North Vietnam and the resistance fighters (Viet Cong), National Front for the Liberation (NLF) of South Vietnam, transport supplies not only via the "Ho Chi Minh Trail" through the Truong Son Mountains from Cambodia (the Ia Drang Valley region), but they also use the South China Sea route along the coast of South Vietnam called the "Ho Chi Minh Sea Route." This effort to move supplies by sea is known by the code name "Market Time." The boats, usually trawlers (falsely registered as fishing vessels), take supplies into the coastal areas of the central and southern parts of South Vietnam, even as far south as the Mekong Delta.

that the National Front for the Liberation of South Vietnam (FLSVN) had been formed on December 20, 1960 to direct the Viet Cong guerilla forces in the south and had as its purpose the overthrow of the Saigon government and the establishment of a "…broad democratic coalition administration…" with the announced objective of "…peaceful reunification of the country." In May 1962 the International Control Commission concluded an investigation of violations of the Geneva Agreements by pointing out that there was "…sufficient evidence to show beyond reasonable doubt…" that Hanoi was sending arms and men to South Vietnam. By the end of 1964 it was estimated that in excess of 40,000 North Vietnamese military personnel had infiltrated into South Vietnam. It was stated in the *Red Flag* on May 4, 1965 that "…the Vietnam question is the focus of the present international class struggle and is a touchstone of the attitudes of all political forces in the world." We must therefore conclude that this is not a civil war.

A fifth major consideration substantiates our commitment to being involved in South Vietnam. Since World War II the United States has undertaken significant responsibilities and commitments to Southeast Asia beginning during the Truman administration. In 1950 the Chinese agreed to supply Ho Chi Minh with military aid. The same year President Truman authorized 35 military personnel to instruct and train South Vietnamese troops. President Eisenhower was reluctant to increase military support. In May 1960 the United States, at the request of the South Vietnamese government, increased the number of advisors to 685. On April 3, 1961 President Kennedy signed the Amity and Economic Relations Treaty. On February 9, 1962 the Military Assistance Command Vietnam (MACV) was created, officially establishing America's commitment to the war effort. Our Senate has approved mutual-defense treaties with South Korea, Japan, Nationalist China, the Philippines, Australia, and New Zealand, and through our Southeast Asia Treaty Organization (SEATO) agreements we are bound to defend Thailand, South Vietnam, Laos and Cambodia. These countries have America's word that we will defend them against an attack by Red China or any other aggressor. Many of these countries are demonstrating their willingness to help block the Red aggression in South Vietnam. South Korea has sent nearly 50,000 troops, the Philippines over 2,000, Thailand slightly over 15,000, Australia approximately 8,000, and New Zealand about 1,000. This clearly points out that to the people of Southeast the "Domino Theory" is really not a theory at all, but a very real life or death consideration.

Under the Southeast Asia Collective Defense Treaty our commitment to the South Vietnamese people was reaffirmed and reiterated by both the Eisenhower and Kennedy Administrations and was supported by Congress with its approval of the Gulf of Tonkin Resolution on August 7, 1964. This Resolution was necessitated following an attack by Hanoi's naval forces on U.S. Destroyers (*Maddox* and *C. Turner Joy*) in International waters in the Gulf of Tonkin in early August 1964. These Resolutions authorized "…all necessary measures…" the President might take "…to repel any armed attack…" against U.S. forces and "…to prevent further aggressions." It also approved "…all necessary

steps including the use of armed force…" which the President might take to help any nation that requests aid…in defense of its freedoms."

The position of the United States was expressed by Secretary of State, Dean Rusk, in a statement on August 3, 1965. He spoke first of America's post war role in defense of peace, freedom and of the right of free choice everywhere. He cited our aid to Greece and Turkey in the face of communist devastated Europe, NATO Defense Alliances in halting aggression in Korea, and support of the United Nations in preserving the Congo's independence. Then he stated, "…had we not done these things—and others— the enemies of freedom would now control much of the world and be in a position to destroy us, or at least to sap our strength, by economic strangulation…. For the same basic reasons that we took all those other measures to deter or repel aggression, we are determined to assist the people of South Vietnam to defeat this aggression." We therefore, had no alternative but to help when South Vietnam asked for our assistance.

The sixth point that must be made is that the goals of the South Vietnamese and of the United States are finally clear. Foreign Minister Tran Van Do on July 22, 1965 outlined them as follows: (1) Dissolution of the National Liberation Front and withdrawal of all North Vietnamese troops. (2) Self determination for an independent South Vietnam. (3) Withdrawal of foreign troops after aggression has ceased. (4) Guarantees for the independence and liberty of the Vietnamese people.

In a news conference on July 28, President Johnson succinctly stated the viewpoint of the U.S.: "We do not seek the destruction of any government, nor do we covet a foot of any territory. But, we insist, and will always insist, that the people of South Vietnam shall have the right of choice, the right to shape their own destiny in free elections in the south, or throughout all Vietnam under international supervision. And they shall not have any government imposed upon them by force and terror so long as we can prevent it."

Finally, we must set forth the prospects for peace in light of the present situation and above all we must not allow these judgments to be altered by minority dissent or by world opinion. General William C. Westmoreland has repeatedly cautioned the American people and the world, that although we are slowly winning and that progress is being made, we must exercise patience, courage and perseverance in order to see this struggle through to a satisfactory conclusion. Anxiety over the Vietnam crisis and its threat to peace has been almost universal and has resulted in efforts by President Johnson, United Nations Secretary General U. Thant, Britain's Prime Minister Harold Wilson, Pope Paul VI, and others, to hasten an end to the conflict, only to be rejected by Hanoi and Peking. President Johnson has said repeatedly, "…the U.S. is ready to hold 'unconditional discussions' with the governments concerned in the interest of arriving at a satisfactory peaceful settlement of the Vietnamese problems…," however, he cautioned in a speech on April 7, 1965, "…we hope that peace will come swiftly. But, that is in the hands of others beside ourselves. And, we must be prepared for a long continued conflict."

My personal misgiving concerning the war in Vietnam are not with our current commitments, but rather with the indecisiveness with which those commitments have been carried out. Barry Goldwater said, "Extremism in the defense of liberty is no vice, moderation in the pursuit of justice is no virtue." Our initial efforts in Vietnam should have been quick, decisive, unfaltering and unmistakable. Victory in Vietnam, and eventually in all of Southeast Asia, will be dependent to a large extent upon the reliability or our treaty commitments and the dependability of our agreements to assist our Southeast Asian Allies in deterring communism in that region of the world. The suggestion of withdrawing to Australia, as advanced by Walter Lippman, would result in mass murder, chaos and would be national suicide for many in South Vietnam. It is true that the U.S. cannot, and should not, be global protectors or international policemen, but we must live up to our agreements.

We must maintain, and even intensify, our military efforts in order to provide security and safety for the South Vietnamese both in the cities and throughout the entire countryside. Whatever military steps are required to achieve these results should be taken, even if it involves increasing the bombing of North Vietnam and increasing the ground forces in the south. It is imperative that we train, equip and modernize the South Vietnamese Armed Forces (ARVN) so they can provide their own national security just as has occurred in South Korea during the past decade.

Since the Special Forces have had significant experience working with the primitive Motagnards and the Vietnamese peasants and since there are other combat units to adequately replace them, I believe it would be both logical and feasible to alter their mission from a combat status to a leadership role in the complex area of pacification, and to be appropriately renamed the Special Pacification Forces. These Special Pacification Forces, along with special units of the ARVN, could be scattered throughout Vietnam to establish and implement a workable plan of social reforms while the other combat units maintain peace and rout the enemy.

The question of a "hot pursuit" as advanced recently by Generals Eisenhower and Bradley should never have become a question at all. It should have been our accepted policy from the first day American troops arrived in Vietnam. You don't play football by giving the opposition the plays, signals, defenses, etc., and we certainly would not advocate a rule whereby a basketball court is marked off allowing an area for the offense to maneuver and function free of opposition. We do not tolerate such ridiculousness in our sports, why should we tolerate it in something as serious as war? We should stop trying to fight a "nice war." I concur with William T. Sherman's comment that "…war is hell!" We should only give cursory credence to international criticism, especially from our European "friends." The United States can be defeated in Vietnam only by being defeated here at home. The war could conceivable have been brought to a satisfactory conclusion already had it not been for the draft card burners, peace marchers and ambitions and/or naïve politicians who have been projecting our image aboard as one of indecision, weakness, restlessness and instability. The North Vietnamese and Peking have certainly taken note of this element of our society. Those who argue for peace by suggesting withdrawal from Vietnam have most certainly given encouragement to the enemy. Those students who apparently enjoy marching in the streets should be given the opportunity of marching in a few rice paddies and see if that affords as much pleasure, and those who choose to burn their draft cards should be given an identification tag a little more resistant to destruction—namely a dog tag. These individuals represent only a very small percentage of our population; however, unfortunately, we must also contend with a much larger section of our citizenry that can readily be identified by their indifference. It seems very peculiar how a proud, productive and progressive nation can spend so much money and expend so many diversified energies to prosecute a war in which so many Americans are dying daily while so many citizens concern themselves not with why we are in Vietnam, or if our freedom is really secure or why our democracy is becoming so rapidly socialized or why inflation is progressively wrecking our economy. Rather, they concern themselves with whether the stock market is up or down, with how to make a fast buck at the expense of others and with schemes to get something for nothing. The often-quoted phrase expressing the view of the late President Kennedy has unfortunately been construed and corrupted by numerous individuals to embody the concept, "Ask not what I can do for my country, but what my country can do for me." It seems if people are not directly involved they feel the responsibility lies with someone else or with the Federal Government. I also believe that the clergy would more nearly fulfill their collective God-ordained purpose by promulgating truth, prayer, peace, patience, compassion and love from the pulpits rather than parading in the streets like a group of maniac reactionaries. I would also include a member of my profession in that group (Benjamin Spock, M.D., a well-known pediatrician, author and social activist).

I believe there will continue to be those who will respond at the proper moment to show forth the greatness of the human spirit, the selfless dedication which gives hope that, in the end, man will attain the peace, freedom and equality for which he has paid so dearly for so long. No matter how tempting it may become to compromise principles and substitute expediency for logical and moral judgments, we must never allow ourselves to confuse selfish pride and egotism with strength and courage, to misjudge indecision and weakness with humility and conservatism, nor to equate progress with liberalism.

If the precepts of fiscal conservatism, political moderation, moral integrity, individual honesty and common sense are utilized prayerfully and dutifully as a guideline, not only for our personal lives, but also for our local, state and national governments and for our diplomacy and foreign policy, regardless of world opinion, then I predict an optimistic future awaits all those who are willing to make the necessary sacrifices today in order to be prepared to meet these challenges. If today our nation began a more logical and resolute program to review, revamp and remold our military and diplomatic policies, we would "…know where are and whither we are tending…" and then "…we could better judge what to do and how to do it."

EPILOGUE

UNION AND LIBERTY

Flag of the heroes who left us their glory,
Borne through their battle-fields' thunder and flame,
Blazoned in song and illuminated in story,
Wave o'er us all who inherit their fame!

Light of our firmament, guide of our Nation,
Pride of her children, and honored afar,
Let the wide beams of thy full constellation
Scatter each cloud that would darken a star!

Empire unsceptred! what foe shall assail thee,
Bearing the standard of Liberty's van?
Think not the God of thy fathers shall fail thee,
Striving with men for the birthright of man!

Yet if, by madness and treachery blighted,
Dawns the dark hour when the sword thou must draw,
Then with the arms of thy millions united,
Smite the bold traitors to Freedom and Law!

Lord of the Universe! shield us and guide us,
Trusting thee always, through shadow and sun!
Thou hast united us, who shall divide us?
Keep us, O keep us the Many in One!

Up with our banner bright,
Sprinkled with starry light,
Spread its fair emblems from mountain to shore,
While through the sounding sky
Loud rings the Nation's cry,—
Union and Liberty! One evermore!

Oliver Wendell Holmes
(Physician, Inventor, Professor, Wit, Autocrat and Poet)
August 29, 1809—October 7, 1894

GLOSSARY OF MEDICAL TERMINOLOGY

Medical conditions encountered in troops or in the indigenous populations during World War II and/or Vietnam, or diagnosed in troops after returning to the U.S or Allied countries.

A

Amebic dysentery (Amebiasis): Diarrhea resulting from ulcerative inflammation of the colon caused by an infection with *Entamoeba histolytica* (Phylum Protozoa). The clinical symptoms range from mild to severe. We frequently encountered amebic abscesses of the liver (other organs could be involved); many were asymptomatic, as far as gastrointestinal symptoms are concerned, until they presented clinically with an "acute abdomen," often very much like appendicitis. The content of the liver abscesses that we encountered had a whitish-yellow, creamy pudding-like consistency rather than the darker, thicker, greenish avocado-paste contents described in Medical textbooks. The color and consistency obviously depends on the age of the abscess. The ones we saw were acute and of short duration. The disease is acquired through fecal contamination of food and water. It has a cosmopolitan distribution, and the eggs are spread by cockroaches, house flies (*Musca domestica*) and poor sanitation.

Anastamosis: An operative union of two hollow or tubular structures, e.g., suturing together of bowel, vein, artery, etc. thereby, reestablishing continuity.

Angiocardiogram (cardioangiography): X-ray imaging of the heart and great vessels made visible by injection of a radiopaque solution.

Anteroinferior (anterior-inferior): In front and below; the front and lower portion.

Aorta: The large artery arising from the heart at the top of the left ventricle that curves downward (aortic arch) passing through the chest and abdomen before branching into the right and left common iliac arteries, and supplying blood to the lungs, heart, kidneys, bowels, pancreas and extremities.

Aortogram (aortography): Radiographic (X-ray) visualization of the aorta and its branches by injection of contrast medium using percutaneous (intravenous) puncture or intra-arterial catheterization.

Arteriovenous fistula: An abnormal communication between an artery and a vein, often due to trauma.

Auscultation: Listening, usually with a stethoscope, to sounds made by the various internal body structures as a diagnostic method.

Autogenous: Self-produced; originating within the body.

Axilla (axillary): Armpit; it contains the axillary artery and vein and the infra-clavicular (below the clavicle) part of the brachial plexus (major nerve complex), and is bounded by large muscles—the pectoralis major anteriorly and the latissimus dorsi posteriorly.

B

Bilateral: Relating to two sides, or both sides.

Brachial Plexus: A network of nerves in the armpits innervating the shoulders, arms and hands.

C

Carcinogenic (cancerigenic): causing cancer.

Carcinoid Tumor: Usually a small slow-growing neoplasm (cancer, malignant tumor) occurring anywhere in the gastrointestinal tract (may even occur in lung and other tissues) with approximately 90% occurring in the appendix with the remainder chiefly in the stomach, other parts of the small intestine, the colon, and the rectum. Those in the appendix seldom metastasize (spread), but other locations frequently spread to involve the liver, but rarely spread above the diaphragm.

Carotid Artery: The common carotid artery branches into the external and internal carotid arteries supplying blood to the head, neck and brain; the right common carotid branches from the brachiocephalic and the left common carotid originates from the aortic arch.

Chloracne: An acne-like eruption due to prolonged contact with certain chlorinated compounds causing comedone (blackhead) formation in sebaceous glands.

Cholera: An acute, epidemic, infectious, diarrheal disease caused by *Vibrio cholerae,* a Gram negative bacteria formerly known as Koch's bacillus. The germ secretes an exotoxin that causes frequent watery stools, often with blood and mucus, and characterized clinically by pain, tenesmus (painful anal muscle spasm), fever, dehydration and even death (when Peyer's patches in the small bowel rupture) if untreated.

Collateral Circulation: Circulation maintained by the development of small anastamosing vessels when the main vessel slowly becomes narrowed and obstructed.

Cutaneous larval migrans: Human infestation of larvae of the dog hookworm, *Ancylostoma braziliense* or *A. caninum*, by penetration of the skin; however, they cannot complete their lifecycle in humans. The trapped larvae may survive for weeks or even months in serpinginous tunnels through the subcutaneous tissue resulting in intense pruritus (itching), erythema (redness) and urticaria (whelps). The condition is sometimes referred to as "creeping eruption" and is a self-limiting problem.

D

Debridement: Excision of devitalized tissue and removal of foreign matter from a wound to decrease infection and permit wound healing.

Decubitus (pl.-tus): A chronic ulcer that develops in pressure areas in debilitated patients confined to bed or otherwise immobilized; bedsore, pressure sore.

Dengue: A viral infection in tropical and sub-tropical regions. It is in the genus *Flavivirus* of the family Togaviridae (Arbovirus). This is the same genus as the Yellow Fever virus and St. Louis Encephalitis virus; however, there is no cross-immunity. The Dengue virus exists in nature as four distinct serologic types. The disease causes high fever (a distinctive saddle-shaped temperature curve), severe muscle and joint pain, lymphadenopathy (swollen lymph nodes), encephalitis with nuchal rigidity (stiff neck) and a non-specific rash. This disease is sometimes called "dandy fever" or "break-bone fever." It is usually transmitted by the mosquito, *Aedes aegypti* (sometimes by *A. albopictus*). The clinical disease ranges from mild to severe (bleeding, shock and death).

Diabetes, type II: Adult onset, usually non-insulin dependent diabetes mellitus.

Dysentery (Gr.dysenteria; dys-, bad; + entera, bowels): Diarrhea usually with fever, cramping, etc. The word is non-specific and may have many causes: bacteria (e.g. *Shigella dysenteriae, Salmonella typhi, Salmonella paratyphi A & B*), viruses, parasites, food poisoning or intolerances, antibiotic usage or induced by radiation and/or chemotherapy, etc.

E

Elephantiasis: Edema, hypertrophy, and fibrosis of the skin and subcutaneous tissue, especially of the lower extremities and genitalia, due to long-standing obstructed lymphatic vessels, caused by the presence of the filarial worm, *Wuchereria bancrofti* (or *Brugia malayi*) of the Phylum Nematoda. These parasitic worms are categorized in two groups based on their adult habitat in the human body: 1) the intestinal roundworms (e.g., the genera Ascaris, Trichuris, Ancylostoma, Necator, Strongyloidies, Enteribous and Trichinella); and 2) the filarial roundworms of the blood, lymphatic tissues and viscera (e.g., the genera Wuchereria, Dipetalonema, Mansonella, Loa, Onchocerca and Dracunculus (some believe that the "fiery serpent" which plagued the Israelites by the Red Sea was caused by Dracunculus [Guinea Worm]). It is spread by ingesting water that is contaminated by copepods (larval stage).

Endoaneurysmorrhaphy (aneurysmorrhaphy): Closure of the sac of an aneurysm to restore the normal lumenal dimensions.

F

Fascia: A sheet of fibrous tissue that encloses muscles and muscle groups.

Fasciotomy: An incision through a fascia, used prophylactically in the treatment of muscular injuries when severe swelling is anticipated which could compromise blood flow.

F.U.O.: Fever of undetermined origin.

G

Giardiasis (Lambliasis): A gastrointestinal disease caused by *Giardia lamblia* (discovered by Leeuwenhoek in 1681), a flagellated protozoa with worldwide distribution. Other parasites in this group are: *Entamoebia histolytica, Dientamoeba fragilis, Trichomonas vaginalis, Isospora belli* and *Balantidium coli.*

H

Hairy Cell Lukemia: A rare, usually chronic neoplasm of the reticuloendothelium system (cells lining the sinusoids of the spleen, lymph nodes and bone marrow).

Hct (abbreviation for hematocrit): a test that separates blood cells from the plasma (the fluid portion of blood).

Hepatitis: There are currently at least four types of hepatitis. The hepatitis A virus (HAV) is a small, RNA-containing virus classified as a picornavirus. It is transmitted primarily through the fecal-oral route; thus, it frequently occurs in small epidemics traced to the ingestion of contaminated food or drinking water. There is a vaccine available. The hepatitis B virus (HBV) is a DNA-containing virus that belongs to a class called hepadnavirus and is transmitted by parenteral exposure (e.g., needle stick, illicit drug use or blood transfusion) or through the broken skin or mucosal exposure (e.g., sexual contact). It is estimated that there are at least 280 million HBV carriers throughout the world. In the U.S., 250,000 or more cases occur annually (0.2-0.4 % of the population are chronically infected). A vaccine is available. Non-A, non-B hepatitis (NANB, hepatitis C) is widely prevalent throughout the world, is spread primarily by parenteral exposure, and accounts for 90-95% of post transfusion hepatitis cases in the world (frequently seen in association with HIV infections). Sexual transmission occurs less frequently than with HBV. Perinatal transmission has been observed. There is no available vaccine. The hepatitis D virus (HDV, or delta agent) is a defective virus that requires co-infection with HBV in order to replicate. It is ubiquitious in nature and is most often found in patients who receive blood transfusions, engage in intravenous drug use or are in close personal contact with infected individuals. Except where vaccines are available and used, there is no specific treatment. All forms of hepatitis may have similar clinical symptoms.

Hepatitus C is usually more severe and is the type responsible for most liver failure and hepatic carcinoma.

Hodgkins Disease: Multiple cell types may be involved (see Non-Hodgkins Disease).

Hypoxia: A decrease below the normal level of oxygen in inspired gases, arterial blood, tissue, etc.

I

Infarction: An area of necrosis (dead tissue) resulting from an insufficiency of the blood supply.

Intraluminal: Within any tube; inside of the bowel, blood vessels, etc.

Ionotrophic: Having an affinity for ions.

J

Japanese B Encephalitis: A Flavivirus infection seen in Japan, Southeast Asia, the South Pacific area, as well as China and India. The case-fatality ratio in the indigenous population approaches 25%. Servicemen who have not been immunized are susceptible. The symptoms include the abrupt onset of headache, confusion, ataxia, slurred speech, tremulousness and confusion. It can be transmitted by mosquitoes and ticks.

Jugular Veins: Major blood vessels draining blood from the head and neck carrying it to the heart.

"Jungle Rot": Macerated skin caused by chronic wetness (trench foot) often associated with peeling, sloughing or even ulceration of the skin that becomes secondarily infected with bacterial (e.g., *Staphylococcus aureus, Pseudomonas aeruginosa, etc.)* and/or fungal infections (*Tinea pedis* or *Candida albicans)*. Other fungi *genera* may be involved (e.g., Trichophyton, Epidermophyton, Microsporum and Scopulariopsis).

K

Kwashiorkor (infantile pellagra): Severe malnutrition due to dietary protein deficiency, seen in children usually one to three years of age, who survive mostly on their mother's milk, and results in anemia, a pot belly and skin changes. In severe cases it can lead to fatty infiltration of the liver, atrophy of the pancreas, renal glomeruli (kidney) changes and death.

L

Laparotomy (celiotomy): Transabdominal incision into the peritoneal cavity.

Leishmaniasis: Caused by parasites in the family Trypanosomidae which includes many genera, only two of which parasitize man. *Leishmania tropica* causes the cutaneous form, while *Leishmania donovani* causes the visceral form. Both are spread by sand flies. *Trypanosoma brucei* (African sleeping sickness) is spread by the tsetse fly (*Glossina palpalis*), and *T. cruzi* (American trypanosomiasis or Chagas' disease), by the reduviid bug (*Triatoma protracta*).

Leprosy (Hansens's Disease): A chronic granulomatous infection caused by *Mycobacterium leprae* (Hansen's bacillus) and usually involving the skin. In the ancient world many various chronic cutaneous diseases were probably referred to as leprosy.

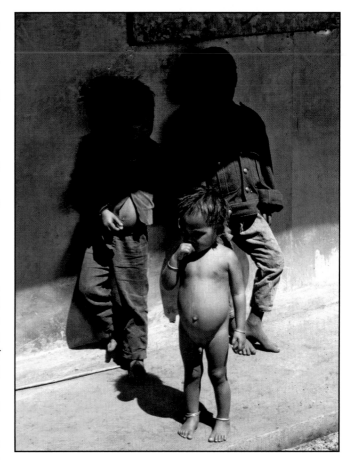

Montagnard children—the small naked child has kwashiorkor disease (infantile pellagra).

Leptospirosis: Aerobic bacteria of the genus Leptospira and comprised of two species: the pathogenic *L. interrogens* and the free-living *L. biflexa*. Approximately 180 serotypes of *L. interrogens* have been isolated from as many as 160 different mammalian species. Leptospirosis is an acute febrile disease of worldwide distribution with both wild and domestic mammals serving as primary hosts. The bacteria gains entrance to the host through the mucosa, conjunctiva or broken skin. The infection results in a hemorrhagic diathesis with involvement of hepatic and renal function, often resulting in transient jaundice. The rarely fatal cases usually results from renal failure. The severe icteric (jaundice) form of the disease is frequently referred to as Weil's disease. The clinical symptoms are characterized by chills, myalgias, severe headache with nausea and vomiting, abdominal pain, bradycardia, adenopathy and nuchal rigidity. A four-fold rise in the OXK (Weil-Felix reaction) titer is considered diagnostic. The disease is world-wide and is spread by human contact with urine from an infected animal. Most cases are mild.

M

Malaria: The disease was known centuries before the etiology was determined. The first attempt to classify this condition was based on the febrile cycle (e.g., quotidian fever [24 hr.], tertian fever [48 hr.] and quartan fever [72 hr.]). The first malarial parasites were seen in 1880, and by 1900 it was known that the disease was spread by the anopheline mosquito. There are four parasite species that involve humans: *Plasmodium falciparum, P. malariae, P. ovale* and *P. vivax*. Although all types may have been present in Vietnam, we primarily saw *P. falciparum* and *P. vivax*, with *P. falciparum* being the one most commonly seen. Although we saw a few cases of hemoglobinuria (blood in the urine—blackwater fever), I do not recall any patient with renal failure. We saw many with varying degrees of hemolytic anemia, and unfortunately there were a few deaths from "cerebral malaria." Those fatal cases resulted from involvement of the heat-controlling mechanism in the brain (hypothalamus). Those patients developed severe headache, hyperpyrexia (extremely high fever), delirium, coma and death in spite of supportive and therapeutic treatment. The clinical manifestation of malaria was the same in World War II as in Vietnam; however, the treatment was different. During World War II, Atibrine, colchicine and quinine were used; while in Vietnam, chloroquine, primaquine, pyrimethamine and Dapsone were the drugs of choice. Dapsone was discontinued after a trial study because of hemolytic anemia and agranulocytosis in a small percentage of cases. A chloroquine-primaquine tablet was taken weekly for prophalyxis. Hydroxychloroquine (Plaquenil) was perhaps used near the end of the Vietnam War, but we did not have it while at Pleiku. Malaria is diagnosed by microscopic identification of the parasite on a Giemsa-stained blood smear.

Melioidosis: Pseudoglanders. An infectious disease of rodents in Southeast Asia and India caused by *Pseudomonas pseudomallei* and is communicable to man. The characteristic lesions are small caseous nodules found throughout the body, which break down into abscesses.

Myocardium: The muscle layer of the heart.

N

Non-Hodgkins Disease (lymphocytic lymphoma): The disease is named for the British physician, Thomas Hodgkins, 1798-1866. The disease involves chronic enlargement of the lymph nodes, spleen and liver, often without leukocytosis (elevated WBC) and associated with anemia. It is considered a malignant neoplasm of lymphoid (Reed-Sternberg cells) tissue and is of uncertain origin. A similar disease occurs in domestic cats.

O

Obtunded: Not fully conscious; to dull, blunt or deaden.

P

Peripheral Neuropathy: A loss of sensory nerve function usually of the lower extremities below the knees. A neuropathy may involve motor, as well as sensory function.

Plague: An infectious disease caused by the bacteria, *Yersinia pestis*. It is characterized by high fever, prostration, petechial eruptions on the skin, lymph node enlargement, pneumonia, hemorrhage and often death if untreated. The clinical forms most seen in humans are the bubonic and pneumonic types. During the middle ages, this pestilence (black death or bubonic plague) caused millions of deaths. It is transmitted to man by fleas that have bitten infected rodents.

Porphyria cutanea tarda: A disorder involving heme biosynthesis, characterized by excessive excretion of uroporphyrins, liver dysfunction and photosensitive cutaneous lesions, with hyper-pigmentation and schleroderma-like changes of the skin.

Q

Quadriplegic (Tetraplegia): paralysis of all four extremities. Paraplegia refers to paralysis of the lower extremities.

R

Radiopaque (radiolucent): Exhibiting relative opacity to, or impenetrability by, X-ray or any other form of radiation.

Round Worms (*Ascaris lumbricoides*): A parasitic nematode of the gastro-intestinal tract generally about the size of the common earth worm. Ascariasis affects more of the world's population than any other parasitic disease. They are the most common cause of intestinal obstruction in children in the tropics. Another nematode, *Enterobius vermicularis* (pin worms), has the same general distribution and contagious probability. Intestinal nematodes that infect the gastrointestinal tract are: enterobiasis (*Enterobias vermicularis* [pin worms]); trichuriasis (*Trichuris trichiura* [whipworms]); ascariasis (*Ascaris lumbricoides* [round worms]); hookworm (*Ancylostoma duodenale* and *Necator americanus*); and strongyloidiasis (*Strongyloides stercoralis*). Extra-intestinal nematodes (Trichinosis) are caused by the ingestion of larvae of *Trichinella spiralis*, the spiral round worm of pigs and bears.

S

Sarcoma: A connective tissue neoplasm (cancerous tumor) that is usually highly malignant and formed by proliferation of mesodermal cells.

Scabes: An Arthropod, *Sarcoptes scabiei* (itch mite, in animals it is referred to as mange), that is cosmopolitan in distribution causing itching and excoriation. It is generally species-specific, and cross-species infestations are usually mild, brief and self-limiting. Human pediculosis is of three types: *Pediculus humanus capitis* (head louse), *P. humanus corporis* (body louse) and *Phthirus pubis* (pubic or crab louse) generally found in the pubic/genital area. All these are found whenever personal hygiene and general sanitation is at a low level.

Schistosomeisis: A trematode (blood fluke) with five species: *Schistosoma mansoni, S. japonicum* (most common with wide distribution), *S. haematobium, S. intercolatum* and *S. mekongi* (the Mekong River Basin). During World War II a large number of troops serving in New Guinea and on the island of Leyte in the Philippines acquired *S. japonicum*. When the cercarial form penetrates the skin, urticaria, rash and itching occurs—referred to as "swimmers itch." Robert Engebrecht, M.D. and Mark T. Cenac, M.D. removed a large bladder stone form a Vietnamese boy at the Pleiku Provincial Hospital. Pathology sections of the stone indicated that

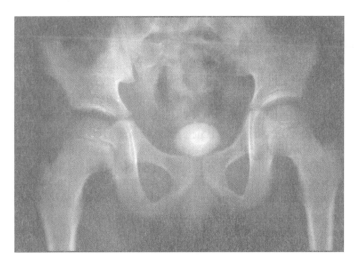

X-ray showing a small hen-egg-sized stone in the bladder of a five-year-old Montagnard boy. The stone blocked the outflow of urine resulting in bilateral hydronephrosis.

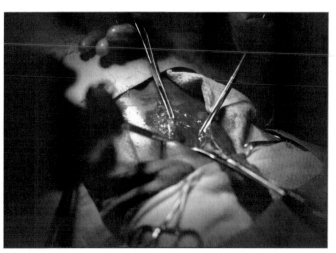

Incision into the bladder.

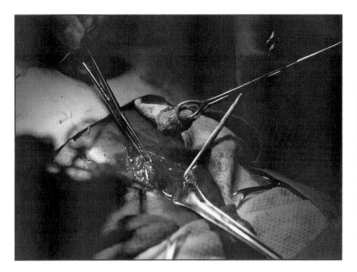

Removal of bladder stone.

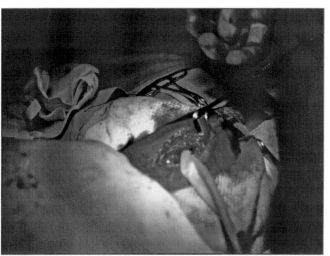

Suprapubic catheter and drain in place.

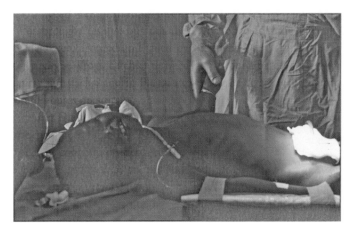

Montagnard boy immediately post-op.

Stone measuring slightly over 3cm. When the stone was sectioned it was determined that schistosomes (eggs and miracidium) had acted as a nidus for the stone.

schistosomes (eggs and miracidium) had acted as the nidus for the stone formation.

Spina Bifida: A limited defect in the spinal column, characterized by the absence of vertebral arches, through which the spinal membranes, with or without spinal cord tissue, may protrude.

Strongyloidiasis: A parasitic worm infection very similar to hookworm. This free-living nematode may live for sometime in soil if temperature and moisture are optimum. There are a number of species that are generally host-specific, although cats and dogs may be infected with the human species, *Strongyloides stercoralis*. Human infection from a canine host has been reported. The filariform larvae penetrate the skin, migrate through the blood vessels to the lungs, are coughed into the throat, swallowed and then eventually invade the small intestine. Eggs from adult worms hatch in the intestine, and the larvae are passed in feces to contaminate the soil; or the larvae can penetrate the bowel wall, again enter the blood stream, go to the lungs, etc., thus creating another cycle. They usually penetrate the skin of the feet between the toes causing a "ground itch" similar to hookworms. Pneumonitis may occur when they pass through the lungs, and while in the small bowel, they may cause diarrhea, malabsorption and ulceration of the bowel. Because of the auto-infectious cycle within the bowel, strongyloidiasis may persist for many years in non-endemic areas if untreated. A study of 600 former British POWs who served in the South Pacific during World War II discovered that eighty-eight (15%) were found to be infected some thirty years after leaving the endemic area. In Zaire, larvae were found in the milk of nursing mothers, and 34% of infants under 200 days of age were infected. A parasite of African monkeys, *S. fuelleborni*, is known to infect humans.

Subdural hematoma: Hemorrhage between the tough, fibrous membrane (dura) forming the outer envelope of the brain and spinal cord and the more delicate fibrous membrane (arachnoid) covering of the brain.

Sulfonamides (sulfa drugs): A group of bacteriostatic (inhibits or retards bacterial growth, but does not kill) drugs containing the sulfanilamide group.

Suprapubic: Above the pelvic bone anteriorly. The technique of inserting a catheter into the urinary bladder through the abdominal wall rather than through the urethra (canal leading from the bladder).

T

Teratogenic: The property or capability of producing abnormal fetal development and malformations.

Tropical Sprue ("tropical diarrhea"): Primary intestinal malabsorption with steatorrhea (passage of fat in large amounts in the feces) occurring in the tropics, often associated with enteric infections and nutritional deficiency, frequently complicated by folate deficiency with macrocytic anemia. A D-xylose absorption test is useful for diagnosis in patients with persistent diarrhea with no demonstrable pathogens.

Typhus: An acute infection and contagious disease caused by rickettsiae, and occurring in two principal forms, epidemic and endemic. The epidemic form caused by *Rickettsia prowazekii* is spread by body lice. The endemic (murine) form is caused by *R. typhi* and is spread by mouse or rat fleas. A milder form, scrub typhus, is caused by *R. tsutsugamushi* and spread by mites (chiggers). The bite produces a papule that ulcerates and heals with a black eschar (see photograph). Clinically, infected patients have high fever, severe headache, dry cough and myalgias.

V

Vasovagal (Vasotropic response): Relating to the action of the vagus nerve upon the blood vessels.

VDRL (abbreviation for Venereal Disease Research Laboratories): A flocculation (precipitation from solution) test for syphilis. Yaws is caused by a spirochete closely related to syphilis. Both diseases were originally designated as separate species within the genus, Treponema, but have been reclassified: *Treponema pallidum* (venereal syphilis), *T. pertenue* (yaws) and *T. endemicum* (endemic syphilis).

W

WBC: A blood test that measures the numbers of the various types of white blood cells in the blood.

Y

Yellow Fever: A hemorrhagic fever scattered throughout the world caused by Arboviruses (e.g. dengue). The vector for the virus is the *Aedes aegypti* mosquito.

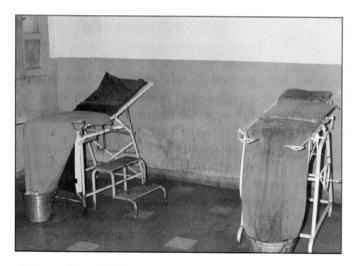

Delivery tables in the Obstetrical Ward at the Pleiku Provincial Hospital.

GLOSSARY OF MILITARY TERMINOLOGY

A

A-1E Skyraider: World War II-type single piston-engine aircraft used for ground combat support.

AATTV: Australian Army Training Team Vietnam.

AK-47: High velocity, 7.62 mm semi-automatic and automatic rifle made in Russia and used by the NVA and VC as their combat assault rifle.

ANZAC: Australian and New Zealand Army Corps.

AO: Area of operation.

Ap: Vietnamese word for village/hamlet.

APO: Army Post Office.

ARVN: Army of the Republic of (South) Vietnam.

B

Base Camp: A unit's tactical field headquarters, operation center and re-supply and refitting location.

Battery: An artillery unit equivalent to a company or a troop.

BLT (U.S. Marines): Battalion Landing Team.

Body Bag: A black plastic bag used to transport dead bodies from the battlefield.

Body Count: The number of enemy dead on a particular battlefield.

BOQ: Bachelor Officers Quarters; Living quarters for officers.

C

Cache: Hidden Supplies.

Central Highlands: Mountainous region of Central South Vietnam.

CIA: Central Intelligence Agency.

CIDG: Civilian Irregular Defense Group, usually Montagnards working with the U.S. Special Forces.

CinCPAC: Commander-in-Chief, Pacific.

Claymore Mine: Antipersonnel fragmentation land mine that delivered fragments in fan-shaped zones about two meters high and fifty meters wide at a range of fifty meters.

CO: Commanding Officer.

CONUS: Continental United States.

Counter Insurgency: Anti-guerrilla warfare.

CRW: Counter-revolutionary warfare.

CTZ: Corps Tactical Zone. Applied to any of the four areas into which South Vietnam was divided for military purposes and designated with a Roman numeral; in July 1970, the CTZs were renamed Military Regions (MRs).

D

DEROS: Date eligible to return from overseas.

DMZ: The demilitarized zone which separated North and South Vietnam along the 17th parallel.

DOW: Date of wounding.

DPC: Delayed primary closure.

Dustoff: Radio call name for the "Huey" medical evacuation helicopters.

DZ: Drop zone.

E

EM: Enlisted men.

ETA: Estimated time of arrival.

F

FAC: Forward Air Controller.

Fire Base: A temporary artillery encampment used for fire support of forward ground operations.

Fire Fight: Engagement with the enemy primarily with the use of small arms.

Flak Vest or Jacket: An armored garment made of steel plates or other bullet-proof materials covered by a padded fabric, designed to protect vital parts of the body from shrapnel.

FSB: Fire Support Base, or simply, fire base.

FULRO: United Front for the Liberation of Oppressed Races.

G

GSW: Gunshot wound.

Gunship: Attack Helicopter.

H

Ho Chi Minh Trail: A network of trails extending from North Vietnam to South Vietnam through the mountains of Laos and Cambodia along which supplies were transported.

I

IRHA: Injuries resulting from hostile action.

Iron Triangle: The Viet Cong-dominated area north of Saigon in the Cu Chi area between the Chi-Tinh and Saigon Rivers.

J

JCS: Joint Chiefs of Staff.

Jolly Green Giant: Sikersky Ch-53 helicopter used for troop and supply transport, rescue, etc.

Jungle Fatigues: Lightweight duty-uniforms designed for wear in tropical climates.

K

KIA: Killed in action.

Klick: Kilometer (1000 meters).

L

Litter: A portable stretcher used to carry the wounded.

LZ: Landing zone for helicopters in a combat area.

M

M-16: Semi-automatic, high velocity rifle used by American Forces.

MAAG: Military Assistance Advisory Group.

MACV: Military Assistance Command, Vietnam.

MASH: Mobile Army Surgical Hospital.

Medevac: Medical evacuation by helicopter (usually Dustoff) or fixed wing aircraft (usually C-130 [Hercules], C-123 [Provider], C-7 [Caribou] or C-141 [to Japan, Philippines, Hawaii or the U.S. Mainland]).

Medic: An enlisted medical technician.

Meritorious Unit Commendation Medal: Recognition awarded to units for exceptionally meritorious conduct in performance of outstanding service for at least six months during a period of military operations against an armed enemy. The degree of achievement required is the same as that which would warrant award of the Legion of Merit to an individual.

MFSS: Medical Field Service School.

MIA: Missing in action.

MP: Military Police.

MPC: Military Payment Certificates.

MUST: Mobile Unit, Self-Contained, Transportable (inflatable surgical hospital).

N

Napalm: The trade name for a mixture of powdered aluminum soap of naphthalene with palmitate, later replaced by "napalm-B," a mixture of polystyrene and benzene solvent to solidify gasoline and used instead of napalm.

NBI: Non-battle injuries.

NCO: Non-commissioned officer.

NVA: North Vietnamese Army.

NVAF: North Vietnamese Air Force.

O

OPLAN: Operation Plan.

P

Pacification: Allied efforts of countering VC influence in the hamlets and villages of South Vietnam.

Phosphorous Grenade: A grenade containing a white, phosphorous filler that burns for about sixty seconds at a temperature of 5000° Fahrenheit.

POW: Prisoner of war.

Presidential Unit Citation: An award made to units of the U.S. Armed Forces for extraordinary heroism in action against an armed enemy. The degree of heroism required is the same as that which would warrant award of the Distinguished Service Cross to an individual.

PRU: CIA-sponsored Provisional Reconnaissance Unit.

"Puff": An AC-47 (DC-3) converted into a gunship with three 7.62 miniguns with rate of fire up to 6000 rounds per minute, per gun, and also equipped to drop flares by parachute—code named "Snoopy."

Punji Stake: A sharp spike of wood, bamboo or steel concealed in a trap and camouflaged by the VC to inflict serious puncture wounds. The tips of the spikes were often contaminated with fecal matter.

PX: Post exchange.

R

R and R: A five-day period of Rest and Recreation (or Recuperation) awarded after six months active duty in a combat zone.

ROK: Republic of (South) Korea forces often referred to as "Rock." Their two divisions in Vietnam were referred to as the "Tiger" and the "White Horse" Divisions.

RPG: Rocket-propelled grenade.

S

SAM: Surface-to-air missile.

SEATO: Southeast Asia Treaty Organization.

Shrapnel: Metal fragments thrown off by exploding bomb, grenade, artillery projectile or mortar round.

T

TAOR: Tactical Area of Responsibility.

TASS: Tactical Air Support Squadron.

Tet: Asian New Year.

TDY: Temporary duty.

Triage: Medical evaluation of the wounded to prioritize or categorize the severity of wounds to determine the order of treatment.

Tunnel Rat: A U.S. soldier who specialized in searching enemy tunnel complexes often accompanied by a Mine/Booby/Tunnel Dog.

U

Units of Military Organization:

Army: A combination of two or more corps consisting of 50,000 or more soldiers, typically commanded by a Lt. Gen. or Gen.

Corps: Two to five divisions, consisting 20,000 to 45,000 soldiers, usually commanded by a Lt. Gen.

Division: Three brigade-sized units consisting of 10,000 to 15,000 soldiers, commanded by a Maj. Gen.

Brigade: Two to five combat battalions consisting of 3,000 to 5,000 soldiers, commanded by a Col. and a Command Sgt. Maj. as senior NCO. Armored cavalry, ranger, and Special Forces units of this size are termed regiments.

Regiment: Two or more battalions.

Battalion: Four to six companies consisting of 300 to 1,000 soldiers, commanded by a Lt. Col. and a Command Sgt. Maj. An armored or armored cavalry unit of equivalent size is called a squadron.

Company: Three to five platoons consisting of 62 to 190 soldiers, commanded by a Major or a Captain and a 1st Sgt. as NCO. An equivalent sized artillery unit is called a battery, while a comparable armored or air cavalry unit is called a troop.

Platoon: Two to four squads or sections totaling 16 to 45 soldiers commanded by a 1st Lt.

Squad: Nine to ten soldiers led by a Sgt. or Staff Sgt.

General Staff

Division
Brigade   Battalion
G-1   S-1 Administration
G-2   S-2 Security
G-3   S-3 Operations
G-4   S-4 Supply (Brigade or Battalion)
Quartermaster (Division)

USARV: U.S. Army Republic of Vietnam.

V

VC: Viet Cong ("Charlie").

Vietnamization: The process of turning over responsibility for the war from U.S. Forces to the South Vietnamese.

VNAF: South Vietnamese Air Force.

W

WIA: Wounded in action.

X

XO: Executive Officer.

"Jolly Green Giant" taking off from 18th Surgical Hospital helipad.

BIBLIOGRAPHY

Andersen, Dean W. *Praise the Lord and Pass the Penicillin, Memoir of a Combat Medic (32nd Division) in the Pacific in World War II.*

Atkinson, Rick. *Where Valor Rests, Arlington National Cemetery.* National Geographic

Bahnsen, (Brig. Gen., U.S. Army, Ret.) John C. "Doc," Jr. *American Warrior.*

Blair, Anne. *Lodge in Vietnam: A Patriot Abroad.*

Bonds, Ray (Editor). *The Vietnam War.*

Bowman, John S. (Gen. Editor). *The Vietnam War Day By Day.*

Bowman, John S. (Gen. Editor). *The Vietnam War (an Almanac).*

Bows, Ray A. (Master Sgt., U.S. Army, Ret.). *Vietnam, Military Lore 1959-1973.*

Brandt, (Lt. Col., U.S. Army, Ret.) Clarke M. *Yeah Kids, I Really Did Go To Vietnam My Vietnam War Memories 1966-1967.*

Breuer, William B. *Retaking The Philippines.*

Brigham, Robert K. *ARVN: Life and Death in the South Vietnamese Army*

Brooks, Richard (Editor). *Atlas of World Military History.*

Brownmiller, Susan. *Seeing Vietnam.*

Buckley, Michael. *Vietnam, Cambodia and Laos.*

Butler, David. *The Fall of Saigon.*

Campbell, James. *The Ghost Mountain Boys.*

Carter, James M. *The Merchants of Blood: War Profiteering from Vietnam to Iraq.*

Coleman, J. D. *Pleiku.*

Conboy, Ken and Ken Bowra. *The NVA and Viet Cong.*

Costello, John. *The Pacific War 1941-1945.*

Craven, Wesley Frank and James Lea Cate (Editors). *The Army Air Forces in World War II, Plans and Early Operations January 1939-August 1942, Vol. I.*

Crawford, Ann. *Customs and Culture of Vietnam.*

Davis, Loyal, M.D. (Editor). *Christopher's Testbook of Surgery.* (Seventh Edition)

Davison, John. *The Pacific War.*

Deppisch, Ludwig M., M.D. *The White House Physician.*

Doyle, Edward, et al. *The Vietnam Experience (The North).*

Dunn, Peter M. *The First Vietnam War.*

Eichelberger, Maj. Gen. Robert L. *Our Jungle Road to Tokyo.*

Evans, A. A. and David Gibbons. *The Compact Time Line of Military History.*

Fall, Bernard B. *Viet-Nam Witness 1953-66.*

Feiler, Bruce. *America's Prophet: Moses and the American Story.* Quote by Carl Westmoreland, Curator of the National Underground Railroad Freedom Center (Cincinnati, Ohio)

FitzGerald, Frances. *Vietnam: Spirits of the Earth.* Photographs by Mary Cross.

Flanagan, John F. *Vietnam Above the Treetops (A Forward Air Controller Reports).*

Gawne, Jonathan. *Finding Your Father's War.*

Giap, General Vo Nguyen. *Memoirs.*

Giap, General Vo Nguyen. *How We Won the War.*

Giap, General Vo Nguyen. *The General Headquarters in the Spring of Brilliant Victory* (Memoirs).

Giap, General Vo Nguyen. *The South Vietnam People Will Win.*

Gilmore, Donald L. with D. M. Giangreco. *Eyewitness Vietnam.*

Hayton, Bill. *Vietnam: Rising Dragon.*

Hensyl, William R. (Managing Editor). *Stedman's Medical Dictionary.* (25th Edition)

Hewitt, Robert L., M.D. *Supporting the Infantry Blue, Diary from a Surgical Hospital (MASH), Vietnam 1966-67.*

Holmes, Richard. *World War II in Photographs.*

Howgood, Barbara J., PhD. *Journal of Medical Biography* (Royal Society of Medicine)

Hubbard, Douglas H., Jr. *Special Agent, Vietnam-A Naval Intelligence Memoir.*

James, D. Clayton. *The Years of MacArthur 1941-1945.*

Kelley, Howard. *Born in the USA-Raised in New Guinea.*

Kelly, Katie. *A Year in Saigon.*

Kelly, William N., M.D. (Editor-in-Chief). *Textbook of Internal Medicine* (Vol. I & II).

Kimball, Jeffrey P. *To Reason Why.*

Kucera, Louis S., Ph.D. and Quentin N. Myrvik, Ph.D. *Fundamentals of Medical Virology.* (Second Edition)

Ky, Nguyen Cao with Marvin J. Wolf. *Buddha's Child: My Fight To Save Vietnam.*

Langguth, A. J. *Our Vietnam, The War 1954-1975.*

Lyles, Kevin. *Vietnam ANZACS, Australian and New Zealand Troops in Vietnam 1962-1972.*

Manchester, William. *American Caesar.*

Markell, Edward K., Ph.D., M.D. and Marietta Voge, Ph.D. *Medical Parasitology.* (Fifth Edition)

Mills, Nick. *The Vietnam Experience (Combat Photographer).*

Moore, (Lt. Gen., U.S. Army, Ret.) Harold G. and Joseph L Galloway. *We Were Soldiers Once—And Young.*

Moore, (Lt. Gen., U.S. Army, Ret.) Harold G. and Joseph L Galloway. *We Are Soldiers Still, A Journey Back to the Battlefields of Vietnam.*

Morris, Eric. *Corregidor: The American Alamo of World War II*

Morris, James M., et al. *History of the U.S. Armed Forces.*

Moskos, Charles C. and John S. Butler. *All That We Can Be.*

Murphy, Edward. *Dak To.*

Murray, Geoffrey. *Customs and Etiquette of Vietnam.*

Olson, James S. (Editor). *In Country: The Illustrated Encyclopedia of the Vietnam War.*

Osborne, Milton. *The Mekong (Turbulent Past, Uncertain Future).*

Pimlott, John. *Vietnam: The Decisive Battles.*

Ray, Sibnarayan (Editor). *Vietnam, Scene From East and West.*

Robbins, Stanley L., M.D. *Textbook of Pathology.*

Rousseau, Marc. *Vietnam.* Philippe Body and Jean-Leo Dugast (photographers).

Rowe, John Carlos and Rick Berg. *The Vietnam War and American Culture.*

Shay, Jonathan, M.D., Ph.D. *Achilles in Vietnam.*

Sheenon, Philip. *Ho Chi Minh City Journal: Hanoi Hannah Looks Back With Few Regrets.*

Shultz, Richard H. Jr. *The Secret War Against Hanoi.*

Simpson, Howard R. *Dien Bien Phu, The Epic Battle America Forgot.*

Smith, Lloyd H., Jr., M.D. and Samuel O. Their, M.D. *Pathophysiology, The Biological Principles of Disease.* (Second Edition)

Smith, Lt. Col. Thomas G. *Fish Heads, Rice, Rice Wine and War: A Vietnam Paradox.*

Souter, Gerry and Janet. *The Vietnam War Experience.* D. M. Giangreco (Editor).

Stanton, Doug. *In Harm's Way* (USS *Indianapolis*).

Steinbeck, John, et al. *Vietnam, We Were There.* Hal Buell (Editor).

Sterling, Eleanor Jane, et al. *Vietnam, A Natural History.*

The American Legion Post 23. *The PaceSetter.* April 2009.

Tiede, Tom. *Your Men at War.*

Tram, Dang Thuy. *Last Night I Dreamed of Peace: The Diary of Dang Thuy Tram (NVA Surgeon).* Translated by Andrew X. Pham.

Vietnam: A Television History, 13 Volumes. Sony; Time Life books.

Westwell, Ian. *1st Infantry Division "Big Red One": Spearhead 6*

Wetterhahn, Ralph. *The Last Battle.*

Wintle, Justin. *The Vietnam Wars.*

Wormenhoven, Lt. Col. Simon, MC. *Papuan Campaign-A Narrative History* Division Surgeon, 32nd Infantry Division. (Medical Department).

Street scene showing houses and a small park/playground at Qui Hoa Leprosarium.

ABOUT THE AUTHOR

Jerry W. Martin, M.D., was born in Providence (Webster County), Kentucky, on November 28, 1935, to Charles R. Martin, Jr. and Rosena Playl Martin. He graduated from Providence High School in 1954 and continued his education at Vanderbilt University in 1954-55 (Sigma Nu), B.S. from Western Kentucky State College, 1958 and M.D. at University of Louisville College of Medicine in 1963 (Alpha Kappa Kappa).

He married Jimmie D. Hobgood on December 18, 1955. They have two daughters, Melissa Martin Johnson, R.N., Mary Elizabeth Martin, B.S., D.V.M. and a son, Charles Stanley Martin, B.S., B.A., M.A., J.D., one grandchild, Elizabeth Johnson Hathaway, B.A., and one great grandchild, Sarah Elizabeth Hathaway.

After engaging in the private practice of Medicine, Surgery, and Obstetrics in Bowling Green, Kentucky for one and a half years, he was drafted into the United States Army, receiving the Reserve Commission of Captain in the Medical Corps on January 15, 1966. Following graduation from the Army Medical Services Officers Basic Course at the Medical Field Service School, Brooke Army Medical Center, Fort Sam Houston, San Antonio, Texas, he was assigned to the 18th Surgical Hospital (MA), then located at Fort Gordon, Georgia (March 14, 1966 to June 16, 1966). While at Fort Gordon, he worked in the Clinics at the Eisenhower Hospital and helped to reestablish, reequip and organize the 18th Surgical Hospital (MA) prior to it being deployed to Pleiku, Pleiku Province, Republic of Vietnam (South) in the Central Highlands. In South Vietnam (Pleiku), the 18th Surgical Hospital (MA) was under the command of the Military Assistance Command Vietnam, U.S. Army Vietnam, 44th Medical Brigade, 55th Medical Group, U.S. Army Support Command (Qui Nhon), and was located in Corps Military Tactical Zone II (II Corps). While serving there from June 24, 1966—June 18, 1967, he was also a member of the Pleiku Medical Association. Upon returning to the U.S., he was appointed Director of the Out Patient Clinic, U.S. Army Hospital, Fort Campbell, Kentucky (July—December 1967). His Honorable Discharge was dated December 11, 1967. For his service in Vietnam he was awarded the Army Commendation Medal, Republic of Vietnam Gallantry Cross, Vietnamese Service Medal (Three Campaigns), Vietnamese Campaign Medal, National Defense Medal. His unit received the Meritorious Unit Citation and a Certificate of Achievement (4th Infantry Division).

While in the private practice of Family Medicine in Bowling Green, Kentucky from 1964-2002, he served as Warren County Medical Society President (1971-72); Kentucky Academy of Family Physicians, (President [1985-86] and Doctor of the Year [1990]); Charter Diplomate, American Board of Family Practice; Warren County Board of Health (1973-80); Chief of Staff, Bowling Green-Warren County Hospital (1970-71); President of Staff (1976-77) and Chairman, Board of Trustees, Greenview Hospital (1978-79); Board of Directors, Warren County Chapter, American Heart Association (1981-97); Kentucky Medical Association's Board of Trustees (1987-93); Board of Directors of KEMPAC (1987-92); American Academy of Family Physicians Bylaws Committee (1993-96), Chairman (1996); Delegate to American Academy of Family Physicians (1992-98); Fellow, Royal Society of Medicine (1992-); Associate Professor, University of Louisville Department of Family Medicine; American Academy of Family Physicians' Delegate to American Medical Association (1996-2008); WKU Team Physician (1968-2002); Physicians Recognition Award (1970-2006); American Academy of General Practice and Founding Fellow, AAFP; Charter Member, American College of Emergency Physicians (1970); Life Member, KMA and AMA.

He served on the Board of Governors, BG-WC Arts Commission (1989-93); Chairman, Research and Resources Committee, Bowling Green-Warren County Bicentennial Commission (1996-98); National Board of Directors, WKU Alumni Association (1999-2003); Co-Founder and Chairman, Board of Directors L.Y. Lancaster-Hugh Puckett Memorial Lectureship Society (WKU, 1980-); Honorary Member W-Club (1994-); Kentucky Museum Advisory Council (1996-2002); WKU Library Advisory Council Board of Directors (2015-); Member, Committee of 75 (WKU's 75th anniversary, 1981); College Heights Foundation Board of Directors (1991-); Hilltopper Athletic Foundation (1968-), Board of Directors (1980-86); WKU Summit Awards (2004 and 2008) and Board of Directors, Cumberland Trace Chapter of the Military Officers Association of America (MOAA).

He has been a member of First Baptist Church since 1964, a Deacon since 1968 (Chairman 1996 and 2002); Chairman, Committee to Commemorate 175th Anniversary (1993); History and Archives Committee (1975-2003), Chairman Bicentennial Celebration Team (1995-2003); former member BG-WC Jaycees, Rotary Club and Chamber of Commerce; member Kentucky Historical Society; Filson Club; Kentucky Ornithological Society; Photography Society of America (1965-), Area Representative (1976-88), District Representative (1988-93); and a member of EQB Literary Club (1982-).

PLEIKU MEDICAL ASSOCIATION
THE MEDICAL FIELD SERVICE SCHOOL

Jerry W. Martin, M.D. sitting in his library with chess set purchased in Hong Kong. His great-granddaughter, Sarah Elizabeth Hathaway, is pictured in the background. Photograph by Tom Brown.

Vietnam Address:
Capt. Jerry W. Martin, M.C.
(05 330315)
18th Surgical Hospital (MA)
APO 96318
San Francisco, Calif.

INDEX

Numerical

100 Flowers and How They Got Their Names 218

A

Aberdeen Bay 108, 109
Aberdeen Floating Restaurant 109
Abrams, Creighton W. 78
Adelaide, South Australia 11
Afghanistan 13
Agent Blue 94, 95
Agent Green 95
Agent Orange 94, 95
Agent Orange Review 95
Agent Pink 94, 95
Agent Purple 94, 95
Agent White 95
Air Force Officer's Club 66
Aitape River 26, 27, 28
Alamo, The 218
Alaska 202
Allen, Joe 138
America For Me 126
American Caesar 24
American Commitment in Vietnam, The 81
American Medical Association's Volunteer Physicians for Vietnam 91
American's Creed, The 16
Amnity and Economic Relations Treaty 42
amputation 180
An Khe 45, 47, 53, 58, 62, 73, 76, 101, 129, 196
An, Nguyen Hu 12
anastamosis 245
Anchorage, Alaska 75, 191
Andersen, Dean 254
Anderson, Bob M.D. 200
Anderson, Charles R. 28
Andrcus, Dr. 62
Andrews, Bob 62
aneurysmorrhaphy 246
angiocardiogram 245
Anh, Nguyen 38, 237
Annam 38, 237, 238
Annamite Mountain 36, 118
Antarctica 21
Antoine's Restaurant 10, 211, 213
ANZUS Treaty 52
aortogram 245
aortography 245
Appalachian Coal Miner's Hospital 13
Arizona 148
Arlington National Cemetery 228, 229
Army Medical Department Museum 217
Army of the Republic of Vietnam 42, 44, 45, 46, 50, 56, 66, 69, 71, 80, 86, 133, 137, 140, 172, 197, 251

Army of the Republic of Vietnam Hospital 8, 51, 59, 87, 98, 117, 129, 130, 193
Arnold, Eddie 107, 201
arterial reconstructions 176
arteriography 175, 178
Artillery Hill 50, 53, 81, 89, 125, 130
Asia 39, 42
Asiatic-Pacific Campaign 148
Association of Marxists Studies 39, 238
Association of Revolutionary Vietnamese Youths 38
Athens, Ohio 228
Atkinson, Rick 254
Atolls, Majura 18
Attu 28
Auburn, Alabama 8
Augusta, Georgia 48, 71, 193, 200
auscultation 177, 245
Australia 20, 21, 24, 42, 51, 52, 74, 140, 142, 242
Australia, Adelaide 21
Australia, Sydney 125
Australian Broadcasting Company Orchestra 93
Austria, Vienna 81
autogenous vein graft 177, 178, 179, 180
Aw Boon Haw 109
axillary approach 97

B

Bac Ho 38
Bad and the Beautiful, The 92
Bagabac 32
Baguio 32
Bahnsen, John Jr. 254
Bailey, Larry 8
Baird, Lois Wilderman R.N. 161, 213, 216
Balete Pass 32
Ban Me Thuot 46, 49, 50, 65, 73, 173, 187
Bang, Trang 140
Bangalore, India 228
Bangkok, Thailand 11, 18, 75, 107, 112, 113, 116, 123, 183
Bardstown, Kentucky 12, 231
Barre, Vermont 228
Bastogn, Belgium 63
Bataan Death March 18, 78
Bataan, Philippines 18, 19, 29, 30
Battle for the Recapture of Corregidor 30
Battle Hymn of the Republic 231
Battle of Buena Vista 231
Battle of Buprang 174
Battle of Dak To 185
Battle of Duc Co, Pleime 174
Battle of Leyte Gulf 19, 29
Battle of Mill Springs 232
Battle of Pavia 16

Battle of Plei Djereng 174
Battle of the Coral Sea 24
Battle of the Ia Drang Valley 12
Battle of Trafalgar 16
Battle-Field, The 232
Battleship *Yamato* 19
Baumgardner, Randy 8
Bayombong 32
Beamon, Ollie M.D. 57
Belinson, Michael M.D. 10, 60, 75, 76, 79, 191, 199, 213, 216, 217, 224
Bellevue, Washington 91
Bengel, India 19
Berg, Rick 255
Bering Straits 21
Berlin 40, 238
Berry, Mary E. 47, 78, 91, 113, 194, 195
Bethesda, Maryland 214
Beyer, General 59
Biak 27
Biak Island, New Guinea 18
Bien Hoa 44, 101, 208
Bien Hoa Air Base 76
Bierman, George W. 47, 48
Bin Laden, Osama 14
Binh Dinh 46, 130, 172
Binh Dong Province 71
Bismarck Archipelago 21
Bivouac of the Dead, The 228, 231, 232
Blair Anne 254
Blamey, General 26
Blue and The Gray, The 232
Blue Beach 25, 27
Body, Philippe 255
Bogadjim 26
Boker, George Henry 232
Bonds, Ray 254
Bonneaux, Colonel 65, 77, 112, 113, 125
Borja, Sally Dawson R.N. 213
Borneo 52
Borrel, A. 119
Boston University 199
Botany: Principals and Problems 218
Bottomside 29
Bowling Green, Kentucky 7, 8, 9, 11, 12, 13, 47, 49, 65, 96, 128, 224, 228, 229, 231, 232, 235, 256
Bowman, John S. 254
Bowra, Ken 254
Bows, Ray A. 254
Bradford, Charles M.D. 30
Brandt, Clarke M. 7, 8, 91, 94, 112, 113, 121, 123, 124, 129, 211, 213, 254
Brannin, Richard 7
Breakneck Ridge 28
Breathitt, Edward T. 72
Breckinridge, John C. 232
Breuer, William B. 254

Bridge of Hope 77, 78
Brigham, Peter Brent 205
Brigham, Robert K. 254
Brink Hotel 44
Brisbane, Australia 21, 24
Brisbane's Amberly Field 22
Britain 40, 107
Brody, Sam 92
Brooke Air Force Base 217
Brooke Army Hospital 197
Brookc Army Medical Center 256
Brookings Institute 56
Brooks, C. T. 232
Brooks, Richard 254
Brown and Root 52
Brown, Edward G. 13, 72
Brown, James 191
Brown, Les 75
Brown, Sheldon M.D. 10, 47, 48, 189, 201, 207, 213, 217, 227
Brown, Tom 7, 86, 257
Brownmiller, Susan 254
Bryant, Anita 75
Bryant, William Cullen 232
Bucher, Dave M.D. 79, 85, 91, 196
Buckberry, Ray 7
Buckley, Michael 254
Buell, Hal 255
Buna 23, 24, 25, 27, 28, 32
Buna Campaign 22, 23, 24
Bunker, Elsworth 64
Burgett, Anthony D.V.M. 68, 69, 184
Burgoyne, Brent 189
Burma 18, 117, 140
Burnman, Daniel 214
Butler, David 254
Butler, John S. 137, 255
Butterfield, Daniel 233

C

Cable, Gerald O. 21
Café du Monde 211
Cagayan Valley 32
Cairo, Egypt 232
California Dahlia Society 216, 217
Call, Major 53
Calley, William L. 53
Calmette, Albert 118
Cam Ranh Airport 126
Cam Ranh Bay 45, 58, 68, 74, 91, 106, 107, 123, 126, 130, 184, 188, 205
Cambodia 34, 35, 36, 38, 39, 40, 41, 42, 45, 46, 65, 73, 75, 81, 91, 112, 117, 119, 120, 124, 125, 126, 129, 132, 140, 185, 186, 214, 236, 237, 238, 239, 241, 242
Camp Alpha 49, 191, 207
Camp Beauregard 20
Camp Bullis 183
Camp Cable 21, 24

Camp Dagupan 33
Camp Enari 9, 79, 91
Camp Evans 148
Camp Holloway 45, 53, 58, 63, 68, 70, 73, 79, 80, 88, 90, 101, 102, 184, 186, 200, 214
Camp Livingston 20
Camp Radcliff 45, 76
Camp Sandy Creek 21
Camp Schmidt 73, 130
Camp Tamborine 21
Camp Woodside 21
Campbell, James 254
Can Tho 43, 101
Canada 40
Canfield, Margaret R.N. 91, 195, 213, 224
Canton 107, 109
Cape Gloucester 18
cardioangiography 245
Cardiovascular Research Institute of the University of California 199
Carigara Bay 29
Carlyle, Thomas 16
Carmon, John 7
Caroline Islands 21, 28, 77
Carpenter, Jared 224
Carson, Callie 47
Carson, Rachael 95
Carter, James M. 254
Casa Rio Restaurant 217
Casarez, Martin 201, 202, 203
Cate, James Lea 254
cecostomy 197
celiotomy 247
Cenac, Mark M.D. 7, 10, 47, 58, 59, 62, 65, 71, 72, 74, 77, 79, 81, 83, 93, 110, 112, 113, 116, 123, 124, 125, 129, 142, 158, 185, 191, 193, 195, 196, 199, 201, 210, 213, 216, 217, 219, 223, 224, 225, 228, 233
Cenac, Nancy 217, 223, 225
Central Highlands 7, 11, 15, 36, 38, 45, 46, 51, 52, 53, 61, 65, 69, 72, 73, 75, 90, 98, 101, 102, 117, 118, 119, 128, 142, 172, 173, 174, 175, 178, 186, 192, 195, 214, 230, 235, 237, 251, 256
Central Pacific Theatre 25
Centre College 231
Chaffee, Roger 84
Chamberland, Charles Edouard 118
Champs Elysees Restaurant 49
Channing—A Study 232
Channing, William Ellery 232
Chao Phraya River 113
Chap, Eugene M.D. 10, 63, 87, 90, 118, 123, 125, 195, 203, 204, 213, 216, 217
Chicago, Illinois 49, 204, 205
China 18, 38, 39, 40, 42, 64, 87, 105, 107, 109, 236, 237, 238, 242
China Beach 45
China Sea 41, 103, 105, 117, 236
China Town 116
Chinghsi, China 38, 238
Cholon 38, 76, 237
Chu Lai 111, 129
Chu Pong Mountains 46, 62
Chulalongkorn University 116

Churchill, Winston 14, 40, 141, 238
Cincinnati, Ohio 254
Civil War 9, 24, 231, 232
Civilian Irregular Defense Group 45
Clark Airforce Base 6, 58, 101
Clark, Mildred Irene 78
Claymore, Mine 251
Cleckley-Thigpen Psychiatric Associates 48
Cleckley, Hervey M.D. 48
Co, Nguyen Huu 64
Cochin, China 38, 39, 237, 238
Cold War 14
Coleman, J.D. 254
Coleman, Minnie Brown 13
Collins, Arthur S. 93
Collins, Daniel J. 175, 178
Colorado River 15
Columbus, Georgia 232
commissurotomy 98
Conboy, Ken 254
Cooper, Sen. John Sherman 128, 235
Cornil, André Victor 118
Corpus Christi Bay 203
Corregidor Campaign 21, 32
Corregidor, Philippines 19, 29, 30, 31, 149, 150
Costello, John 254
Counsels and Ideals from the Writings of William Osler 17
Craven, Wesley Frank 254
Crawford, Ann 254
Crispa-Vega, Sergeant 208
Cronkite, Walter 133, 136
Crowell, Lieutenant Colonel 53
Cu Chi 209
Culinary Institute of America 220, 221, 222, 223
Cuoi, Little 87
Custer, George Armstrong 45
Czaplicki, Eugene Boleslaw 63

D

Da Lat 119
Da Nang 38, 45, 49, 50, 52, 68, 101, 133, 196, 203, 209, 237
Da Nang Air Base 50, 76
Dac To 56
dacron graft 178
Dahl, Anders 218
Dai Co Viet 38
Dai, Bao 39, 238, 239
Dai, Emperor Bao 39, 40
Dak To 53, 71, 73, 187
Dalat 101
Dallas, Texas 49, 230, 232
Damone, Vic 75
Danville, Kentucky 231
Darlac 65
Davis, James 137
Davis, Loyal M.D. 254
Davison, John 254
De Gaulle, President 44
de Meneses, Jorge 22
debridement 176, 178, 179, 205, 208, 246
Decatur, Stephen 16
Declaration of Honolulu 74
Declaration of Peace 74
Dee, Sandra 49
Delano Hall 214

delayed primary technic 176
Democratic Republic of Vietnam 36, 39, 40, 237, 238
Den, The 109
Deppisch, Ludwig M.D. 254
Desert Storm 215
Devotions upon Emergent Occasions 232
Dexter, Judy 78, 82
Dickey, James 106
Diem, Ngo Dinh 34, 40, 65, 239
Dien Bien Phu 34, 39, 133, 238
Dietz, Deborah 216, 217
Diller, Phyllis 75
Dinh, Sergeant 120
direct exploration 178
direct suture 176, 177, 178
Dirge for a Soldier 232
Do, Minister Tran Van 44, 242
Dobadura 22
Domino Theory 42, 183
Don Dien Michelin 75
Doner, Sergeant 196
Dong Ha 132, 133
Dong, Lao 42, 241
Dong, Pham Van 81
Donmuang 112
Donne, John 230, 232
Douglas, Kirk 92
Downing, Joy 7
Doyle, Edward 254
Dragon Mountain 9, 75, 79, 90, 110, 111
Dragon Mountain Base Camp 91
Dragon's Back Peninsula 109
Drake, Daniel 17
Drang River 46, 62, 90
Drea, Edward J. 27
Driniumor River 26, 27, 32
Dripps, Robert M.D. 59, 183
Drummer Boy of Shiloh, The 5
Drury's Milan Room 217
Duan, Le 42, 241
Duc Co 45, 53, 77
Duc, Thish Quang 40
Duclaux, E. 119
Dugast, Jean-Leo 255
Dugway Proving Ground 195
Dulles, John Foster 75
Duluth, Minnesota 215
Dunn, Pat 78, 82, 83
Dunn, Peter M. 254
Duval, Jack 12, 13

E

Eagle's Nest 109
East Indies 21
Ecker, Judy 216, 217, 219, 223, 225, 226, 227
Ecker, Roger M.D. 10, 57, 75, 85, 142, 153, 161, 195, 196, 200, 213, 216, 217, 219, 227
Eichelberger, Robert L. 24, 26, 254
Eifler, C. W. 56, 59, 75
Eisenhower Hospital 48
Eisenhower, Dwight D. 12, 34, 40, 42, 44, 75, 76, 137, 183, 200, 238, 242
Eisenhower, John 76
Eisenhower, Mary 76
Eisenhower, Milton 76
Elegy for a Dead Soldier 5, 15
Ellison, Mary 183
Ellison, Norig M.D. 51, 183, 216

Ely, Minnesota 193
Emerson, Ralph Waldo 16
Enari, Mark N. 91
endoaneurysmorrhaphy 176, 177, 246
Engebrecht, Mary 225, 226
Engebrecht, Robert M.D. 10, 47, 48, 49, 71, 82, 117, 153, 156, 159, 205, 206, 213, 216, 217, 224, 225, 226
Engels 39
Enuol, Y B'ham 65
Ethnic Minorities Solidarity Movement 65
Europe 44
European War 21
Evans, A.A. 254
Evans, Dale 92
Evers, Sergeant 63
extensive laceration 180

F

F. Edward Hébert School of Medicine 214
Falk, Stanley 24
Fall, Bernard B. 81, 254
fasciotomy 157, 246
Fat Man 11
Feiler, Bruce 254
Fera, Rita 75
Fiji 77
Finch, Francis Miles 232
Finschhafen 25
First Baptist Church 13
Fishback, Malcolm T. 132
FitzGerald, Frances 254
Flanagan, John F. 254
Flint, Michigan 189
Flynn, James 7
Ford, Gerald R. 56, 57, 96, 97
Fort Albert Sydney Johnson, Kentucky 9, 232
Fort Benning, Georgia 69, 190, 195
Fort Bragg, North Carolina 12, 47
Fort Campbell, Kentucky 12, 128, 191, 235, 256
Fort Carlson, Colorado 190, 195
Fort Devens, Massachusetts 199
Fort Dix, New Jersey 183
Fort Douglas, Utah 195
Fort Gordon, Georgia 11, 15, 33, 46, 47, 48, 49, 53, 57, 63, 69, 72, 121, 123, 124, 149, 190, 193, 205, 207, 228, 230, 256
Fort Jackson, South Carolina 195
Fort Leavenworth, Kansas 208
Fort Lee, Virginia 205
Fort Lewis, Washington 93, 149, 202, 209
Fort Mason, California 21
Fort McArthur, California 190
Fort McNair, Washington, D.C. 214, 215
Fort Mills, South Carolina 29
Fort Monmouth, New Jersey 101
Fort Riley, Kansas 195
Fort Sam Houston, Texas 46, 53, 75, 183, 185, 190, 191, 192, 193, 195, 197, 205, 217, 256
Fort Sill, Oklahoma 195
Fort Wolters, Texas 190, 196
Fortuna Hotel 113
Four Seasons Restaurant 203
Four Voices from Shiloh 5

France 40
Franciosa, Anthony 49
Francis I 16
Frankfort Cemetery 231, 232
Frankfort, Kentucky 231
Franklin, Gary 217, 226, 227
Franklin, Lori 217, 226, 227
Fredericksburg, Texas 218
Free World Military Assistance
  Forces 50
Freedman, Philip M.D. 91, 104
Freedom Bird 126, 127, 188, 194
French Croix de Guerre 9
French-Indochina War 184
Freneau, Phillip 232
Fukuoka, Japan 33
FULRO Ceremony/Festival 3, 9,
  46, 64, 65, 72, 172, 173, 174
Fulton, Robert C. 7, 13, 133, 209
Fulton, Virginia 13

G

Gable, Clark 126
Gabriel, Sister 91
Galen 17
Galloway, Joseph L. 12, 255
Garcia, Alfredo 137, 201, 202,
  203, 208
Garden Encyclopedia, The 218
Garner, James 49
Garrison, Fielding H. 232
Gawne Jonathan 254
Geelvink Bay 25, 27
Geneva 36, 40
Geneva Accords 40, 239
Geneva Conference 40
Geneva Convention 14
Geneva Peace Talks 40
George Bush Gallery of the Pacific
  War 218
Georgetown University 128, 215,
  235
Georgetown, Kentucky 128, 235
Georgi, Johann 218
Gettysburg Address 228, 232
Gettysburg, Pennsylvania 5
Ghost Mountain Boys 22
Gia Dinh 76
Giangreco, D. M. 255
Giap, Vo Nguyen 39, 42, 136, 238,
  241, 254
Gibbons, David 254
Gilbert Islands 18, 21, 28, 77
Gill, William H. 28, 32
Gillis, Samuel Peters M.D. 10, 57,
  79, 83, 85, 123, 124, 153, 156,
  182, 205, 206, 213, 216, 219,
  221, 224, 233
Gillis, Sandra 219, 221, 225, 233
Gilmore, Donald L. 254
Glasgow, Kentucky 12
God Save The Flag 232
Godfrey, Arthur 92
Goforth, Virgil M.D. 79, 85, 91
Golden Gate Bridge 196
Golden Gate Park 216, 217
Goldwater, Barry 148, 243
Gona Campaign 24
Goodacre, Glenna 229
Goodenough Island 25
Gooding, Ron 203
Goodwine, Tom CRNA 78, 79,
  188
Gordon, Maurice K. 13

Gouldthorpe, Barbara R.N. 78, 82,
  185, 216
Graham, Billy 76
Grand Canyon 15
Grand Palace 115
Grand Rapids, Michigan 195
Grapes of Wrath, The 78
Great Britain 21
Greece 44, 242
Green Hell 26
Grill, The 109
Grissom, Gus 84
Guadalcanal 24
Guam 12, 18, 19, 28, 49, 75, 205
Guerrytown, Alabama 232
Gulf of Siam 36, 236
Gulf of Tonkin 34, 36, 42, 242
Gulf of Tonkin Resolution 44

H

Haan, William 20
Hai 84
Haiphong 118
Hall, Robert 59
Hallam, Arthur Henry 228
Halmahera Island 27
Hames, Bill 83, 91, 185
Hamilton-Juliano, Mary R.N. 78,
  87, 190, 204, 213
Hamit, Harold F. 178
Han Giang River 138
Hancock Bank and Trust Company
  8
Hancock, Kenneth Wayne 190
Hanks, Tom 215
Hanks-Rizzo, Vivian CRNA 216
Hanoi 36, 39, 42, 44, 74, 118,
  120, 126, 136, 237, 238, 241,
  242
Hanoi-Haiphong 35
Hariko 22, 23
Harkins, Paul D. 42, 52
Harkless, PFC 196
Harrell, O'Neal 13
Harrow School 14
Hart, Frederick 229
Hartford Hospital 183
Hartman, Bob 24
Harvey 17
Hashimoto, Mochitsura 11
Hatch, Ron CRNA 78, 79, 153
Hathaway, Elizabeth Johnson 8,
  86, 256
Hathaway, Eric William 8, 144
Hathaway, Sarah Elizabeth 257
Hawaii 49, 100, 193, 205
Hawaiian Islands 21
Hay, Colonel 78
Hays, Anna Mae 78
Hays, Will S. 5
Hayton, Bill 254
Haywood, Cheryl J.D. 222
Health Science Center's Kornhauser
  Medical Library 75
Heath, Mary Lee 78, 82
Heatherton, Joey 75
Heaton, Leonard D. 12, 74, 75,
  76, 78
Heilbronn, Germany 195
hematocrit 246
Hensyl, William R. 254
Hernandez, Raquel M.D. 200
Hero and Leander 16
Heston, Charleton 129

Hewitt, Robert M.D. 3, 7, 10, 13,
  58, 75, 79, 82, 84, 98, 99, 100,
  112, 122, 123, 129, 130, 142,
  153, 156, 175, 178, 185, 186,
  189, 191, 192, 200, 211, 213,
  214, 216, 217, 222, 224, 254
Hildebrand, Captain 132
Hines, Duncan 12
Hines, Virginia 206
Hiroshima, Japan 19
Ho Chi Minh City 95, 120, 126,
  216
Ho Chi Minh Trail 41, 45, 94,
  130, 183, 241, 251
Hoan, Vu-Ngoc 98
Hoang, Bac Si 87
Hobgood, Jimmie D. 256
Hoc Tap 42, 241
Hodgkins, Thomas 248
Hoisington, Elizabeth P. 78
Holden, William 109
Hollandia, Netherlands 26, 27, 28
Hollingsworth, James F. 140
Hollis, Chaplain 13, 72, 82
Hollis, General 62
Holloway, Charles E. 45
Holmes, Oliver W. 17, 232, 244
Holmes, Richard 254
Hon Me Islands 42
Hon Ngu Islands 42
Hong Kong Hilton Hotel 108,
  110, 203
Hong Kong International Airport
  109
Hong Kong Island 109
Hong Kong, China 11, 18, 19,
  105, 107, 109, 110, 119, 192,
  198, 201, 203, 257
Honolulu International Airport 49
Honolulu, Hawaii 49, 74, 107,
  183, 191
Hope, Bob 75
Hopkins County History 13
Hosking, Georgi 217
Hosking, Wayne M.D. 8, 10, 15,
  47, 48, 49, 70, 71, 79, 85, 87, 98,
  99, 106, 153, 156, 183, 189, 191,
  192, 200, 201, 207, 213, 216,
  217, 218
Hostellerie La Fregate 102, 103
Hotel Thayer 219, 220, 224
Houlton, Colonel 63
Hound of Heaven, The 232
House of Lords Pub 219
Houston, Texas 46
Howard University 81
Howe, Julia Ward 231
Howgood, Barbara J. 254
Huang, Tang Ming 87
Hue 34, 39, 40, 50, 68, 133
Hughes, Carl W. 76
Hulsey, Admiral 28
Hunter 17
Huntley, Chet 93
Huong, Thu 126
Huong, Trang Van 41
Hurricane Katrina 216
Hyde Park, New York 220

I

I Have A Rendezvous with Death
  232
Ia Drang Valley 8, 12, 41, 46, 62,
  101, 121, 172, 228, 230, 241

Imphal 19
In Flanders Fields 232
In Memoriam 228, 232
In Touch 79
India 40, 62, 75
Indochina 36, 40, 120, 238
Indochinese Communist Party 39
Indochinese War 39
Indonesia 105, 140
internal fixation 179
International Commission for
  Supervision and Control 40
International Conference in Geneva
  237
International Control Commission
  42
intramedullary nailing 179
Iraq 13
Irian Jaya 22
Iron Triangle 130, 252
Iwo Jima, Japan 19, 77

J

J.A. Jones Construction 52
Jade Lotus Room 109
James, D. Clayton 254
Japan 18, 19, 21, 33, 39, 42, 58,
  66, 78, 123, 126, 198, 202, 212,
  242
Japanese Garden of Peace 218
Japanese Room, The 212, 213
Jarai 45
Jardin du Roi 218
Jaskowski, Margaret R.N. 78, 185,
  213, 216, 228, 233
Jenicek, Col. 76
Jenkins, Felix M.D. 47, 48, 56,
  70, 71, 79, 82, 85, 96, 106, 153,
  158, 185, 189, 192, 196, 201,
  217, 222
Jenmin Jih Pao 77
Jenner 17
Jericho: The South Beheld 106
Johnson, Harold Keith 78, 134,
  138
Johnson, James Weldon 233
Johnson, Jane 133
Johnson, Lyndon B. 12, 34, 40,
  44, 45, 52, 74, 78, 81, 95, 137,
  183, 242
Johnson, Melissa Martin R.N. 86,
  256
Johnston, Albert Sidney 231
Jonathan, Shay M.D. 255
Jones, David M.D. 96
Jones, Dick M.D. 91, 102, 207
Jones, Jim R.N. 78, 82, 83
Jones, Thomas Jr. 80
Juliano, Joseph M.D. 10, 47, 48,
  78, 83, 87, 118, 159, 189, 190,
  196, 204, 213, 217

K

Kafoglis, Nick M.D. 13
Kaiser 22
Kaku, Michio 124, 129, 130
Kalb, Walter 136
Kanchanaburi National War
  Cemetery 115, 116
Kanoya 33
Kapsner, A.L. 46
Karlsruhe, Germany 195
Keeling, William 133, 134, 135,
  138, 209

Keller, Helen 15
Kelley, Howard 254
Kelly, Charles L. 47
Kelly, Katie 254
Kelly, William M.D. 254
Kendrick, Douglas B. 76
Kennedy, John F. 5, 16, 34, 40, 42, 44, 64, 81, 94, 148, 183, 242, 243
Kenner Army Hospital 205
Kentucky 191
Khanh, Nguyen 41, 65, 239
Khe Sanh 133
Khe, Lai 203
Khiem, Tran Thien 41
Khontum 73
Kilburn, H.L. 46
Kimball, Jeffrey P. 254
King, Martin Luther Jr. 17
King Philip II 218
Kinnard, Harry 45, 46, 63
Kirkland, Ron 137
Kitasato, Shibasaburo 119
Klaus, R.M. 46
Klebs, Theodor 118
Kleiger, R.E. 46
Knang, Nang Quan 81, 84, 92
Koch, Robert 118, 119
Kokoda Track 26
Kokura 33
Kontum 13, 45, 46, 50, 53, 63, 71, 81, 91, 98
Kontum Hospital Fund 91
Kopff, R.G. Jr. 46
Korea 40, 44, 105, 238, 242, 243
Korean War 78, 177, 192, 205
Kotlarz, Wanda 204
Kowloon 110
Kowloon Peninsula 107, 109
Kowloon Public Pier 109
Kramer, C.H. 46
Kravatz, A.S. 46
Kreiner, John 66, 68, 102, 187, 216, 217, 218
Kublai Khan 38
Kucera, Louis S. 254
Kwagalein 28
Kwai River 115, 116
Kwajalein 18
Ky, Nguyen Cao 6, 41, 64, 65, 74, 76, 172, 174, 239, 254
Kyoto, Japan 75
Kyushu, Japan 33

L

Labiche, H.M. Jr. 46
Lackland Airforce Base 69
Laennec 17
Lai Khe 3, 132, 182, 195, 201, 208
Lake Bien Ho 51, 118, 155
Lake Cushman 91
Lamesa, Texas 208
Lan 120, 192
Langguth, A.J. 254
Langley 18
Laos 35, 36, 38, 39, 40, 42, 45, 91, 132, 140, 236, 237, 238, 239, 242
laparotomy 247
Larson, Stanley 93, 99, 214
Lau Ong Nam 120
Lavaux, Switzerland 118
Lawson, William Bennett III 8

Lazorchak, Joseph F. 47, 49, 82, 83, 188
Le Meridian Hotel 211
Leacock, Fred M.D. 82
League for the National Union of Vietnam 39
Lee, Bob 195
Lee, Robert E. 16
Lee, William 64, 81, 82
Lefkowitz, M. 46
Leigh, Vivien 126
Leitchfield, Kentucky 13
Lemnitzer, Layman L. 94
Lenin 39
Leonard, Phillip M. 195, 216, 226, 227, 233
Letter to a Mother 5
Lexington, Kentucky 8, 13
Leyte 19, 28, 29, 32, 33, 142, 150
Leyte Campaign 21, 28, 29
Leyte Gulf 19
Leyte, Philippines 12
Leyte-Samar Campaign 29
Liberty Printing 7
Lieberman, H. 46
ligation 176
Lin, Maya Ying 228
Lincoln, Abraham 5, 14, 228, 232
Lincoln Memorial 228
Lindem, Peggy 201, 215
Lindem, M.C. (Tony) M.D. 46, 47, 48, 49, 51, 56, 60, 61, 71, 74, 79, 85, 94, 106, 121, 123, 156, 159, 193, 194, 195, 201, 205, 206, 207, 215, 216
Lingayen Beach 29
Lingayen Gulf 19, 29, 33
Linnaeus, Carolus 218
Lippman, Walter 243
Literary Club 12
Little Boy 11
Littman, D.B. 46
Loan, Nguyen Ngoc 76, 140
lobectomy 96
Loc, Vinh 3, 54, 64, 82, 89, 113, 174
Lodge, Henry Cabot II 64, 140, 197
Loëffler, Friedrich 118
London, England 219
Long Binh 71, 130, 195, 208
Long, Gia 38, 237
Longfellow, Henry Wadsworth 230, 232
Lord, T.J. 46
Los Angeles International Airport 216
Los Angeles, California 190, 216
Louisville, Kentucky 12
Lowson, James A. 119
Loyola Law School 190
Luzon Campaign 29
Luzon, Phillipines 19, 21, 28, 29, 30, 32, 33, 142, 150
Lyerly, D. 46
Lyles, Kevin 254

M

Mabilao 29
MacArthur, Douglas 16, 18, 19, 21, 22, 26, 28, 29, 30, 31, 32, 75, 78, 186
Macauley, Kathy 7
Madisonville, Kentucky 13

Magim 46
Mai 120, 192
Majestic Hotel 39
Malasia, Pa Nang 202
Malay Peninsula 22
Malaya 18, 52
Malaysia, Singapore 107, 140
Malinta Hill 30
Malinta Tunnel 30
Malogne House 214
Man Could Get Killed, A 49, 200
Man Mo Meal Island 109
Man of LaMancha 17
Man, Chu Huy 45
Manaoog-San 29
Manchester, William 24, 255
Mang Yang Pass 45, 73, 102, 103
Manicom, R.E. 46
Manila Bay 29
Manila, Philippines 18, 19, 29, 49, 74, 118, 126
Mansfield, Jayne 84, 92, 204
Marble Palace 115
Marburg University 118
Mariana Islands 11, 18, 19, 21, 28, 77
Marine Memorial Club and Hotel 216
Markell, Edward K. 255
Marlowe, Christopher 16
Marshall Islands 18, 21, 28, 77
Marshall, George C. 75
Martin, Charles Stanley 256
Martin, Charles Jr. 256
Martin, Jerry M.D. 2, 4, 5, 10, 14, 17, 46, 47, 48, 70, 71, 73, 74, 79, 84, 85, 87, 93, 106, 109, 118, 124, 141, 156, 185, 186, 189, 193, 194, 206, 213, 216, 217, 219, 222, 224, 226, 227, 231, 233, 256
Martin, Jimmie 8, 12, 128, 219, 225, 226, 227
Martin, Mary Elizabeth 256
Martin, Rosena Playl 256
Martino, Tony 92
Marx 39
Massey, Robert A. 59, 129
Matthews, Thomas S. 232
McAuliffe, Anthony 63
McCain, John 214
McCarthy, Merrick F. 5
McCloud, Dr. 129
McCormack, John W. 136
McCrae, John 232
McCullough, Col. 62
McDonald, Jean Marie 222, 225, 227
McDonald, T.J. 46, 190
McDonald, Terry M.D. 10, 91, 188, 213, 222, 224, 227
McDowell, Ephram 17
McGinnis, Marge R.N. 78, 83, 212, 213, 214, 216
McNamara, Robert S. 40
McNurney, Jules J. 128
McVay, Charles Butler III 11
Medford, Bill 102, 187
Medical Civic Action Program 51
Medical Field Service School 256
Meharry Medical College 189
Mekong Delta 42, 44, 65, 67, 84, 101, 241
Mekong River 36, 38, 43, 119, 237

Memoirs 136
Memorial Walk 218
Memphis, Tennessee 228
Menger, W. A. 218
Menger Bar 219
Menger Hotel 218, 226, 227
Menzies, Robert 52
Mercouri, Melina 49
Merecki, E.A. 46
Meridith, Don 93
Merrill's Marauders 18
Metcalf, Col. 133
Mexican War 231
Mexico 22
Meyer, Mark 58, 75
Meyer, Richard J. 101
Meyers, Gilbert 6
Michie Stadium 224
Michigan 6, 20, 212
Middleside 29
Midway 77
Midway Island 18
Milenta Hill 32
Military Assistance Advisory Group 42
Military Assistance Command Vietnam 42, 45, 52, 64, 68, 71, 77, 80, 81, 98, 101, 174
Military Assistance Command Vietnam Headquarters 11
Military Officers Association of America 12
Military Payment Certificates 61, 62
Military Provincial Health Assistance Program 51
Military Revolutionary Council 41
Mill Valley, California 199
Millay, Edna St. Vincent 230, 232
Miller, Pat CRNA 58, 78, 79, 118
Miller, Ray L. 56
Mills, Nick 255
Mills, Robert 128, 235
Milne Bay 23, 25
Milton, John 16
Milwaukee, Wisconsin 33
Mindanao 27, 28
Mindanao Sea 29
Mindoro, Philippines 19, 29
Minh, Guong Van 41, 239
Minh, Ho Chi 34, 38, 39, 42, 81, 126, 136, 237, 238, 241, 242
Minh-Quy Hospital 91
Minnesota 192, 193
Mississippi 182
Mitchum, Robert 92, 204
mitral valvulotomy 98
Mizell, Major 58
Moji 33
Molenga House 215
Moluccas 22
Mon-Khmer 38
Montana, Little Bighorn 45
Moore, D.C. 46
Moore, Francis M.D. 205
Moore, Harold G. 8, 12, 46, 255
Moore, J. William 12
Morehead, C.D. 46
Morgan, Russell 13
Morning Walk, A 15
Morotai 27, 28, 32
Morotai Campaign 27
Morris, Eric 255
Morris, James M. 255

Morrison-Knudsen 52
Moscow, Russia 38, 237
Moskos, Charles C. 137, 255
Moving Wall Vietnam Veterans
   Memorial 229
MSTS *Gordon* 196
Mufson, A.S. 46
Munch, R.V. 46
Muong 45
Murphy, Edward 255
Murray, Geoffrey 255
My Lai 34
My Tho 43

N

Nagasaki, Japan 19
Nakhon Phanom Royal Thai Air
   Base 77
Napa Valley 216
Nashville, Tennessee 49, 128
Nass, Bernard (Ben) 47, 82
Nassos, Mary Ann 225
Nassos, Tassos M.D. 10, 79, 91,
   213, 216, 224
National Assembly Hall 116
National Front for the Liberation of
   South Vietnam 40, 42
National Institute of Health 68
National Liberation Committee for
   Vietnam 39
National Museum of the Pacific
   War 218
National Naval Medical Center 214
National Security Action
   Memorandum 40
National Security Council's
   Memorandum 42
Neidballa, R.G. 46
Nelson, I.J. 46
Nelson, Viscount Horatio 16
Nesson, Ron 56, 57
Netherlands 21
Neuva Guinea 22
Nevins, Marty 116
New Guinea 21, 22, 23, 24, 25,
   26, 27, 28, 142, 150
New Guinea Campaign 26, 27,
   148
*New Guinea-The U.S. Army
   Campaigns of World War II* 27
New Mexico 36, 237
New Orleans, Louisiana 13, 75,
   142, 207, 211, 212, 216
New Otani Hotel 198
New Pleiku Air Base 61, 65, 76,
   77, 79, 90, 93, 112, 113, 130
New Pleiku Airport 50, 58, 75,
   112, 126
New York 93, 199, 215
New York City, New York 195
New York Hospital-Cornell Medical
   Center 195
New York Times 35, 192
New Zealand 42, 51, 52, 74, 113,
   242, 251
Newsday Magazine 78
Newsweek 68, 212
Ngo, Trinh Thi 126
Nha Trang 49, 52, 67, 68, 90, 91,
   96, 101, 102, 118, 119, 120, 182
Nha Trang Airport 102
Nha Trang Bay 102
Nhi, Trung 237
Nhu, Madame 89

Nhu, Ngo Dinh 40, 102, 239
Nice, France 81
Nicholasville, Kentucky 8, 12
Nichols, E.A. 46
Nick, Utah 140
Nicklaus, Jack 48
Nielsen, Jon 92
Nimitz, Chester W. 18, 19, 21,
   28, 218
Niu Lang Bian 101
Nixon, D.D. 46
Nixon, Richard M. 34, 35, 78,
   133, 137
Norfolk, Virginia 16
Normandy 63
North Vietnam 34, 35, 36, 41, 45,
   74, 77, 81, 130, 173, 183, 215,
   236, 237, 241, 243
Norton, Major General 9, 62, 75
Norwood, B.G. 46
Nutter, Jean 12
Nutter, Raymond T. 8, 9, 12, 65,
   66, 116
NVA 45, 46, 50, 53, 60, 73, 77,
   91, 117, 120, 122, 125, 129,
   130, 132, 133, 136, 137, 140,
   201, 251

O

O'Callaghan, T. 46
O'Dell, Lieutenant Colonel 59
O'Donnell, Texas 202, 208
O'Hara, Theodore 231
O'Riordan, C.P. 46
Oahu, Hawaii 6
Oakland, California 53, 191
Oakland, Kentucky 12
Observer, The 68
*Ode on the Death of the Duke of
   Wellington* 16, 232
Okinawa, Japan 19, 45, 50, 77,
   133, 196
Old Talbert Tavern 12
Oldham, Johnny 9
Olsen, C. 46
Olson, James S. 255
Olympia 91
Operation Attleboro 74
Operation Bolo 81
Operation Francis Marion 186
Operation Homecoming 215
Operation Irving 46
Operation Junction City 93
Operation MacArthur 131, 186
Operation Masher/White Wing 46
Operation Michaelmas 26
Operation Paul Revere 46, 60
Operation Paul Revere I 56
Operation Paul Revere II 53, 60,
   122
Operation Paul Revere IV 72, 73,
   77
Operation Pershing I 46
Operation Pershing II 46
Operation Plan 252
Operation Ranch Hand 94
Operation Sam Houston 186
Operation Thayer II 46
Operation Villa Verde Trail 33
Operations Plan 42
Orehek, Don 6, 8, 92, 93, 217,
   218
Orehek, Suzanne 217, 218
Ormoc Valley 29

Osborne, Milton 255
Osler, William 17
Osmena, President 33
Other Side of Eden, The 79
Ottumwa, Iowa 190
Our Jungle Road to Tokyo 24
Outlaw, Hazel 76
Owen Stanley Mountains 22, 24

P

Pacific Architects and Engineers 52
Pacific Combat Zone 218
Pacific Stars and Stripes 68
Pacific War 21, 32
Paducah Tilghman High School 13
Paducah, Kentucky 13
Page Communications 71, 130
Page Communications Engineers,
   Inc. 101
Page, William Tyler 16
Pagoda, Xa Loi 40
Pakistan 183
Palaus 28
Palou Islands 21
Pappas, S.G. 46
Papua 24, 25, 26, 142, 149, 150
Papuan 22
Papuan Campaign 20, 21, 24, 148
Papuan Peninsula 22
Paradise Lost 66, 70, 71, 79, 82,
   185, 188, 193, 199, 211
Paris, France 13, 34, 35, 119, 218
Parker, J.L. 46
Pasteur, Louis 17, 118
Patton, George S. 63
Pearl Harbor, Hawaii 14, 18, 21,
   75, 77
Peers, William R. 9, 75, 93, 94,
   110, 111, 214
Peking 39, 126, 242
Pentagon 35
People's Liberation Armed Forces
   41
Perley, Jules M.D. 79, 111, 152
Pershing, John Joseph 5
Philadelphia General Hospital 190
Philadelphia, Pennsylvania 77, 232
Philippine Islands 6, 18, 19, 21,
   25, 27, 28, 29, 33, 42, 58, 74,
   101, 149, 197, 205
Philippines 140, 242
Phillips, M.W. 46
Phu Bai 132
Phu Bon Province 65
Phu Lam 101
Phu Tai Valley 53
Phu Yen 172
Phu Yen Province 45
Phuc, Kim 140
Phy My 130
Pimlott, John 255
Pinamopoan 29
Pitoe 27
Plasczynski, Janet 217
Plasczynski, Leo R.N. 57, 78, 83,
   188, 191, 196, 199, 203, 223,
   224
plaster immobilization 179
Platt, B.B. 46
Plaza of the Presidents 218
Plei Me 45, 46, 172
Plei-Djereng 172
Pleiku 3, 6, 7, 8, 9, 10, 11, 12, 13,
   15, 45, 46, 47, 48, 49, 50, 52, 53,

54, 55, 56, 57, 59, 60, 62, 63, 64,
   65, 66, 68, 70, 71, 72, 73, 74, 75,
   76, 77, 79, 80, 81, 84, 87, 88, 89,
   90, 91, 95, 96, 97, 98, 99, 101,
   102, 104, 106, 107, 110, 117,
   122, 124, 126, 128, 130, 140,
   141, 142, 148, 151, 172, 175,
   178, 182, 183, 184, 185, 186,
   187, 189, 190, 191, 192, 193,
   195, 196, 197, 199, 200, 203,
   204, 205, 210, 211, 212, 218,
   219, 225, 226, 227, 228, 230,
   235, 256
Pleiku Air Base 76
Pleiku Airfield 185
Pleiku City 9, 12, 13, 45, 46, 50,
   51, 63, 73, 75, 77, 89, 228
Pleiku Medical Association 8, 13,
   51, 59, 85, 87, 90, 98, 129, 193,
   197, 256
Pleiku Province 8, 50, 53, 65, 111,
   142, 228, 235, 256
Pleiku Provincial Hospital 13, 51,
   52, 56, 57, 58, 59, 87, 89, 98,
   250
Ploger, Robert R. 62
pneumonectomy 92
Poland 40
Pollak, M.J. 46
Polly, Peking 9
Pongani 22
Pope, Alexander 16
Port Moresby 22, 23, 24, 25
Poticha, Stuart M.D. 46, 91
Pounds, Dwight 7, 229, 231
Powell, Jose 225
Practitioner of Medicine 17
Prayer of Maimonides 232
Presidents, The 56
Princeton University 232
Providence High School 256
Providence St. Peter Hospital 91
Providence, Kentucky 256
Psalm of Life, A 80, 232

Q

Quang Duc 65
Quang Tri 3, 132, 134, 135, 137,
   138, 139, 148, 149, 182, 191,
   201, 202, 203, 208, 209
Quang Tri Province 7, 13, 132,
   133, 142
Quang Tri Provincial Hospital 133
Quat, Phan Huy 41
Quebec 28
Qui Hoa Leprosarium 9, 105, 255
Qui Nhon 9, 45, 47, 48, 52, 53,
   57, 58, 62, 63, 67, 68, 70, 73, 75,
   76, 84, 90, 91, 101, 102, 103,
   104, 105, 106, 117, 130, 182,
   184, 185, 193, 194, 195, 196,
   197, 199, 200, 203, 207
Qui Nhon Bay 45
Quincy, Massachusetts 215
Quixote, Don 17
Quoc, Nguyen Ai 38, 39, 237, 238

R

Rabaul, New Guinea 28
radical debridement 97
radical prostatectomy 96
radiographic 245
Rama, King 113
Rameriz, Sandy 156, 227

Ranck, James B. 63, 83, 91, 203
Rangoon, Burma 112
Rawls, Lou 106
Ray Sibnarayan 255
Raye, Martha 12, 66, 92, 130, 203
Raymond International 52
reconstructive plastic surgery 164
Red Beach 27, 45
Red China 42
Red Flag 42, 241, 242
Red River 237
Reed, Margaret Teresa Yvonne 12
Reed, Walter 17, 76
Reeder, Delbert 13
Reflections at the Wall 15, 214, 215, 228, 229, 233
Regimental Room 216
Reichenberger, J.A. 46
Reid, S.H. 46
Renascence 232
Repose 98
Republic of Korea 53
Republic of Vietnam 8, 9, 11, 34, 40, 41, 46, 48, 53, 64, 76, 111, 130, 148, 195, 228, 235, 237, 239, 241, 256
Repulse Bay 109
restorative arterial surgery 176
Retes, Ynigo Ortiz de 22
Revitalizing A Nation 16
Rhode Island College School 215
Rhodes, Gene 9
Richards, Jodie 219
Richardson, Sara Hill 12
Richtsmeier, Ron 223, 225
Richtsmeier, Judy Dexter RN 57, 58, 213, 223, 224, 226
River Rendezvous, A 15
Robbins, Stanley M.D. 255
Rock Force Corregidor 30
Rogers, Roy 92
Rohs, H. 46
Roosevelt, Franklin D. 20
Roosevelt, Theodore 13, 18, 19, 136, 219
Rosen, Jack 92
Rosenberg, Jerry M.D. 13, 51, 129, 158
Rousseau, Marc 255
Roux, Emile 118
Rowe, John Carlos 255
Rumsfeld, Donald H. 52
Rush 17
Rusk, Dean 44, 242

S

Saidor 25, 26, 32
Saidor Campaign 25
Saigon 9, 11, 34, 35, 36, 38, 39, 40, 41, 44, 49, 52, 53, 56, 61, 64, 65, 66, 67, 68, 71, 75, 76, 79, 81, 90, 93, 100, 101, 107, 116, 118, 120, 126, 137, 184, 185, 190, 191, 195, 201, 202, 205, 216, 237
Saipan 18
Salk, Jonas 17
Salt Lake City, Utah 195, 215
Sams, B.F. 46
San Antonio River Walk 217
San Antonio, Texas 6, 8, 46, 58, 191, 193, 197, 206, 217, 226, 227, 256
San Diego, California 47

San Francisco Bay 217
San Francisco Bay Cruise 217
San Francisco International Airport 49
San Francisco, California 11, 13, 21, 49, 185, 196, 199, 205, 216, 217
San Jose Mindoro Philippine Islands 31
San Pedro, California 190
Sanananda 24, 28
Sanananda Campaign 24
Santa Barbara, California 18
Santa Monica, California 190
Sara Norasingh Theatre 116
Sartorius, Patrick M.D. 57, 91, 199
Sasebo 33
Saturday Review 81
Savannah, Georgia 53
Schachner, S.H. 46
Schmidt, Richard H. 46, 130
Schueing, Ruby Britsch R.N. 213
Sclesinger, Arthur Jr. 184
Scott, Jack M.D. 128, 235
Scranton, Pennsylvania 130
Sea Palace Floating Restaurant 108
Seattle-Tacoma International Airport 128
Seattle, Washington 128
Seeger, Alan 232
Sevenson, Sandy 225
Severino, R.M. 46
Seymour, E.L.D. 218
Sha Tin Floating Restaurant 109, 110
Shangai 18
Shapiro, Karl 5
Sheenon, Philip 255
Shek-O 109
Sherpe, Howard 100
Shore, R.T. 46
Shueing, Ruby Britsch R.N. 224
Shultz, Richard Jr. 255
Shumchum River 109
Shurtleff, Thurman L. 47
Sikes, Douglas W. 8
Silent Spring 95
Simond, Paul-Louis 119
Simpson Howard R. 255
Sinatra, Nancy 93
Sinemi Plantation 22, 23
Sinemi-Buna Trail 22
Singapore 140
Sio 25
Sioux 45
Skinner, Marcheta VanMeter 12
Skyroom Restaurant 216
Slabisak, Chuck 195
Slocum, Harvey M.D. 59
Smith, Bedell 9, 40, 239
Smith, David E. 76
Smith, Don M.D. 75
Smith, Lloyd Jr. 255
Smith, Othar O. 12, 13
Smith, Patricia M.D. 13, 90, 91
Smith, Thomas G. 255
Soberg, David 49, 63, 83
Soc Trang 43, 66, 123
Socialist Republic of Vietnam 86
Socialist Revolution in North Vietnam 42
Solomon Islands 21, 28
Solzhenitsyn, Aleksandr 14
Somerset, Kentucky 232

Sometimes 80
Souter, Gerry 255
Souter, Janet 255
South Carolina 203
South China Sea 36
South Korea 42, 51, 74, 197
South State Construction Inc. 13
South Vietnam 6, 7, 9, 12, 34, 35, 36, 40, 41, 42, 44, 45, 46, 51, 52, 53, 65, 68, 71, 74, 85, 86, 94, 100, 117, 126, 129, 132, 133, 136, 137, 140, 148, 173, 186, 205, 208, 228, 230, 236, 237, 239, 241, 242, 251, 252, 256
South Vietnamese Armed Forces 243
Southeast Asia Collective Defense Treaty 44
Southeast Asia Treaty Organization 42, 52, 81, 136, 242, 252
Southern Philippines Campaign 148
Soviet Union 40
Spanish American War 219
Spellman, Cardinal 76
Sperland, Major 191
Spice Islands 22
Spiller, Cora Jane Hines 12
Spiller, Robert E. 7, 12
Spitzer, N.C. 46
Spock, Benjamin M.D. 243
Spurling, Jerry 71
St. John's Hospital 190
St. Joseph College 231
St. Louis Cathedral 211
St. Louis, Missouri 13, 128
St. Petersburg, Russia 218
Stanton, Doug 255
Star Ferry Pier 109
Stars and Stripes 78, 81, 192
Steelman, Trent 224
Steger, Byron L. 78
Steinbeck, John 78, 255
Steinbeck, John IV 79
Sterling Eleanor Jane 255
Stetcher, Ann R.N. 78, 117
Stevens, Thomas H. 31
Stewart, Elaine 92
Stewart, New York 219
Stinnott, Edmund W. 218
Stoner, Daniel 217
Stovall, Thelma L. 72
Strader, Charles Wesley 8, 11
Strangers in the Night 49
Stratton, Richard A. 214, 215
Street Without Joy 81
Stuart, Ted M.D. 10, 46, 47, 48, 63, 101, 102, 103, 207, 213, 216, 217, 221, 224
Stuart, Toni 217, 221, 225
Sullivan, Father 72
Sulu Sea 29
Summers, Harry G. 186
Suorez, Capt. 135
superclavicular approach 97
Supporting the Infantry Blue Diary from a Surgical Hospital 7, 100
Surigao Straits 28, 29
Suu, Phan Khoc 41
Suzie Wong Hotel 109
Suzuki, Premier 19
Swarzkopf, H. Norman 12
Sweeney, Charles 19
Swenson, Craig 193

Swenson, Orville M.D. 10, 46, 47, 48, 49, 58, 71, 79, 82, 118, 141, 193, 201, 213, 215, 216, 217, 224, 225
Swenson, Sandy 193, 215
Swenson, Stanley 141
Swietnicki, F. 46
Swink, J.E. 46
Sydenham 17
Sydnor, Wallace 9
Sylvester, Maj. 134, 138
Syracuse University 81

T

Tachikawa Airbase 198
Tacoma, Washington 47, 48
Tadji 27
Tan Son Nhut International Airport (Air Base) 49, 52, 56, 66, 75, 76, 77, 101, 116, 184, 191
Tan Thoi 44
Tang Dynasty 38
Tatom, John M.D. 47, 48, 57
Taumorong 172
Tay Nguyen Campaign 45
Tay Ninh 75
Tay Ninh City 93
Temple of Fame, The 16
Tennyson, Alfred Lord 16, 228, 229, 232
Teranishi, Irv 216, 217, 219, 225
Teranishi, Pat Johnson R.N. 6, 8, 78, 194, 207, 211, 212, 213, 214, 216, 217, 219, 222, 224, 226, 227, 233
Terry, Robert D. 101
Tesser, S. 46
Texas 93, 208
Thailand 18, 34, 42, 51, 74, 77, 101, 117, 140, 242
Thanatopsis 232
Thanh Hoa Province 215
Thanh, Nguyen Tat 38
Thayer Hotel 224, 225
Their, Samuel M.D. 255
These Boots Are Made for Walkin' 93
Thieu, Nguyen Van 34, 35, 41, 64, 137, 174, 197, 239
Thigpen, Corbett M.D. 48
Tho, Nguyen Ngoc 41, 239
Thompson, Francis 232
Thompson, Jim 113
Thompson, Ron CRNA 78, 79, 82, 83, 153, 185, 213
thoracotomy 156
Thoreau, Henry David 106
Three Faces of Eve, The 48
Thua Thien Province 132
Thuy, Nguyen Vinh 39
Tibbets, Paul 19
Tiede, Tom 255
Tierney, Marian 78
Tiger Balm Gardens 108, 109, 110, 203
Tilghman, Lloyd 13
Till, E.W. 46
Time Magazine 68, 98
Tinian 19
Titi 195
To the Memory of the Brave Americans 232
Tokyo Bay 19
Tokyo International Airport 128

Tokyo, Japan 18, 68, 77, 119, 126, 128, 130, 191, 198
Tomkiewicz, T. 46
Tonkin 38, 39, 237, 238
Topside 29, 30
Tourane 38
Townsville's Archer Field 22
Trac, Trung 237
tracheostomy 155
Tram Dang Thuy 255
Travis Airforce Base 75, 191, 207, 216
Tre, Ben 6
Tripler Army Hospital 195
Troiano, G. 46
Truluck, Charles 203
Truman, Harry S. 5, 15, 19, 34, 42, 183, 242
Trung Nguyen 45
Truong Quoc Dung 56
Truong Son 118, 172
Truong Son Mountains 41, 241
Tse-tung, Mao 39, 238
Tsimshatsui 109
Tulane 185
Tulane University School of Medicine 13, 142, 211, 213
Turkey 44, 242
Tuy Hoa 45, 68
Ty, Bac Si 87, 204

U

U.S. "Doolittle" 18
U.S. Army Center of Military History 28
U.S. Army Vietnam 50
U.S. Constitution 14
U.S. Military Academy 219, 224, 225
Ulmer, R.H. 46
Uniform Services University of the Health Sciences 214
Union Station 214
United States 40, 42, 74, 77, 195, 242, 243
University of Berlin 118
University of Georgia Medical School 48
University of Kentucky 13
University of Kentucky Medical Center 13
University of Louisville College of Medicine 9, 12, 13, 74, 75, 256
University of Paris 118
University of Southern California 190
University of Virginia 191
University of Washington Medical School 91
Uselton, Russell W. 47, 48, 49
USNS *General Edwin D. Patrick* 53
USNS *Walker* 48
USS *Buckner* 47
USS *C. Turner Joy* 44, 242
USS *Cecil F. Doyle* 12

USS *Enterprise* 18
USS *Hornet* 18
USS *Indianapolis* 11, 12, 19, 21
USS *Maddox* 42, 44, 242
USS *Missouri* 19
USS *Ticonderoga* 44, 215

V

Vakas, J.L. 46
Valerio, Oscar M.D. 78, 83, 87, 123, 152, 153, 188, 204
Valley Forge 215
Van Hoa 45
Van, Duong 41
Van Dyke, Henry 126
Vanderbilt University 91, 256
Vandergriff, W.L. 46
VanMeter, Joseph W. 12
VanMeter, Phillip P. 12
Vann, John 44
Vecchione, J. 46
vein grafts 176
Venereal Disease Research Laboratories 250
venous patch angioplasty 178
Victoria Bay 107, 109, 110
Victoria Peak 107, 109, 110, 203
Vien Duc Anh Bae Ae Orphanage 105
Viet Cong 34, 40, 41, 42, 44, 45, 46, 50, 53, 56, 60, 62, 65, 66, 72, 76, 77, 79, 80, 81, 89, 91, 92, 98, 102, 103, 112, 117, 118, 121, 129, 130, 132, 136, 137, 140, 159, 160, 161, 162, 172, 173, 183, 191, 194, 195, 201, 202, 239, 241, 242, 251, 252
Viet Minh 39, 42
Viet Minh National Front 39
Viet-Nam Witness and the Two Vietnams 81
Vietnam 3, 6, 7, 8, 9, 11, 12, 13, 34, 35, 36, 38, 39, 40, 42, 44, 45, 47, 48, 49, 50, 52, 58, 61, 62, 63, 64, 68, 69, 72, 73, 76, 77, 78, 79, 81, 84, 85, 86, 87, 93, 94, 95, 96, 100, 101, 105, 117, 118, 120, 126, 127, 128, 133, 136, 137, 140, 148, 150, 151, 175, 176, 177, 178, 180, 183, 184, 185, 186, 190, 191, 192, 193, 194, 195, 196, 197, 198, 199, 200, 201, 203, 204, 205, 206, 207, 209, 210, 211, 212, 213, 215, 216, 228, 230, 235, 236, 237, 238, 239, 241, 242, 243
Vietnam Counteroffensive Campaign 57
Vietnam Journal 100
Vietnam Veterans Memorial 36, 81, 214, 228, 229, 231, 233
Vietnam War 3, 5, 6, 7, 11, 12, 14, 34, 36, 77, 86, 94, 95, 117, 126, 141, 142, 145, 184, 192, 211, 215, 228, 229
Vietnam Women's Memorial 229

Vietnamese Workers Party 39
Vigano, Father 119
Villa Verde Trail 30, 32
Vincente-Mapandan 29
Vinh Loc 172
Vinh Loc, Maj. Gen. 225
Virchow, Rudolf 17
Visayan Islands 28
Von Leewenhoek 17
Voncanon, J.W. 46
Voss, H.E. 46

W

Wake Island 18, 49, 205
Wall That Heals 7
Wall, J.W. 46
Walsh, John 189
Walter Reed Army Institute of Research 175
Walter Reed Army Medical Center 75, 76, 175, 182, 196, 199, 214
Walton, John K. 47, 91
Waltzer, Arthur M.D. 91, 104
Wanigela 22
War of Independence 14
Warren County, Kentucky 7
Warren Front 22
Washington, D.C. 6, 7, 40, 56, 68, 74, 75, 76, 81, 96, 100, 136, 175, 182, 183, 196, 199, 214, 215, 228, 229, 231
Washington Monument 228
Waters, John K. 101
Watson, T.R. 46
WBC 250
We Are Soldiers Still 12
We Were Soldiers Once...And Young 12, 15, 46
Weaver, Pat R.N. 78, 82, 117
Weber, B.C. 46
Wechsler, H. 46
Weinberger-Powell Doctrine 186
Weiner, I.J. 46
Weis, F.R. 46
Welch, Phillip H. 71, 85, 125
Wells, Diana 218
Wells, Robert J. 133
West, Jim 138
West Hartford, Connecticut 200
West Point, New York 16, 196, 219, 220, 224, 225, 226
West Point Military Academy 220
Western Kentucky State College 256
Western Kentucky University 7, 9, 12, 128, 232
Westmoreland, William C. 6, 12, 16, 42, 44, 45, 46, 59, 62, 75, 78, 93, 99, 136, 197, 211, 214, 236, 242
Westwell, Ian 255
Wetterhahn, Ralph 255
Whalen, E.W. 46
Wheeler, Earle 78
White, Ed 84
White Beach 25

White House 57, 101
White Plains, New York 219
Whither We Are Tending 128, 235
Whittier, John Greenleaf 16
Wicks-Varina Lumber and Builders Supply 48
Wier, James A. 9, 53, 56, 74, 75
Wilde, Oscar 218
Wilderman, Lois R.N. 224, 227
Wilhelmsland 22
Williams, P.E. Jr. 46
Williamson, Walter A. 232
Wilson, Harold 242
Wilson, Nancy 106, 201
Windsor, David 217
Wingate, General 18
Winslow, Clive CRNA 213, 215, 216
Winters, Jonathan 92
Wintle, Justin 255
Wirts, H.K. 46
Wisconsin 20
Witche, Lt. 59
Wittenberg, James 198
Woehler, T.R. 46
Wolf, Marvin J. 254
Wolff, L.H. M.D. 112
Woolridge, William O. 78
Wordsworth, William 136
World Is Too Much With Us, The 137
World Trade Center 14
World War I 9, 13, 20, 22, 29, 68, 189
World War II 3, 5, 7, 9, 11, 13, 14, 16, 18, 20, 21, 22, 24, 32, 36, 42, 44, 60, 76, 77, 93, 95, 112, 113, 126, 142, 145, 148, 149, 150, 175, 192, 230, 237, 242, 251, 254
World War II Memorial Monument 5
Wormenhoven, Simon 255

Y

Y Bih Alio 65
Yalau Plantation 26
Yale University 228
Yamaguachi 33
Yamashita, General Tomoyuki 33
Yaumati Typhoon Shelter 109
Yawata 19
Yeah Kids I Really Did Go To Vietnam My Vietnam War Memories 1966-1967 7
Yellowstone Bar 88
Yersin, Emile John Alexandre 118, 119, 120
Yogada, A. 46

Z

Zig-Zag Pass 30
Zimov, Lieutenant Colonel 58
Zollicoffer, Felix K. 232

Top left, clockwise: Madame Nhu's summer home in Pleiku. A young Vietnamese boy peeping through his yard fence sucking on a piece of hard candy I given him (photo won numerous awards at juried exhibitions). View looking north from atop the water tower. The rainfall visible beyond the communicat antennae is approximately over Lake Bien Ho. Sunset over the Chu Pong Cambodian Mountains made from our BOQ (this photograph won multiple aw in numerous juried exhibitions).